T0224929

Microsoft Word Secrets

The Why and How of Getting Word to Do What You Want

Flavio Morgado

Apress®

Microsoft Word Secrets: The Why and How of Getting Word to Do What You Want

Flavio Morgado
Rio de Janeiro, Brazil

ISBN-13 (pbk): 978-1-4842-3077-0
https://doi.org/10.1007/978-1-4842-3078-7

ISBN-13 (electronic): 978-1-4842-3078-7

Library of Congress Control Number: 2017957541

Cover image designed by Freepik

Managing Director: Welmoed Spahr
Editorial Director: Todd Green
Acquisitions Editor: Gwenan Spearing
Development Editor: Laura Berendson
Technical Reviewer: Ralph Mercurio and Massimo Nardone
Coordinating Editor: Nancy Chen
Copy Editor: Brendan Frost
Artist: SPi Global

Distributed to the book trade worldwide by Springer Science+Business Media New York, 233 Spring Street, 6th Floor, New York, NY 10013. Phone 1-800-SPRINGER, fax (201) 348-4505, e-mail orders-ny@springer-sbm.com, or visit www.springeronline.com. Apress Media, LLC is a California LLC and the sole member (owner) is Springer Science + Business Media Finance Inc (SSBM Finance Inc). SSBM Finance Inc is a **Delaware** corporation.

For information on translations, please e-mail rights@apress.com, or visit http://www.apress.com/ rights-permissions.

Apress titles may be purchased in bulk for academic, corporate, or promotional use. eBook versions and licenses are also available for most titles. For more information, reference our Print and eBook Bulk Sales web page at http://www.apress.com/bulk-sales.

Any source code or other supplementary material referenced by the author in this book is available to readers on GitHub via the book's product page, located at www.apress.com/9781484230770. For more detailed information, please visit http://www.apress.com/source-code.

Printed on acid-free paper

To Bia
For your help and patience to support me
Whenever I need you by my side
Dear love…

Table of Contents

About the Author

Flavio Morgado is a Food Engineer with a MSc. degree in Food Science and Technology. He is also a VBA Professional developer, a technical writer, an English-to-Brazilian Portuguese technical translator, and a professor of Epidemiology, Statistics, and Medical Informatics at UNIFESO, a health sciences university in Rio de Janeiro, Brazil. Flavio has written more than 30 books, including *Programming Excel with VBA* (Apress), and has translated an equal number. He also loves animals and the exquisite nature of the surrounding rainforest, and when he is not teaching, writing, or developing, he can be found running or riding his mountain bike through the Teresopolis Mountains, followed by his 11 dogs, or spending time on the stunningly beautiful beaches of Cabo Frio in Rio de Janeiro.

About the Technical Reviewers

Ralph Mercurio is a director with Capeless Solutions, which focuses on Microsoft 365 and SharePoint, in the areas of infrastructure, development, and migration. Ralph has over 13 years of experience working in technology in a variety of roles and across many industries.

Massimo Nardone has more than 23 years of experience in Security, Web/Mobile development, Cloud and IT Architecture. His true IT passions are Security and Android.

He has been programming and teaching how to program with Android, Perl, PHP, Java, VB, Python, C/C++, and MySQL for more than 20 years.

He holds a Master of Science degree in Computing Science from the University of Salerno, Italy. He has worked as a Project Manager, Software Engineer, Research Engineer, Chief Security Architect, Information Security Manager, PCI/SCADA Auditor, and Senior Lead IT Security/Cloud/SCADA Architect for many years.

His technical skills include: Security, Android, Cloud, Java, MySQL, Drupal, Cobol, Perl, Web and Mobile development, MongoDB, D3, Joomla, Couchbase, C/C++, WebGL, Python, Pro Rails, Django CMS, Jekyll, Scratch, etc.

He worked as visiting lecturer and supervisor for exercises at the Networking Laboratory of the Helsinki University of Technology (Aalto University). He holds four international patents (PKI, SIP, SAML, and Proxy areas).

He currently works as Chief Information Security Office (CISO) for Cargotec Oyj and he is member of ISACA Finland Chapter Board.

Massimo has reviewed more than 40 IT books for different publishing companies and he is the coauthor of *Pro Android Games* (Apress, 2015).

Acknowledgments

This book was written to inspire people to produce better text documents. Many times I had to search the Internet for a better understanding of a typographic term or to acquire more knowledge about the many Microsoft Word features and capabilities. So I would like to thank the following typographic- or Microsoft Word–oriented Internet sites (in alphabetical order):

- Additive Tips: `http://www.addictivetips.com/category/microsoft-office/`

- bonfx: `http://bonfx.com/best-sans-serif-fonts/#`

- Business Writing: `http://www.businesswritingblog.com`

- Butterick's Practical Typography: `http://practicaltypography.com`

- Canva Design School: `https://designschool.canva.com/`

- Creative Market: `https://creativemarket.com/`

- Discover.TYpography: `https://www.typography.com/`

- Dummies.com: `http://www.dummies.com/software/microsoft-office/word`

- Exljbris Font Foundry: `https://www.exljbris.com/`

- Font Space: `http://www.fontspace.com`

- Fonts.com: `www.fonts.com`

- Graham Mayor: `http://www.gmayor.com/replace_using_wildcards.htm`

- I Love Typography: `http://ilovetypography.com/`

- Microsoft Office Support: `https://support.office.com`

- Slide Bean: Best Times New Roman alternatives: `https://slidebean.com/blog/best-times-new-roman-alternatives`

ACKNOWLEDGMENTS

- Tech Republic: http://www.techrepublic.com/blog/10-things/10-cool-ways-to-get-more-from-words-find-and-replace-feature/

- The Book Designer: https://www.thebookdesigner.com/

- Tips.net: https://word.tips.net/index.html

- Translation Journal: http://translationjournal.net/Featured-Article/using-ms-word-s-advanced-find-and-replace-function.html

- True-Type Typography: http://www.truetype-typography.com

- Web Typography: https://johndjameson.com/

- Word Articles: http://www.wordarticles.com/

- Write Content Solutions: http://www.write.com/content-solutions/

Introduction

As soon as I published my first Apress book, *Programming Excel with VBA*, my very talented editor, Gwenan Spearing, asked me "What's next?" I then proposed writing a book about Microsoft Word because in my opinion it is probably the most used software in the world, while it is also probably the least understood. She promptly asked me to prepare a Table of Contents about how the book would approach the topic with a different concept than that used in other books on the market.

My first approach was to write a small, concise book, of 200 pages at most, to teach Microsoft Word basics, using a very fast and direct approach. As you can see, I failed at that. The book became bigger than expectations. But I think it is much better also. Some issues deserved more attention and some options needed to be clarified while others needed a step-by-step approach.

Since Microsoft Word is indeed an advanced typographic tool, I made the decision to teach it by covering the typography component. And I added chapter exercises.

It was a pleasure to produce this book for you, reader. So here is the result, and I truly hope that you like it—or even better, that you learn from it.

Although it offers extreme simplicity in its usage, Word also has deep typographical knowledge and rules, so anyone can play Gutenberg in their own way. While Word is easy to use, it is often misunderstood because it is so rich in typographic tools.

And it is due to being so ambitious in its intentions—to be a typographic tool as easy to use as it is powerful in its effects—Word sometimes becomes misunderstood. Who never gets mad about a Word document that

- Refuses to obey the formatting options that need to be applied?

- Seems not able to format text into a table?

- Cannot hold the position of title headers and other items (such as figures) as the document is edited?

- Or so many other "simple" things we want to do but have difficulty executing?

What's in the Book

This book was written to try to make sense of Microsoft Word as a typographic tool, and as such, it breaks the knowledge behind well-formatted and printed documents into 12 successive chapters that will solidly build your knowledge on the very simple typographic principles behind Microsoft Word interface, spread through its powerful Ribbon tabs or its many (and sometimes very hidden) dialog boxes, options, and features.

The chapters present a succession of knowledge that requires you to read them linearly, from the first to the last, and then go back at random whenever necessary, with each chapter having one or more exercises so you can practice the knowledge gained so far.

And by the end, I surely expect that you will suddenly have that strong feeling of final mastery.

Screenshots are from Windows 7 and Word 2016 versions. You may see small differences from the ones you see on your computer. Much of this book can be used with earlier versions of Word.

So what is in the book?

- **Chapter 1, Brief Introduction to Word and File Extensions** is a very small chapter that makes a simple Microsoft Word presentation: how its interface is organized, the names the book uses to refer to some specific interface components, and a brief introduction to file extensions.

- **Chapter 2, Hidden Characters, Inheritance, and Paragraph Formatting** talks about hidden characters and how Microsoft Word uses them to set simple typographic concepts, like paragraphs, line breaks, and tabulation characters. You will be also introduced to the controls found in the Home tab of the Ribbon and the Paragraph dialog box (alignment, indentation, spacing, and text flow controls).

- **Chapter 3, Character Attributes** discusses another basic issue regarding text formatting—the font and characters you choose to present your documents. You will learn about the different font types, how to install and use them, And how to take advantage of the controls found in the Home tab of the Ribbon and the Font dialog box to produce text documents that may rival the ones formatted by professional typographers.

- **Chapter 4, Select, Find, and Replace Text Characters** gives you a solid introduction to a feature already touched on in previous chapters: Find and Replace text in a document. By using the tools offered by Microsoft Word, you will wake up your abilities to quickly format any kind of document, by finding the desired text and applying the desired formatting options.

- **Chapter 5, Quick Document Formatting with Styles** explains what a style is and how you can use it to quickly apply standardized formats to the text. You will be introduced to the Styles Gallery and the different interfaces to manage styles. It also talks about the Normal style, its strong inheritance behavior, and how you can create and manage the styles available in a document.

- **Chapter 6, Using Recommended Styles** talks about the philosophy behind the usage of a determined set of styles treated by Microsoft Word as Recommended, and how you can take advantage of using them, along with the Design tab and the Styles Set gallery to quickly apply or change the appearance of a text document.

- **Chapter 7, Using Heading Styles** introduces you to the all-important Heading1 to Heading9 styles that you can use to hierarchically format the headings (title and subtitles) of your document. It shows how to take advantage of the Paragraph > Outline level property, how to collapse and expand the document text, how to quickly navigate inside the text using the Navigation Pane, and how to automatically create the document's Table of Contents. You will also have a brief introduction to Microsoft Word Outline view and how use it to quickly change the position of large text blocks inside the document.

- **Chapter 8, Page Formatting** discusses page formatting, which is the essence of any document's final appearance. You will learn how to select page sizes and margins and how to use the Header and Footer areas to propagate information on the document. You will learn how to number pages and use different Header/Footer options for the First, Even and Odd pages, producing different types of popular documents (like e-books, PDF files, and books printed on both sides of the paper).

- **Chapter 9, Section Breaks** approaches how Microsoft Word allows changing the page formatting options inside a document using Section Breaks, which is a special hidden character. You will learn how to change page size orientation and vertical alignment for just one page, how section inheritance propagates through the document, and how to set or break links between sections. You will also be introduced to formatting text into columns and controlling the page number shown on different document pages.

- **Chapter 10, Formatting Tables** uses all the knowledge gathered so far to show that each table cell can be considered as an independent document which is affected by the Normal style and all available formatting options. This chapter teaches how you can create and format tables that will surely obey your document formatting, and also approaches how you can use formulas to calculate table values.

- **Chapter 11, Creating and Using Templates** discusses how you can use the typographic knowledge revealed in previous chapters to create a Microsoft Word Template that can be reused to reproduce the same document appearance in different files. You will learn how to use ready-made templates, the importance of the Normal.dotm template, and where templates are stored on your hard drive. You will also learn how to can create, use, and associate or insert an existing document to a template so you can take advantage of its style sets and all of its formatting options (including page formatting).

- **Chapter 12, Master and Subdocuments** explores how Microsoft Word allows managing different documents as a single entity using the Outline view and the Master/Subdocument approaches. You will also be introduced to how you can create an Index (glossary) at the end of the document, and how you can take advantage of all the knowledge discussed on this book (formatting, hidden character, styles, section breaks, templates...) to produce a consistent format in long documents of any size, produced by one person or many different people.

This Book's Special Features

This book has two main special features: the Attention box and the Exercises it proposes to explore the issues approached in each chapter and its sections.

Attention   This box will call your attention to important information regarding the issue being discussed, and sometimes will even explain some unexpected Microsoft Word behavior. Use as a tip to enhance the knowledge under discussion.

Exercises: These were produced with the intention to make you practice the concepts approached in previous sections, the current chapter, or previous chapters. They become increasingly difficult from Chapter 2 to Chapter 12, and will give you the opportunity to test how a Microsoft Word document reacts or can be changed by following its steps.

They use fragments or the entire texts of classic and famous books, all of them considered as public domain.

Website Extras

Each chapter points to the Internet (https://github.com/apress/msft-word-secrets) and file you must download to have access to the documents proposed in the chapter exercises.

Each chapter has its own compressed .ZIP file whose content you can extract using Windows Explorer or a number of freeware software packages (iZarc, WinZip, WinRAR, and even Internet Explorer) to a desired folder (I am supposing that you will create a book folder in your \Documents folder, and recommend that you use a different folder for each chapter file.)

Your Feedback Is Very Important

Before you continue with the reading, I would like to say that your opinion is very important to me. I really don't know how many of you will write me to give any comment but I hope I can answer everyone and, whenever it's possible, resolve questions or problems that arise.

Since I have many other duties, sometimes it may take a little while before I can answer you, but I promise to do my best. Please feel free to write me at the following e-mail address:

flaviomorgado@gmail.com

CHAPTER 1

Brief Introduction to Word and File Extensions

This book does not intend to teach you how to use Microsoft Word. It supposes that you already have some knowledge about it: how to open, change, and save documents, and how you can format text.

This very brief chapter is just a primer about Microsoft Word interface, so you can easily associate some terms cited throughout these book chapters.

Figure 1-1 details some items of the Microsoft Word interface and how they are cited in the chapters.

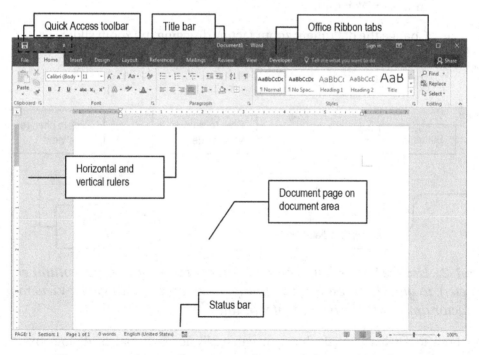

Figure 1-1. *The Microsoft Word 2016 interface and the names of its main items, as cited in this book*

© Flavio Morgado 2017
F. Morgado, *Microsoft Word Secrets*, https://doi.org/10.1007/978-1-4842-3078-7_1

Microsoft Word commands are mainly found in the Ribbon tabs and the many dialog boxes derived from its commands.

But some can also be executed from different parts of it Interface, like

- **Title bar**: shows the name of the current document and has the Quick Access tool bar for common file operations.

- **Ribbon**: the tabbed control that allows access to Microsoft Word commands.

- **Ruler**: shows page dimensions using the desired units and gives access to the Page Setup and Tab dialog boxes.

- **Document area**: shows the current selected document page (or document content, according to the View mode selected).

- **Status bar**: where each item can give access to different dialog boxes by clicking the text it shows, such as the following (Figure 1-2):

    - Navigation Pane, Word count, Idiom, or Zoom dialog boxes.

    - Change Microsoft Word view mode (to Page Layout, Reading mode, or Web mode).

    - Change the document zoom factor (dragging the zoom slider) or show the Zoom dialog box (by clicking the percent zoom factor indicator).

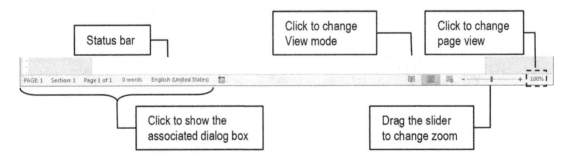

Figure 1-2. *Use the Status Bar to read document information (page number, word count, etc.), to quickly access specific dialog boxes, and to change the View mode or zoom factor applied to the document window*

The book text will always cite how you can easily access a specific dialog box whenever important to make you more productive in using Microsoft Word interface.

A Note About Word File Extensions

For those of you that still do not understand what a file extension is, here comes a good explanation about how to see or hide them, and why I talk so much about them in the book.

For your information, every file you create using a computer has two parts in its name: the name itself and a file identification code that uses three or more characters and is appended to the name by the program that creates it. To separate the name from its file extension, Windows (and most operational systems) uses a dot, like this:

filename.ext

Where

- filename: Is the name you give to the file, which can be up to 255 characters;

- ext: The file extension that the program appends to the file—generally a three-letter combination that is associated with the program name (but can have more than three characters).

Microsoft Word, for example, traditionally used the file extension .DOC up to Word 2003 version, but by the time that Microsoft moved in the direction of Office 2007, the world had changed: there were many pressures on Microsoft to force it adopt an open file structure standard to save its Office files using what is called an "XML schema," so any programmer could easily open its files.

So all Office 2007 suite programs standardize their file structure to XML (e**X**tended **M**arkup **L**anguage) adding an extra "X" character to each program file extension: the standard Microsoft Word .DOC file extension (and file format) changed to .DOCX (did you guess that the last X comes from XML?).

That's why throughout this book I always refer to Microsoft Word files using their four-letter file extension (like the new standard .DOCX Word file, .DOCM for an macro enabled document, or .DOTX and DOTM for a template or macro enabled template).

Attention   Although .DOTM files are cited in the text, Macro codes are not approached in this book.

Do Not Change a File Extension

That's it: the file extension identifies the file type.

And somewhere inside Windows there is a file extension table that associates every file extension to an executable program. This way, Windows can also associate the file with a special icon, and whenever you double-click the file, Windows looks in extension inside the file extension table for the appropriate program to open it, and if it finds a match, opens the program with the desired file.

Attention   Many people naively believe that changing one file extension to another also changes the file type. This is not true and always leads to disasters. For example, Adobe Reader uses the now very popular .PDF extension. If you change any Microsoft Word file extension from .DOCX to .PDF, Windows will quickly change its icon from a Word document file to a PDF file, but you will not change the expected file structure. The Adobe Reader program (the one normally associated to a .PDF file extension) will not be able to open the file—and even if it does, it is more than probable that you will just see garbage instead!

Showing File Extensions

You normally can't see the file extensions using Microsoft Word Open or Save as dialog box, or in any Windows Explorer window, because Microsoft Windows hides them to protect the file extensions from being inadvertently changed by the users, so the correct program can always open the file whenever the user double-clicks it!

But this is just an option in Windows interface, and as such, it can be turned on and off. To turn on file extensions exhibition in your Windows 7, follow these steps:

1. Open the Control Panel from the Start menu and double-click Folder Options to open the Folder Options dialog box.

2. In the Folder Options dialog box, select the View tab and uncheck Hide extensions for known file types.

3. Click OK to close the Folder Options dialog box.

Attention   In Windows 10, open File Explorer and use the View Tab Options command to show the Folder Options dialog box.

From now on, all file extensions will appear in all folders!

Attention   Be careful not to delete the file extension, if exhibited, whenever you rename a file using Windows Explorer.

About This Book's Figures

All figures used in this book come from Microsoft Word 2016 version and Microsoft Windows 7 system environment. Small differences perceived on your computer may be due to a different Windows or Word version.

Anyway, most of the dialog boxes pictured in this book have had the same appearance and formatting since Microsoft Word 2000.

CHAPTER 2

Hidden Characters, Inheritance, and Paragraph Formatting

Every word processor—Microsoft Word included—bases its inner workings on hidden characters and the basic principle of inheritance to copy the format applied to whatever is under the cursor to what comes next. To format its text paragraphs, Microsoft Word uses three main hidden characters:

¶ indicates an Enter key pressed in the document, used to represent the end of a text paragraph.

→ indicates a Tab key pressed in the document, used to displace the text to the next tabulation mark.

↵ indicates a Shift+Enter key combination pressed in the document, used to manually break a text line.

In this chapter, you will see how these hidden characters and formatting inheritance impact Microsoft Word text, why it is so important to control the text flow, and how to take advantage of knowing that they were inserted in the text to gain precise control over any .DOC or .DOCX text document. The document sited on the Exercise section can be found by downloading the Chapter02.zip file from this Internet address:

```
https://github.com/apress/msft-word-secrets
```

F. Morgado, *Microsoft Word Secrets*, https://doi.org/10.1007/978-1-4842-3078-7_2

Hidden Characters and Inheritance

Whenever you open Microsoft Word 2016 it presents you the "New Template" screen from where most people select the first, default Blank document template (earlier versions of Word just show the blank document template, Figure 2-1).

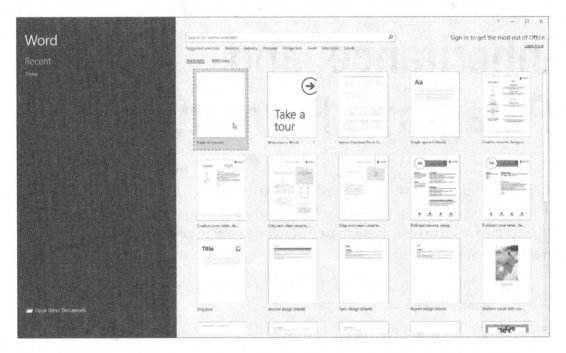

Figure 2-1. *Microsoft Word New Template selection screen*

Attention   You can make Microsoft Word 2016 go straight to a blank page without showing its New Template screen by unchecking the "Show the Start Screen when this application starts" option, found in File ➤ Options ➤ General ➤ Startup Options area.

After selecting the first Blank document template, Microsoft Word will offer you the new, white page of an apparently blank document, into which no text has yet been inserted (Figure 2-2).

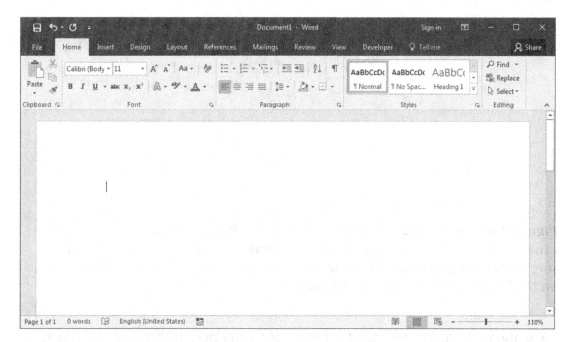

Figure 2-2. *This is the Microsoft Word blank page obtained whenever you select the Blank document template*

The page seems to be clean, but it isn't, and you can confirm this by clicking the Show/Hide button of the Paragraph area of Microsoft Word Ribbon (the one that has the "¶" character paragraph mark, also known as *pilcrow*). This command will make Word show all possible hidden characters and breaks inserted in the document. Since the document is still empty you will see just one ¶ character, which indicates a single, blank paragraph inserted in the text (Figure 2-3).

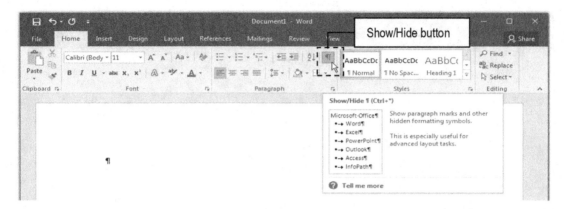

Figure 2-3. *This figure shows the ¶ (pilcrow) hidden paragraph character that exists in every Word blank document, as an indication that it has at least one single text paragraph. To show/hide such characters, click the Show/Hide button on the Paragraph area of the Ribbon again.*

Attention   From now on, I will refer to the Microsoft Word Ribbon just as "Ribbon."

Each of these three hidden characters has an importance inside any Microsoft Word document and will be discussed in the next sections of this chapter. But to really understand why they are important we first need to learn about another serious issue: paragraph formatting inheritance.

Paragraph Formatting Inheritance

For the sake of the next explanations, I will leave the Show/Hide button selected in next figures. Supposing that you are on the blank page of a new document, if you begin to type anything, the typed text will appear using the default Calibri, 11 pt, regular font. If you select the Bold formatting button in the Font area of the Ribbon and continue typing, everything after that will be bold formatted. Keeping the Bold option pressed and selecting the Italic formatting button, now everything will be bold and italic, until you deselect these attributes before typing anything again (Figure 2-4).

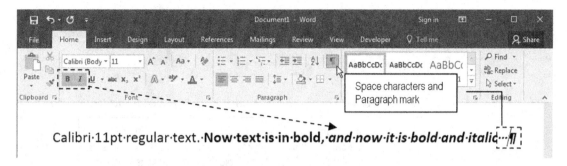

Figure 2-4. *Whenever you change any font properties, these properties will remain active for whatever you type, constituting the first inheritance level of any word processor*

This is the first word processor inheritance level: font properties. Whenever you apply a font property to the text, everything you type will continue to be formatted using such properties, until another set of properties is selected. Note in Figure 2-4 that when the Show/Hide option is selected, Microsoft Word also shows a second hidden character: the dot character "·", in the middle of the text line, for each space you typed with your keyboard space bar (I put a sequence of three space characters at the end of the text so you can see them).

When you press the Enter key and continue to type, you will realize that a new ¶ paragraph character will appear in the text, and that all precedent formatting attributes will be copied from the previous paragraph to this new one. This is the second level of inheritance: *each paragraph receives the same formatting options of its predecessor.*

Press the Enter key repeatedly to insert as many lines of text as you want, and note that Microsoft Word will add a new ¶ paragraph mark for each Enter key you press, each one inheriting the same formatting options of its predecessor (Figure 2-5).

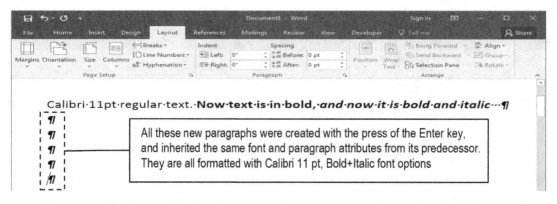

Figure 2-5. *Whenever you type the Enter key, a new hidden ¶ paragraph mark is inserted into the document, each one receiving by inheritance the same formatting options of its predecessor!*

And if you now uncheck the Show/Hide option of the Paragraph area of the Ribbon, you will see that all hidden characters (the ¶ paragraph marks and "·" characters for each space typed) disappear from the text view. They are all still there, but now you can't see them anymore (Figure 2-6).

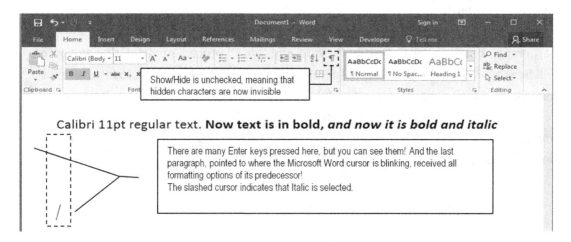

Figure 2-6. *After unchecking the Show/Hide button of Microsoft Word Paragraph area on the Ribbon, all hidden characters disappear from the user view! They are still there, but now are invisible!*

This very simple operation has a deep impact on Microsoft Word document behavior, because most people do not understand this *inheritance* in paragraph formatting or realize that each space character and Enter key continues to exist in the document, allowing some unexpected behaviors, since the current paragraph formatting is always copied to the next when an Enter key is pressed. Through the next sections, this book will explore this concept whenever possible, trying to explain why the user of Microsoft Word thinks that it works poorly when it doesn't.

Paragraph Formatting

Text paragraphs are the main component of any document, and Microsoft Word offers in the Font and Paragraph areas of the Home tab of the Ribbon many important controls as shortcuts to both the Font and Paragraph dialog box options. Among other things, you can control the font properties, alignment, line spacing, space before and after, and text flow. Figure 2-7 shows the main Paragraph controls that will be detailed in the next sections (Font controls will be analyzed in Chapter 3).

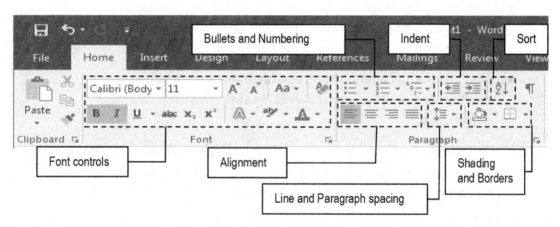

Figure 2-7. *The Paragraph area of the Home tab with its many paragraph controls*

Text Alignment

Alignment controls how each text paragraph aligns to the page margin, and just as any other text processor, Microsoft Word allows a choice between Left, Center, Right, and Justify alignments. The correct use of text alignment is a matter more of taste than of science, but it's necessary to follow some simple rules if you want your documents to look better and to be as legible as possible.

Although there is no scientific research to sustain this argument, most typographers believe that reading is improved when the correct alignment is used, so follow these simple principles:

- A "ragged" edge happens at the right of a Left alignment, at left of a Right alignment, and at left and right of a Center alignment. It is referring to the undulating shapes created by the white space along the opposite side of text alignment.

- Center alignment has double ragged edges (at left and right) that impede reading speed and comprehension.

- Use Center alignment just for chapter titles that begin on a new document page, or to present the author name that may appear right before or after the document title.

- Don't use Center alignment on document section titles, because the reader may lose them when reading. Section titles must be always Left aligned.

- The straight (or "hard") left edge and ragged right edge combination of standard Left alignment tends to performs best for readers because it helps the eye find the start of the next line when it leaves the end of the last one.

- Use Right alignment just on special paragraphs (like signatures or citation credits).

- The effect of full-justified text—which produces straight left and right edges of a text block—results in uneven space between words, which may be harder to read: the uniform shape of the justified paragraph block makes it easier for the eye to get lost when returning from the end of one line to the start of another.

- Justify alignment works best on multicolumn layouts, because small-width columns don't make the reader lose the position of the next line.

- Long documents with Justify alignment (like books) may feel boring and tiring to read, and that is why some desktop publishers choose Left alignment in textbooks to improve text readability.

- Justify alignment may be used when the audience is mainly composed of people that are acquainted with it, like lawyers, teachers, and so on.

Attention   I will issue my opinion here. I personally dislike Justify alignment, and unless it is mandatory, I do not use it in anything I produce. As I said before, it is a matter of taste.

Now that you have some clues about how to use text alignment, let's give more attention to Justify alignment because sometimes it may be a source of unexpected Microsoft Word behavior.

Justify Alignment

Although it is not recommended in long text documents, Justify alignment is the most frequently desired paragraph attributes, where all paragraph text lines but the last are perfectly aligned to the left and right page margins. When you ask Microsoft Word to Justify any text paragraph, its inner algorithm does something like this:

1. Count the number of words found in each line of text.

2. Count the number of character spaces need to stretch the line to the right text margin.

3. Divide the number of character spaces by the number of words minus 1, to know how many spaces must be inserted between each word.

4. Insert extra spaces between each word but the last, making the text left and right aligned, or in a word, justified!

Figure 2-8 shows the first paragraph of James Fenimore Cooper's *The Last of the Mohicans* using two different alignments: Left and Justify. It uses a Microsoft Word document page with the Show/Hide button checked, with the text formatted using the default Calibri 11 pt font, and 160% zoom so you can best understand what happened to the text. The "·" characters you see between the words are the spaces typed to separate them.

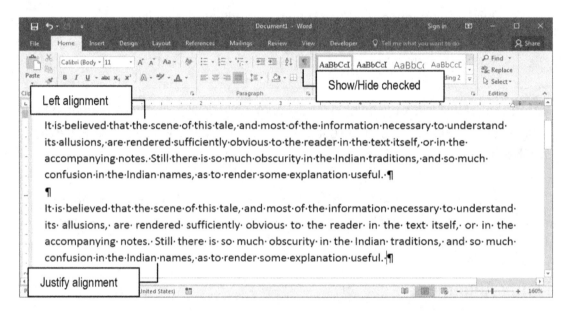

Figure 2-8. *Two versions of the same paragraph: the first is left aligned, the second justified. The Microsoft Word Show/Hide option is checked and the zoom is 160%.*

Look at the second Justify alignment paragraph of Figure 2-8 and note that its second and third lines received extra spaces between its words to guarantee that they were equally separated, so the first and last word of each line are perfectly left and right aligned to the page margins.

Also note that Microsoft Word did not insert any hidden characters to Justify the text: justification was made by using a kind of "empty space" between the words, so they become harmonically separated in each line of text (Figure 2-9 gives a bigger zoom to the justified paragraph so you can better appreciate the justifying effect).

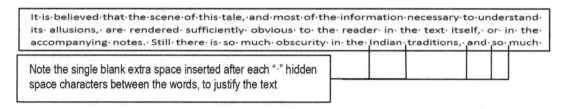

It·is·believed·that·the·scene·of·this·tale,·and·most·of·the·information·necessary·to·understand·
its· allusions,· are· rendered· sufficiently· obvious· to· the· reader· in· the· text· itself,· or· in· the·
accompanying· notes.· Still· there· is· so· much· obscurity· in· the· Indian· traditions,· and· so· much·

Note the single blank extra space inserted after each "·" hidden
space characters between the words, to justify the text

Figure 2-9. *Microsoft Word inserts empty spaces (not hidden characters) to further separate the words of each text line, so it can Justify any text paragraph!*

If the justified paragraph has many words, the effect may be quite good. But if it hasn't, which happens in special cases—like in text using column layout with narrow columns, or when there are other special hidden characters inserted in the text—the effect may be very surprising. This is especially true when the text has Manual line break characters.

Manual Line Break

Besides the fact that you can press the Enter key to insert a new document paragraph, or in typographic words "insert a paragraph break," sometimes you may want to (or inadvertently) break a line inside a paragraph without inserting a new ¶ pilcrow hidden paragraph mark in the text. This kind of operation is typographically called a "Manual Line Break," and Microsoft Word does this by inserting the hidden Manual line break character ↵ whenever you press Shift+Enter.

Attention   From now on, every time you see the "+" character concatenating two or more keys to be pressed, it means that you should keep pressing the first one(s) and then press the next. In this case, press and hold Shift and then press Enter once.

We can insert a line break in the middle of the second line of the same justified paragraph used in the last example by simply pressing Shift+Enter after the word "obvious." Figure 2-10 shows what happens to the justified text after the insertion of such Manual line break character.

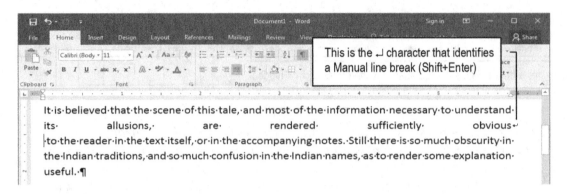

Figure 2-10. *Justified paragraph after the insertion of a Manual line break character (↵) in the middle of its second text line (after the word "obvious")*

Did you notice how spaced words become in the second text line after the insertion of the ↵ Manual break line? Using the rule stated in the last section, Microsoft Word counted the words, counted the number of space characters needed to get to the right margin, and put these equal blank space characters between each word, so the first and last word of the second line become perfectly spaced—or in typographic jargon, justified.

This is very relevant, because if you have a single ↵ Manual line break character inserted in a single justified paragraph and begin to type anything in this paragraph without being aware of this situation, Microsoft Word may present you with very odd behavior.

Figure 2-11 shows what happens in such cases (note that hidden characters are shown). When the two words "Demystifying Word" are typed in the first line of the justified paragraph that has a Manual line break, Microsoft Word tries to equally space the two words, make them bounce around on the screen, putting the first left aligned and the second (and last) word, right aligned!

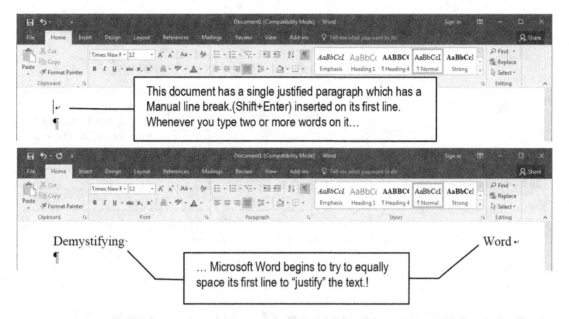

Figure 2-11. *Whenever an empty justified paragraph has a Manual line break as its first character, Microsoft Word will try to Justify each typed word, making them bounce around the screen as you type them!*

Do you get it? Now, imagine the very moments when this happens without any knowledge about these possibilities and being unaware of such hidden characters.

Attention   In my experience, orienting university students to produce technical articles, it is quite common to see sequential Manual line break characters separating each text line inside a paragraph as a proof that the text was copied from Internet web sites or Adobe Acrobat PDF files. So, that is the truth: whenever you click Show/Hide command to show hidden characters and find Manual line breaks separating text lines, it came from the Internet or another source of electronic information.

Too easy to find cheating!

Microsoft Word offers the "File ➤ Options ➤ Advanced ➤ Layout options for <document name>, Don't expand character spaces on a line that ends with Shift+Enter" option to avoid expanding a justified paragraph that has a Manual line break character created by pressing Shift+Enter (Figure 2-12).

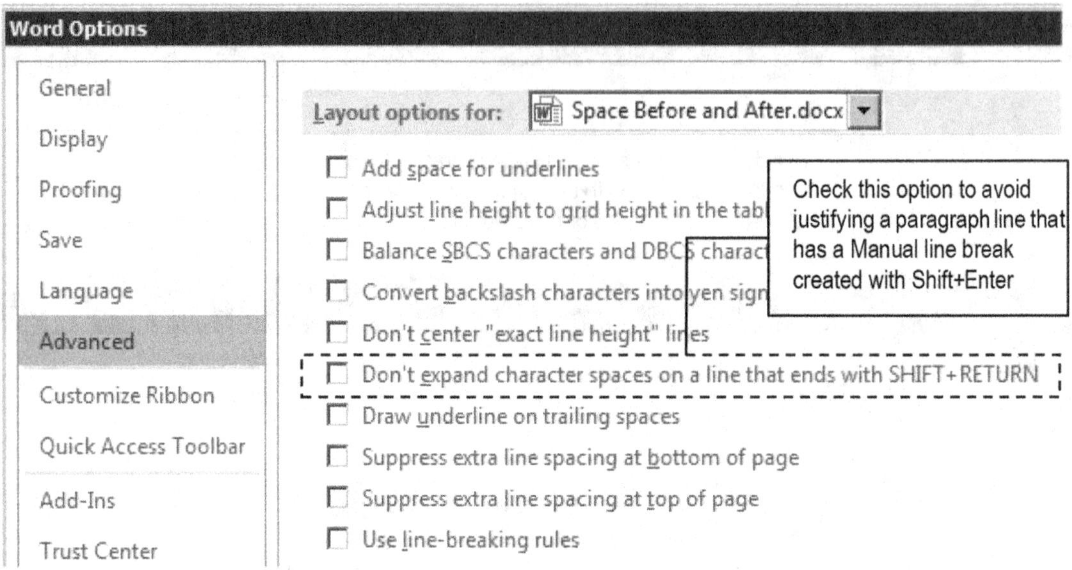

Figure 2-12. *Check the File ➤ Options ➤ Advanced ➤ Layout options for <document name>. Don't expand character spaces on a line that ends with Shift+Return option, to avoid justifying a line that has a Manual line break created with Shift+Enter in a justified paragraph.*

Other Paragraph Attributes

Besides alignment, every paragraph has many different attributes related to a typographic issue. To fully understand them, it is needed to understand some basic typography concepts.

Baseline, Descender and Ascender Lines

Every Font obeys typography rules when it draws its letters, and Microsoft Word uses such rules to implement control over characters and paragraphs you type in the document.

Figure 2-13 shows how the characters are built inside a Font based on five imaginary straight lines.

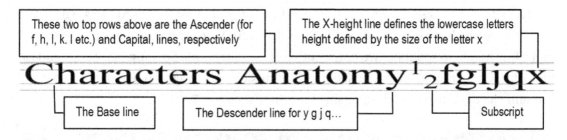

Figure 2-13. *The anatomy of all characters in a Font obeys some typographical principles that determine the size of its lowercase and uppercase letters, and the appearance of some special letters that have ascenders (like f, h, k, and t) or descenders (like g, j, p, and q).*

- **Baseline**: the lines where all characters lie down.

- **X-height**: right above the baseline, defines the size of the lowercase letters by the size of the "x" letter.

- **Capital line**: above the x-height line; defines the size of uppercase letters (which is not always the same height as the ascender).

- **Ascender line**: next above the Capital line; defines the size of ascenders, a vertical stroke that extends above the x-height line for some lowercase letters, like b, f, h, and t.

- **Descender line**: defines the size of descenders, which are vertical strokes or tails that hang below the baseline for some lowercase letters, like g, j, p, and q.

Keeping in mind that such font attributes are fixed to each font (like Calibri, Times New Roman, or Arial), let us examine how they affect the way Microsoft Word works by exploring some paragraph attributes.

Line Spacing

Line spacing, typographically called *leading*, is the space that Microsoft Word uses to separate the current line of text from the previous inside the same or different paragraphs. Line spacing = 1 is typographically defined as *120% the size of the greatest font used in a single line.* Or more specifically, it calculates 20% of the height between the Ascender and Descender lines for current text line and uses this space to separate it from the previous text line of text.

Note that I italicized the words "120% the size of the greatest font used in a single line"!

This means that when you use Line Spacing = 1.5, Word adds 50% more space, or half a line height to separate two consecutive lines. When Line Spacing = 2, Words adds a blank line between every two consecutive lines inside the paragraph. Figure 2-14 shows the same justified text paragraph, using Line Spacing = 1, 1.5, and 2.

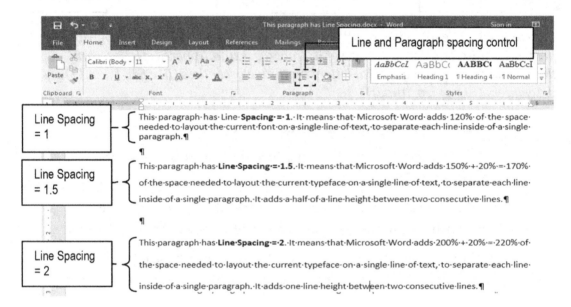

Figure 2-14. *Line spacing 1, 1.5, and 2 applied to the same paragraph to insert space between paragraph text lines*

Since I told you that the Line spacing control is granted regarding 120% of the greatest font size used in a single line, Figure 2-15 shows what happens to a text paragraph using Line spacing = 1 and that has just one of its characters with a greater size! Just the selected "t" letter has font Calibri, 24, while all other characters of the entire paragraph has font Calibri, 11.

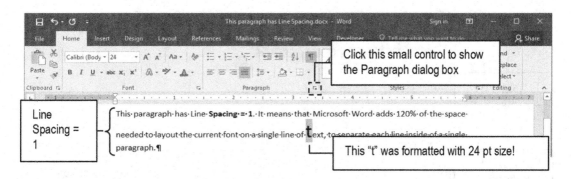

Figure 2-15. *This figure shows that Microsoft Word uses the 120% rule based on the largest font size found in any single character (the selected "t," formatted with a 24 pt size), to define what is considered as Line spacing = 1, to separate the second line of text from the first*

Attention   Regarding Line spacing, the opposite is also true: if **all characters** of an entire line of text have a font size smaller than the paragraph font size, this line spacing will be smaller than the others.

This odd behavior always happens when you insert some small image as a character inside any text line, or use a different font type to define the appearance of a single character. In case that you are wondering if different fonts of the same size occupy the same vertical space: the answer is yes, they do. Calibri 12 seems to be greater than Times New Roman 12 because its X-height line is at an upper position, but they have the same height distance between their Ascender and Descender lines for a 12 pt size.

Microsoft Word allows precise control over the Line spacing applied to each paragraph using the Paragraph dialog box, which can be selected in three ways:

1. Click the Line and Paragraph Spacing control in the Paragraph area of the Home tab and select the Line Spacing Options...; or

2. Click the very small square at the bottom right of the Paragraph area of the Home tab of Word Ribbon (see Figure 2-15); or

3. Right-click the desired paragraph and select Paragraph... in the context menu.

You will receive the traditional Microsoft Word Paragraph dialog box, which is quite the same since Word 2000 or even older versions (Figure 2-16).

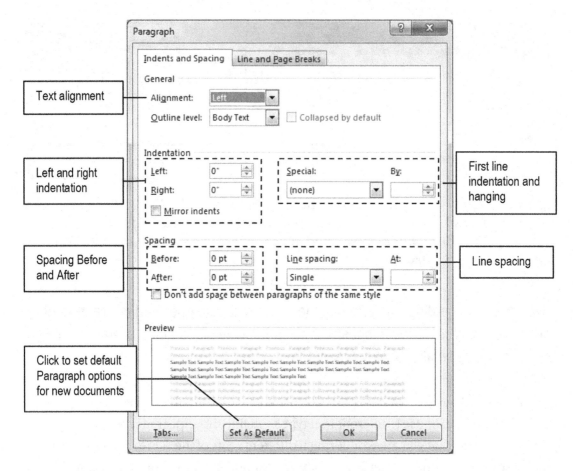

Figure 2-16. *Microsoft Word Paragraph dialog box*

In the General area at the top of the Paragraph box you find the Alignment control (to allow selecting the left, center, right, or Justify alignments), and the Outline level (which will be explained in the "Outline Level" section of Chapter 7). In the Spacing area, you will find the Line spacing control, which offers these options:

- **Single**, **1.5 lines, and Double**: Applies Line spaces 1, 1.5, and 2, respectively.

- **At least**: Does not allow that line spacing to go below the specified level, even when font size is smaller.

- **Exactly**: Keeps line spacing at an exact size, not increasing it whenever one or more characters inserted in the text receive a bigger font size than that specified for the entire paragraph. When selecting this option, the upper part of such bigger characters may be missing in the line they reside.

- **Multiple**: Allows selecting any line space you want (besides 1, 1.5, or 2), using real values with one-decimal precision (like Line spacing = 3 or 1.7).

If we apply Line spacing = Exactly = 11 pt to the paragraph shown in Figure 2-15, with the big 24 pt "t" inside a paragraph formatted with Calibri 11 pt size, this big letter will lose its vertical stroke, while all paragraph lines will receive Line spacing = 1 (Figure 2-17).

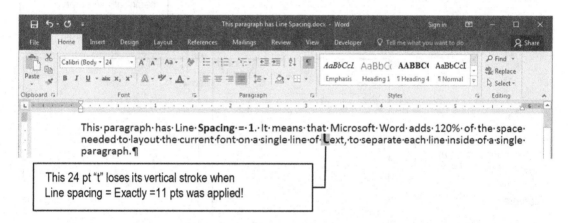

Figure 2-17. *Microsoft Word allows you to apply a permanent line spacing using the Exactly option, which will define a precise amount of line spacing, independently of the characters size found in each text line. In such cases, the bigger characters may lose their vertical strokes.*

Attention   As you may note in the last example, Line space = 1 is equal to Line Space = Exactly = 11 pt for a paragraph formatted with 11 pt size. In other words:

Line spacing = Line spacing Exactly in pt ÷ Font size in pt.

By applying a Line Spacing = Exactly = 18 pt for a 12 pt font paragraph, you will apply Line spacing = 18 ÷ 12 = 1.5.

As you might be wondering, current line spacing is also inherited by the next paragraph when you press Enter.

Space Before and After Paragraphs

Many people have the (strange) habit of pressing Enter twice at the end of each paragraph to insert an empty row of the same line spacing between two consecutive paragraphs, as a visual clue to show where one paragraph ends and the other begins.

When they do this they also insert a pair of hidden paragraph characters preventing Microsoft Word from precisely controlling the text flow between document pages, because this extra empty paragraph may become the first paragraph of the next page displacing the text from the top margin (Figure 2-18).

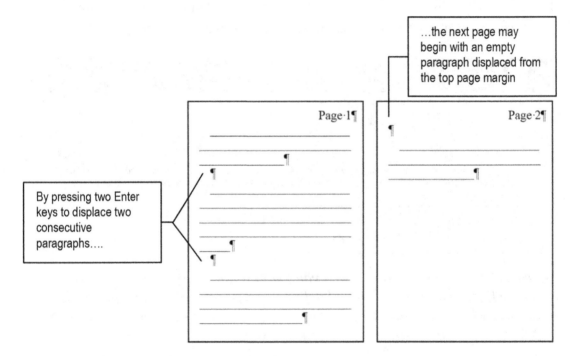

Figure 2-18. *By using two consecutive Enter keys to insert a white space between two consecutive paragraphs, the document may get pages where the first paragraph is an empty text row, displacing the text from the top margin by the current line spacing.*

As a rule of thumb, **never type two Enters** to separate text paragraphs. Instead, use the Before and After options of the Paragraph dialog box shown in Figure 2-16, or the Before and After options of the Spacing area of the Layout tab on the Ribbon, shown in Figure 2-19.

- Use the Space Before to separate the current paragraph from the previous. It is most used to displace special paragraphs like section, figure, or table titles from the previous paragraph in the document text (also called body text).

- Use the Space After to separate the current paragraph from the next. It is most used to displace the document text paragraphs (body text) whenever the text doesn't use indentation in its first row.

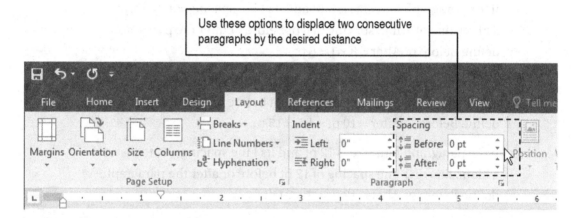

Figure 2-19. *Use the Spacing ➤ Before and After options of the Layout tab to displace characters by specific values, instead of pressing Enter key two or more times to create such white space*

You can define the After and/or Before spacing options using different measuring units by specifying the desired suffix:

- By using single real numbers without a unit suffix the Before and After options are specified in points.

- Use 1 in to define it in inches;

- Use 1 cm to define it in centimeters (1 inch equals 2.54 cm).

- Use 12 pt to define it in typographic Point units.

Attention   A point is defined as 1/72 of an inch (about 0.353 mm), or 1/12 of a pica (another common typographic measure).

Whichever the unit you use, Microsoft Word will always convert Spacing Before and After values to typographic points units and show it accordingly, and since spacing Before and After are paragraph properties, they will be inherited by the next paragraph whenever you press Enter.

To guarantee that the Before and After spacing options are proportional to the Line spacing used by the paragraph, set them with the same paragraph point size multiplied by the Line spacing used on it.

Let me explain better:

- If the paragraph font size is 8 pt and its Line spacing = 1, to insert a blank line of 1-line spacing of 8 pt before or after the paragraph, define Before or After = 8 × 1 = 8 pt.

- If the paragraph font size is 10 pt and its Line spacing = 1.5, to insert a blank line of 1.5-line spacing of 10 pt before or after the paragraph, define Before or After = 10 pt × 1.5 = 15 pt.

- If the paragraph font size is 12 pt and its Line spacing = 2, to insert a blank line of 2-line spacing of 12 pt before or after the paragraph, define Before or After = 12 pt × 2 = 24 pt.

Do you get it?

Attention   The rule of thumb is as follows: To insert an empty line before or after the current paragraph, the Spacing Before or After options must be proportional:

Paragraph font size × Line spacing

Figure 2-20 shows how any Microsoft Word document uses the Before and After Space options to displace text paragraphs from its neighbors.

How Microsoft Word Implements Paragraph Spacing

Giving closer attention to Figure 2-20, you will realize that Microsoft Word doesn't use both the Space After and Before options to displace two consecutive paragraphs.

The third paragraph of this figure (the "New Section Title (16 pt, Line spacing = 1, Before = After = 16pt)" paragraph that uses bold characters) is displaced by just 16 pt from the previous paragraph (the "New paragraph (inherited from previous)" which has the Space After = 12 pt option).

By the typographic rule of paragraph spacing we expect that it will be spaced by 28 pt from its predecessor: 12 pt from the Space After option of the precedent paragraph plus 16 pt from the Space Before of this paragraph.

But it isn't.

Since Microsoft Office 2003, Microsoft Word has begun to philosophically implement the Space paragraph options to displace the current paragraph from its neighbors. I think they had a great discussion to take this decision, which seems to work this way:

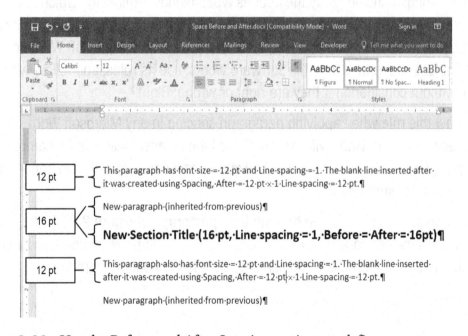

Figure 2-20. *Use the Before and After Spacing options to define an extra space that must exist before or after any text paragraph, so it can be visually separated from the previous or next paragraph without pressing the Enter key extra times*

To displace two successive paragraphs where one employs the Space After option and the other employs the Space Before option (vice versa), use the greatest values of both options.

Using this thought, Microsoft Word acts philosophically correct, since it uses the greatest defined space (after or before) to space two successive paragraphs, to guarantee that the greatest space is always used.

But from the objective point of view, Microsoft Word fails to be precise: instead of using the options defined by the user, it "thinks" which is the best and then applies it.

Attention   I researched this with other popular word processors. Corel WordPerfect does not have options to define Space Before and After paragraphs. The word processors of the free software LibreOffice and OpenOffice, like the professional desktop publishing software QuarkXPress and PageMaker, are very objective: they sum the Space After and Before options to displace two consecutive paragraphs.

From my programmer point of view (I am again issuing an opinion here) Microsoft Word is wrong: it should apply the options typed without "thinking" which is the best, or have a clear option to not add space before and/or after for two successive paragraphs when their values are equal . But since this is a Microsoft Word book, we must just understand how the software works, use its rules, and follow with them, without considering if they are right or wrong. Right?

So, follow this rule when applying paragraph spacing in any Microsoft Word document: Microsoft Word will always discard the smallest value when comparing the Space After and Space Before of two successive paragraph. If both options are equal, it will not sum them.

Let's be practical: to guarantee that the third paragraph of Figure 2-20 is 28 points spaced from the previous one, define Space Before = 28 pt (Microsoft Word will discard the Space After=12 pt implemented in the previous paragraph).

To avoid that the first paragraph spacing problem shown in Figure 2-17 happens when the text flows between two successive pages, Microsoft Word offers in the "File ➤ Options ➤ Advanced ➤ Layout options for <document name>" options, the "Suppress extra line spacing at bottom of Page" and "Suppress extra line spacing at top of page" options. Check both to guarantee a perfect text flow for body text paragraphs that implement the Space Before and After options (Figure 2-21).

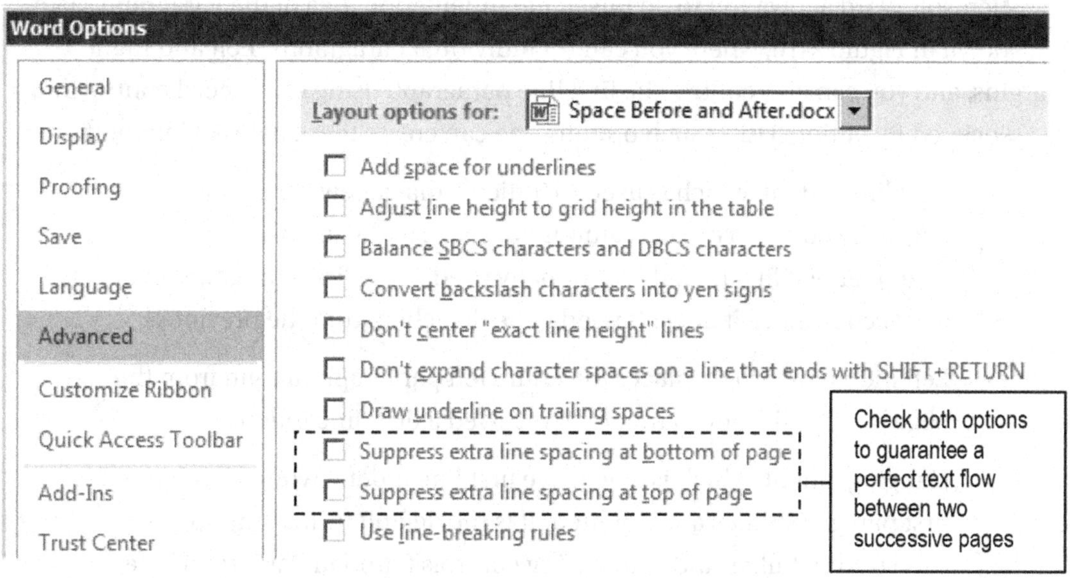

Figure 2-21. *Use Microsoft Word File ➤ Options ➤ Advanced ➤ Layout options for <document name> > Suppress extra line spacing at bottom of page and/or Supress extra line spacing at top of page options to guarantee a perfect text flow between document pages whose body text implements the Space Before and After options*

Attention   Although Microsoft Word offers these two options for suppressing extra line spacing at the bottom or top of a page, it seems to me that it really does not implement such space when the page breaks, so both options seem to be unnecessary.

Paragraph Indentation

Every printed page has a predefined margin that defines where the text of the document will appear on the page, but on a full text page we may eventually need to indicate where each paragraph begins by adding an extra space in it first line, creating what is called a *First line indent*. Other times we must give an emphasis to some special text paragraphs from the body text by detaching then from the page left and/or right margins.

Microsoft Word allows you to do this in the Indentation area of the Paragraph dialog box shown in Figure 2-16, where you can set individual paragraphs' Left and Right margins, and you can also control the first line paragraph using the Special control and its associated By option. Using such options one can create these types of indentations:

- First line indent, which is used to indicate that a new paragraph begins by adding a defined amount of space to the left of the first character of it first line. It is optionally used in the first paragraph of any section since it doesn't need to be detached from the previous.

- Left indent, which displaces the entire left paragraph margin from the page left margin—even though it received a First line indent.

- Hanging indent, which is a negative first line indent, when all but the first paragraph lines are indented. It is the default formatting style used by the Bullets and Numbering controls found in Paragraph area of the Home tab of the Ribbon.

- Right margin indent, which displaces the entire paragraph right margin from the page right margin.

Attention   As a good formatting practice, choose just one effect to signal the beginning of a new paragraph: Paragraph spacing or First line indent. Don't use both!

The English version of Microsoft Word uses inches to define the Indentation options found in the Paragraph dialog box (Figure 2-16) and in the Layout tab of the Ribbon (Figure 2-19), but you can change this default measurement unit to centimeters, millimeters, points, or picas using the Show measurement option, found in the Display area of the Advanced dialog box, which you can show using the File ➤ Options ➤ Advanced command (Figure 2-22).

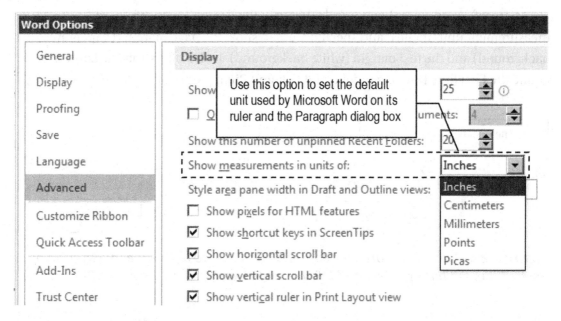

Figure 2-22. *Microsoft Word allows defining the desired unit to be used in its ruler and the many Paragraph dialog box options using the option File ➤ Options ➤ Advanced ➤ Display ➤ Show measurement units.*

Showing and Using the Ruler

Since it may be difficult for most of us to *think* in terms of inch values to define the desired paragraph indentation, Microsoft Word offers a horizontal ruler that is hidden by default in its interface and can be set to visible by checking the Ruler option in the Show area of the View tab of the Ribbon (Figure 2-23).

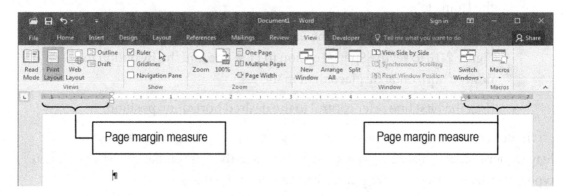

Figure 2-23. *Check the Ruler option in the Show area of the View tab to make Microsoft Word display a horizontal ruler with a scale that uses the application default unit measure.*

Microsoft Word ruler shows a scale that uses the default Microsoft Word measurement unit (inches) and specific areas to show the page margins (dark gray background) and the text margin (white background). It also offers specific controls to define the First line, Hanging indent, and Left and Right paragraph indent (Figure 2-24).

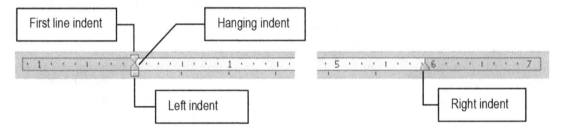

Figure 2-24. *Microsoft Word rule controls allow you to define the indentation of the first line, all but first line, and left and right margin*

Apply Paragraph Indentation

Most people employ one of these two bad habits to indent the first paragraph line to signal that a new paragraph begins:

1. Type a defined number of spaces (4 to 6 spaces); or

2. Type a Tab character.

Never do that. To apply a First line indent to any text paragraph you can

- use one of the default five options exposed in the Paragraph area of the Home tab.

- use the Indentation area of the Paragraph dialog box shown in Figure 2-16 to set the Special option to First line and the By option to desired horizontal displacement in inches.

- drag the First line ruler control to the desired horizontal position.

In both cases, whenever the paragraph has the appropriate indentation, you may leave inheritance to take care of copying its format to the next paragraph whenever you type Enter to create a new paragraph with the same indentation.

Default Indentation Options

Microsoft Word has five default options in the Paragraph option of the Home tab of the Ribbon to allow insert an indent in any paragraph: Bullets, Numbering, Multilevel List, Decrease indent, and Increase indent (Figures 2-7 and 2-25).

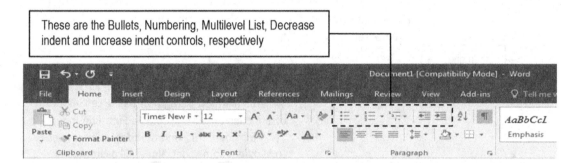

Figure 2-25. *Microsoft Word offers the Bullets, Numbering, Multilevel List, Decrease indent, and Increase indent controls in the Paragraph area of the Home tab. They may change the Left, Right, Special, and By options found in the Indentation area of the Paragraph dialog box reflecting on the position of associated ruler controls.*

Each one may change the Left, Right, Special, and By options of the Indentation area of the Paragraph dialog box shown in Figure 2-16 (or the Indent Left and Right options of the Paragraph area of the Layout tab of the Ribbon, shown in Figure 2-19). The Bullets, Numbering, and Multilevel list controls automatically create a hanging indent in the paragraph, while the Decrease and Increase indent changes the Left Indentation option of the paragraph (for further tips about this issue, see section "Bullets and Numbering" later on in this chapter).

Figure 2-26 shows many different paragraph indentations produced by dragging Microsoft Word ruler controls to specific positions (as you drag any of the ruler controls, Word will show a vertical dashed line to allow precise text alignments), or by using the Numbering tool.

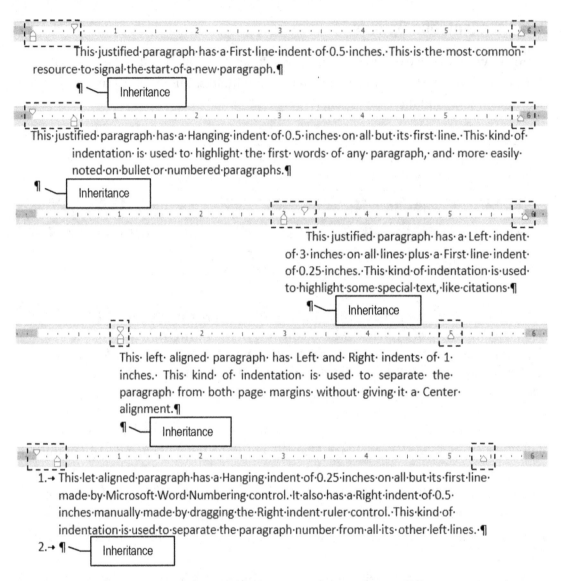

Figure 2-26. *Drag Microsoft Word ruler controls to achieve different types of text formation. You can left indent just the first line, all lines but the first, or all left or right lines. When you press Enter, the next paragraph will inherit all these format options!*

Attention   After each paragraph had been indented, an Enter key was pressed to create a new, identically formatted paragraph, so you can better appreciate inheritance in action. The *pilcrow* ¶ character that represents the inherited paragraph is always right under the ruler First line indent control for the paragraph that precedes it.

Although is quite easy to drag the ruler controls to achieve a desired effect, it may be difficult to use Microsoft Word default inches unit to make the same adjustments in the Paragraph dialog box controls (or in the associated controls of the Paragraph, Indentation options of the Layout tab).

For example, the last numbered text paragraph of Figure 2-26 (the one with a hanging indent produced by Microsoft Word Numbering control) received the values shown in Figure 2-27. Quite complex to consider such numbers without any typographic knowledge, isn't it?

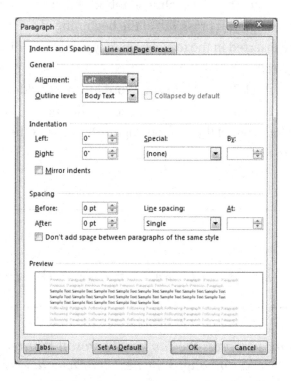

Figure 2-27.   *You can easily implement the Autonumber feature by a click of a mouse; define these values in Microsoft Word Paragraph dialog box: Special = Hanging, By = 0.25.*

Paragraph Tabulation

Most of you that are reading me now may never have used a typewriter machine to produce a page of text. This old technology has a special way to easily allow the creation of tables on a printed page using three special keys:

- an "Add tabulation" key that allowed to define specific horizontal page positions on the paper;

- a "Tabulator" key that makes the typewriter carriage to fast jump to the next tabulated position;

- a "Clean up tabulations" key to redefine the tabulation positions.

It is interesting that although many people used the typewriter, most of them were unaware how to use these three keys to produce tables. That is why the first computers produced received a Tab (Tabulator) key right above the All Caps key: it was to mimic the old typewriter keyboard, and smooth the transition from one technology to another.

Most interesting is the fact that today almost nobody knows the usefulness of the Tab key. They just know that when you press Tab at the beginning of a new paragraph, a fixed amount of space will be inserted in the text, which may vary depending on the horizontal position where it is inserted.

Every time you press the Tab key, Microsoft Word inserts a hidden → (Tab character): the right arrow that you see in text whenever you check the Show/Hide option of the Paragraph area in the Home tab of the Ribbon. Figure 2-28 shows the insertion of five tab characters and numbers 1 to 5 after each tab.

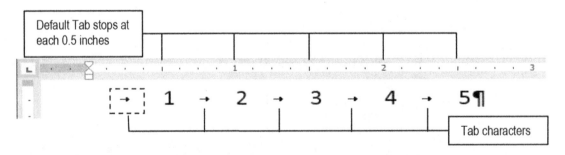

Figure 2-28. *Every time you press the Tab key, Microsoft Word inserts a hidden "→" tab character in the text and aligns the next character at each 0.5-inch position on the ruler.*

Attention   If Word doesn't insert a Tab key at the beginning of any paragraph—displacing its First line indent control instead—press Ctrl+Tab to do it!

Note how the → Tab characters force these numbers to be perfectly left align below the respective 0.5, 1.0, 1.5, 2.0, and 2.5 inch positions of the ruler. This behavior is because Microsoft Word is factory defined to space each Tab stop by 0.5 inches in the horizontal position.

You can check or change the default tab position by clicking the Tabs button located at the bottom right of the Paragraph dialog and inspecting the Default tabs option (Figure 2-29).

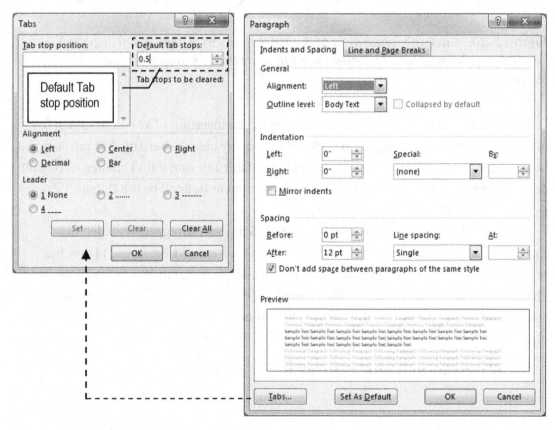

Figure 2-29. *This is the Tabs dialog box, where the Default Tab stop option is factory set to 0.5 inches*

Besides the default Tab stops, you can set the horizontal rule position (and type) of each Tab stop to wherever you want just by clicking the white area of the ruler. When you click, Microsoft Word will insert a Tab stop character of the tab type selected at the right of the ruler, and will horizontally displace all the remaining text in the same row. Figure 2-30 shows what happened to the numbers' positions in the text when a left default Tab stop was inserted in the ruler at about 0.75 inches.

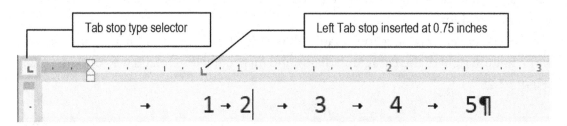

Figure 2-30. *Click the white area of the ruler to insert a default left Tab stop. Note how the text is horizontally repositioned to obey the Tab stop position and tab character order.*

Note that number 1, which was left aligned by the insertion of a Left tab stop at 0.5 inch position, is now left aligned at 0.75 inches, exactly below where the left Tab stop was inserted in the ruler. Also note that every other default Tab stop didn't change its default position, being exactly below each 0.5 inch increment as defined by the Default Tab stops value (at 1.0, 1.5, 2.0, and 2.5 inches).

If the first Left Tab stop now positioned at 0.75 inches is dragged to the left or right, the number character that is at the left of this Tab stop (the number 1) may be repositioned on the screen, eventually displacing all the remaining text of this row. Figure 2-31 shows what happens when the 0.75 inch Left Tab stop shown in Figure 2-30 was moved to 1.5 inches: all other tab aligned numbers were also right displaced to the next default Tab stop position on the ruler (at 2, 2.5, 3, and 3.5 inches).

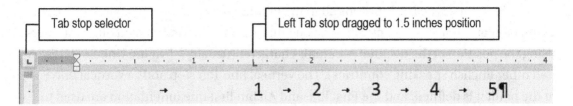

Figure 2-31. *When you drag any Tab stop along the ruler, all printed characters to its left that are preceded by hidden tab characters have their position affected. This figure shows the effect of dragging the left Tab stop to the 1.5-inch position.*

Attention   You can also insert Tab stops at a specific horizontal position of the page by double-clicking anywhere on the page's white space. The selected type of Tab stop will be inserted in the ruler. Press Esc or Ctrl+Z to undo such operation.

Types of Tab Stops

Microsoft Word has seven types of Tab stops, according to what is selected in the Tab stop selector located at the left of the ruler, out of the page borders (see Figure 2-32). Every time you click this tab selector it changes its icon, cyclically returning to the default Left Tab stop. You can select the types of Tab stops shown in Figure 2-32.

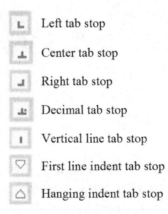

Figure 2-32. *Microsoft Word Tab stop types defined when you click the Tab stop selector at the right of the ruler*

The first three types of Tab stops align the tabulated text to the left, center, and right of the tabulation mark, respectively. The decimal Tab stop is used to right align numbers using the position of the decimal separator character (usually "." in the United States and other English speaking countries). The vertical line Tab stop adds a vertical line at the point it is defined, and the First line and All but first line indentation are used to click the ruler to reposition the associated ruler controls (they have the same effect of dragging the First line or All but first line rule controls on the rule). Figure 2-33 shows how these different Tab stops impact on the tabulated.

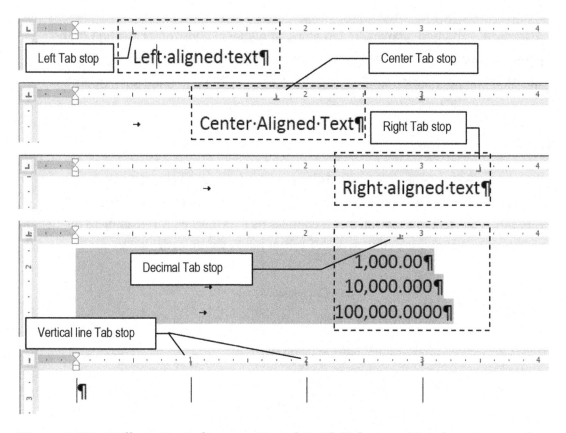

Figure 2-33. *Different text alignments made with Tab stops. Note how text can be aligned to the left, center, or right of a Tab stop, and how numbers can be perfectly aligned to its decimal character separator.*

All those Tab stops were created to allow the design of precise tables, which was fully surpassed by Microsoft Word Tables capability (see next section). And now that you have some basic understanding about how Tab stops work, just follow this very simple rule:

NEVER type two successive tab characters. One is always enough since you set a Tab stop at the appro priate position on the ruler**.**

Attention   Note that when you add a Center aligned Tab stop, type a Tab character to put the cursor down the Tab stop and type anything; the text will be center distributed as you type. Conversely, when you add a Right aligned Tab stop and type some text, the text will grow to the left and keep aligning its last character to the right Tab stop position.

Precise Text Alignment with Tab Stops

Have you ever tried to align different text columns on the screen using spaces to perfectly separate them, only to note that they later became totally misaligned when printed?

This happens due to the different horizontal spaces used by different characters implemented by the Microsoft Windows installed fonts (we will see more about Fonts in Chapter 3).

Most modern computer fonts are "proportionally spaced," which means that each character occupies just the space it needs, while the typewriter font (and some special Windows fonts) are "mono spaced": each character occupies the same horizontal space.

On proportionally spaced fonts, the "l" (L lowercase) and "i" characters are the narrowest ones, and the "M" (uppercase) is the largest; the space character occupies its own horizontal space. Since different rows has different letters and space characters, you can't separate words using a defined amount of space characters and expect that they will be correctly aligned when printed!

This is the best utility for Tab stops: to perfectly align text columns in different paragraphs. Note that thanks to inheritance, you can put many different Tab stops at specific positions and produce new, identical paragraphs with the same Tab stops just by pressing the Enter key.

Let's suppose you want to create a three-column text to produce a basic table to correctly align text and numbers. The first column begins at the left paragraph margin and does not need a Tab stop (is Left aligned by default). The second column begins at 2 inches and is also Left aligned. The third column begins at 4 inches and is where numbers of different magnitudes are to be typed, perfectly aligned to their decimal points. Figure 2-34 shows how this basic paragraph alignment can be defined in Microsoft Word ruler using Tab stops.

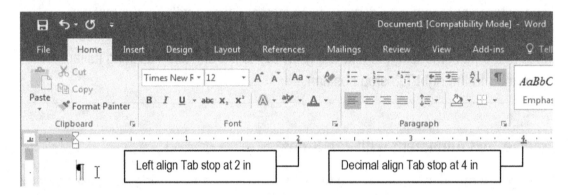

Figure 2-34. *A simple paragraph with two Tab stops: a left Tab stop at 2 in and a decimal Tab stop at 4 in*

Follow these instructions as a simple exercise:

1. Type any word at the beginning of the paragraph.

2. Press tab to jump to 2 inches (first Tab stop) and type another word.

3. Press tab again (second Tab stop) and type a number.

4. Press Enter and repeat steps 1 to 3 to insert two other perfectly aligned text rows.

Figure 2-35 shows how this simple exercise must appear in my Microsoft Word interface. Note that all three rows of text were perfectly aligned at left margin, at 2 inches and 4 inches on the ruler and will surely print as you see them on the screen!

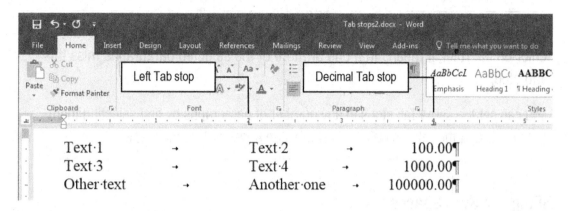

Figure 2-35. *Text aligned by different tab stops attributed to the first paragraph and copied to the next by inheritance when Enter is pressed*

Also note that there is just one Tab key pressed between each text column, and that the text precisely aligns with the next Tab stop position. And you want to change the position of a Tab stop of many paragraphs at once, you must first select them and then drag the desired Tab stop to a new position on the ruler. The text of all selected paragraphs will immediately be repositioned on the screen (Figure 2-36).

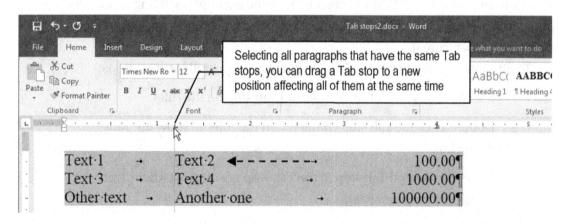

Figure 2-36. *Select all paragraphs with the same Tab stops and drag a Tab stop to easily reposition any text column aligned to it*

Attention   If the selected paragraphs have one or more Tab stops with a fade color on the ruler, it means that one or more of the selected paragraphs miss this Tab stop.

You can set the same Tab stops to any number of paragraphs by first selecting them before clicking the ruler to define each Tab stop horizontal position type.

Filling Tab Stop Spaces

Chances are that you may need to insert trailer characters (like dots or underscores) as visual clues to associate text with numbers in the same text row, to create the common text formatting we see in some accounting tables or in any book's analytical index.

If you ever did it, you probably noticed that although the page numbers seem to be perfectly aligned on the screen they don't aligned well on the printed page.

You should NEVER try to type leading or trailing dots to fill a text gap in an attempt to try to align them. Instead you must place a tab character at the appropriate ruler position and indicate for Microsoft Word to precede it by the appropriate filling characters (a space character is the default Tab character filling type, but you can also use dots, dashes, or underscores).

To fill a tabulation gap with a different character type, follow these steps:

1. Use the mouse to define the desired Tab stop on the ruler.

2. Double-click the Tab stop character on the ruler to show the Tabs dialog box.

3. Select the desired Tab stop in the Tab stop position list (identify it by its position in inches).

4. Eventually change its alignment type in the Alignment area (see Figure 2-29 for alignment types).

5. Change its leader character by selecting one of the possible four options in the Leader area.

6. **VERY IMPORTANT:** click Set to redefine the Tab stop before closing the Tabs dialog box.

Repeat steps 3 to 5 for every other Tab stop you want to change and then close the Tabs dialog box to apply the desired format to the selected paragraphs.

Attention   You can easily show the Tabs dialog box by double-clicking any tabulation mark on the ruler.

To remove a Tab stop from the selected paragraphs, click the desired Tab stop and drag it out from the ruler to the document area, or double-click it to show the Tabs dialog, select it from the list and click Clear to remove it.

Figure 2-37 shows what happened after these operations had been applied to the decimal Tab stop defined at 4 inches in Figures 1.29 and 1.30. Note that now leading dots fill the space created by the decimal Tab stop automatically created by the Tab stop. And if you drag the Tab stop with leading dots to the right, all selected paragraphs that have it will be affected, adding or removing leading dots to the new specified position.

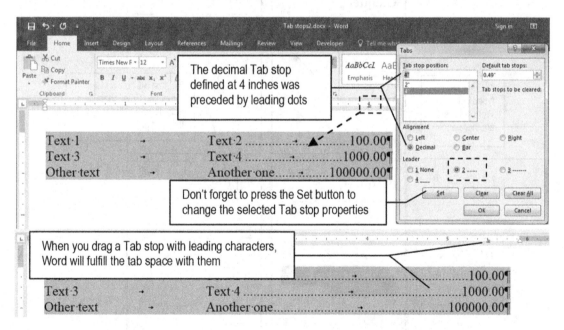

Figure 2-37. *Double-click any Tab stop to invoke the Tabs dialog box, where you can select any of the Tab stops on the list and change its alignment or leader character. Don't forget to press the Set button to define each Tab stop property before closing the Tabs dialog box.*

Text Flow

Programmers call text "a string" because its successive character sequence resembles a long string of letters. With this thought in mind, it is quite obvious that whenever more text is inserted or deleted at any text position of a Microsoft Word document, this text string will grow or shrink. Text inserted or deleted at the beginning or at the middle of the document's *text string* will displace the remaining text toward the string end.

For example, how many times have you caught yourself typing many Enter keys at the end of a page just to reach the beginning of the next page?

As you may be wondering now, this kind of action inserts many hidden ¶ characters into the text, leading to an undesirable consequence on the document: the remaining text will reflow down under, eventually sending these sequences of empty paragraphs to the beginning of another page. Figure 2-38 shows a diagram of what happens to the text in such occasions.

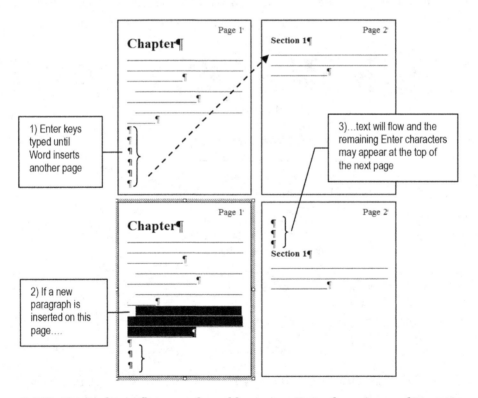

Figure 2-38. *Typical text flow produced by many Enter keys pressed to get a new page. Note that when a new paragraph was added to the first page, the Enter keys were displaced to the second page, inserting three empty lines of text at the beginning of the next page.*

Page Breaks

From now on, every time you want to reach a new page in any document, insert a Page break by pressing Ctrl+Enter. Microsoft Word will insert a hidden Page Break character that can be seen by checking the Show/Hide option of the Home tab of the Ribbon. It will be represented as a dashed line where you can read "Page break" to indicate each Ctrl+Enter typed.

If you type some text *before* the page break character, the remaining text will reflow until the page break pass to the other page (Figure 2-39).

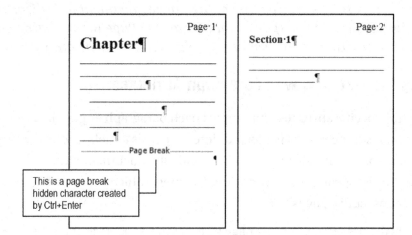

Figure 2-39. *Press Ctrl+Enter to insert a page break, forcing Microsoft Word to create another page in the document. All remaining text will reflow to the new page(s).*

Watch the Status Bar

Many people may inadvertently insert one or more Ctrl+Enter characters in the text, inserting many white space pages that seems coming from nowhere...

Keep an eye on Word Status bar to see how many pages the document already has. Figure 2-40 shows a three-page document with the Show/Hide option checked, allowing you to see two page breaks that generate a three-page document. Word status bar shows Page 3 of 3 because the text insertion cursor is at page 3.

Figure 2-40. *Microsoft Word showing a three-page document as indicated by the status bar (cursor at page 3). Note that it has two Page Break characters (Control+Enter) inserted at text beginning, which creates two empty pages.*

Controlling the Text Flow with Paragraph Attributes

Besides control-specific attributes that impact each paragraph appearance, Microsoft Word and most text processors also offer different options to define another very important task: controlling the way text flows along the document pages.

Typographically speaking, it is considered a typographical error whenever text flows through two consecutive pages and

1. only the first line of the last page's paragraph appears at the bottom of the page, continuing printing at the top of the next page: this lone row at the end of a page is called an orphan row; or

2. only the last line of the last page's paragraph appears at the top of the next page: this lone row at the beginning of the page is called a widow row); or

3. any title section paragraph prints alone at the bottom of the page, while the first section paragraph prints alone at the top of the next page; or

4. a chapter title paragraph does not begin on a new page. It is misplaced printed in the middle of the last precedent chapter page.

Figure 2-41 visually explains when these typographic errors may happen whenever the text flows through the document pages. Microsoft Word controls how text flows between document pages to avoid such errors using the Lines and Page Breaks tab of the Paragraph dialog box (Figure 2-42), which offers these text flow controls. They are as follows:

- **Widow/Orphan control**: to avoid the occurrence of the first two situations pictured in Figure 2-40.

- **Keep with next**: to avoid the occurrence of the third situation pictured in Figure 2-40 (section title not printed on the same page of its first paragraph).

- **Keep lines together**: to avoid that any paragraph suffers a break in the lines between page breaks (normally used in special situations like contract clauses, bibliographic references, etc., when the paragraph text must be printed on the same page).

- **Page break before**: to avoid the occurrence of the fourth situation pictured in Figure 2-40 (chapter title not printed on a new page).

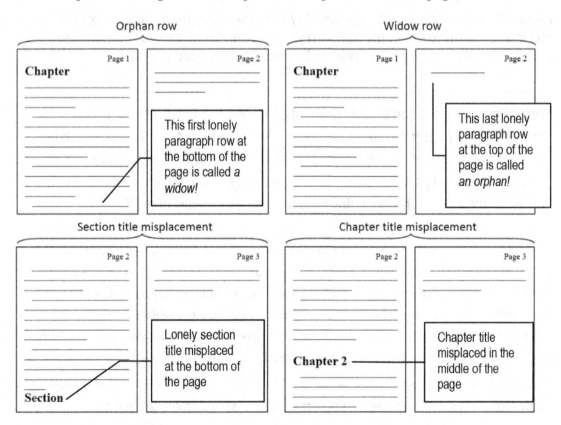

Figure 2-41. *Common typographic text flow errors that may arise in incorrectly formatted text documents, when the text flows between two consecutive pages (note the page numbers).*

Figure 2-42. *The Line and Page Breaks tab of the Paragraph dialog box offers text flow controls to avoid the appearance of widow and orphan rows, and to guarantee that certain paragraphs will begin on a new printed page*

Attention   There is some disagreement about the definitions of widow and orphan: what one source calls a widow another calls an orphan. The explanation given so far is the most prevalent on the Internet and I will follow it. Since Microsoft Word has a single command to control both Widow and Orphan rows at once, for the sake of this book this discussion doesn't really matter!

If you understood how these options work, you may now perfectly understand why it is so important to avoid pressing two or more successive Enter keys to separate two consecutive text paragraphs. By using just one Enter you can surely trust that Microsoft Word will perfectly control the text flow of the entire document whenever you insert more text in any part of it. Otherwise, it will try to control empty text paragraphs inserted by many consecutive hidden ¶ characters, and the text flow will always be a mess...

Attention   You will see how to implement this text flow rules in Chapter 4.

Line Numbers and Hyphenation

Line numbers are mostly used in contracts, script, code documentation, and some English tests to allow precise references to specific lines of text (text boxes, figures, and tables are counted as a single line).

Hyphenation is a Microsoft Word resource that can automatically hyphenate words when they fall in the hyphenation zone (the right page or column margin). It is typically used in Justify aligned text or columnated text to avoid the extra spaces inserted by justification.

Both Line Numbers and Hyphenation commands can be found in the Page Setup area of the Layout tab of the Ribbon and are very easy to implement.

The Suppress line numbers and Don't hyphenate options found in the Formatting exceptions area of the Line and Page Breaks tab of the Paragraph dialog box can be checked to avoid that such formation is applied to the selected paragraphs.

Borders and Shading

Typographers refer to lines that separate paragraphs as *rules*, and borders all around them as *boxes*. Microsoft Word calls them borders. Such formatting resources can be associated to a background color to detach the entire paragraph, to call the reader's attention to important things in the text (like the Attention notes you see everywhere in this book). They can be applied to pages, paragraphs, and tables.

Before applying a border to a paragraph, verify if there is a need to use it in this specific paragraph: don't forget that you can use paragraph spacing and indentation to do the job.

Microsoft Word allows you to add borders to the selected paragraph(s) using the Shading and Border controls found in the Paragraph area of the Home tab of the Ribbon or using the Page Border command found in the Page Background area in the Design tab of the Ribbon. Both commands may display the traditional Borders and Shading dialog box, which allow adding borders and shading to the entire page (using the default selected Page Border tab) or to just the selected paragraphs (using the Borders tab, Figure 2-43).

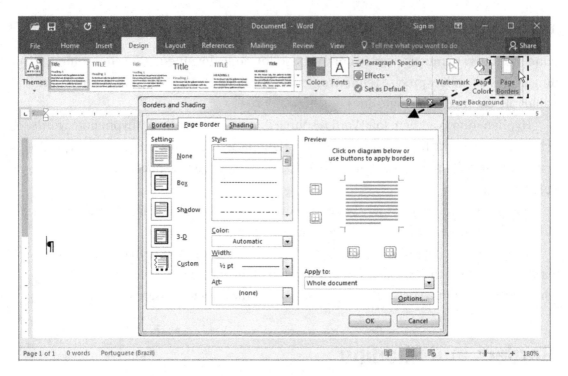

Figure 2-43. *Use the Page Borders command found in the Design tab to show the Borders and Shading dialog box, from where you can add different borders and shading to text paragraphs.*

Attention   The Borders and Shading dialog box opens with the Page Border tab selected by default, which is quite similar to the Borders tab. If you do not select the Border tab, the borders will be added to the page, instead of the paragraph.

To add a paragraph border, you must first select the Borders tab and then use one of these two methods:

- Use the Setting area at left of the Borders tab to define which type of border must be added to the selected text paragraphs. You can remove all borders (by selecting None) or add a simple box (all four borders are identical), a shadow, or a 3D border.

- Select the style, color, and width combo box to define the desired border appearance.

Using the Shading tab, select a Fill color to be used as the paragraph background color (or define a pattern).

To add borders and shading to any paragraph, follow these instructions:

1. Click the desired paragraph (or select them), show the Borders and Shading dialog box, and click Borders tab.

2. Define the border style, color, and width and click the Preview area at the top and bottom borders (or its associated buttons at the left of the paragraph preview).

3. Click the Shading tab and select the desired Fill color (I selected "White, Background 1, Darker 15%").

4. Press OK to close the dialog box and apply the desired border (Figure 2-44).

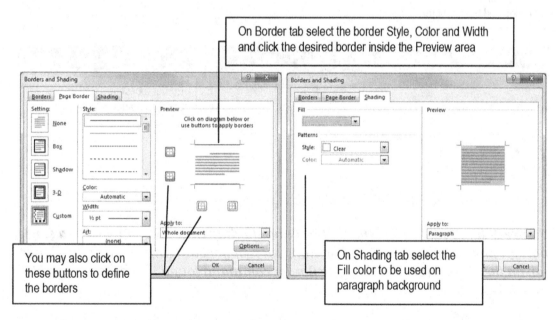

Figure 2-44. *Use the Borders tab to define the border style, color, and width, and click the Style area to which border will receive it. Use the Shading tab to define the Fill color used in the paragraph background.*

Figure 2-45 shows a simple text paragraph that received the borders and shading defined by Figure 2-44, and that can be also set or confirmed using the Border and Shading controls of the Home tab of the Ribbon: black straight lines of 1/2 pt width in the top and bottom borders, with a White, Background 1, Darker 15% fill.

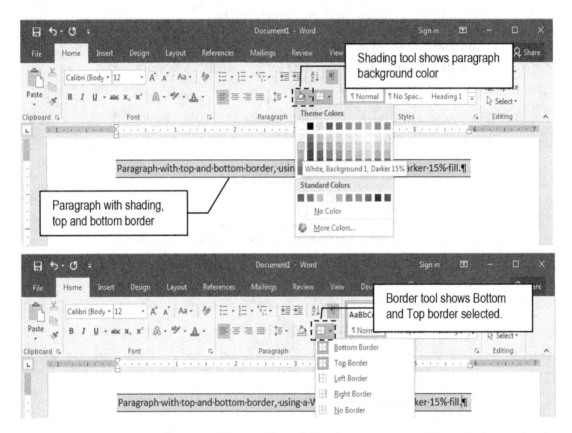

Figure 2-45. *Borders (top and bottom) and shading Gray 15%) applied to a single paragraph using the Border and Shading tools of the Paragraph area of the Home tab on the Ribbon (or with the Page Border command found in the Design tab of the Ribbon)*

Figure 2-46 shows what happens when two Enter keys were pressed: inheritance copied all paragraph formatting to the new ones, but now the top and bottom borders were added to just the first and last paragraphs in the sequence, respectively.

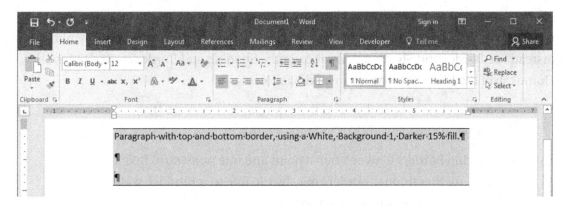

Figure 2-46. *Borders and shading inheritance keep the top and bottom borders just on the first and last paragraphs of the sequence, respectively*

Figure 2-47 shows what happens when the intermediate paragraph of Figure 2-46 has its Left indent control of the ruler dragged to 0.5 inches: now that each paragraph has a different layout, Microsoft Word applies top and bottom borders to each one, although they all share the same background color.

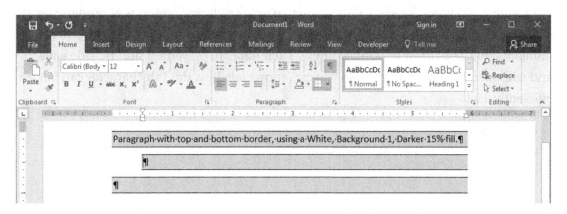

Figure 2-47. *If any paragraph inside a sequence of borders and shading formatting changes its left or right indentation margins, it breaks the inheritance and all different paragraphs receive their own borders.*

You must never make rules and borders using old typewriter habits that employ repeated typographic characters, like punctuation, hyphens, dashes, or math symbols: instead use Border and Shading dialog box or the Shading and Border controls of the Home tab of the Ribbon, being aware of the following:

- these paragraphs really need this typographic resource (try paragraph spacing and/or indentation first).

- use thin borders between half a point and one point size. Take into account that thinner borders may be too fine to reproduce well in an office printer or computer screen.

- avoid using thicker borders because they are counterproductive, creating *noise* that may diminish the attention to the information inside. Think that your reader needs to see the data, not the lines around it.

- solid borders work best; dots, dashes, or double lines are unnecessarily complicated.

Figure 2-48 shows the same data formatted using different amounts of borders: they share the same tabulation marks to align the text (but the first table also uses Vertical tabulation marks to draw its vertical lines). Their data are presented side-by-side with and without it hidden characters so you can appreciate how the Tab character can be efficiently used.

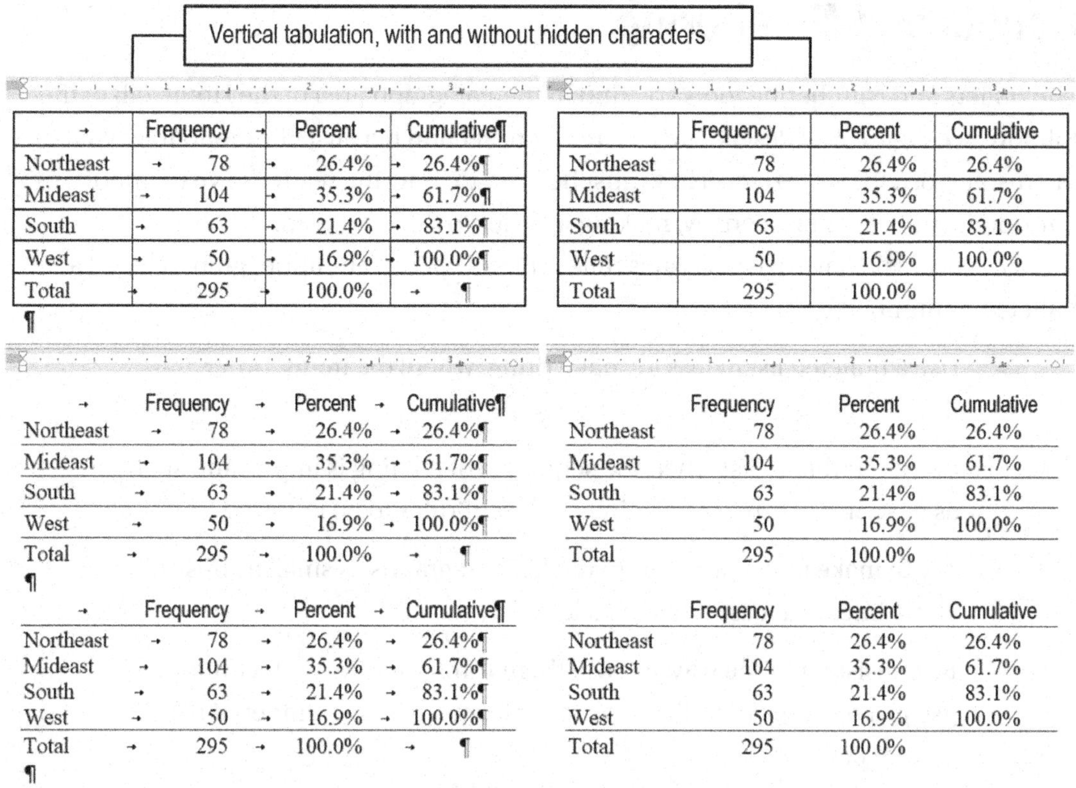

Figure 2-48. *The same data formatted with the aid of Tabulation marks and Tab characters using different amounts of borders. The left version shows the hidden characters; the right version hides them. All but the first table share the same Tabulation characters (the first table also has Vertical tabulation to generate its vertical lines). Which is the best?*

Look at the ruler and note that the first table, created using tab characters, has also Vertical tabulation marks to generate its vertical lines. The second table doesn't have the top and bottom borders or the vertical lines; the last table has just a bottom border behind its first row and top border above its last row (the total row).

Which one seems best formatted to you? I think that you might now understand that sometimes less formatting may give a better finish!

Attention   These tabulated data can also be easily produced using Microsoft Word Tables, which will be discussed in Chapter 5.

Bullets and Numbering

The Bullets and Numbering tools you find in the Paragraph area of the Home tab of the Ribbon (see Figure 2-7) deserve an independent section because they tend to work as Microsoft Word thinks is right. They must be used to draw the reader's eye to important information the text must convey, making it easier to find and read.

Whenever you have a list of issues that demand special attention, grant it using a bulleted or numbered list:

- Use a bulleted list in less formal writing, where the items' order doesn't matter.

- Use a numbered list when the sequence of reading is important, such as describing steps, instructions, or event rules to be followed.

- Try to make bullet and numbered list paragraphs as small as possible. Three lines is a reasonable max length.

- Be consistent in the way you use them throughout your document: use just one type of bullet or number format for the numbered lists in your document.

- When applying Bullets or Numbering tool to a set of paragraphs, try to use only up to the third level of numbering: more levels can add confusion for the reader.

Both the Bullets and Numbering tools creates hanging indents in the paragraphs where they are applied and require that you type at least one character so its format can be used and copied to the next paragraph by inheritance, whenever you press Enter. Otherwise, an empty standard paragraph will be created.

Changing Bullets and Numbering Levels

Bullets and Numberings can have different levels, which can be created by pressing the Tab key at the beginning of a level do demote it, or Shift+Tab on any sublevel bullet to promote it.

Figure 2-49 shows a simple paragraph created using the Bullets tool, which received the first bullet level. After the Enter key is pressed, inheritance takes care to create another bulleted paragraph of the same level. When the Tab key is pressed at the beginning of this new paragraph, the new paragraph is demoted to the second bullet level, which is also inherited by the next paragraph when Enter is pressed. Keep pressing Enter and Tab to see different bullet levels appear in your document, each one indented to the level immediately above it (press Shift+Tab at the beginning of any sublevel bulleted paragraph to promote it to the level immediately above it).

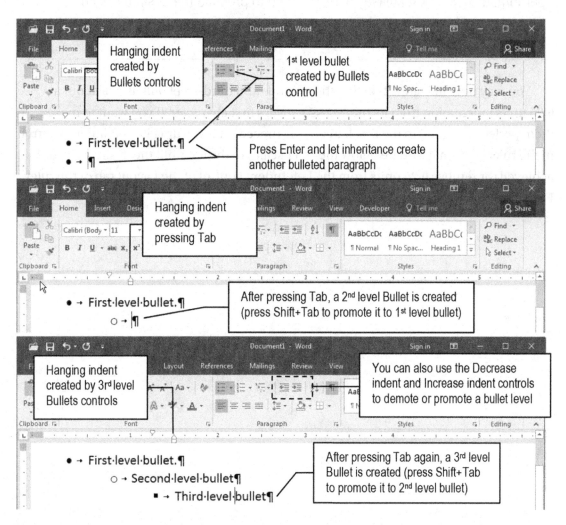

Figure 2-49. *Create different bullet levels by pressing Tab (to demote) and Shift+Tab (to promote) at left of the first bullet paragraph character, or use the Decrease indent or Increase indent controls.*

Attention   Instead of pressing Tab or Shift+Tab at the first character of a bulleted paragraph, you can also use the Decrease indent or Increase indent controls of the Paragraph area of the Home tab of the Ribbon to demote and promote the bullet level (these controls don't require that you put the cursor at the first character paragraph: just click it anyway and use them to produce the desired result).

Microsoft PowerPoint bullet lists work the same way.

You may note in Figure 2-49 that the second- and third-level bullets use about a 0.25 units indentation from its predecessor level's first character. If you want to make them perfectly aligned to the first letter of the precedent level, drag its Left indent control in the ruler (the small square below the ruler scale) to the left until the desired position is achieved (or remove 0.25 units from the Left Indent control of the Layout tab of the ruler, Figure 2-50).

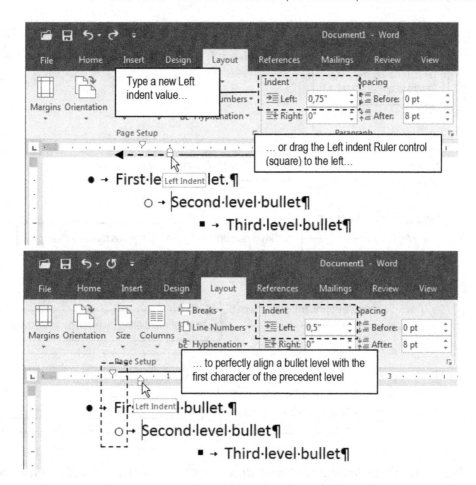

Figure 2-50. *Drag the Left indent of any second- or third-level bullet paragraph until it stays perfectly aligned to the first letter of the precedent level*

The same is true when you use the Numbering tool to create a numbered list: after you type anything in the first numbered paragraph and press Enter, its format is copied to the next paragraph by inheritance, and whenever you press the Tab key at the beginning of a numbered text paragraph, it changes its level and numbering system (Figure 2-51).

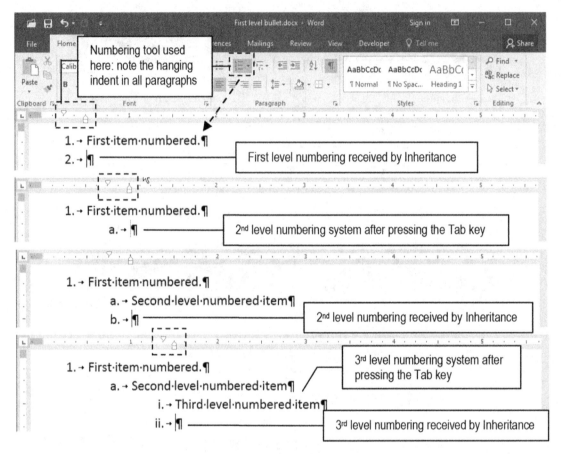

Figure 2-51. *The Numbering tool also allowscreation of a multilevel numbering system by pressing Tab to demote the paragraph number (or Shift+Tab to promote it). Each numbered paragraph has a deep indentation relative to its precedent level, using a hanging indent format.*

Attention   The same rules used to demote and promote Bullet levels apply to numbered paragraphs.

Note however that the Multilevel list tool does a different indentation than the Numbering tool. The Numbering tool adds deep indentation for all its sublevels, while the Multilevel list doesn't: it numbers the text paragraphs creating a perfect indent in its sublevels, where the number of the next level is perfectly positioned to the hanging indent alignment of the level that precedes it (Figure 2-52).

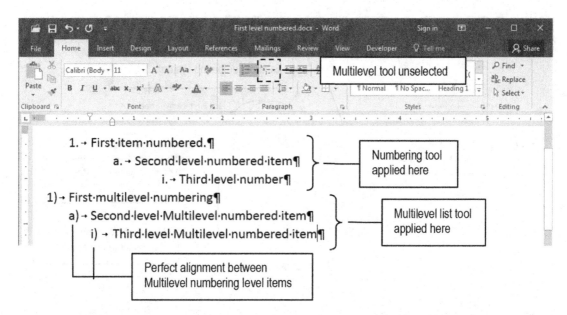

Figure 2-52. *The Multilevel list tool creates a perfect indentation between different levels of numbering (also achieved by pressing Tab at the beginning of a numbered paragraph). It does not add a Left indentation to the first-level paragraph (it is perfectly aligned to the page margin).*

Attention   Although we can select the Multilevel list tool to apply a different type of paragraph numbering, it does not remain selected in the paragraphs that has received its formatting options: Microsoft Word keeps showing the Numbering tool selected instead.

The Multilevel list tool also offers different types of numbering system that can be selected by clicking its small arrow. To change any paragraphs already numbered by a different numbering system, just select the desired paragraphs and apply a different numeration to them (Figure 2-53).

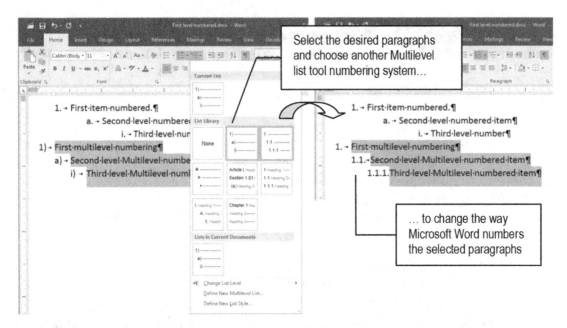

Figure 2-53. *Use the Multilevel list tool to choose another numbering system to any number of selected paragraphs, according to the indentation paragraph levels.*

Changing Paragraph Numbers

In my practice of producing long text documents using Microsoft Word (like this book you are reading), both the Numbering and Multilevel list tools may inadvertently change the first number of some spaced numbered paragraphs in the document: an automatically numbered paragraph that must begin on 1 subtly follows the next number of the last numbered paragraph, well above it in the text, even though it has many other text paragraphs in between them.

Other times the number system restarts when it shouldn't: I just need that it continues to numerate from the last numbered paragraph (which is especially true in some "follow the next instructions" lists).

To force Microsoft Word to restart to numbering the paragraphs the way you want:

- Click the Numbering tool and select Set Numbering value... command; or

- Right-click the first numbered paragraph and the context menu that appears select Set Numbering value... command

Both options will bring the Set Numbering Value dialog box (Figure 2-54), which will allow to select one of the following.

- **Start a new list**: which will restart paragraph numbering from 1;

- **Continue from previous list**: which will give to the selected paragraph the next number used in the last numbered paragraph above (at any point of the document);

- **Set value to**: which allows you to indicate which number must be used to number the selected paragraph.

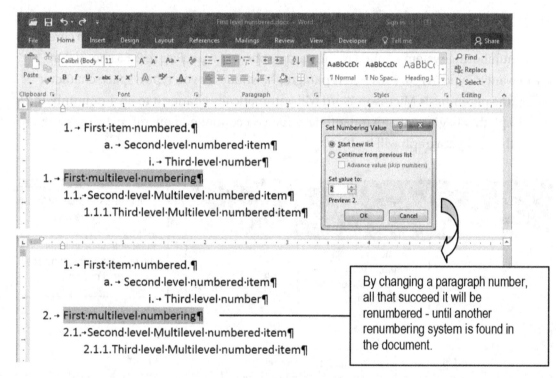

Figure 2-54. *Right-click any autonumbered paragraph and choose Set Numbering value to restart its numeration from any value. All paragraphs that follow will be renumbered until Word's find another restarting point.*

Attention   Whenever you change the autonumber applied to a paragraph in a Microsoft Word document, each paragraph that follows it will automatically change its number to the next used in the sequence, until it finds a paragraph which is set to restart numbering from 1.

Although the Numbering tool and Multilevel list tools seem the same, they aren't: Microsoft Word will continue from previous list from the last numbered item applied to the Numbering *or* Multilevel list tool (each tool holds its own number system sequence).

There may be such moments that you don't want to let Microsoft Word take care of the numbering system applied to the paragraphs you type. Figure 2-55 shows that if you want to type "A)" to start a new paragraph, whenever you type a space character before the parenthesis Microsoft Word will automatically change it to an autonumbered paragraph that begins with an indented A) that you cannot edit anymore. By pressing Enter, the next paragraph will be B).

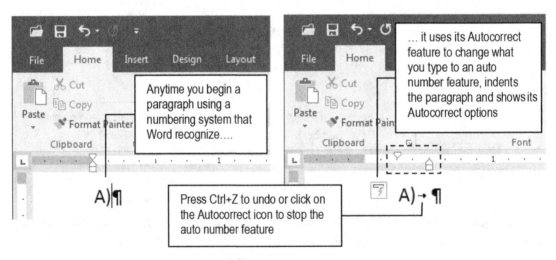

Figure 2-55. *To undo any Microsoft Word Autocorrect action (like change any paragraph number system to an autonumbered paragraph), press Ctrl+Z, or click the Autocorrect icon and disable this feature*

If you want to disable such behavior you can do one of the following:

- press Ctrl+Z to undo the last Autocorrect operation (by pressing Enter, the next paragraph will be a blank one).

- uncheck the Automatic numbered lists option found in the AutoFormat As You Type tab of the Autocorrect dialog box (found by clicking the "File ➤ Options ➤ Proofing ➤ Autocorrect options..." button of the Word Options dialog box, Figure 2-56).

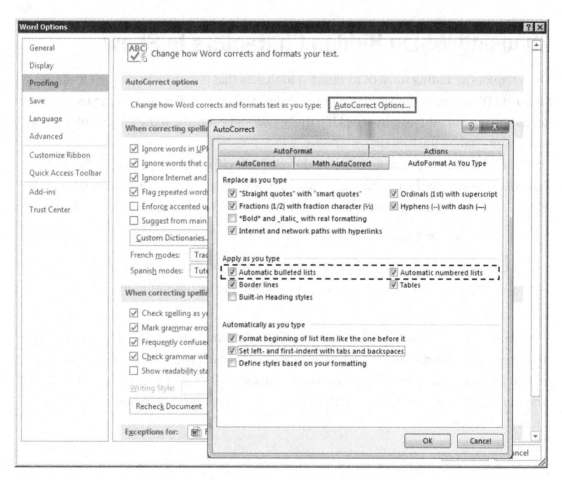

Figure 2-56. *Use the Automatic bulleted lists and Automatic numbered list of the AutoCorrect dialog box to control whether Microsoft Word will automatically create bullets and numberings as you type some special characters at the beginning of a new paragraph*

- click the Autocorrect icon that appears at the left of the paragraph and choose one of the following options:

  - **Undo Automatic Numbering**: disable the last autonumbering applied (same as pressing Ctrl+Z).

  - **Stop Automatically Creating Numbered Lists**: uncheck the Automatic numbered lists option in the Autocorrect dialog box.

  - **Control AutoFormat Options**: show the AutoCorrect dialog box.

Choosing Which Hidden Characters to Show

This chapter (including most of its figures) indicates that it may be important to show Microsoft Word's hidden characters in the text so you can control whether to use them or not as you type or edit text, by checking the Show/Hide control of the Paragraph section of the Home tab of the Ribbon.

Instead of showing each possible hidden character (like the space bar "·" characters that *pollute* how your document text is viewed in Microsoft Word interface), you may choose what hidden characters must be permanently shown in your Microsoft Word copy:

1. click File ➤ Options ➤ Display

2. Use the Always show these formatting marks on the screen area to check which hidden characters you want to be permanently visible.

In *my* Microsoft Word copy I always check the Tab characters and Paragraph marks (the Object anchors option is checked by default), so I can always view where a Tab →, an Enter ¶, or a Shift+Enter ↵ were pressed in the text and fix it as necessary (Figure 2-57), whether or not I selected the Show/Hide control of the Paragraph section of the Home tab of the Ribbon.

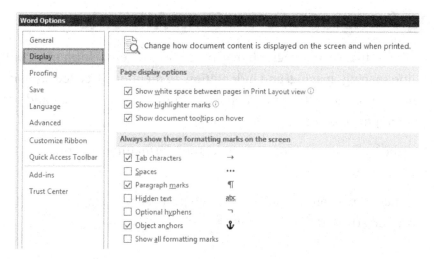

Figure 2-57. *The Microsoft Word Options dialog box offers for its Display settings the possibility of choosing which hidden characters may be permanently shown in your documents. I suggest checking Tab characters and Paragraph marks.*

The options that your Word copy must always show is now a matter of *taste*.

Attention   Throughout these many years I have helped many different people (friends, teachers, students, writers…) to fix their Microsoft Word documents. Everyone that I helped, when viewing the document in my Microsoft Word interface, become frightened by the appearance of the pilcrow ¶ character after each Enter they pressed in the document. They immediately said: "What are those symbols in my document?"

You may feel strange at the beginning when they are always turned on, but in the long run, they may become absolutely necessary to take control of any Word document.

If you disable the Automatic numbered lists option, Microsoft Word will permanently stop using it in all other documents until the option is checked again.

Copying Paragraph Formatting Attributes

Now that you know that each paragraph may have many different formatting options (alignment, line spacing, spacing, and indentation, to mention just a few...), it is interesting that you can copy the paragraph formatting options you want and paste them into other paragraphs by using two different methods:

- Use the ¶ character to copy just paragraph formatting (no Font properties are copied).

- use the Format Painter tool to copy and paste all paragraph formatting (including all its Font properties).

Copying Just Paragraph Formatting (No Font Properties)

If you want to copy just Paragraph dialog box options (plus Borders and Shading, Bullets and Numbering), use the ¶ character to convey this formatting information by following these steps:

1. Check the Show/Hide control in the Paragraph area of the Home tab of the Ribbon.

2. Select just the ¶ character from the paragraph that has the information you want to copy and press Ctrl+C to copy it to Clipboard (optionally, you can right-click and choose Copy, or click the Copy control in the Clipboard area of the Home tab).

3. Select just the ¶ character in the destination paragraph (the one to be formatted) and press Ctrl+V to paste (optionally, you can right-click and choose Paste, or click the Paste control in the Clipboard area of the Home tab).

Figure 2-58 show these operations in action, to copy just the Paragraph formatting (Alignment, Line spacing, Spaces, Indentation, Borders and Shading) from a source to a destination paragraph. Note that the paragraph destination does not change its Font properties.

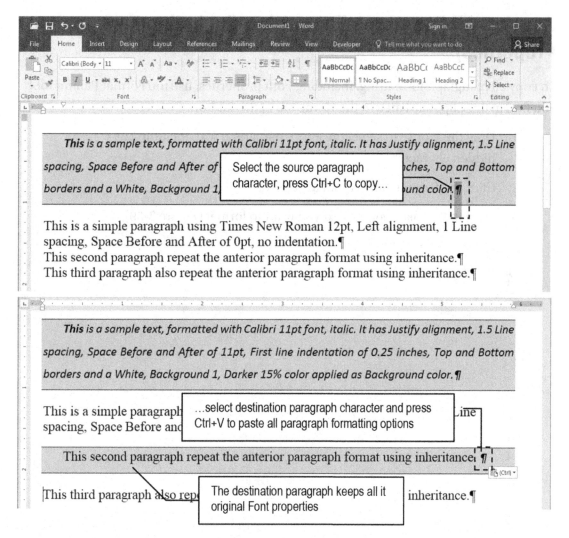

Figure 2-58. *Use Clipboard to copy all paragraph formatting options between two paragraphs: select the pilcrow character of the source paragraph and press Ctrl+C to copy it; select the pilcrow character of the destination paragraph and press Ctrl+V to paste. No Font properties are copied using this method.*

Copying All Paragraph Formatting (Including Font Properties)

To copy all paragraph formatting, including Font properties, use the Format Painter tool you find in the Clipboard area in the Home tab of the Ribbon:

1. Drag the mouse to select the entire paragraph text, including its ¶ hidden character.

2. Click the Format Painter tool to copy.

3. Drag the mouse over the text you want to format (Figure 2-59).

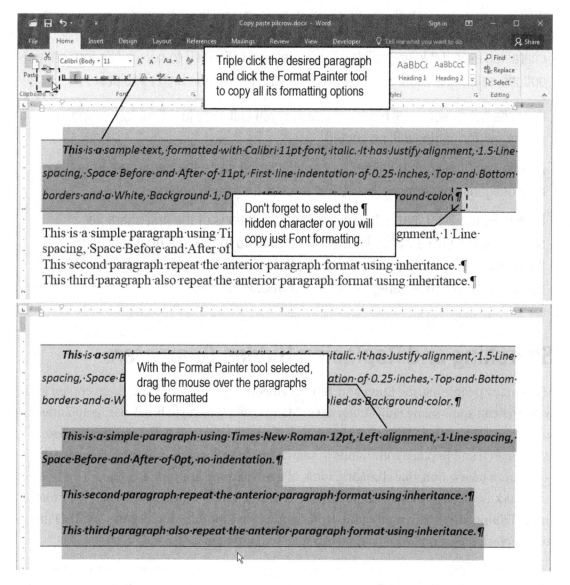

Figure 2-59. *Use the Format Painter tool to copy and paste all paragraph formatting: select the entire text of the the source paragraph (triple-click it, or drag the mouse to include its ¶ hidden character), click the Format Painter tool to copy, and drag the mouse over the destination paragraphs to paste.*

Attention   Triple-click any paragraph to easily select it (including its hidden ¶ character, even if it is not visible). Then, press Ctrl+Shift+C to copy all its formatting options, select the destination paragraphs, and press Ctrl+Shift+V to paste it.

If you do not select the ¶ hidden character, you will copy just Font formatting: no paragraph formatting will be copied.

Double-click the Format Painter tool to lock it and paste the paragraph format to noncontiguous paragraphs. Press Esc or click it again to unlock it.

Note in Figure 2-59 that if the Font formatting options of the first character selected will be used by the Format Painter tool to format the destination paragraphs (just the first "**This**" word in the source paragraph used bold, while all the text of destination paragraphs were formatted in bold).

Searching and Replacing Hidden Characters

Since many people use the Enter and Tab keys incorrectly, and since some text copied from web sites can show many Shift+Enter keys (Manual line breaks) to break paragraph lines when pasted in Microsoft Word documents, it is good to know that you can use Microsoft Word Search and Replace commands to search for these characters in a document and sometimes take action, like changing some of them to more appropriate ones.

This kind of search can be made by selecting the Find ➤ Advanced Find... command in the Editing area at the right of the Home tab of the Ribbon, which shows Word's Find and Replace dialog box with its Find tab selected by default.

Attention   The Find and Replace dialog box has three tabs: Find, Replace, and Go To. You can also show it using a single click by selecting the Replace command that is also found in the Editing area of the Home tab of the Ribbon.

Click the More>> button of Find and Replace dialog box to expand it, check that the cursor is inside the Find what text box, and then click the Special button at its bottom to show the special Find what options it offers for searching (Figure 2-60).

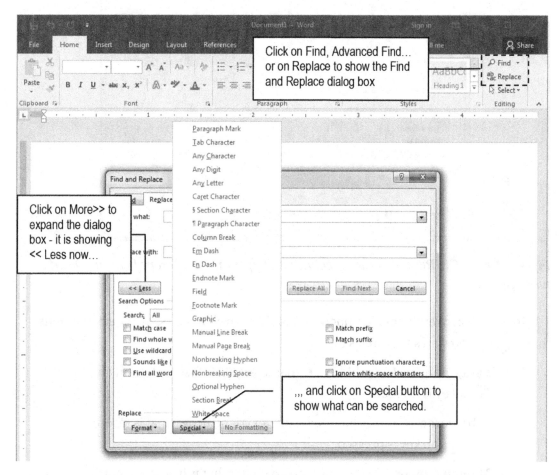

Figure 2-60. *This is the expanded view of Word's Find and Replace dialog box, from where you can select some special characters to search inside any document*

Attention   The Special Find and Replace list options also change for both the Find what and Replace with check boxes when the Use wildcards option is checked (Figure 2-61). Its uses will be seen in the "Making Wildcard Searches" section of Chapter 4).

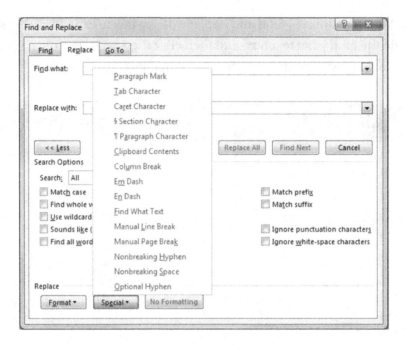

Figure 2-61. *The Replace with Special list of options is different from the Find what list*

To make a conventional Find operation for hidden characters, the Special options that we are interested so far are as follows:

- **Paragraph Mark**: the hidden ¶ character that is inserted when an Enter key is pressed.

- **Tab Character**: the → hidden character (right arrow) that is inserted when a Tab key is pressed.

- **Manual Line Break**: the ↵ hidden character that is inserted when Shift+Enter keys are pressed.

- **Manual Page Break**: the hidden dashed line with "Page Break" in the middle that is inserted when Ctrl+Enter keys are pressed.

- **White Space**: the vertical center aligned dot "·" hidden character, which represents an empty space that is inserted when the Space key is pressed.

Attention   Do not confuse the Paragraph Mark and ¶ Paragraph Character options: the first means the hidden character inserted by Microsoft Word to indicate that an Enter key was pressed; the second is the real pilcrow ¶ character inserted by the user in some legal documents by using Microsoft Word Symbol command (which is commented on in Chapter 3).

These Special search options are translated into a sequence of two characters (character case counts) where the first is always a caret ^. Table 2-1 shows all of them.

Table 2-1. *Text Character Sequence for Some Special Search Options Found in Microsoft Word Search and Replace Dialog Box*

Special search to	Character sequence
Paragraph Mark	^p
Tab Character	^t
Manual Line Break	^l
Manual Page Break	^m
White Space	^w

Let us see how can we take advantage of using such hidden characters in a search and replace operation to fix a messy text document produced with Microsoft Word.

Exercise

Extract "The Last of the Mohicans, Introduction and Chapter1.docx" file from Chapter02.zip and open it in your Microsoft Word copy. This is a small, eight-page document that has just the Introduction and Chapter 1 of the famous book *The Last of the Mohicans* by James Fenimore Cooper published in 1840.

Attention   This document was prepared by me to resemble some Microsoft Word documents which I had already received and that bring confusion to anyone who tries to fix them without a deep understanding of what is really going on inside the text. I did not really find it as it is presented: it was purposely produced to be used as a didactic example.

When you open it for the first time in a typical Microsoft Word environment, it must seem quite well formatted, as shown in Figure 2-62, which shows its title, author credit, Introduction section title, and three of its first text paragraphs.

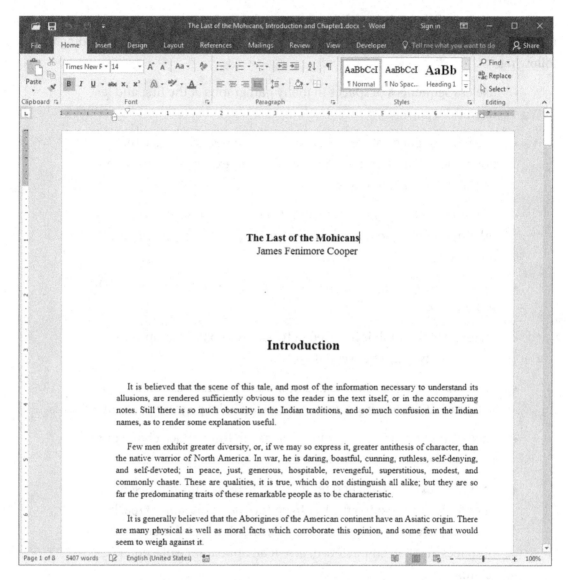

Figure 2-62. *This is the appearance of "The Last of the Mohicans, Introduction and Chapter1.docx" file, which can be extracted from Chapter02.zip, when opened in a regular Microsoft Word interface. It seem to be a nice text document, but it isn't…*

But when you click the Show/Hide control of the Paragraph area in the Home tab of the Ribbon, you will notice that it has a lot of *trash* inside it (Figure 2-63), including the following:

- useless sequences of spaces in many paragraphs at the first and last document page;

- useless sequences of Tab characters and spaces to displace the book title and author name in two different text lines to give then an apparently Center alignment;

- the "Introduction" (at page 1) and "Chapter 1" (at page 4) section titles also use sequences of spaces and Tab characters to give them an apparently Center alignment;

- each paragraph begins with a six-space sequence to create a First line indentation;

- an empty paragraph is inserted between two text paragraphs to create empty space between then;

- each paragraph line ends with a Manual Line Break character, which will prevent the text from correctly flowing if the page size is changed;

- each phrase inside a paragraph begins with three space characters to detach it from the precedent phrase;

- scroll the text to page 3 and note that there is an enormous sequence of Enter keys pressed in the last Introduction paragraph to reach the next page where Chapter 1 begins, and that it also makes use of spaces and Tab characters to give it an appearance of Center alignment.

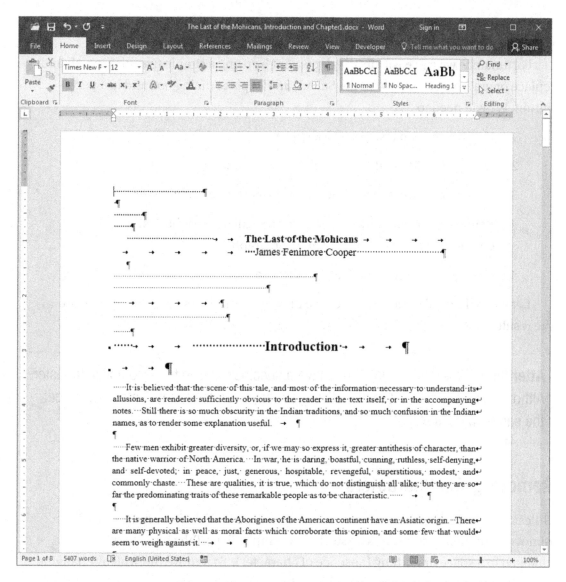

Figure 2-63. *This is the appearance of "The Last of the Mohicans, Introduction and Chapter1.docx" file when the Show/Hide tool is checked, revealing the trash inadvertently inserted into the text: sequences of spaces and Tab charaters, text lines ending with Manual Line Breaks, two Enter characters to separate paragraphs, and many other additions...*

If we consider that the entire book could be formatted this way, one can imagine the work that must be made to fix such a mess by hand, one-by-one...

Fortunately, we can easily fix the document by using a simple five-step search and replace operation with the aid of the Search and Replace dialog box and its Special button. We will need to

1.   Change any Tab character to a space;

2.   Change any Manual Line Break to a space character;

3.   Change any two-space sequence to just one space character;

4.   Remove the remaining spaces that may still exist as the first character at the beginning of any paragraph.

5.   Change any two Enter characters to one;

Let us do them all (follow the exercise on your computer so you can appreciate the result)!

Attention   This kind of task must have a specific order to be accomplished faster. Although you can make it in any other, you may need to repeat some tasks to get the same final result.

Removing Tab Characters

Unless the document has some tables or another use for Tab characters, it is safe to remove all of them, which is the case of the example. Each Tab character must be changed to a space or nothing (absence of character). To remove them all by changing them to nothing, do a Replace command with the following steps:

1.   select the Find what option and type a ^t (or select the Special ➤ Tab Character option);

2.   leave the Replace with option empty;

3.   click the Replace all button and watch Microsoft Word replace 37 occurrences of Tab characters with nothing, effectively removing them from the text (Figure 2-64).

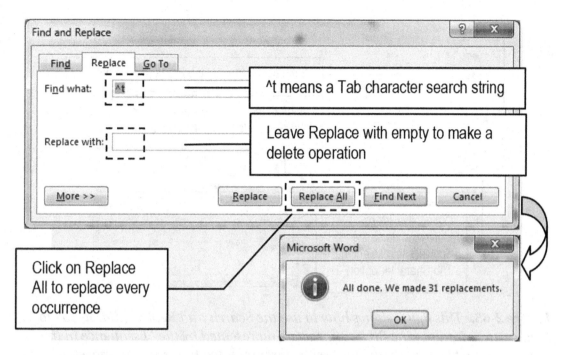

Figure 2-64. *This figure shows how to use the Search and Replace dialog box remove any Tab character (represented by the ^t sequence in the Find What text box) from the text (represented by the empty Replace with option).*

Removing Manual Line Break Characters

All manual line break characters must be changed by a Space character, or the last word at the end of a line will glue to the first word of the next line. To change them all, do another Replace command with the following steps:

1. select and clean the Find what option, then type a ^l (or select Special ➤ Manual Line Break option).

2. in the Replace with option, type a Space character (optionally, type ^w or select the Special ➤ White space option).

3. click the Replace all button; Microsoft Word must replace 306 occurrences of Manual Line Break characters with a Space character, effectively fixing the text flow whenever the page size or its margins are changed (Figure 2-65).

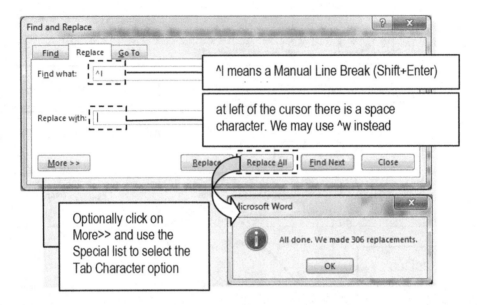

Figure 2-65. *This figure shows how to use the Search and Replace dialog box to replace any Manual Line Break character (represented by the ^l sequence in the Find What text box) with an empty space (represented by a space at the left of the cursor inside the Replace with option - we could also use ^w to represent the space character).*

Changing Two Successive Space Characters to Just One

Now is time to search for any two successive space characters and change them to just one. Since there is a lot of successive space characters, this operation must be repeated until no two space characters are found:

1. Select and clean the Find what option and type two successive space characters (optionally, you can type ^w^w or select the Special ➤ White space option twice).

2. Select and clean the Replace with option and type a single space character (optionally, type ^w or select the Special ➤ White space option).

3. Click the Replace all button and watch Microsoft Word make 699 replacements in its first pass through the text to change two successive spaces to just one space character (Figure 2-66).

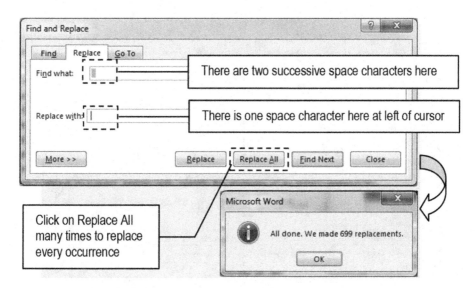

Figure 2-66. *This figure shows how to use the Search and Replace dialog box to replace two successive space characters with just one (you may use Find What =^w^w and Replace =^w instead). The Replace All operation must be successively repeated until it returns "All done. We made 0 replacements."*

4. Close the first warning message of 699 replacements and click the Replace all button again. This second Replace all operation will make 183 replacements.

5. Repeat step 4 successively, while Microsoft Word makes 105, 34, 17, 8, 2, and at last 0 replacements, as an indication that there are no more occurrences of two successive space characters in the document (Figure 2-67).

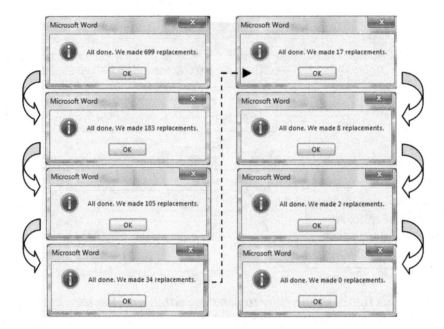

Figure 2-67. *Press Replace all sucessively to make all replacement operations needed to replace each two sucessive space characters with just one, until there are no more to replace.*

Remove the Space Character That Begins Any Paragraph

After changing two successive spaces by only one space, any paragraph that used a space character sequence to create the First Line indent effect will hold a single space at its beginning (and many may also have it at its end). So it is time to remove these lonely beginning spaces by searching for a paragraph character followed by a space character (`p) and then replacing with just a paragraph character:

1. select and clean the Find what option, then type a "^p " (without the quotes), or optionally type ^p^w, or successively select Special ➤ Paragraph Mark and Special ➤ White space options).

2. in the Replace with option and type ^p (or select the Special ➤ Paragraph Mark option).

3. click the Replace all button; Microsoft Word must replace 67 occurrences of a Paragraph character followed by a space with just a Paragraph character in its first pass through the text.

4. Repeat step 1 until there are no more occurrences of a Paragraph character followed by Space character (Figure 2-68).

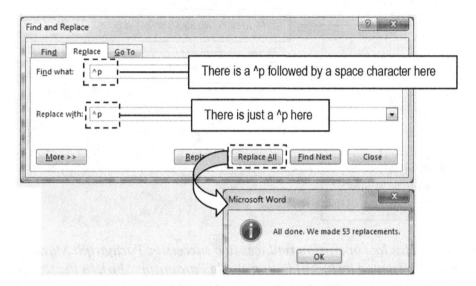

Figure 2-68. *This figure shows how to use the Search and Replace dialog box replace a Paragraph Mark character followed by a space characer (^p) with a single Paragraph Mark character (^p). You may also use ^p^w in the Find what option. The Replace All operation should be repeated until no Paragraph Mark character followed by a space characer be found in the document.*

When this operation ends, the text must be now very clear from strange typing habits—just the first document paragraph will remain with a space character.

Changing Two Successive Enter Characters to Just One

The last operation is to replace two successive paragraph characters (^p^p) with just one paragraph character (^p) following these last instructions:

1. Select and clean the Find what option, then type a ^p^p (or select Special ➤ Paragraph Mark option twice).

2. Confirm that the Replace with has just a ^p (a single Special ➤ Paragraph Mark option).

3. Click the Replace all button; Microsoft Word must replace 81
   occurrences of a Paragraph character followed by a space with just
   a Paragraph character in its first pass through the text (Figure 2-69).

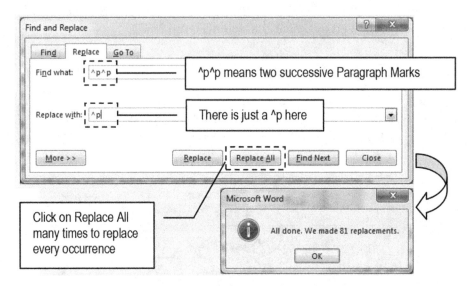

Figure 2-69. *This last operation replaces two successive Paragraph Mark characters (represented by ^p^p) with a single Paragraph Mark in the text. The Replace all operation must be repeated until there are no two successive Paragraph Mark characters in the document.*

4. Repeat step 3 until there are no more occurrences of a Paragraph
   character followed by Space character.

As you click Replace all, Microsoft Word will replace 23, 13, 7, 5, 4, and 3; my Microsoft Word copy keeps returning 3 occurrences forever, without any explanation (Figure 2-69).

When you finish these operations, the text will be quite clean, just needing to be better formatted by applying some of the paragraph attributes cited in this chapter (Figure 2-70).

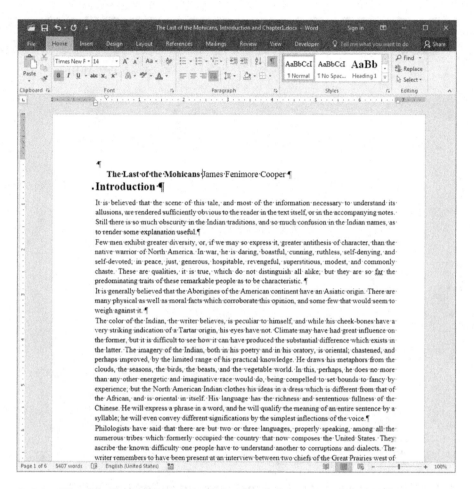

Figure 2-70. *The final appearance of the file "The Last of the Mohicans, Introduction and Chapter1.docx" after removal of all its useless characters using Microsoft Word Search and Replace Special features*

Figure 2-71 shows the first paragraphs of "The Last of the Mohicans, Introduction and Chapter1 Formatted.docx" file, which can be extracted from Chapter02.zip file. Titles were centralized and received Spacing Before and After = 50 pt. Body text received a First line indentation = 0.25. All paragraphs received Line spacing = 1. The document page was changed from Legal (8.5x14) to A4 (8.27x11.69). And it keeps flowing very well through the document pages.

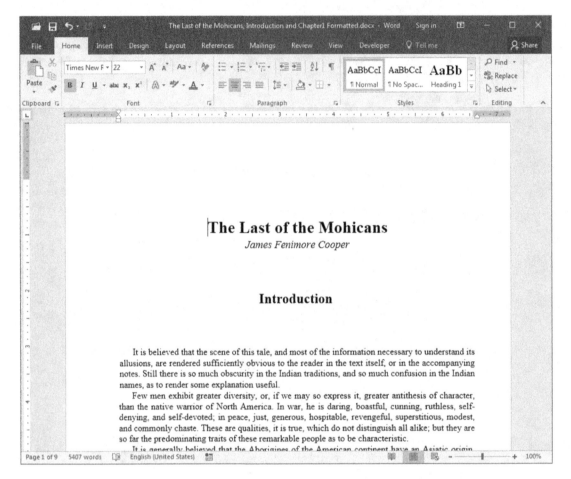

Figure 2-71. *This is "The Last of the Mohicans, Introduction and Chapter1 Formatted.docx" file, which you can also extract from Chapter02.zip file. Its book title and author name received different font sizes, all title paragraphs received Space Before and After = 50, and all Body text received a First line indentation =0.25. Page size was changed to A4 so you can appreciate how the document text flows perfectly when is well formatted.*

Compare Figures 2-71, 2-70, and 2-63 and take your own conclusions. Quite cool, isn't it?

Summary

Microsoft Word uses four special hidden characters to control the paragraph formatting of documents when you press the Enter key to create a Paragraph Break, the Shift+Enter keys to create a Manual Line Break, the Tab key to insert a Tabulation Character, and the Ctrl+Enter keys to insert a Page Break. All of these hidden characters—and many other types of code inserted in the document—can be seen by checking the Show/Hide control found at the top right corner of the Paragraph area of the Home tab of the Ribbon.

Using paragraph attributes, you can set to each paragraph the text alignment, line spacing, spacing before and after, indentations, and special options to control the text flow between document pages.

All of these formatting options are automatically copied to the next paragraph when you press the Enter key using inheritance: the next always inherits the previous attributes.

Once you know about these hidden characters and how they impact text flow, you can use Microsoft Word Search and Replace Special features to find and change them to more appropriate characters, allowing the text processor to perfectly control how the text flows between document pages.

In this chapter, you learned the following:

- How Microsoft Word, like any other text processor, uses inheritance to transfer one paragraph formatting option to the next when you press the Enter key.

- How hidden characters are used to signal special text breaks, such as paragraph breaks, manual line breaks, and page breaks.

- How to control many different paragraph attributes using the Microsoft Word Paragraph dialog box.

- How to effectively use the Tab key associated with Microsoft Word ruler tabulation marks to perfectly align text in different paragraphs.

- How the tabulation marks of one paragraph are always inherited by the next when an Enter key is pressed.

- How to create perfectly formatted tables using the Tab key and tabulation marks.

- How to easily open the Tabs dialog box by double-clicking any tabulation mark on the ruler.

- How to fill the space between a Tab character and a tabulation mark using four different types of trailing characters.

- How Microsoft Word controls text flow using special properties found in the Line and Page Breaks of the Paragraph dialog box.

- How and when to use Bullets and Numberings in the document.

- How to set or restart the autonumbering feature of the Numbering and Multilevel List tools found in the Paragraph area of the Home tab of the Ribbon.

- How to copy paragraph formatting options using both Copy/Paste and the Paste Formatting tool found in the Clipboard area of the Home tab of the Ribbon.

- How to use Microsoft Word Search and Replace Special features to remove unwanted and useless characters inserted in a document so the text can perfectly flow between document pages.

In the next chapter, we will talk about Character Attributes and how to effectively use all the typographic power of the Microsoft Windows operating system to make your documents look better.

CHAPTER 3

Character Attributes

Character attributes relate to precise typographic control of text formatting of the letters and words, and consequently to the whole appearance of the text paragraphs of your document.

It includes everything that may affect the appearance of the characters on the page, including the characters itself, the font selection and its attributes (like point size, bold, italic, underline, caps size, etc.), letter spacing and vertical displacement, kerning, and some other subtleties that may be seen in certain types of documents.

To really make the best use of Microsoft Word to format your documents by manipulating character attributes, it is necessary to understand some basic typographic knowledge and how Microsoft Windows allows them to be implemented using Fonts.

The documents used to generate some book figures and the ones sited on the Exercise section can be found by downloading Chapter03.zip file from this Internet address:

```
https://github.com/apress/msft-word-secrets
```

Typeface and Font Classification

Typographers historically refer to a Typeface as an entire family of fonts (like Arial) reserving the word *Font* to refer to a specific font type, size, and weight (like Arial, 12 pt, Bold): this distinction made sense in the letterpress age, when each font was physically associated with a drawer of metal type. Not any more: nowadays in the Computer Age, the word Font often means a whole family of styles of any size. So, whenever somebody talks about the Calibri font, he or she is talking about all the different styles in which it can be presented in a document.

There are many different font types and ways to categorize them. They can be associated with four main groups according to their appearance: serif, sans serif, script, and decorative.

Let us explore how these different font classifications can impact the appearance of your document.

© Flavio Morgado 2017
F. Morgado, *Microsoft Word Secrets*, https://doi.org/10.1007/978-1-4842-3078-7_3

Serif and Sans Serif Fonts

For those of you that have never heard about "serifs," they are the tiny tails on the main strokes of the letters which are supposed to help to lead the eyes from left to right. Figure 3-1 shows two graphic representations of letter "A": with serifs (using the Times New Roman font) and without serifs (using the Calibri font).

Figure 3-1. *Representations of letter "A" using a font with serifs (Times New Roman) and without serifs (sans serif) (Calibri)*

Attention   Many sans serif fonts are named receiving the "Sans" suffix, like "Comic Sans," "Gil Sans," "Lucida Sans," and so on.

One of the secrets of creating good document appeal is to combine sans serif and serif fonts in a single document: one for the section titles and another for the body text. This strategy will be explored in the section "Combining Fonts" later in this chapter.

Script and Decorative Fonts

Script (or calligraphy) fonts tend to mimic some beautiful handwritten styles, commonly seen on marriage invites and certificates, while decorative fonts can have many different types and are used in advertising or to add a special feeling to some types of documents. Figure 3-2 shows two other graphic representations of the letter "A" using a script font (Kunstler Script) and a decorative font (Algerian).

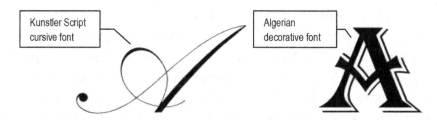

Figure 3-2. *Representations of letter "A" using an script font (Kunstler Script) and a decorative font (Algerian): both with serif!*

Symbol Fonts

Inside the decorative group, we may find Symbol fonts that offer symbols instead of letters, like Webdings, Wingdings, and so on. Figure 3-3 shows the graphic representation of letter "A" when using these three symbol fonts.

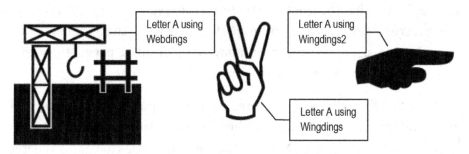

Figure 3-3. *Representations of letter "A" using three symbol fonts: Webdings, Wingdings, and Wingdings2*

Attention   Use Microsoft Windows Character Map applet (found at Start button ➤ All apps ➤ Windows Accessories ➤ Character Map) to select and copy to clipboard any character associated to a symbol font, like Wingdings.

Monospaced and Proportionally Spaced Fonts

Different letters need different amounts of horizontal space on a printed page. Take for example the Occidental alphabet letter "M" (the widest alphabet letter) and compare it to the Occidental alphabet letter "I" (the thinnest): they need different amounts of horizontal space on a printed page.

Typographers refer to all fonts where each character occupies just the space it needs (with great difference between lowercase and uppercase letters) as proportionally spaced, while fonts in which each character occupies the same horizontal space (for both its uppercase or lowercase letters) are referred to as monospaced.

Most Microsoft Windows fonts are proportionally spaced (each letter occupies just the space it needs), but you will also find installed by default a serif monospaced font called Courier New.

Monospaced fonts are used only when there is a need to correctly position different rows of text in the same text column (like programming language editors do, or programming books use to print code that the reader must follow) or when you have a need to create an antique, typewriter-produced feeling for your text.

```
Take for example this paragraph. It was typed using the serif, monospaced
Courier New font, and you can surely replace it with many other monospaced
fonts available on the Internet, like American Typewriter, Consola, Love
Letter Typewriter, Monaco, and so on. Note, however, that whenever a
monospaced font is used, it may need many more printed pages than what is
needed to print the same text using a proportional font.
```

Figure 3-4 shows the alphabet using three popular proportional fonts (the serif Times New Roman, and the sans serif Arial and Calibri) and one monospaced font (the serif Courier New), all set to a 14 pt size. Note that all four paragraphs have a Tab character after the Font name and a left tabulation mark at 1.75 inches on the ruler to guarantee that each alphabet begins exactly at the same horizontal page position. Also note that the monospaced font Courier New needs many more horizontal spaces to represent the same alphabet letters!

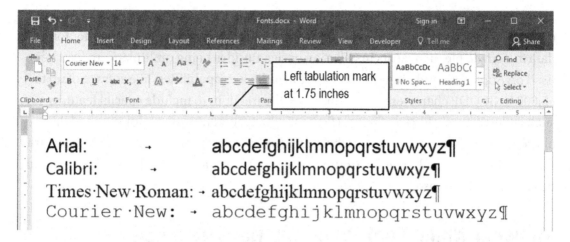

Figure 3-4. *Different alphabets typed with two sans serif (Arial and Calibri) and one serif (Times New Roman) proportionally spaced fonts, compared to one serif monospaced font (Courier New). Note how the monospaced font on the last text row needs much more horizontal space to represent the entire alphabet.*

Font Technologies

There are three main font technologies, which emerged at three different moments in time. You may find all of them to download as font files:

- Adobe PostScript Type 1

- TrueType

- OpenType

The Adobe Postscript Type 1 font was the first digital font, developed in the early 1980s. It is based on Adobe's PostScript printing technology, which is a programming language developed for high-resolution output, and has long been viewed as a reliable choice by professional designers, publishers, and printer manufacturers. Each postscript font consists of two different files: one to be seen on the screen and another to be sent to the printer (postscript printers expect to receive the postscript font instructions before printing).

The TrueType format was jointly developed by Apple and Microsoft about six years before the appearance of Adobe PostScript because both manufacturers early perceived that they needed to have its own font technology to not be controlled by an outside company (like Adobe), since it's such a key issue. They contain both the screen and printer font data in a single file, which makes them easier to install, and they can be used on both PC and Macintosh computers.

99

The OpenType format is the latest font technology to be introduced. It is a joint effort of Adobe and Microsoft, and like TrueType, contains both the screen and printer font data in a single file to make its installation easier. Besides being multiplatform (can be used on Apple, PC, and Linux), it has several exclusive capabilities, like storage of up to 65,000 UNICODE characters, which provides the freedom to include special features such as small caps, old-style figures (figures is the typographic name for numerals), alternate characters, different alphabet types (like Chinese, Arabic, etc.), and other extras that previously needed to be distributed as separate fonts and special characters that can be explored by Microsoft Word 2016.

Knowing Which Font Types You Have Installed

It may be interesting to know which font types you have installed on your Windows system so you can eventually select them to take advantage of all formatting available in Microsoft Word 2016 (as you will see in the section "Using Character Attributes" later in this chapter). To install a new font on your system, you must show the Windows Font folder (Figure 3-5), using one of these two methods:

1. Click Start ➤ Control Panel ➤ Appearance and Personalization ➤ Fonts, or

2. Open the Windows Explorer (click its icon on Windows taskbar or press Windows key+E), expand Computer ➤ Local disk (C:) ➤ Windows, and click the Font folder.

Attention   The Windows key is the one between the left Ctrl and Alt keys with the Microsoft symbol on it.

Figure 3-5 shows the default view for the Microsoft Windows Font folder.

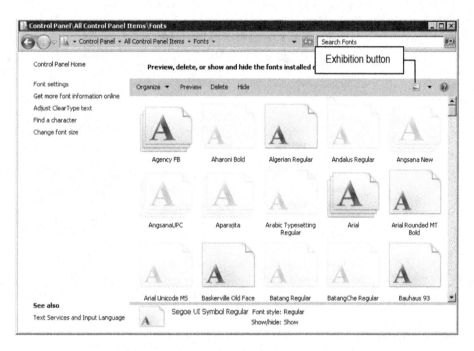

Figure 3-5. *The Microsoft Windows Fonts folder in your default view. Click its Exhibition icon and change its view to Details!*

In the Windows Font folder, you can list fonts installed by type following these instructions:

1. Click the View icon over the top right side of the Windows Font window and select the Details view.

2. Right-click the header column to show other column options and select Font Type in the context menu (Figure 3-6).

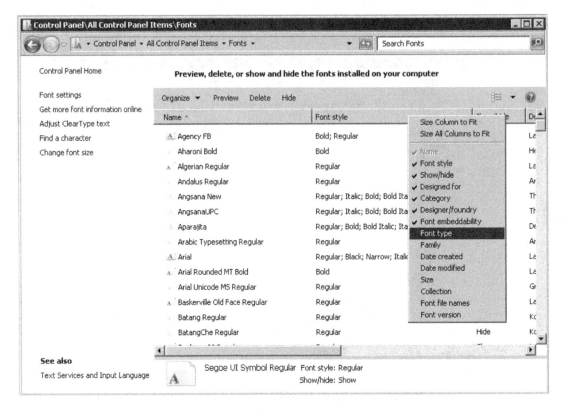

Figure 3-6. *After selecting the Details view, right-click any column header and show Font Type in the context menu. The Font Type column will be added as the last column header to the right.*

3. The Font Type column will be added as the last column header. You may eventually click the Font type header column and drag it to the left of the font name to be easier accessed.

4. Click Font Type header to classify fonts by type, or click the Font Type arrow and check the font type that must be shown by the Windows Font window (Figure 3-7).

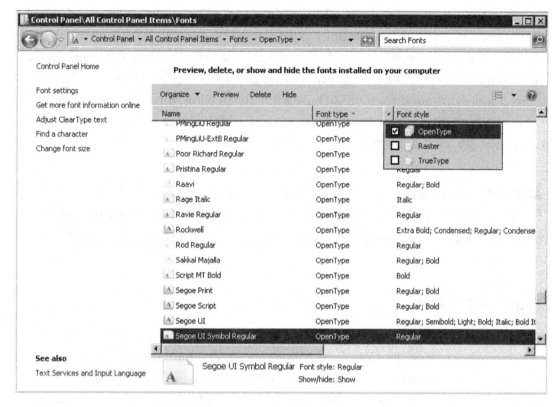

Figure 3-7. *Drag the Font Type column to the left of the Name column so you can easily select font types*

System Fonts

System Fonts are the ones that everybody has installed by a default installation of Microsoft Windows and/or Microsoft Office suite. They are considered by typographers and professional designers as despicable, mainly because they are

1. optimized for screen readability and not for print.

2. overexposed in the sense that they are used all time in almost every Word document;

3. not very well made, lacking finishing details.

Yes, I am talking about Times New Roman and Arial, the most used fonts in the world.

I personally don't dislike the combination or usage of Times New Roman/Arial fonts, but whenever you have the opportunity to get some professionally formatted text that feels like it has something like an undistinguished beauty, it is because it does not make use of system fonts: instead, it probably uses a professional set of serif/sans serif fonts.

So, if you want your documents to have a different feeling when others read them, you must rely on different serif and sans serif fonts, and the Internet is full of possibilities (see section the "How to Install Fonts" later in this chapter).

Attention   There are many fonts with very interesting path histories, like Times New Roman and Arial, which was the reasons for their selection as default system fonts for Microsoft Windows. Google it to find more information about this interesting issue.

Combining Fonts

To give a good impression, you must combine serif and sans serif fonts in the text, which is more a matter of taste than a science: something like combining colors, tie and shirt, purse and shoes... Anyway, there is an agreement that the use of a san serif font for chapter and section titles and a serif font for body text works better, mainly because it is supposed that the serifs helps the eye to follow the text.

As far as I know, all Microsoft Office documents that I have read used Arial in their chapter and title sections and Times New Roman in the body text. The idea is to create contrast to perfectly define when the paragraph is a title and when it is normal text (or body text).

Do some homework and try to find new fonts that may cause your documents to stand out from the crowd. Since there are a lot of different fonts to try, you must use simple rules to not overuse them in your document:

1. If possible, try to avoid the default Arial/Times New Roman combination: choose another pair of sans serif/serif fonts searching the Internet, and eventually buy some.

2. In text documents, try to use no more than three different fonts (one for chapter titles, one for section titles, and one for body text).

3. Never use script, fancy, or decorative fonts in your text documents: keep the simple serif/sans serif classical combination because... it is enough.

How to Install Fonts

There are thousands of Internet sites that offer free fonts for your usage. Note however that to have the best results you may need to buy some professional fonts. And once you have downloaded the desired font, you may receive an entire typeface font family (like the bold, italic, underline, and narrow variants) on a single zip file.

To install such fonts in Microsoft Windows, you must

1. Download the font (you may receive a compressed file that needs to be expanded to free the font files).

2. Select all downloaded font files and copy them to Clipboard (press Ctrl+C).

3. Navigate to the C:\Windows\Fonts folder. Microsoft Windows will change the folder appearance.

4. Right-click inside the C:\Windows\Fonts folder and select Paste to install the font.

Attention   You may need to close and open Microsoft Word so the installed fonts appear in the font list.

Using Special Characters

Special characters are those special symbols that don't exist on your keyboard, like the © (copyright) and ™ (trademark) symbols, currency symbols (¢, £, ¥), typographic symbols (§, ¶, etc.) and many others that you may regularly use in text.

Special Text Characters

Microsoft Word allows the use of some special characters as you type your text. Table 3-1 lists some of them.

Table 3-1. *Special Characters That You Can Type Inside a Microsoft Word Document*

Character name	Shortcut	Usage
Nonbreaking space	Ctrl + Shift + Space	Avoid separation of two words by a line break
Nonbreaking hyphen	Ctrl + Shift + _	Avoid separation of two hyphenated words by a line break
En-dash –	Ctrl + Num -	Used to separate text instead of the default hyphen
Em-dash —	Ctrl + Alt + Num -	Used in a special way to indicate dialog
Optional hyphen	Ctrl + -	The hidden character that may break a word at the end of a line
Ellipsis …	Ctrl + Alt + .	The … ellipsis character must be used instead of three dots …

Attention   The Num - expression used in Table 3-1 means the "-" character found on the numeric keypad found at the right of any PC keyboard, not the hyphen found near the Backspace key.

A nonbreaking space (Ctrl+Shift+Space) has the same width of the space character typed with the spacebar, but it prevents the text from flowing to a new line or page. A nonbreaking hyphen is the same: it has the same width of a regular hyphen but doesn't let the text flow from its position on one line to the next.

Use the nonbreaking space or the nonbreaking hyphen whenever two words (spaced or hyphenated like United States or Coca-Cola) or two successive punctuation characters (like the open and closing parenthesis after an Excel function name, like Sum()),, must not be broken at the end of a line: the entire expression must be always printed together on the same line.

About the size difference between the hyphen, en-dash, and em-dash, the hyphen is the shortest of them, and must be used to concatenate a compound word that represents two intimately related things, like fractions or ordinal numbers (three-quarters), to set words prefixed by ex-, self-, cross-, or all- (like ex-wife), and in numerous other situations.

The em-dash normally has the width of capital letter H, approaching the size of three successive hyphens ---, while the en-dash is half of its size (approaching the size of two successive hyphens --).

Use the en-dash to connect two things that are related by a range in substitution of the typical *from...to...* construction, like page numbers (pages 97–123), a span between two years, months, or days (207-2017, January–June, 23-31), etc.

Use the em-dash whenever you want to insert a break between parts of a sentence, to signal a personal speech in romances, to indicate duplicate citations on the same paragraph, or to put a nice pause in text to simulate a natural conversation between people. It is normally used at the beginning or in the middle of dialogs, like the next text (it has been italicized to call it to your attention):

> *— As I was saying, bla, bla, bla.... and he continued talking endlessly until Sara stood up and went to her room: — What is wrong, Sara? You don't like my stories? ...*

Attention   Some people believe that the origin of the em-dash and en-dash lies within the typographic widths of capital letters M and N, respectively. But this isn't so: the em-dash comes from the measure of the height of a piece of type used by a traditional metal font, while the en-dash always had half of its size. They were bigger in the past and in the Computer Age they became narrower.

Microsoft Word always changes single hyphens typed in the middle of a phrase to an en-dash character. In case it fails (and it sometimes does), type the Ctrl+Num - character.

The ellipsis is a single character that should be used in professionally formatted text instead of typing three successive dots. Since most of us have a strong addiction to typing three dots, use Microsoft Word Replace command to change three successive dots with the Ctrl+Alt+. character.

Symbols Command

Microsoft Word offers the Symbols dialog box (found in the Symbols area at the right border of the Insert tab of the Ribbon) to help you search and select the appropriate symbol you want to use in your document (Figure 3-8).

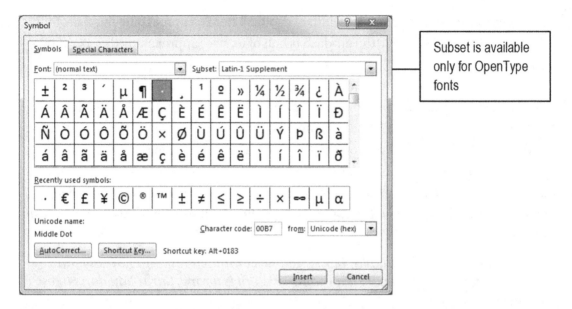

Figure 3-8. *Use the Symbol dialog box to select any symbol that may exist in any font and insert it into your document*

It is quite simple to use the Symbol dialog box:

- Select the desired font;

- In case it is an OpenType font, the Subset combo box appears to help you select specific subsets of characters inside the font (the list options may vary according to the font selected);

- Click the desired character and choose Insert (or press its associated shortcut key that appears at the bottom of the dialog box).

Attention   Use the Symbol dialog box to explore symbol fonts like Webdings, Wingdings, and so on.

The Symbol dialog box also offers the Special Character tab, from where you can select popular special characters and quickly insert them into your document – like the ones mentioned in Table 3-1 and shown in Figure 3-9.

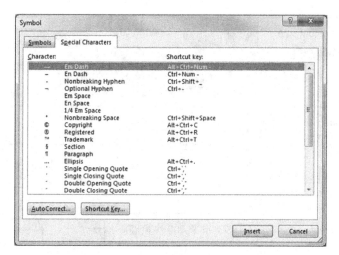

Figure 3-9. *The Special Character tab of the Symbol dialog box offers shortcuts to popular special characters you may need to insert into the document*

Optionally, you can also

- use AutoCorrect to associate a short name or nickname to the character so whenever you type it and press the space bar, Microsoft Word automatically changes it to the associated character (or character sequence).

- associate a Shortcut key to a special character (shortcut keys must be prefixed by Ctrl, Shift, Alt, or any combination of these keys).

Using Character Attributes

Microsoft Word uses the Font area of the Home tab of the Ribbon to allow control character attributes for any amount of text (Figure 3-10). You can select the font type, size, and most attributes by a single click of the mouse on the appropriate control, or by calling the Font dialog box (Figure 3-11), which offers traditional controls to these and other character attributes.

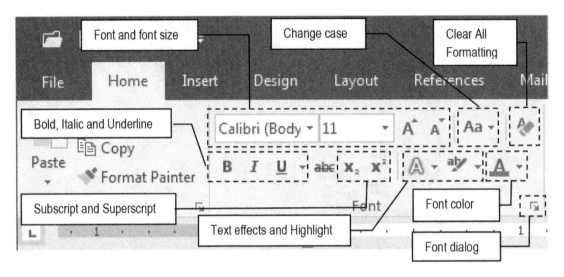

Figure 3-10. *Use the Microsoft Word Font area controls to change character attributes*

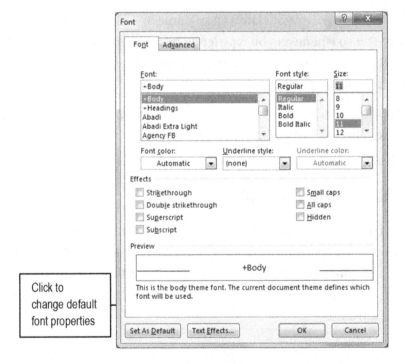

Figure 3-11. *The Font dialog box, from which you can select character attributes*

Attention   Click the Set as Default button of the Font dialog box to change the default font properties used by Microsoft Word to this and other new documents.

We will now explore each Font dialog control so you can make better use of them.

Font and Font Size

Now that you have a basic understanding about the different font types available in your Windows system, select the text first and use the Font combo box in the Font area of the Home tab of the Ribbon (Figure 3-10), or use the Font list box of the Font dialog box (Figure 3-11) to apply it to the selected font. Keep the text selected and use the Font size combo box to select the size.

Since Microsoft Word versions 2010, up to 2016, the default font selected is Calibri 11 pt, a sans serif font that appeared as an alternative to Arial (which is still present as a system Font). And by your knowledge gathered so far about inheritance, you may already know that once a font is selected in a blank paragraph, inheritance will take care to use it until another font is selected.

The point size selected for a text document must follow simple rules:

- The most comfortable point size range for body text is between 10 pt and 12 pt.

- Not every font appears equally when selecting the same point size (for instance, Arial or Calibri 12 are bigger than Times New Roman 12 pt).

- You can type intermediate half-point sizes in the Font Size combo box (try 10.5, 11.5, 12.5 etc.).

- Use a bigger font for headings.

- Use up to 14 or 16 pt size for the highest-level headings. Then, diminish the point size for subheadings by 1 or 0.5 points. Considering that if the headings are formatted using a sans serif font like Calibri, while the body text uses a serif font (like Times New Roman) it is probably bigger than the body text of the document.

- Use the Increase font size and Decrease font size controls of the Font area of the Home tab of the Ribbon to easily increase or decrease the selected text by one point up to 12 pt, and by two points above it (or their associated shortcuts Ctrl+Shift+> and Ctrl+Shift+<).

Font Color

Microsoft Word can change the text color of your documents by both using the Font color tool, found in the Font area of the Home tab of the Ribbon (Figure 3-10), or the Font Color option, found in the Font tab of the Font dialog box.

Although there are a lot of colors to choose from, be judicious when you need to apply colors by following some simple rules:

- Always use black for the body text: it is the better reading color for large amounts of text.

- Use colors in special text paragraphs, like chapter or title sections, headers, footers, and footnotes.

- Use colors for special characters and effects, like bullets, numberings (color just the number), and borders.

- Use a small set of colors in text: two or three colors at maximum. Less is more!

- Try to use shades of one single color (changing brightness) than multiple color tones.

- Avoid the use of close values or complementary colors in text, because they tend to decrease the contrast.

- It is better to use light colors instead of dark ones. The human eye is more prone to perceive subtle differences in light colors than darker.

- Once colors have been chosen for specific text paragraphs, keep consistency in their application through your entire document.

- Take a walk around the bookstore and study some colored books to get good ideas of how to use color in text.

- And never forget that a colored book is costlier to print than a black-and-white one.

Underline, Bold, and Italic

Underline, Bold, and Italic are text attributes used to highlight text that can be selected both in the Font area of the Home tab of the Ribbon (Figure 3-10) and in the Font style list box of the Font dialog box (Figure 3-11). Microsoft Word has simple shortcuts to Bold, Italic, and Underline:

- Press Ctrl+U to activate/deactivate Underline.

- Press Ctrl+B to activate/deactivate Bold.

- Press Ctrl+I to activate/deactivate Italic.

Underline

In typewriter days, text had no way to be highlighted using bold or italic: one had to go back and retype an underscore below the typed text to emphasize it. That is why Microsoft Word and every other text processor offer Underline as a text highlight option: it is a strange way to be linked to the past.

And if you look at the Microsoft Word Font area in the Home tab of the Ribbon, you will note that you have not just the U control to underline text, but may also have arrows to select different underline types and colors.

Although Microsoft Word offers so many ways to underline text, don't do it. It's is like using typewriter technology in computer times: use just Bold or Italic instead.

Bold and Italic

Bold and Italic are the preferred tools to give emphasis to the text, and are mutually exclusive: use one or another, never both. And since they are text properties, once you turn them on, they will be used on everything next to it due to character formatting inheritance!

Follow these simple rules to use Bold and Italic:

- Use bold in headings if they are less than one line long;

- Use Bold whenever you want your text to scream;

- Use italic for a subtle, gentle emphasis;

- NEVER use Bold and Italic together: take one or another;

- Use bold and italic as little as possible in body text, or you will lose the point;

- On Serif fonts, both Bold and Italic work well, but Italic doesn't work well on San Serif fonts.

Attention   Some fonts may have a bold style and a semibold style, while others can be heavier than bold, using "black" or "ultra" in its name. Use them just on large sizes for headlines or chapter titles. They don't work well in body text and should never be used there.

Subscript and Superscript

Superscript and Subscript are typographic resources that use a point size smaller than the text of the same line and appear above and below the main line of text, respectively. They can be selected both in the Font area of the Home tab of the Ribbon (Figure 3-10) and in the Effects area of the Font dialog box (Figure 3-11).

Superscripts are the small characters that appear partially above the x-line (see Figure 2-13), and are commonly used in mathematical or chemical formulas (like Einstein's famous equation $E = mc^2$) or to signal footnotes or endnotes in the text (like this one[1]—look to the end of this page).

Subscripts are the small characters that appear partially below the baseline (see Figure 2-13) and are used just in mathematical and chemical formulas (like the famous water chemical formula H_2O).

Microsoft Word offers the Subscript and Superscript tools in the Font area of the Home tab of the Ribbon (see Figure 3-8). Just click any of them and type: inheritance

---

[1]This is a footnote.

will take care to continually create subscript or superscript characters until you click the same tool again.

You can also use keyboard shortcuts to turn on/off subscript or superscript:

- Press Ctrl + Shift+ + to activate superscript characters;
- Press Ctrl + = to activate subscript characters;
- Press again any one of these two shortcuts to remove the subscript/ superscript and return to the normal text size.

Attention   If you accidentally activate subscript or superscript characters and want to remove this formatting option from the text, select the text first and press Ctrl+= twice: the first time everything will format as subscript; the second type will remove it.

Some professional OpenType fonts offer Subscript and Superscript character sets that may be slightly heavier than a smaller character should be, so that they're more legible. They can also be partially positioned above the Ascender or Capital letters of the font (for superscripts).

Change Case

The names uppercase and lowercase come from Gutenberg time, when printers kept the type for those letters in different drawers of a desk: they put the capital letters in the upper type cases, and the small letters for more frequent use in the lower type cases.

Everybody has already had the experience of typing a good amount of text and suddenly realizing that it was all typed using uppercase due to the Caps Lock key being inadvertently pressed.

Microsoft Word offers the Change case tool in the Font area of the Home tab of the Ribbon (see Figure 3-8) from where you can fix what you type, changing the case of the selected text letters. This easy-to-use tool works like this:

- Select the text first. For each sentence found in the selected text (a sentence is considered the text from one period, exclamation point, or question mark to the next);
- Click on the Change case tool and select one of its options:

- Sentence case: just the first letter of the first word of the sentence is in uppercase.

- lowercase: all characters in the sentence are in lowercase.

- UPPERCASE: all characters in the sentence are in uppercase.

- Capitalize Each Word: each word of the sentence begins in uppercase;

- tOGGLE cASE: for each word, alternate uppercase and lowercase each time the command is selected.

Attention   When Caps Lock key is pressed, a light appears on your keyboard. By using Shift while Caps Lock is pressed, things will change places and the keyboard will now type in lowercase.

Using Shift+F3 to Change Case

You can also use the Shift+F3 function key shortcuts to change case of the selected text. Supposing that the text is entirely in uppercase, each time you press Shift+F3 the text goes:

- from UPPERCASE to lowercase;

- from lowercase to First Word Of Each Letter In Uppercase;

- from First Word Of Each Letter In Uppercase to UPPERCASE

Try it for yourself; it's quite easy!

All Caps

All caps is short for "all capitals" and is an option in the Effects area of the Font dialog that changes lowercase to uppercase in the selected text. It is equivalent to pressing the Caps Lock key of your keyboard and typing everything in uppercase, or selecting the text and pressing Shift+F3 until all letters change to uppercase.

The use of uppercase letters in regular text may lead the reader to lose interest in reading because it turns the words into a monotone sequence of big rectangles that decrease the speed and ease of reading; on the other hand, the varying size of the lowercase letters—short and tall letters, ascending and descending glyphs—makes reading less challenging, allowing the eyes to read entire words by shape, instead of letter sequence.

Don't ever use uppercase letters in body text. Use it only in chapter and section titles and headlines shorter than one line, in headers and footers, or judiciously in very small phrases whenever you want to give emphasis to the text, but in this latter case, try to use Small caps (Figure 3-12).

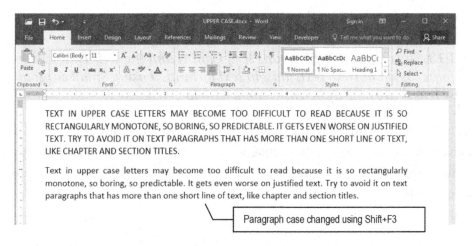

Figure 3-12. *Two version of the same text paragraph, with uppercase (all caps) and lowercase letters*

Attention   Whenever you feel prone to use uppercase letters in text paragraphs, try to detach them from the text using borders or by changing their background color or font size. But if you really need to use uppercase letters, also apply some positive character spacing and kerning to improve legibility (see "Scale, Character Spacing, and Kerning" later in this chapter.

Small Caps

Small caps are another option in the Effects area of the Font dialog box that creates short capital letters having the size of lowercase letters (Figure 3-13).

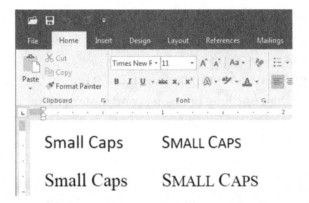

Figure 3-13. *Text typed using the sans serif Calibri and the serif Times New Roman fonts. At left normal text, at right text formatted using Small caps: all the lowercase letters are now uppercase letters with lowercase size.*

Text in Small caps can be used as alternative to uppercase, bold, and italic to detach text or give it emphasis or some distinctiveness, and that is why it is so frequently used for business cards of law firms' names. Although it may be less jarring than all caps, try to avoid its use in larger amounts of text: use it judiciously in title and subtitle sections where all words begin with a capital letter, or it will lose its impact (Figure 3-14).

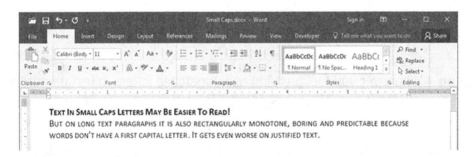

Figure 3-14. *Use Small Caps effect on small section titles (up to a line long) where all words have first letters in uppercase*

Strikethrough, Double Strikethrough, and Hidden

The Effect options ~~Strikethrough~~, ~~Double strikethrough~~, and Hidden are digitally used by Microsoft Word whenever its Track Changes options are checked in the Tracking area of the Review tab on the Ribbon.

Whenever you check the Track Changes option—which is excellent to track changes of shared documents created by different people at the same time, or the ones that are suffering a digital copy desk service—Microsoft Word will use the ~~Strikethrough~~ effect to format deleted text, and the ~~Double strikethrough~~ effect to format moved text. Both options will also receive the Hidden effect so you can select the Original or No Markup options to hide them from view.

Attention   These options should not be used to format your documents since they may make the text unreadable.

Scale, Character Spacing, and Kerning

Scale, Character spacing, and Kerning are typographic resources to control the space horizontally occupied by any amount of text. They are frequently used in desktop publishing to make the text fit into a defined amount of space on the page (like newspapers do), and/or to avoid text paragraphs ending in split words or the appearance of orphan or widow lines.

Microsoft Word offers in the Character Spacing area in the Advanced tab of the Fonts dialog box fine adjustments for changing Scale, Character space, and Kerning (Figure 3-15).

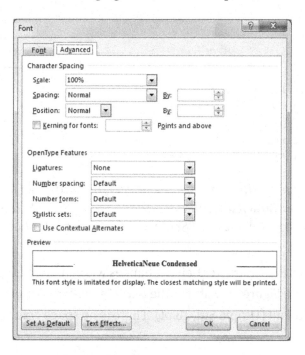

Figure 3-15. *The Advanced tab of the Fonts dialog box, where you can find adjustments for character spacing and kerning*

Scale

Character scale stretches or shrinks the width of letters and the space in between them in a block of text: there is no change to the height of the letters, so they keep the same point size regarding line spacing.

Character space = 100% means a normal character size for the selected font. Amounts below 100% diminish the character's width, while those greater than 100% increase it. Figure 3-16 shows how the expression "Character Scale" looks at different amounts of scale. Note how the horizontal space is affected by Scale: a Scale = 50% uses half the horizontal space required by Scale = 100% (normal character size), which is half the size of Scale = 200%.

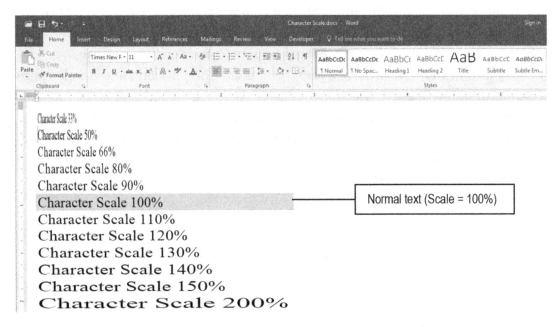

Figure 3-16. *This figure shows how Scale affects the character width for the selected text. A Scale = 50% uses half the horizontal width of Scale = 100% (normal text), which is also 50% the width of Scale = 200%. Character height is not changed!*

Although it seems that character height changes with an increase or decrease in the Scale value, they don't. Figure 3-17 shows the letter "a" with scales of 50%, 100%, and 200% for the selected font (Utopia Std, 18 pt). There is no space character between these characters.

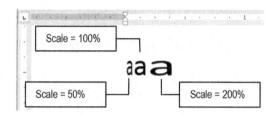

Figure 3-17. *Character scale does not affect character height: the characters keep the same font size regarding line space, while changing its horizontal dimension.*

When applying character Scale, you can type the desired amount of scale using integer values. Don't use too much or too small scale values when there is a need to stretch or shrink the text, respectively. Select the text and employ small increases or decreases until you get the desired effect. A well-done scale factor should be almost imperceptible to the reader.

Note however that Scale always distorts the type, producing undesirable results in printed text. That is why some fonts may include variations having a suffix like "condensed" or "expanded" that are designed with different horizontal spreads than the one applied to the plain style, and this font version will perform better when printed.

Spacing

Spacing, also called *letterspacing* or *tracking*, changes just the horizontal space between characters while keeping their proportions the same. No distortion is applied to the type. This control affects text legibility because small amounts of added spacing make characters emerge and be easily recognizable, which is especially true for smaller font sizes.

Microsoft Word uses Spacing = Normal to designate the default font character space. It uses the words Condensed and Expanded to smaller or greater space values, respectively.

Character spacing is used in accordance with changes made in Font size, Font weight (normal, bold), and letter case. There is a direct relationship between letter case, font size, and character spacing. Larger font sizes need smaller character spacing, and vice versa. The same is true for uppercase letters: their default space is designed to be the minimum necessary, and they will show better using an expanded character spacing.

Conversely, there is an inverse relationship between font weight and letter space: light typefaces are well complemented by using expanded character spacing, while bold typefaces go better by pulling letters close together.

Follow these rules to correctly use Character spacing in text:

- Normal text (between 10 and 12 pt) should have Character Spacing = Normal.

- Large text size (> 12 pt) may be improved by a Character Spacing = Condensed.

- Smaller text size (< 10 pt) goes better with Character Spacing = Expanded.

- Use between 5–12% of the point size to increase character spacing without making noticeable alterations in text flow (for a 12 pt size font this means Spacing = Expanded between 0.6–1.4 pt).

- Use no less than 5% of point size to decrease character spacing, or the text characters will begin to be huddled, seeming to fall one over the other (for a 12 pt size font this means Spacing = Condensed not greater than 0.6 pt).

- Do not add too much space. If letters are spread too far apart, having space enough to fit more letters in between, it is because the Expanded effect is overused.

- Conversely, do not remove too much space. If letters begin to touch each other on their glyphs, it is because the Condensed effect is overused.

Figure 3-18 shows how character spacing impacts the sans serif Arial Narrow font and the serif Times New Roman font formatted using different character spacing options (from condensed to expanded). Look how text becomes huddled at greater condensing and how it grows at greater expansions.

-1.4pt	CHARACTERSPACING	CHARACTERSPACING	-1.4pt	Condensed
-1.0pt	CHARACTER SPACING	CHARACTER SPACING	-1.0pt	Condensed
-0.6pt	CHARACTER SPACING	CHARACTER SPACING	-0.6pt	Condensed
0.0pt	CHARACTER SPACING	CHARACTER SPACING	0.0pt	Normal
+0.6pt	CHARACTER SPACING	CHARACTER SPACING	+0.6pt	Expanded
+1.0pt	CHARACTER SPACING	CHARACTER SPACING	+1.0pt	Expanded
+1.4pt	CHARACTER SPACING	CHARACTER SPACING	+1.4pt	Expanded

Figure 3-18. *Different character spacing options and how they affect text legibility*

Position

Position, typographically called *baseline shift*, allows raising or lowering the baseline of selected text without making any change to its size or appearance. It is considered a great typographical tool to vertically displace text characters and create special text effects that are quite subtle, and not available inside the font character set.

Microsoft Word Position command must be set to Normal (at the baseline), Raised (above the baseline), or Lowered (below the baseline), using increment values of 0.5 pt size.

Some examples of using Position:

- **Diagonal fractions**: use less than 10% of the Font size to raise and lower fraction items, while diminishing the font size by 1 pt for numerator and denominator, to avoid affecting the paragraph baseline displacement too much. The **12/19** fraction, which can be formatted as $^{12}/_{19}$ in this line, formatted with Utopia, 9 pt, by using Utopia 8 pt and Position = 1 pt to raise the numerator and lower the denominator (note that the line spacing of this paragraph was not affected).

- **Raise the @ symbol**: use 2 pt size to raise the @ symbol in e-mail addresses so the inferior part of the @ character be positioned at the baseline: the **flaviomorgado@gmail.com** became **flaviomorgado@gmail.com** where the @ character received Position = Raised = 1.5 pt for a 9 pt font.

- **Lower the ™ trademark symbol:** use Position = Lowered = 1.5 pt on the trademark symbol to align it to the x-line (height of lowercase letters): **Apress books™** becomes **Apress books™.**

It is also used to create a ^{j}a^{g}g^{e}d, ^{j}u^{m}p^y visual text effect by raising or lowering intermediate characters, or even vertically repositioning parentheses, braces, brackets, bullets and other special characters commonly found in text (like @, $, ©, ™, etc.).

Attention   The Position option impacts the line spacing the same way as font size, meaning that if the Line space option of the Paragraph dialog box is not set to the Exactly option, the paragraph line where any character changes its vertical displacement may show a bigger line space.

Kerning

Kerning refers to adjusting the space of some specific pairs of characters so they can occupy less space and achieve a subtle, pleasant result, usually imperceptible to user eyes. It is most perceptible when using large font sizes (>14 pt), although it can be applied to any font size. It is applied when a letter has a diagonal or horizontal glyph that can serve as a *hatch* to the next letter, like WA, Wa, VA, Va, Ti, Ta, Yi, Ya ...

Kerning is typographically considered as a good formatting practice and is recommended to be imposed to any text size. This is so true that most OpenType fonts may have tenths or hundreds of specific kerning pairs encoded inside it.

Microsoft Word offers the Kerning for fonts option in the Character Spacing area of the Advanced area of the Font dialog box (see Figure 3-15) unchecked by default. When you check it, you can select the smallest font size to where kerning must be applied (Microsoft Word offers 20 pt size as the default value, because kerning in small font size can make it difficult to correctly discriminate some pairs of letters).

Figure 3-19 shows some letter encounters with and without kerning, and how the word WAVE can change its appearance with and without kerning.

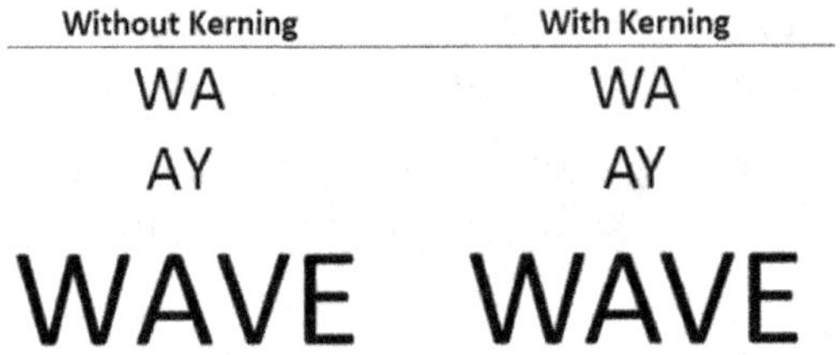

Figure 3-19. Subtle kerning text adjustments for WA, AY, and WAVE

Attention   Professional desktop publishing programs, such as Quark XPress and Adobe InDesign, allow the user to define precise kerning controls in many different units.

OpenType Features

The OpenType Features area, found in the Advanced area of the Font dialog box, is logically applied to just OpenType fonts. It allows turn on the usage of alternate characters to the selected text, in case the options were implemented in the selected font.

Attention   See section "Knowing Which Font Types You Have Installed" earlier in this chapter to learn how you can identify the OpenType fonts installed on your computer.

If you are wondering if every OpenType font implements each OpenType feature, the answer is no. Some fonts implement no features, others implement just some, and almost none implement them all.

So, how you can know before trying these features? Simple: use the Symbol dialog box to explore the font character set.

Attention   See section "Symbols Command" earlier in this chapter to learn how you can evoke and use the Symbol dialog box.

To simplify our example, let us use the Calibri font: one of the most popular OpenType fonts (and one that already become a System font), Calibri was introduced with Microsoft Office 2007 so Microsoft Word could implement many of the OpenType Features offered by the Advanced tab of the Font dialog box.

By opening the Symbol dialog box (found in the Insert tab ➤ Symbols area) and selecting the Calibri font in the Font combo box, you will note that its subset combo box has an extensive list of OpenType features to select, among which you will find "Space modified letters," "Superscripts and Subscripts," "Currency Symbols," "Number forms," "Alphabetical Presentation Forms," to mention just a few (Figure 3-20).

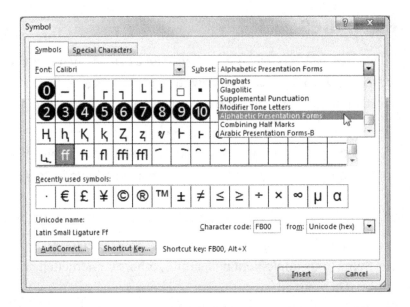

Figure 3-20. *The Symbol dialog box with the Calibri font selected, showing part of its extensive subset of OpenType features (like the "Alphabetic Presentation Forms," popularly known as "ligtures")*

Ligatures

Ligature is the word used to indicate when glyphs from two or more characters collide. It is quite common in handwriting, when two characters have some of their strokes merged with one above or inside another, becoming a single letter. It is a typographic resource that may evoke an arcane way of printing that gives an old-fashioned look to the text; it's a matter of taste whether to use it or not.

The character that best represent a ligature is the ampersand (&), which represents the ligature of letters *e* and *t*, forming the Latin word *et* (which means *and*).

In the metal typesetting times, some letters for specific fonts may have created a problem when put together, like the ff, fi, fj, fl encounters, but this problem doesn't happen anymore in most digital fonts.

The Ligature options are as follows:

- **None**: no ligatures.

- **Standard Only**: combine just certain pairs of letters (like fi).

- **Standard and Contextual**: combine certain pairs of letters contextually positioned before or after them.

- **Historical and Discretionary**: more used on ck, sp, st, and rt letter pairs to give a decorative or fancy appeal.

- **All**: apply all types of ligatures whenever is possible.

Figure 3-21 shows the Font dialog box in which the Calibri font was selected, and a pair or trio of letters like ff, fi, fl, ffi, ffl was typed in the text, without and with ligatures, so you can see how the OpenType Feature Ligatures = Standard Only (the one offered by this font) appears in the Preview area of the Font dialog box and when applied to the text. Instead of the two letters typed, Microsoft Word changes the two typed characters to a single one in which the individual component letters are joined together by their glyphs.

Attention   Use font size up to 20 pt to see the effect in the Preview area of the Font dialog box.

Since a ligature uses a single character, it must not be used with the Spacing option, because the internal space of the letters associated will not change.

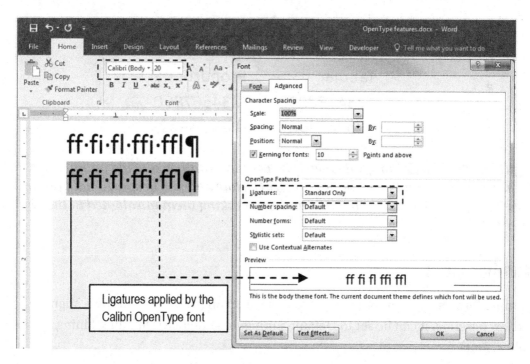

Figure 3-21. *The Calibri font OpenType Featere Ligatures = Standard Only option set to some pairs or trios of letters. Note how the two or three letters were replaced with a single one that runs them together by joining their glyphs.*

Attention   Ligatures are best used in some script fonts, like Gabriola, which is installed by default with Microsoft Word 2007 or later versions, and the reader is invited to use it to explore more about this issue.

Number Spacing

Number spacing is a typographic resource that allows a choice between Default, Tabular, or Proportional spacing between the numbers (Default = Tabular for the Calibri font).

Tabular is used when there is a need to precisely align numbers using the same text column in different lines of text, like in financial reports. Proportional makes each number occupy just the space it needs, so they will not align well in two different lines of text; this is preferable for numbers in the text or headlines.

Figure 3-22 shows two sets of numbers, one using the OpenType Feature Number spacing = Tabular (Default) and Proportional options. Note how the Tabular option misaligns the text between two different text lines.

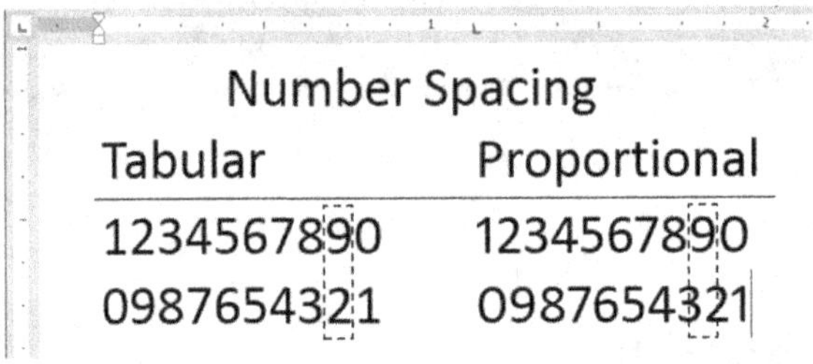

Figure 3-22.   *The Calibri font OpenType Feature Number spacing option set to Tabular (at left) and Proportional (at right). Note how the Proportional option uses just the space required by each number, making them misaligned in the two lines of text.*

Number Form

Number form is a typographic resource that can change the way numbers align to the text baseline. It can be set to Default, Lining, or Old-style (Default = Lining in the Calibri font).

Lining means that each number is aligned to the baseline, with all having the size of an uppercase letter. The Old-style option produces numbers with different heights and baseline alignments: some are the size of lowercase letters (normally 1, 2, and 0), others are the size of uppercase letters (normally 3, 4, 5, 6, 7, 8, and 9), and they have different baseline alignments (3, 4, 5, 7, and 9 are positioned below the baseline, while 6 and 8 are positioned on it).

The Lining option can be used in any situation but goes better with uppercase letters. The Old-style option is preferred in body text with lowercase letters.

Figure 3-23 shows how the OpenType Feature Number Form appears for the Calibri font using Lining (Default) and Old-style options. Letters ABcep were put together to show how the Old-style option makes numbers the size of uppercase and lowercase letters, and how some align below the baseline (with letter p descender line) or at the baseline.

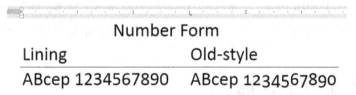

Figure 3-23. *The Calibri fontOpenType Feature Number Form with the Lining (Default) and Old-style options. Note how Old-style uses different alignments and baseline displacements (uppercase and lowercase letters—one with a descender— were inserted to allow alignment comparisons for the OpenType Old-style numbers).*

Stylistic Set

Stylistic set refers to specific alternate character sets that were built at specific positions inside the Unicode font. Each set consists of different characters' styles grouped by similar variations of glyphs, and although the OpenType standard reserves space to implement up to 20 possible different Stylistic sets, it is rare to find a font that implements more than six of them.

The Stylistics set options are identified by numbers (Stylistics set=1 to Stylistics set =20) and are applied to certain characters at the beginning or end of words, according to the option selected.

It is normally used in certain OpenType script fonts (like Gabriola, installed by default with Word 2016) to give a flourish to the text, presenting an old-fashioned appearance typically found for marriage invites and other types of official certificates.

Table 3-2 shows how the Gabriola font changes its appearance with Stylistics set = 2, 4, 5 and 6 (options Default and 1, 2, and 3 look the same).

Table 3-2. *Different Stylistic Set Options Applied to a Default Text Using the Gabriola Font*

Stylistics set	Gabriola font example
Default	Once Upon a Time… The Script Gabriela Font added some Flourish to its Text.
2	Once Upon a Time… The Script Gabriela Font added some Flourish to its Text.
4	Once Upon a Time… The Script Gabriela Font added some Flourish to its Text.
5	Once Upon a Time… The Script Gabriela Font added some Flourish to its Text.
6	Once Upon a Time… The Script Gabriela Font added some Flourish to its Text.

Use Contextual Alternates

This option allows Microsoft Word to automatically apply alternate characters when special letter encounters are found in the text, so it can use specific OpenType alternate characters to improve both spacing and ligature connections. Whenever this option is checked *and* the OpenType font implements the feature, Microsoft Word can select specific alternate characters to the beginnings and ends of some words, or to some others that are next to punctuation or at the end of a paragraph.

The Text Effects Tool

Text Effects tools are located in the Font area of the Home tab of the Ribbon (Figure 3-10). It allows the selection of predefined color and font options, or the specification of the Outline, Shadow, Reflection, Glow, Number Styles, Ligatures, and Stylistics set to be applied to the text, as a shortcut to the same options found in the Font dialog box (Figure 3-24).

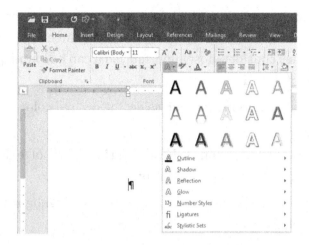

Figure 3-24. *The Text Effects tool allows a quick access to the OpenType Features found in the Advanced tab of the Font dialog box. Some options will be available just when the text selected uses an OpenType font that implements the effect (such as Number Sytles, Ligatures, and Stylistic Sets).*

These coloring options, which can change letter outline and foreground colors, are seldom used in cursive text document formatting, but are very useful for posters, banners, and other fancy or decorative one-page publications.

Some of its options (like OpenType features) become enabled only when the cursor or selected text is formatted with an OpenType font. And since you can select a lot of different options, one by one, Microsoft Word also offers the Clear All Formatting tool (see Figure 3-10) to return the selected text to its default appearance.

Attention   Use the Text Effects tools as the simplest way to verify if the selected font is an OpenType one, and if it implements the desired OpenType Features: an OpenType face will enable Number Styles, Ligatures, and Stylistic Sets options.

Text Highlight

Besides some specific options found in the Text Effects tool (like Outline, Shadow, Reflection, and Glow), the Text Highlight tool is the only tool that does not has an equivalent command inside the Font dialog box.

Text highlight is used to mimic the highlight pens used to mark text, detaching important parts from the text that surround it: this is a resource used by many people to highlight whichever they consider most important, so it can be found quickly.

Its usage is straightforward:

- Click the Highlight tool arrow and select the desired color (default is bright yellow);

- Select the text first and then click the Text Highlight tool to detach it and automatically deselect the tool; or

- Click (or double-click the tool to lock it) and then highlight multiple parts of the document

To remove the highlight applied to the text you can

- Select the Highlight tool color used;

- Select the text and again apply the Highlight tool with the same color (or select the No color option);

- Use the Clear All Formatting tool (see Figure 3-10).

But when you have a large text document full of highlights and you want to remove then all, you can use one of these two strategies:

1. Press Ctrl+A to select the entire document text and apply the Text Highlight tool twice: the first time will apply highlight to the entire text, and the second time will remove it;

2. Use the Replace dialog box to find any highlighted text and change it to normal text (see section "Find and Replace Font Attributes" later in this chapter).

Attention   The Shading tool, found in the Paragraph area in the Home tab of the Ribbon (see Figure 2-7), can also be used to highlight text with the same bright yellow default color used by the Highlight tool. Whenever this happens, you will not be able to remove the highlight using the Highlight tool; while it may seem to be the same formatting, it really is not. So, whenever you can't remove text highlighting using the Highlight tool, try to use the Shading color tool instead, using the same technique cited before: apply it twice to the entire text: the first time will paint all text background with the selected color, while the second time will remove it.

To remove text highlight made with the Highlight tool, use the tool No Color option, apply the same highlight color twice, or use the Replace command to find and replace it.

Text Highlight with the Shading Tool

It is also possible to highlight text with the Shading tool using the same bright yellow color defined by default in the Highlight tool. The final result will look the same, but the formatting applied is different, and it may be difficult to remove it in case you do not understand what has happened to the text.

Try to follow these steps using any text document:

1. Click the Shading tool arrow and select the same bright yellow color used by the Highlight tool;

2. Select the text to be highlighted;

3. Click the Shading tool to highlight the text.

The only difference you may perceive to indicate that the Shading tool was used to highlight text happens whenever the hidden pilcrow paragraph character ¶ was also highlighted, because Microsoft Word will highlight the text until it reaches its right indent character on the ruler (which is usually aligned to the right page margin).

Figure 3-25 shows the "Text Highlight.docx" Microsoft Word document (which you can extract from Chapter03.zip file), showing text paragraphs highlighted with the same bright yellow color using both the Highlight and Shading tools. They look the same, don't they?

Note however that the second highlighted paragraph has its background highlighted to its right margin indent, as a clear indication that this formatting was made using the Shading tool.

The problem with the Shading tool is that its formatting is not easily removed: you must select exactly the same text highlight to remove it by applying its No Color option.

Let me be clear: if you select more text than the one that was originally highlighted with the Shading tool and apply to it a No Color option with the Shading tool, you *will not remove the highlight!* (Open the document and try for yourself).

But it gets even more complicated when both options were simultaneously used in selected text: you can't remove the highlight using just the Highlight or the Shading tool—you must use both!

When this happens, you have two choices:

- Use the Clear All Formatting tool;

- Use the Format Painter tool.

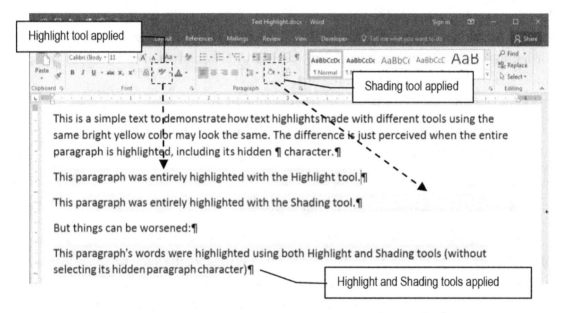

Figure 3-25. *Text highlighted using the Highlight and Shading tool (or both simultaneously). When these tools use the same color, you cannot disinguish which formatting was applied to the text, which makes it harder to remove.*

Use the Clear All Formatting Tool

The Clear All Formatting tool (Figure 3-10) is supposed to remove every text formatting applied by the Font and Paragraph dialog boxes, returning the text to its original state. Just click the Clear All Formatting tool to select it and drag it over the text to

- Bring to the text the default paragraph font (the one applied to its first character, which is stored in the hidden ¶ character).

- Remove bold, italic, underline, subscript, superscript, character spacing, OpenType features, and so on. Text will use the regular font size and appearance.

- Remove any paragraph formatting: line spacing, alignment, spacing before and after, flow properties.

- Remove any tabulation marks.

- Remove any Shading and Border options.

It is almost perfect to remove formatting options, except for the fact that it doesn't remove Highlight tool options: this format will remain in the text. (See for yourself!)

Use the Format Painter Tool

The easiest way to remove undesirable text format while keeping the format you want is to use the Format Painter tool (Figure 3-10) to copy the source format and apply it to a target text, following these steps:

- Select the text that has the desired source format.

- Click the Format Painter tool to copy all its formatting options (double-click it to lock the tool).

- Drag the mouse over the target text.

Using this simple method, you can easily remove both the Highlight and Shading tools with a click of the mouse!

Drop Cap

Drop Cap is the typographic resource used to enlarge one or more letters that begin a new paragraph (like this large letter "D") to signal that the text has a new beginning. It is commonly used to open a paragraph or a report, and was used from the 4th century in codex books created by scribes and monks as a visual clue to clearly define when a new section or idea started in the text.

The large letter "D" that begins the first paragraph of this section is called a *Drop Cap* because it grows down into the text, taking up the left space of the initial text lines below it.

It is called an *Initial* when the character size grows above the baseline of the first paragraph line where it resides (like this large letter "I" you see here).

Since this text effect has both font and paragraph formatting, affecting the letter dimension and the paragraph left indent, respectively, Microsoft Word implements it using the Drop Cap tool found in the Text area of the Insert tab of the Ribbon (Figure 3-26).

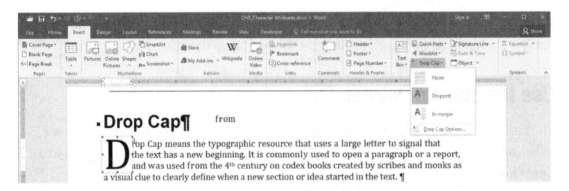

Figure 3-26. *Microsoft Word Drop Cap tool found in the Text area of the Insert tab of the Ribbon offers two options to left indent the paragraph that receives the Drop Cap letter: Dropped and In Margin.*

Microsoft Word enables the Drop Cap tool whenever the text is over a text paragraph with at least one single character typed, and as Figure 3-25 implies, it offers three different options:

- Dropped: is the most common usage, where it creates a first line indent to all lines affected by the drop cap letter;

- In Margin: left indent all paragraph lines, leaving the drop cap paragraph floating alone in the text;

- Drop Cap options: show the Drop Cap dialog box from where you can better define the appearance of the drop cap letter (Figure 3-27).

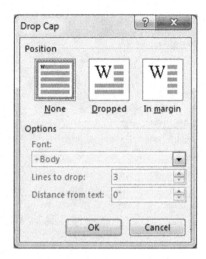

Figure 3-27. *The Drop Cap dialog box allows you to control the drop cap type and its appearance, including its font, the lines to drop, and the distance from text*

Use the Drop Cap dialog box to control the drop cap appearance, including the position, the number of lines to drop, and the distance from the text. And as Figure 3-26 shows, Microsoft Word adds a frame with handles around the first letter used by the drop cap to detach it from the text and make the remaining text flow around it.

Use the next tips to remove and format drop cap letter from the text:

- To remove and replace a drop cap letter, just apply again the Drop Cap command. Alternatively, you can click the drop cap frame border and press the Delete key–but you will need to retype the first paragraph letter.

- Drag the drop cap frame handles to increase/decrease the drop cap size.

- Double-click the drop cap frame border to show the Frame dialog box, from which you can select other frame options (Figure 3-28).

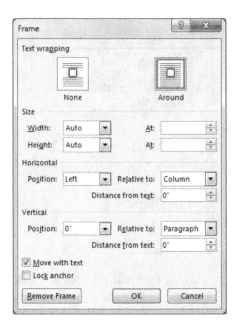

Figure 3-28. *Double-click the drop cap frame margin to show the Frame dialog box, where you can precisely control the frame properties. Use the Remove Frame button to remove the frame, and consequentely the drop cap effect.*

- To use more than one letter as a drop cap, first select the letters and then apply the drop cap command. Alternatively, click the drop cap frame and type more letters.

- There is no rule on what font may be used for the drop cap–you can use the same paragraph font. But you may have better effects using decorative fonts.

- Avoid using drop caps of less than 3 lines in height: they aren't effective in calling the reader's attention or adding drama to the text.

- Avoid using drop caps of more than 7 lines in height.

- Don't use drop caps with center or right aligned paragraphs.

Find and Replace Font Attributes

Microsoft Word allows you to use the Find and Replace dialog box to search for specific text formatting and eventually remove it or replace it with another formatting option. This operation does not require that any character be searched or replaced.

Click the Replace command found in the Editing area at the right of the Home tab of the Ribbon to show the Find and Replace dialog box, click More to expand it and select the Format button, and note that it offers options to define Font, Paragraph, and so on; see the options shown in Figure 3-29.

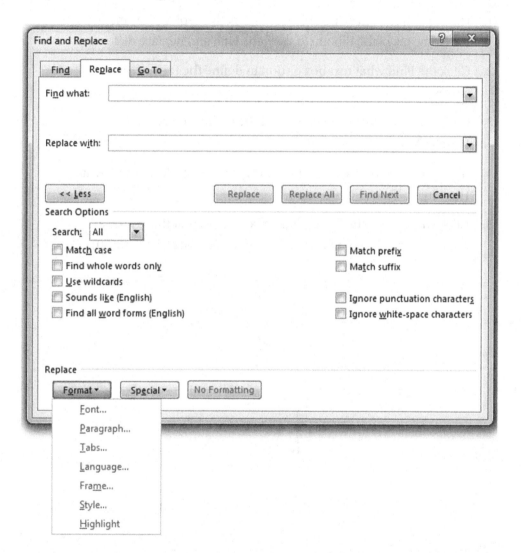

Figure 3-29. *Use the Format button options of the Find and Replace dialog box to select specific Font, Paragraph, Tabs, Language, Frame, Style, and Highlight formatting for both the Find what and Replace with options.*

Each one of these options will bring the associated dialog box, from which you can choose the formatting option that you want to find and/or replace.

Let us suppose that you have a text document where the section title paragraphs were formatted with Arial, 14 pt, Underline, Left aligned and you want to change them to Times New Roman, 16 pt, Bold text, Center aligned. You can easily change the formatting options applied to all these section title paragraphs by following these steps:

1. Highlight the text to be changed and select the Replace command in the Home tab of the Ribbon to show the Find and Replace dialog box.

2. Click the Find what text box option to define the format to be searched.

3. Click the More>> button to expand the dialog box and select Format ➤ Font.

4. In the Font dialog box, select the format to search for: Font = Arial, Font Style = Bold, Font size = 14.

5. Click OK to close the Font dialog box and see that these format options were placed below the Find what text box (Figure 3-30).

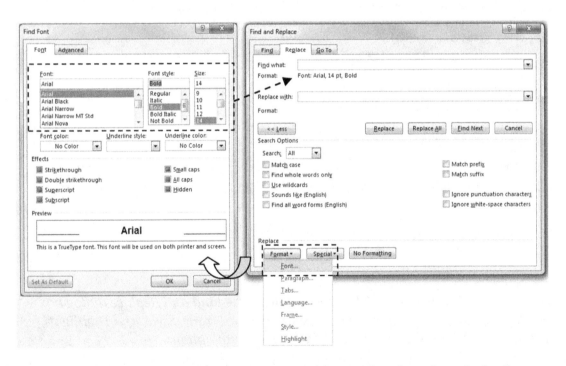

Figure 3-30. *Use the Format ➤ Font option of the Find and Replace dialog box to define within the Find what text box the font formatting options that must be searched for in the text (Arial, 14 pt, Bold).*

6. Click the Replace with text box option to define the replacement format and click the Format ➤ Font option again.

7. On the Font dialog box, select the replacement format: Font = Times New Roman, Font Style = Regular, Font size = 16.

8. Click OK to close the Font dialog box, and click Format ➤ Paragraph to show the Paragraph dialog box.

9. In the Paragraph dialog box, select Alignment = Center and press OK to close it and see how these formatting options were placed below the Replace with text box (Figure 3-31).

10. Click Replace all to make all possible replacements.

Note in Figures 3-30 and 3-31 that the check box options found in the Font and Paragraph dialog boxes are grayed and checked by default. This formatting convention means that the option will not be removed in case it is already set, and neither set case it is not applied. Figure 3-31 also shows that the Page break found before in the Pagination area of the Line and Page Breaks tab of the Paragraph dialog box was checked (it is not grayed anymore), meaning that this option should be set by the Replace with option. See Figure 3-31.

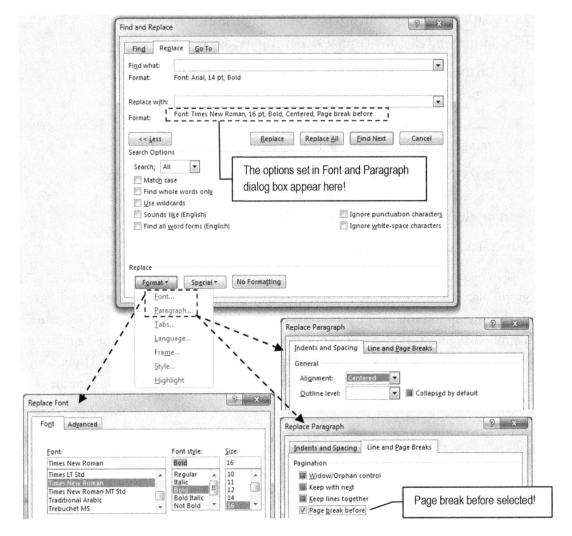

Figure 3-31. *Use the Format ➤ Font option of the Find and Replace dialog box again to define within the Replace with text box the new font formatting options that must be applied to the text (Times New Roman, 16 pt, Bold).*

Use these tips to search and replace text formatting:

- The font or paragraph attribute selected in the Find what text box doesn't need to be selected in the Replace with text box: if you search for a font you don't need to replace it.

- To search and remove markups made with the Highlight tool, click the Find what text box and select Format ➤ Highlight, then click the Replace with text box and select Format ➤ Highlight twice.

- Use the No Formatting button to remove any formatting of the Find what and Replace with text boxes.

Exercise 1

The objective of this exercise is to quickly format a document with specific text formatting options using Microsoft Word's Replace command:

Extract "The Adventures of Tom Sawyer Chapter 1-3 Unformatted.docx" file from Chapter03.zip and open it in Microsoft Word. This is a small document of 11 pages with the first three chapters of the famous Mark Twain book *The Adventures of Tom Sawyer*, published in 1856.

When you open it for the first time in Microsoft Word, it may be similar to what you see in Figure 3-32.

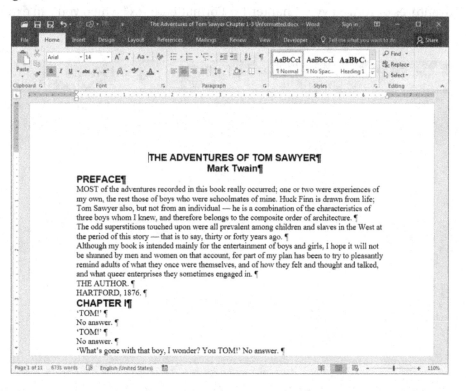

Figure 3-32. *This is "The Adventures of Tom Sawyer Chapter 1-3 Unformatted. docx" file that you can extract from Chapter03.zip.*

Note that its first two chapter titles (Preface and Chapter1) are formatted with Arial, 14 pt, Bold font, and that the body text is formatted with Times New Roman 12: two typical System fonts.

143

Apply the document text formatting options using Microsoft Word Replace command:

- Section titles (book title and chapter titles):

  - **Font**: Verdana, 16 pt, Bold.

  - **Paragraph**: Spacing Before = 24 pt, Page break before.

- Body text (paragraphs formatted with Times New Roman font):

  - **Font**: Georgia, 11 pt.

  - **Paragraph**: Justify alignment, First line indent = 0.3, Line spacing = Single, Widow/Orphan control.

- Apply a Drop Cap to the first paragraph of every section.

Figure 3-33 shows Microsoft Word using a two-page view for this document version ("The Adventures of Tom Sawyer Chapter 1-3 Formatted.docx", which you can extract from Chapter03.zip) that received all proposed changes.

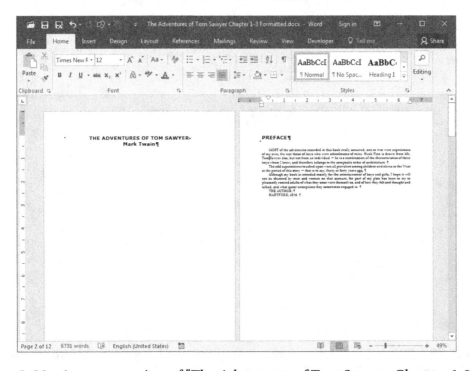

Figure 3-33. *A two-page view of "The Adventures of Tom Sawyer Chapter 1-3 Formatted.docx" file at the end of the proposed exercice. Title sections automatically begin at a new page due to the Page break before option applied by the Replace All command.*

Note that book title and author name print on the same page because they are separated by a Manual Line Break to keep them in the same paragraph, while PREFACE begins on the second page due to having the Page break before option set.

Attention   To change the section title's formatting, search just for the Arial font. Then use the No Formatting button to clear the formats in the Find what and Replace with text boxes. To change the body text, search just for Times New Roman font. In both cases, use the Replace with text box to apply the desired format to titles and body text.

Exercise 2

The objective of this exercise is to fix document problems using Microsoft Word's Replace command.

Extract "The Adventures of Tom Sawyer Chapter 1-3 Bad Format.docx" file from Chapter03.zip and open it in Microsoft Word. This is also an 11-page document with just the first three chapters of Mark Twain's book *The Adventures of Tom Sawyer*, but it is now full of trash: hidden characters, bad formatting, highlights made with the Highlight and Shading tools.

When you open it for the first time in Microsoft Word, it may be similar to what you see in Figure 3-34 (supposing that the Show/Hide tool is unselected).

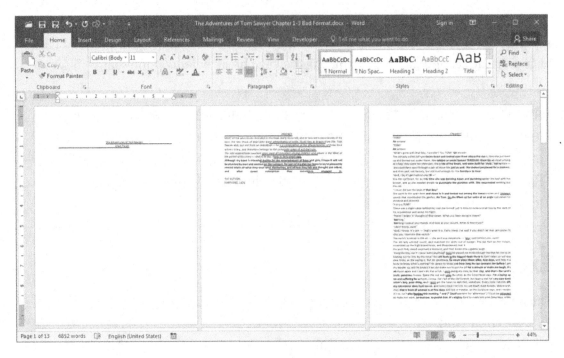

Figure 3-34. *This is "The Adventures of Tom Sawyer Chapter 1-3 Bad Format. docx" file that you can extract from Chapter03.zip.*

To fix this document using Microsoft Word Replace command, you must

1. Click the Show/Hide button to show the document's hidden characters and explore the document to recognize where unnecessary characters were inserted.

2. Use the Exercise section tips of Chapter 2 to remove all unnecessary hidden characters from the text.

3. Select all the document text (press Ctrl+A) and use the Clear All Formatting tool to remove all its unnecessary formatting.

4. Select all the text again and use the Highlight tool twice to remove all highlights applied to the text (you will need to reselect the text using the Ctrl+A shortcut between these two successive operations).

5. Apply Bold formatting to book and section title words and then use Exercise 1 rules to format the text.

146

Summary

Microsoft Word uses typographic principles to apply many different character formatting options to the text, using both the Font area of the Home tab of the Ribbon and the Font dialog box, which can be evoked any time using the right mouse button.

To make good use of such tools, you must understand the differences in the font types and how to use them, combining both serif and sans serif fonts to achieve better results, and use some typographic tips so your documents look better when printed.

As with paragraph formatting options, you can also use the Find and Replace dialog box to quickly change formatting options throughout the entire text.

In this chapter, you learned the following:

- Microsoft Word is a sophisticated typographic tool that uses many professional features to format the text.

- Typeface and fonts are not the same typographically, but are the same for computer usage.

- Fonts can be classified into four main groups: serif, sans serif, script, and decorative.

- Fonts can be monospaced or proportionally spaced.

- How to combine fonts so your documents have the most appeal to readers.

- What is considered a System font and how to install new fonts onto your Microsoft Windows system.

- How to insert symbols and other special characters into the text.

- How to use font attributes to format the text, making a better use of font type, size, style (underline, bold and italic), and color.

- Why you should not use underline formatting: use bold or italic.

- How to use Ctrl + = to apply subscript and Ctrl + + to apply Superscript (or use the associated tools of the Home tab of the Ribbon).

- How you can easily change the text caption using both the Shift+F3 shortcut and Change Case tool.

- How to use All caps and Small caps effects.

- What Character space is and how to use it (Scale, Spacing, Position, and Kerning).

- What OpenType features are (Ligatures, Number spacing and form, Stylistics set) and how to implement them in the text.

- Text can be highlighted using both the Highlight tool and the Shading tool (using both together makes them more difficult to remove).

- You can use the Clear All Formatting tool to remove most text formatting options, but not Highlight format done with the Highlight tool.

- Highlighted text formatted with the Highlight tools can be easily removed by this same tool or using the Format button of the Find and Replace dialog box.

- You can easily change text formation for Font, Paragraph, Tabs, and Highlight using the Find and Replace dialog box.

In the next chapter, we will explore how to apply consistent formatting options to the text using the concept of text Styles.

CHAPTER 4

Select, Find, and Replace Text Characters

Microsoft Word documents can be quite long, and whenever this is the case you may need to move and search through the text to find and select specific characters, words, text sequences, sentences, and paragraphs, and then move them, copy them, and/or apply the desired formatting options to them.

In this chapter you will learn how to move through the text, select, find, and replace text strings to easily format them.

The documents used as examples and the ones cited in the Exercise sections can be found by downloading Chapter04.zip file from this Internet address:

`https://github.com/apress/msft-word-secrets`

Moving Through and Selecting Text

As most professional software does, Microsoft Word obeys to Microsoft Windows system rules regarding the use of keyboard keys to move or select text:

- **Home, End**: go to beginning and end, respectively.

- **Arrows**: make a discrete movement in the arrow's direction.

- **Page Down, Page Up**: make a large move, down or up relative to the window size and zoom applied.

- **Ctrl**: (control key) multiply the movement made with Home, End, Arrows, Page Down, and Page Up.

- **Shift**: turn on the text select mode with Home, End, Arrows, Page Down, and Page Up.

F. Morgado, *Microsoft Word Secrets*, https://doi.org/10.1007/978-1-4842-3078-7_4

This seem quite obvious but most people do not know how to take advantage of these keys, nor do they try them to realize what they do regarding moving through a Microsoft Word document. Let us see them in action: extract "The Count of Monte Cristo, Alexandre Dumas, Chapters 1-5.docx" from Chapter04.zip file, a 31-page document that shows the first five chapters of the famous novel created by Alexandre Dumas (in collaboration with Auguste Maquet) in 1844, and open it in Microsoft Word (Figure 4-1).

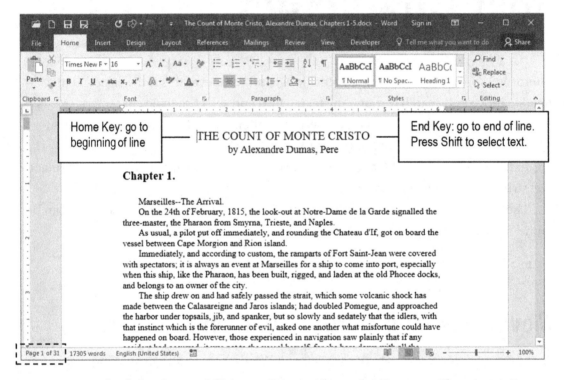

Figure 4-1. *The "The Count Of Monte Cristo, Alexandre Dumas, Chapters 1-5. docx" document that you can extract from Chapter04.zip file, opened in Microsoft Word*

Look to the status bar and note that it has 31 pages.

Using Home and End Keys

Supposing that the text cursor is positioned at the beginning of the document (at left of the first word of the first document paragraph), make simple tests pressing Home and End keys:

- **End**: go to the end of line.

- **Home**: return to the beginning of line.

Since Shift turns on text selection, you will see the following (supposing that you are at the beginning of the first document paragraph):

- **Shift+End**: select text from cursor position to the end of the line.

- **Shift+Home**: select text from cursor position to the beginning of the line.

Since Ctrl is the multiplication move key, you will see the following (supposing that you are at the beginning of the first document paragraph):

- **Ctrl+End**: go to the end of the document (Figure 4-2).

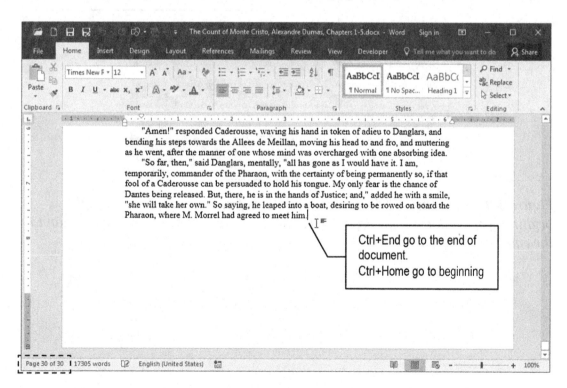

Figure 4-2. *Press Ctrl+End to go to the end of the document. Press Ctrl+Home to go to the beginning.*

- **Ctrl+Home**: go to the beginning of the document.

And since Shift turns on text selection and Ctrl is the multiplication move key:

- **Shift+Ctrl+End**: select text from cursor position to the end of the document.

- **Shift+Ctrl+Home**: select the text from cursor position to the beginning of the document (Figure 4-3).

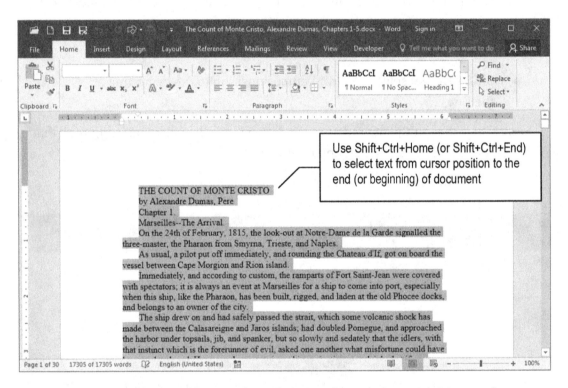

Figure 4-3. *Press Shift+Ctrl+Home to select text from current position to the beginning of the document. Press Shift+Ctrl+End to select from current position to the end of the document.*

Using Arrow Keys

The use of arrow keys alone is no mystery: Left and Right arrows move the text cursor a character at a time, while Down and Up arrows move the text cursor a text line at a time in the arrow's direction.

Since Shift turns on text selection, pressing Shift+Arrow key will do the following:

- **Left, Right arrows**: select one or more characters in the arrow's direction.

- **Down, Up arrows**: select one or more text lines in the arrow's direction, up to the text column where the selection begins.

Since Ctrl is the multiplication move key:

- **Ctrl+Left, Ctrl+Right arrows**: move to the beginning of the next word in the arrow's direction.

- **Ctrl+Down, Ctrl+Up arrows**: move to the beginning of the next paragraph in the arrow's direction.

And by pressing Shift+Ctrl:

- **Shift+Ctrl+Left, Shift+Ctrl+Right arrows**: select one word at a time in the arrow's direction.

- **Shift+Ctrl+Down, Shift+Ctrl+Up arrows**: select one paragraph at time in the arrow's direction.

Using Page Down and Page Up Keys

Page Down and Page Up keys have an unanticipated behavior for the length of move through the text, because Microsoft Word, along with most other professional software packages, considers *a page* what you are currently seeing on the screen: or in other words, Page Up and Page Down relates to *a screen page*.

And since what you are seeing is relative to the window size and state (restored, maximized), and zoom factor applied to the document, whenever you press Page Down or Page Up the document window will displace *a screen page* in the direction of the key pressed (down or up), and this is not a perfectly predictable move.

Since Shift turns on selection:

- **Shift+Page Down, Shift+Page Up**: should select what Microsoft Word considers as one *screen page text* at a time in the key direction (it has erratic behavior according to the page view used and cursor position in the document).

- **Ctrl+Page Down, Ctrl+Page Up** will have different behavior if:

  - **No search had been made in the document**: in this case, it will move to the beginning of the next or previous page according to the page key direction.

  - **Any search had been made in the document**: in this case, it will select the text found by the last Find operation in the document.

Attention   Microsoft Word 2016 has a bug here, because whenever you perform any Find operation in the document, even if you clean up the Find what text box (either in the Navigation pane or in the Find and Replace dialog box), it will no longer use Ctrl+Page Down and Ctrl+Page Up to go to the beginning of the next or previous page: it will try to do the search again and you will need to close and open Microsoft Word again to reestablish the normal Ctrl+Page Up and Ctrl+Page Down behavior.

- **Shift+Ctrl+Page Down, Shift+Ctrl+Page Up**: should select the next or previous page text, as Microsoft Word 2003 or previous versions did, but does nothing, as if no keys had been pressed.

Attention   Press Ctrl+A to select the entire document text.

Use the Navigation Pane ➤ Pages option to show page thumbnails and go to a specific page (see the section "The Navigation Pane" later in this chapter).

Selecting Text with Mouse

Selecting text with the mouse is quite obvious: just click and drag to select the desired, contiguous text. But by correctly positioning the mouse pointer and pressing the Shift and Ctrl keys, you can also select different amounts of text:

- Click the text to position the cursor inside the paragraph.

- Double-click to select the word under the cursor.

- Triple-click to select the paragraph.

Since Shift turns on selection:

- Press and hold Shift to select between two consecutive click points.

- Double-click to select a word, press and hold Shift, and click to select consecutive words

- Triple-click to select a paragraph, press and hold Shift, and click to select consecutive paragraphs.

Using the mouse, the Ctrl key is used to make noncontiguous selections:

- Double-click to select a word, press and hold Ctrl, and keep double-clicking words to randomly select them.

- Triple-click to select a paragraph, press and hold Ctrl and keep triple-clicking to select noncontiguous paragraphs.

- Press and hold Ctrl, double-click to select a word, triple-click to select a paragraph to add to the current selection.

Selecting Sentences

The Ctrl key is also used to select sentences, but Microsoft Word 2016 has a different behavior from previous versions:

- Click inside any paragraph that has more than one sentence.

- Press and hold Ctrl and click to select the sentence (Figure 4-4).

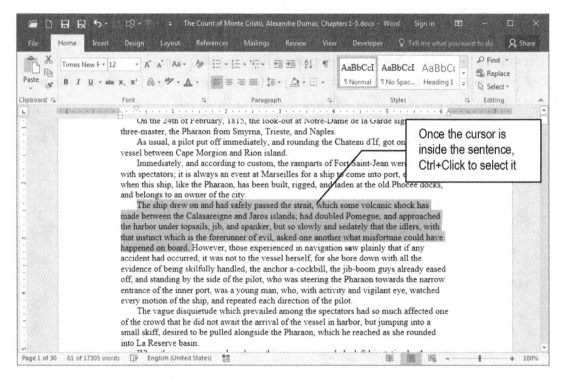

Figure 4-4. *Click the sentence to position the text cursor; press and hold Ctrl and click again to select the sentence*

Attention   On previous versions of Microsoft Word, you could keep pressing Ctrl and click to continue selecting other sentences. The 2016 version obliges you to click anywhere in the desired sentence to position the text cursor inside it before you press Ctrl and click it again to select the sentence.

Selecting Text by Clicking the Left Margin

By clicking the left margin of the page, you can select different amounts of text. Point the mouse to the left margin of any paragraph until the text cursor turns a right pointing arrow and:

- Click at left margin to select a line.

- Double-click at left margin to select the paragraph.

- Triple-click at left margin to select the entire document (same as Ctrl+A, Figure 4-5).

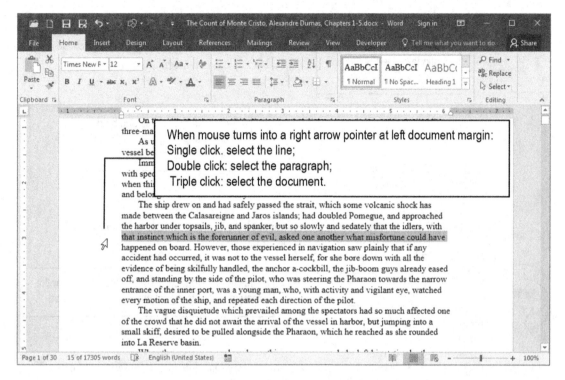

Figure 4-5. *Point the mouse cursor at the left document margin until it turns into a right-pointing arrow. Click to select the line, double-click to select the paragraph, and triple-click to select the entire document.*

Copy or Move the Selected Text

You can move the text selected, even if it is a noncontiguous selection, by using the keyboard or the mouse.

To move and copy the text selection with the mouse:

- Click and drag the text selection to move it to a new position.

- Press and hold Ctrl, and click and drag the text selection to copy it to a new position (Microsoft Word will add a "+" sign near the cursor to signal the copy operation, Figure 4-6).

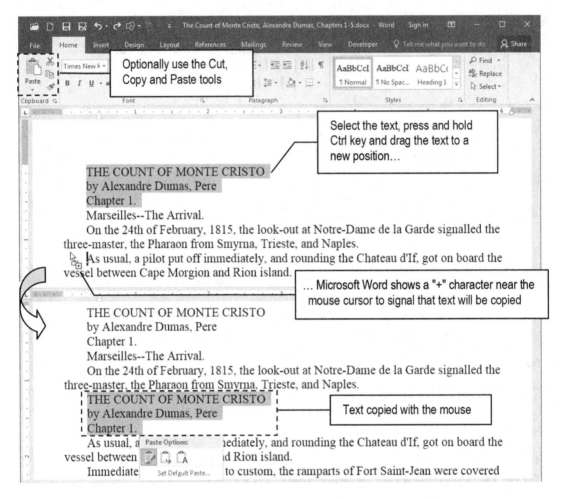

Figure 4-6. *Select the desired text, press and hold Ctrl key, and drag it to a new position. Microsoft Word will show a small "+" character near the mouse pointer to signal that you are making a text copy instead of performing a move operation.*

To move and copy the text selection with the keyboard (or with the aid of the Clipboard area of the Home tab of the Ribbon):

1. Select the desired text.

    - Press Ctrl+X (or click Cut in the Clipboard area of the Home tab of the Ribbon) to remove the text to clipboard, or

    - Press Ctrl+C (or click Copy in the Clipboard area of the Home tab of the Ribbon) to copy the text to clipboard

2. Click the destination position.

3. Press Ctrl+V (or click Paste in the Clipboard area of the Home tab of the Ribbon) to paste the text from clipboard.

Find Text Characters

Microsoft Word offers more than one way to find text character sequences in the text, using the tools found in the Editing area of the Home tab of the Ribbon, from which you can click Find to expand its menu options and select

- Find: to show the Navigation pane with the Results option selected, from which you can make a quick document search (or use the Ctrl+F shortcut).

- Advanced Find: to show the Find and Replace dialog box, with the Find tab selected (or use the Ctrl+H shortcut).

- Go To: to show the Find and Replace dialog box with the Go To tab selected.

Attention   Use the Go To tab of the Find and Replace dialog box to go to the desired page number: type the page number and press Enter to show it.

Press F5 at any time to display the Find and Replace dialog box with the Go To tab selected.

The Navigation Pane

By pressing Ctrl+F, you can quickly show the Navigation Pane with the default Results view, which will appear by default docked at the left side of Microsoft Word document window (Figure 4-7).

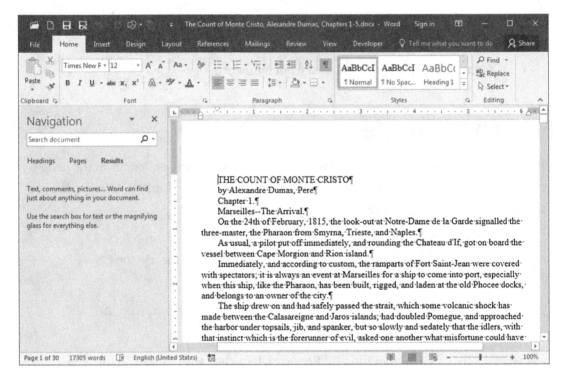

Figure 4-7. *Click the Find tool of the Editing area in the Home tab of the Ribbon (or press Ctrl+F) to show the Navigation Pane with the Results option selected*

Attention   Click and drag the Navigation pane title bar to undock it and make it float over the Microsoft Word window.

Click the text box inside the Navigation pane, type anything you want, and Microsoft Word will make a quick search in the document for this text string. All results found are highlighted in the document and show inside the Navigation pane as a list of items. The document text will also be displaced to show the first occurrence found.

Using the Navigation pane, it may be quite easy to select specific chapter and section titles inside the document, as long as they have some word in common (like the word "Chapter," commonly found in romances and many other documents to indicate the beginning of a new chapter).

Figure 4-8 shows how you can easily find all occurrences of the word "Chapter," to easily format the document's chapter title paragraphs.

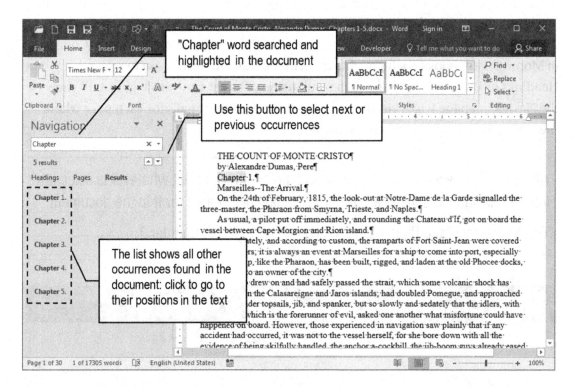

Figure 4-8. *Type whatever you want to search in the Navigation pane and Microsoft Word will instantly search and highlight each occurrence in the document, while the Navigation pane list will show all paragraphs in which it appears*

Below the text box is shown the number of items found (five results for the word "Chapter"), while the paragraph where those items were found is shown in the Navigation pane list (note that it shows occurrences of "Chapter 1" to "Chapter 5").

Click the small arrows located below the right side of the Navigation pane text box to go to each occurrence found in the document, or click any item of the list to go to the document place where the occurrence found resides (scroll the list if necessary to show more items found).

If there are too many occurrences of what is searched, the Navigation pane will not show them in the list: it will warn you to use its Pages option to show page thumbnails of where each result is. You can then click each page to displace the text to this specific position.

Figure 4-9 shows what happens when you try to search for the article "the" using the Navigation pane: it finds 1,254 occurrences in the first five chapters of the "Count of Monte Cristo" book text, highlights them in the text, and warns you to select the Headings or Page options to see each result using different contexts. Figure 4-10 shows the Navigation pane Pages view, which presents page thumbnails for each page where the search found the desired text characters.

Attention   Select any text you want and press Ctrl+F to put whatever is selected into the Navigation pane text box and automatically search for it in the document.

The Navigation Pane Headings view will be discussed in Chapter 7.

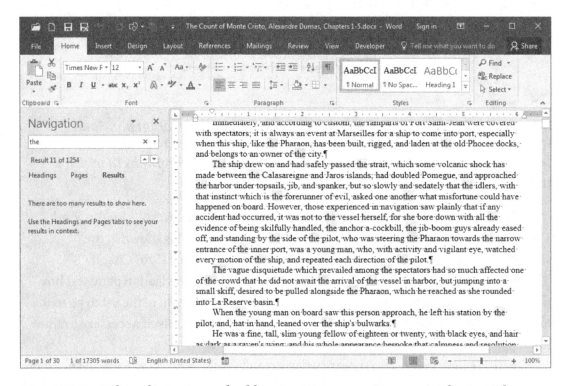

Figure 4-9. *When the text searched has too many occurrences in the text, the Navigation pane indicates the count but does not show them as a list of items. Instead, it shows a warning message asking you to use its Headings and Pages options.*

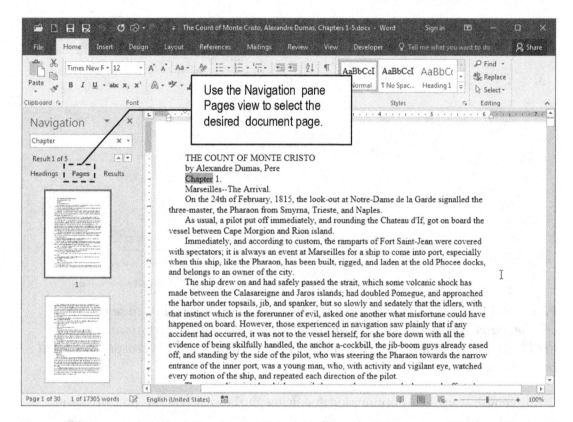

Figure 4-10. *The Navigation pane Pages view shows page thumbnails of each page where the text result was found*

Setting Find Options

The Navigation pane allows configuring how the search will be made by clicking the magnifying glass (or the small triangle pointing down located at the right side of its text box) to reveal a pop-up menu to define what you want to search and set searching options for character sequences (Figure 4-11).

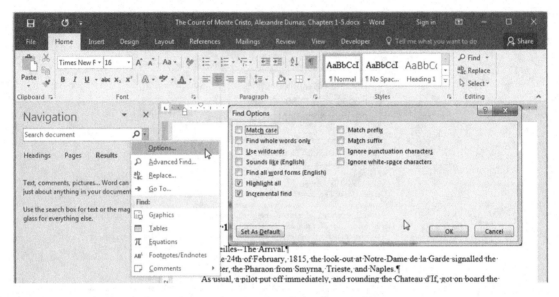

Figure 4-11. *Click the right side of the Navigation pane text box to select what will be searched (below the Find area), or select the Option... command to show the Find Options dialog box, from which you can define how Microsoft Word will perform the search.*

By choosing any of the options located below the Find area of this pop-up menu (Graphics, Tables, Equations, Footnotes/Endnotes, or Comments), if any had been inserted in the document, Microsoft Word will instantly jump to the first option found and you will need to use the small buttons located below the text box to go to the next and previous items that may exist.

Click Options to show the Find Options dialog box and define further character search options, which exhibit most of the options found in the expanded view of the Find and Replace dialog box (see Figure 3-30).

To test the Navigate pane Find Options, I will use the "The Count Of Monte Cristo, Alexandre Dumas, Chapters 1-5.docx" document as an example, considering that just one search option is checked at a time, and that the text cursor is located at the beginning of the document (press Ctrl+Home to return to the beginning of the document between each search; otherwise, Microsoft Word will begin from the current cursor position). Use the next and previous buttons located below the right side of the Navigation pane text box to select the results shown.

Attention   Whenever you choose Options to show the Find Options dialog box and click OK to close it, Microsoft Word inadvertently clears the text you are searching for.

Two of the Find Options dialogs relate just to the Navigation pane and the way it shows the search results (and are checked by default):

- **Highlight All:** highlight the text found in the document (with a yellow highlight, default option).

- **Incremental Find**: search as you type, without the need to press Enter (by unchecking it, you will need to press Enter to begin the search).

Two options make the search more specific to whatever you type:

- **Match case**: search for words using an exact combination of upper and lowercase characters. (e.g., typing "**count**" will return 19 results including: "**count**", "**counts**", "**count**enance", "ac**count**able", "**count**ry", etc., but will not find "Count").

- **Find whole words only**: search for a character sequence that begins a sentence or has a space before and after it. (e.g., typing "**count**", "**COUNT**" or any other case combination returns 2 results, including: "**COUNT**" and "**count**").

Two other search options for words that begin or end with the text sequence are as follows:

- **Match prefix**: find text sequences that begin with the characters typed (type "**count**" to return 15 results, including: "**COUNT**", "**count**enance", "**count**ry".)

- **Match suffix**: find text sequences that end with the characters typed (type "**count**" to return 5 results including: "**count**" and "ac**count**".

One option is used to make pattern searches:

- **Use wildcards:** perform complex searches based on wildcard character patterns. The most known wildcards are the interrogation mark "?" to find any single character (type "**Th?s**" to return 103 results, including "wi**th s**pectator", "**this**", "**thos**e", "**thus**", etc.); and the asterisk "*" to find any character sequence until it reaches a space character (type "**Th***" to return 1931 results, including "**the**", "24**th**", "with", "this", "wor**thy**", etc.

Attention   Wildcard searching options are explored on the section "Making Wildcard Searches" later in this chapter.

Two options make the search using phonetic or contextual word variations (which disable Match case, Find whole words only, Match prefix, and Match suffix options):

- **Sounds like (English):** find phonetic variations of the term searched (type "**sun**" to return 38 results, including: "**seen**", "**sewn**", "**Son**", "**son**", "**soon**".

- **Find all word forms (English):** find English word variations commonly found in verb conjugations, gerunds, etc. (type "**go**" to return 52 results including: "**go**", "**going**", "**gone**", "**went**").

Two search options for just the words typed, not considering any punctuation or spaces between them, are as follows:

- **Ignore punctuation characters**: search for two ore more consecutive words, ignoring punctuation (like .,;:?!) between them (type "**M de**" to return 3 results, including "a**m d**etermined", "**M. de** Villefort"

- **Ignore white space characters**: search for two or more consecutive words ignoring one or more spaces between them.

Using Advanced Find

The Advanced Find option found when you click the Find command in the Editing area of the Home tab of the Ribbon shows the previously seen Find and Replace dialog box with the Find tab selected (use the Ctrl+H shortcut).

By clicking the More>> button, the dialog box expands to show the same options found in the Find Option dialog box accessed by the Navigation pane, but also shows the Format and Special buttons already discussed in Chapter 2 (Figure 4-12).

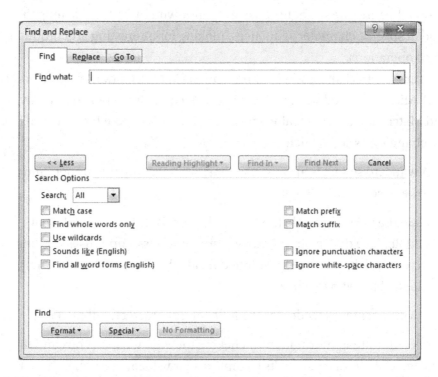

Figure 4-12. *The Advanced Find option found in the Find command in the Editing area of the Home tab of the Ribbon shows the Find and Replace dialog box with the Find tab selected by default. By clicking the More>> button, the dialog box expands and shows the same options found in the Find Options dialog box accessed by the Navigation pane.*

Since both the Navigation pane and the Find tab of the Find and Replace dialog box can make most character search options—including wildcard searches—and considering that the Find and Replace dialog box is the only way that you can also make replacement operations, it will be used through the remainder of this book as the preferred way to make searches in any Microsoft Word document.

Attention   The Search Options of the Find and Replace dialog box relate to the Find Options dialog box: any option set in one dialog box (including the Find what text box) is already set in the other.

Making Wildcard Searches

Wildcard searches are important because they allow you to find character patterns in the text instead of specific character sequences, making for interesting and productive Find and Replace operations.

Whenever you check the Use wildcards option (in Find Options or Find and Replace dialog box), Microsoft Word will disable the Match case, Find whole word only, Match prefix, and Match suffix options (along with the Navigation pane Incremental find), while also changing its search behavior:

- A wildcard search is always case sensitive, meaning that upper- and lowercase letters differ.

- As in the normal search, the Special button found in the Find what and Replace dialog box shows two different sets of options according to whether the cursor is positioned inside the Find what text box or the Replace with text box.

- It will consider as wildcards the following characters: ?-*!<>@()[]{}.

You can confirm that information by clicking the Find what text box and then clicking the Special button to show its list options for wildcard searches. Note that the first nine listed options (from "Any Character" to "0 or More Characters," which show their associated wildcard characters to the right) allow you to build pattern searches (Figure 4-13).

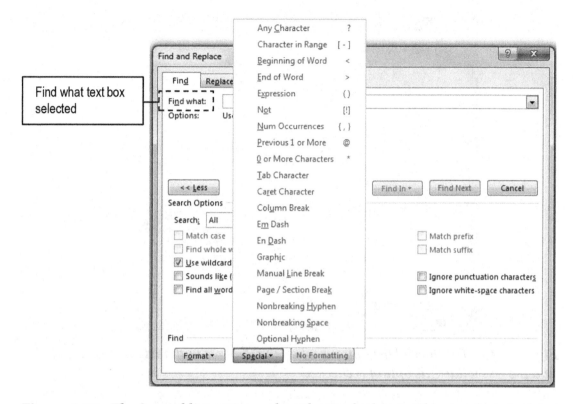

Figure 4-13. *The Special list options when the Find what text box is selected and the Use wildcards option is checked*

Attention   Look with more attention to the Find what Special list options and note that it has no provision to search for the Paragraph mark character (^p) used in the regular Find and Replace operations already performed in some of this book's exercises.

By clicking the Replace tab with text box and clicking the Special button, the list option presented is totally different. Now just the first list option ("Find What Expression") can be used for a pattern replacement (and at its right its associated wildcard character is also presented), while the "Find What Text" appears as an alternative for replacing what is found (Figure 4-14).

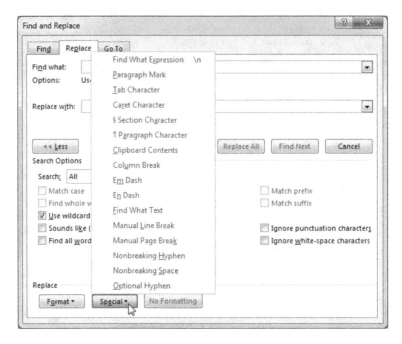

Figure 4-14. *The Special list options when the Replace with text box is selected and the Use wildcards option is checked*

This interface behavior change has two important meanings:

- To search for any wildcard character as a single text character that may exist in the text, you must precede the desired wildcard character by a backslash character "\". (e.g., to search for the asterisk "*" on the text you must type *).

- You can't reuse the wildcard characters used in the Find what text box in the Replace with text box.

Wildcard characters are not easy to understand at first because they produce a kind of *low-level search language*: a kind of encrypted text that is very scary for most people. The next sections will try to make sense of wildcards and leave a registry of how you can use them to create regular expressions to make character pattern searches and take advantage of them whenever necessary.

Microsoft Word Wildcards

To effectively make wildcard search and replacement operation, it is necessary to understand each possible wildcard syntax so you can build expressions that can find the character patterns that you are looking for and eventually perform the desired replace operation. Table 4-1 shows all Microsoft wildcards you can use in the Find what text box, along with their usage and meaning.

Table 4-1. *Microsoft Word Wildcards Allowed in the Find what Text Box*

Wildcard	Usage	Meaning
^13	Paragraph mark	Find a paragraph break (like ^p in regular search)
?	Single character	Find anything in the character position
*	Multiple characters	Find anything
@	Last character and its reoccurrences	Find reoccurrence of the character before @
<	Beginning of a word	Find words beginning with what comes next to <
>	End of a word	Find words ending with what comes before >
[]	List of characters	Find what is inside the brackets (in any order)
[!]	List of no characters	Ignore what is inside the brackets after the [! (in any order)
[-]	Characters in range	Find characters in the alphabetical order of the range (e.g., [P-T] or [0-9])
[!-]	Ignore characters in range	Ignore characters in the alphabetical order of the range (e.g., [!a-z] or [!RST])
{n}	Num of occurrences	Find n successive occurrences of the character that precedes the {
{n,}	At least num of occurrences	Find at least n successive occurrences of the character that precedes the {
{n,m}	n or m occurrences	Find n or m occurrences of the character that precedes the {
( )	Define pattern sequence	Use parenthesis to define what is searched and manipulated with the Replace with text box.

Attention   The ^p sequence used to search for a paragraph break in a regular Find operation is not allowed when Use wildcards option is set. As Table 4-1 implies, you need to use the ^13 sequence instead (and this is not shown on the Special list options).

Find Wildcard Patterns

The next list briefly explores each of these wildcards using the "The Count Of Monte Cristo, Alexandre Dumas, Chapters 1-5.docx" document as an example, considering that just the Use wildcards options is checked and that the quotes are not typed. You can practice using both the Navigate pane and the Find and Replace dialog box, selecting its Find tab. Note however that just the Navigate pane will detach the finding options with the yellow color and show how many results had been found for each example.

- Type "**^13**" to find 568 results, meaning that this book has 568 paragraphs. Since this is a hidden character it will not be highlighted by the Navigation pane (but will be selected if you use the Next or Previous buttons).

- Type "**?hat**" to find 288 results, including "**Chat**eau", "t**hat**", "w**hat**", "**hat**", "**hat**e", etc.

- Type "**we***" (with a space suffix, necessary to stop the search at the end of the word) to find 200 results, including "bet**ween** ", "**were** ", "Ho**wever** ", "t**wenty** ", "**we** ", "t**wenty-four** ", "to**wer** ", "lo**wer**," "lo**wered** ", etc.

Attention   Typing "*we" or "*we " (with a space suffix), everything is selected, because Microsoft Word will find everything before the first "we", then everything after it and before the next "we"... till the end of the file.

- Type "**o@**" to find 5676 occurrences of the letter "o" alone or in succession like in "l**o**ok", "b**oo**m", "p**oo**r", "g**oo**d", "d**oo**r", etc.

- Type "**<wh**" to find 325 results of words that begin with "wh", including "**wh**en", "**wh**ich", "**wh**at", "**wh**o", "**wh**ole", "**why**", "**wh**en", "**wh**im", "**wh**om", "**wh**ere", etc.

- Type "**st>**" to find 182 results of words that end with "st", including "lo**st**", "mo**st**", "re**st**", "again**st**", "la**st**", "mu**st**", "ju**st**", "almo**st**", "hone**st**", etc.

- Type "**<[yw]**" to find 1631 results of words that begin with "y" or "w" lowercase letters (search is case sensitive), including "**w**ith", "**w**here", "**w**hen", "**y**oung", "**y**ou", etc.

- Type "**<[YW]**" to find 183 results of words that begin with "Y" or "W" uppercase letter, including "**W**ell", "**Y**es", "**Y**ou", "**W**ho", "**W**hy", "**W**ell", etc.

- Type "**[yw]>**" to find 1173 results of words that end with "y" or "w" lowercase letters, including "b**y**", "Februar**y**", "immediatel**y**", "speciall**y**", "narro**w**", "sa**w**", "follo**w**", etc.

- Type " **?[wzk]?**" to find 282 results of words that begin with any letter (there is a space before the "?" wildcard) followed by the "w", "z", or "k" lowercase letters followed by any letter, including "li**ke**?", "d**wo**n", "cro**wn**d", "besp**oke**", "**we**", "cre**w**", "se**wn**", "ma**ke**", "li**ke**", etc.

- Type " **t[!h]?**" to find 757 results of words that begin with a "t" lowercase letter (there is a space before the "t" letter) that isn't followed by the "h" lowercase letter, and ends with any letter, including "**to**", "**top**sails", "**tow**ards", "**tur**ned", "**ta**lk", etc.

- Type " **m[!a-p]?**" to find 170 results of words that begin with an "m" lowercase letter (there is a space before the "m" letter) and is followed by any letter different then the lowercase letters "a" through "p", followed by any other letter, including "**muc**h", "**mus**t", "**my**", "**mys**elf", "**mut**tered", "**mur**mured", etc.

Attention   The [-] wildcard represents a range of character that obeys the ASCII or ANSI character sequence found in any font. This sequence normally establishes this order: numbers (0-9), followed by uppercase letters (A-Z), followed by lowercase letters (a-z). This means that to search for any upper- or lowercase Latin letter you need to use a wildcard pattern like [A-z]. You can confirm this order by inspecting the Symbol dialog box character list (Insert tab ➤ Symbol ➤ Show Symbol).

- Type "**<?o{2}**" to find 166 results of words that begin with any letter followed by two successive "o" lowercase letters, including "**too**", "**doo**r", "**goo**d", "**loo**king", "**too**k", "**soo**n", etc.

- Type "**<[dgl][!o{2}]?**" to find 752 results of words that begin with "d", "g", or "l" lowercase letters not followed by two successive "o" lowercase letters, including "**la**", "**la**den", "**la**den", "**li**ke", "**gu**ys", "**le**ft", "**le**aned", "**gr**eat", "**ga**ve", etc;

Find and Replace Wildcard Patterns

Using all the preceding operations, case you need to operate in the text found, you must employ the Replace command found in the Editing area of the Home tab of the Ribbon to show the Find and Replace dialog box, considering that:

- By leaving the Replace with text box empty (with no formatting options set) the Replace all command will remove all results found;

- By leaving the Replace with text box empty and selecting any formatting option (like bold, italic, highlight, etc.) the Replace all command will just change the format of all results found;

- To keep the text pattern found and aggregate it with some added text, click the Replace with text box and click Special ➤ Find what text option. Microsoft Word will add ^& as the replacement operation wildcard, which means each pattern found.

- To remove any of the wildcard patterns searched, embrace them with the ( ) operator and then use their number with the \n syntax in the Replace with text box.

- By using the ( ) wildcard pattern count operator to isolate wildcard patterns, you can just use \n wildcards up to the number of ( ) wildcards used in the Find what text box (e.g., the presence of two ( ) wildcards means that you can use \1 and \2, but not \3, or Microsoft Word will generate an error).

- When ( ) wildcard pattern count operator is used, not using one of the \n possible replacement wildcards means *removing* that wildcard pattern in the replacement operation (e.g., (^13)([a-z]) searches for a paragraph break and paragraphs that begin with a lowercase letter; by using \2 on the Replace with text box, the replacement operation will remove any paragraph mark before a paragraph and join the lowercase letter to the previous paragraph).

Try the next exercise:

- Type "**(Edmond) (Dantes)**" (there is a space between the two names) in the Find what text box.

- Type /2 /1 in the Replace with dialog box (there is a space between the two wildcard replacement patterns).

- Click Replace all to change eight results.

This is equivalent to finding every occurrence of "Edmund Dantes" and replacing with "Dantes Edmund".

Attention   You can always undo the last Find and Replace operations by clicking the text and pressing Ctrl+Z (or selecting the Undo arrow in Microsoft Word Quick Access Toolbar located in the left corner of its title bar.

Exercise 1

The objective of this exercise is to use the wildcard pattern search to fix bad formatting in documents.

For the record: since the Microsoft Office 2007 release, Microsoft Word has been able to easily create PDF files (using the File ➤ Export ➤ Create PDF/XPS command), the so-called Portable Document Format developed by Adobe and widely used to generate read-only files and also open PDF files nicely, converting them to the docx format, as long as the original PDF file has no encryption or protection.

But since many people don't know that, it is quite common to use a PDF printer third-party software (like CutePDF, PDFWriter, PDF Redirect, etc.) to generate PDF files even from inside Microsoft Word!

There is no problem with such PDF printer results because PDF files are almost always used for reading and eventually printing using the Adobe Reader, Fox Reader, and many other free PDF readers.

The problem arises when somebody opens such a PDF file and then copies and pastes its contents inside a Microsoft Word document. The document text may look nice enough, but it isn't. It may become full of paragraph breaks in each of its lines.

Extract "The Count of Monte Cristo, Alexandre Dumas, Chapters 1-5, Bad Formatting.docx" document from Chapter04.zip file, and open it in Microsoft Word. This document was created by a copy/paste process from "The Count of Monte Cristo, Alexandre Dumas, Chapters 1-5.pdf" file (that you can also extract from Chapter04.zip), which was produced by printing the associated Microsoft Word document in one of those PDF printers from Microsoft Word 2016 interface.

Click the Show/Hide tool found in the Home tab of the Ribbon to show its hidden characters and note that the document text is a mess: each text line is broken using a Paragraph break character (Figure 4-15).

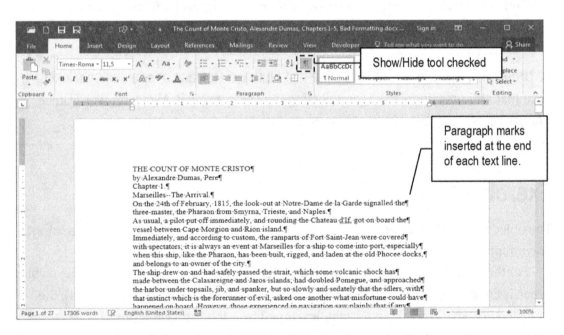

Figure 4-15. *This is "The Count Of Monte Cristo, Alexandre Dumas, Chapters 1-5. Bad Formatting.docx" document open inside Microsoft Word with the Show/Hide tools checked to show its hidden Paragraph marks*

Attention   The PDF files created by Microsoft Word using the File ➤ Export ➤ Create PDF/XPS command do not produce this kind of paragraph break for each text line.

Make a wildcard pattern search to quickly and easily correct this not-uncommon situation, producing a perfect document by removing the Paragraph marks of each text line and keeping them when the text has a paragraph break

Checking for Paragraph Breaks

Looking with more attention at the "The Count of Monte Cristo, Alexandre Dumas, Chapters 1-5, Bad Formatting.docx", you will realize that every *real* paragraph break in the document:

- ends with a period, exclamation point, question mark, or double quote.

- has the next line beginning with an uppercase letter.

You can check this by making a wildcard search with the Navigation pane (Ctrl+F) using the Use wildcards option and the ["\!\?]^13 wildcard as search pattern, which means:

- ["\.\!\?] searches for any of characters inside the brackets (".!?).

Attention   Note that since "!" and "?" are wildcards they need to be preceded by the backslash "\" to be found as text character. Otherwise, Microsoft Word will complain that the search pattern has invalid characters.

- ^13 searches for a Paragraph break after any of the previously found characters.

Figure 4-16 shows that this Find operation results using the Navigation Pane returned 578 results in the document, which were highlighted in the text.

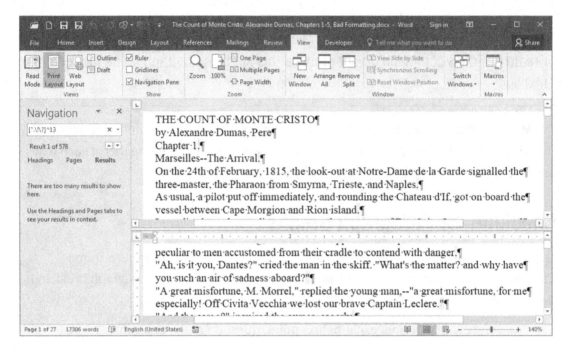

Figure 4-16. *Using the Navigation pane, you check the Use wildcards option (expand the text box and click Options) and use the [".\!\?]^13 pattern to find each Paragraph mark that really defines a paragraph break*

Attention   The document received a 140% zoom and was divided to show two different areas (using the View ➤ Split command, which was renamed to Remove Split) so you can show the period (.) and double quote (") characters (followed by the ¶ Paragraph mark) selected in the text.

Fixing Line Breaks

To make the change and fix the text, you need to do the opposite: fix the normal line breaks by changing every incorrect paragraph mark by a space. Or in wildcard search jargon, search for Paragraph mark characters followed by any lowercase letters and change them to a space followed by the lowercase text found. Follow these steps:

1. Click the Replace command found in the Editing area of the Home tab of the Ribbon to show the Find and Replace dialog box.

2. Click More>> and check Use wildcards option.

3. In the Find what text box, type "(^13)([a-z])" (without the quotes).

4. In the Replace with text box, type a space and "\2." The Find what text box must receive the " \2" wildcard pattern (there is a space before \2 wildcard replacement option).

5. Click Replace all button.

Microsoft Word will replace every Paragraph break followed by a lowercase letter by a space followed by the lowercase letter found (the \2 wildcard, Figure 4-17).

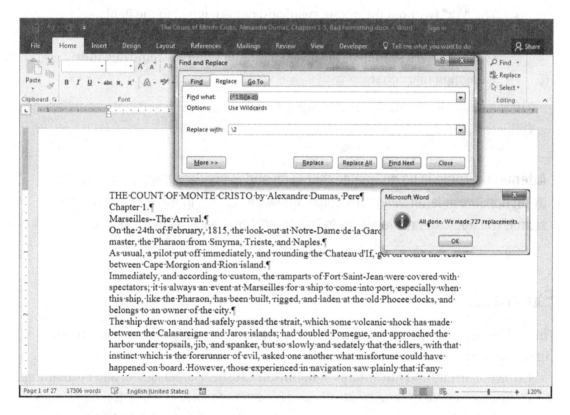

Figure 4-17. *To fix the text, use the Find and Replace dialog box with the Use wildcards options checked. In the Find what text box, type (^13)([a-z]), and in the Replace with text box type, " \2" (without the quotes, with a space preceding the \ character). Click Replace all to make 727 replacements.*

And as explained before, this wildcard search and replace option works this way:

- The **(^13)([a-z])** wildcard pattern typed in the Find what text box defines two different wildcard patterns:

    - **(^13)** search for a Paragraph break (the Replace with text box recognizes it as \1 wildcard pattern).

    - **([a-z])** search for any lowercase letter (the Replace with text box recognizes it as \2 wildcard pattern).

- The " **\2**" (without the quotes) wildcard pattern typed in the Replace with text box replaces whatever was found by a space followed by the second pattern searched (the lowercase letter), literally removing the Paragraph mark character.

The document is now ready to be formatted using other search and replace operations. Quite cool, huh?

Attention   There is no guarantee that each and every Paragraph mark followed by an uppercase letter will really begin a new paragraph in the text. But such a search will approximate very well to the original text paragraph breaks.

Exercise 2

This objective of this exercise is to use a wildcard search to remove unwanted, hidden characters that insert line breaks in the text.

Extract "The Life and Adventures of Robinson Crusoe, Daniel Defoe, Bad Formatting. docx" document from Chapter04.zip file and open it in Microsoft Word. It is a 151-page document with the original text of the famous 19th-century book of Daniel Defoe.

Click the Show/Hide button and note that this is a document copied from a PDF file previously created with a PDF Printer (not with Microsoft Word File ➤ Export command): every line of text ends with a Paragraph mark (Figure 4-18).

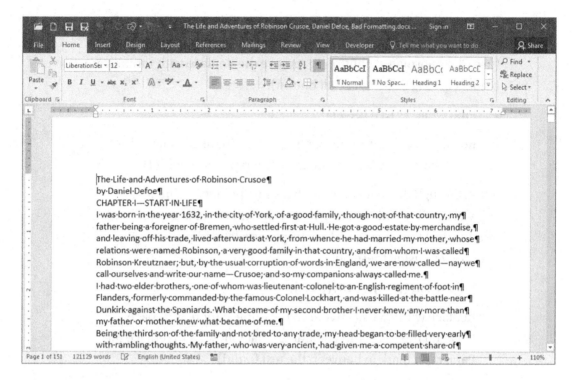

Figure 4-18. *This is the 151-page "The Life and Adventures of Robinson Crusoe, Daniel Defoe, Bad Formatting.docx" document that you can extract from the Chapter04.zip file*

Scroll through the text and note that it seems that this document begins its paragraphs using just an uppercase letter (no paragraph seems to begin with a " or — character). Do the next exercise list:

- Check the Use wildcard option (either in the Find Options or Find and Replace dialog box).

- Use the Navigation pane to search for each chapter title using wildcards (use CHAPTER*^13) pane and use the list results to quickly move for each of the 20 chapter titles (note the word CHAPTER in uppercase).

- Use the Replace command to find every chapter title paragraph and replace its format with these formatting options:

  - **Font**: Garamond, 16 pt, Bold.

  - **Paragraph**: Alignment = Centered, Spacing After = 24 pt, Page break before.

- Remove all 5,666 unwanted line breaks by finding any Paragraph mark *not followed* by an uppercase letter using these options (use Clear Formatting button to remove the Replace with formatting before clicking the Replace all button):

    - Find what: **(^13)([!A-Z])**

    - Replace with: **" \2"** (without the quotes, there is a space before the \ character to substitute the Paragraph mark found).

- Scroll through the text and note that some paragraph breaks are still wrong: they end with a lowercase letter and a Paragraph mark, and the next line begins with an uppercase letter. Fix these 152 occurrences using these options:

    - Find what: **([a-z])(^13)([A-Z])**

    - Replace with: **"\1 \3"** (without the quotes; there is a space between the 1 and the \ character that follows it to replace the Paragraph mark in between the text found);

Attention   This last operation will wrongly affect the book title and author name (which became a single paragraph), joining it with the first chapter title; this will need to be manually broken by an Enter key and centered.

- Uncheck the Use wildcard option to search for every body text paragraph (in Find what option, set these Font properties:Calibri 12 pt) and replace it with these formatting options (in Replace with option set these Font properties):

    - **Font**: Trebuchet MS, 11 pt.

    - **Paragraph**: Alignment = Justified, First line indent = 0.3, Line spacing = Single, Widow/Orphan control.

The document must now have 142 pages, and must be similar to the one you found by extracting "The Life and Adventures of Robinson Crusoe, Daniel Defoe, Formatted. docx" from Chapter 04.zip file, which received all these formatting options plus a manual change in the book title and author name formatting (Figure 4-19).

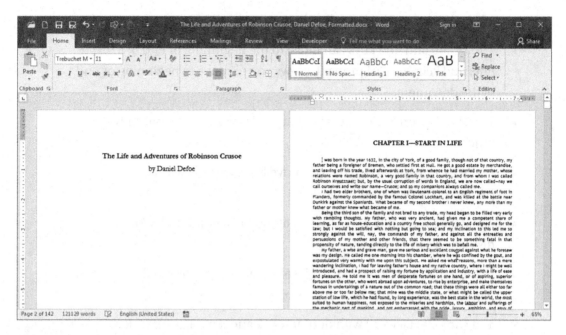

Figure 4-19. *The "The Life and Adventures of Robinson Crusoe, Daniel Defoe, Formatted.docx" document with the suggested formatting options applied using search and replace techiques*

Summary

Microsoft Word allows you to quickly move and select the text of any document by using the Home, End, Page Up, Page Down, and arrow keys. With the aid of Ctrl, Shift, and Alt alone or together and the mouse, you can easily move or select the text you want and apply simple operations like cut, copy, paste, and format.

It also offers two different ways to search the document: using the Navigation pane and using the Find and Replace dialog box, with the Find or Replace tab selected.

You can make simple searches using different search options or make complex character pattern searches using wildcard characters.

In this chapter you learned the following:

- The Home and End keys can move to the beginning or end of a text line, and keeping Ctrl pressed allows you to move to beginning or end of the document.

- The Shift key turns on text selection, and Ctrl key is the multiply movement key.

- Using Ctrl+Arrows key, you can move from word to word or paragraph to paragraph.

- The Page Down and Page Up keys alone make Microsoft Word displace a screen of text.

- Using Ctrl+Page Down or Ctrl+Page Up, you can move to the beginning of the next or previous page.

- You can select a word with double-click and a paragraph with a triple-click.

- Ctrl+A selects the entire document.

- By moving the mouse cursor to the left margin, a single click selects the text line, a double click selects the paragraph, and a triple click selects the text.

- Ctrl+Click selects sentences.

- You can move the text selected by dragging it with the mouse, or copying it by keeping Ctrl pressing while dragging it.

- By keeping Alt left pressed, clicking and dragging the mouse through the text, you can make a columnar selection.

- You can make search operations using either the Navigation pane (Ctrl+F) or the Find tab of the Find or Replace dialog box.

- The Navigation pane highlights the text found in the document.

- Both interfaces have advanced search options that may restrict (whole word, match case) or extend what is searched (match prefix or suffix, sounds like, English word forms).

- Wildcard searches are the most powerful search option because they operate based on search patterns.

- The ^p associated to a Paragraph mark in a normal search can't be used in a wildcard search: use ^13 instead.

- The ( ) is used to identify wildcard patterns typed on the Find what text box, that are operated with \n option in the Replace with text box (where n represents the ( ) count).

In the next chapter, you will learn how you can create quick and consistent formatting options through one or many documents using Styles.

CHAPTER 5

Quick Document Formatting with Styles

After all this talk about typography, paragraph and text formatting in Chapters 2 and 3, you are probably thinking that text formatting is a very laborious and complicated task, very prone to errors due to the difficulty of equally implementing the same formatting in similar paragraphs scattered across the pages of long text documents.

Fortunately, this is not true! You can attribute many different formatting options to a style, name it, and then apply it to the same paragraph type to easily standardize the text format. By using different styles in a single document (for title, headings, body text, quotes, etc.), you can create what is called an "visual editorial standard" for a document, and then easily apply it to different documents that must share the same formatting options, making what is technically called "Desktop Publishing."

In this chapter you will learn everything about styles: how to create, apply, change, and manage them in Microsoft Word documents.

The documents used as examples and the ones cited in the Exercise sections can be found by downloading Chapter05.zip file from this Internet address:

```
https://github.com/apress/msft-word-secrets
```

The Style Gallery

You already know that each new empty document opened in Microsoft Word has an empty paragraph, but chances are that you never noticed that this empty paragraph is formatted with the Normal style.

© Flavio Morgado 2017
F. Morgado, *Microsoft Word Secrets*, https://doi.org/10.1007/978-1-4842-3078-7_5

You can confirm this information looking to the Style Gallery found in the Style area of the Home tab of the Ribbon: the large control area full of "AaBbCcDd" items that Microsoft Word uses to show the selected style and a partial list of the styles available in the current document, where the Normal style is selected by default.

Each style name shown is formatted in the Style Gallery using its current font options (font, size, color, spacing, borders, etc.) so you can anticipate the appearance that each one will give to the text when selected (Figure 5-1).

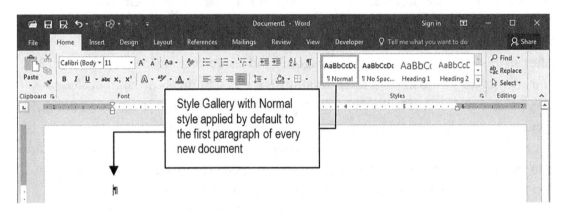

Figure 5-1. *The Normal style is applied by default to the empty poragraph found in every new Microsoft Word document*

Attention   The Style Gallery width changes accordingly as the Microsoft Word window width changes. It may show more or fewer styles in its first row depending on the monitor size, screen resolution, and window state (restored, maximized) you are using.

Click the small arrow at the bottom right of the Style Gallery to expand it and exhibit some other styles available for this document. Note that it also offers three different commands: Create a Style, Clear Formatting, and Apply Styles.

Figure 5-2 names some important elements of the Style Gallery.

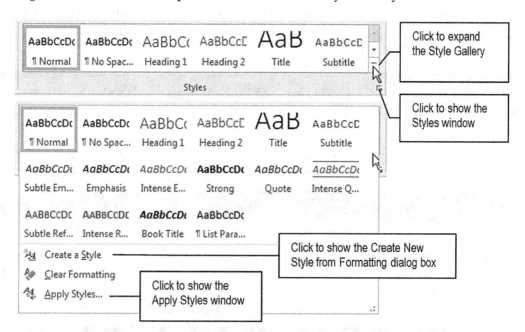

Figure 5-2. *Click the bottom right arrow of the Style Gallery to expand it and show some other styles available in the document, and its three command options*

Figures 5-1 and 5-2 show the Style Gallery with the Normal style selected, meaning that the current text paragraph is formatted, or associated to it.

Having the cursor positioned inside any text paragraph, you can easily see how it will look when receiving another style by just pointing the mouse over the desired style. Drag the mouse over the styles in the Style Gallery and note that some styles change the appearance of the entire text paragraph, while others change the appearance of just the word where the cursor is positioned.

By clicking any style you change the text association to it, meaning that the desired text is now formatted, or associated to the style chosen.

Try to successively click Heading 1, Heading 2, Title, and Subtitle (available in the first Style Gallery row) and notice how the selected paragraph immediately changes its appearance (font, size, color, etc.) by receiving all of the style format (Figure 5-3).

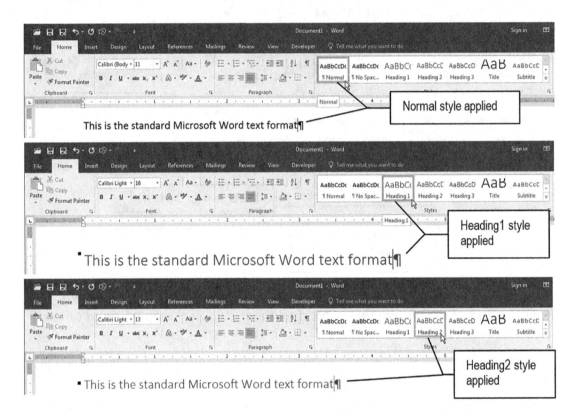

Figure 5-3. *Click anywhere in the text and select a new style to apply all its formatting options to the entire text paragraph: there is no need to select the text when selecting paragraph formatting styles*

Now try to select one or more words and select a style such as NoSpacing, Heading1, or Emphasis in the Styles Gallery. Note that for most styles just the selected text will be formatted with the style options, while for a few, the entire paragraph is formatted. When just the selected words are formatted, the entire paragraph keeps its default formatting options. Figure 5-4 shows a Normal style paragraph that received the Heading1 style in some of its words. It remained formatted with Normal style while some words received the Heading1 style.

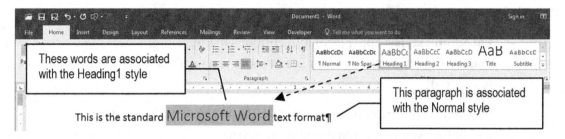

Figure 5-4. *You can apply some styles to just the selected text. In this case, the entire paragraph will be kept associated to its default style (Normal style in this case), while the selected words will receive the font formatting associated to the applied style.*

And as a last exercise, click the mouse inside any word (don't select its characters, however) and drag the mouse over the styles named Subtle Em..., Emphasis, Intense E... and Strong, Subtle Ref..., Intense R... or Book Title (you may need to expand the Style Gallery to find them), and note that for these styles, just the word where the cursor is positioned receives the style format (Figure 5-5).

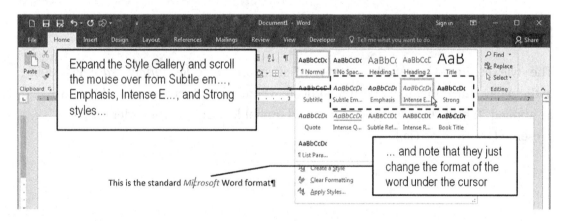

Figure 5-5. *Some styles apply their formatting options to just the word under the cursor (or to the selected text). They are called character styles.*

This style behavior is possible because there are three main types of styles:

- **Paragraph styles**: apply formatting options to the entire text paragraph (whether or not some text inside it is selected).

- **Character styles**: apply formatting options to the word where the cursor is positioned (or to the selected text).

- **Linked (paragraph and character)**: apply formatting style to the entire text paragraph if nothing is selected, or to just the selected text (as character styles do).

Attention   As you will see later, Microsoft Word also allows the creation of Table styles (a single style name that can be applied to different table parts), and List styles (which can be used to format bullets and numberings, using different formatting options for the bullet/number and text parts).

Recommended Styles

The style set offered by default in the Style Gallery are called *Recommended* styles. Most of them have meaningful names that indicate where in the document text they must be applied. Table 5-1 shows their names and probable usages in the order they are presented by the Style Gallery.

Table 5-1. *Default Microsoft Word Styles Shown by the Style Gallery in Their Presentation Order*

Style Name	Type	Usage
Normal	Paragraph	Format the body text of the document
NoSpacing	Paragraph	Format the body text with line spacing = single
Heading1, Heading2	Linked (paragraph and character)	Format chapter title and first subtitle level.
Title, Subtitle	Linked (paragraph and character)	Format the document title and subtitle)
Subtle Emphasis, Emphasis, Intense Emphasis	Character	Give emphasis to words using italic and/or color
Strong	Character	Give emphasis to words using bold
Quote, Intense Quote	Linked (paragraph and character)	Give emphasis to words using bold
Subtle Reference, Intense Reference	Character	Give emphasis to words using small caps and/or bold and color
Book Title	Character	Give emphasis to book title words using bold and italic

The Styles Window

You may now wondering how you can easily differentiate styles by their usage: it is a paragraph style, a character style, or a linked style? The best way to do this is to click the (very) small square button located at the bottom right corner of the Style area of the Home tab of the Ribbon (see Figure 5-2) to show the Styles windows (Figure 5-6).

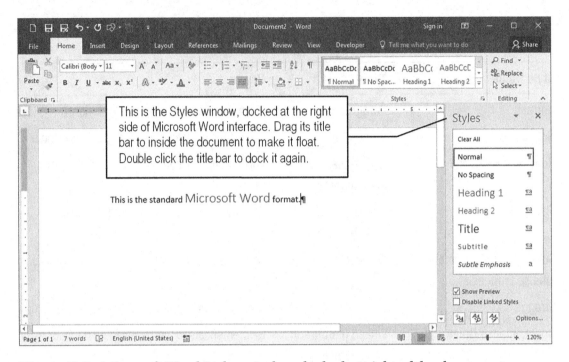

Figure 5-6. *Microsoft Word Styles window docked at right of the document area*

Microsoft Word Styles window is used to manage styles and by default shows the styles in the same order that they appear in the Style Gallery. It may appear as first docked at the right side of the document, but you can make it float over the Microsoft Word interface by clicking and dragging its title bar (where you read "Styles") inside the document window. To dock it again, double-click its title bar (Figure 5-7).

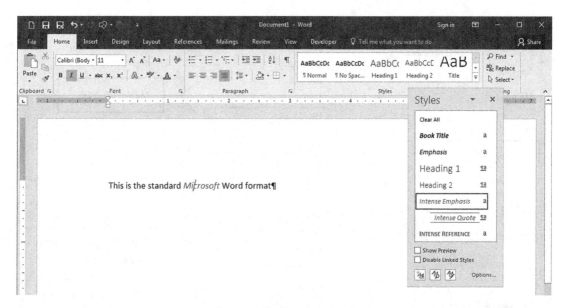

Figure 5-7. *The Styles window floating over the document, after being dragged by its title bar*

Attention   The Styles window does not change the text appearance when you scroll the mouse through its styles, as the Style Gallery does. You must keep the Show Preview option checked to see the style appearance in the list, or click the style to format the text.

The Styles window may show styles using different presentation formats. By default it has the Show Preview option checked so you can see each style name formatted using its own style options. It shows at the right of each style name a small icon that indicates the style type (Figure 5-8):

¶ Paragraph style

a Character style

¶a Linked (paragraph and character) style

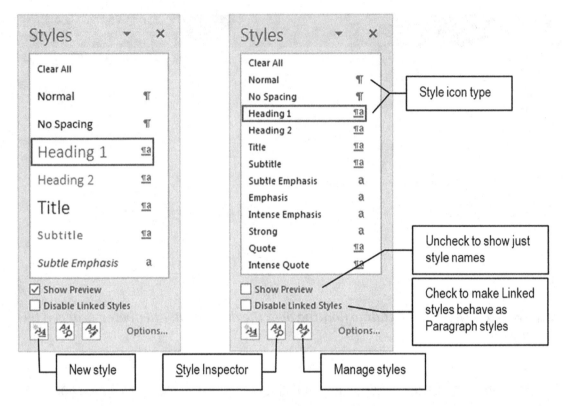

Figure 5-8. *The Styles window in its floating state. It has icons to the right of the styles to indicate their type, and can show/hide the stype formatting.*

It also offers two main options:

- **Show preview**: enable/disable the preview format applied to the style name (checked by default).

- **Disable linked styles**: when checked, make styles defined as Linked (paragraph and character) behave as Paragraph styles: their formatting options will be always applied to the entire paragraph, whether or not some text has been selected.

The Styles window is the place from where you can best manage the styles available in any document. It allows you to create new styles and inspect and manage the styles that appear inside it. It also allows personalization, giving you the chance to select which styles must be shown and in which presentation order. It is also resizable when it is floating over the document, so you can extend or shrink both its height and width by dragging its borders or corners (try it).

The Style Pane Dialog Box

Click the Options... link located at the bottom right corner of the Styles window to show the Style Pane Option dialog box from where you can define how the styles are presented in the Styles window list (this option doesn't apply to the Style Gallery, Figure 5-9).

Figure 5-9. *The Style Pane Options dialog box, which allows changing styles shown by the Styles window and their presentation order*

The Style Pane Options dialog box may be too complex to be fully understood all at once, so I will teach about it throughout the book as its various functionalities need to be brought forward. For the sake of the present discussion, try to use some of these options:

- **Select styles to show**: use this combo box to choose which styles will appear in the Styles windows:

    - **Recommended**: show the same styles that appear in the Style Gallery.

    - **In use**: show just the styles that have been applied in the current document (even if they are not applied anymore).

    - **In current document**: show all styles stored inside this document, having been applied or not.

- **All styles**: show all styles available, including the ones stored in the document template and that are not visible in the Style Gallery (an enormous list of styles is available for use).

- **Show how list is sorted**: define the order that the styles appear in the Styles window:

  - **Alphabetical**: style names in ascending order.

  - **As Recommended**: style names use the same order presented by the Style Gallery.

  - **Font**: style names sorted in ascending order by the font name it uses;

  - **Based on**: style names sorted by the style on which they are based (if any).

  - **By type**: style names sorted by its type name (Character, Linked, and Paragraph types).

Attention   As you will see later in this book, Microsoft Word allows implying style inheritance by making a style be based on another one. This means that if some formatting attribute is changed in the base style, all other styles that are based on it will instantly receive that attribute.

By changing the Select styles to show option, you can limit or expand the style list. For example, for the document shown in Figure 5-6 (which uses just the Normal and Heading1 styles) use the "In use" option to show just these two styles in the Styles window (Figure 5-10).

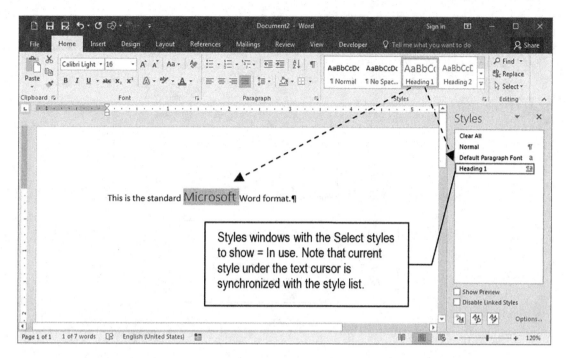

Figure 5-10. *The Styles windows showing just the styles in use in the document sorted "As Recommended" (Normal and Heading 1, same Style Gallery sort order). The Clear All and Default Paragraph font are always shown.*

But when you select the "All styles" option, the Styles window will show all styles available both in the document and in the template upon which it's based: the style list will be populated by many style names that do not appear in the Style Gallery. Figure 5-11 shows the "All styles" option in action, keeping the Show how list is sorted = As Recommended.

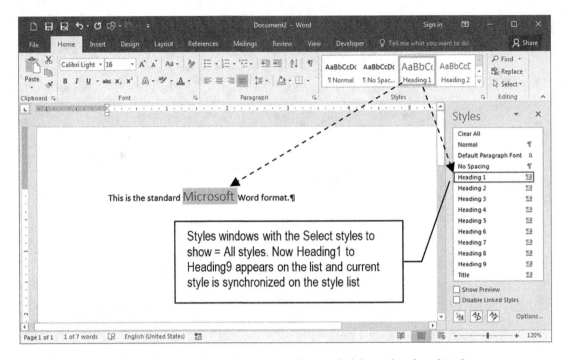

Figure 5-11. *The Styles window showing all available styles for the document, sorted "As Recommended." Note that now you see Heading1 to Heading9 styles.*

The Normal Style

As Figure 5-1 shows, every new Microsoft Word document has just a single text paragraph formatted with the Normal style. And since almost nobody realizes this or even knows what styles are, probably most Word documents created use just the Normal style, which makes it the most used style in the world.

Open any document you already produced in Microsoft Word (or any document cited on the Exercise sections of Chapters 2 and 3), scroll through the text, and note that every paragraph is formatted using just the Normal style. This phenomenon will probably repeat in almost all Microsoft Word documents you have at hand.

And since the Normal style is so used, you can quickly change the format of a text document without making any text selection by just updating the Normal style properties.

Updating the Normal Style

Microsoft Word allows the Normal style properties to be changed in three different ways:

1. With the Font and Paragraph dialog box.

2. Using Match Selection option.

3. Using the Modify style dialog box.

The first option affects just the Normal style—and all other styles that are based on it, which makes it so special—while the second and third options can be used by any other style.

Updating Normal with the Font and Paragraph Dialog Boxes

The most easiest and complete way to update the Normal style is using the "Set as Default" button found in the Paragraph and Font dialog boxes.

By changing Font and Paragraph dialog box options and clicking their Set as Default button, you will receive a warning message that allows you to define if the changes made will be applied to this document only or to every other new document created with Microsoft Word (Figure 5-12).

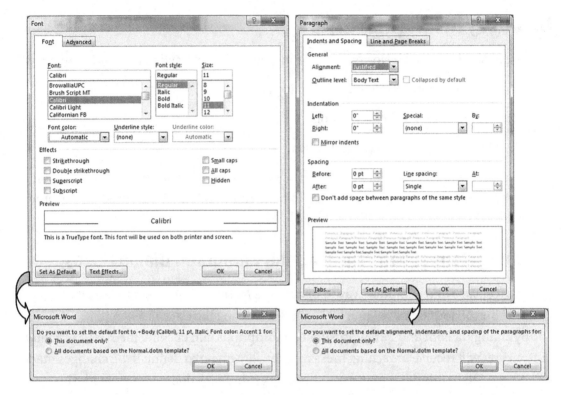

Figure 5-12. *Use the Set as Default buttons of the Font and Paragraph dialog box to redefine the appearance of the Normal style to the current or any other new Microsoft Word document*

Attention   Each dialog box will show a short description of the new Font and Formatting options that will be used by the Normal style.

Updating Styles by Match Selection

The second way you can update the Normal or any other style of the Style Gallery is quite simple:

1. Apply the style (or the desired style) to a text paragraph.

2. Change all formatting to this paragraph (font, paragraph, border, color, language, etc.).

3. Right-click the style name in the Style Gallery and choose "Update <style> to Match the Selection" command.

The style in use will be immediately changed to match the paragraph formatting options, and all other paragraphs that received this style will reflect such changes. Figure 5-13 shows how you can locally change a Normal paragraph style, right-click the Normal style in the Style Gallery, and choose Update Normal to Match the Selection, affecting all other Normal style paragraphs in the text.

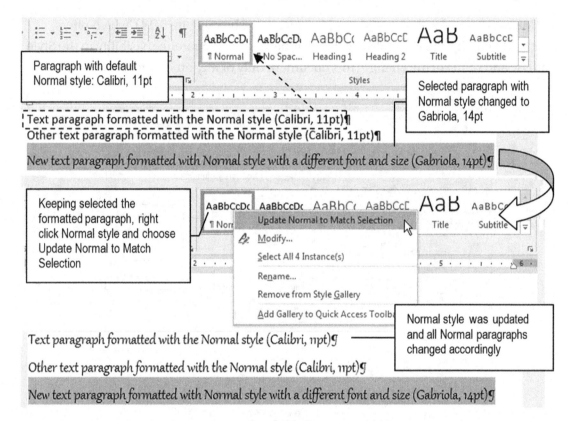

Figure 5-13. *Apply the desired style to any text paragraph, right-click its name in the Style Gallery, and choose Update <style> to Match the Selection to update the style format. All paragraphs that received the style will be automatically formatted to reflect the style.*

Attention   There is no need to select the entire paragraph text to change it with the Match the Selection option: click anywhere inside the paragraph, right-click its name in the Style Gallery, and choose Update <style> to Match Selection.

Updating with the Modify Style Dialog Box

The third method used to update a style is by using the Modify Style dialog box:

1. Right-click the style name in the Style Gallery;

2. Select the Modify.... command.

Microsoft Word will open the Modify Style dialog box (Figure 5-14), which offers controls to change the Normal style name, inheritance, appearance, visibility in the Style Gallery, and scope of the change (this document only or any other new document).

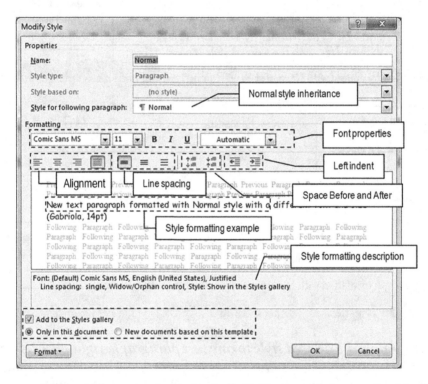

Figure 5-14. *Right-click any style in the Style Gallery and choose the Modify... command to show the Modify Style dialog box*

Use the Properties area to change Normal style name, type, and inheritance properties:

*   **Name**: the style name (as appears in Style Gallery and Styles windows).

*   **Style type**: choose between Character, Paragraph, and Linked (character and paragraph). This option is disabled for styles already created.

- **Style for following paragraph**: define the style inheritance, or the style applied in the next paragraph when you press Enter in any paragraph formatted with this style. By default, any Normal style paragraph generates another Normal style paragraph.

Use the Formatting area of the Modify Style dialog box to change the style appearance:

- **Font properties**: font, size, bold, italic, underline, and color.

- **Paragraph properties**: alignment, line spacing, increase/decrease the Space Before and After (by 6 pt each time), and increase/decrease Left indentation by the default tab stop value.

In the middle of the Modify Style dialog box, the white text box shows a preview example of current style formatting options. At the bottom left area of the Modify Style dialog box you can also define if the style must be shown in the Style Gallery and where the scope of the change it undergoes must be stored:

- **Add the style to the Style Gallery:** check to make the style appear in the Style Gallery. This option appears checked for all recommended styles already shown in the Style Gallery.

- Define where the changes must be stored:

  - **Only in this document**: the style change affects just this document text-it will not be applied to new Microsoft Word documents.

  - **New documents based on this template**: affects every new document created with Microsoft Word Normal.dotx template (the standard document template).

Also note that at the bottom left corner of the Modify Style dialog box, there is a Format button that expands when you click it, showing other style formatting options (Figure 5-15). Using the Format button, you can access the Fonts, Paragraph, Tabs, Border, Language, Frame, Numbering, Language, Shortcut key, and Text Effects dialog boxes to format the style.

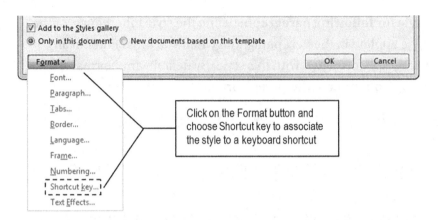

Figure 5-15. *Use the Format button of the Modify Style dialog box to bring the associated Microsoft Dialog box, from which you can select further style options*

Associate the Normal Style with a Shortcut Key

From my point of view, the best way to apply some Microsoft Word styles is by associating them to a mnemonic shortcut key, so you can quickly apply them without needing to locate them using the Style Gallery or the Styles window.

For more than two decades I have been using Microsoft Word with its Normal style associated to the Ctrl+Space shortcut key, because it is quite easy to apply and remember, but you can select any other Ctrl, Shift, and/or Alt + letter combinations to create your preferred shortcut key. Just follow these steps:

1. In the Modify Style dialog box, click Format ➤ Shortcut key... command.

2. Microsoft Word will show the Customize Keyboard dialog box for the Normal style (or the style name you are editing), with focus on the Press shortcut key text box.

3. Press the shortcut key you want to associate to the style (press the Alt, Ctrl, Shift key combinations first and then type the desired character).

4. Microsoft Word will show the shortcut key typed in the Press new shortcut key option (Ctrl+Space). Note that below the Current keys option there is an indication if the desired shortcut is already assigned to another Microsoft Word command or style (Figure 5-16).

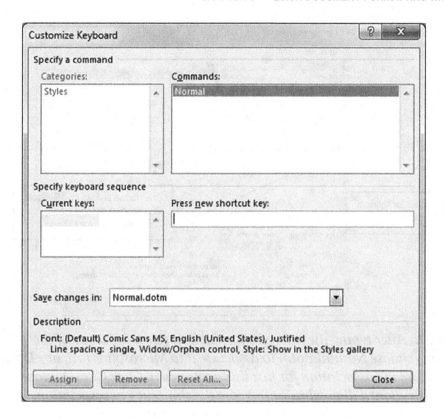

Figure 5-16. *Use Format ➤ Shortcut key... command of the Modify Style dialog box to show the Customize KeyBoard dialog box to associate a shortcut key to the style you are editing. Note that below Current keys option (which is empty), there is an indication if the typed shortcut key is currently assigned to another Microsoft Word command.*

    5.   Since the Assign button has the focus, press Enter to assign the desired shortcut key to the selected style (or click the Assign button), to transfer the shortcut key to the Current keys option (Figure 5-17).

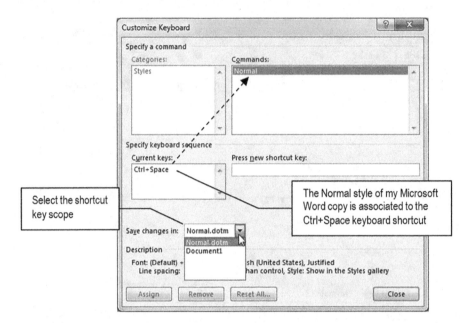

Figure 5-17. *After typing the desired shortcut key, select the scope of the association (choose Normal.dotm to associate it to Microsoft Word, or <Document name> to store the association for just this document). Click Close to close Customize KeyBoard dialog box and create the shortcut key association.*

6. Use the Save changes in option to define the shortcut scope:

    -   **Normal.dotx**: select this option to make the style shortcut available to every Microsoft Word document.

    -   **<Document name>**: use this option to store the shortcut style inside this document (it will not work in other documents).

7. Since the Close button received the focus, press the Enter key (or click the Close button) to close the Customize Keyboard dialog box, associate the style to the keyboard shortcut, and return to the Modify Style dialog box (Figure 5-17).

When you close the Customize Keyboard dialog box, the focus will return to the Modify Style dialog box. To really complete the keyboard shortcut association, you must close the Modify Style dialog box by clicking its OK button.

From this point on, try to use the associated keyboard shortcut in the text to apply the Normal style.

Attention   From this point on in this book, I will suppose that you are using Ctrl+Space keyboard to apply the Normal style whenever necessary.

Global and Local Formatting

You already know that the Normal style is the default style used to format new documents, and that you can change the text formatting options for any amount of text, without the use of styles: just select the text and use the Font and Paragraph dialog box, for example.

What happens when you change the style applied to a text paragraph is that you apply a *global* formatting, and when you select text and change its formatting options, you apply a *local* formatting (like Figure 5-13 did before updating the Normal style using the Match the Selection option).

In Microsoft Word and many other professional software packages, local formatting has precedence over global formatting: a very reasonable decision meaning that the local formatting applied to the text will remain unchanged by a global formatting change.

In other words, if a text paragraph has the Normal style applied, and part of its text has a different formatting option (some of its characters or words received bold, italic, another character spacing, color, language, etc.), whenever you change the global formatting option (the style), this change *will not affect* the local formatting option applied to the selected text.

Let make this clear: if a Normal style paragraph needs some words to be formatted using italic, when you apply a Quote style formatted with regular font (not italic), the italicized words will remain italic.

Take on the next simple exercise:

1. Type two different text paragraphs using the default Normal style.

2. In one of these paragraphs, select some of its words and change the font used and some of its attributes (like bold, italic, color, size, etc.).

3. Using the techniques described in the previous section, change the Normal style font to a different font used either by the style or to the text words changed in step 2.

The paragraph words that received the local font and attribute changes will not be automatically updated to reflect the new font associated to the Normal style. Or in other words, the local font formatting applied to some words of the Normal paragraph style will have precedence over the global font now used by the Normal style (Figure 5-18).

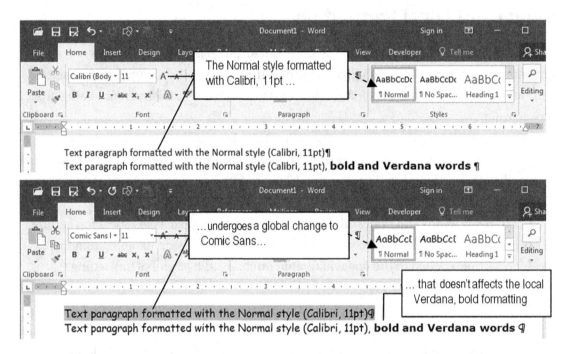

Figure 5-18. Changes made in the Normal style do not apply to local text formatting. In this figure, the Normal style font was changed from Calibri to Comic Sans, and the bold and Verdana words were not affected.

So we can write a simple inheritance law to make a Global style change:

> *Any change made to a specific style attribute will also be made in all text formatted with this style (or any other style that is based on it) unless the text (or the style based on it) has this attribute locally defined.*

Those global changes made in the Normal style may impact other recommended Microsoft Word styles that are based on it, leading to unexpected changes in other document paragraphs; this may make you feel that you have little control over text formatting.

Normal Style Inheritance

To understand the Normal style inheritance, inspect any recommended styles that may be affected by changes made to the Normal style: Heading1, Heading2, Title, Quote, and Intense Quote:

1. Right-click the style in the Style Gallery.

2. Choose Modify... to show the Modify Style dialog box.

3. Note that in the Property area, the Style based on property is defined to Normal.

Attention   By right-clicking any style in the Style Gallery or the Styles window, you can select Modify… to inspect its properties without applying it to the text.

Figure 5-19 shows the Modify Style dialog box evoked to the Heading1 style.

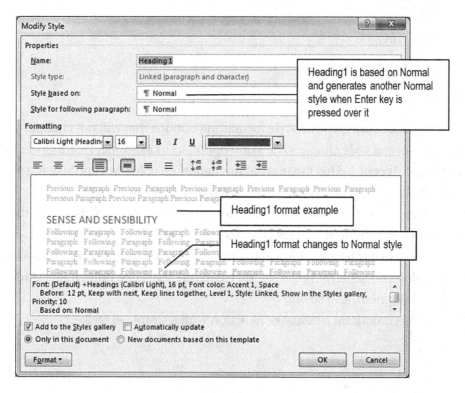

Figure 5-19. *The Modify Style dialog box evoked for the Heading1 recommended style*

Note that Heading1 has these style Properties set:

- **Style** Type = Linked (character and paragraph) (disabled).

- **Style based on** = Normal.

- **Style for following paragraph** = Normal.

Now look to the style example area and see its format appearance. Also look to the style description area and note the specific formatting option it received, which made it different from the Normal style upon which it is based:

- Font: (Default) +Headings (Calibri Light), 16 pt.

- Font color: Accent 1.

- Space Before: 12 pt

- Keep with next

- Keep lines together

- Level 1

- Style: Linked

- Show in the Style Gallery

- Priority: 10

These differences are the local style formatting options that will not change whenever the Normal style changes the same options. For example, Heading1 has the blue color called Accent 1. This means that no matter the color you apply to normal, Heading1 will always be a blue, Accent1 color (local style formatting).

But note that this style has no first-level indent option defined. This means that if the Normal style first-level indent value is changed, the Heading1 first-level indent level will be affected, because it is based on Normal. The same is true for other font and paragraph formatting options not locally applied to the Heading1 style, like Bold, Italic, Underline, Line spacing, Alignment, and so on.

Let us see this inheritance behavior in action with a simple exercise.

Exercise 1

The objective of this exercise is to confirm the Normal style inheritance.

Extract the "Sense and Sensibility, Jane Austen Chapters 1-3 Calibri 11pt.docx" Microsoft Word document from Chapter05.zip file and open it in Microsoft Word. It should be similar to what you see in Figure 5-20 if you checked the Paragraphs mark option in the Display area of the Word Options dialog box (see the section "Choosing Which Hidden Characters to Show" in Chapter 2 for more information).

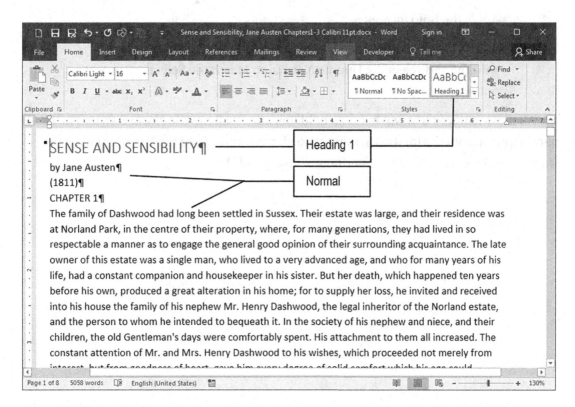

Figure 5-20. *The "Sense and Sensibility, Jane Austen Chapters1-3, Calibri 11pt. docx" Microsoft Word document extracted from Chapter05.zip. The first paragraph is formatted with the recommended Heading1 style, and all the remaining text is formated with the default Normal style (Calibri, 11 pt)*

Note that it is entirely formatted with default Microsoft Word Normal style (Calibri, 11 pt, left aligned, Line spacing = 1.15). It also has its first chapter ("Sense and Sensibility") formatted with the Heading1 style.

Let's quickly apply a Bold formatting to the entire text just changing the Normal style applied to the second paragraph:

1. Triple-click the second text paragraph formatted with the Normal style to select it (or select just the pilcrow ¶ character, if is visible, because paragraph formatting options are stored there).

2. Apply the Bold format.

3. Right-click the Normal style either in Style Gallery or in the Styles window and select the Update Normal to Match the Selection option.

All the document text will become bold, because it all has the Normal style. The first paragraph formatted with the Heading style also becomes Bold because it is based on Normal, and received Bold by inheritance (Figure 5-21).

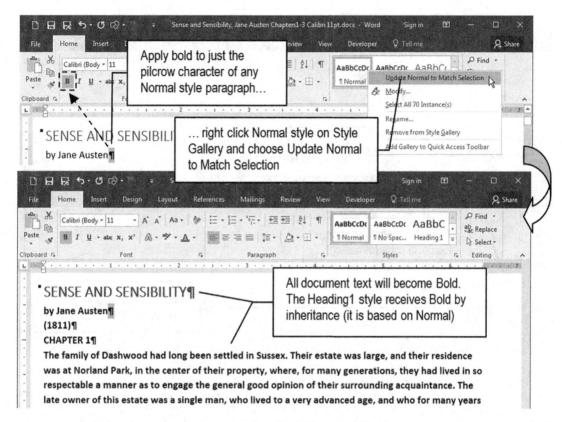

Figure 5-21. *If you apply Bold to the entire text of any Normal style paragraph (or just to its hidden pilcrow ¶ character), by updating the Normal style to Match Selection, all Normal style pagraphs and the ones based on it (like Heading1) will receive bold by inheritance*

Now try to make a Normal style change that will not propagate to any "based on Normal" style (like Headings1):

1. Select any word of a Normal style paragraph and change its color (select Red, for example).

2. Right-click the Normal style in either Style Gallery or the Styles window and select the Update Normal to Match the Selection option.

The red color applied to the text will change the default Normal style color, which will affect all Normal styles. But since Heading1 is formatted with the Accent 1 blue color, it will not react to the new Normal style color: its local formatting has precedence over global formatting option of the style that it is based on (Figure 5-22).

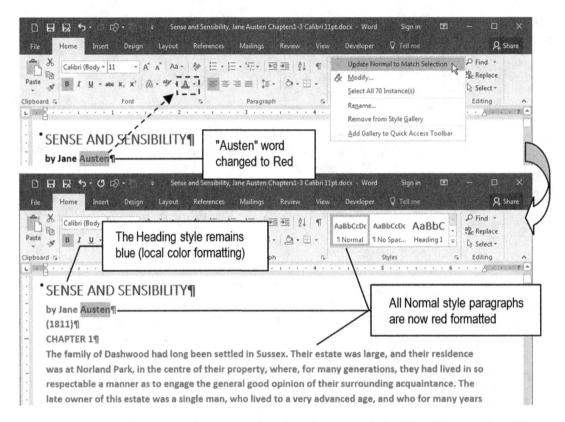

Figure 5-22. *By changing the Normal style color to red, the Heading1 style will not be affected because it specifies its own color (local formatting)*

Creating New Styles

You can create your own set of styles to format your documents using one of these methods almost in the same way that's used to modify an existing style:

- **Create from selection**: first format a text paragraph with all desired attributes and then associate them to a style name

- **Create from scratch**: evoke the Create a New Style from Formatting dialog, define the text attributes using the Format button, and then apply them to the text

I think the first option is preferred because you can format a text paragraph the way you want, applying all desired options like Font, Paragraph, Border, Shades, Color, Language, and so on, until it has the desired appearance, and then evoking the previously discussed Modify Style dialog box, using one of these methods:

- Use the Create Style command offered by the expanded Style Gallery (see Figure 5-2), which will show the Create a New Style from Formatting dialog box, from which you must type the new style name and choose Modify... (Figure 5-23)

Figure 5-23. *You can create a new style by either expanding the Style Gallery and selecting the Create a Style command, which will show the Create the New Style from Formatting dialog box, or clicking the New Style button of the Styles window*

- Click the New Style button of the Styles window

Attention   If you click OK in the Create a New Style from Formatting dialog box shown by the Create a Style command, the style will be created using the Style Type = Linked (character and paragraph), which cannot be changed anymore. Use the Modify button instead to allow control of this property before the style is created.

Both options will end up showing the previously discussed Modify Style dialog box using the selected paragraph formatting options as a base for the new style being created, showing on its title bar the expression "Create a New Style from Formatting," to remember that this style still doesn't exist (Figure 5-24).

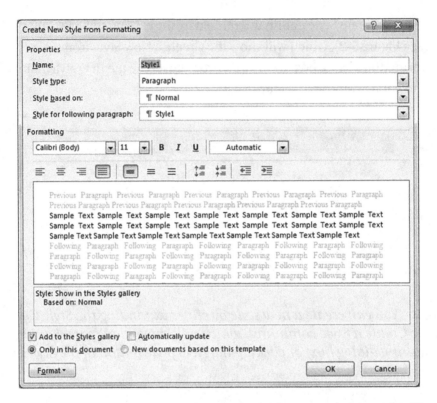

Figure 5-24. *Whenever you try to create a new style, Microsoft Word will end up showing the Modify Style dialog box with the "Create New Style from Formatting" title, and showing all Properties options enabled*

The "Create New Style from Formatting" dialog box will inherit all current paragraph formatting options, associate them to their formatting commands (font, size, bold, italic, underline, color, alignment, line spacing, space before and after, and left indent), and show the details in the style description area (see Figure 5-19 for a better description).

To create a new style, follow these instructions:

1. Format the text with the desired properties (you can change them later).

2. Show the "Create New Style from Formatting" dialog box and type the style name (default name is Style1, if it doesn't exist).

3. Select the style Properties: Style type, Style based on, Style for the following paragraph.

4. Change the basic formatting options using the dialog box control or click the Format button located to the bottom right to show additional formatting dialog boxes.

5. Finally, associate a shortcut key to the style.

6. IMPORTANT: click OK to create the style.

All new styles will appear at the first positions of the Style Gallery.

Figure 5-25 shows the Style1 style created using the default options you see in Figure 5-24 (a perfect copy of the Normal style) appearing at the right of the Normal style in the Style Gallery, at the bottom of the Styles windows, and selected in the Apply styles window (because it was applied to the default, empty paragraph of the new document).

Figure 5-25. *New styles appear at right of the Normal style in the Style Gallery, in the current sort order of the Styles window, and selected in the Apply Styles window, because it is also applied to the selected paragraph*

Removing, Adding Styles from Style Gallery

You can remove or add the styles you created (or any other style) from the Style Gallery, following one of these options:

- To remove a style, right-click it either in the Style Gallery or in the Styles window, and choose Remove from Style Gallery. The style will not be deleted, and will continue to appear in the Styles window.

- To add a style to the Style Gallery, right-click it in the Styles window and select Add to Style Gallery.

Deleting a Style

Deleting an existing style is quite easy:

1. Right-click the desired style either in the Style Gallery or in the Styles window;

2. Select Delete <style name>...

Microsoft Word will show a dialog box to confirm the style deletion, and by accepting the confirmation, the style will be deleted and all paragraphs formatted with it will receive the Normal style.

Attention   You can undo the style deletion pressing Ctrl+Z (or choosing the Undo command at the Quick Access Toolbar located at the top left corner of Microsoft Word title bar).

Exercise 2

Let's try to create some styles with a practical example. Extract "Sense and Sensibility, Jane Austen Chapters1-3.docx" file from Chapter05.zip the and open it in Microsoft Word.

Note that this document has just eight pages when you extract it from Chapter05.zip file, and is entirely formatted using just the Normal style that was updated to Times New Roman, 12 pt, Line spacing = single.

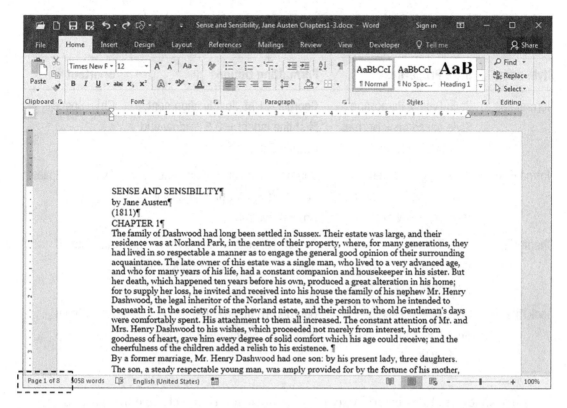

Figure 5-26. *The basic version of "Sense and Sensibility, Jane Austen Chapters1-3. docx" Microsoft Word document, as you can extract from Chapter05.zip file*

Our target is to format this document text using four different paragraph styles:

- **Normal**: already applied to the entire text document.

- **NormalFirst**: must be applied to the first body text paragraph of each chapter.

- **ChapterTitle**: must be applied to the chapter titles.

- **BookTitle**: must be applied to just the Book title.

These paragraph styles must be formatted as specified in Table 5-2.

Table 5-2. *Paragraph Styles That Must Be Used to Format the "Sense and Sensibility, Jane Austen Chapters1-3.docx" Microsoft Word Document*

Style name	Style Properties	Formatting Options	Shortcut
Normal	Style Type = Paragraph Style based on = Normal Next Style = Normal	Georgia, 11 pt, Justify alignment, First line indent = 0.5, Widow and Orphan Control	Ctrl+ Space
NormalFirst	Style Type = Linked Style based on = Normal Next Style = Normal	Georgia, 11 pt, Justify alignment, Space After = 11 pt, Widow and Orphan Control	Alt+ Ctrl+ Space
ChapterTitle	Style Type = Linked Style based on = Normal Next Style = NormalFirst	Calibri, 16, bold, Center alignment, Space After = 1 Page break before	Alt+ Ctrl+C
BookTitle	Style Type = Linked Style based on = Normal Next Style = Normal	Georgia, 18 pt, bold, Center alignment, Space Before = 2 in	Alt+ Ctrl+B

Since styles can be affected by style inheritance, let us first change the Normal style so you can see how the text can be affected by this change.

Changing the Normal Style from Selection

The style applied to the body text is the most important because it will be used to format the biggest part of the document. This document uses the Normal style to format the body text, so we may begin by changing the first text paragraph to the formatting standards proposed by Table 5-2 and then updating the Normal style to match the paragraph style.

Follow these steps:

1. Select all the text for the first body text paragraph (the one below Chapter1 that begins with "*The family...*").

Attention   To easily select an entire text paragraph, triple-click it or point the mouse to its left border, and when the mouse pointer changes to a right pointing arrow, and double-click it.

---

2. Using the Font area of the Home tab of the Ribbon, apply to the selected paragraph the Georgia, 11 pt font, and a Justify alignment.

3. Show the Paragraph dialog box (right-click it and select Paragraph...), and define Indentation, Special = First Line, By = 0.5.

4. Click the Line and Page Breaks tab of the Paragraph dialog box and check Widow/Orphan control option (Figure 5-27).

5. Press OK to close the Paragraph dialog box and return to the document.

6. Right-click the Normal style in the Style Gallery and choose Update Normal to Match Selection option to update it.

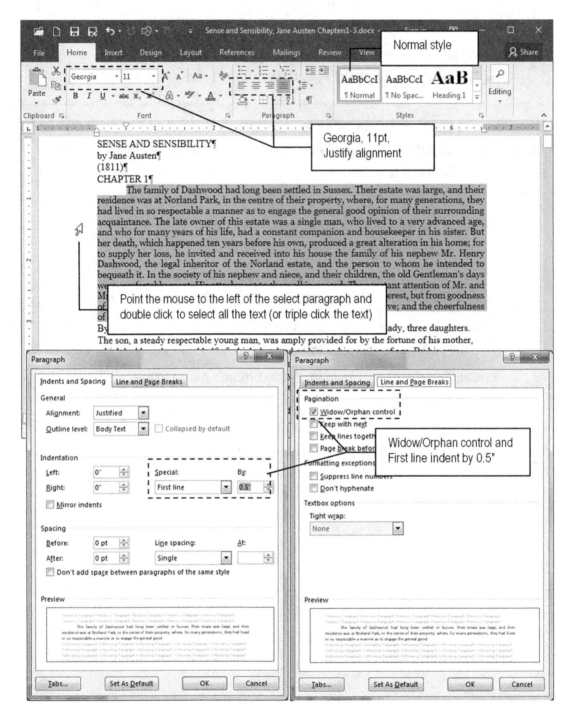

Figure 5-27. *Select all the text of the first body text paragraph and change its formatting options to Georgia, 11 pt, Justify alignment, First line indent = 0.5, Widow/Orphan control*

Microsoft Word will update the Normal style and the entire document will receive the new formatting options, since all its paragraphs were formatted with the Normal style. Note that since the font size was changed to a new, small standard, the document will shrink and will now exhibit 7 pages: 1 page less (Figure 5-28).

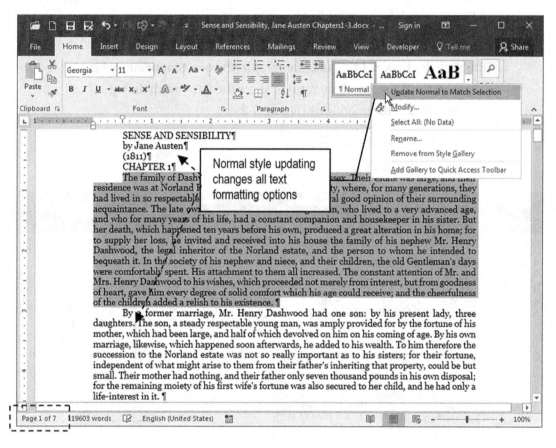

Figure 5-28. *Once you have defined the body text format for the document, right-click the style applied to the text in the Style Gallery and choose Update <style> to Match Selection option. This figure updates the Normal style to a new standard, changing the appearance of the entire document.*

Attention   On some occasions, you may need to select the entire text (press Ctrl+A) and apply the Normal style (press Alt+Space if you assigned it this shortcut) to guarantee that changes made in the Normal style will be applied to the entire document.

Creating NormalFirst Style

Now the Normal style was already formatted, let us use it as the template to create the NormalFirst style: the one that must be used to format the first paragraph of each chapter. As proposed by Table 5-2, it must have the same Normal font formatting options, no First line indent, and Space After = 11 pt.

To easily create the NormalFirst style, follow these steps:

1. Right-click Chapter 1 first text paragraph (the one that begins with *"The family..."*), select Paragraph to show the Paragraph dialog box, and define these options (Figure 5-29):

    - Indentation, Special = None.

    - Space, After = 11 pt.

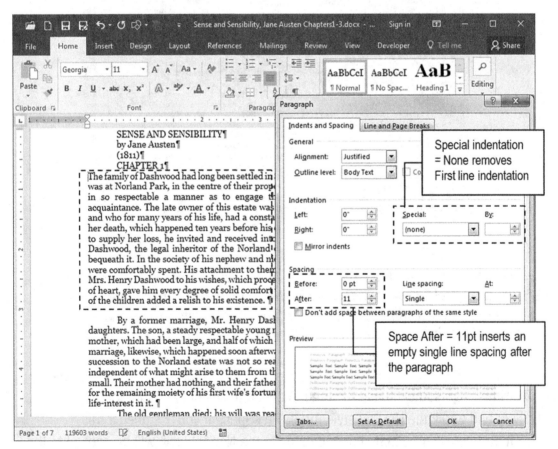

Figure 5-29. *The NormalFirst style must have no First line indentation and Space After = 11 pt (to create an empty space proportional to an 11 pt single line spacing)*

2. Press OK to close the Paragraph dialog box and return to the text.

3. Expand the Style Gallery (see Figure 5-2) and select the Create a Style option to show the Create New Style from Formatting dialog box (Figure 5-30).

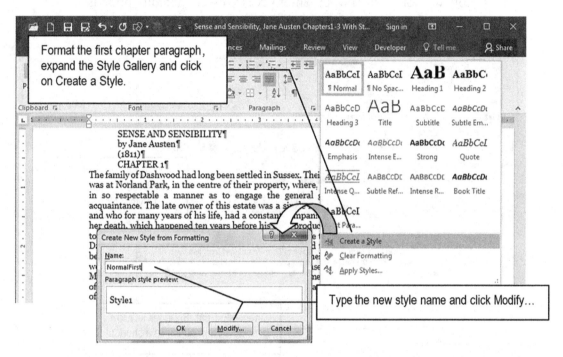

Figure 5-30. *After you format the first Chapter 1 paragraph (no Left indent and Space before = 11 pt), expand the Style Gallery and select the Create a Style option to show the Create a New Style from Formatting dialog box*

4. In Create New Style from Formatting dialog box, select the Name text box and type NormalFirst to name the new style.

5. Click Modify to show the expanded Create New Style from Formatting dialog box and define these options in the Properties area:

    - **Name**: NormalFirst (the style name as it will appear in the Style Gallery, Styles, and Apply Styles windows).

    - **Style type**: Linked (paragraph and character) (to allow its application either to the text selected or to the entire paragraph.

- **Style based on**: Normal (the style from which it will inherit all other formatting options not implemented by this style; choose None to create styles with no inheritance).

- **Style for following paragraph**: Normal (the next style that follows NormalFirst when Enter key is pressed: default option is the same style name being created, Figure 5-31).

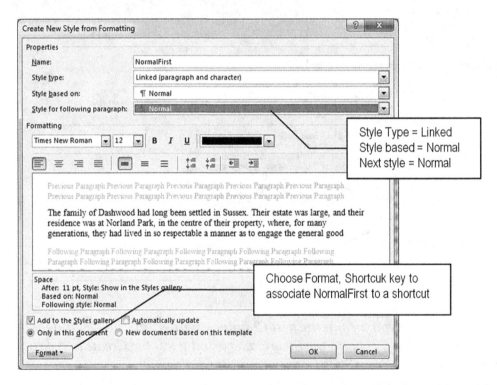

Figure 5-31. *The NormalFirst style must be based on Normal style and have the Style for the following paragraphs defined to Normal*

6. In the Create New Style from Formatting dialog box, click Format ➤ Shortcut key to show the Customize Keyboard dialog box and attribute the Ctrl+Alt+Space shortcut to the NormalFirst style (Figure 5-32).

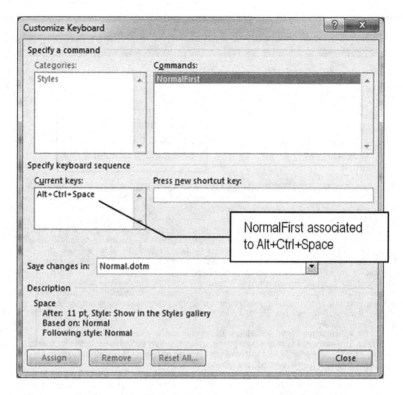

Figure 5-32. *Associate the NormalFirst style to the Alt+Ctrl+Space shortcut*

7. Click OK to close the Customize Keyboard dialog box and return
    to the Create New Style from Formatting dialog box.

8. Click OK to close the Create New Style from Formatting dialog box.

Since the Add to the Style Gallery option was selected by default, the style will appear
in the Style Gallery, and will be selected as an indication that it has been applied to the
selected paragraph (Figure 5-33).

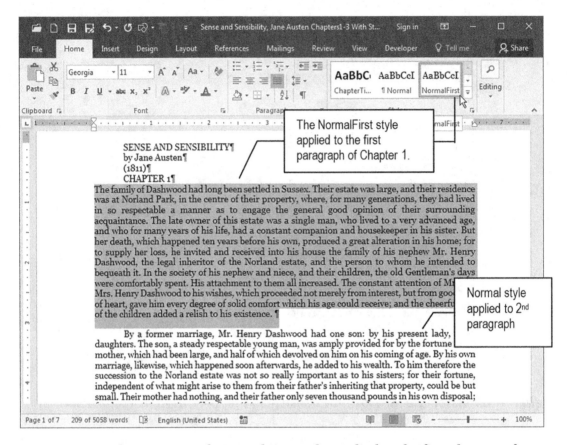

Figure 5-33. *The just-created NormalFirst style applied to the first chapter of Chapter 1. Note that is has no First line indent (as the Normal style paragraphs that surround it have), but has a space afterward that separates it from the next*

Attention   Once a style is added to the Style Gallery, you can remove it by right-clicking its name and selecting Remove from Style Gallery command. The style will not be deleted: it will just not be shown anymore by the Style Gallery.

Creating ChapterTitle Style

The ChapterTitle style must also be created by example and applied to all chapter enunciator paragraphs using Microsoft Word Replace command.

Follow these steps to create ChapterTitle style:

1. Select the Chapter 1 text paragraph (triple-click it) and apply the desired formatting options (use Home tab of the Ribbon and/or the Font and Paragraph dialog boxes):

    - Calibri, 16, bold;

    - Center alignment;

    - Indentation, Special = None;

    - Space After = 1.

    - Page break before.

Attention   Since the Chapter 1 paragraph is formatted with the Normal style, it received by inheritance a First line indent = 0.5 that must be removed!

---

2. The Chapter 1 text paragraph must now begin on document page 2, since it has the Paragraph dialog box Page break before option set.

3. Follow steps 3 to 8 used early in the section "Creating NormalFirst Style" to create ChapterTitle style from the selection.

4. Using the Create New Style from Formatting dialog box, set the following style Properties (Figure 5-34):

    - **Name**: ChapterTitle;

    - **Style type**: Linked (paragraph and character);

    - **Style based on**: Normal;

    - **Style for following paragraph**: Normal;

    - **Shortcut**: Alt+C.

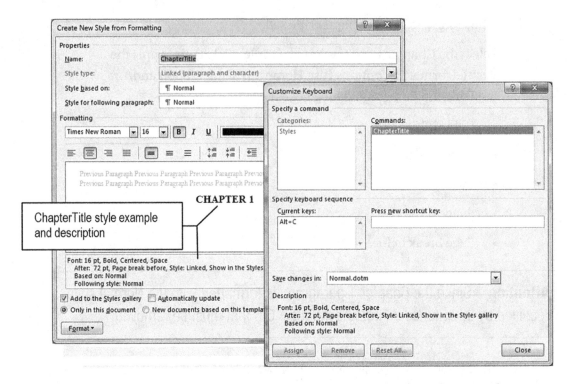

Figure 5-34. *The Create New Style from Formatting dialog box showing the ChapterTitle properties and the associated keyboard shortcut. Note the style description with all its specific properties, plus the entire Normal style on which it is based.*

When you close the Create New Style from Formatting dialog box, Microsoft Word will apply the ChapterTitle style paragraph to the "Chapter 1" paragraph, and will show the style selected in the Style Gallery (because the Add to Style Gallery option was selected by default). Note that now "Chapter 1" begins on Page 2, the next style is NormalFirst followed by Normal, and the document now has 8 pages again (Figure 5-35).

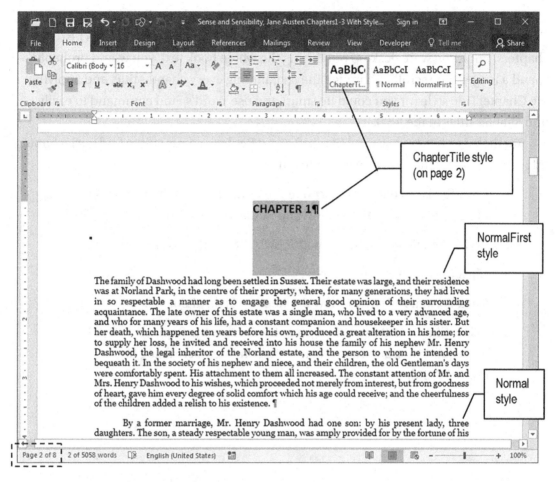

Figure 5-35. *The ChapterTitle style applied to "Chapter 1" paragraph. Since the style has the Page break before option set, it forces the paragraph formatted with it to begin on a new page. Also note that it has a Space Before = 1" to separate it from the next paragraph (formatted with NormalFirst style).*

Replacing Chapter Titles with the ChapterTitle Style

Now that ChapterTitle style is created and associated to the Alt+C style, you can easily scroll through the text to find another chapter paragraph, click to select it, and press Alt+C to apply its Chapter title style, an operation that will automatically format the chapter title and insert a new document page.

This operation can be easily accomplished in "Sense and Sensibility, Jane Austen Chapters1-3 With Styles.docx" document, since it is just 8 pages long and has just 3 chapters. But if you were desktop publishing the whole book text, you would probably spend a longer time scrolling through the text, finding every chapter title, and applying the ChapterTitle style (or you could be smart and use Word's Find command to easily find chapter titles in the text).

But there is a better way: use Microsoft Word Replace command to find each chapter title and apply the ChapterTitle style following these steps:

1. Click Replace command found in the Editing area of the Home tab of the Ribbon to show the Find and Replace dialog box.

2. In the Find what text box, type "CHAPTER" (without quotes).

3. Click the Replace with text box.

4. Click Format ➤ Style to show the Replace Style dialog box.

5. Select ChapterTitle style and press Ok to close the Replace Style dialog box and return to the Find and Replace dialog box (Figure 5-36).

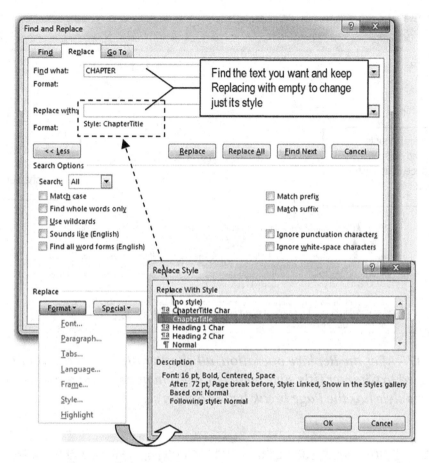

Figure 5-36. *Use the Find and Replace dialog box to search for "CHAPTER" and replace it with the ChapterTitle style*

6. Under the Replace with text box you will now read Style: Chapter title. Press Replace all to make the desired style change just in chapter title paragraphs.

When you close the Find and Replace dialog box, the document will have 11 pages. Scroll through the text until you find "Chapter 2" paragraph and note that it begins on a new page, having 1 inch of space to separate it from the next, first chapter paragraph.

Click the first paragraph of Chapter 2 and press Ctrl+Alt+Space to apply the NormalFirst style. Do the same with the first paragraph of Chapter 3 (Figure 5-37).

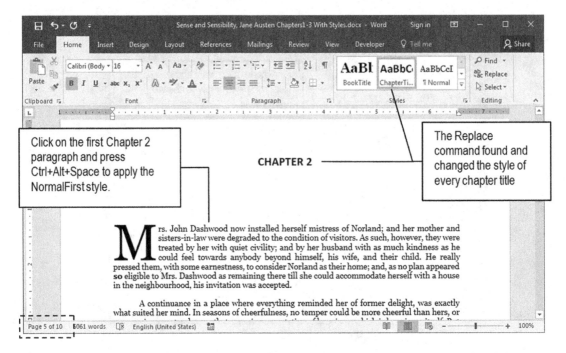

Figure 5-37. *After the Replace operation, all chapter title paragraphs had their style changed to ChapterTitle style, which makes them begin on a new page because this style has the Page break before option set*

Attention   Before doing such a "find and replace" operation, you must be pretty sure that what you are searching for exists just in independent text paragraphs, or the replace operation can make a mess by applying the replacement style to the wrong paragraphs.

Inserting a New Chapter Title

To see how style properties are important to paragraph inheritance, do this experiment:

1. Go to the end of the document (press Ctrl+End) and if necessary, insert a new paragraph.

2. Type Chapter 4 in the new paragraph at the end of the document and press Alt+C to apply the ChapterTitle style (or click this style in the Style Gallery).

3. The "Chapter 4" paragraph will jump to a new page (due to the ChapterTitle style having the Page break before option set). The document will now have 11 pages.

4. Press Enter to insert a new NormalFirst style paragraph (due to the ChapterTitle style having the Style for following paragraph = NormalFirst).

5. Press Enter in the first, empty NormalFirst paragraph to insert a new Normal style paragraph (due to the NormalFirst style having the Style for following paragraph = Normal) (Figure 5-38).

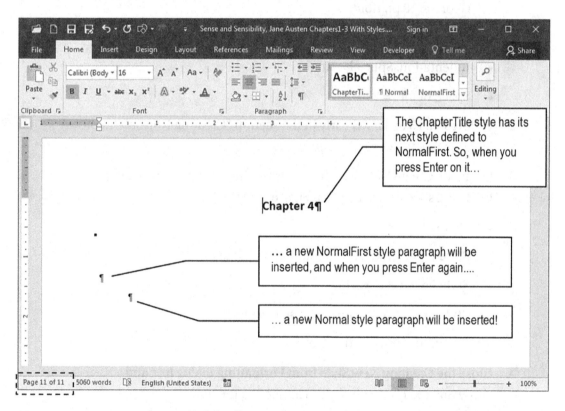

Figure 5-38. *Go to the end of the "Sense and Sensibility, Jane Austen Chapters 1-3. docx" document (press Ctrl+End), type Chapter 4, and press Alt+C to apply the ChapterTitle style, which will force the paragraph to begin on a new page. Press Enter to automatically insert a NormalFirst style and press Enter again to insert a Normal style (both inserted by style inheritance).*

Cool, isn't it? Using the appropriate style properties, you can easily write and desktop publish the document at the same time!

Creating and Applying the BookTitle Style

The last style you need to create to format the "Sense and Sensibility, Jane Austen Chapters1-3.docx" document is the BookTitle style. You do not really need to create it unless you are supposed to use the same document formatting options to format other similar public domain books. But is a good exercise to practice with styles, so follow these instructions to create it:

1. Select the first document paragraph (the book title: triple-click it) and format it according to the specifications of Table 5-1:

   - Georgia, 18 pt, Bold;

   - Center alignment;

   - Indentation, Special = None

   - Space Before = 2 in

2. Follow steps 3 to 8 used early in the section "Creating NormalFirst Style" to create BookTitle style from selection.

3. Using the Create New Style from Formatting dialog box to set the following style Properties (see Figure 5-34):

   - **Name**: BookTitle.

   - **Style type**: Linked (paragraph and character).

   - **Style based on**: Normal.

   - **Style for following paragraph**: Normal.

   - **Shortcut**: Alt+Ctrl+B.

4. Close the Creating New Style from Formatting dialog box and verify that the BookTitle style is applied to the text.

5. Center align the author name and year paragraphs, and remove the first line indentation (received by inheritance from the Normal style).

Figure 5-39 shows the "Sense and Sensibility, Jane Austen Chapters1-3 With Styles. docx" document (that you can also extract from Chapter04.zip file) with the BookTitle style applied to its first paragraph.

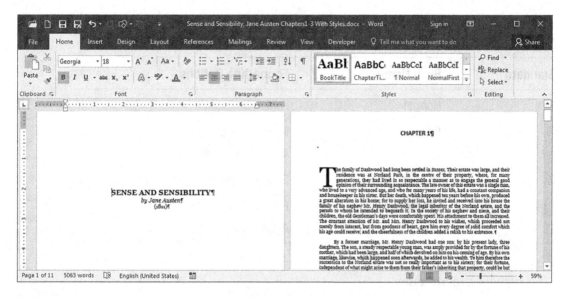

Figure 5-39. *The "Sense and Sensibility, Jane Austen Chapters1-3 With Styles. docx" document showing the BookTitle style applied to the first document paragraph and a drop cap of 4 lines height applied to the first paragraph of each chapter.*

This document has all the formatting options proposed for it, while also has a drop cap character with a height of 4 lines applied to every NormalFirst paragraph that begins a new chapter.

Cool, huh? Can you also make such changes in the "Sense and Sensibility, Jane Austen Chapters1-3.docx" document?

Exercise 3

The objective of this exercise is to make changes to the appearance of the "Sense and Sensibility, Jane Austen Chapters1-3 With Styles.docx" document by changing its Normal and ChapterTitle styles formatting options to Standards 1 and 2 proposed by Table 5-3, which uses a pair of serif/sans serif fonts to format the text:

Table 5-3. *Paragraph Styles That Must Be Used to Format the "Sense and Sensibility, Jane Austen Chapters1-3.docx" Microsoft Word Document*

Standard	Style Name	Formatting Options
1	Normal	Font = Constantia
	ChapterTitle	Font = Century, 22 pt Alignment= Right
2	Normal	Font = Franklin Gothic
	ChapterTitle	Font = Cambria, 20 pt Alignment = Left

Try these experiments:

1. Use the Modify to Match Selection option to change the styles' format (apply the standards to a single paragraph and then update the style to match its formatting options).

2. Change the Normal style first and watch:

   • The BookChapter and NormalFirst style updates by inheritance.

   • The NormalFirst paragraphs lose their Drop Cap (you will need to rebuild them manually).

3. Change ChapterTitle first and then change Normal. Note that since ChapterTitle is based on Normal, it will lose the font formatting options when Normal is updated.

4. Change the font used by Normal and ChapterTitle styles for each standard (e.g., for Standard 1, Normal = Century, ChapterTitle = Constantia, 22).

5. Make your own choice of fonts and paragraph options to change ChapterTitle and Normal styles based on the typographical knowledge you've gathered so far from this book.

Conclusion

Microsoft Word styles are the heart of text processing operations, because they allow implementation of complex formatting options in different text paragraphs by a click of the mouse.

The styles offered by the Styles Gallery are called Recommended styles, and you can use them to change the appearance of your text. Or you can create a new set of styles giving them names that are more significant to the task at hand.

The Normal style is the default style used by most Microsoft Word documents, and is quite common to see long text documents using just the Normal style applied to all paragraphs.

Local formatting options have precedence over global formatting options, which affect style inheritance this way: any formatting change made in a base style carries through to the styles based on it, as long as these based styles do not locally implement other formatting.

And this is what explains the strong inheritance behavior for Normal.dot changes: most recommended styles (and new styles) are frequently based on it.

Summary

On this chapter you learned:

- Style is a name place to store a predefined set of formatting options that can be applied at once to the text.

- Microsoft Word calls "Recommended" the default style set offered by the Styles Gallery found in the Home tab of the Ribbon.

- The Style Gallery allows you to quickly format text by clicking any style it shows.

- You can expand the Style Gallery to show more styles or some commands to allow you to create or apply styles.

- You can show the Styles window using the small square that sits at the bottom right corner of the Styles area of the Ribbon.

- You can use the Styles window option to show all the styles that exist in the current document and present them in different sort orders.

- Both the Style Gallery and the Styles window can be used to change, insert, and modify styles.

- Both the Style Gallery and the Styles window show the current style applied to the text as long as it's visible in its style list.

- You use the Style Gallery to show the Apply Styles windows.

- Just the Apply Styles window synchronizes the style used in the text.

- Formatting options can be considered as local or global.

- Microsoft Word gives precedence to local formatting options over global ones.

- Normal style is the most used style in the world.

- Normal style is the base for many other recommended styles (or new created styles), unless it is manually changed.

- You can easily change the text formatting by just changing the Normal style.

- Styles have properties that allow them to be based on other styles, and a style applied to one paragraph will and select the style for the next paragraph that follows.

- You can associate any style to a shortcut key so it can be easily applied as you write, without need for taking your hands off of the keyboard.

In the next chapter, we will explore Microsoft Word Recommended styles and how to use the Design tab controls to easily change the appearance of any text document.

CHAPTER 6

Using Recommended Styles

Microsoft Word calls the styles shown by default in the Quick Style Gallery as *"Recommended"* because it offers different tools at the Document Formatting area of the Design tab of the Ribbon to professionally change any document appearance that makes use of them to format the text.

In this chapter, you will learn how to use the Recommended styles along with the Design tab tools to quickly and professionally change the appearance of any text document created with Microsoft word.

The documents cited in this chapter and the Exercise sections can be found by downloading Chapter06.zip file from this Internet address:

`https://github.com/apress/msft-word-secrets`

Recommended Styles

The Design tab of the Ribbon offers tools at the Document Formatting area of the Design tab of the Ribbon to professionally change any document appearance that makes use of Microsoft Word Recommended styles to format the text (Figure 6-1).

© Flavio Morgado 2017
F. Morgado, *Microsoft Word Secrets*, https://doi.org/10.1007/978-1-4842-3078-7_6

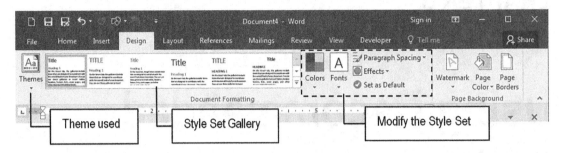

Figure 6-1. *The Design tab of the Ribbon is used to change the appearance of "Recommended" style set*

Note that the same interface defined by the Style Gallery to show single style formatting options is now used by the Style Set Gallery to show the formatting options of three special Recommended styles: visual examples of the Title, Heading1, and Normal styles format are shown in each option of this control (Figure 6-2).

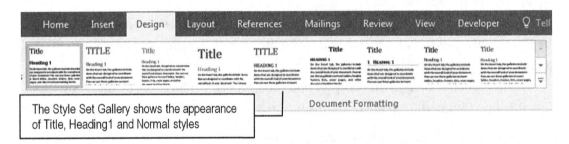

Figure 6-2. *The Style Set Gallery of the Design tab of the Ribbon shows the format that will be applied to the Title, Heading1, and Normal Recommended styles*

And this is not all: among the tools that you can use to change the Recommended styles formatting options, you will also find:

- **Themes**: to change all formatting options.

- **Colors**: to change the color palette options.

- **Fonts**: to change the fonts options.

- **Paragraph spacing**: to change the spacing options.

- **Set as Default**: to set the selected options as the default formatting standards for new documents.

As cited in Table 5-1, each Recommended style has a name that indicates its main usage, and if you follow these recommendations, it will be quite easy to professionally format and change the appearance of any text document produced with Microsoft Word.

And since you may now have a better understanding of styles and how to create, modify, and use them, let's see a practical example of Recommended styles usage and how you can use Microsoft Word Design tab tools to format a document.

Using Recommended Styles

To have an easier understanding of how Microsoft Word Design tools interacts with Recommended styles, extract file "Microsoft Word Recommended Styles.docx" from Chapter06.zip file and open it in Microsoft Word. Note that this document uses the recommendations for usage cited in Table 5-1, where each style name was applied to specific paragraphs of words (Figure 6-3).

For example, the Title style was applied to the first document paragraph; Subtitle was applied to the paragraphs that follow it. Character styles were applied to some words that represent the styles. To help you see the association made to each paragraph and some words, they were named and formatted with the associated style it received.

Style Themes

A Theme is a specific combination of fonts and formatting options used to format the recommended style set.

Using the Design tab, you can select different style themes to apply to any document that uses the Recommended style set to format titles, subtitles, headings, body text, quotes, and so on. The default Themes used in a new, empty Microsoft Word document is called "Office."

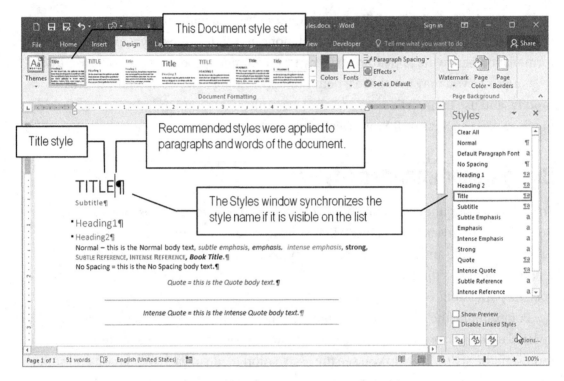

Figure 6-3. *The Microsoft Word Recommended Styles.docx file has paragraphs and words already formatted with the Recommended style set*

By default, the Office theme is associated to the This Document style set: the first Style Set gallery item. Every other item of the Style Set Gallery has a name associated with it, like Basic (Elegant), Basic (Simple), Basic (stylish), Black and White (Capitalized), and so on.

To easily change the appearance of the Office theme applied to the document, click any style set.

Figure 6-4 shows the Microsoft Word Recommended Styles.docx file appearance after it has received the Shaded style set. Note that the This Document style set thumbnail was updated to reflect the style set in use.

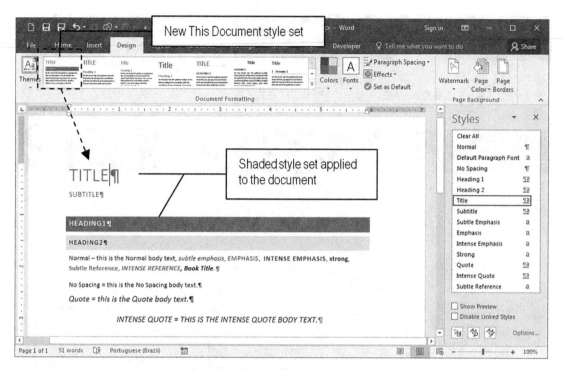

Figure 6-4. *Use the Style Themes tool of the Document Formatting area of the Design tab of the Ribbon to easily change the appearance of any document formatted using the default "as Recommended" styles in the text*

Like the Quick Style gallery does to show more styles, you can expand the Style Set Gallery to expose other style sets available by clicking the small arrow located at the bottom of its scroll bar (Figure 6-5).

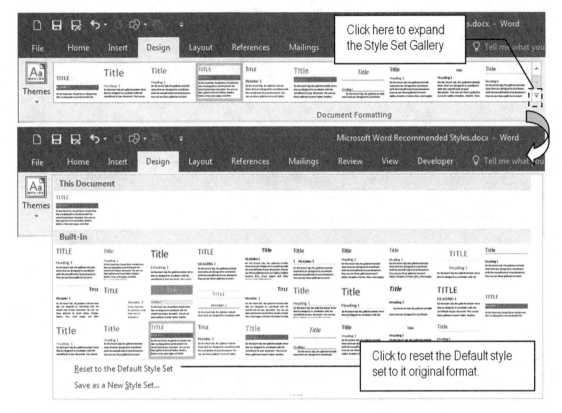

Figure 6-5. *Expand the Style Set Gallery to reveal other style sets, reset to the default style, or save the current style set as a Microsoft Word Template dotx file.*

There will be two commands:

- **Reset to the Default Style Set**: return the document appearance to the default theme style set.

- **Save as a New Style Set...**: click to save the current style set as a new Microsoft Word Template. The new Style Set will appear as the second style theme in the beginning of the Style Set Gallery.

Attention   Templates will be discussed in Chapter 11). By default, they are saved in the C:\Users\<username>\AppData\Roaming\Microsoft\QuickStyles folder.

To remove a saved style set, right-click on the Style Set Gallery and chose Delete. Microsoft Word will delete the associated file from your disk and remove it from the Style Set Gallery.

Theme Colors

You can change the style set appearance by applying a different color palette using the Colors option of the Document Formatting area of the Design tab of the Ribbon: just click the Colors button to expand it and drag the mouse over the available color palettes to see how the Recommended styles area changed and the text is affected. Click the desired color palette to make the change permanent (note that not all styles are affected by a new color palette, Figure 6-6).

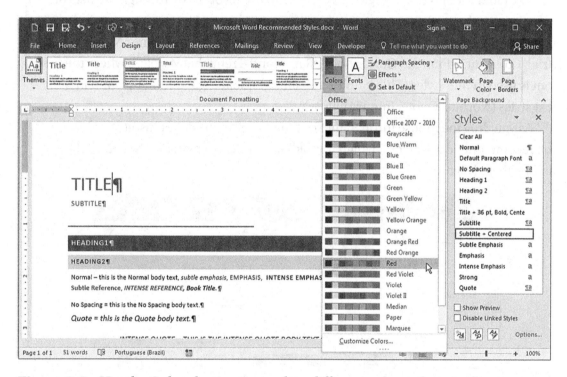

Figure 6-6. *Use the Colors button to apply a different color palette to the recommended styles applied to the text. Note however that not all styles will be affected by the new palette*

Attention   Select the Office color palette to reset the recommended styles to the default color theme.

Theme Fonts

Like the Colors button, use the Fonts button to apply different font combinations to the current style set. The button also expands when you click it and shows different font pairs professionally combined to format the document title, subtitle, and body text.

Each font theme has a name. The default font theme is called Office, there is an Office 2007-2010 theme, and the other themes are named according to the font or font combination used by the theme.

Most font themes use a single sans serif font, but if you scroll through the list you will note that there are some sans serif/serif combinations (like Century Gothic-Palatino Linotype, TV Cen MT-Rockwell, etc.) or serif/sans serif fonts (like Times New Roman-Arial, Constantia-Franklin Gothic book, Garamond-TrebuchetMs, etc.), where the first font is used in title styles (Title, Subtitle, Heading1, Heading2) and the second in body text styles (Normal, Quote, Intense Quote).

As you drag the mouse through the font themes proposed, Microsoft Word changes the recommended styles font, which immediately reacts to better allow you to choose among them (Figure 6-7).

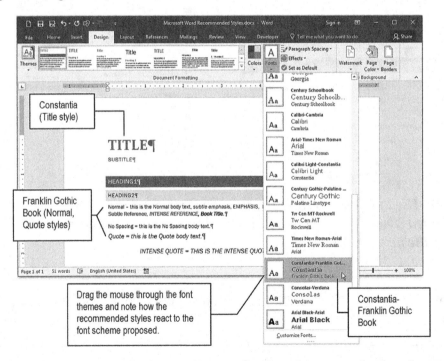

Figure 6-7. *Use the Font button to change the font theme applied to the Title/Body text recommended styles. Some font themes use a single font, while others offer pairs of serif/sans serif or sans serif/serif fonts (the first applied to title styles).*

Paragraph Spacing

Using the Paragraph spacing button, you can change paragraph Space Before/After and Line spacing options for all recommended styles at once. There is a default paragraph spacing for each style set, and other spacing themes called No paragraph space, Compact, Tight, Open, Relaxed, and Double.

Use them to insert/remove space between text paragraphs so it can best fit into fewer or more document pages as needed (Figure 6-8).

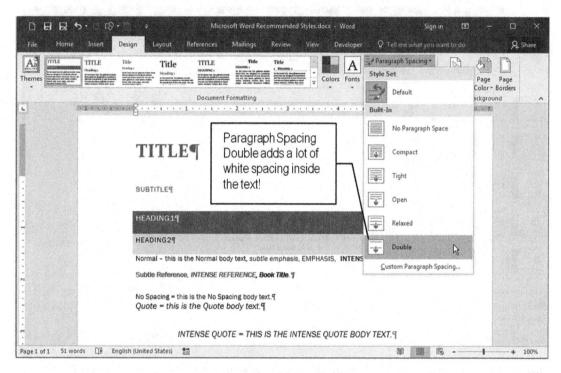

Figure 6-8. *Use the Paragraph Spacing button to easily change the Space and Line Spacing of all recommended paragraph styles, and easily make the text fit the desired number of pages*

Set as Default

Use this option to make the current formatting options become the standard format for new documents. It will affect all recommended styles and will become the default appearance for every new Microsoft Word document.

Theme Button

Use the Theme button to select an entire new theme (combination of font type, font, color, and paragraph spacing options) or to save the current options to a new theme.

The Theme button offers named themes, where the default is called Office. As you scroll through the list the recommended styles react to them, offering new ways to professionally format any document that uses this basic Microsoft Word style (Figure 6-9).

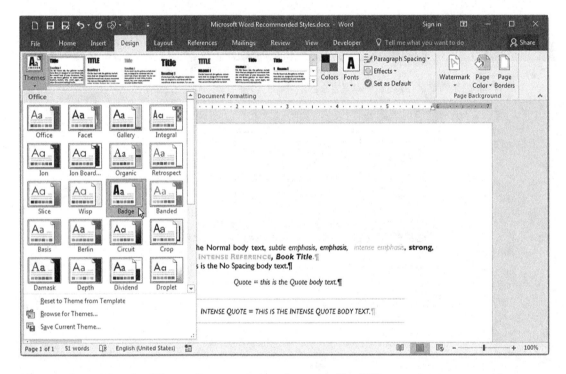

Figure 6-9. *Use the Theme button to apply a totally different theme set to the recommended styles used in the document. You can also modify a theme and save it for future usage.*

Attention   To reset the recommended styles format to the original standards used by Microsoft Word, use the Theme button to select the default Office theme, expand the Style Set Gallery, and select Reset to Default Style Set (Figure 6-5).

Finding the Style Applied to the Text

The Microsoft Word Recommended Styles.docx file is a good opportunity to show you that although Microsoft Word offers both the Quick Style Gallery and the Styles window to show/manage styles, both interfaces may fail to show which styles is in use by the text (character styles) or paragraph (paragraph styles) when you click the mouse to position the text cursor on it.

To see how this may happen, first change the Styles window appearance to make it show all the styles inside the document sorted in alphabetical order by following these steps:

1. Show the Styles window by clicking the small square located at the bottom right of the Styles area in the Home tab of the Ribbon (see Figure 5-2).

2. In the Styles window, uncheck the Show preview option, click Options... to show the Style Pane Options dialog box, and set these options:

   - **Select styles to show**: All styles;

   - **Select how list is sorted**: Alphabetical.

3. Close the Style Pane Options dialog box and click the first paragraph of the Microsoft Word Recommended Styles.docx file (the one with "Title" word formatted with the Title style).

Depending on the size of your screen, size of the Microsoft Word window, and your resolution, you may note that the style used by the text/paragraph selected may not be selected and may not be shown in either the Quick Style Gallery or the Styles window (Figure 6-10).

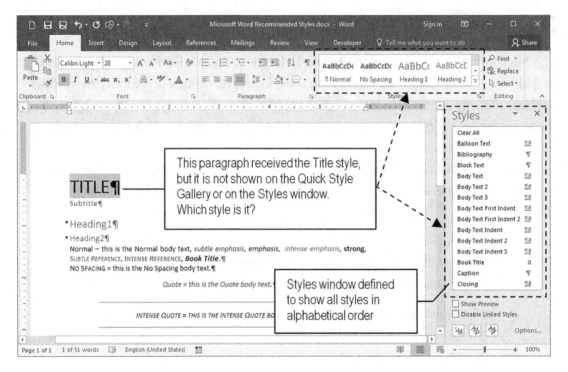

Figure 6-10. *Sometimes the size of Microsoft Word window doesn't allow synchronyzation the style used by the selected text/paragraph in the Quick Style Gallery or the Styles window*

In fact, the Styles window did synchronize the selected Title paragraph style, but it doesn't scroll the list to show what it selected: you have to do it manually to discover which style this paragraph has.

Don't worry! Microsoft Word also offers the Apply Styles window that shows a combo box that reacts like the one used by Microsoft Word 2003 or older versions (expand the Quick Style Gallery and click the Apply Styles... command, see Figure 5-2).

By default the Apply Styles window is anchored at the right side of the Microsoft Word interface, but is can be dragged inside the document window to float over it, so you can better position it anywhere of the screen and always know which style is in use (Figure 6-11).

Attention   From my point of view, I rather use the Apply Styles window to format text because it always show the style in use, and allow to reapply the style by either click on the Reapply button or by selecting again the style from the list. By keeping the Auto Complete style names option checked, you can also type the style initials on the list to easily find it by its name. Or open the Styles window to insert, modify and manage styles.

Although it is not specified, the Apply Styles window shows the same styles currently shown by the Styles window.

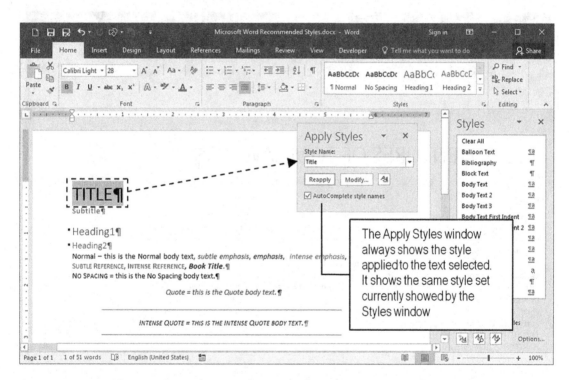

Figure 6-11. *The Apply Styles window can float over Microsoft Word window and always show the style in use when you click the text. It also allows you to reapply and modify the selected style, or show the Styles window.*

Exercise 1

The objective of this exercise is to use the Design tab Style Set Gallery to quickly change the appearance of a document formatted with Recommended styles.

Extract file "The Adventures of Tom Sawyer Chapter 1-3 Recommended Styles.docx" from Chapter06.zip file and open it in Microsoft Word.

Explore the file by clicking its title ("The Adventures of Tom Sawyer"), subtitle ("Mark Twain"), chapter titles ("Chapter1", "Chapter 2", and "Chapter 3"), and any body text paragraphs ("'Tom!'") and note that they were formatted using the Recommended styles Title, Sutbtitle, Heading1, and Normal, respectively (Figure 6-12).

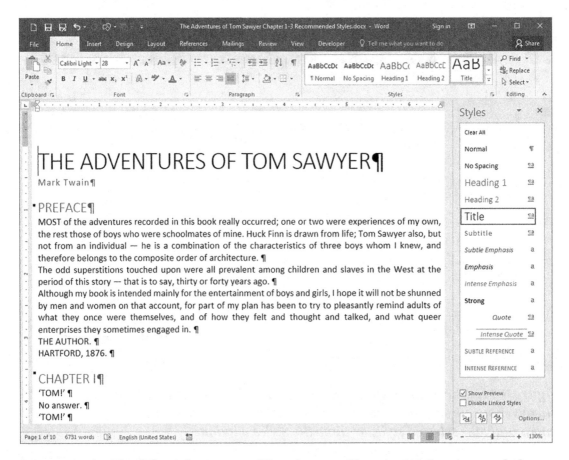

Figure 6-12. *The "The Adventures of Tom Sawyer Chapter 1-3 Recommended Styles.docx" file uses the Recommended styles Title, Subtitle, Heading1, and Normal to format the document title, subtitle, chapter titles, and body text, respectively.*

Follow these tips to easily change this document format:

- Click the Design tab of the Ribbon and scroll the mouse over the Style Set Gallery themes to see how the text quickly changes its formatting options to fit the Style Theme under the mouse.

- Click any colored Style Set Galley to change the document appearance (and redefine the This Document theme: the first Style Set theme). Figure 6-13 shows the Lines (simple) theme applied to the document.

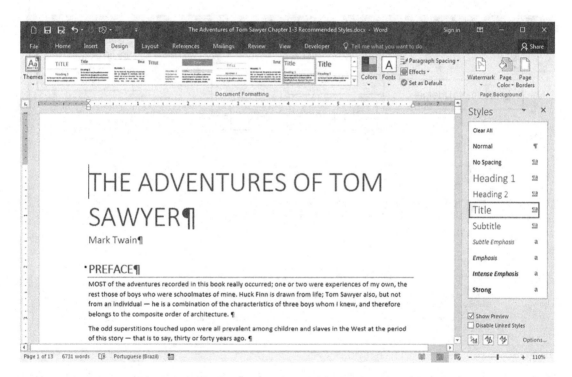

Figure 6-13. *The Line (simple) theme applied to the document*

- Having chosen a colored Style Set theme (any theme that has the Title style colored), click the Color option and scroll the mouse through the color palettes available and note how the document changes its appearance.

- Click any Color palette to redefine the Recommended styles colors and note how the This Document theme changed to reflect the selected color palette.

- Click the Fonts button and select another font theme and watch how the document changes the font used by its title (Title, Subtitle, and Heading1) and body text (Normal) styles. Figure 6-14 shows the Orange red color palette and the Constantia-Franklin Gothic Book font themes applied to the document.

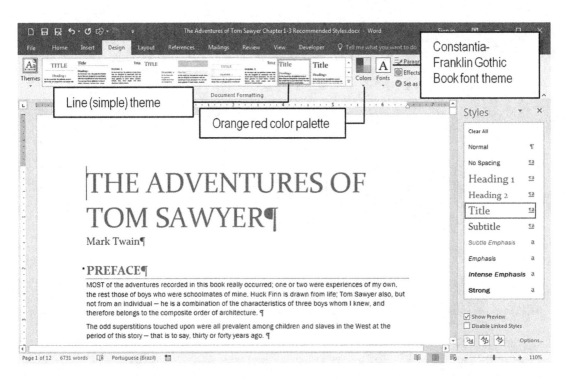

Figure 6-14. *The Orange red color palette and Constantia-Franklin Gothic Book font theme applied to the document that received the Line (simple) theme*

- Try to use new Paragraph spacing options and note how they impact on the document appearance and its page count (look the page count in the Microsoft Word status bar).

- Save this formatting option as a new Style Set expanding the Style Set Gallery and selecting Save as New Style Set... option. Note that Microsoft Word will add the style set saved as the second item of the Style Set Gallery (Figure 6-15 shows the Test Style Set saved).

Figure 6-15. The Test Style Set saved on the disk, appearing as the second style set theme

- Right-click the saved style set in the Style Set Gallery and select Delete to remove it from the gallery and delete it from the disk.

- Changes everything made by selecting an entire theme using the Themes button (located at left of the Design tab). Figure 6-16 shows the Badge theme applied to the document.

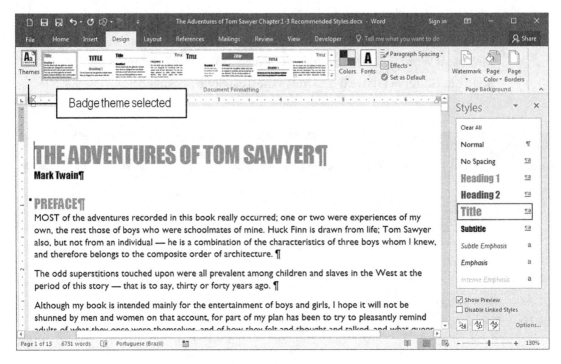

Figure 6-16.   *The Badge theme applied to the document. Each theme selected uses its own set of font, color, and paragraph spacing. Try to apply a new Style Set to the theme selected to produce different variations of it.*

- As a last exercise, reset the document formatting options to the default style set using the Reset to the Default Style Set command found by extending the Style Set Gallery (see Figure 6-5), applying the Office theme for both Font and Color palettes, and selecting the Default Paragraph Spacing option.

Attention   You can make your own theme by selecting the Design tab options, and also changing the Recommended styles formatting options to your preference. When it is done, save the theme to the disk using the Save as Style Set command found in the extended Style Set Gallery (see Figure 6-5).

Creating and Applying a Dialog Style

Authors and editors uses different typographic rules to signal the speech of a character or personage.

In the "Adventures of Tom Sawyer Chapter 1-3 Recommended Styles.docx" file you may note that every character speech begins and ends with a single quote character (as the 10th 'Tom!' paragraph shows in Figure 6-12). But also note that single quote characters are commonly used in the text to detach from words (do a Find operation by a single quote character and see for yourself).

As another exercise we must create a Dialog style to format every speech paragraph and, using Find and Replace techniques, apply this style to all other text speech paragraphs found in this document. Follow these steps to create the Dialog style:

1. Triple-click the first 'TOM!' speech character to select it (or point the mouse to its right and click to select the entire text line).

2. Apply Italic to the entire paragraph text.

3. Drag the Left indent control of the Ruler (the small square that sits in the gray area of the Ruler) to the first stop point to create a Left indent of 0.13 (show the Paragraph dialog to confirm, Figure 6-17).

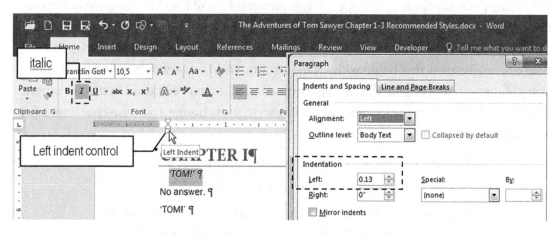

Figure 6-17. *Select the first speech paragraph, apply Italic to all its characters, and drag the Left indent Ruler control to the right to the first Ruler position, creating an Indentation Left = 0.13 (show the Paragraph dialog to confirm the Left indentation value).*

4. Using the techniques described in the section "Creating New Styles" from Chapter 5, use the Create from Selection technique to create the Dialog style based on the formatted paragraph (Figure 6-18).

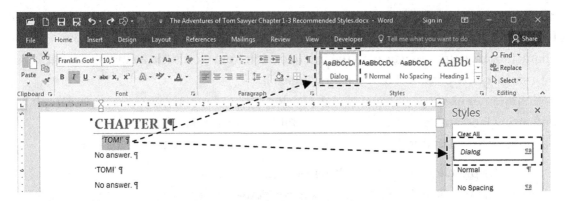

Figure 6-18. *The Dialog style created from selection, applied to the first text speech*

Now it is time to apply the Dialog style to all other text speech paragraphs. Since this document also uses the single quote to detach some words inside paragraphs, if we use the Find and Replace dialog box to search for a single quote character and apply the Dialog paragraph, many nonspeech text paragraphs will also be formatted using the Dialog style.

We need to find a way to unequivocally apply the Dialog style to just the speech paragraphs: the ones that begin with a single quote. Or in other words, we must replace every paragraph that begins with a single quote by a character not used in the document (like the { left brace), apply to them the Dialog style, and change again the character used by a single quote. Follow these steps:

1. Click Replace command found in the Editing area of the Home tab of the Ribbon to show the Find and Replace dialog box.

2. Click the Find What text box, click the More button to expand the dialog box, click Special button, and select Paragraph Mark option (Microsoft Word will use ^p to find the paragraph marks).

3. Type the single quote. 'The Find What dialog box will become ^p'.

4. Click Replace with, click Special ➤ Paragraph Mark option (Microsoft Word will use ^p as replacement text).

5. Type { (left brace). The Replace with dialog box will become ^p{.

6. Press Replace All to find and replace all occurrences (Figure 6-19).

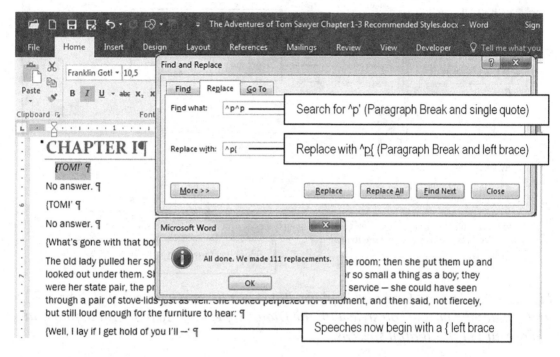

Figure 6-19. *Use the Find and Replace dialog box to search for every paragraph that begins with a single quote (^p') and replace it by a Paragraph Break and a left brace (^p{). Press Replace All to find and replace all 111 paragraph speechs.*

7. Click the Find what text box delete its content and press the { left brace character.

8. Click the Replace with text box, delete its content, click More>> to expand the dialog box, click Format ➤ Style, and select the Dialog style.

9. Press Replace All button to find all 111 occurrences of { left braces and apply the Dialog style (Figure 6-20).

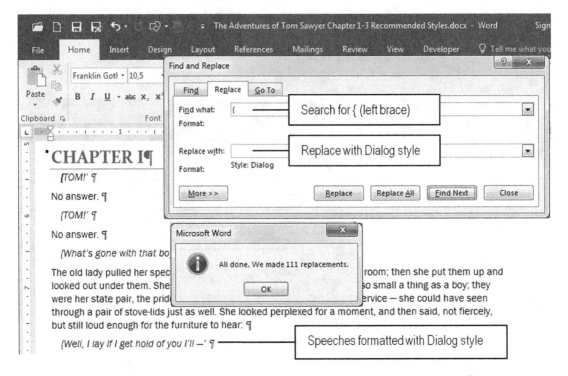

Figure 6-20. *Use the Find and Replace dialog box to search for every { left brace and replace the paragraph style with the Dialog style. Press Replace All to find and replace all 111 paragraph speechs.*

10. Finally, replace every { left brace by a single quote: in Replace with text box type ' (single quote) and press Replace All to change all occurrences (there is no need to clear the No Formatting button, Figure 6-21).

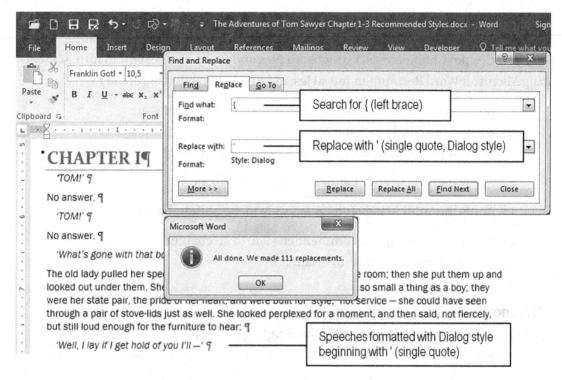

Figure 6-21. *To make every Dialog style paragraph begins with a single quote, use the Find and Replace dialog box to search for { (left brace) and change it to ' (single quote).*

Attention   Extract "Adventures of Tom Sawyer Chapter 1-3 Recommended Styles Formatted.docx" file from Chapter06.zip to see the final appearance of this document.

Exercise 2

The objective of this exercise is to apply the Recommended styles to a document and use the Design tab Style Set Gallery to quickly change its appearance.

Inside Chapter06.zip you will find two public domain book extracts: "Sense and Sensibility, Jane Austen Chapters1-5.docx" and "The Last of the Mohicans, James Fenimore Cooper Chapters 1-5". Extract both files and follow the next list to format them using Microsoft Word Recommended styles and the Design tab tools of the Ribbon:

1. Apply to the entire document the Normal style (both files are entirely formatted with the No Spacing style, which is not affected by most Design tab tools, like Font, Color, and Spacing).

2. Apply the Title Recommended style to the book title.

3. Apply the Subtitle Recommended style to the author name.

4. Apply the Heading1 Recommended style to all chapter titles (Introduction, Chapter 1 to Chapter 5)

Attention   use the methods discussed in Chapter 4 to find each chapter title paragraph and replace its text using the Heading1 format.

---

5. Update the Heading1 style, setting the following formatting options in the Paragraph dialog box:

    - Space After = 24 pt.

    - Break page before.

6. Both files use a single quote or a double quote to begin a text speech. Create a Dialog style and apply it to just these paragraphs using Find and Replace techniques.

7. "The Last of Mohicans" uses the * (asterisk) character to signal a quote. Use Find and Replace techniques to find these paragraphs and apply them the recommended Quote style.

8. Use the Design tab options to change the formatting options of one of these documents using a typographic standard that pleases you. Save this standard using the "Save as New Style Set" option and apply it to the other document, so they are equally formatted.

9. Delete the Style Set from the Style Set Gallery.

Attention   You can extract formatted versions of both files from Chapter06zip file. Their file names are suffixed with the word "Formatted."

Conclusion

Microsoft Word Recommended styles are useful to allow quick document formatting that can be easily changed using the tools found in the Design tab of the Ribbon.

By correctly applying the Title, Subtitle, Heading1, Heading2, Quote, Normal, and other Recommended styles, you can quickly apply a new formatting theme to the document, change its font options, color palette, and/or paragraph spacing, change the Recommended styles formatting, and save and reuse the theme in other documents.

Summary

In this chapter you learned:

- Recommended styles have this name because they are used by some Microsoft Word tools to easily format any document.

- You can apply a theme set using the Style Set Gallery found in the Design tab of the Ribbon.

- The Style Set Gallery uses the first item to show the This Document Style set, and all other items have names associated to previously saved style sets.

- Once you use a Style theme set, you can change its formatting options by applying different Font themes, Color palettes, and/or Spacing options that change some key formatting options of the Recommended styles.

- The current style theme set applied to the document is associated to the Document Style set: the first Style Set Gallery item.

- Any style set can be saved as a document template to be reused later.

- The last saved style set appears as the second style theme set in the Style Set Gallery (the first is always the Document Style set).

- You can use the Themes control to apply previously saved themes.

- Once you select any of the Themes available, you can apply any of the Style Themes set found in the Style Set Gallery.

In the next chapter, you will learn how to use the Recommended Heading styles (Heading1 to Heading9) to format document chapter and section tittles, apply automatic section titles numbering, create a document map, use Microsoft Word Outline view, and automatically generate the document TOC (Table of Contents).

CHAPTER 7

Using Heading Styles

Among the Recommended Styles, the so-called Heading styles are intrinsically related to some important Microsoft Word features to format and manage documents.

In this chapter, you will learn how to effectively format your documents using some Microsoft Word advanced features that are based in the correct usage of Heading styles.

The documents cited in this chapter and the Exercise sections can be found by downloading the Chapter07.zip file from this Internet address:

```
https://github.com/apress/msft-word-secrets
```

Why Are Heading Styles Important?

The expression Heading styles means the Recommended styles Heading1 and Heading2 normally shown in the Microsoft Word Styles Gallery; but goes from Heading1 to Heading9 as one can see on the fully expand view of the Styles window.

They are important because when they are correctly applied to the document section titles, Microsoft Word can

- Hierarchically number the heading paragraphs.

- Quickly navigate through the document using it headings.

- Easily change the document format with the Design tab.

- Generate the document's Table of Contents.

- Use the Outline view to manipulate the text.

Each of these features can be done just because Heading1 to Heading9 styles have the Paragraph Outline level property set to the appropriate hierarchical level each style represents.

269

© Flavio Morgado 2017
F. Morgado, *Microsoft Word Secrets*, https://doi.org/10.1007/978-1-4842-3078-7_7

Outline Level

Outline level is the last of Microsoft Word Paragraph dialog box options to need a comment in this book, and is associated to the hierarchy that the title paragraph has in the text.

By default, Outline Level 1 must be used for first-level title hierarchy (chapter titles or first-level section titles), Level 2 for the second sublevel, Level 3 for the third, and so on; up to nine different hierarchy levels are allowed to hierarchically define the document structure.

You can easily perceive how Microsoft Word uses Heading styles to control hierarchy of the document by extracting the "Heading1 to 3.docx" document from the Chapter04. zip file, or by following these steps to create a Heading formatting document:

1. Open an empty Microsoft Word document.

2. Press Ctrl+F to show the Navigation pane and click it Headings view option.

3. Type "Heading 1" in the first paragraph and apply the Heading1 style (note that the "Heading1" text appears in the Navigation pane).

4. Press Enter to insert another paragraph, type "Heading2", and apply the Heading2 style (Microsoft Word 2016 will instantly show the "Heading2" text in the Navigation pane while the Styles Gallery begins to show the Heading3 style to the right of the Heading2 style).

5. Once more, press Enter to insert another paragraph, type "Heading3", and apply the Heading3 style (once again, Microsoft Word 2016 will show the "Heading3" text in the Navigation pane while the Styles Gallery begins to show the Heading4 style).

Attention   Every time you apply a Heading style to the text, the next heading style level in the hierarchy is shows in the Styles Gallery (e.g., If you apply Heading2, Heading3 will become visible to it right).

Figure 7-1 shows a Microsoft Word document with three text paragraphs that received Heading1, Heading2, and Heading3 styles, with the Navigation pane showing the Headings view. Note how each Heading style is indented from the previous or next heading level.

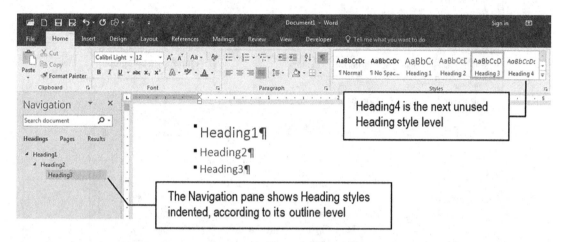

Figure 7-1. *When Microsoft Word Heading styles are applied to title sectionl paragraphs, they appear in the Navigation pane Headings view, and the next Heading level still not applied to the text will appear in the Style Gallery list*

Attention   You can also show the Navigation pane by clicking the Navigation pane option in the Show area of the View tab of the Ribbon.

This is possible because each Heading style is associated to a different Outline level: Heading1 receives Outline level = Level 1; Heading2 received Outline level = Level 2, etc. This can be confirmed by right-clicking any Heading style name visible in the Styles Gallery and choosing Modify to show the Modify Style dialog box, from which you can read in the style description the Outline level the style received.

Figure 7-2 shows the Modify Style dialog box for the Heading1 style. Note that it description shows "Level 1" as the outline level set.

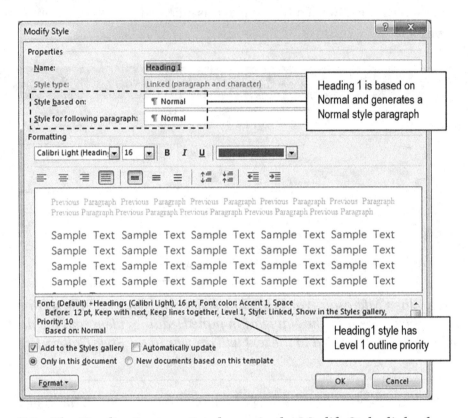

Figure 7-2. *The Heading1 properties shown in the Modify Style dialog box (right-click the style name in the Styles Gallery and choose Modify). Note that the style description shows that it has "Level 1" outline priority.*

Select the Format ➤ Paragraph option in the Modify Style dialog box to show the Paragraph dialog box for the Heading 1 style and note that in has Outline level = 1, which is also disabled, meaning that this property can't be changed for any Heading style (Figure 7-3).

Attention   Inspecting other Heading style properties, you will notice that Heading2 to Heading9 will receive Outline levels 2 to 9, respectively. In other words, the Outline level is associated to the Heading style number.

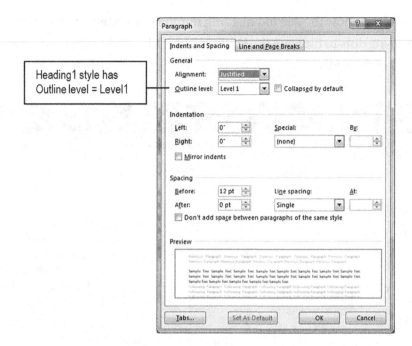

Figure 7-3. *The Paragraph dialog box for the Heading 1 style shows that in has Outline level defined to Level 1*

Attention   Not just Heading styles will appear in the Navigation pane: any paragraph that has it Outline level property set to anything different from Body Text will appear in the Navigation pane.

Numbering Heading Styles

Having any paragraph title in which a Heading style was applied, click the Multilevel List tool located in the Paragraph area of the Home tab of the Ribbon and choose any numbered list that uses Headings (look to it names). All Heading style paragraphs will automatically receive the associated numbering system, where each Heading receives the prefix defined to it Outline level property.

Figure 7-4 shows how the second heading numbering system shows the paragraph hierarchy by using dots to indicate the Outline level (1 for first Level 1, 1.1 for first Level 2, 1.1.1 for first Level 3, etc.).

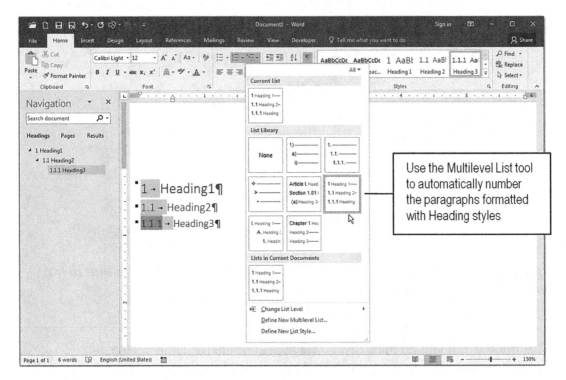

Figure 7-4. *The Multilevel List tool can automatically number each Heading style formatted paragraph of the document, which is also shown in the Navigation pane*

By continuing to insert more section titles and reapply styles Heading1 through Heading3 (or higher levels), the section title numbering system is restarted. Copy and paste multiple copies of the paragraphs formatted with Heading styles to see how Microsoft Word numbers them according to the system selected in the Multilevel List tool and the Outline level associated to the Heading style (Figure 7-5).

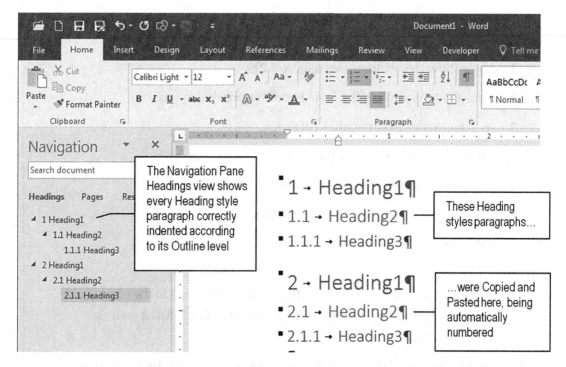

Figure 7-5. *New Heading style paragraphs automatically receive the correct number or letter according to the current Multilevel Numbering system selected, and you can remove or change the number system at any time. The Navigation pane reflects in it Headings view all paragraphs formatted with Heading styles.*

Heading Styles Shortcut

In is quite easy to apply Heading styles by clicking the desired style located in the Styles Gallery or the Styles window (although the Styles window may require you to scroll it style list), but you can become more productive by associating each Heading style to a keyboard shortcut, because you will no longer need to perform such an operation by pointing and clicking the mouse.

Use the Alt+*n* combination keys where *n* relates to the Heading style number, so you can easily associate each Heading style to a mnemonic key combination, very easy to press: Alt+1 apply Heading1, Alt+2 apply Heading2, and so in, until Alt+9 to Heading9.

Follow these steps to apply shortcuts to all Heading styles in your Microsoft Word copy:

1. Show the Styles window (see Figure 5.2);

2. Click Options to show the Style Pane Options dialog box.

3. In Select Styles to show, click All styles.

4. Click OK to close the Style Pane Options dialog box.

5. Scroll the Styles window list to show the Heading1 style.

6. Right-click Heading style and select Modify.

7. Click Format ➤ Shortcut and associate Heading1 to Alt+1 shortcut.

8. Repeat steps 5 to 7 to associate Heading2 to Heading9 to the associated Alt+n key (associate Alt+2 with Heading2, Alt+3 with Heading3, etc.).

Once each Heading style is associated to an Alt+n key, try to change the style applied to any text paragraphs by pressing it keyboard shortcut. You will become more productive in desktop publishing the text while writing in; it's easy to change Heading styles without even taking your hands off of the keyboard.

Attention   To effectively work with Heading styles in the text, keep the Navigation pane with the Headings view selected and look to it indentations: they reflect the current hierarchy applied to all document Heading paragraphs and are the best way to know if you are applying the correct Heading style to the current text paragraph.

Collapsing and Expanding Heading Styles

In is supposed that between two heading styles, an undetermined amount of text will be inserted to compose the body text of the document. By applying Heading styles to the text, you can easily navigate through in by using either the Navigation pane or the document window itself.

In the Document window, click any paragraph formatted with a Heading style to put the text cursor in in and note that Microsoft Word shows a small slanted triangle at it left: the same small triangle shows in the Navigation pane (Figure 7-6).

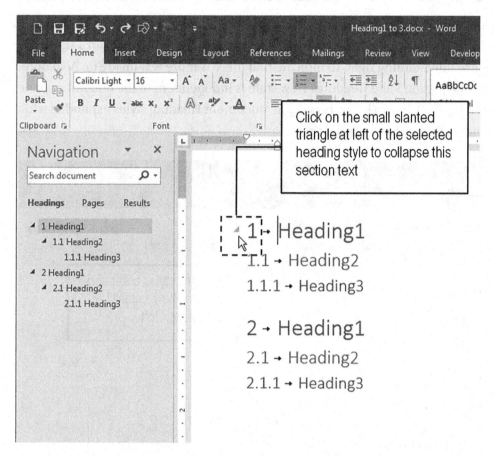

Figure 7-6. *Use the small triangles pointing down at the left of any Heading style to collapse/expand the document text or the Headings view of the Navigation pane*

This small slanted triangle allows you to collapse/expand the text inside two successive Heading styles applied to the document, so you can easily navigate through the text no matter how much text is inserted between them. Click any collapsed Heading style triangle to show it content again.

Attention   Triangles are shown next to the Heading styles that have text of a lower hierarchy inside in.

Note that when the text inside a Heading style is collapsed, the triangle keeps appearing at the left side of the Heading style paragraph, changing from a slanted triangle to one pointing right, to indicate that there is more text inside in. Also note that the Navigation Pane Headings view state is independent of the document pane view (Figure 7-7): in can keep showing all document Heading styles expanded while the Document window is collapsing them.

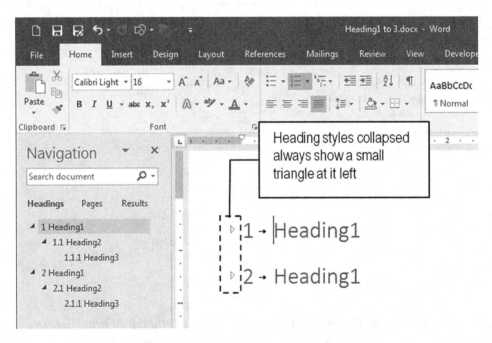

Figure 7-7. *The Navigation pane view is independent of the Document window view. When any Heading formatted paragraph is collapsed, Microsoft Word keeps showing the triangle at it left, which changes to a triangle pointing right.*

Changing Heading Styles Prefix

If any paragraph formatted with a Heading style is deleted or receives another Heading style level, all remaining Heading paragraphs will be automatically renumbered, according to it Outline level. For example, if the second Heading 1 paragraph is deleted (the one numbered as 2), the 2.1 paragraph will become 1.2, and 2.1.1. will become 1.2.1 (Figure 7-8).

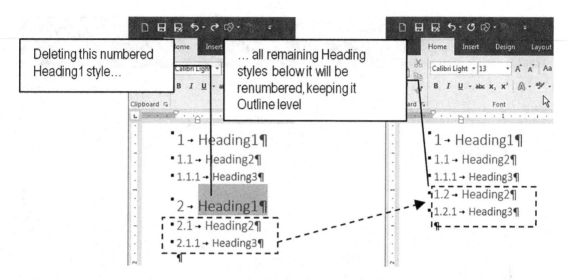

Figure 7-8. *Microsoft Word renumbers heading styles according to their Outline level: each paragraph receives the number, letter, or symbol associated to the current number system*

And if you change the numbering system using other options found in the Multilevel List tool, all paragraphs will change their numbering prefixes.

Figure 7-9 shows the first Heading numbering system in action, applying a paragraph prefix for each Heading level style: the first Heading1 style paragraph is prefixed with "Chapter 1" text, the first Heading2 style paragraph is prefixed with "Section 1.01", the first Heading3 style with "(a)", etc. (the words "Heading1", "Heading 2", and "Heading3" next to each prefix constitute the paragraph text typed in the document).

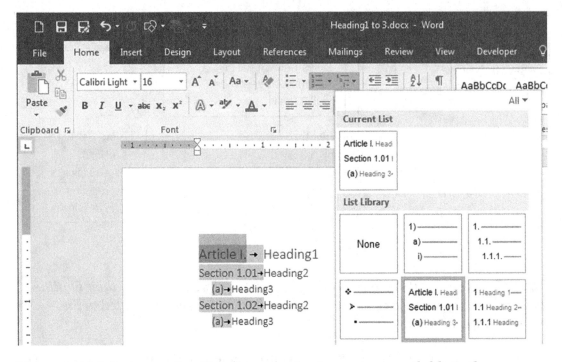

Figure 7-9. *Select any other Headings numbering system available in the Multilevel List tool to change the prefix associated to each Outline level*

Renumbering Heading Styles

To change the prefix associated to any Heading style paragraph, use the mouse and the Multilevel List tool to change any Heading paragraph number prefix applied by the Multilevel List tool using the mouse.

Follow these steps:

1. Click the desired paragraph to place the text cursor in.

2. Click the Multilevel List tool to expand in list.

3. Point the mouse to the Change List Level item to expand in list and click the desired level.

Be aware that you can apply any Outline level to any paragraph in the text: Microsoft Word will not care if some previous Outline level is missing.

Figure 7-10 shows that the first paragraph (where "Heading1" was typed) received the Heading2 style, and now is prefixed with "Section 1.01", while the third paragraph (where "Heading 3" was typed) received the Heading1 style and is now prefixed with "Article 2" when their Heading styles were changed. The Styles Gallery shows the style applied to the text, while the Navigation pane shows it indentation level. The expected "Article 1" prefixed paragraph does not appear anymore in the document.

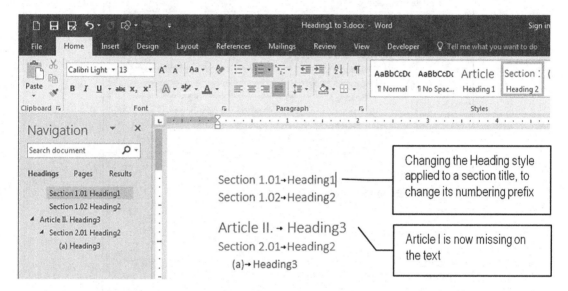

Figure 7-10. *Change the Heading style applied to a section paragraph to affect the section titles numbering system for the whole document*

Define a Multilevel List

You can learn how Microsoft Word can number and renumber Heading style paragraphs by studying the way in produces the formatting applied to any Heading style formatted paragraph, like the ones shown in Figure 7-9.

Follow these instructions:

1. Apply any Multilevel List tool option for Heading styles to one or more Heading style formatted paragraphs.

2. Click any formatted Heading style paragraph, expand the Multilevel List tool, and select the Define New Multilevel List... option.

Microsoft Word will show the Define new Multilevel list dialog box, from which you may note how each Heading style is composed. Figure 7-11 shows how the "Article n" prefix is applied to any Heading1 style paragraph, while also show the sequence of "numbering" applied to all other Heading styles (Heading2 to Heading9).

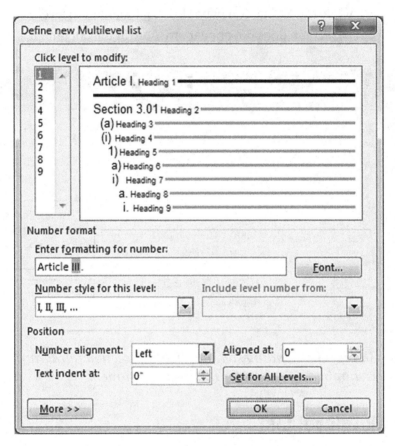

Figure 7-11. *The Define new Multilevel list dialog box, from which you can inspect and understand how any Multilevel List option is created to enumerate the Heading style paragraphs*

At the top left of this dialog box you can click the number (1 to 9) associated to each Heading style and select in in the list box at it right. The numbering properties associated to the Heading style are shown in the Number format area below them, from which you can select one of the following:

- **Enter formatting for number**: Insert a text prefix to precede the Heading style text. Note that in has the style numbering option in gray, indicating that this is a Microsoft Word calculated field that will produce the autonumbering feature.

- **Font**: Show the Font dialog box from which you can use any character attributes (including color) to format the Heading style prefix.

- **Number style for this level**: Choose the number style that must be applied to each Heading style. You can select between different numbering systems (including Arabic, upper- or lowercase Roman, upper or lowercase alphabetic, and many others), or use bullets, pictures, etc.

Attention   You can reinsert the autonumbering gray indicator by selecting another option in the Number style.

- **Include level number from**: This option (unavailable for Heading1) allows inclusion of the number of any superior Heading style to the Heading style selected (Heading2 can include Heading1's last number; Heading3 can include Heading1's and/or Heading2's last number, and so in).

- **Position**: This indicates how the text prefix will be aligned before the Heading style paragraph text (Left (default), Center, or Right alignment).

- **Aligned at**: Use to indicate the Left indentation applied to the Heading style level.

- **Text indent at**: Use to indicate the Hanging indent alignment applied to the Heading paragraph.

- **Set for all levels**: Makes all Heading style levels left aligned the same way, with no indentation between them.

Click the More>> button of the Define new Multilevel list dialog box to expand it left side and show further options to define and create new multilevel numbering lists (Figure 7-12).

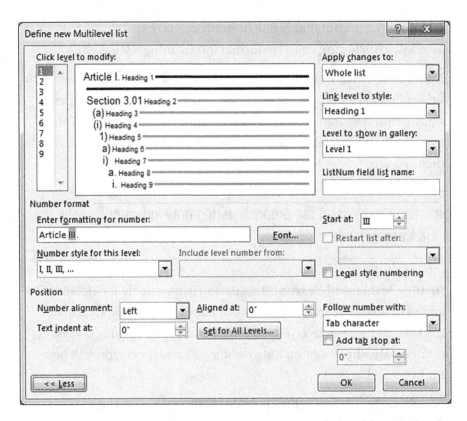

Figure 7-12. *The expanded view of the Define new Multilevel list dialog box, which expands the right side to show options from which you can further define how the changes will be applied in the numbering system*

- **Apply changes to**: Use in to define the scope of the changes made to the multilevel list:

    - **Whole list**: All document Heading style paragraphs will be affected.

    - **This point forward**: Previous Heading styles in the document will not be affected by the changes.

    - **Current paragraph**: Just the current Heading style paragraph will be affected.

- **Link level to style**: This option links the Heading style to the numbering system.

- **Level to show in gallery**: Indicates the level prefix to show in the Styles Gallery for the associated Heading style.

- **ListNum field list name**: Very technical setting; allows attributing a name to a Heading level so you can use in with Microsoft Word LISNUM field (by typing "myliststyle" to allow use of {LISTNUM "myliststyle" \1 }.

Attention   Microsoft Word does many of it tricks to insert document information in the text (like autonumbering paragraphs, inserting page number, system date and hour, etc.) using Fields (using the Quick parts command of the Insert tab of the Ribbon). These fields are always embraced by curly brackets, followed by it specific syntax, like {LISTNUM "myliststyle" \1}.

Microsoft Word uses Ctrl+F9 to insert the field's curly brackets, and Alt+F9 to alternate the field view (field code) with field value. Try in!

- **Start at**: Define the starting number for the first item of the list (default is 1).

- **Restart list after**: Define the Heading Outline level where the current Heading level number must be restarted (unavailable for Heading1). By default, Heading2 restarts from 1 after every new Heading1 style, and so in.

- **Legal style numbering**: This option applies when the numbering system uses both Roman and Arabic numerals: Roman numerals used for higher level paragraphs (Chapter titles) will be changed to Arabic numerals in the current level paragraph (Chapter Section title).

  Example: Heading1 uses "Article I" prefix (with Roman numeral for higher level); if Heading2 uses Include number from: Level 1 option, and is prefixed with "Section" text, in may be numbered as "Section I.01". By checking the Legal style numbering option, in will be numbered as "Section 1.01" instead (no Roman numeral on current level).

- **Follow number with**: Indicates the character to follow the text prefix (and number), before the Heading style paragraph text. Default is a Tab character that will align in the next default tab stop (at every 0.5 in the Ruler or at the position defined by the Add tab stop at option). You can also set in to a Space character or nothing.

- **Add tab stop at**: Define the horizontal ruler position of the next "Tab character"used by the Follow number with option.

Create a New Multilevel List

Use the Define a New List Style… option found in the Multilevel List tool options to create a new numbering system to be used in Heading style paragraphs. In will show the Define New List Style dialog box (which is very similar to the New Style dialog box), from which you can define the multilevel style name options (Figure 7-13).

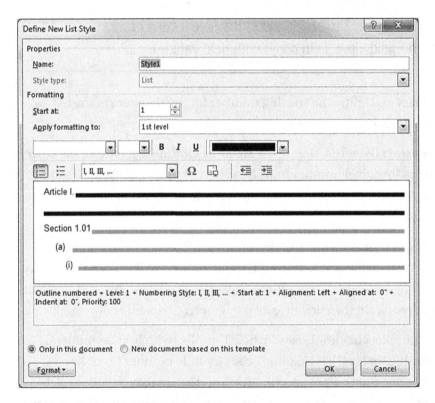

Figure 7-13. *Use the Define New List Style… command found in the Multilevel List tool to show the associated dialog box, from which you can create a new numbering system*

You can use these options to define a new numbering system:

- **Name**: Associate the new numbering system to a style name, which will be sequentially numbered as Style1, Style2, etc. (you can't use a name already used). The style name will appear only when you expand the Multilevel List tool and point to the Lists Style area.

- **Formatting area**: Show basic options found in the Define new Multilevel list dialog box to define the stating number and Outline level, some character options (font, size, bold, italic, underline, and color), whether in will receive numbers or bullets, symbols or pictures, and it left indent. Also define if this numbering system will be stored inside this document or in the associated document template.

All the Formatting area options can be set by clicking the Format button at the bottom of this dialog box and selecting the Numbering option, which will show the Define new Multilevel list dialog box in Figures 7-11 and 7-12, from which you can fine-tune the desired Heading numbering system.

Quickly Navigating with Heading Styles

Since most people don't know what the Outline level property does, or about the Navigation Pane Headings view, in is not unusual to find body text paragraphs that received some Outline level options appearing in the Navigation pane Headings view: they were inadvertently formatted with Outline Level 1 to Level 9, probably selected out of pure curiosity when the user, trying to make sense of such properties, noted that nothing happened to the text and left in applied to the body text.

Let us see an example of such formatting: extract the "The Count of Monte Cristo, Alexandre Dumas, Chapter 1-4 Bad Outline level.docx" document from Chapter07.zip file and open in in Microsoft Word.

Note that in has just the first 28 pages of the famous Alexandre Dumas book, where Title, Subtitle, and Heading styles were applied, along with the Elegant Style Set available in the Style Set Gallery found in the Design tab of the Ribbon (Figure 7-14).

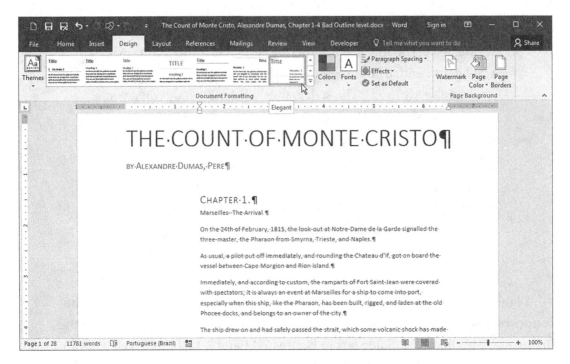

Figure 7-14. *This is "The Count of Monte Cristo, Alexandre Dumas, Chapter 1-4 Bad Outline level.docx" document, extracted from Chapter07.zip, which received the Title, Subtitle, and Heading Recommended styles (plus Normal for the body text), and was formatted with the Elegant Style Set, found in the Style Set Gallery of the Design tab of the Ribbon.*

The document seems to be quite well formatted, but when you show the Navigation pane with the Headings view selected (check the Navigation pane in the Show area of the View tab of the Ribbon, or press Ctrl+F and click Headings), you will note that in has a lot of body text paragraphs that received some Outline level property (as the file name implies, Figure 7-15).

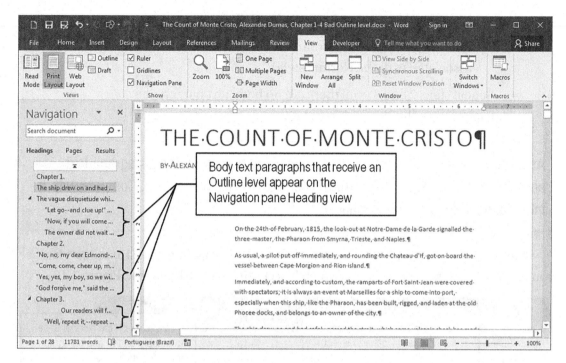

Figure 7-15. *Use the Navigation pane Headings view to search for body text paragraphs that inadvertently received some Outline level property. Use the pane to quickly move through the document (by clicking any chapter heading) or easily select these badly formatted paragraphs.*

Exercise 1

The objective of this exercise is to fix "The Count of Monte Cristo, Alexandre Dumas, Chapter 1-4 Bad Outline level.docx" document by manually changing any body text paragraphs that received an Outline view by reapplying the Normal style.

Follow these steps:

1. Press Ctrl+F to show the Navigation pane and click the Headings option.

2. In the Navigation pane, click any body text paragraph that is not a Chapter title and appears in its Headings view.

3. Microsoft Word puts the text cursor at the beginning of such paragraphs in the Document window. Reapply the Normal style to remove it Outline level using one of these options:

- Click the Normal style in the Styles Gallery, or

- Press Ctrl+Space (the recommended shortcut that should be associated with the Normal style).

4. Repeat steps 2 and 3 until there are no body text paragraphs appearing in the Navigation pane.

Attention   Before reapplying the Normal style, right-click the paragraph text and choose Paragraph in the Context menu to see it Outline level. Compare with it indentation in the Navigation pane.

The body text paragraphs will disappear from the Navigation pane Headings view as you reapply them the Normal style (which has Outline level = Body text, Figure 7-16).

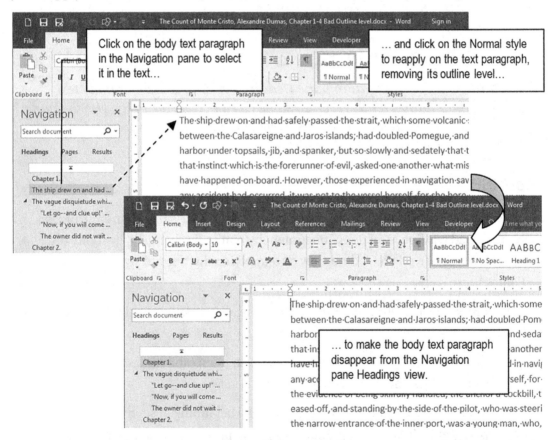

Figure 7-16. *In the Navigation pane, click any body text paragraph to select in the Document window and reapply the Normal style to redefine in Outline level to Body text and remove in from the Headings view*

Exercise 2

The objective of this exercise is to fix "The Count of Monte Cristo, Alexandre Dumas, Chapter 1-4 Bad Outline level.docx" document using the Replace command to automatically apply the Normal style.

Follow these steps:

1. Click the Replace command in the Editing area of the Home tab of the Ribbon to show the Find and Replace dialog box.

2. In the Find what text box, click in Format ➤ Style to show the Style dialog box and select the Normal style.

3. In the Replace with text box, click Format ➤ Style to show the Style dialog box and select the Normal style.

4. Press Replace all to find each Normal style paragraph and reapply the Normal style.

The body text paragraphs will disappear from the Navigation pane Headings view (Figure 7-17).

Attention   "The Count of Monte Cristo, Alexandre Dumas, Chapter 1-4 Heading styles.docx" document has a fixed version of the first four chapters of the famous Alexandre Dumas book, where just the Heading styles have the Outline level property defined. In was also formatted using the Formal style set found in the Style Set Gallery of the Design tab of the Ribbon.

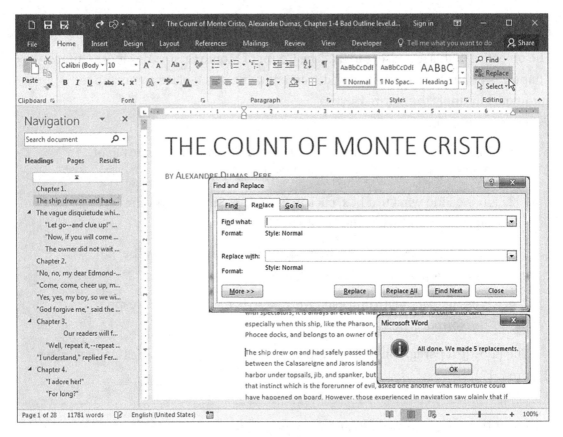

Figure 7-17. *Use the Replace command to find each Normal style paragraph and replace in with a Normal style (reapply style). Microsoft Word will reaply the Normal style to all Normal formatted paragraphs, restituting the Outline level = Body text property.*

Attention   Microsoft Word gives incorrect messages regarding the number of paragraph styles found and replaced in the document.

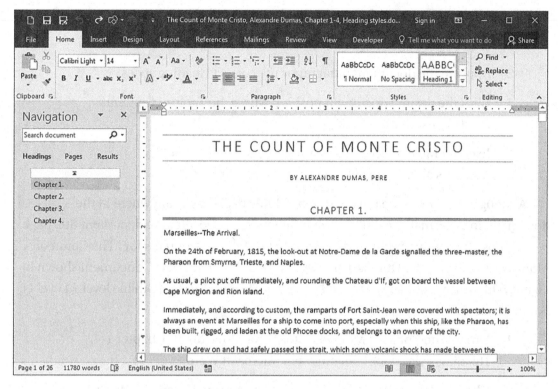

Figure 7-18. *"The Count of Monte Cristo, Alexandre Dumas, Chapter 1-4 Heading styles.docx", where just Heading styles have an Outline level, using the Formal style set*

Creating TOC: Table of Contents

As you can see, Heading styles alone with the aid of the Outline level property creates the document TOC (Table of Contents), which is automatically shown in the Navigation pane Headings view.

So, to create any document's Table of Contents, Microsoft Word just need to find those text paragraphs that have an Outline level property set and present them in a list, with or without their page numbers, wherever you want in the document.

Attention   Microsoft Word may use every paragraph that has an Outline level property set to compose the Table of Contents. So be aware that you must inspect the Navigation pane to guarantee that no body text paragraph is inadvertently formatted with some Outline level defined.

The entire process needed to create the document TOC is as follows:

1. Show the Navigation pane (Ctrl+F, click Headings view).

2. Apply to the document paragraphs the correct Heading styles.

3. Click the desired document position where the Table of Contents must be inserted.

4. Execute Table of Contents command found in the Table of Contents area of the References tab of the Ribbon.

Although you can create the document's Table of Contents anywhere in the document, in is normally inserted in an independent page after the document title page.

Suppose that we are interested in creating the Table of Contents for "The Count of Monte Cristo, Alexandre Dumas, Chapter 1-4, Heading styles.docx" document shown in Figure 7-18, which is already formatted using just Heading1 styles (Outline level = Level 1). Follow these steps:

1. Open "The Count of Monte Cristo, Alexandre Dumas, Chapter 1-4, Heading styles.docx" document in Microsoft Word.

2. Click the beginning of the "Chapter1" paragraph (Microsoft Word will insert the Table of Contents before the selected paragraph).

3. Click the Table of Contents command found in the Table of Contents area of the References tab of the Ribbon and select the first TOC style proposed.

Microsoft Word will run through all the document pages searching for paragraphs that have the Outline level set, and will insert the document's Table of Contents at the desired document position (Figure 7-19):

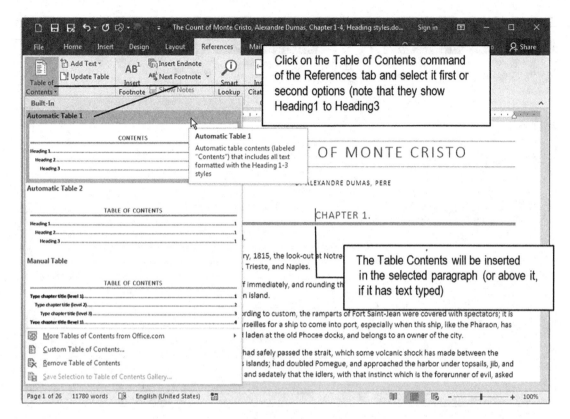

Figure 7-19. *To create the Table of Contents for the "The Count of Monte Cristo, Alexandre Dumas, Chapter 1-4, Heading styles.docx" document, click the paragraph that will receive in and click the Table of Contents command found in the References tab of the Ribbon.*

Figure 7-20 shows the final result: all Heading1 style paragraphs that identify the first four chapters of the "The Count of Monte Cristo, Alexandre Dumas, Chapter 1-4, Heading styles.docx" were found and inserted in the document's Table of Contents along with the page number where each one appears (this document shows the page number in the bottom right of the page).

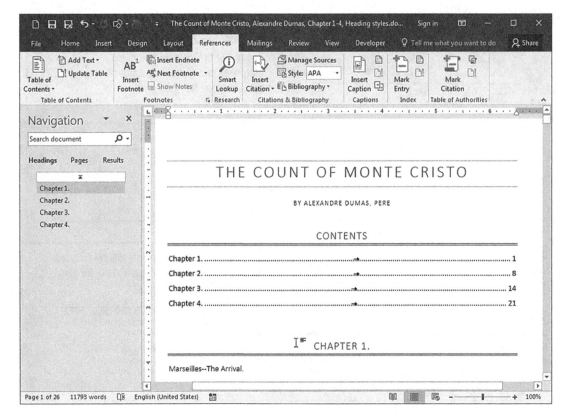

Figure 7-20. *The "The Count of Monte Cristo, Alexandre Dumas, Chapter 1-4, Heading styles.docx" with the Table of Contents automatically created by Microsoft Word*

Fast, huh? How many times have you spent precious minutes (or hours) manually creating a document's Table of Contents?

Understanding the Table of Contents

Let's study what Microsoft Word did to understand how to better manipulate any of the automatically created Table of Contents.

- **Table of Contents is an object inserted in the text**: Click the Table of Contents and note that Microsoft Word surrounds in as a single object that can be easily deleted.

- **Table of Contents is a calculated field**: Press Alt+F9 and note the field code used by Microsoft Word to create the Table of Contents. Press Alt+F9 again to recalculate in and show it pages again (Figure 7-21).

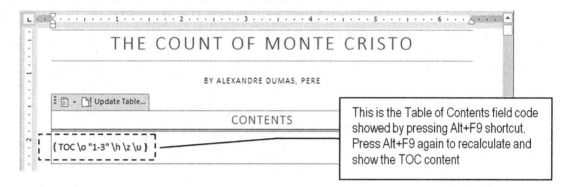

Figure 7-21. *Press Alt+F9 to alternate from Field code view and Field value view. This figure shows that the Table of Contents is a Microsoft Word calculated field. The Alt+F9 key combination forces the field to be updated.*

Attention   When you press Alt+F9 to show Microsoft Word Field codes, you are actually checking the Show field codes instead of their values option found in the File ➤ Option ➤ Advanced ➤ Show document content area of the Word Options dialog box.

- **Table of Contents entries are hyperlinks**: Ctrl+click any table entry to instantly move to this part of the document (you can also use the Navigation pane to do this).

- **Table of Contents uses special styles**: Both the Table of Contents title and it text paragraph are formatted with special styles. Expand the Style Gallery, click the Apply Styles… command to show the Apply Styles window, and inspect them.

- The CONTENTS title was formatted using the TOC Heading style
  and has the same formatting used by Heading1 style (Figure 7-22).

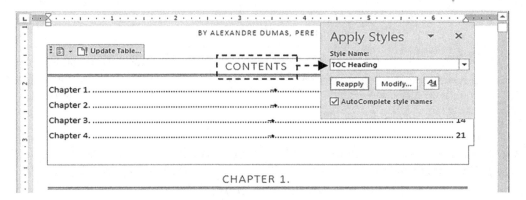

Figure 7-22. *The Table of Contents is an object that uses special styles to format it components: it title (CONTENT) is formatted using the TOC Heading style*

- The chapter titles formatted with Heading1 style received the
  TOC1 style (point the mouse to the left of each Table of Contents
  entry, click to select the entire paragraph, and check the style in
  the Apply Styles window, Figure 7-23).

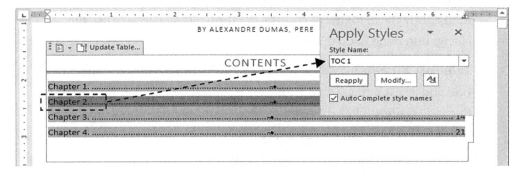

Figure 7-23. *Each index entry is formatted with a TOCn style, where n is associoated with the paragraph Ouline level (e.g., Heading1 receives TOC1, Heading2 receives TOC2, etc.)*

Attention   Just the Apply Styles window synchronizes the paragraph style when you click in in the text. The Styles window will also show in, but you will need to make in show all document styles (Options ➤ Select styles to show = All styles) and scroll it style list to see the style name selected.

There is a TOC*n* style for each Heading*n* Recommended style (TOC1 to Heading1, TOC2 to Heading2, etc.). This is one of the reasons that Microsoft Word has so many styles inserted in any document.

- **TOC1 style is based in Heading1 style**: Use the Modify... button of the Apply styles window to show the Modify Style dialog box and note that it Style is based in = Heading1.

- **TOC entries uses a Right tab stop and leading dots**: Click any TOC entry and double-click the Right tab stop located at the right paragraph margin to show the Tabs dialog box (Figure 7-24).

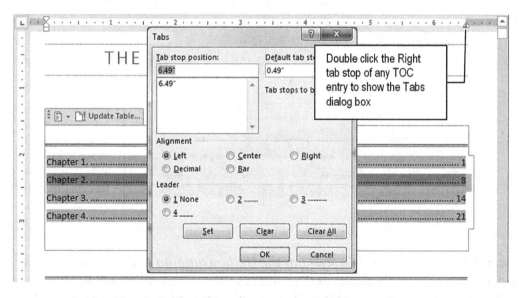

Figure 7-24. *Double-click the Right tab stop positioned at the right margin of any TOC entry and note that in is fulfilled with dot leaders between the end of the entry text and the page number*

- **TOC*n* styles updates automatically**: Show the Modify Style dialog box for TOC1 style (or any other TOC*n* style) and note that in has these properties: Style based in = Normal and Automatically update checked. This means that in may inherit most Normal style changes, and that changes made to any paragraph formatted using TOC1 will instantly reflect in the style.

For example, drag the Chapter 1 table entry Right tab stop to the left to a new position and note that the entire Table of Contents will be reformatted (Figure 7-25).

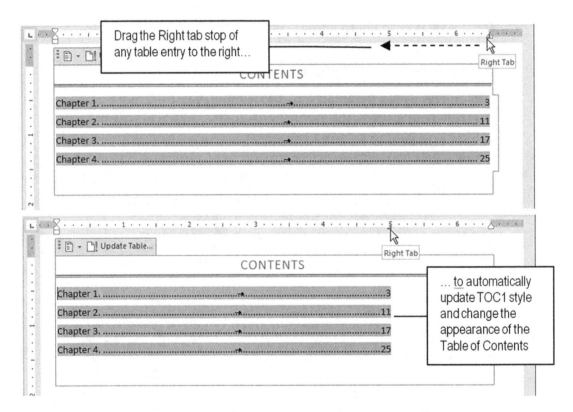

Figure 7-25. *Since any TOCn style has the Update automatically option set, any change made to a TOCn paragraph updates the style property, immediately reflected in all paragraphs formatted with in. This figure changes the position of the Right tab of the first table entry, changing the entire Table of Contents appearance.*

As you can see, the knowledge gathered so far in this book has begun to pay dividends. Many formatting details discussed in previous chapters may now make sense to you.

Attention   Field codes appear with a gray background due to the Field Shading = As Select option found below the Show field codes instead of their values found in the File ➤ Option ➤ Advanced ➤ Show document content area of the Word Options dialog box.

Updating the Table of Contents

The automatically created Table of Contents may need to be updated for many reasons; the most probable ones are changes in the document by insertions, deletions, or changes in the body text or section titles formatted with Heading styles, which may impact the document page count or Table of Contents composition.

Whenever necessary, you can update the Table of Contents by first clicking the Table of Contents to select in (in will become grayed) and using one of these methods:

- Press the F9 function key.

- Click the Update Table command located above the Table of Contents object.

Both options will make Microsoft Word show the Update Table of Contents dialog box, from which you can select:

- **Update page numbers only**: Table of Contents entries will not be changed, just their page numbers; or

- **Update entire table**: to rebuild the Table of Contents.

Attention   Although the Table of Contents is a Microsoft Word calculated field, in entries are fully editable: you can insert paragraphs and text between them, change the entry titles, and so on. By selecting the first options, all changes manually made by you will be kept. The Updated entire table options rebuilds in, discarding any changes manually made to in.

Let us see this in practice still using the "The Count of Monte Cristo, Alexandre Dumas, Chapter 1-4, Heading styles.docx" document, performing these steps:

1. Right-click the "Chapter 1" paragraph (formatted with Heading1 style) and choose Paragraph in the context menu to show the Paragraph dialog box.

2. In the Paragraph dialog box, select the Line and Page Breaks tab and check the Page break before option (Figure 7-26).

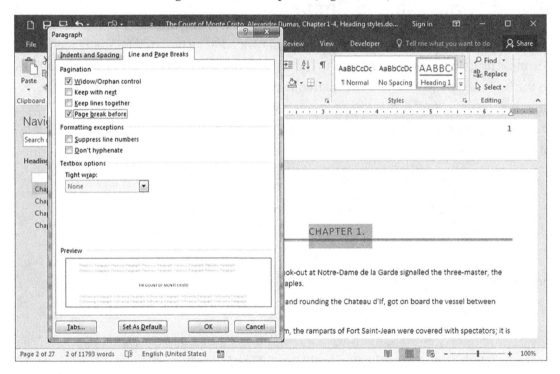

Figure 7-26. *Right-click "Chapter 1", choose Paragraph in the context menu, and in the Paragraph dialog box select the Page break before option*

3. Close the Paragraph dialog box and note that now "Chapter 1" begins in a new page (in will now print in page 2, increasing page count to 27).

4. Right-click the Heading1 style in the Styles Gallery and choose Update Heading1 to Match Selection option (Figure 7-27).

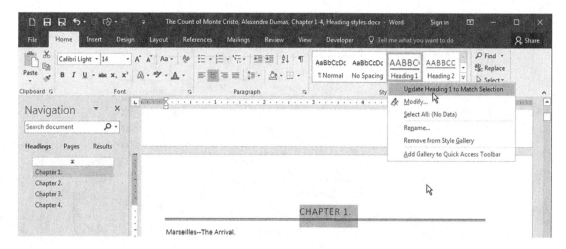

Figure 7-27. *Once "Chapter 1" paragraph formatted with Heading1 style has the Page break before option set, right-click Heading1 style in the Styles Gallery and choose Update Heading1 to Match the Selection option, to make every Heading1 style begin in a new page.*

5.   All other chapter titles formatted with the Heading1 style (or based in in) will now begin in a new page.

Attention   Since "CONTENT" header formatted with TOC Heading style is based in the Heading1 style, in will also receive the Page break before by inheritance, and will now print in page 2; Chapter 1 will print in page 3, and the page count will increase from 27 to 30.

---

6.   Click the Table of Contents and use one of the methods proposed in the preceding (press F9 function key or click Update table command above the Table of Contents object) to show the Update Table of Contents dialog box, select one of it options, and press Enter to update the document's Table of Contents (Figure 7-28).

Attention   Extract "The Count of Monte Cristo, Alexandre Dumas, Chapter 1-4, Heading styles with TOC.docx" document from the Chapter07.zip file. It Heading1 style was formatted with the Page break before paragraph option, thus inserting it Table of Contents in the document's second page (due to inheritance).

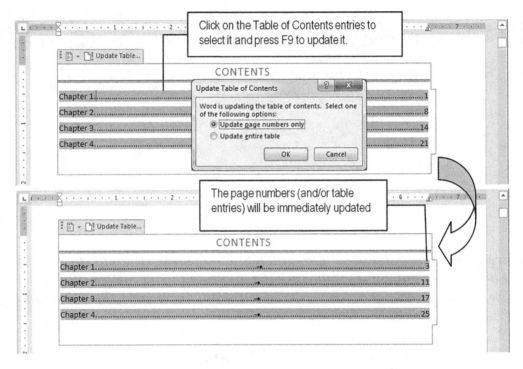

Figure 7-28. *To update the Table of Contents, click it entries (they will become grayed), press F9, and show one of the options available: update just the page numbers or update the entire table*

Attention   There is no way to control the appearance of "CONTENT" or "TABLE OF CONTENTS" paragraph above the automatically generated Table of Contents, whenever you use one of the first options proposed by this command. However, you can change this paragraph text or even manually delete in from the text (in will be reinserted whenever you need to rebuild the Table of Contents).

Deleting a Table of Contents Object

You can delete a Table of Contents object inserted in any document in two different ways:

- Use the Remove Table of Contents command found in the Table of Contents command of the Reference table or in the context menu found in the Table of Contents object header.

- Use the mouse to select the title and table entries of the Table of Contents object (they will become grayed, with the table entries using a deep gray color) and press Delete.

Custom Table of Contents

Microsoft Word continues to support it standard way of creating a Table of Contents using the Custom Table of Contents... command found in References tab, Table of Contents command list, which will show the Table of Contents dialog box, which offers the same interface employed by all Microsoft Word versions prior to Microsoft Office 2007 (Figure 7-29).

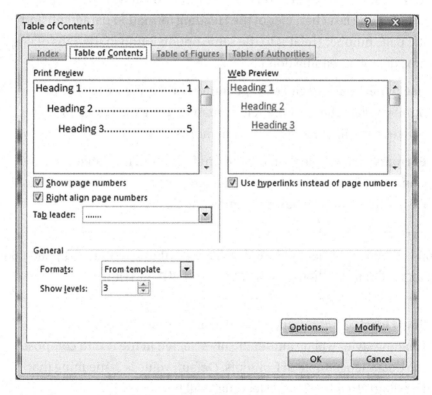

Figure 7-29. *The Custom Table of Contents... command shows the Table of Contents dialog box from which you can control how Microsoft Word will create the Table of Contents for the document*

The Print Preview list shows the TOC appearance, while the Web Preview list shows in if you save the document with the HTML format. You also have these options:

- **Show page numbers**: Uncheck to hide the page numbers for the Heading styles found in the document (this option must be unchecked when you are formatting a document to be converted to some e-book format, like e-pub or MOBI formats).

- **Right align page number**: Makes the page numbers appear aligned to the right page border by inserting a Right tab stop in each TOC*n* style. Uncheck to make the number appear next to the Heading formatted paragraph text.

- **Tab leader**: Allows selection of the way Microsoft will fill the space between the last character of the Heading formatted paragraph and the page number (relates to the same option found in the Tabs dialog box; default is leading dots).

- **Use hyperlinks instead of page numbers**: Suppresses the page number when the document is formatted using the HTML format (since they will not make sense anymore).

- **Formats**: Allows selection of different formats to the Table of Contents (default is From template, but you can select among Classic, Distinctive, Fancy, Modern, Formal, and Simple).

Attention   When you select different options from the Formats list, Microsoft Word changes the formatting options of styles TOC1 to TOC9.

- **Show levels**: Uses numbers 1 to 9 to allow selection of which Heading styles will be automatically selected in the text to compose the document's Table of Contents. Default value is 3, meaning that Heading1, Heading2, and Heading3 will be used.

- **Options**: Shows the Table of Contents Options dialog box that allows associating numbers 1 to 9 to the styles that must be used to compose the Table of Contents. Default association is Heading1 = 1, Heading2 = 2... until Heading9 =9, according to the Show levels option selected (Figure 7-30). Use this option to compose other types of Tables of Contents, like Chapter TOC, List of Tables, List of Figures, etc.

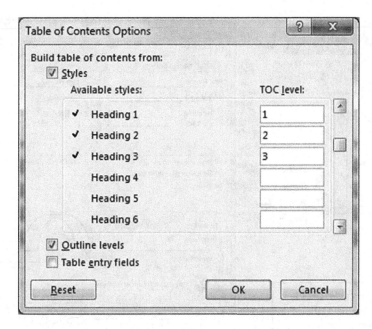

Figure 7-30. *Use the Table of Contents Options dialog box to create Table of Contents using any styles available in the document*

Whenever you use the Custom Table of Contents... command to show the Table of Contents dialog box and click OK to close in, Microsoft Word will check if the document already has a Table of Contents object inserted. If this is true, in will select the first Table of Contents object found and will ask if you want to replace in. Use "Yes" to replace the existing Table of Contents by the new options selected. Use "No" to insert another Table of Contents object in the document at the text cursor position (Figure 7-31).

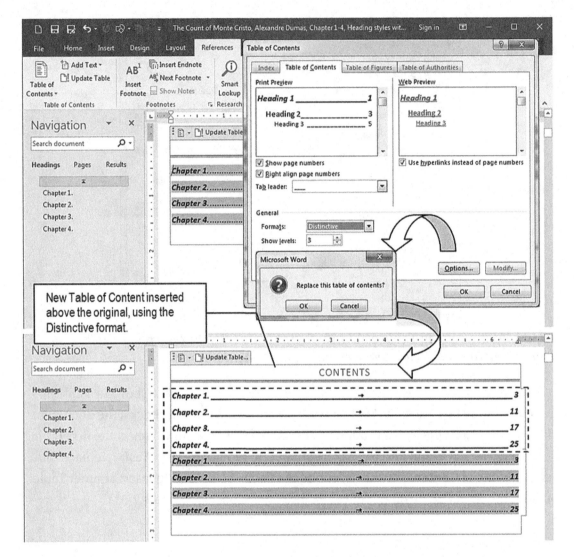

Figure 7-31. *By answering "No" when Microsoft Word asks to "Replace the Table of Contents?", a new Table of Contentes is created at the cursor position, with no title, and with the desired format and options chosen*

Exercise 3

The objective of this exercise is to quickly format a document using Recommended styles and create two Table of Contents: one for the chapters and another for it figures.

Extract "The Count of Monte Cristo, Alexandre Dumas, Chapter 1-4, Ilustrated.docx" document from Chapter07.zip file and open in in Microsoft Word.

Scroll through this document's pages and note that in has some of the figures used to illustrate the original edition (created by G. Staal, J.A. Beauce, and other eminent French artists of the late 19th century), followed by a figure description paragraph, formatted in bold.

You must format this document by following these specifications:

1. Apply Title and Subtitle styles for the document title and author name, respectively.

2. Join each "Chapter n" paragraph with the next to produce the most concise Table of Contents and apply the Heading1 style, which must be changed to begin in a new page.

3. Make Microsoft Word automatically number each image description using "Figure n: " as prefix (where n represents the figure count).

4. Guarantee that each figure and it paragraph description appear center aligned in the same page.

5. Create the document's Table of Contents for chapter titles and the "List of Figures" for figure descriptions, keeping both indexed in the first page (after the author name).

Let's get started!

Join Two Paragraphs and Apply Heading1 Style

This is a very simple task to do manually in such a small document: you just need to put the text cursor at the end of each "Chapter n" paragraph (press End key), type a colon followed by a space (": "), and press Delete to remove the Paragraph break and join in with the chapter title that comes next.

But if the document has all it chapters, this manual operation may take a long time to accomplish. Let's do in using a Find and Replace wildcard operation:

1. Click the Replace command in the Editing area of the Home tab of the Ribbon to show the Find and Replace dialog box.

2. Click More>> to expand in and check the Use wildcards option.

3. Click Find what text box and type: **(Chapter*)(^13)(*13)**
   (Chapter*) to find each chapter title; * finds it number, **(^13)** finds a Paragraph break that follows in, and the second **(*^13)** finds the next text paragraph and it Paragraph break.

4. Click Replace all text box and type: **\1: \3** "**\1:** " without quotes, represents the **(Chapter*)** wildcard used in the Find what text box, followed by a colon and a space; **\3** represents the **(*^13)** wildcard that selects the next paragraph and it Paragraph break.

5. While in the Replace all text box, click Format ➤ Styles and choose Heading1.

6. Press Replace all to replace all for occurrences in the text and apply the Heading1 style (Figure 7-32).

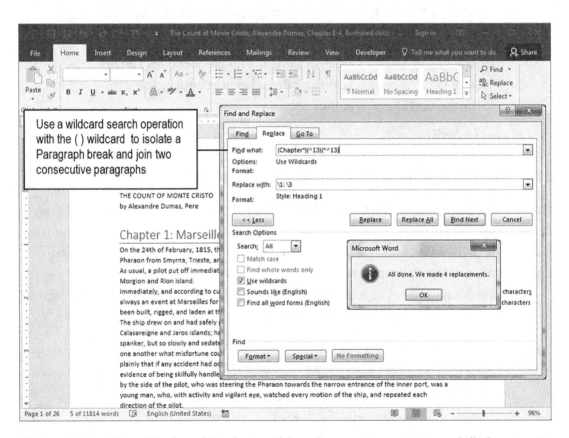

Figure 7-32. *Use a Find and Replace wildcard operation to join each "Chapter n" paragraph with the next, while also formatting in with the Heading1 style*

These six steps join each chapter title with the chapter description and apply the Heading1 style. Now make the Heading1 style begin in a new page:

1. Right-click any Heading1 style formatted paragraph, select Paragraph in the context menu, click the Line and Page Breaks tab, and check the Page break before option.

2. Close the Paragraph dialog box.

3. Right-click Heading1 style in the Style Gallery and choose Update Heading1 to Match the Selection option (Figure 7-33).

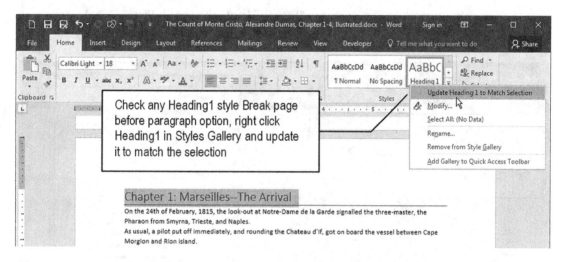

Figure 7-33. *Right-click any Heading1 formatted paragraph, show the Paragraph dialog box, and check the Page break before option. Then, right-click the Heading1 style in the Styles Gallery and choose Update Heading1 to Match Selection.*

The document will now have 28 pages with each chapter and description printing in a single line of text and beginning a new page.

Makes Image and Description Print in Same Page

To guarantee that each image paragraph and the paragraph description that follows in print in the same page you need to create two new styles:

- **FigureCaption**: bold, center aligned, numbered with prefix "Figure n". Shortcut key Shift+Alt+F.

- **Figure**: center aligned with the Keep with next paragraph property selected. Style to follow = ImageCaption. Shortcut key Alt+F.

To create the FigureCaption style, follow these instructions:

1. Scroll through the document and click any figure description paragraph (in bold, after each figure).

2. Center align this description paragraph.

3. Click the Numbering tool found in the Paragraph area of the Home tab of the Ribbon and select the Define New Number Format... command to show the Define New Number Format dialog box.

4. In the Define New Number Format dialog box, click the beginning of the Number format option and type "Figure " (note the space, Figure 7-34).

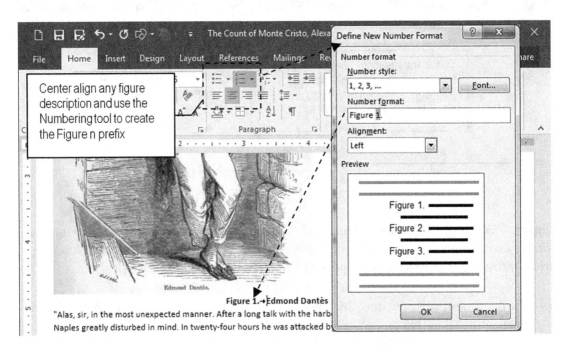

***Figure 7-34.** Use the Numbering tool to create the Figure n prefix so each figure description is automatically numbered*

Attention   If you inadvertently delete the numbering field in gray, just select a Number style option to insert in again in the Number format option.

5. Press Enter to close the dialog box and apply the "Figure 1" prefix to the selected figure description.

6. Drag the hanging indent control of the Ruler to the right so the numbering field is correctly positioned near it prefix.

7. Click the Layout tab and set the Spacing, After property to 6 pt.

8. Using the Styles window New Style button, create the FigureCaption style and attribute the Shift+Alt+F shortcut to it.

And once the FigureCaption style is created, it is time to create the Figure style to be applied to each Figure paragraph, following these steps:

1. Click any figure paragraph and center align in.

2. Right-click the figure paragraph, select Paragraph in the context menu, click the Line and Page Breaks tab, and check the Keep with next option.

3. Using the Styles Window New Style button, create the Figure style and attribute the Alt+F shortcut to it.

Now apply the Figure and FigureCaption styles to each figure and figure description found in the document using one of these two methods:

- **Apply styles manually**: Scroll through the document, click each figure found, and press Alt+F shortcut; click each figure description paragraph below in and press Shift+Alt+F.

- **Apply Figure style using Find and Replace**: Press Ctrl+H to show the Find and Replace dialog box:

  - In Find what text box, select Special ➤ Graphic (to use the ^g graphic code).

  - In Replace with text box, select Format ➤ Style to show the Replace Style dialog box and select the Figure style.

  - Press Replace all to replace all 12 occurrences of graphics in the document.

Now manually apply the FigureCaption to each figure description paragraph:

  - Click More>> button to expand the Find and Replace dialog box; click and check the Use wildcards option.

  - In Find what text box, type *^13.

  - Click Format ➤ Font and select Bold.

  - In Replace with text box, select Format ➤ Style to show the Replace Style dialog box and select the FigureCaption style.

  - Press Replace all to replace all 12 occurrences of figure description paragraphs in the document.

Attention   This search and replace operation works just because each figure caption was formatted with bold.

Create the Document's Table of Contents

Now that the document has already been tagged with Heading1 and FigureCaption styles, in will be easy to create the document's Table of Contents and List of Figures indexes by just following these steps:

1. Place the text cursor at the beginning of the "Chapter 1 - Marseilles - The Arrival" paragraph.

2. Click References ➤ Table of Contents and select the first Table of Contents option to generate the document's Table of Contents for chapter titles (Figure 7-35).

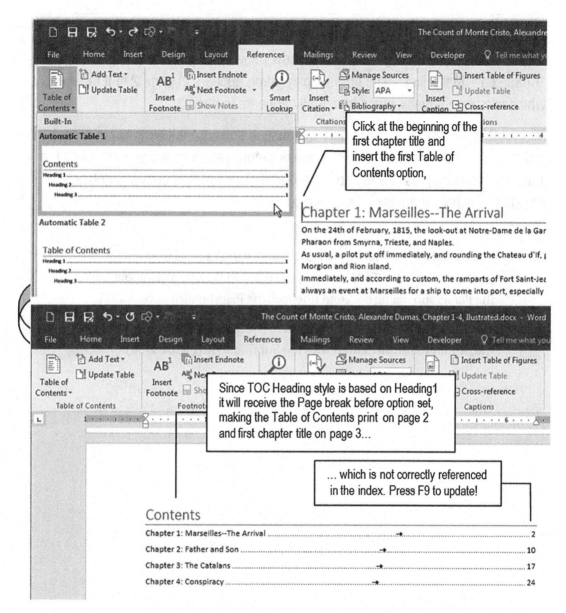

Figure 7-35. *Click the beginning of "Chapter 1: Marseilles - The Arrival" paragraph, select References ➤ Table of Contents command, and select the first option to insert a Table of Contents above the first chapter title. Note that Microsoft Word put the wrong page number in the index (in does not consider that "Contents" TOC title is based in Heading1 and has the Page break before option set).*

Attention   Since the Heading1 style has the Page break before option set, the Table of Contents will be generated in a new page. Note that in Figure 7-35 the "Chapter 1 - Marseilles - The Arrival" paragraph appears in page 2 in it table entry, which is a wrong guess, since in actually appears in page 3.

Microsoft Word 2016 has a bug here because in does not take into account that the "CONTENTS" may have the Page break before paragraph option set. Click the Table of Contents, press F9 to show the Update Table of Contents dialog box, and update the index, whenever is necessary.

3. Right-click the "Contents" paragraph above the Table of Contents (formatted with the TOC Heading style), select Paragraph to show the Paragraph dialog box, and uncheck the Page break before option.

4. The Table of Contents will now print in the first document page, below the Author name formatted with the Subtitle style (Figure 7-36).

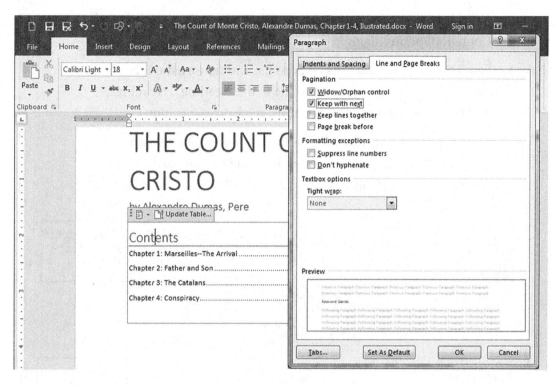

Figure 7-36. *Right-click the "Contents" Table of Contents title paragraph formatted with the TOC Heading style, choose Paragraph to show the Paragraph dialog box, and uncheck the Page break before option to make the Table of Contents print in the first document page.*

Attention   If necessary, click the Table of Contents and press F9 to update the index page numbers.

Create the List of Figures

To create the list of figures below the Table of Contents, in is necessary to inform Microsoft Word that just the FigureCaption style must be used to create the List of Figures index. Follow these steps:

1. Click below the last TOC entry and type "List of Figures".

2. Click References ➤ Table of Contents and select the "Custom Table of Contents…" command to show the Table of Contents dialog box.

3. In Table of Contents dialog box, click Options to show the Table of Contents Options dialog box.

4. Scroll the Table of Contents Options list and remove the 1, 2, and 3 TOC*n* style associations made to the Heading1, Heading2, and Heading3 paragraphs (they must have no association).

5. Click FigureCaption style association box and type 1, to associate in with TOC1 style (just FigureCaption style must be used to generate the List of Figures index, Figure 7-37).

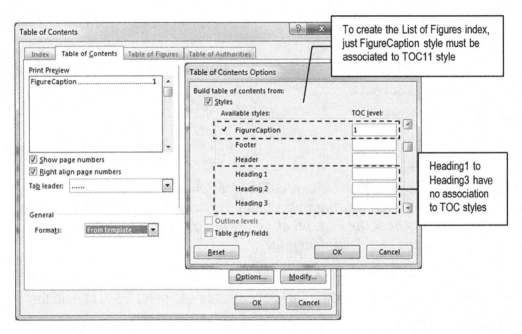

Figure 7-37. *Use the Table of Contents Option dialog box to break the Heading1, Heading2, and Heading3 style associations to TOCn styles and associate just the FigureCaption style to TOC1 style by typing 1 at it right*

6. Click OK to close the Table of Contents Options dialog box and click OK again to close the Table of Contents dialog box.

7. Microsoft Word will ask if you want to replace the already existing Table of Contents (Figure 7-38).

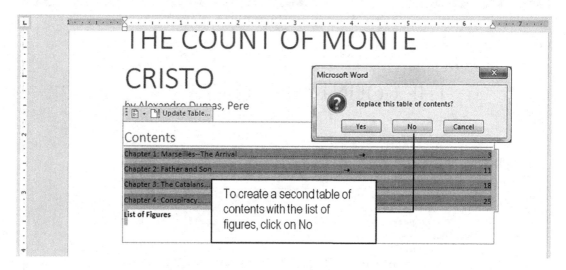

Figure 7-38. *When the Table of Contents dialog box is closed, Microsoft Word will ask if you want to replace the existing Table of Contents. Click No to keep the original Table of Contents and create the new List of Figures index, using just the FigureCaption styles at the cursor position.*

8. Click No to generate a new List of Figures index below the Contents index in the first document page, using just the FigureCaption styles found in the text (Figure 7-39).

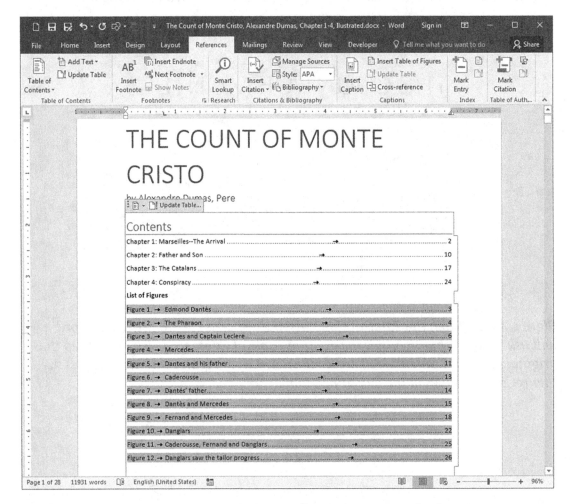

Figure 7-39. *The document now has two tables of contents: the first uses Heading1, Heading2, and Heading3 styles (the last two styles have no occurrences in the text) and the second uses just the FigureCaption styles*

Attention   Press F9 in the List of Figures index and update it page numbers whenever necessary.

Now use the Design tab of the Ribbon to apply different Style set to the document and quickly reformat in. Note that you may need to update their TOCs after such operations.

Attention   "The Count of Monte Cristo, Alexandre Dumas, Chapter 1-4, Illustrated Formatted.docx" document found inside the Chapter07.zip file has all the formatting proposed by this exercise, plus the Lines (Distinctive) style set applied using the Design tab of the Ribbon.

Try to follow the figures by pressing Ctrl and clicking the List of Index entries.

Exercise 4

The objective of this exercise is to format a document with Recommend styles, fix in with a wildcard search, and produce it Table of Contents.

Extract the "American Declaration of the Rights and Duties of Man.docx" document from Chapter07.zip file and open in in Microsoft Word. In has the well-known Bogotá Declaration proposed by nations of the Americas at the Ninth International Conference of American States in Bogotá, Colombia, in April 1948.

Click the Show/Hide tool in the Home tab of the Ribbon to show the document's hidden characters and note that the document has six pages and the addition of two consecutive Enters for each paragraph break (Figure 7-40).

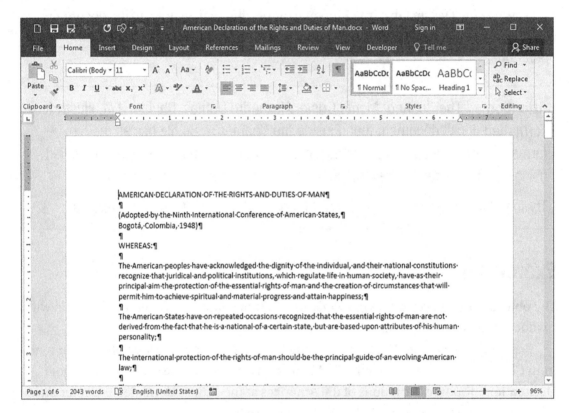

Figure 7-40. *This is "American Declaration of the Rights and Duties of Man.docx" document, which you can extract from Chapter07.zip file. In has no formatting and shows the addition of two successive Enter keys for each paragraph break.*

Format this document by following these steps (use Exercise 3 tips if necessary):

1. Apply Title and Subtitle styles to it first and second paragraphs.

2. Scroll the text to locate the next "AMERICAN DECLARATION OF THE RIGHTS AND DUTIES OF MAN":

   - Press Ctrl+Enter to insert a page break before this paragraph.

   - Apply the Title style and Subtitle style to the "Preamble" paragraph that follows in.

3. Make a Find and Replace operation to replacing two consecutive Enter keys with just one Enter key:

   - Press Ctrl+H to show the Find and Replace dialog box.

   - **Find what**: ^p^p

   - **Replace with**: ^p

   - Press Replace all to replace 68 occurrences.

4. Join this document's "CHAPTER" paragraphs with the text paragraphs that follow them using a Find and Replace with wildcard operation (which is case sensitive):

   - Expand the Find and Replace dialog box and check Use wildcards option.

   - **Find What**: (CHAPTER*)(^13)(*^13)

   - **Replace with**: \1: \3

   - With cursor in the Replace with text box, click Format ➤ Style and select **Heading1** in the Replace Style dialog box

   - Press Replace all to replace 2 occurrences

5. Join this document's "Article" paragraphs with the text paragraphs that follow them using another Find and Replace with wildcard operation:

   - **Find What**: (Article [0-9]*)(^13)(*^13)

> **Attention**   Since there are some "Article" (there is a space after) words inside some body text paragraphs, use (Article [0-9]*) to search for "Article"! words followed by a space and a number.

- **Replace with**: \1: \3

- With cursor in the Replace with text box, click Format ➤ Style and select **Heading2** in the Replace Style dialog box

- Press Replace all to replace 38 occurrences (Figure 7-41)

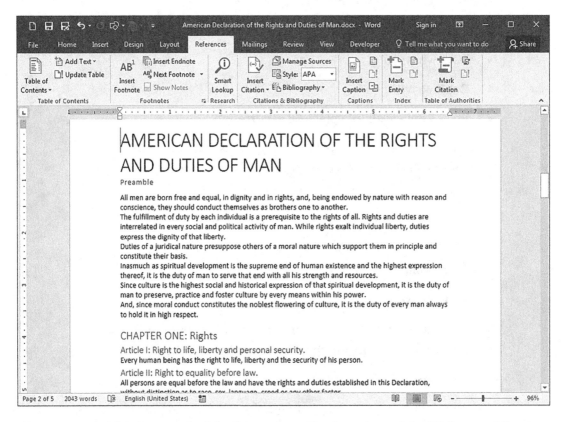

Figure 7-41. *This is page 2 of the "American Declaration of the Rights and Duties of Man.docx" document after receiving the Title, Subtitle, Heading1, and Heading2 paragraphs using a wildcard Find and Replace operation*

6. Click on begin of "CHAPTER ONE: Rights" paragraph (the first Heading1 paragraph) and insert the first Table of Contents option using the References tab, Table of Contents command.

7. Right-click any Heading1 paragraph, check the Page break before option in the Paragraph dialog box, and use the Update Heading1 To Match Selection option to update the style. The Table of Contents will now print in page 2.

8. Click any TOC2 style inside the Table of Contents and use the Layout tab (or the Paragraph dialog box) to set Spacing After = 0. Since TOC2 has the Update automatically style option set, the Table of Contents will shrink and fit into a single page.

9. With the Table of Contents selected, press F9 to update the page numbers (Figure 7-42).

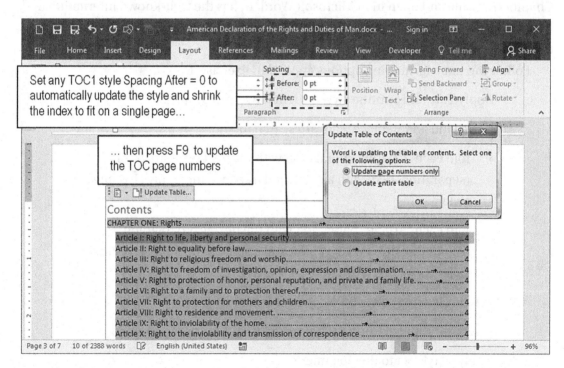

Figure 7-42. *Once the Table of Contents has been inserted into the document, click any TOC2 style (any Article entry) and set the Layout tab Spacing After= 0, to make the index fit into a single page. Press F9 while the index is selected to update the page numbers.*

Attention   "The American Declaration of the Rights and Duties of Man Formatted. docx" document that you can extract from Chapter07.zip file has the formatted version proposed by this exercise, after receiving the Black and White (Classic) Style set found in the Design tab of the Ribbon (the style set removes the Page break before option of Heading1 that needs to be reapplied).

Exercise 5

The objective of this exercise is to quickly format a document with Recommended styles, join paragraphs with a wildcard search, generate it Table of Contents, and format with the Style Set gallery.

Extract the "European Convention of Human Rights.docx" document from Chapter07.zip file and open in in Microsoft Word. In has the well-known international treaty to protect human rights and fundamental freedoms in Europe, drafted in 1950 by the then newly formed Council of Europe.

Follow the same formatting options applied in Exercise 4:

1. Apply Title and Subtitle styles to it first two paragraphs.

2. Use a Find and Replace wildcard search to:

   - Join each "Chapter" paragraph with the next text paragraph (separating them with a colon and a space) and apply Heading1 style

   - Join each "Article" paragraph with the next text paragraph (separating them with a colon and a space) and apply Heading2 style

3. Set the Heading1 style Break page before option.

4. Insert the Table of Contents before the first "Chapter" paragraph.

5. Apply a Style set to the document.

Attention   The "European Convention of Human Rights Formatted.docx" document found inside Chapter07.zip file received all these formatting options and the Simple Style set, found in Design tab.

Using the Outline View

Once your document is structured using the Recommended Heading styles, you can get more control over headings and the text itself using Microsoft Word Outline view: a powerful way to move text around and control the heading levels spread through the document.

To effectively use the Outline view, in is necessary that you have a document formatted with Heading styles of many levels, so this time I will use as example the "European Convention of Human Rights Headings.docx" document, which you can extract from Chapter07.zip file; this document was formatted using Heading1 to Heading4 for it section titles, and it received the Minimalist Style set found in the Design tab (Figure 7-43).

Attention   For those of you that are interested in how to apply Heading1 to each "CHAPTER n" paragraph and Heading2 to the text that comes next, with a Find and Replace wildcard operation, here goes the tip: first format each "CHAPTER n" paragraph and the next with bold (Find what: (CHAPTER*^13)(*^13)), Replace with: Bold), then change just "CHAPTER" paragraphs to Heading1, not bold (Find what: (CHAPTER*^13), Replace with: Heading1, Regular). Finally, replace what is still bold with Heading2 (Find what: Normal style, Bold, Replace with: Heading2, Regular).

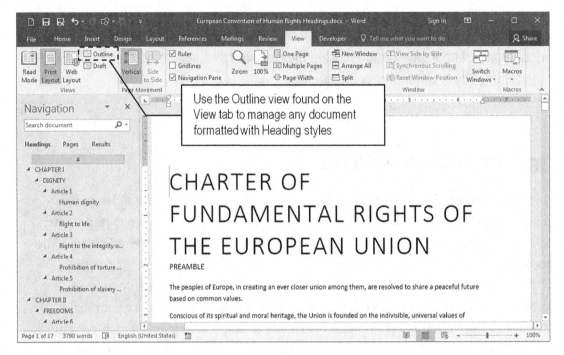

Figure 7-43. *This is the "European Convention of Human Rights Headings.docx" document, which you can extract from the Chapter07.zip file; it has Heading1 to Heading4 Recommend styles applied to key text paragraphs (look to the Navigation pane Headings view).*

To active the Microsoft Word Outline view, click the Outline view command found in the Views area of the View tab of the Ribbon. Microsoft Word will show and activate the Outlining tab next to the File tab and will put small circles at left of each body text paragraph (Figure 7-44).

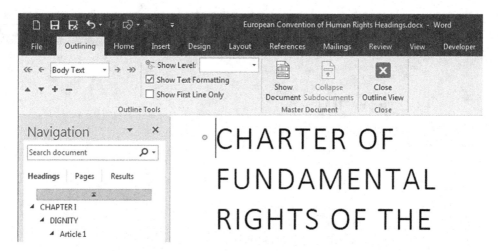

Figure 7-44. *The Outlining tab shown with the Outline command in the View tab offers tools to manage Heading styles and it contents*

Attention   To deactivate Microsoft Word Outline view, click the Close Outline View button of the Outlining tab and use the Views area options of the View tab by clicking the Print Layout button located in the Microsoft Word status bar's right side.

Selecting Outline Levels

Use the Show Level list of the Outlining tab to decide which outline levels must be shown. Each level selected shows the level selected and all precedent levels. For example, by selecting Level 1, just Heading1 paragraph styles are shown. Selecting Level 2, Heading1, and Heading2 paragraphs is shown.

Figure 7-45 shows Microsoft Word Outline view exhibiting the Heading1 and Heading2 style paragraphs applied to the "European Convention of Human Rights Headings.docx" document. Note that each heading level received a ⊕ symbol to it left as an indication that you can expand in to show the text inside the heading. Also note that the Navigation pane Headings view is not affected by the Outline view Show Level option.

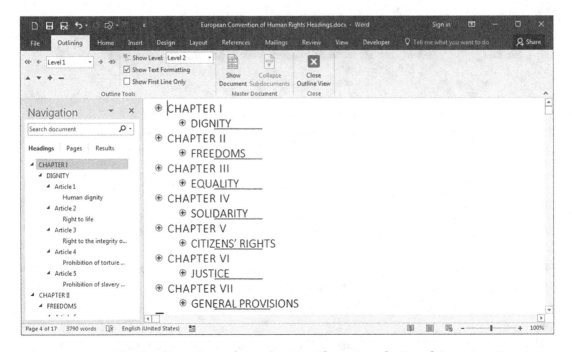

Figure 7-45. *The Outline view after selecting Show Level= Level 2 option. In now shows just Heading1 and Heading2 style paragraphs.*

Note that the Outlining tab has these options below the Show Level list:

- **Show Text Formatting**: checked by default, allows you to show the text formatting applied to each Heading style in the Outline view;

- **Show First Line only**: unchecked by default, shows just the first body text line inside each Heading style.

To partially reveal other possible headings inside a collapsed Heading style shown in Outline view, click the heading and use the + collapse button located in the Outlining tab (use the - collapse button to collapse in again). Figure 7-46 shows the "DIGNITY" paragraph expanded showing all Heading3 paragraphs that exist inside in. Click the + button again to show all Heading4 styles.

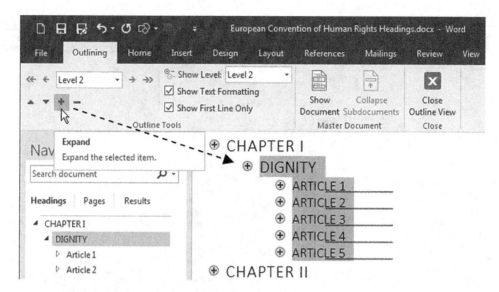

Figure 7-46. *Use the Expand and Collapse buttons of the Outlining tab to partially expand and collapse any Heading style*

To reveal all the text inside any Heading style, double-click the ⊕ symbol to it left (or use the Expand + button of the Outlining tab). Figure 7-47 shows the "DIGNITY" paragraph formatted with Heading2 style expanded with the Show First Line option checked. Note that all it subheadings (Heading3 and Heading4) are now shown in the Document window.

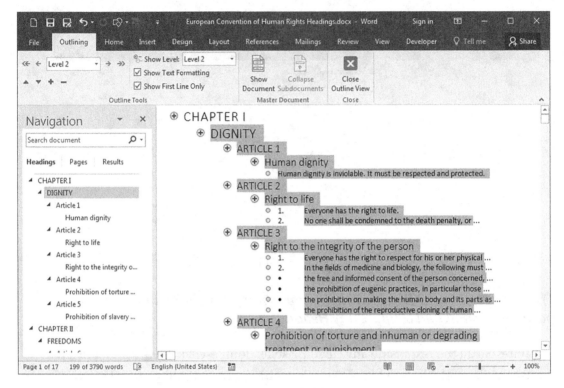

Figure 7-47. *Double-click the ⊕ symbol to the left of any Heading style in Outline view to expand in and show it contents. This figure has the Show First Line Only checked, showing just the first body text line of each Heading4 style.*

If you double-click any Heading style to expose all it contents, use the - collapse button of the Outlining tab to collapse the body text and show it lowest Heading level (in this case, Heading4 paragraphs). Keep pressing - button in the Outlining tab to collapse the headings.

Promoting and Demoting Outline Levels

The Outline view is perfect when you want to organize your thoughts by changing the outline levels of one or many headings at once using the Outlining tools to promote or demote Heading styles (Figure 7-48).

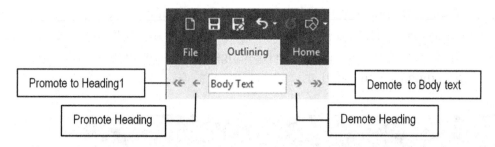

Figure 7-48. *Use the Outlining tab tools to promote or demote Heading styles in the Outline view*

As you can see, you can use the Promote button to make Heading2 become Heading1, or instantly promote any Heading style to Heading1. Or use the Demote button to make Heading1 become Heading2 or demote any Heading style to Body text (with Normal style).

There are simple rules to promote or demote any Heading style.

- Click the Heading text to act just in in (it subheadings must not be grayed).

- Click the Heading ⊕ symbol to select all it contents to act in in and all it subheadings (if any).

Suppose for example that you want to insert a new "ABOUT DIGNITY" Heading2 style before the "DIGNITY" paragraph and demote the "DIGNITY" Heading2 and all it content to a lower outline level. Using the Outline view you just need to follow these steps.

1. Click at left of the "DIGNITY" Heading2 paragraph and press Enter to insert another Heading2 paragraph before in (the Navigation pane will show this new empty Heading2 style).

2. Type "ABOUT DIGNITY" into the paragraph text.

3. Click the ⊕ symbol at left of the "DIGNITY" paragraph to select all it content.

4. Use the Demote right-pointing arrow of the Outlining tab to demote in to Heading3 (all the Heading3 styles inside will be demoted to Heading4, and the Heading4 will be demoted to Heading5, Figure 7-49).

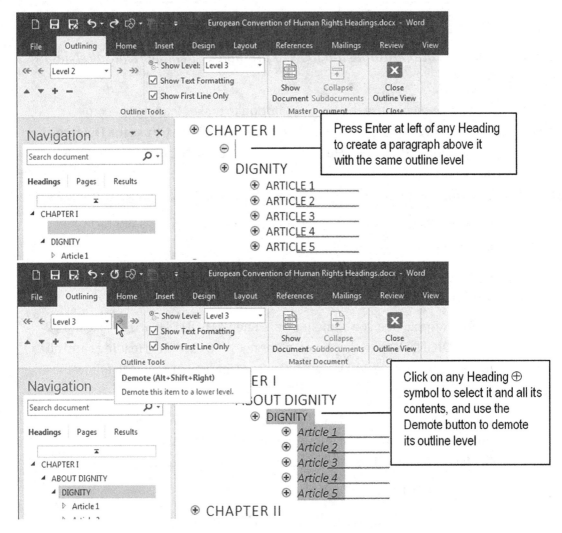

Figure 7-49. *Use the Outline view to insert new Heading styles and reorganize the Heading levels with the Promote and Demote tools found in the Outlining tab*

Moving Heading Contents

Using the Outline view, you can move large blocks of text to a new position without needing to select, copy, and paste text in the document; instead, you can use the Move down and Move up tools found in the Outlining tab.

In quite simple to use, and they obey the same rules as the Promote and Demote tools:

1. If just the Heading style is selected (it content *is not grayed*), just it text will be moved.

2. If all the Heading style and it contents are selected (they are all grayed), all the text will be moved.

The easiest way to move Heading and contents is to first collapse in and then use the Move up or Move down tools of the Outlining tab, or just drag the Heading with the mouse to a new position and... *voilà!* All text will be repositioned inside the document.

Figure 7-50 shows how you can move "CHAPTER I" and all it contents below the CHAPTER II content. Easy, isn't in?

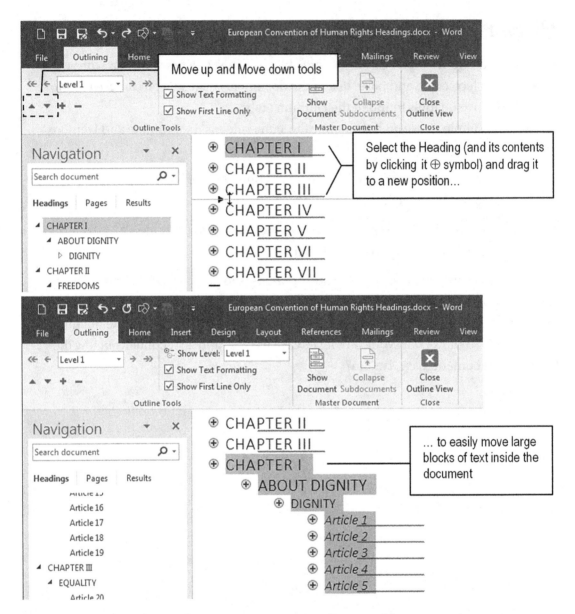

Figure 7-50. *Use the Outline view to move Headings and in contents to a new position inside the document. Collapse the desired Heading first, click the ⊕ symbol at left, to select all it contents and drag in with the mouse to a new position (or use the Move up and Mode down tools of the Outlining tab).*

Conclusion

Heading styles are among the most powerful of the Microsoft Word tools to format and organize the text.

They are based in the Outline level property found in the Paragraph dialog box to hierarchically define Heading precedence in the text. By using Heading1 to Heading9 to format your document chapter and section titles, you can take full advantage of the Navigation pane and the Design tab tools, automatically create Table of Contents indexes, and use the Outline view to easily restructure your thoughts by changing Heading levels and moving large blocks of text with simple mouse operations.

Summary

In this chapter you learned:

- Heading styles goes from Heading1 to Heading9, and are associated with the Paragraph ➤ Outline level property.

- You can use the Multilevel list tool to easily number Heading styles and produce a consistent numbering system inside any document.

- Each Heading style has a small triangle to it left in the Document pane that allows collapsing or expanding it contents.

- Using the Navigation pane (Ctrl+F) Headings view you can write very well-structured documents formatted with Heading1 to Heading9 styles.

- After applying Headings view to create the hierarchical structure of any document, you see it Table of Contents being created in the Navigation Pane Headings view.

- The Navigate Pane Headings view allows you to quickly move to any document chapter or section using a single mouse click.

- Using the References ➤ Table of Contents command, you can easily create the document's Table of Contents with or without the page numbers, using different index presentation styles.

- You can create Table of Contents with or without a heading associated to the TOC Heading style, using it automatic options or the Custom Table of Contents... command.

- Table of Contents entries are formatted with TOC*n* styles associated with the Heading*n* style found in the document (e.g., TOC1 with Heading1).

- To show the TOC Heading or TOCn styles in the Styles window, you must click Style ➤ Options and make in use the Select styles to show = All styles option.

- The Apply styles window is the only style interface that automatically synchronizes the style used in any text paragraph.

- Using the Table of Contents Options dialog box, you can define what Outline levels (1 to 9) will be associated to each paragraph style and create different Table of Contents indexes (like "List of Figures" of "List of Tables").

- How to easily format text documents using Heading styles and the Find and Replace with wildcard options.

- How to use Microsoft Word Outline view to show, format, and move large blocks of text using the Outlining tab tools.

In the next chapter you will be presented with how Microsoft Word formats document pages by using the Page Setup dialog box options and breaking the document into sections.

CHAPTER 8

Page Formatting

Microsoft Word pages are easy to configure once you understand how it works and can differentiate types and usage. In this chapter, you will learn how to take the most from the Page Setup dialog box and the usage of the page Header and Footer areas to achieve better results in your document formatting and exporting.

You will learn how to create and manage different types of Header and Footer, how to correctly insert page numbers (and page count), and how to produce nicely formatted e-books, PDF files, and booklet printing using Microsoft Word options.

The documents cited in this chapter and the Exercise sections can be found by downloading the Chapter08.zip file from this Internet address:

```
https://github.com/apress/msft-word-secrets
```

Types of Documents

Text documents differ one another in the types of pages they use, and for the sake of this discussion they can be considered as

- **Single-page documents**: print on just one side of the paper and one or two types of pages: the first page and the others.

- **Mirror page documents**: print on both page sides and have two or three types of pages: the first page, odd pages (front), and even pages (back).

- **Complex documents**: may have different types of pages, not just changing which side of the paper they print on, but also presenting different page sizes and orientations.

Microsoft Word deals with such page variability inside any text document using the Page Setup dialog box (and its three tabs) to configure the pages, and the hidden Section break character to indicate where one page type begins and another ends.

© Flavio Morgado 2017
F. Morgado, *Microsoft Word Secrets*, https://doi.org/10.1007/978-1-4842-3078-7_8

The first step to master how to format different page sizes is to understand the Page Setup dialog box and how each document page is constituted.

Page Setup

Whenever you open a new, blank document in Microsoft Word, you receive a new blank page; the size of this page is associated to the page size defined in your default printer, so the first action to produce any printed document is to configure its page size: the medium in which it will be printed and becomes alive.

This is done using one of these methods:

- Using the Size command found in the Page Setup area of the Layout tab to select one of the already set-up page sizes (Figure 8-1).

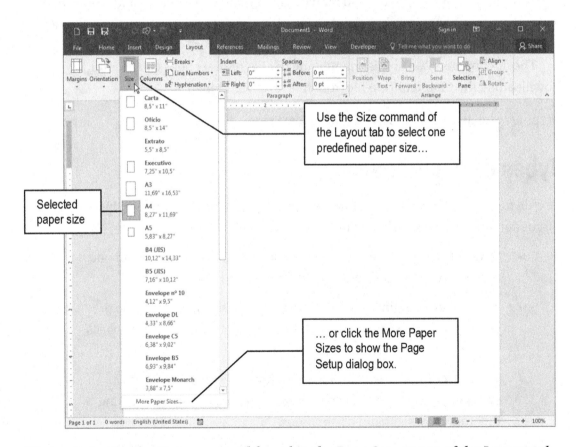

Figure 8-1. *Use the Size command found in the Page Setup area of the Layout tab to select a predefined paper size or click on More Paper Sizes... to show the Page Setup dialog box*

- Using the Page Setup dialog box, which can be shown by different methods:

    - Double-clicking the ruler (the easiest way).

    - Using the Size ➤ More Paper Sizes… command found in the Page Setup area of the Layout tab.

    - Clicking the small Page Setup button found in the Page Setup area of the Layout tab.

    - Using the File ➤ Print ➤ Margins ➤ Custom Margins… command.

Using any of these methods, you can change the options or show the Page Setup dialog box with the Paper tab selected (Figure 8-2), from where you use the Paper size area to select any of the page sizes presented by the Layout tab Size command (see Figure 8-1) or use the Width and Height text boxes to create a Custom Size.

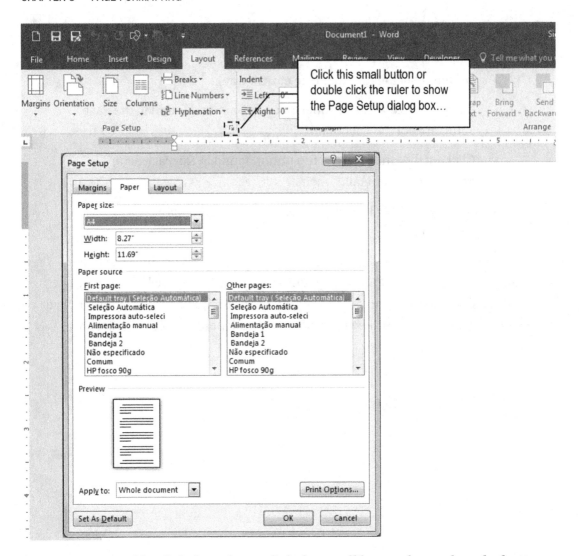

Figure 8-2. *Double-click the ruler or click the small button located on the bottom right side of the Page Setup area of the Layouo tab to show the Page Setup dialog box with the Paper tab selected*

Attention   The Paper tab also allows selection of the printer tray used by the first page and other pages of the current document.

Paper orientation is selected in the Margins tab.

And once you have defined the paper size, it is time to adjust the document's margins and header and footer sizes.

Margins, Header, and Footer

As seen in any other text-processing software, every Microsoft Word page has three main areas:

- Margins and the space inside them (where the document prints).

- Header: the space above top margin.

- Footer: the space below the bottom margin.

The text you type in any Microsoft Word document will appear inside the document margins of each document page, but whatever you type or insert in the Header or Footer areas will appear on every document page (that is why the Headers and Footers are used to convey document information like page number, page count, date printed, etc.).

Microsoft Word hides these areas from your eyes but you can get a hint about the size of these areas by

- Using the horizontal and vertical ruler.

- Setting two options found in the Show Document Content area of the Advanced option found in Word Options dialog box (File ➤ Options ➤ Advanced):

  - Show text boundaries

  - Show crop marks.

Attention   It is not obvious to most people that both the Header and Footer are special document page areas, because everything you put in them will appear on every document page. They are mostly used to convey the page number, page count (page n of m), or other document information, like printed date, produced by, and so on.

Figure 8-3 shows how the white page looks when Crop marks are shown (appearing at the top left and bottom right page corners). It also shows the text boundary around the first empty page paragraph (with the Show/Hide tool checked so you can see the hidden Paragraph break character).

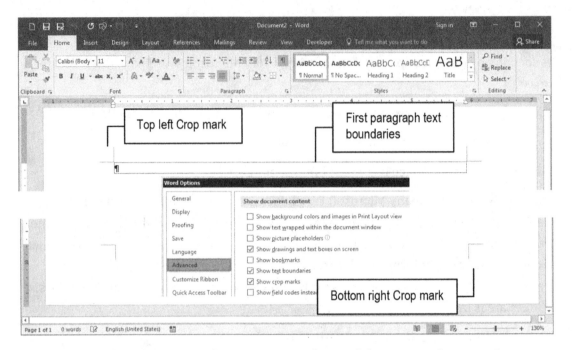

Figure 8-3. *The white page of a new Microsoft Word document showing Crop mark and Text boundary options set for its first paragraph. These options allow you to set the positions of the Header, Footer, and Page margins (top, left, right, and bottom margins).*

Accessing the Header and Footer Page Areas

There is more than one way to access the document page Header and Footer areas:

- Double-click the Header and Footer area (identify it by the dark gray area of the ruler, which is above the top crop mark or below the bottom crop mark).

- Use the Header ➤ Edit Header (or Footer ➤ Edit Footer) commands found in the Header and Footer area of the Insert tab of the Ribbon.

Whenever you access the Header or Footer area, Microsoft Word activates its content and deactivates the document content (the text of which becomes grayed), while it also activates and shows the Header & Footer Tools Design tab on the Ribbon, where you will find tools to manipulate this special document page area (Figure 8-4).

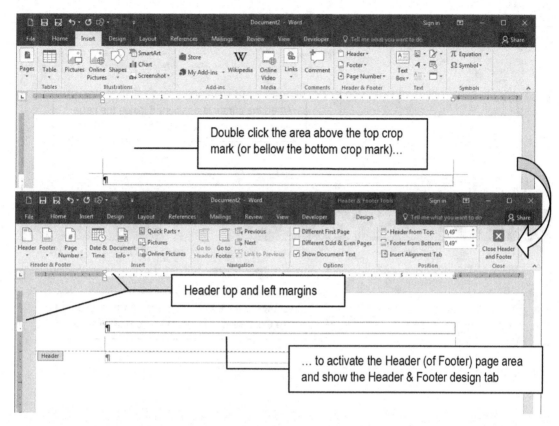

Figure 8-4. *Double-click the page area above (or below) the top (or bottom) crop mark to activate the page Header (or Footer). Microsoft Word will show the Header & Footer Design tab where you can find tools to manipulate this important document page area.*

Once the page Header or Footer area is activated, you can alternate between the Header and Footer areas using the Goto Footer (or Goto Header) commands found in the Navigation area of the Header & Footer Tools Design tab of the Ribbon (Figure 8-5).

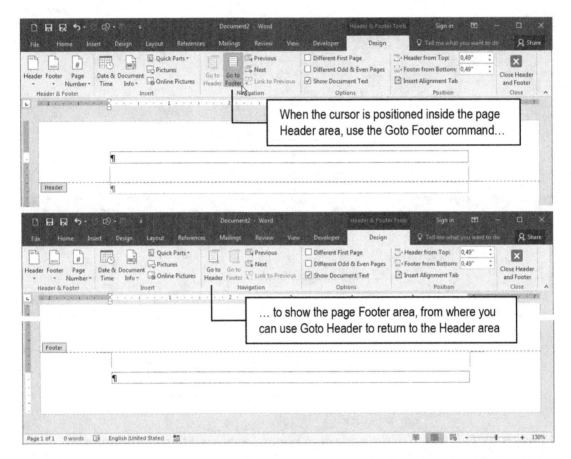

Figure 8-5. To alternate between the page Header and Footer areas, use the Goto Footer and Goto Header commands found in the Navigation area of the Header & Footer Tools Design tab on the Ribbon

Change Page Margin Size

Now that you know that the document page has the special areas called Margins, Header, and Footer, it is interesting to note that Microsoft Word has a dark gray area on its horizontal and vertical rulers to define the space used by its Left, Right, Top, and Bottom page margins, which also appear in the Header and Footer areas.

Since the page is the same for the entire document, whenever you change its margins, the entire document will obey these new margin values. And once more, this can be done in three different ways:

- Setting page, Header, and Footer margin sizes interactively, by dragging its Ruler guides (Left, Right, Top, and Bottom).

- Using the Layout and the Header & Footer Tools tabs.

- Using the Page setup dialog box.

Configuring Margins Using the Ruler

You can easily change the pages and header margins using the mouse to drag the ruler margin handles: they can be found where the horizontal and vertical ruler dark gray and white areas met.

Just point the mouse cursor to the ruler's dark gray edge, until the mouse cursor changes shape to west-east arrow for both the left and right margins, or to a north-south arrow for the top and left margins, and then drag it to a new position.

Attention   The vertical ruler can be just shown in the Print Layout view (default Microsoft Word view), if the Show vertical ruler in Print Layout (found on Advanced ➤ Display area of the Word Options dialog box) is checked. The dark gray area that represents the top and bottom page margins on the vertical ruler is shown just if the Show white space between pages in Print Layout (Display ➤ Page Display area) of the Word Options dialog box is checked (Figure 8-6).

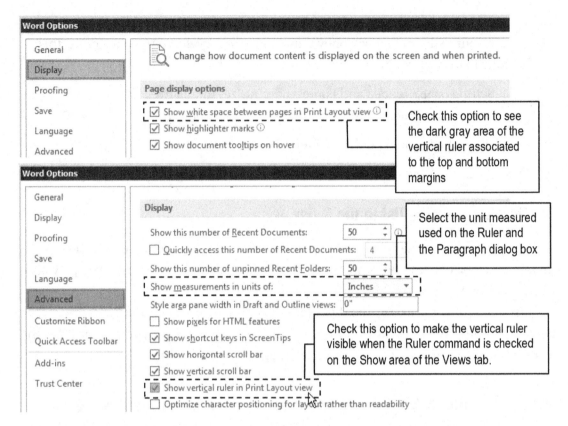

Figure 8-6. *Check the Show white space between pages in Print Layout view (Display ➤ Page display options) and Show vertical ruler in Print Layout vie (Advanced ➤ Display options) of the Word Options dialog box (File ➤ Options) to ensure that the vertical ruler will appear correctly on the screen. Use the Show measurements in units of option to define the ruler unit measure.*

Figure 8-7 shows the mouse cursor positioned to change each page margin. Note that the horizontal ruler indicates the size of the left and right margins in its dark gray area, using the measurement unit defined by the Show measurements in units of option found in the Display area of the Advanced tab of the Word options dialog box (File ➤ Options ➤ Advanced), while the vertical ruler just shows it for the bottom margin (and I have no clue why Microsoft Word behaves this way).

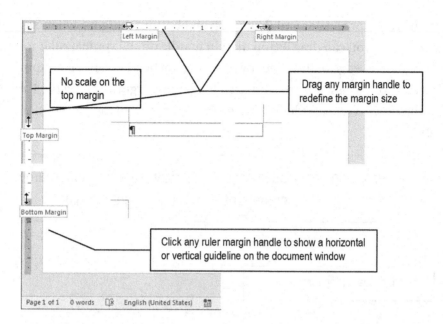

Figure 8-7. *Point the cursor to the dark gray edge of the horizontal or vertical ruler to find the left, right, top, and bottom margin handles*

You may experience some difficulty in finding the left margin handle on the horizontal ruler, because it stays in between the First line indent and the Hanging indent controls. Be patient and try to correctly position the mouse cursor until the mouse cursor changes to a west-east arrow.

To change any margin size, just click the mouse on the ruler margin handle and drag it to a new position (Microsoft Word will show a horizontal or vertical dashed line in the document window).

Attention   Be aware that whenever you change any margin size, this change will affect the entire document forcing the text to reflux along its pages, meaning that you may need to update any Table of Contents object that may exist in it.

The same is true for Header and Footer top and bottom margins: whenever the Header is activated, you can drag its top margin handle on the vertical ruler to change its distance from the top edge of the page (by dragging the header vertical bottom margin handle, you change the associated document top page margin), or drag the Footer top margin handle on the vertical ruler to change its distance from the page bottom edge (Figure 8-8).

Attention   By dragging the Header or Footer horizontal left or right margin handles, you will change the document page's left and right margins.

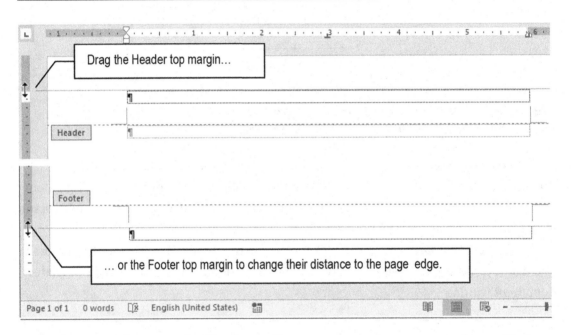

Figure 8-8. *By dragging the Header or Footer top margins, you can change their distance from the page edge. Note that by dragging the Header (or Footer) bottom margin, you increase the Header (or Footer) height, but change the page top (or bottom) margin position.*

Attention   The changes made by dragging the Header or Footer top margins on the vertical ruler can also be made using numerical values typed into the Header from top or Footer from bottom controls found in the Position area of the Header & Footer Tools Design tab (see Figures 8-4 and 8-5).

Configuring Margins Using the Layout Tab of the Ribbon

The Layout tab of the Ribbon offers the Margins command in its Page Setup area, from which you can select different margin profiles using the mouse. It will change the left, right, top, and bottom margins (and probably adjust the Header and Footer top margins) to give to your document a new appearance (Figure 8-9).

You can select among

- **Normal**, **Narrow**, **Moderate,** and **Wide**: to quickly change the size of the document margins and give it a new appearance;

- **Mirrored**: to create margins for documents printed on both paper sides (front and back), which produces odd and even pages whose margins are mirrored (left margin of an even page is the right margin of an odd page).

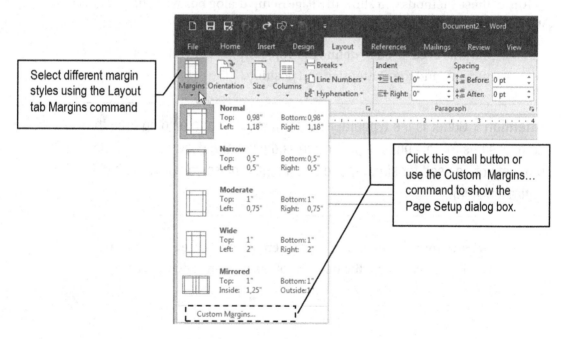

Figure 8-9. *Use the Margin command found in the Page Setup area of the Layout tab to easily change your document margins using different margin styles*

Configuring Margins Using Page Setup Dialog Box

The most traditional way to configure the document page margins is using the Margins tab of Microsoft Word Page Setup dialog box, which can be shown using different methods:

- By double-clicking the ruler and selecting the Margin tab (the easiest way).

- By using the Margins ➤ Custom Margins... command found in the Page Setup area of the Layout tab (see Figure 8-9).

- By clicking the small Page Setup button found in the Page Setup area of the Layout tab (see Figure 8-9).

- By using the File ➤ Print ➤ Margins ➤ Custom Margins... command.

Any of these methods will show the Page Setup dialog box with the Margins tab selected (Figure 8-10), which offers these options:

- **Margins area**: used to define the Top, Bottom, Left, and Right margins, and the Gutter size and position.

Attention   Gutter is the typographical term for the page binding area that compensates for this unused paper part and gives the document real margins (it must not be used for single-page documents unless you plan to bind it by its entire left side).

- **Orientation**: alternates the page orientation between Portrait and Landscape, changing the position of the margins and the gutter.

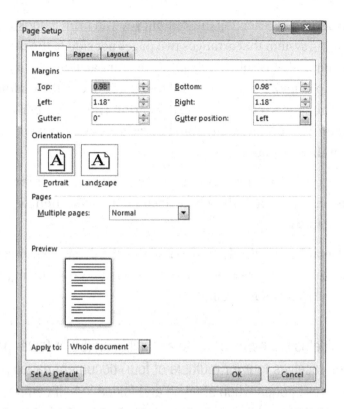

Figure 8-10. *The Page Setup dialog box with the Margins tab selected. Use it to precisely define the page margins, gutter size and position, page orientation, and number of pages used in the document (or when it is printed).*

- **Multiple pages**: allows you to define if the document margins will change according to the document type:

  - **Normal**: document prints just on front of paper, having just one type of margin.

  - **Mirror margins**: document prints on both sides of paper, changing margin positions to the front or back of paper.

  - **2 pages per sheet**: document prints two pages on a single paper side.

- **Book Fold**: by selecting this option, you can print a booklet: a printing system that arranges two pages per side of the paper (creating what is called a *signature* of four pages into a single sheet of copy). These pages will then be folded in the middle and grouped to constitute the final print. The Sheets per booklet option defines how many consecutive pages will be printed on each sheet of paper.

- **Apply to**: this option appears in every Page Setup tab to indicate if the options set will apply to the whole document, this section, or from this point forward.

- **Set as Default**: click this button to redefine the default page size and margins used by Microsoft Word in every new document (it will change the Normal.dotx template).

Attention Booklet is the name given to a small book (50 or fewer pages) where each paper page receives four (or multiple of four) document pages printed in front and back. These pages when stacked and folded in half compose the correct booklet page sequence, and the pages are stapled on the fold. You need a front and back printer to have better results.

Formatting E-books

Many people ask how to format a document in Microsoft Word so it can be used by an e-book reader (like the popular Amazon Kindle). It is important to know that this is more a matter of text formatting; there's no need to bother with the page setup applied to the Microsoft Word document, because e-reader devices are quite variable in screen size and resolution.

In general, you must follow these formatting rules to create good-quality Microsoft Word documents that will be nicely read on most e-book devices:

- **Body text**: Font is unimportant because each reader has its own fonts. Format the Normal style with 10 pt size and a System font like Arial, Times New Roman, or Calibri.

Paragraph alignment is unimportant because most e-readers use Left alignment. To detach each paragraph, apply a First line indent = 0.2 or a Space After = 6 pt size and Line spacing = single.

- **Title, subtitle and section titles**: Must be formatted with Title and Subtitle and the Heading styles, which must be no larger than 16 pt size. Heading1 can have the Page break before option set.

- **Bold, Italic, Underline, and font formatting**: Can be used at will.

- **Header and Footer**: Must be removed like in any new empty document.

- **Page size, Margins, and Alignment**: Must not be taken into account because these values will be ignored by the e-book converter.

- **Table of Contents**: Must be generated using the Custom Table of Contents... command and with the Show page number option unchecked (index entries must not be followed by page numbers; since page size is variable, page numbers do not make sense).

Once the document is correctly formatted you must save it on the disk and use an e-book converter software (like Calibre, GooReader, 2EPUB, etc.) to convert it to some popular e-book formats, like *epub* (preferred document format for Android and iOS devices, Kobo eReader, Barnes & Noble Nook, and Amazon Kindle Fire) or the also popular MOBI format (preferred document type for Kindle devices).

Simulating Kindle Paperwhite Screen

Since the first and most popular e-reader is Kindle, with Kindle Paperwhite having one of the smallest screens available (about 7"), you can use the Page Setup dialog box to simulate how the document will appear on the Kindle screen using these values (Figure 8-13):

- Page size; 3.5 × 4.75.

- Margins: 0.2 all around.

Exercise 1

The objective of this exercise is to format a document to be used as an e-book and export it to Kindle MOBI format using Calibre free software.

You can verify how to format a document to be transformed into e-book by extracting "Sense and Sensibility, Jane Austen eBook.docx" from the Chapter08.zip file and opening it in Microsoft Word. It has the full text of the famous 1811 Jane Austen book.

Follow these steps to verify how this document was formatted for e-book publication:

1. Verify that the document uses 174 pages to show the full book text using the current page size.

2. Double-click the ruler to show the Page Setup dialog box (or use the Margins and Size commands found in the Page Setup area of the Layout tab) and verify that:

   - Page size = Letter (8.5 × 11.5).

   - Margins = Normal (Top = Bottom = 0.98, Left = Right = 1.18).

3. Verify that the document has clean Header and Footer areas.

4. Explore the document text formatting:

   - Book title and Author name received Title (Calibri 16 pt) and Subtitle (Calibri 11 pt) styles, both center aligned (Figure 8-11).

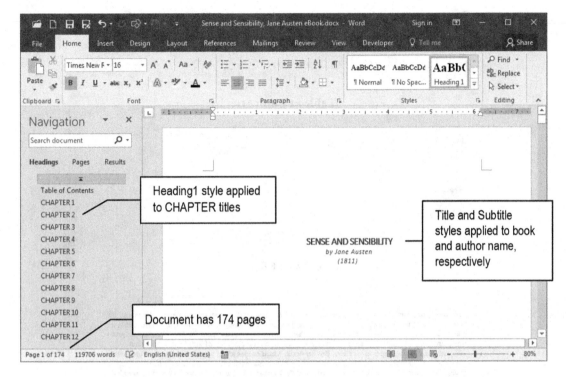

Figure 8-11. *This is "Sense and Sensibility, Jane Austen eBook.docx", which you can extract from Chapter08.zip file. It has the full book text presented in a 174-page document, formatted with Letter page size and Normal margins.*

- All "CHAPTER n" title sections received Heading1 style (Times New Roman 16 pt, center aligned, Space After = 24 pt, Page break before).

- Body text received Normal style (Times New Roman, 10 pt, left aligned, First line indent = 0.06, Widow/Orphan control.

5. The document's Table of Contents uses just the Heading1 style without page numbers for its index entries (Figure 8-12).

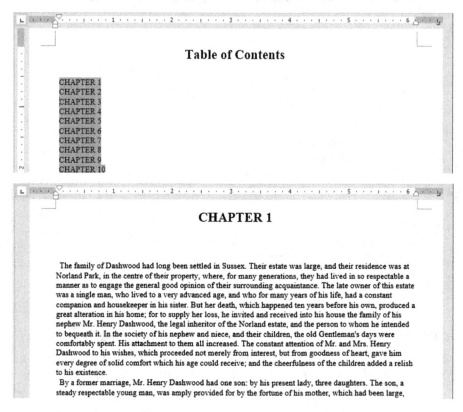

Figure 8-12. *The "Sense and Sensibility, Jane Austen eBook.docx" document's Table of Contents has no page numbers. Each "CHAPTER" section was formatted with Heading1 style (Times New Roman 16 pt, Page break before). Body text was formatted with Normal style (Times New Roman 10 pt, First line indent = 0.06).*

6. Use the Page Setup dialog box to simulate the Kindle Paperwhite screen (Figure 8-13):

    - Page size; 3.5 × 4.75.

    - Margins: 0.2 all around.

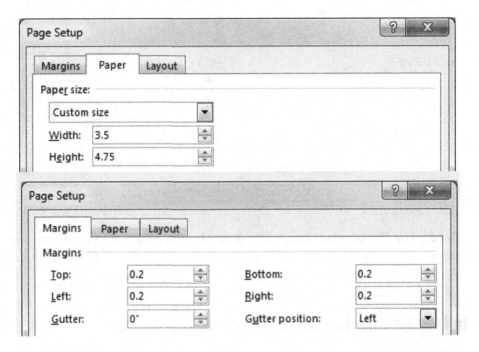

Figure 8-13. *Use the Page Setup dialog box to simulate a Kindle Paperwhite screen (of 7"), using a Paper size Width = 3.5 and Height = 4.75. Define 0.2 margins all around the page.*

Once you change the Paper size for simulating the Kindle Paperwhite screen, note that the page count increased to 573 pages!

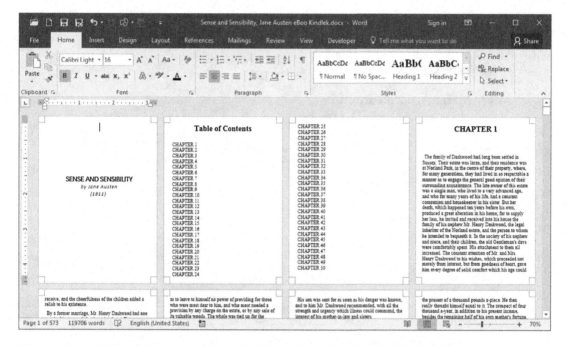

Figure 8-14. The "Sense and Sensibility, Jane Austen eBook Kindle.docx" document, formatted with a 3.5 × 4.75 page size and 0.2 of margins, now with 573 pages, makes a good simulation of a Kindle Paperwhite screen.

Tips to Use Calibre to Produce E-books

Calibre is a free software e-book converter that you can download from this web site:

`https://calibre-ebook.com/download`

Open the Calibre interface and follow these steps to use a Microsoft Word document to produce an e-book:

1. Click the Add Books tool and select the Microsoft Word document file (Calibre will add it to the beginning of its list of files).

2. Click the Edit Metadata tool and fill the Title and Author name (click the arrows at the right of each field to fill the Title sort and Author sort text boxes).

3. If this is a book that already exists on the Internet, use the Edit Metadata dialog box Download Metadata button to search for its metadata.

4. The Calibre Download Metadata dialog box may found in different sources of book metadata. Click the desired metadata and press OK to close the dialog box.

5. Calibre will try to recover book covers from the Internet. If found select the desired book cover in the Download Metadata dialog box.

6. Close the Edit Metadata dialog box to return to Calibre interface and click the Convert Books tool.

7. The selected book metadata will appear in Convert Books dialog box.

8. In the Convert Books dialog box top right corner, select the Output format (MOBI for Kindle, EPUB for other e-readers).

9. Click OK to convert the document.

Calibre creates the Documents, Calibre Library folder where you will find the Author name folder (as defined in steps 2 through 4) with a different folder for each book converted. There you will find your MOBI or EPUB file, ready to be transferred to your e-reader.

Changing the Document Layout

A Microsoft Word document can print differently according to the selections made in the Layout tab of the Page Setup dialog box (Figure 8-15).

- **Section**: This option allows configuration of which type of section this page belongs to. Normally a document has just one section which begins on a new page (default option).

Attention   Section and its types were discussed earlier in Chapter 9, "Section Breaks".

- **Different odd and even**: allows defining if the odd and even pages will have different Header and Footer areas (which is desirable in documents that will be printed on both sides of the paper).

- **Different first page**: allows defining if the first document (or section) page will have a different Header and Footer area.

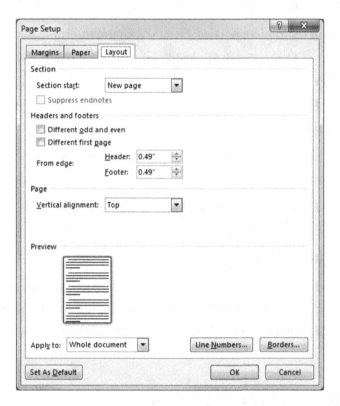

Figure 8-15. *Use the Layout tab of the Page Setup dialog box to configure how Microsoft Word manages the document page Header and Footer and the vertical alignment of the text*

- **From edge**: use the Header and Footer options to change the top margin—or distance from page edge—for the Header and Footer areas (as you can do by dragging their top handles on the vertical ruler or by changing the Header from top or Footer from bottom options found in the Header and Footer Design tab, see Figures 8-4 and 8-5).

- **Vertical alignment**: define how the text will be vertically aligned on each page of this document section. Default is Top, meaning that text begins to print on the top page margin (you can select center bottom or Justify vertical alignments).

Header and Footer for Normal Documents

For the sake of this discussion a *Normal* document is one formatted with Multiple Pages = Normal in the Margin tab of the Page Setup dialog box, intended to be printed using just the front of the page.

Figure 8-16 shows Normal documents A, B, C, and D, which have different numbering options (and consequently different types of pages) according to the state of the Different odd and even and Different first page options found Page Setup dialog box Layout options:

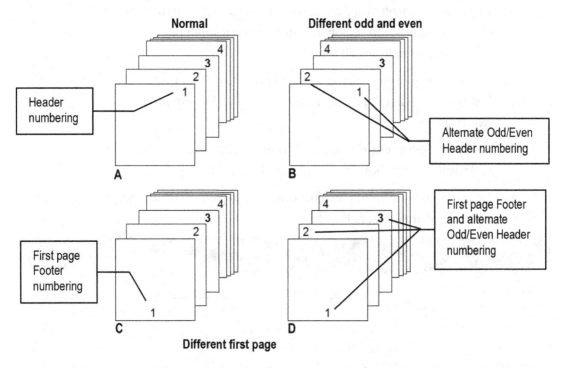

Figure 8-16. *Normal document types (A, B, C, and D) numbered according to the state of the Different odd and even Layout option (right column) and the Different first page option (lower row)*

- **Document A**: pages numbered on the top right side of the page (single page with a Header)

- **Document B**: pages numbered alternating the top left and top right side of the pages (two page types, with an Odd Page Header and an Even Page Header)

- **Document C**: first page numbered on Footer (center aligned). All others numbered on the top right side of the page (two page types, with a First Page Header and a Header)

- **Document D**: first page numbered on Footer (center aligned). All others pages numbered alternating the top left and top right side of the pages (three page types, with a First Page Header and an Odd Page Header and an Even Page Header)

You can reproduce such behavior in Microsoft Word following the next steps:

1. In a new Microsoft Word document, double-click the ruler to show the Page Setup dialog box and format a small page size of 2 × 2, with 0.2 margins all around.

2. Close the Page Setup dialog box and press Ctrl+Enter twice to insert two hidden Page break characters (the document must have two pages).

3. Show the document Header area (double-click the top page area) to activate it and show the Header and Footer Design tab.

4. Note that the document has just one type of page (with a Header and Footer area, Figure 8-17).

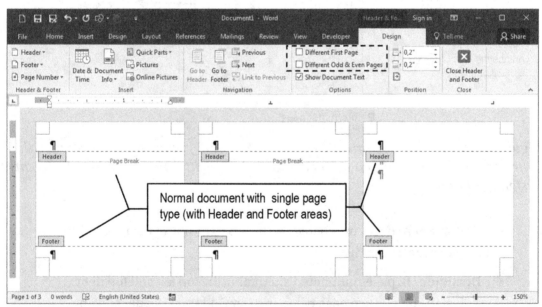

Figure 8-17. *A normal document with two page breaks and a single type of page has just a Header and a Footer area*

5. Check the Different first page options located in the Options area of the Header and Footer Design tab and note that now the first page has the First Page Header and First Page Footer areas, while all other pages have the Header and Footer areas (Figure 8-18).

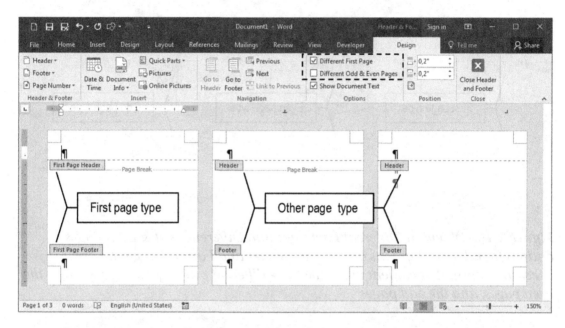

Figure 8-18. *A normal document with the Different first page option set has the First Page Header and First Page Footer areas on its first page, while all other pages have just the Header and Footer areas*

6. Check the Different Odd & Even Pages options located in the Options area of the Header and Footer Design tab and note that now the document has on its first page the First Page Header and First Page Footer areas, on its second page the Even Page Header and Even Page Footer, and on its third page the Odd Page Header and Odd Page Footer areas (Figure 8-19).

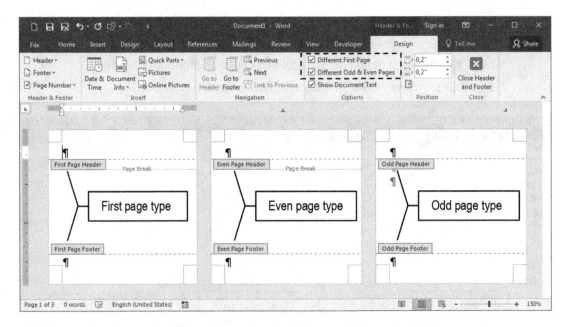

Figure 8-19. *When the Different First Page and Different Odd & Even Pages options found in the Options area of the Header and Footer Design tab are checked, a normal document will have three different page types: the first page, the even pages, and the odd pages*

Follow these tips to navigate to the different types of pages produced by the Different first page and Different Odd & Even Pages options using the Navigation area of the Header & Footer Design tab tools:

- When the Header is activated and selected, use the Go To Footer button to select the Footer of the same page (vice versa with the Go To Header button).

- Press the Next button to go forward on the different page Headers or Footers.

- Press the Previous button to go backward on the different page Headers or Footers.

- Keep the Show document text selected to see the document text grayed (deactivated) when the Header/Footer is activated.

Inserting Header/Footer Objects

You can consider the Header and Footer page areas as mini text editors where you can insert anything, from a single text line, to a table, figure, shape, or object. What you must consider is that everything inserted in the Header or Footer areas will appear on every page of the same type (every normal page, first page, odd or even pages).

You can confirm that by activating any document Header (double-click the top of page Header area) and using the Shapes tool located in the Illustrations area of the Insert tab to insert any kind of shape into the page (Figure 8-20).

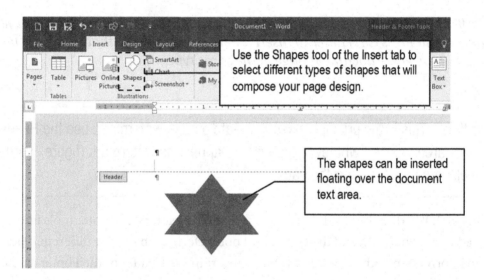

Figure 8-20. *Whatever you insert into the Header or Footer page areas will appear behind the text of every document page of the same type (even if it is floating in the document text area)*

Close the Header area (double-click the document text area) and note that although the star shown in Figure 8-20 was inserted in the page Header area, it is floating outside the Header area over the document text area (inside the document margins). Press Ctrl+Enter to insert another document page and note that it now appears at the same position, behind the text of any document page of the same type (Figure 8-21).

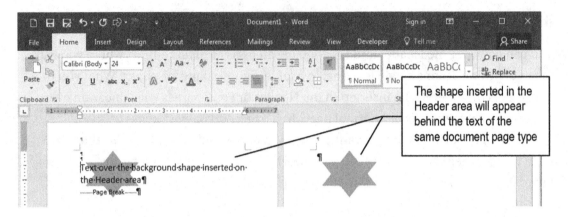

Figure 8-21. *Type some text and note that the shape was positioned behind the document text. Press Ctrl+Enter to insert a new page and note that the shape will now appear on every document page of the same type.*

Attention   This is the principle used to create a page watermark: use the Header or Footer area to insert whatever you want to appear as watermark (figure, word art, table, etc.) floating over the page.

Microsoft Word explores this concept offering the Header and Footer tools found in the Header and Footer area of the Header & Footer Design tab to offer different types of built-in information and shapes that you can insert in the Header or the Footer area of your document (Figure 8-22).

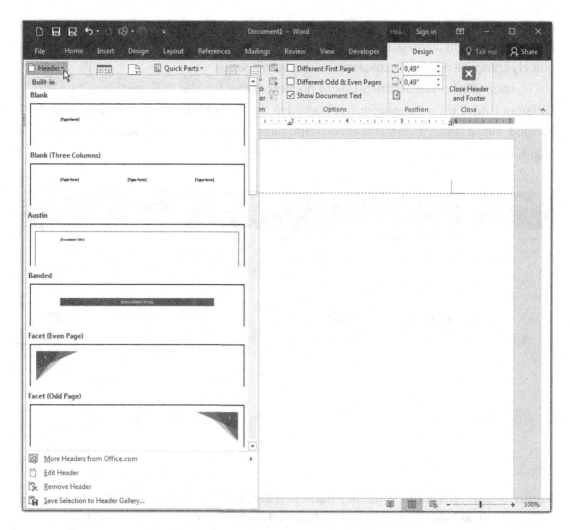

Figure 8-22. *Use the Header and Footer tools found in the Header & Footer design tab to select different built-in texts and objects that you can insert in your document Header or Footer areas to compose its pages*

Attention   The Header and Footer commands are also found in the Head & Footer area of the Insert tab of the Ribbon, whenever the document text is active.

Each available built-in Header and Footer option has a name, and some of them were specifically tailored to be inserted in the First Page Header, Even Page Header, Odd Page Header, or normal Header.

You will find items to insert page number, author name, document title, date, etc., left, center or right aligned; it's a matter of choice and taste to select what is available to quickly compose nice and professional formatting pages.

Figure 8-23 shows a Microsoft Word document that has the Different First Page and Different Odd & Even Pages options checked in the Layout tab, receiving the built-in Banded, Faced (Even page), and Faced (Odd page) inserted into its first, even, and odd pages, respectively.

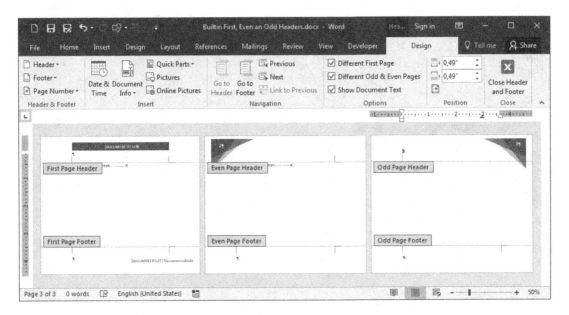

Figure 8-23. *This is the "Builtin First, Even and Odd Header.docx" document, which received built-in formatted options on its first, even, and odd pages*

Inserting Header/Footer Page Numbers

The document information most used in the Header or Footer area of Microsoft Word documents is page numbering, which must be inserted as a calculated field in the Header or Footer page areas, so it can appear on all document pages.

To number the document pages, use the Page Number control found in the Header & Footer area of the Insert tab (or in the Header & Footer Design tab that appears whenever the Header/Footer area is activated, Figure 8-24).

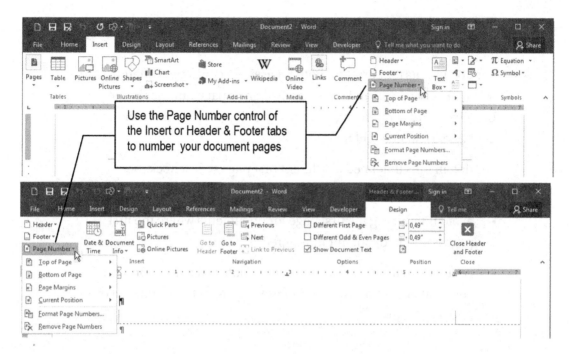

Figure 8-24. *Use the Page Number control found in the Header & Footer areas of the Insert tab or the Header & Footer Design tab shown when the Header/Footer is activated*

You can select to put the page number calculated field at any of the following locations:

- **Top of Page**: meaning the page Header.

- **Bottom of Page**: meaning the page Footer.

- **Page Margins**: positioned at the left or right page margins.

- **Current Position**: where the text cursor is positioned, either in the Header/Footer area or in the document text.

As with the Header and Footer tools, there are many different page numbering options to choose from (Figure 8-25), and you must select them according to the page side (right or left), desired style, and state of the Different First Page and Different Odd & Even Pages options found in the Header & Footer Design tab:

- For Normal documents printed just on one side of the page, insert a right aligned page number in the Header or Footer area.

- For documents that print on both page sides, check the Different Odd & Even Pages option and insert a left aligned page number in the Even Page Header (left page) and a right aligned page number in the Odd Page Header (right page).

- For documents that need a different first page style, check the Different first page option and:

  - avoid numbering the first page for documents where the first page is counted, but not numbered.

  - center align the page number in the Footer area using one of the center aligned options found in the Page Number ➤ Bottom of Page command.

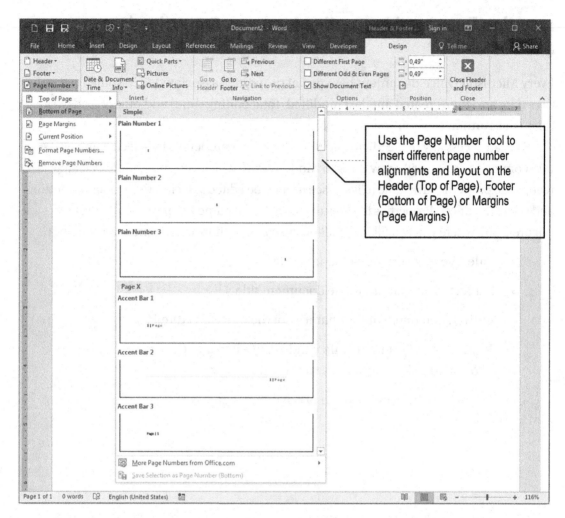

Figure 8-25. *Use the Top of Page, Bottom of Page, or Page Margin options of the Page Number control to select between different numbering alignment and styles*

Inserting Document Properties for Cover Page, Header, and Footer

Every Microsoft Office document has special properties associated to it, some read only (like date and time created and last modified, total editing time) and others read/write (like Title, Author, Description, Tags, etc.)

You can access any of the Microsoft Word document properties by selecting the File ➤ Info command, which will show the Info window, from which you can explore or change the read/write properties available (click to see if it can be edited), or click the Properties button and select Advanced Properties to show the <document name ➤ properties dialog box (Figure 8-26), where you can fill in the following types of information (and many others):

- Title: use to insert the document title.

- Subject: complement to the document title.

- Author: document author name (not the one who edited it).

- Tags: appears just in the Info window, use it to add document information like author name publication, year, etc.

- Comments: brief description of document content.

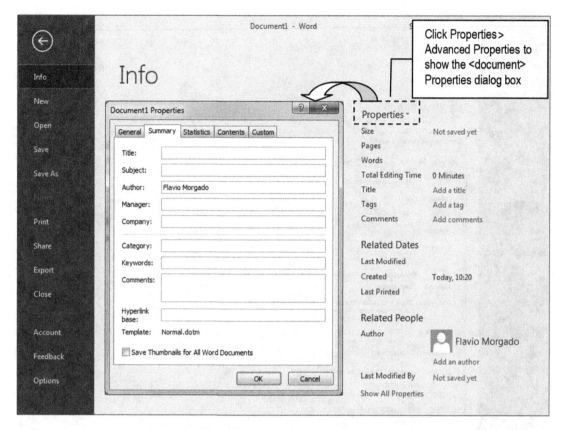

Figure 8-26. *This is Microsoft Word File* ➤ *Info screen, from where you can inspect and change some document properties, or click Properties* ➤ *Advanced Properties to show the <document name> properties dialog box*

The information you insert for the document properties will be used by the Cover Page (Pages area), Header, and Footer (Header & Footer area) commands found in the Insert tab of the Ribbon to generate special cover pages, header and footer content, already formatted with professional building blocks.

Figure 8-27 shows the Info window and Properties dialog box for the "Sense and Sensibility, Jane Austen eBook.docx" document, which identifies the document properties Title, Tags (just in Info window), Author, Keywords and Comments properties set.

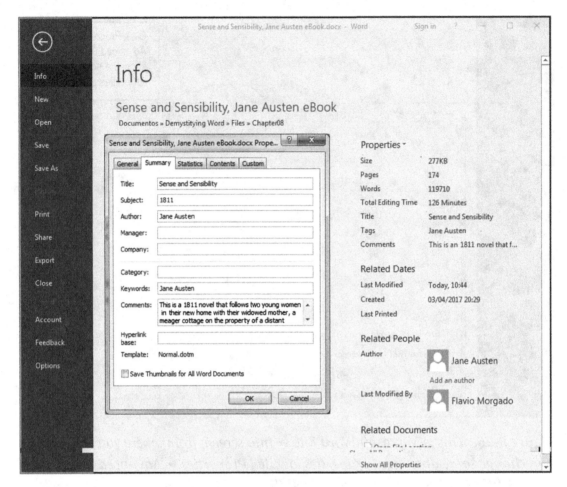

Figure 8-27. *This is the "Sense and Sensibility, Jane Austen eBook.docx"*
document Properties, which can be used by the Cover Page, Header, and Footer
commands of the Insert tab to generate professionally formatted pages, along with
header and footer information

Inserting Cover Pages

By selecting the Cover Page command found in the Pages area of the Insert tab of the
Ribbon, you can select different page styles to compose the document's first page, which
will take advantage of the document Properties you entered to identify the document:
Title, Tags, and Author.

Figure 8-28 shows the built-in Austen cover page style, which uses the document
Title and Subject properties to compose the cover title, inserting the Author property at
the bottom of white rectangle.

Attention   Press Alt+F9 to alternate between field code and field value to see which document property is used in each Page Cover area.

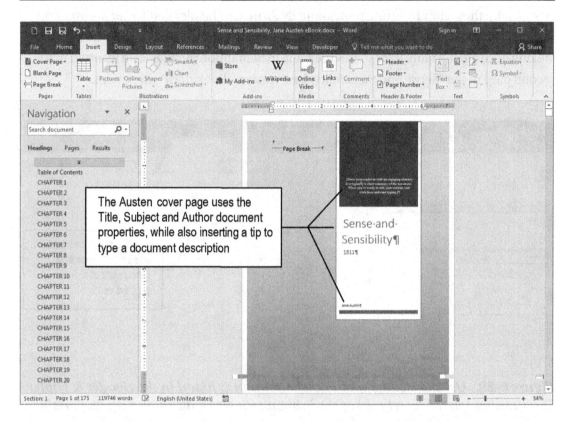

Figure 8-28.   *The built-in Austen cover page used to create a cover page for the "Sense and Sensibility, Jane Austen eBook.docx" document. It uses the document Properties (File ➤ Info) to automatically insert the document Title, Subject, and Author fields into the formatted cover.*

Attention   The built-in Cover Pages reserve places to type another document properties like document description, year, e-mail, and so on. You can insert this information or remove the field from the cover.

Inserting Header/Footer Information

The same is true for the Header and Footer commands found in the Header & Footer area of the Insert tab of the Ribbon (which can also be found in the area of the Header & Footer Design tab): they allow inserting professionally formatted header and footer information that takes advantage of the document Properties inserted by you, to easily create a nice-looking document. Figure 8-29 shows the built-in Semaphore header style inserted in the second page of the "Sense and Sensibility, Jane Austen eBook.docx" document.

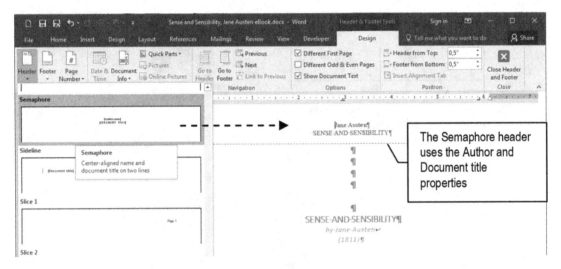

Figure 8-29. *Use the Header and Footer commands found in the Header & Footer Tools Design tab (or Insert tab) of the Ribbon to insert built-in and professionally formatted header and footer information that takes advantage of the document properties you entered*

Attention   The Built-in Cover Page designs are associated to the built-in Header and Footer designs: there is a Semaphore Cover page, Header, and Footer design that you must apply together to get the best formatting effect for your document.

Now it is your turn to try the Cover Page, Header, and Footer option to quickly create different document cover, header, and footer layouts for your documents! Try it!

Formatting Header/Footer Information

Whenever you have a new, empty Header or Footer area active, you have in fact a mini text processor where you can insert any text information needed to format your page headers.

Figure 8-30 shows a new empty Header, with its default empty paragraph (note the pilcrow ¶ character), which is formatted by default as left aligned with two tab stops: a Center tab stop positioned in the middle of the page and a right tab stop positioned on the right page margin. Although you can insert your own tab stops in any Header paragraph, these default tab stops are there to help you easily insert three different pieces of Header information aligned at left (press Tab), center (press Tab), and right margin.

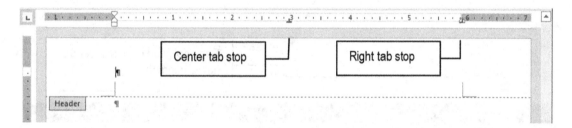

Figure 8-30. *Default Header/Footer paragraph, formatted with a left alignment and two tab stops: a Center tab in the middle of the page and a Right tab on the right page margin*

When you use the Page Number control to insert a Header/Footer left, center, or right aligned page number, Microsoft Word inserts a new paragraph at the Header/Footer area, inserts a Page number field in it, and changes the paragraph Alignment to Left, Center, or Right according to your page number selection: it does not require any tab character to make use of these tab stops (Figure 8-31).

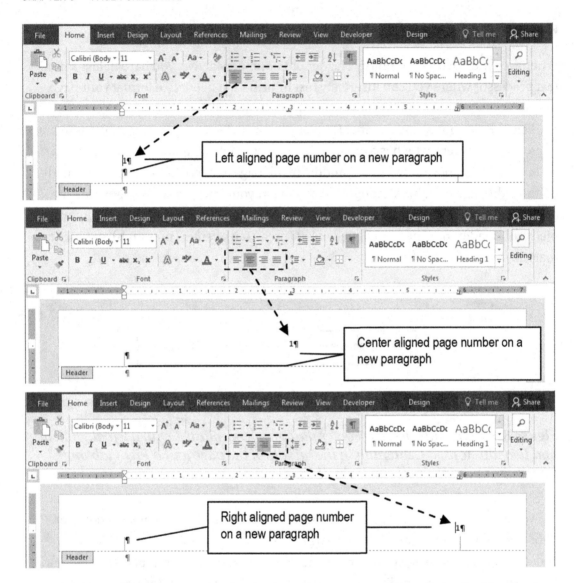

Figure 8-31. *The Page Number control inserts a new paragraph in the Header/Footer, inserts a Page number field, and aligns the paragraph according to the number alignment selected*

This is important because if you want to compose the Header, you will do better using a Left aligned paragraph that can take advantage of using Tab stops to produce the desired effect.

Extract the "Formatted Header and Footer.docx" document from Chapter08.zip file, open it in Microsoft Word, double-click its Header area, and note how its Header paragraph was formatted to present the document title ("Microsoft Word Secrets"), chapter title ("Formatting Header Paragraphs"), and page number (Figure 8-32).

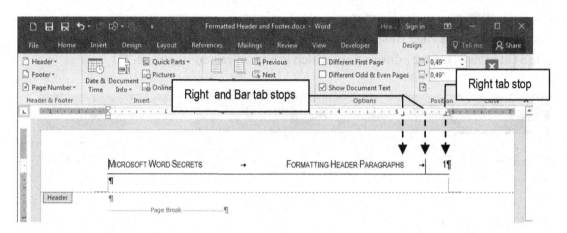

Figure 8-32. *This is the "Formatted Header and Footer.docx" file which you can extract from Chapter08.zip file, format its Header area using three tab stops (Right tab, Bar tab, and Right tab) and hidden Tab characters to perctly align them on the page*

The Header paragraph was composed by using these steps:

1. The Header paragraph was Left aligned

2. The desired information was typed (document and chapter names), separated by a Tab character. Another Tab character was inserted to separate the Chapter name from the page number and formatted with Small caps.

3. The page number was inserted using the Page Number tool and selecting the Current Position ➤ Plain Number option.

4. The default Center tab stop was dragged away from the ruler.

5. A Right tab stop was inserted on the ruler and dragged to correctly position the Chapter name.

6. The Bar tab stop was inserted and positioned on the ruler (the Right tab stop located at the Right paragraph margin was already there).

7. The Border tool found in the Home tab of the Ribbon was used to add a Bottom border to the Header paragraph.

While the Header & Footer Design tab is shown, check the Different Odd & Even Pages options and note that the Header will become Odd Page Header. Since the document has three pages created by two Manual Page Breaks, press the Next button in the Navigation area of the Header & Footer Design tab to navigate to the second page and show the Even Page Header: note how its paragraph was formatted to convey the same Odd Page Header information, which is now mirrored (Figure 8-33).

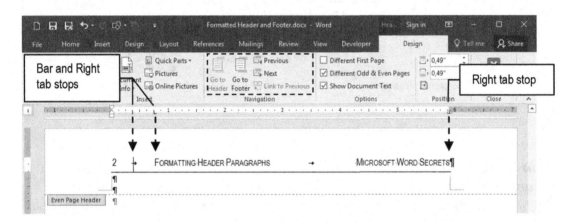

Figure 8-33. *The "Formatted Header and Footer.docx" document Even Page Header is also Left aligned, and it has Bar, Left, and Right tab stops to perfectly mirror the Header (now Odd Page Header) formatting and text presentation*

Now the Even Page Header is a mirrored view of the Odd Page Header. It is still Left aligned with the page number filed inserted as its first character. It then has a Tab stop, the Chapter title, and the Book title, separated by a tab stop. Now a Bar tab and a Left tab stop were inserted on the ruler to correctly position the Even Page Header information (the Right tab located in the right paragraph margin was already there).

Click the Previous button in the Navigation area of the Header & Footer design tab to return to the first document page and check the Different First Page options. Note that the Odd Page Header changed to First Page Header. Click the Go to Footer control in the Navigation area of the Design tab and look how the First Page Footer was formatted (Figure 8-34).

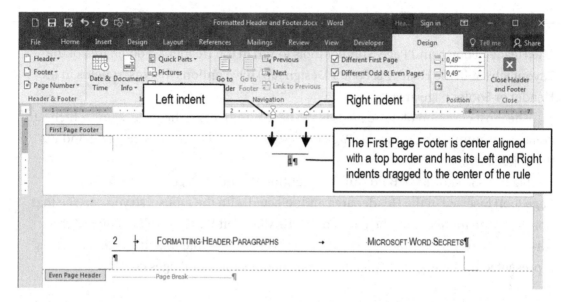

Figure 8-34. *The "Formatted Header and Footer.docx" document First Page Footer is center aligned with a top margin, and it had its Left and Drag indent dragged to the center of the ruler to create this simple effect*

The First Page Footer was created by following these steps:

1. The Footer paragraph was center aligned.

2. The page number was inserted using the Page Number tool and selecting the Current Position ➤ Plain Number option.

3. The Border tool found in the Home tab of the Ribbon was used to add a Bottom border to the Header paragraph.

4. The paragraph Left and Right indents on the ruler were dragged to the center of the page to create the small border above the page number.

Attention   It is interesting to note that once a Header, Even Page Header, and First Page Header are formatted in the document, they will remain there, ready to be used; you can also hide them by unchecking the Different First Page and Different Odd & Even Pages options.

Using Calculated Fields

The Header, Footer, and Page Number tools found in the Header & Footer area of the Layout tab (or in the Header & Footer Design tab) have options that insert fields in the Header or Footer page area.

The most common of these fields is the Page number and the Page count, which can create page numbering using the *Page x of y* style, where *x* is the page number and *y* is the page count.

Figure 8-35 shows the Bold Number 1 option (found in Page Number ➤ Top of Page tool) inserted in the Header area and selected with the mouse, so you can see that both the page number and the page count are Microsoft Word calculated fields (press Alt+F9 to show the field codes instead of their values and note that the page number is represented by the Page field, and the page count by the NumPages field).

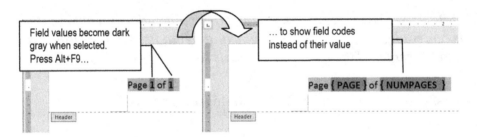

Figure 8-35. *The Page Number insert the page number and page count on the Header or Footer areas using calculated fields (Page and NumPages, respectively). Press Alt+F9 to alternate between the field value and field code*

Microsoft Word has many different field codes that can insert useful system (date, time, folder) and document (page, page count, words count, document name, author, etc.) information. You can show all available fields by selecting the Quick Parts tool Field... option (found in both the Header & Footer Design tab and the Insert Tab of the Ribbon), which will show the Field dialog box, from where you can select a field category and a field value to be inserted anywhere in the document text.

Figure 8-36 shows the Field dialog box with the NumPages field selected in the Field names list (which is part of the Document Information category), and the many format and numeric formats it offers.

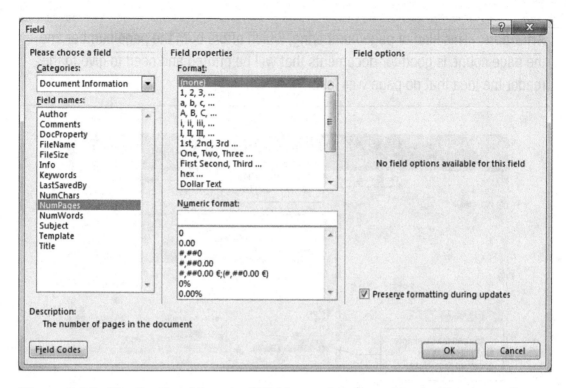

Figure 8-36. *Use the QuickPart tool Field... option (found in the Text area of the Insert tab of the Ribbon) to show the Field dialog box, from where you can select many different types of system and document information to insert into the document as a calculated field*

Use these fields to compose better Header and Footer numbering systems. For example, the Page Number tool has the Accent Bar 1 (left aligned) and Accent Bar 2 (right aligned) numbering option which respectively insert the **n |** Page or Page **| n** (where *n* is the page number) nicely formatted styles of page numbering (the Page word received a Calibri font with character spacing Expanded = 3 pt, using the Advanced tab of the Font dialog box). By using the NumPages field found in the Field dialog box, you can change them to **n of m |** Page or Page **| n of m**, where m represents the NumPages field (Figure 8-37).

Attention   This kind of page numbering, which offers both the page number and the page count, is good for documents that will be printed and need to give to the reader the idea that no page was lost.

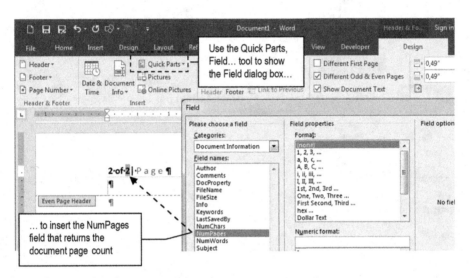

Figure 8-37. *Use the Field dialog box to insert different types of system/document ionformation into the Header and Footer areas of your documents. This figure shows how the Numpages field was inserted in the Even Page Header to format the Accent Bar 1 Page Number ➤ Top of Page numbering option.*

Attention   The "Header & Footer with Accent Bar and NumPages field.docx" document found in Chapter08.zip has such page numbering formatting inserted in the First, Even, and Odd page Header and Footer areas.

Saving New Page Number Formats

Once you have created a new page number format, you can save it so it can be reused later in new documents. To save changes made to the AccentBar 1 page number style shown in Figure 8-33, follow these steps:

1. Select the entire Header/Footer row that has the number format you want to save.

2. Use Save Selection as Page Number... option found in the Page Number tool Top of Page, Bottom of Page, or Current Position options to show the Create New Building Block dialog box (Figure 8-38):

- Name: use it to give a consistent name to the page number format.

- Gallery: define the Page Number command where the page number format must appear (Top of Page, Bottom of Page, Current Position).

- Category: choose the category that best fits to the page number style that's been saved.

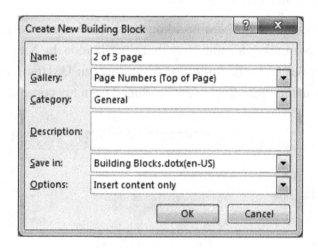

Figure 8-38. *The Create New Building Block*

- Description: use it to give a brief description of the page number style that's been created.

- Save in: use Building Blocks.dotx (en-US) to save it so that it's available in all Microsoft Word documents. Use Normal.dotx to have it available to all documents based on this template only.

- Options: define how the building block will be inserted in a document. This option will have no effect in page number formats inserted on Header/Footer areas:

  a. **Insert content on its own page**: place the building block on a separate page with page breaks before and after the building block.

  b. **Insert in own paragraph**: place the building block into its own paragraph.

  c. **Insert content only**: place the building block as a word sequence inside a sentence.

Figure 8-39 shows the Create New Building Block fulfilled to create a variation of the Accent Bar 1 page number format. Note that since it adds the NumPages field, it was saved as Accent Bar 1.1 in the Building Blocks.dotx (en-US) template, so it can be available in any Microsoft Word document produced from my computer.

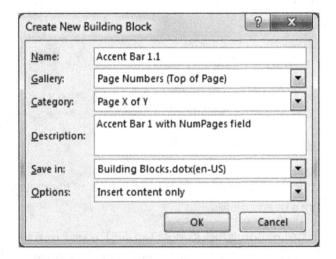

Figure 8-39. *When creating new page number formats based on existing page numbers, use a name variation so it can appear next to the same page number in the Page Number tool options.*

Attention   To remove any page number format inserted, right-click it in the Page Number tool gallery and choose the Organize and Delete... option to show the Building Blocks Organizer dialog box, from where you can change, edit, or delete any available building block.

Formatting PDF Files

PDF—Portable Document Format—is an industry standard created by Adobe to generate electronic read-only documents that can be opened by Adobe Reader, Fox Reader, Nitro PDF Reader, PDF-Xchange Editor, and many other free software packages available on the Internet.

Although you print a PDF file from any Microsoft Windows program by installing and using a PDF Printer program (like CutePDF, DoPDF, PDFCreator, etc.), Microsoft Word can easily create PDF documents using its File ➤ Export command (which also allows you to create an XDF file).

Attention   XDF is the XML version of a PDF file, which was once supposed to become the most used electronic, read-only file type—a forecast that has been confirmed so far.

In general, you must follow these formatting rules to create good-quality PDF files from Microsoft Word documents:

1. Use a popular page format (like Letter or A4).

2. Use Heading styles (Heading1 to Heading9) to format chapter and section titles.

3. Add Header and Footer information for the first page, odd and even pages to

   - Identify the document title on each page.

   - Add page number and page count to each page.

By using Heading styles, you can use Microsoft Word File ➤ Export command and click the Create PDF/XPS button to show the Publish as PDF or XPS dialog box and define the PDF options desired (Figure 8-40).

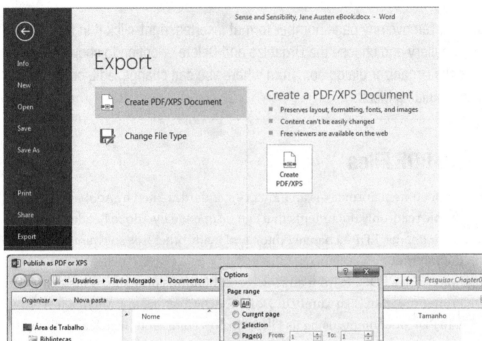

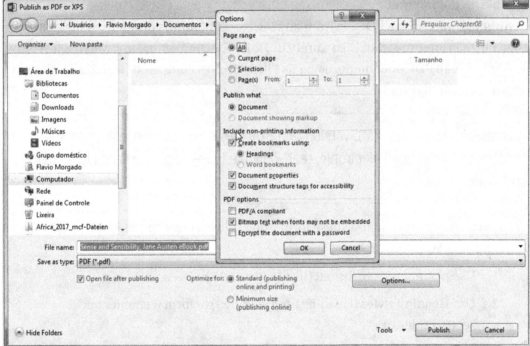

Figure 8-40. *Use Microsoft Word File ➤ Export ➤ Create PDF/XPS Document to show the Publish as PDF or XPX dialog box. Click Options and select Create bookmarks using Headings option to create the PDF Table of Contents (Bookmarks).*

The Create PDF/XPS Option dialog box offers these options:

- **Standard (publishing online and printing)**: document receives the best quality output.

- **Minimum size (publish online)**: document receives minimum image quality settings.

- **Options**: use this button to show the PDF Options dialog box, from where you can use

  - **Page Range area**: decide which pages must be exported to the PDF file.

  - **Publish what**: only document text or text and markups (if any).

  - **Include nonprinting information**:

    a. **Create bookmarks using**: select **Headings** to use Heading styles to create the PDF Table of Contents.

    b. **Document Properties**: save all document properties in PDF, like author name, date created, etc.;

    c. **Document structure tags for accessibility**: tags are for accessibility; they indicate the structure of a document so it can be read for persons with disabilities. They communicate the reading order and determine exactly which items will be read.

  - **PDF Options**:

    a. **PDF/A Compliant**: PDF/A is a new electronic document standard that guarantee that the final PDF will preserves its visual appearance over time independent of the tools that will be used in the future to open it.

    b. **Bitmap text when fonts may not be embedded**: convert text to bitmap when it is not possible to insert the font information in the document.

    c. **Encrypt document with a password**: protect the document with a password, which will be needed to open and read it.

Attention   Whenever your document has Heading styles applied to its chapter and section titles, define the Create bookmarks = Headings. This will make the PDF reader software exhibit the Bookmarks pane, from where you can navigate through the PDF document just like you do using Microsoft Windows Navigation Pane Headings view.

Exercise 2

The objective of this exercise is to produce a nicely formatted PDF file using the "The Last of the Mohicans.docx" document, which you can extract from the Chapter08.zip file; this contains the entire text of the famous James Fenimore Cooper book published in 1826.

Note this document's formatting options:

- Letter paper size with 1" margins all around.

- Formatted with the Black and White (Capitalized) Style set.

- The first two paragraphs received the Title and Subtitle styles (for book title and author name, respectively).

- Heading1 style formatted with Paragraph ➤ Page break before option checked.

- Table of Contents object inserted in its first page because the CONTENT paragraph (formatted with TOC Heading style, which is based on Heading1 style) has its Page break before option unchecked (Figure 8-41).

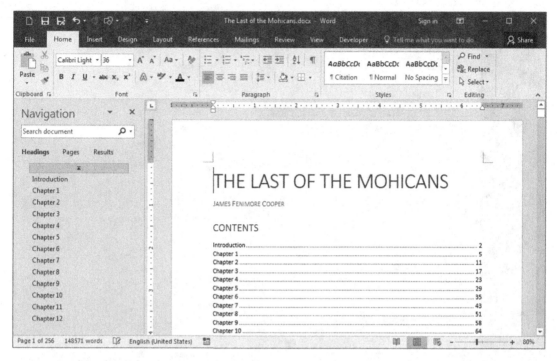

Figure 8-41. *This is "The Last of the Mohicans.docx" document, which you can extract from the Chapter08.zip file with the full book text spread over 256 Letter-size pages (using 1" margins all around and formatted with the Black and White (Capitalized) Style set, with Heading1 style formatted with the Paragraph ➤ Page break before option set)*

The final PDF must have Header/Footer information and Bookmarks to allow easy navigation and better page format whenever necessary.

Attention   The Page Cover, Header, and Footer text and designs proposed in this exercise were chosen solely for educational reasons.

Open "The Last of the Mohicans.docx" document in Microsoft Word and follow these steps:

1. Use the File ➤ Info ➤ Properties ➤ Advanced Properties to show the document Properties dialog box and note how some of its key properties were defined (Title, Subject, Author, Tags, Figure 8-42).

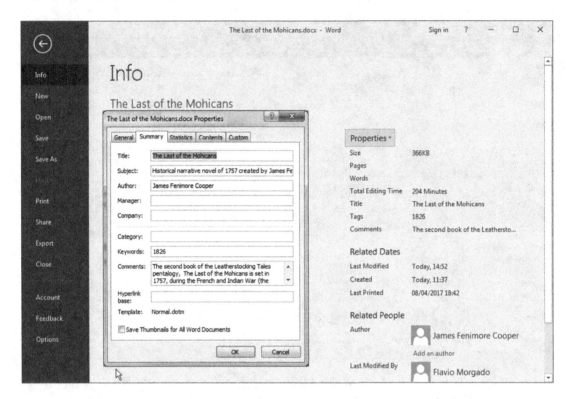

Figure 8-42. *This is "The Last of the Mohicans.docx" document Info window and Properties dialog box. Note the Title, Subject, Author, and Keywords properties.*

2. Use the Insert ➤ Page Cover command to insert the built-in
    Filigree cove page and note how it takes advantage of the Title,
    Subject, and Author name (Figure 8-43).

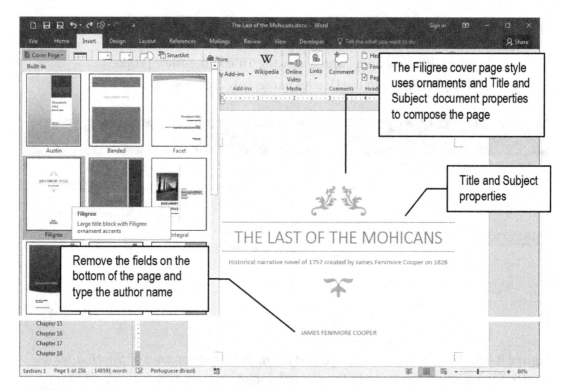

Figure 8-43. Use the Cover Page command found in the Insert tab to insert a Filigree style cover page into the document. Remove the fields inserted in the bottom of the page and type the author name (James Fenimore Cooper).

Attention   Delete the fields inserted by the Filigree cover page at the bottom of the page (Date Company name and Company address) and insert the author name (James Fenimore Cooper) in their place.

3. Double-click page 2 Header area to activate it, and check the Different first page (must be checked) and Different Odd & Even pages options.

Attention   Whenever you insert a Cover Page, Microsoft Word will automatically set the Different first page options and use some unexpected mechanism to number this cover page as page 0 (zero). That is why the next page has an Odd Page Header (page number 1). It seems to be a bug…

4. Use the Header tool found in the Header & Footer Tools Design tab and use the Header ➤ Top of page option to insert right aligned Filigree header (which uses the Title and Author property fields right aligned to the Header paragraph, Figure 8-44).

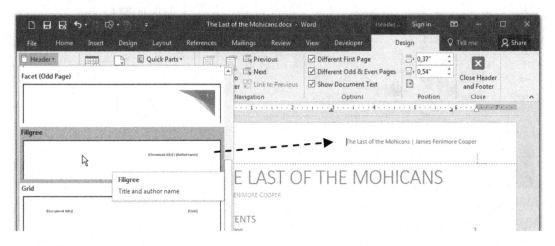

Figure 8-44. *Use the Next button found in the Navigation area of the Header & Footer Tools Design tab to go to the second document page and use the Header command to insert a Filigree header style*

5. Left align the Filigree header, select its entire text (click at right of paragraph to select it), and change its color to black.

6. Press End twice to go to the end of the paragraph header (at right of the Author field), and press Tab to tabulate to the Right tab stop (note that it's not aligned to the right margin).

7. Drag the Right tab stop on the ruler to align it to the right margin and use the Page number tool ➤ Current position command to insert the Accent Bar 2 header style (Figure 8-45).

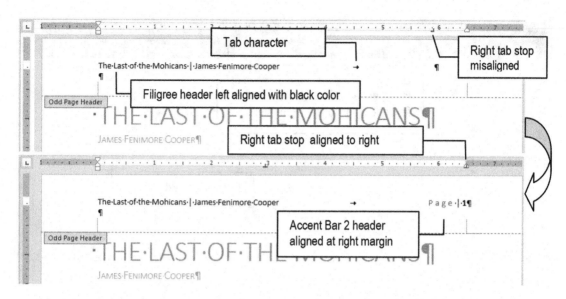

Figure 8-45. *Use the Header tool Top of page command to insert a Filigree header (which uses the Title and Author document property fields), which must be left aligned. Press Tab and use the Page Number tool, Current Position command to insert an Accent Bar 2 page number style and drag the Right tab stop on the ruler to right align the page number.*

8. Once the Accent Bar 2 header is inserted, press End to go to the end of the line, type " of " (note the spaces before and after), and use the Quick parts tool, Field... option to show the Fields dialog box from where you must insert the NumPages field to the right of the header text.

9. Add a bottom border to the Odd Page Header text (Figure 8-46).

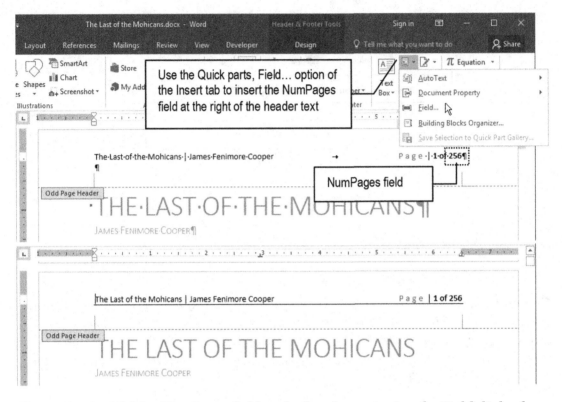

Figure 8-46. *Add the NumPages field to the header text using the Field dialog box, which can be shown by selecting the Quick parts tool, Field...option found in the Insert tab*

10. Click the Next button found in the Header & Footer Tools Design tab to show the Even Page Header (3rd document page, where you find the "Introduction" chapter).

11. Repeat steps 4 to 8 to create the Odd Page Header, noting that since this is an even (left) page, you must

-   Left align the Accent Bar 1 (followed by " of " and the NumPages field) with the left page margin.

-   Use two Tab characters to separate the "Page" expression at right of the page count (NumPages field) from the Filigree header, which must be right aligned with the right page margin (Figure 8-47).

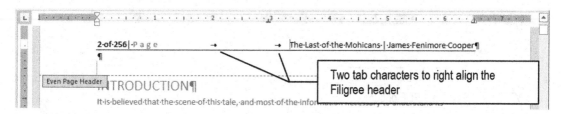

Figure 8-47. *Create the Even Page Header as a mirrored view of the Odd Page Header you see in Figure 8-46: insert the Filigree header style as usual, but now you must use the Accent Bar 1 page number style (followed by the NumPages field).*

Attention   You can delete the center Tab stop in the middle of the ruler scale and use just one tab character to right align the author name.

---

12. Save the document and use the File ➤ Export ➤ Create PDF/XPS button to show the Publish as PDF or XPS dialog box (see Figure 8-40).

13. In the Publish as PDF or XPS dialog box click the Options button to show the Options dialog box.

14. Check the Create Bookmarks using Headings options.

15. Close the Options dialog box and click Publish in the Publish as PDF or XPS dialog box to generate the PDF file in the desired folder (usually the folder from where you open the Microsoft Word file).

You can extract "The Last of the Mohicans for PDF.docx" and "The Last of the Mohicans for PDF.pdf" documents from Chapter08.zip file to see Microsoft Word and PDF versions of this exercise. Figure 8-48 shows how the PDF file will look when opened in Adobe PDF Reader DC 2017, with the Bookmarks option showing all "Chapter" section titles, formatted with Heading1 styles.

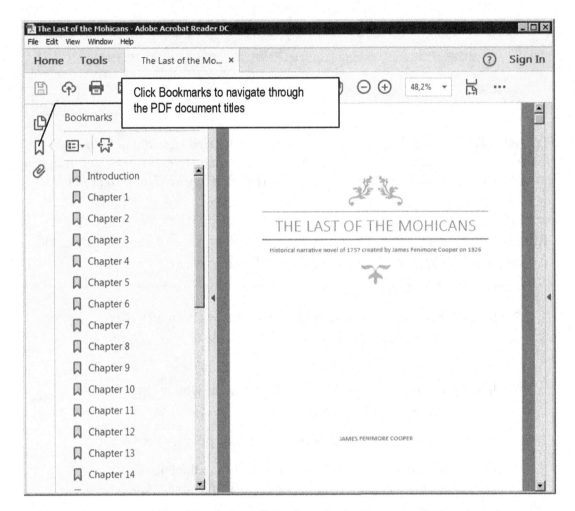

Figure 8-48. *This is Acrobat Reader DC 2017 screen showing "The Last of Mohicans for PDF.PDF" file, which has Bookmarks created by using Heading1 styles in the original Microsoft Word file.*

Formatting Booklets

The term Booklet is usually attributed to a small book made up of to 40 pages, where each sheet of paper is printed on front and back, receiving two pages on each paper side (constituting what is called *a four-page signature*), usually having an outer cover page made up of paperboard (or any other paper of bigger grammage).

To compose a booklet, we can print these four-page sheet signatures and

- individually fold them in the middle, composing a notebook of one sheet of paper; the booklets are then stacked in the right order, receiving staples or spirals to bind the booklets, or;

- stack each four-page signature in the right order, and fold the stacked sheets in the middle to compose a single notebook that is then stapled together in the middle to bind the booklet.

Attention   A variation of this process is to create notebooks of up to ten stacked four-page signatures folded in the middle, which are stacked with other similar notebooks that will be spiral bound to compose the final booklet.

Microsoft Word creates booklets by printing sheet signatures of four document pages, choosing which document pages will be printed on each sheet signature side according to the Sheets per page option that appears whenever you set Multiple Pages options to Book Fold (found in the Page Setup dialog box, Margins tab, Figure 8-49).

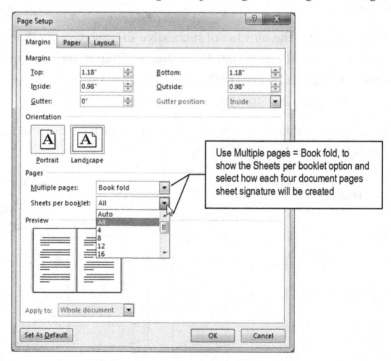

Figure 8-49.   *Whenever you select Multple pages = Book fold in the Margins tab of the Page Setup dialog box, Microsoft Word will show the Sheets per booklet option to allow selection of how each sheet signature of four document pages will be created*

The Sheets per booklet options are as follows:

- **All**: default value, includes all document pages to compose the sheet signatures, which need to be stacked and folded in the middle to compose the final booklet.

- **Auto**: includes up to 40 successive document pages to compose notebooks of up to ten sheet signatures (of four pages each), which need to be stacked and folded in the middle. The notebooks will be then stacked together to compose the final booklet.

- **4**: use four successive document pages to compose sheet signatures that create notebooks of single sheets of paper. The single-page notebooks are then stacked together to compose the final booklet.

- **8**: uses eight successive document pages to compose sheet signatures, which create notebooks of two successive sheets of paper that need to be stacked together and folded in their middle. The two-page notebooks are then stacked together to compose the final booklet.

- **12** to **40**: indicates the number of successive sheet signatures that will create notebooks of a multiple of four sheets of paper that need to be stacked together and folded in their middle (12 = 3 sheet signatures, 16 = 4 sheet signatures, 40 = 10 sheet signatures).

Figure 8-50 shows how this process works using an eight-page document as example and the Sheets per booklet = 4 successive pages.

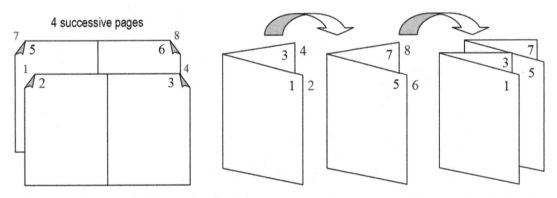

Figure 8-50. *How the Sheets per booklet = 4 option influences the printing process of an 8-page document using booklet signatures of 4 pages*

As you can see, when Sheets per booklet = 4 pages, each sheet of paper will receive four successive document pages. At the left side of the figure you can see that on the first printed sheet signature of four pages (front page), the internal side of the page will receive pages 2 and 3, while the outer side (back of page) will receive pages 1 and 4. The second printed sheet signature will receive pages 5 and 6 (front) and 7 and 8 (back). Since each sheet signature is composed by four successive pages, each one must be folded in the middle to compose a single notebook of four successive document pages, which will then be stacked to bring the right document page sequence to the final eight-page booklet.

Figure 8-51 shows how this process works for the same eight-page document with Sheets per booklet = 8 successive pages.

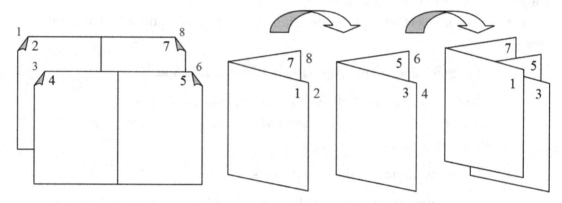

Figure 8-51. *How the Sheets per booklet = 8 option influences the printing process of an 8-page document using booklets of 4-page signatures*

This time things are completely different. When Sheets per booklet = 8 pages, each sheet signature will no longer receive four successive document pages. Since it will use 8/4 = 2 sheet signatures to create each notebook, each sheet signature will receive the page numbers that will give the right page sequence when two successive page signatures are stacked and folded.

At the left side of the figure you can see that on the first printed sheet signature of four pages (front page), the internal side of the page will receive pages 4 and 5, while the outer side (back of page) will receive pages 3 and 6. The second printed sheet signature will receive pages 2 and 7 (front) and 1 and 8 (back). Since these two page signatures must be stacked and folded together to create a two-page notebook made up of eight successive pages, that will bring the right document page sequence to the eight pages of the final booklet.

> **Attention**   Microsoft Word uses the Sheets per Booklet = Auto = 40 pages as a maximum value, because 40/4 = 10 sheet signatures is the maximum number of pages that can be stacked and folded together without creating too much bulk.

If you have long text documents like *Sense and Sensibility* or *The Last of the Mohicans*, which have more than 150 pages (according to page size, margins, and formatting options used), and want to print them and bind them into booklets, you must set Sheets per booklet = Auto or 40, to not end up with many sheets of paper to stack and fold, which will not work for staples or even for the final document paper fold itself, unless if you plan to cut the sheet of papers in the middle using a professional paper cutter, and spiral bind them together.

Whenever you select Multiple pages = Book fold to produce a booklet, Microsoft Word will

- Change the document's page Orientation to Landscape.

- Change page width to half the original height of the paper size selected (if the original page size was Letter, 8.5 × 11, the document page will receive a width = 5.5).

- Double the number of document pages.

- Print the document as expected, but not show how the pages will be printed, either in document view or in the File ➤ Print window.

So, follow these rules whenever you want to produce an appropriate booklet printing:

- Use a font size between 10 pt and 12 pt for the body text.

- Use a font size not bigger than 16 pt for chapter and section titles.

- Change page margins to half the original size.

- Set the Different Odd and Even options in the Headers and footers area of the Layout tab of the Page Setup dialog box.

- Set Sheets per booklet = All, if you plan to cut the sheet signatures in half, using a professional paper cutter.

- Set Sheets per booklet = Auto, if you plan to spiral bind the final booklet, to create notebooks of up to 10 successive sheet signatures (of four pages each).

- Print the book using a PDF printer (like CutePDF) so you can store and see the final result before printing the book (the File ➤ Export to PDF/XPS option will not work this time).

- Use a double-side printer for better results. If you don't have such a printer, print all the odd pages first, invert the printed stack of sheets, put them on the printer tray again (with printed side up), and print all the even pages.

Exercise 3

The objective of this exercise is to show you how to produce a booklet using Microsoft Word and a PDF Printer software to store and show the final result, so it can be easily reprinted in the future. It uses the "European Convention of Human Rights.docx" document, which you can extract from the Chapter08.zip file.

Formatting Tips

Open the "European Convention of Human Rights.docx" document in Microsoft Word and note that the document has 13 pages, receiving Title, Subtitle, Heading1, and Heading2 styles formatted with the Simple style set (selected from the Design tab Style Set gallery). Heading1 style was changed by checking the Paragraph ➤ Page break before option, and Heading2 style was changed by checking the Paragraph ➤ Keep with next option (Figure 8-52).

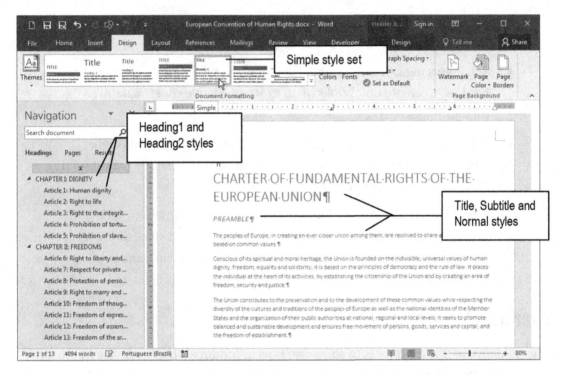

Figure 8-52. *The "European Convention of Human Rights.docx" received styles Title, Subtitle, Heading1, Heading2 (see the Navigation pane), and Normal. It was formatted with the Simple style set selected in the Design tab's Style Set gallery.*

Double-click the ruler to show the Page Setup dialog box, and note in the Page tab that it is formatted with a Letter size page (8.5 × 11), and in the Margin tab that it has Top, Bottom, and Outside margins = 0.5 and Inside margin = 1, with Multiple Pages = Mirror Margins (the inside margin is bigger than outside). In Layout tab note that it has Different odd and even and Different first page options checked, which gives it different first page, odd, and even page headers (Figure 8-53).

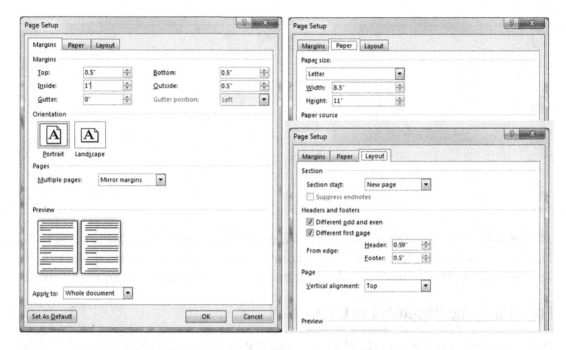

Figure 8-53. *Double-click the ruler to show the Page Setup dialog box and note that the "European Convention of Human Rights.docx" document uses a Letter page, with 0.5" Top, Bottom, and Outside margins, and 1" inside margin, with Different odd and even and Different first page header options checked*

Close the Page Setup dialog box, press Page Down key to move to page 2, and note that it has a Table of Contents. Look to page 2 and 3 headers and note they received the modified Accent Bar 1 and 2 header styles (by adding the NumPages field), and that there is just one Right tab stop positioned at the inside margin of the Even Page Header and likewise at the outside margin of the Odd Page Header (right margin of both page types).

With the Show/Hide button selected in the Home tab of the Ribbon, note that both the Odd and Even Page Header text received just one Tab character to correctly align its text (Figure 8-54).

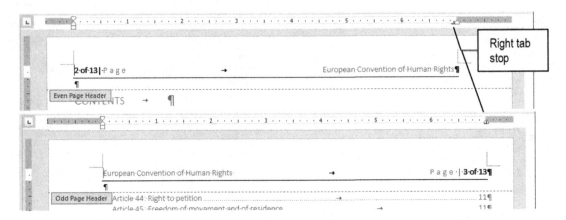

Figure 8-54. *The Even and Odd Page Headers for the "European Convention of Human Rights.docx" document has just one Right tab stop positioned at the inside even page margin and outside odd page margin (right margin of both page types)*

Formatting the Document to Booklet

To convert this document to a booklet and print a PDF of it, follow these steps:

1. Double-click the ruler to show the Page Setup dialog box, select the Margins tab, and set these options:

    - Multiple Pages = Book Fold.

    - Sheets per booklet = All

2. Note that page Orientation changes to Landscape and becomes disabled, and page margins Top and Inside exchange their values (Top = 1" and Inside = 0.5", Figure 8-55).

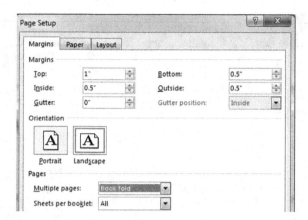

Figure 8-55. *When Multiple pages is changed to Book Fold, page Orientation changes to Landscape and Top and Inside margins exchange their values. Paper side remains Letter.*

3. Close the Page Setup dialog box, look at the ruler scale, and note that although the document paper size is still Letter (8.5 × 11), the document page width is now half of the height of a Letter size page (5.5″), and its height is the page size width (8.5″). The document text reflux has increased its page count to 23 pages (Figure 8-56).

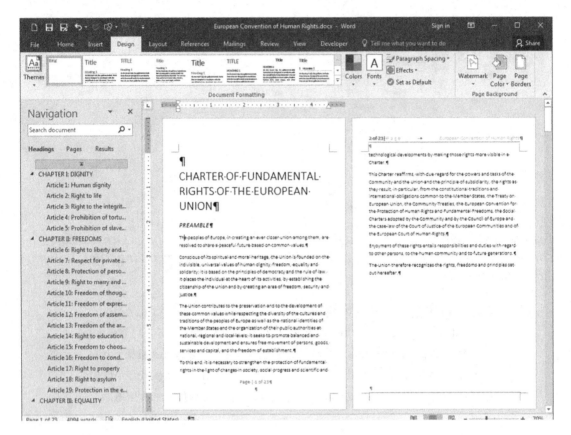

Figure 8-56. *When the Page Setup ➤ Margins ➤ Multiple pages command is changed to Book Fold, the document page remains the same, but it changes its orientation to Landscape with each document page changing its width to half the page height and its height to the page width*

4. Select File ➤ Print and note that Microsoft Word does not show the final appearance of the booklet's four-page signature (although it will print correctly if you try, Figure 8-57).

5. To see how each page (front or back) will be printed, you must select a PDF printer from the Printer list. If you don't have a PDF printer installed, you can select the Microsoft XPS document writer, which will print a XPS document (XML Paper Specification).

6. The PDF or XPS printer selected will ask for a folder and file name to save the final file (CutePDF writer will offer to save it with the same file name using the PDF extension).

7. Open Windows Explorer (press Window key+E), navigate to the folder where the XPS or PDF file was saved, and double-click it to show how its booklet pages were generated.

Figure 8-57 shows the XPS Viewer window with the "European Convention of Human Rights.xps" document opened, showing its first two pages, which must be printed on a single sheet of paper, using front and back printing (duplex printing).

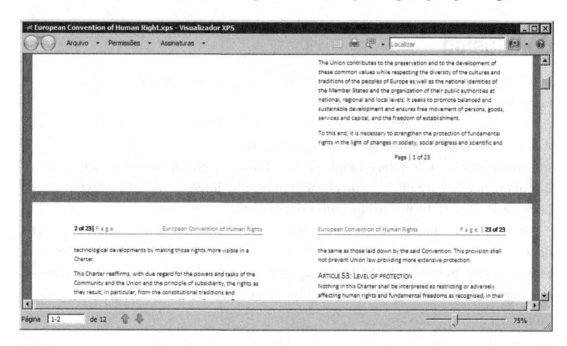

Figure 8-57. *This is the "European Convention of Human Rights.xps" document opened in Microsoft Windows XPS Viewer, showing the first two XPS pages, which must be printed on a single sheet of paper, using front and back. Page 1 (front) has an empty page (booklet's last page) and document page 1. Page 2 has document pages 2 and 23, side by side.*

Since Figure 8-55 used Sheets per booklet = All, all pages were used to generate the final print, and that is why the first XPS page (front) has a white page at left and document page 1, while second XPS page has document pages 2 and 23 side by side.

To create the final booklet, you just need to print all 12 pages of the XPS or PDF document using a front and back printer, fold the final print in the middle, and add its staples to the fold (don't forget the paperboard cover!).

Attention   The Chapter08.zip file has both the "European Convention of Human Rights Booklet.docx" Microsoft Word document and the "European Convention of Human Rights.xps" XPS booklet printing, which you can extract to see how they were created.

Conclusion

In this chapter, we discussed page formatting: size, orientation, margins, and header and footer areas.

You learned how to access these areas using a double-click, and how to format them using the ruler controls or the page setup dialog box.

Microsoft Word offers the Header & Footer Tools Design tab full of important tools that allow creation of a different first header page, and different odd and even pages for documents that can be printed on both sides of paper.

We also talked about how to create well-formatted e-books, how to export good PDF documents (using the Table of Contents to generate the PDF BookMarks), and how to create booklets by setting the Multiple pages option to Book Fold, and the differences that may arise by selecting the Sheets per booklet options.

Summary

In this chapter you learned:

- That you can open the Page Setup dialog box by double-clicking the ruler.

- That every document page has three main independent areas: the Header, the Footer, and the space between the margins.

- That everything you put in the Header will appear on all document pages that has this header.

- That you can create different headers for the first, odd, and even document pages.

- That Microsoft Word has page styles to insert as document cover pages.

- That each Microsoft Word document has properties that can be set using the File ➤ Info command, which will be automatically inserted in these page styles.

- That the Header and Footer commands found in the Insert or Header & Footer Tools Design tabs can be used to automatically insert professionally formatted text that uses these document properties (like Title, Author, etc.).

- How to use the Header and Footer Tools Design tab commands to move from header to header or footer to footer, and how to alternate between the page Header and Footer areas with a click of the mouse.

- That the Page Number tool found in the Insert or Header & Footer Tools Design tabs can be used to generate different page numbers located in page Header, Footer, or margins.

- How to use the Insert ➤ Quick Parts ➤ Field... tool to show the Field dialog box from where you can select different document information fields that can be used in your document text.

- That you can use Alt+F9 to alternate between field value and field code.

- How to produce a Page x of y header, where x is the page number and y is the page count.

- How to use the Header and Footer tab stops to best align the Header and Footer text.

- How to professionally format a Microsoft Word document to produce nice PDF files.

- How to use the File ➤ Export to PDF/XPS tool and its Options dialog box to create PDF files that use document Headings to create PDF Bookmarks.

413

- How to take advantage of Microsoft Multiple pages option found in the Page Setup dialog box Margins tab to produce nice formatting.

- How to use the Sheets per booklet option to produce different booklet styles using a four-page signature.

In the next chapter, you will learn about how to use Section Breaks to create different document sections that can have different page formatting options (like numbering, orientation, and vertical alignment).

CHAPTER 9

Section Breaks

Although Microsoft Word doesn't have a "page style" resource, which is commonly found in other popular text processors (like BROffice, LibreOffice, or professional desktop publishing tools like Quark XPress and Adobe InDesign), it can produce different page styles in a single document by dividing the document into sections.

In this chapter, you will learn how to use the different types of Section Breaks to control page formatting and have greater control over the document text flow, including the use of columns, numbering, page size, orientation, and vertical alignment. All the documents cited in this chapter can be found by downloading the Chapter09.zip file from this Internet address:

```
https://github.com/apress/msft-word-secrets
```

What Is a Section Break?

Section Break is the traditional way that Microsoft Word uses to allow changes to the text flow and alignment inside a single page or to use different page formatting options in a single document, including page numbering.

There are two main types of section breaks:

- **Continuous**: used to change the text flux inside a page, allowing the creation of columnated text.

- **Page break**: used to insert a new page, allowing page numbering control inside the document.

Every Microsoft Word document has at least one section called "Section 1". Earlier versions showed this information by default on the Status bar, but this gave more confusion than explanation, and since the advent of Microsoft Office 2007, this information is no longer available by default: but it is still there!

415

To show section number information, right-click Microsoft Word status bar to show the Customize Status Bar menu and click Section at the top of the list to see that the word "Section 1" appears at the left of the page number (Figure 9-1).

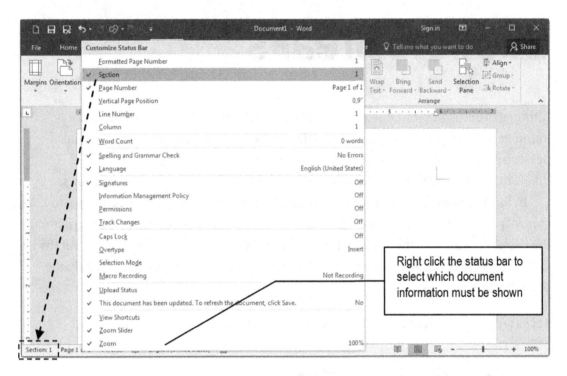

Figure 9-1. *Right-click Microsoft Word Status bar to show the Curstomize Status Bar pop-up menu and click Section to see section number information for any document*

Inserting Section Breaks

You can insert a Section Break, or in other words, create another section in any Microsoft Word document, by using the Section Breaks area of the Breaks tool found in the Page Setup area of the Layout tab of the Ribbon (which can also be used to insert Page Breaks, Figure 9-2).

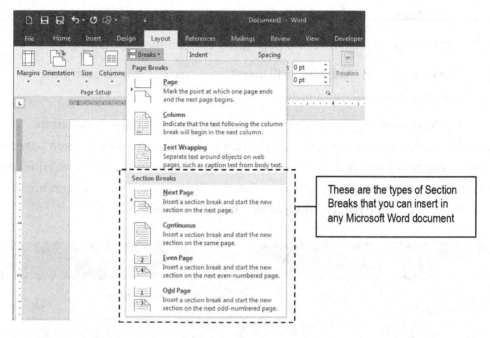

Figure 9-2. *Use the Breaks tool found in the Layout tab of the Ribbon to select different types of section break to be inserted in the current position of the document and create another section*

Types of Section Breaks

You can select among these types of Section Breaks to insert into a document:

- **Continue**: type of section break used to produce text columns on the document page.

- **Next page**: type of section break that is also a page break, in the sense that the next page begins on a new document section.

- **Even page**: type of section break that is also a page break, but makes the next page receive the next even number available.

- **Odd page**: type of section break that is also a page break, but makes the next page receive the next odd number available.

For those who are wondering why there are so many different types of section breaks, you may note that some Section Breaks are also page breaks (the ones that have the word "page" on it), and these will work this way:

- **Continue**: doesn't break the document into another page.

- **Next Page**: will insert a new page using consecutive numbering.

- **Even Page** and **Odd Page**: will insert a new page that will receive the next even or odd numbering.

The "Different Section Breaks.docx" document, which you can extract from Chapter09.zip, has all four types of section breaks: Continue, Next Page, Even page, and Odd page. Figure 9-3 shows the first document page (Page 1) with the Show/Hide tool checked, so you can see that this page has Continuous and Next Page section breaks, one after another, with some paragraphs inserted in between them.

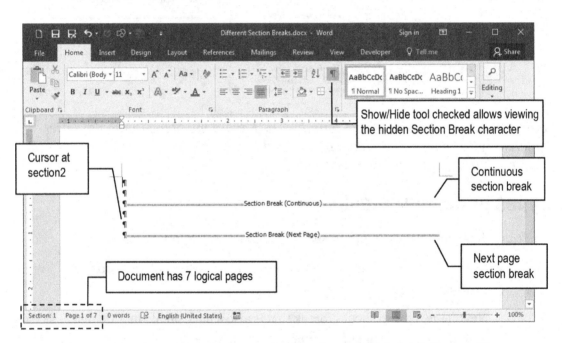

Figure 9-3. *The "Different Section Breaks.docx" document has all possible section break types. Page 1 has a Continuous and a Next page section break. They are visible because the Show/Hide tool is checked in the Home tab of the Ribbon.*

Attention   Although the Section Break appears as a double line with a title showing the section break type, I use the term "Section Break Character" because you can select the section break in the text as you do to select any single text character: press Shift+Right arrow or drag the mouse over it.

Note that the document first page shown on Figure 9-3 has the text cursor positioned in a Section 2 paragraph (continuous section) and that it has seven logical pages (Status bar indicates Page 1 of 7). Do the following exercise using the "Different Section Breaks. docx" document:

- Press Ctrl+Page Down on page 1 to go to page 2 (even page); note that the Status bar considering it as Section 3, Page 2 of 7, and that it has a Section Break (Even Page) (Figure 9-4).

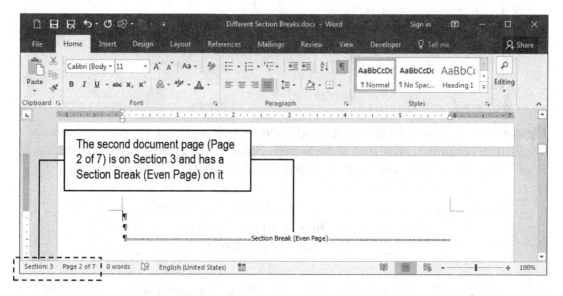

Figure 9-4. *The second page of "Different Section Breaks.docx" document, numbered as Page 2 of 7, has an Even Page section, being part of Section 3*

- Press Ctrl+Page Down in Section 3, Page 2 of 7 to go to the next page and note that the Status bar considered it as Section 4, Page 4 of 7 (even page). There is no page 3 due to the Section Break (Even Page) inserted in *physical* page 2, and it has another Section Break (Next Page) inserted (Figure 9-5).

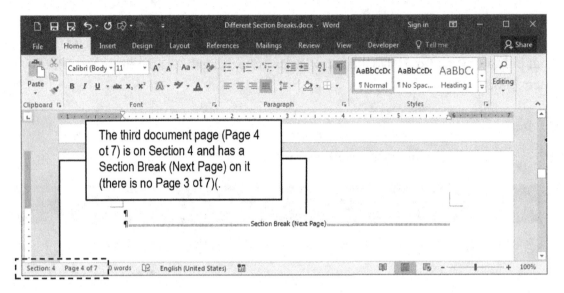

Figure 9-5. *Section 4, Page 4 of 7 of "Different Section Breaks.docx" document is the 3rd physical document page due to the Section Break (Even Page) inserted in Section 3, Page 3 (there is no Page 3 of 7). It also has a Section Break (Next Page) inserted*

- Press Ctrl+Page Down in Section 4, Page 4 of 7 (*physical* page 3) to go to next page and note that the Status bar considered it as Section 5, Page 5 of 7, which also has a Section Break (Odd Page) (Figure 9-6).

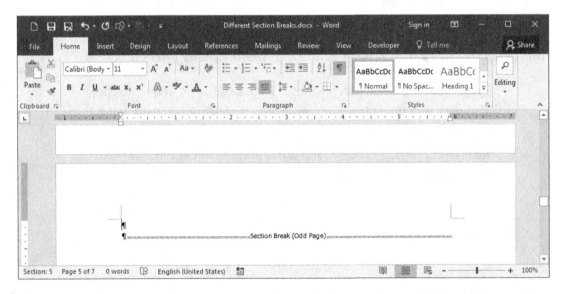

Figure 9-6. *Section 5, Page 5 of 7 of "Different Section Breaks.docx" document is the 4th physical document page and has a Section Break (Odd Page) inserted*

- Press Page Down in Section 4, Page 5 of 7 to go to the last document page and note that the Status bar considered it as Section 6, Page 7 of 7 (*physical* page 4). There is no page 5, due to the Section Break (Odd Page) inserted in logical Page 5 of 7 (Figure 9-7).

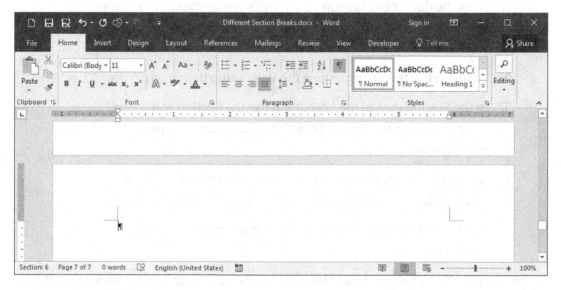

Figure 9-7.   *Section 6, Page 7 of 7 of "Different Section Breaks.docx" document is the 5th physical document page due to the Section Break (Odd Page) inserted in Section 5, Page 5 of 7, and has a Section Break (Next Page) inserted*

You may note that I am using the term *physical page*, because different page breaks can lead to a disagreement between the real page sheet printed and its *logical* page number.

Whenever any Microsoft Word document *logical* even page number receives an Even Page section break, the next page will miss the next sequential odd number, receiving instead the next *logical* even number. The same is true for when any *logical* odd number page receives an Odd Page section break; the next page will be the next odd number, and the even page number in between them will not exist in the document.

Changing Section Break Type

You can change the section break type by two ways:

- Deleting the hidden Section Break character and inserting another Section Break of the desired type; or

- Using the Page Setup dialog box to change the Section Break type.

Both methods will work, but the first one (delete and insert another Section Break) may lead to losing some section information (like section Header/Footer text), which is not recommended. So, use the Page Setup dialog box to change the section type following these steps:

1. Click the document Section where you want to change the Section Break type (look to Microsoft Word Status bar to recognize the section number).

2. Double-click the Ruler to show the Page Setup dialog box.

3. In the Section area of the Layout tab use the Section star control to select the type of section (it will show the current type of break used by this section).

4. Look to the Apply to option located at the bottom of the Page Setup dialog box and confirm that it is set to "This section".

5. Press OK to close the Page Setup dialog box and change the section type.

Figure 9-8 shows how you can change the 6th page of the "Different Section Break. docx" document from Odd Page to New Page, effectively inserting a Page 6 of 6 in the document (which does not exist due to the Section Break (Odd Page) inserted on Page 5).

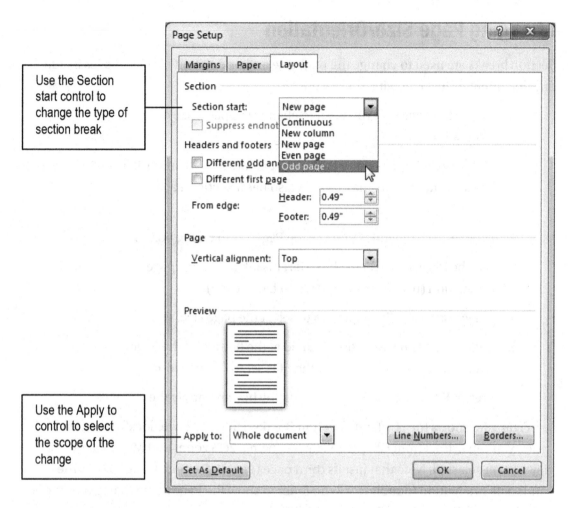

Use the Section start control to change the type of section break

Use the Apply to control to select the scope of the change

Figure 9-8. *Whenever you need to change any Section break type, use the Page Setup dialog box instead of delete and reinsert a new Section Break*

Attention   To apply the same breaks to the entire document, press Ctrl+A to select the document text and use Section start option located in the Apply tab of the Page Setup dialog box to define the default Section Break type. The Apply to combo box must show "Selected Sections" to indicate that all selected sections will be affected by this change.

Changing Page Size/Orientation

Section breaks are used to change the page size and orientation of select pages inside any document by just following these steps:

1. Locate the page that you want to change the page size or orientation.

2. Make sure it has a Section Page Break before it (and unless it is the last document page, make sure it also has a Section Page Break after it).

3. Double-click the Ruler to show the Page Setup dialog box.

4. Use the Page Setup dialog box Margins tab to change page orientation (usually from Portrait to Landscape).

5. If necessary, use the Paper tab to select the page size.

6. Look to the Apply to option located at the bottom of the Page Setup dialog box and confirm that it is set to "This section".

7. Press OK to close the Page Setup dialog box and apply the change.

Figure 9-9 shows the "Different Section Breaks, Different Page.docx" document, which you can extract from Chapter09.zip file, with a 20% zoom and Many Pages view option selected. Note that just its third page (Page 4, Section 4, Page 4) has the Landscape orientation (double-click the Ruler to show the Page Setup dialog box and note that just this page has this orientation).

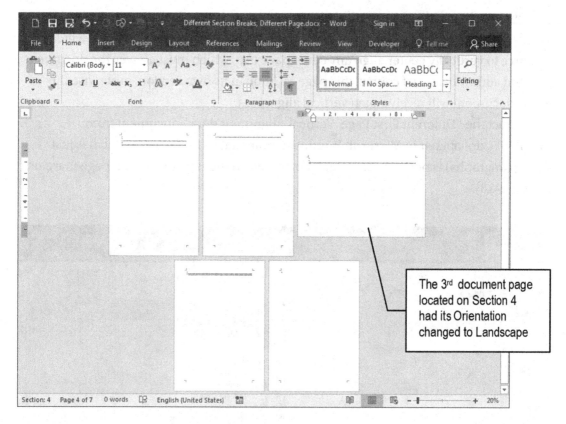

Figure 9-9. *This is the "Different Section Breaks, Different Page.docx" document, which has a single page of different orientation*

Attention   Double-click the zoom tool at the right of Microsoft Word status bar to show the Zoom dialog box, from where you can select the Many pages option.

Whenever you need to use a page of different size in any document, be careful to select the printer tray from where this page size must be drawn. Note that this kind of selection may lead to printing problems with printers that do not have multiple trays from which they can draw pages.

Changing Page Vertical Alignment

Section Breaks are also fine to change page vertical alignment, which is a document resource seldom used on purpose but commonly activated unintentionally, leading to odd behaviors in the document.

You can change the page vertical alignment using the Vertical alignment option found in the Page area of the Layout tab of the Page Setup dialog box, and it is a great resource to vertically center align any cover page text, which must convey the document title and author name. Of course, this page must be in its own section, otherwise the entire document will receive such vertical alignment.

Extract the "Different First Page, Vertical Alignment.docx" document from Chapter09.zip, open it in Microsoft Word, and note that its first page (which has just three paragraphs) is perfectly center aligned between the top and bottom page margins (Figure 9-10).

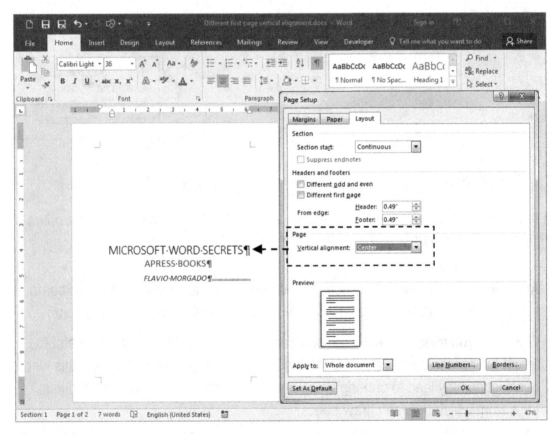

Figure 9-10. *This is the "Different First Page vertical alignment.docx" document you can extract from Chapter09.zip. Its first page has just three paragraphs center aligned between the top and botton page margins, using the Vertical Alignemnt command found in the Layout tab of the Page Setup dialog box.*

Section Inheritance

You already know that the Section Break is a hidden Microsoft Word character that is not part of the paragraph: it is positioned in between two paragraph breaks, can be viewed whenever you check the Show/Hide tool in the Paragraph area of the Home tab of the Ribbon, and can produce a numbering change in the document pages according to the type of section break inserted.

So you must be aware that whenever you insert a section break into a document:

1. A new section is created below the current section, receiving consecutive numbering (Section 2, Section 3, etc.).

2. All page formatting options (including Header/Footer formatting and text) are inherited by the new section from the previous section.

3. The hidden Section Break character holds all the formatting options used to format the section below it, until it finds another section break or the end of the document.

Let's see a practical example of how this happens. Extract "Section Inheritance.docx" document from Chapter09.zip file and open it in Microsoft Word. Note that it has just a single page, with the Header text "Section 1 FIRST PAGE HEADER". Double-click the Header area and note in the Header & Footer Tools Design tab that both the Different First Page and Different Odd & Even Pages options are checked, meaning that this document has three different types of headers (first, even, and odd page, Figure 9-11).

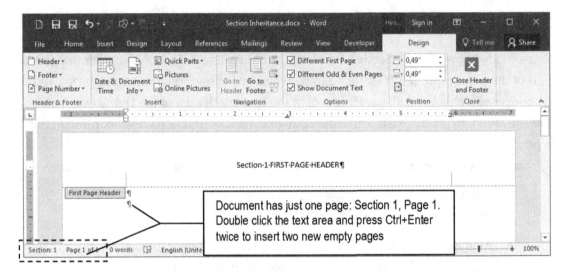

Figure 9-11. *The "Section Inheritance.docx" document, which you can extract from Chapter09.zip file, has just one page and the text "Section 1 FIRST PAGE HEADER" inserted in its First Page Header. It has the Different First Page and Different Odd & Even Pages options checked.*

Double-click the text area and press Ctrl+Enter twice, to insert two new empty pages in the document (one even [page 2] and one odd [page 3]). Use Ctrl+Page Up and Ctrl+Page Down to show the beginning of each document page and see that both the odd and even pages already have Header text inserted (Figure 9-12).

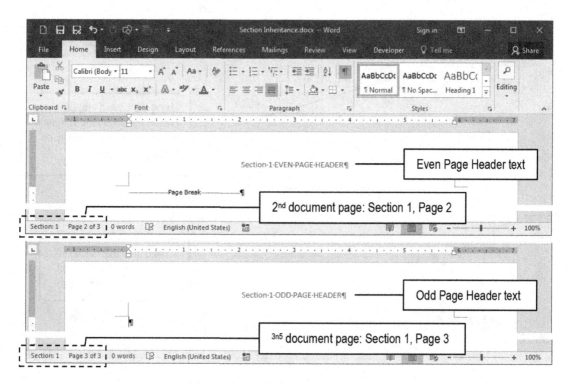

Figure 9-12. *Press Ctrl+Enter twice in the "Section Inseritance.docx" document to insert two new pages (even and odd) and note that its Section 1 already stores its Even and Odd Page Header text*

Although "Section Inheritance.docx" has no "Section 1" section break hidden character, it still stores the information regarding the text for its headers area somewhere inside the document, as you may realize by inserting two new pages in the document to reveal the Even and Odd Page Header texts.

Supposing that you are on the third empty document page, press Enter to insert a new paragraph and use the Layout ➤ Breaks ➤ Next Page command to insert a section break hidden character that will break the document into a new section (Section 2), inserting its fourth document page. Double-click Section 2, Page 4 Header area and note that it is named First Page Header - Section 2 (Figure 9-13).

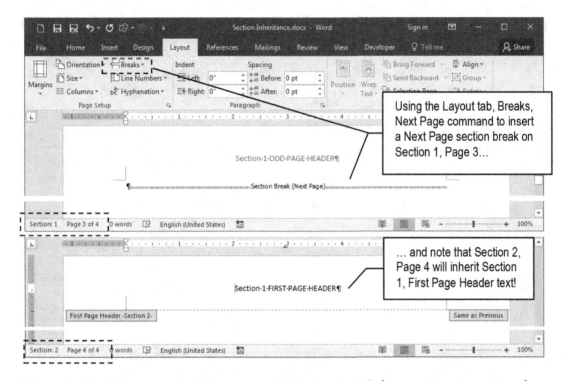

Figure 9-13. *Whenever you insert a new Section Break (even a Continuos one), the next section will inherit all previous section formatting options. Since Section 1 has the Different First Page option checked, Section 2 will also has a First Page Header, inheriting Section 1 First Page Header text.*

As you can see, Section 2, Page 4 begins another document section that inherits all Section 1 formatting options: since Section 1 has the Different First Page option checked, Section 2 will also have it, inheriting not only the section formatting but also the default "Section 1, FIRST PAGE HEADER" text!

Once more, while the cursor is at Section 2, Page 4 first paragraph, press Ctrl+Enter twice again in Section 2, Page 4 to insert two new empty document pages (odd page 5 and even page 6), and note that they both inherited the Section 1 Odd Page Header and Even Page Header texts (Figure 9-14).

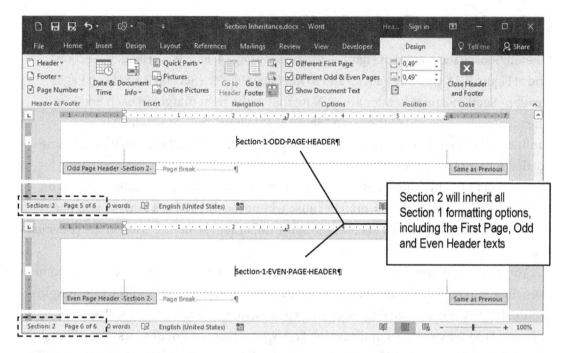

Figure 9-14. *By inserting two new empty pages in Section 2 (pages 5 and 6), since Section 1 has the Different Odd & Even Pages option checked, they will also inherit Section 1 Odd and Even Page Header texts*

And this behavior will continue, on and on, as new section breaks are inserted in the document.

Attention   Even if the Different First Page option is checked, the Continuous section break creates a new document section that does not generate a new First Page Header, but creates Odd and Even Page Headers if the Different Odd & Even Pages option is checked.

Linked Header/Footer Sections

Carefully look at the bottom of Figure 9-13, showing Page 4, First Page Header - Section 2, and at Figure 9-14, showing Pages 5 and 6 Odd Page Header - Section 2 and Even Page Header - Section 2 page header areas. Note that at the right margin of each Section 2 header (pages 4, 5, and 6) there is a "Same as Previous" indicator, which is a confirmation of section inheritance in the sense that the current section has the same header/footer of the previous section.

This section inheritance behavior is quite desirable for most documents based on chapters (like books, manuals, etc.) because whenever you insert a new section page break, it recreates in the new section the same document structure used in the previous section.

You can appreciate this behavior by extracting "Page Numbers Only.docx" document from file Chapter09.zip, which was formatted using a A5 page size and Narrow margins (defined in Layout tab, Size and Margins tools), having the Different First Page and Different Odd & Even Pages options checked, where the document's First Page Footer, Even Page Header, and Odd Page Header received the Circular page number style (using the Insert tab, Page Number tool).

It has six pages, divided by a Next Page section break inserted in Section 1, Page 3, which makes Section 2, Page 4, First Page Footer inherit the Section 1, Page 1, First Page Footer (the same behavior for Section 2 pages 5 and 6, Figure 9-15).

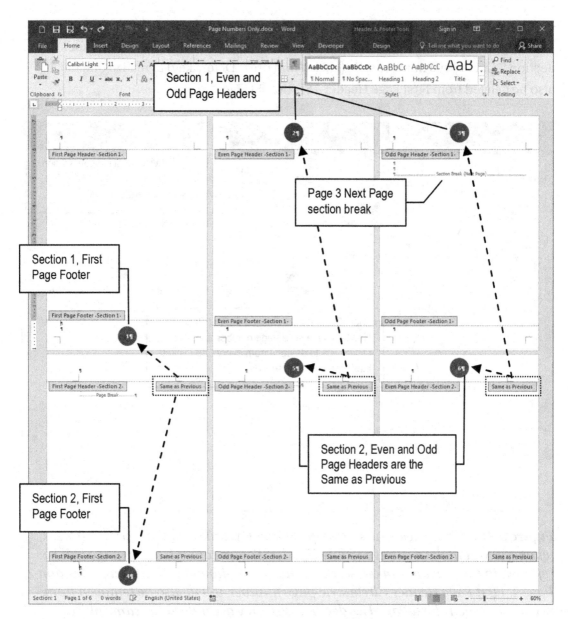

Figure 9-15. *This is the "Page Number Only.docx" document, which you can extract from Chapter09.zip file. It has six pages and two sections, using three different page types per section (First Page, Even and Odd pages), which had received the Circular page number style on its First Page Footer, Even and Odd Page Header*

When Microsoft Word tells us that a Header/Footer is "Same as Previous" it is not kidding: it is indeed the same content! Try for example to delete First Page Header - Section 2 Circle page number style (click it and press Delete key) to realize that it will also be deleted from First Page Header - Section 1 (Figure 9-16).

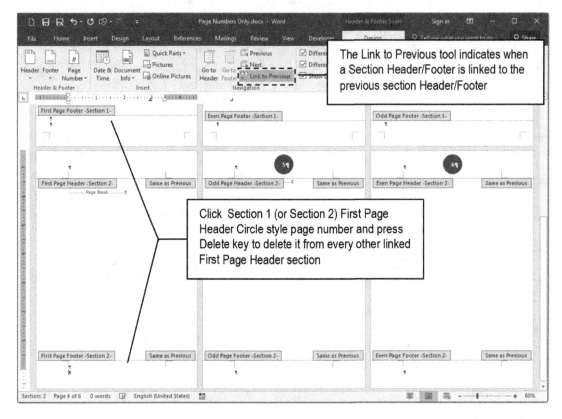

Figure 9-16. *Since each new section page break is linked to the section before, whenever you make a change in any Header/Footer content, this change will be reflected in the previous linked section. This figure shows that by deleting Section 2, Page 4, First Page Header Circle style page number, it will also be removed from Section 1, Page 1, First Page Header, because they are indeed the same object*

The same is true for any other Header/Footer content that shows the "Same as Previous" title at its right side.

This linked header/footer content is the default Microsoft Word behavior for every new section created, but you can break such linkage using the Link to Previous tool found in the Navigation area of the Header & Footer Tools Design tab (Figure 9-17).

Figure 9-17. *Use the Link to Previous tool found in the Navigation area of the Header & Footer Tools Design tab to break the link between the two consecutive sections, allowing the creation of different types of Header/Footer in each document section*

Breaking Section Link

The Link to Previous tool found in the Navigation area of the Header & Footer Tools Design tab allows breaking the link that may exist between two consecutive sections' Headers and Footers (including the First Page, Odd Page, and Even Page Header/ Footer). It is important to note that you can break the link between two consecutive Header sections while keeping the link between its Footer sections (and vice versa).

We need to break a section link to the previous section whenever the headers of the two consecutive sections must be different, which mostly happens in some types of publications (e.g., books and manuals) where the Header/Footer area conveys the chapter name that begins each new book section.

Take any book from your library and look at its headers (technical books are more prone to make such formatting). Note that some of them will change the Header/Footer areas of the odd/even page to give information about which chapter title the page belongs to. More commonly, books use the even page header (left page) to convey the chapter title, and the odd page header to convey the book or section title.

To create such complex even/odd page headers in which text content changes according to the chapter or section title, it is imperative to use unlinked section breaks, with each one holding its own information. And you will better understand this process by following the steps of the next exercise.

Automatically Inserting Section Breaks

Look again to Figure 4-14 and note that the Find and Replace dialog box does not offer in the Replace with text box Special button an option like "Section Break", meaning that you cannot easily search for text and automatically insert a Section Break before or after it.

But we can do this by using the Clipboard Contents option found in the Special button, using a Find and Replace operation, following these steps:

1. Insert the desired Section Break type in the text.

2. Select the Section Break on the page and cut it to Clipboard (press Ctrl+X, Figure 9-18).

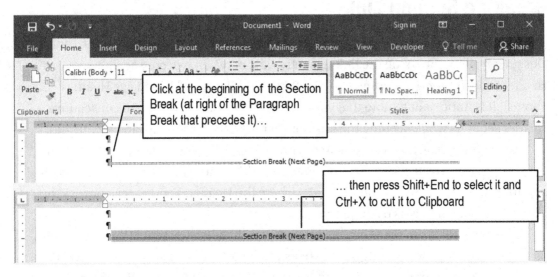

Figure 9-18. *To automatically insert Section Breaks of the same type in the text, insert the first Section Break, click at its left, press Shift+End (or Shift+Right arrow) to select it, and press Ctrl+X to cut it to Clipboard*

3. Press Ctrl+H to Show the Find and Replace dialog box.

4. In the Find what text box, type whatever you want to search for.

5. In the Replace with dialog box, use the Special ➤ Clipboard Contents (^c) and Special ➤ Find What Text (^&) to insert the Clipboard content before the Find what text search.

Section Breaks and Spacing Before

You may not have noticed, but whenever any paragraph has its Spacing Before options set to any amount of spacing and it also has the Page break before option checked, it does not obey the Spacing Before on the new page.

To me, this seems to be a bug in Microsoft Word.

The good news is that this behavior disappears whenever this paragraph is preceded by a Section Break of any type.

Try the next experiment:

1. Open a new, blank document in Microsoft Word and check the Show/Hide tool in the Home tab of the Ribbon.

2. Press at least an Enter key to insert a second paragraph.

3. For this second paragraph, show the Paragraph dialog box (right-click it and select Paragraph) and set these options:

    -   Spacing Before = 40.

    -   Page break before = checked.

4. Close the Paragraph dialog box and note that this paragraph begins on another page, but does not implement the Spacing Before = 40 pt.

5. With the next page paragraph still selected, insert any type of Section Break before it.

The paragraph will now implement the Spacing Before = 40 pt (Figure 9-19).

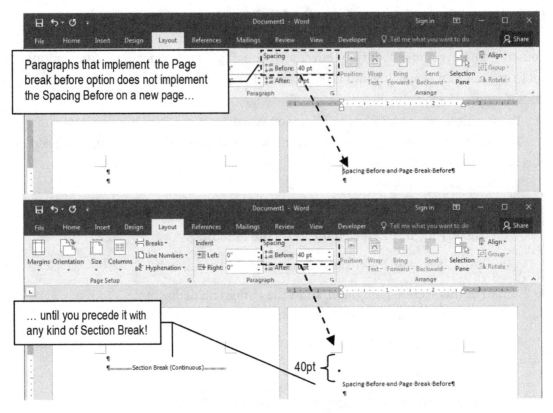

Figure 9-19. *Insert a Section Break of any kind before a paragraph that must begin on a new page to make its Spacing Before option be implemented on that page*

Exercise 1

The objective of this exercise is to exemplify how to create different even/odd page headers for a document that uses mirror margins, having different first page, even and odd headers in each book section. It will use the "European Convention of Human Rights.docx" file, which you can extract from Chapter09.zip file.

Open the "European Convention of Human Rights" document from the Chapter09. zip file in Microsoft Word and note that it is formatted with a Letter size paper (8.5 × 11) and Normal margins (choose with the Size and Margins tools of the Page Setup area of the Layout tab). It received the Title, Subtitle, Heading1, and Heading2 styles and was formatted with "Lines (Distinctive)" style set (choose in the Style Set Gallery found in the Design tab), which produced an 11-page document.

It has the Different First page and Different Odd & Even Pages options checked, which respectively received the Accent Bar Bottom, Accent Bar 1, and Accent Bar 2 header styles (choose with the Footer and Header tools found in the Header & Footer Tools Design Tab) (Figure 9-20).

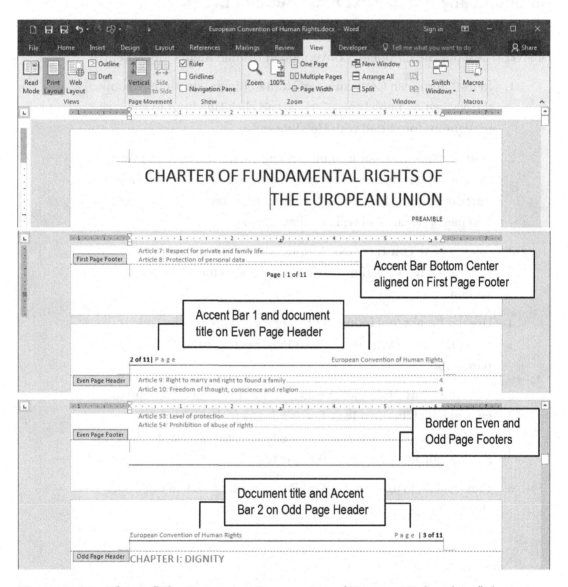

Figure 9-20. *This is "The European Convention of Human Rights.docx" document extracted from the Chapter09.zip file. It has an Accent Bar Bottom page number on its First Page Footer, and Accent Bar 1 and 2 page numbers on its Odd and Even Page Headers.*

You must insert a Next Page Section Break before each document chapter title and unlink each new section from the previous to produce personalized headers to each chapter, showing the chapter number at its even and odd pages.

Automatically Add a Next Page Section Break

Follow these instructions to add a Next Page Section Break before "CHAPTER 1: DIGNITY" text of "The European Convention of Human Rights" document:

1. In the "European Convention of Human Rights" document, show the Navigation pane (press Ctrl+F) and click Headings to show all paragraphs formatted with Heading styles.

2. Double-click the ruler to show the Page Setup dialog box, select the Paper tab, and change page Height = 5 to force the creation of new document pages, so each chapter may have first, even, and odd pages (document will now have 32 pages).

3. Click "CHAPTER 1: DIGNITY" entry on Navigation page (formatted with Heading1 style) to select it in the document window.

4. Use the Breaks tool found in the Page Setup area of the Layout tab of the Ribbon to insert a Next Page Section Break before this paragraph.

5. With the Show/Hide tool checked in the Home tab of the Ribbon, click at left of the Next Page Section Break (or at right of the pilcrow Paragraph Break that preceded it) and press Shift+End (or Shift+Right arrow) to select it in the text.

6. Press Ctrl+X to remove the Next Page Section Break to Clipboard (Figure 9-21).

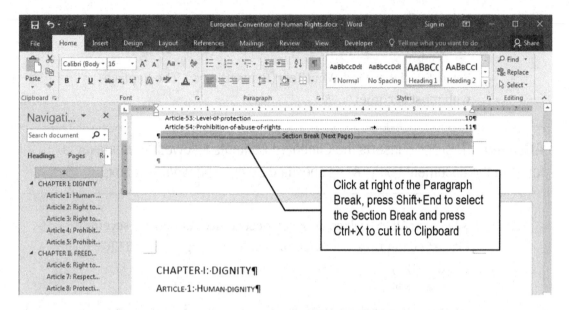

Figure 9-21. Insert a Next Page Section Break before the "CHAPTER 1: DIGNITY" text, select it in the text, and press Ctrl+X to cut it to Clipboard

Now use the Find and Replace dialog box to make a normal search for every "CHAPTER" text formatted with Heading1 style and precede it by the Next Page Section Break inserted in Clipboard.

Follow these steps:

1. Use the Replace command (Ctrl+H) found in the Editing area of the Home tab of the Ribbon to show the Find and Replace dialog box.

2. Click Find what and use these search parameters to find all Heading1 style "CHAPTER" text paragraphs:

    • Find what: CHAPTER

    • Select Special ➤ Style ➤ Heading1 on Find Style dialog box.

Attention   The parenthesis pair allows use of the \n wildcard in the Replace with text box.

---

3. Click the Replace with text box and use these options:

    - Select Special ➤ Clipboard Contents (to insert a ^c)

    - Select Special ➤ Find What Text (to insert a ^&). The Replace
      with must become: ^c^&

Attention   The ^c^& inserts the Clipboard Contents followed by whatever is
found in the document text (^&) as specified by the Find what text box.

---

4. Press Replace All to replace all seven occurrences and insert seven
    Next Page Section Breaks, one before each Heading1 "CHAPTER"
    text (Figure 9-22).

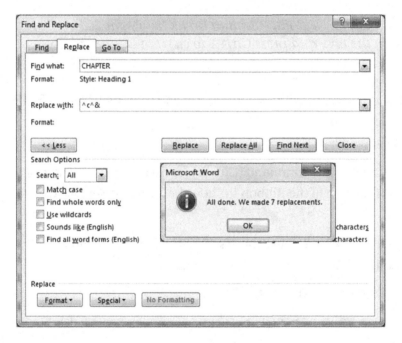

Figure 9-22. *Make a normal Find and Replace operation to search for each
Heading1 "CHAPTER" text paragraph and insert the Next Page Section Break that
is inside Clipboard before each occurrence found*

Break Section Links and Personalize Headers

The document will now have 35 pages spread across eight sections after you inserted all seven Next Page Section Breaks before each of its seven "CHAPTER..." paragraphs (Figure 9-23).

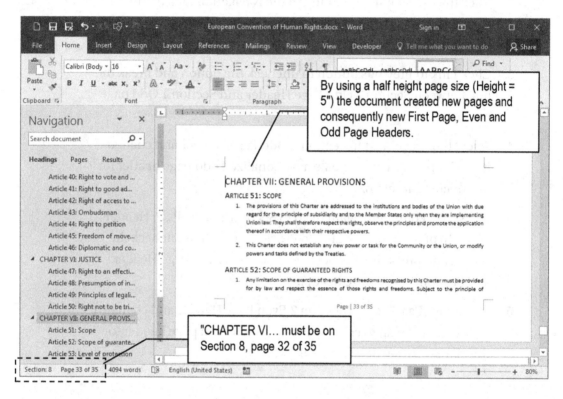

Figure 9-23. *After inserting a Next Page Section Break before each Heading1 "CHAPTER..." title, the document must have 35 pages, and "CHAPTER VII..." must be in Section 8, Page 32 of 35*

Attention   By inserting new sections in the document, they will all inherit the same First Page, Even and Odd Page Header text: all sections will have the Link to previous option set.

443

It is time to break the link between each section so each one can have its own Header text. Follow these steps:

1. Press Ctrl+Home to go to the first document page; double-click its Header area.

2. Click the Next command found in the Navigation area of the Header & Footer Tools Design tab, until you reach Section 2, Odd Page Header (Page 9 of 35).

3. Click Link to Previous button to uncheck the option and break the link between Section 2 Odd Page Header and Section 1 Odd page header.

4. Select the "Page" text in Section 2 Odd Page Header and change it to "Chapter I" text, to create a personalized odd page header for this document section.

5. Press Next command again to go to Section 2, Even Page Header (Page 10 of 35) and click Link to Previous button to uncheck the option and break the link between Section 2 Even Page Header and Section 1 Even page header.

6. Select the "Page" text in Section 2 Even Page Header and change it to "Chapter I" text, to create a personalized even page header for this document section (Figure 9-24).

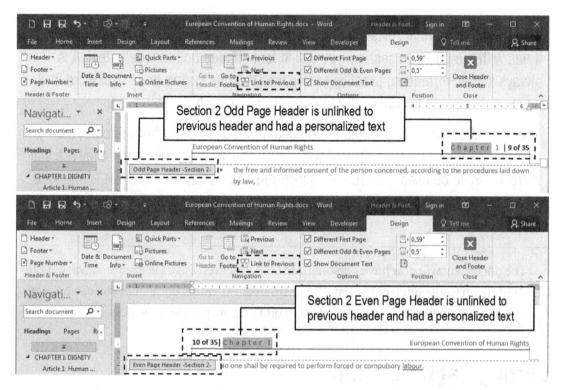

Figure 9-24. *Uncheck the Link to Previous command found in the Navigation area of the Header & Footer Tools Design tab to break the link between Section 2 and Section 1 Odd Page Headers and change the "Page" work to "Chapter I"*

7. Repeat steps 6 to 9, searching for the next section's Odd and Even page headers, breaking its link with the previous section and creating personalized "Chapter n" titles in its headers (note that they will inherit the precedent "Chapter n" title).

8. When all chapter sections' odd and even page headers are personalized to show the chapter numbers in their headers, click the Close Header and Footer button at the right of the Header & Footer Tools Design tab (or double-click the document text) to select the document text.

9. Press Ctrl+A to select the entire document text and double-click the Ruler to show the Page Setup dialog box and change the Page Height = 11 to make the pages have a Letter size again (or use the Size ➤ Letter command in the Layout tab of the Ribbon).

Attention   If you inadvertently change any header text before breaking the link it has with the previous section, you will in fact change both headers' text. It is always a good formatting practice to use the Previous button to go backward in document sections to confirm that they were adequately personalized.

Note that after you changed again the document page Height from 5 to 11, the text will reflux and many chapters' odd/even headers will disappear—they are still there, ready to be used if more text is inserted, the document Style Set is changed, or you press Ctrl+A to select the document text and change its page size and margins.

The document will now have personalized Odd and Even Page Headers for each chapter (the "European Convention of Human Rights Unlinked Headers.docx" that you can extract from Chapter09.zip file has these personalized odd and even section headers).

Setting Page Columns

Another usage for Section Breaks is to produce columnated text using two or more columns to make the text flow across the document page, which can be formatted by following two simple steps:

1.   Select the text you want to flow in columns.

2.   Choose the desired column count using the Columns tool found in the Page Setup area of the Layout tab of the Ribbon.

If you do not select any amount of text, all the document text will be columnated until you insert another Section Break and define it as a single column text.

Let us see follow a simple example with the "European Convention of Human Rights Unlinked Headers.docx" used in the last section; this document has a Preamble section that must be flow in two columns inside the first document page.

Follow these instructions:

1.   In the "European Convention of Human Rights Unlinked Headers. docx" document, select all the paragraphs inside the "Preamble" section (begin with "The People..." and end before the "Contents" paragraph).

2. Click the Columns tool in the Layout tab and select Two columns.

Voilà! All the "Preamble" paragraphs (not including the "Preamble" text formatted with Subtitle style) will instantly flow in two columns on the same page (Figure 9-25).

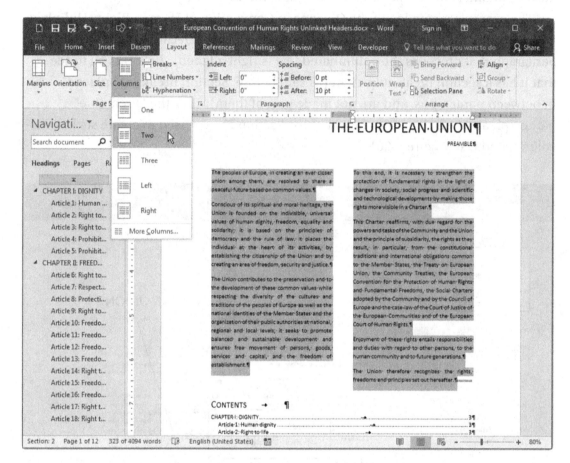

Figure 9-25. *To make the text flow into columns inside a page, select the text first and then use the Columns tool found in the Page Setup area of the Layout tab to define how many columns you want (by not selecting any text, the entire document—or current section—will be columnated)*

Attention   By not selecting any amount of text, all the document text—or current section, if there is any Section Break—will be columnated.

To understand what really happens when you ask Microsoft Word to format text using columns, click the Show/Hide tool in the Home tab of the Ribbon and search for the two Continuous section breaks that were inserted in the document: one before the first and another after the last columnated paragraphs.

The example created with the "European Convention of Human Rights Unlinked Headers.docx" document is very didactic for this purpose because the "Preamble" paragraph that precedes the columnated text is right aligned, allowing you to see that it has a section break at its right (as said before, Section Breaks are placed in between paragraphs, and are not made part of them): click the "Preamble" paragraph and Left align it to show the two Section Breaks used to create such columnated text (Figure 9-26).

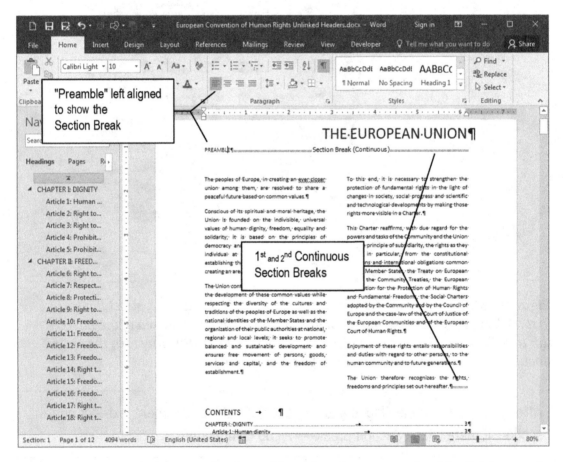

Figure 9-26. *Check the Show/Hide tool found in the Home tab of the Ribbon and eventually change some paragraph alignment so you can see the two Continuous Section Breaks that encompass the columnated text*

And once the text is columnated, you can play with it using the Columns tool:

- Press Ctrl+Shift+Enter to insert a hidden Column break character, allowing control of where a given column ends (use this technique to define the column height).

- Use the Columns tool to select Three, Left, and Right commands and change the way text is columnated (Left and Right creates different column widths with the narrowest at left or right, respectively).

- Select More Columns... to show the Columns dialog box from where you can choose further column formats (Figure 9-27).

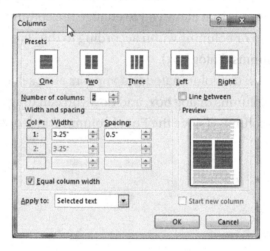

Figure 9-27. *Use the Columns ➤ More Columns... command to show the Columns dialog box from where you can choose more column formatting options*

Among the possibilities that the Columns dialog box offer to format columnated text, you will find:

- **Number of columns**: allows defining up to twelve columns per section.

- **Line between**: check to insert a vertical line that separates the columns.

- **Width and spacing**: use to precisely define each column width.

- **Equal column width**: use to make all columns have the same width.

Note that whenever you have a columnated text and click any text column, Microsoft Word ruler will show controls that allow you to change the column margins (and consequently the column or columns width according to the state of the Equal column width option of the Columns dialog box).

Figure 9-28 shows how the columnated text appears after selecting the Line in between option of the Columns dialog box, and how you can drag the left column's right margin to narrow both columns (since the Equal column width option is checked).

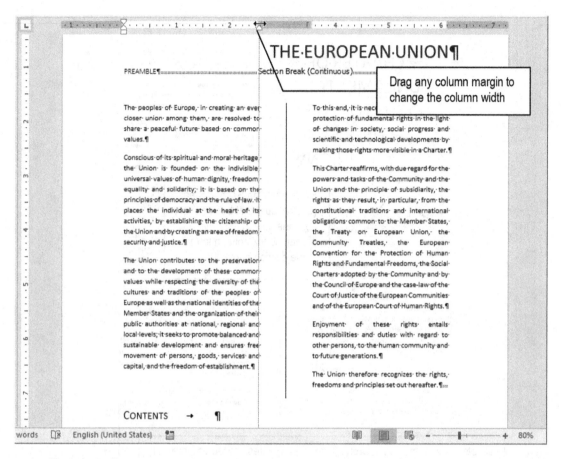

Figure 9-28. *Using the Line between width and dragging any column margin, we can interactively change one or all column widths (according to the Equal column width option stated in the Columns dialog box)*

How Column Information Is Stored

Column formatting information is stored inside the section, meaning that the top Section Break is the one responsible for storing how the text that comes before it will be formatted.

This is important because if you delete the top Section Break that begins any columnated text, all the text above it will receive the same column formatting, effectively propagating the columnated text to the previous document section.

You can see an example of such propagating by deleting the Section Break (Continuous) that is at the right of the "Preamble" paragraph: the text before it will also be columnated (Figure 9-29).

451

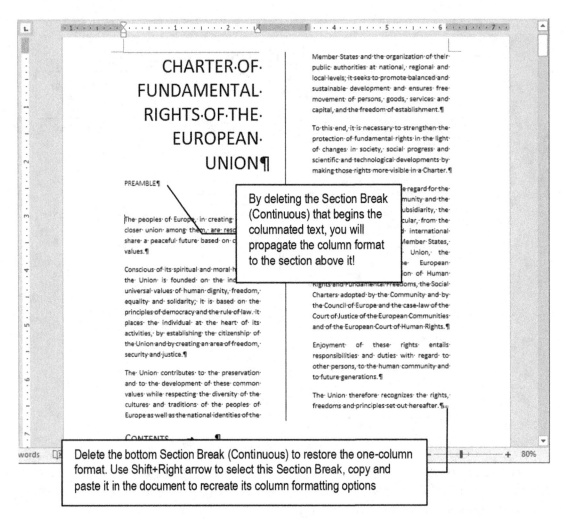

Figure 9-29. By deleting the Section Break (Continuous) that begins the columnated text, you will effectively propagate the same column formatting to the previous document section. By deleting the Section Break (Continuous) at the bottom of the columnated text, it will return to the default one-column format

Attention   Since the column formatting is copied to the previous section whenever the top Section Break is deleted, it is clear that the column formatting is stored in the bottom Section Break. Select the bottom section break (place the text cursor at the left of the Section Break and press Shift+Right arrow), copy it, and paste it in any other single column document part to recreate the same column formatting above this place. Try it!

The European Convention of Human Rights Unlinked Headers & Columns.docx" document, which you can extract from Chapter09.zip, has the columns and diving lines shown in Figure 9-29.

The lesson here is quite simple, if you want to remove column formatted text from any document: first remove the bottom Section Break (Continuous) that ends the columnated text, effectively propagating the one-column format to the section above (the columnated one), and then remove the Section Break (Continuous) that was used to begin the columnated text!

Numbering Complex Documents

For the sake of this discussion, I will consider as a "complex document" one that needs to change page numbering style and/or page count, whether or not its first page (which is usually the document cover) is counted or numbered.

Such complex documents also need to be divided by Section Breaks to perfectly control their page numbering and number style. Figure 9-30 shows some examples of how they look for both Normal (printed in one side of paper) or Mirror documents (printed on both side of paper), which may have the Different first page option set, allowing numbering or counting the first page (cover).

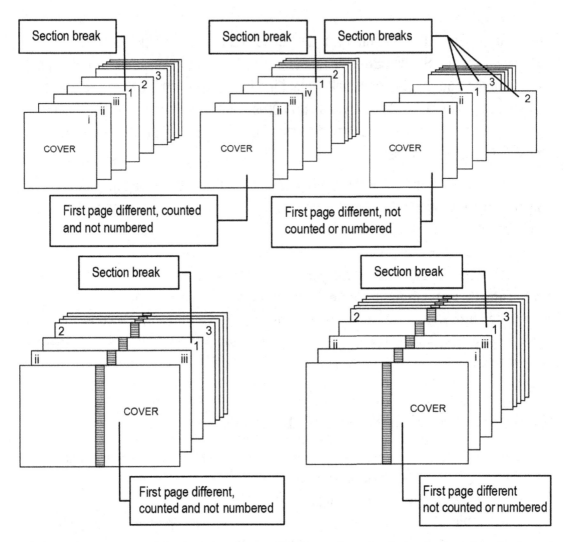

Figure 9-30. _Normal (printed in one side of page) and mirror (printed in both sides of page) documents that have complex formatting_

All document examples number their first pages using Roman numeral styles, restarting the page numbering at some point using Arabic numerals, and with one or more pages whose Orientation was set to Landscape.

Also note that in Figure 9-27, the spot where each page breaks must be placed to change the page numbering style from Roman to Arabic numerals, restarting the page count or changing some page Orientation to Landscape.

Renumbering Pages

Figure 9-30 shows different ways to count and/or number the first document page. Its top left example counts and numbers all it pages, including its cover page, using Roman numerals, and then inserts a Section Break to restart page counting using Arabic numerals.

This document numbering style can be imposed by using the Microsoft Word Format Page Numbers... option found in the Page Number tool found in the Header & Footer area of the Insert Tab of the Ribbon, which will show the traditional Page Number Format dialog box (Figure 9-31).

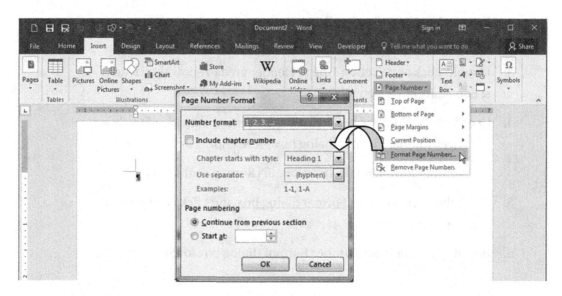

Figure 9-31. *Use the Page Number ➤ Format Page Numbers... command to show the Page Number Format dialog box, from where you can control the number format style and each section's first page number*

You have the following options to format the document or section page numbers:

- **Number format**: use to select different numbering systems (Arabic, Letters, Roman uppercase or lowercase).

- **Include chapter number**: this option works with Heading styles that use the Numbering tool to automatically number them. When you check it, you can select which Heading style number will be used and add a separator to prefix the page number.

- **Page Numbering**: use this area to select which page number must be associated to the first section page:

  - **Continue from previous section:** default option, allow consecutive page numbering from section to section.

  - **Start at:** allow changing the section's first page number, ignoring all precedent pages.

Based on the knowledge gathered so far, you may anticipate that to create two different numbering styles in any document, you must:

1. Use the Page Number tool to insert a page number in the Header.

2. Insert a Next Page Section Break to separate the two different numbering section styles.

3. Double-click any Section 1 page Header area to show the Header & Footer Tools Design tab.

4. Use the Page Number ➤ Format Page Number command to show the Page Number Format dialog box for Section 1 and define:

   - Number format = I, II, III or i, ii, iii (Roman numerals).

5. Close the Page Number Format dialog box and click Next button to show Section Header.

6. Evoke again the Page Number Format dialog box for Section 2 and define:

   - Number format = 1,2,3 (Arabic numerals).

   - Start at =1

7. Close the Page Number Format.

You can see an example of such page numbering style by extracting the "Cover Counted and Numbered, Different number styles.docx" document from Chapter09.zip file and opening it in Microsoft Word.

This document has six pages, with a Next Page Section Break inserted into its third page, receiving these formatting options in its two sections (Figure 9-32):

- **Section 1**: Number format = i, ii, iii (lowercase Roman numerals).

- **Section 2**: Number format= 1,2,3, Start at = 1

Showing the Logical Page Number on Status Bar

Microsoft Word may cause some confusion regarding the Even and Odd Page Headers and the even/odd page numbers whenever the we use the Page Number Format dialog box to restart any Section numbering.

You may eventually find the document on a *logical* even page (like page 2 or ii) while the Header title area shows "Section 2, Odd Page Header" (vice versa for odd page numbers).

For those moments, you can show the logical page number associated to this physical page in Microsoft Word Status and take a better decision about how to format a given Header/Footer text:

1. Right-click the Status bar to show the Customize Status Bar pop-up menu.

2. Check the Formatted Page Number option.

From this point on, Microsoft Word will begin to show "Page n" page number as its first Status Bar information, where n is the logical page number. Use it to guarantee that you are at an even and odd page and correctly align the right header/footer even and odd page text (Figure 9-33).

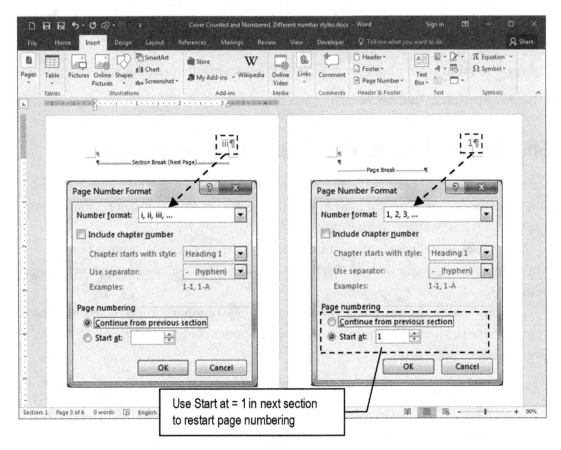

Figure 9-32. *This is the "Cover Counted and Numbered, Different number styles. docx" document showing its third and fourth pages, separated by a Next Page Section Break. It uses different numbering styles and page renumbering between its two sections*

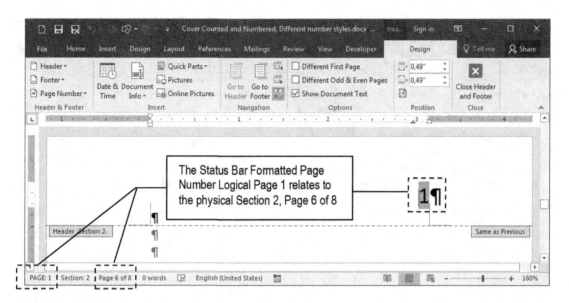

Figure 9-33. *Right-click the Status bar to show the Customize Status Bar context menu and click Formatted Page Number to show the logical page number as additional important page information*

Hiding First Page Number

The Figure 9-30 top middle example differs from the top left example just because it doesn't show the cover page number, while still counting it as Page i (1).

This can be easily accomplished in "Cover Counted and Numbered, Different number styles.docx" document by using the Previous command found in the Navigation area of the Header & Footer Tools Design tab to show Section 1 Header and checking the Different First Page option, which will make Microsoft Word show the First Page Header, which does not receive a page number (Figure 9-34).

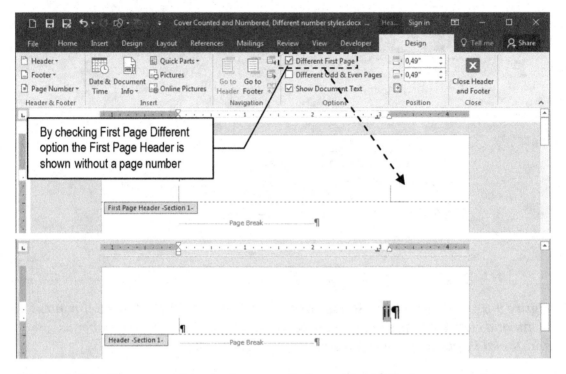

Figure 9-34. *To remove the any document's (or section's) first page number, just check the First Page Different option and remove its page number*

Not Counting the First Page

The Figure 9-30 top right example differs from the top left and middle examples because it doesn't count or show the cover page number, which is an effect that is very simple to achieve by following these steps:

1. Insert a Next Page Section Break in the first document page (Section 1, cover).

2. In Section 2 (2nd page), show the Page Number Format dialog box and set Start at = 1.

Attention You cannot set the Start at option to a negative number, but can set it to 0 (zero) as long as you use the default Number Format = 1,2,3 (Arabic numerals). But you cannot set Start at = 0 when a section uses Roman or Letter numbering system.

So, to make a document not count or show any number on its first page, restarting page numbering from 1 on its second page (using any numbering system), you need to

1. Insert a Next Page break on its cover page (Section 1).

2. Format Section 2 with: any Number Format and set these options:

    • Different First Page = *unchecked.*

    • Link to Previous = *unchecked.*

    • Start at = 1.

Figure 9-35 show this effect in the "Cover Counted and Numbered, Different number styles.docx" document, which received a New Page Section Break on its first page and these formatting options for Section 2:

• Different First Page = *unchecked*

• Link to Previous = *unchecked.*

• Number Format = i, ii, iii (lowercase Roman numerals).

• Start at = i.

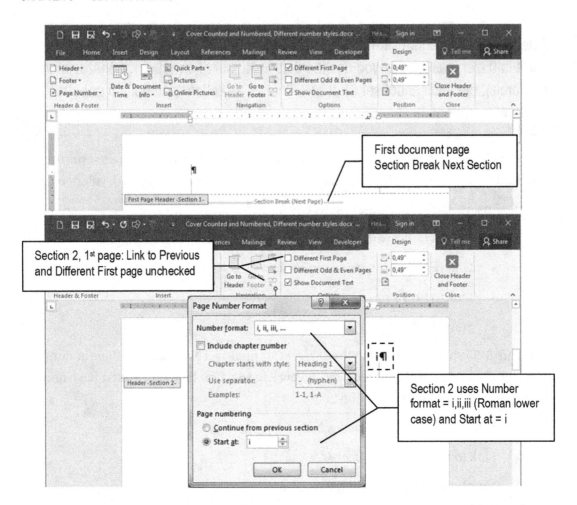

Figure 9-35. *To not count or number the cover and start numbering at the 2ⁿᵈ document page, you need to insert a Next Page Section Break in the first page, and in Section 2, first page (2ⁿᵈ document page) set Number Format = i, ii, iii and Start at = i*

Attention   Complex documents with Mirror margins obey the same rules. Since they mostly use Odd Page Section Breaks to begin a new chapter, they tend to lack some page numbers (as Figure 9-30 shows in its two bottom examples, which has empty "even" pages at left of page number "1").

Exercise 2

The objective of this exercise is to show how you can format a Microsoft Word document using columns and different number systems (Roman and Arabic numerals) to number its pages, having the chance to see how some formatting options can add complexity to the document regarding its section count.

It will use the "Moby Dick, Herman Melville.docx" document that you can extract from the Chapter09.zip file, which has the famous 1851 Herman Melville novel (this book was a commercial failure at the time it was published). It needs 325 A4 pages to spread its introduction, 135 chapters, and an epilogue.

It has no Section Break (has just Section 1), uses Title, Subtitle, Quote, Heading1, Heading2, and Normal Recommended styles, plus the Citation style created by myself (to format some special paragraphs found in book introduction) and was formatted with the Basic (Elegant) Style set (Figure 9-36).

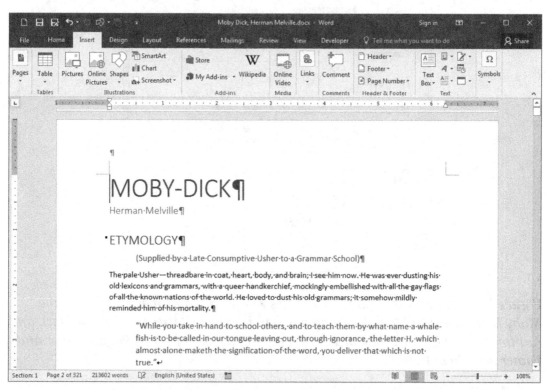

Figure 9-36. *This is the "Moby Dick, Herman Melville.docx" document that you can extract from Chapter09.zip file, with Herman Melville's famous 1851 novel published in full text. It uses Recommended styles (Title, Subtitle, Quote, Heading1, Heading2, Normal) and was formatted using the Basic (Elegant) style set.*

Insert a Cover Page

Let us begin formatting the "Moby Dick, Herman Melville.docx" document by changing its first page: it has Properties that allow you insert a built-in Cover Page as the first document page:

1. Click File ➤ Info Properties ➤ Advanced Properties to show the Moby Dick, Herman Melville Properties dialog box and inspect the document properties (Figure 9-37).

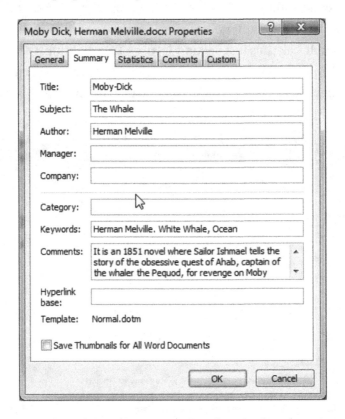

Figure 9-37. *Use File ➤ Info ➤ Properties ➤ Advanced Properties to show the Moby Dick, Herman Melville dialog box and note how it uses the Title, Subject, and Author fields to identify the document allowing the use of Cover Page, Header and Footer built-in objects*

2. Return to the document page and use the Insert ➤ Cover Page tool to select a built-in page. This exercise will use the Ion (Dark) cover page due to its blue detail that resembles the ocean.

3. Inspect the built-in cover page and how it uses the Title, Subject, and Author fields to define some document properties.

    • At the top of the Ion (Dark) page there is a small control showing year 1900: click it and type the book publication year (1851).

    • At the bottom of the Ion (Dark) page there are two controls to type the Company name and Company address. Use or delete them at will (I typed in the Apress name and address, Figure 9-38).

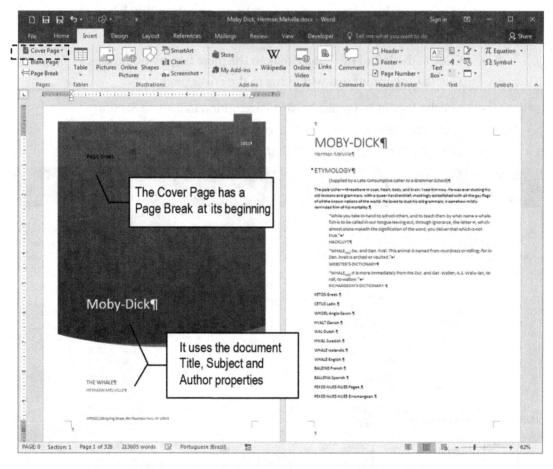

Figure 9-38. *Use the Insert ➤ Cover Page ➤ Ion(Dark) tool to insert a built-in cover page that uses the Title, Subject, and Author document properties to personalize the first page*

    • Double-click the Ion (Dark) cover page Header area to show the Header & Footer Tools Design tab.

4. Execute the Page Number ➤ Format Page Numbers... command to show the Page Number Format dialog box.

5. Note that now the document Section 1 has these properties (and the Status Bar, Formatted Page Number = Page 0, Figure 9-39):

   - Number format: 1,2,3 (Arabic numerals).

   - Page numbering: Start at = 0.

6. The built-in page inserted as the first document page *must not* be counted or numbered, so you need to change the Page Break it has on its top to a Section Break (Next Page):

   - Click at the left of the Page Break in the page begin and press Delete (document text will reflux to the cover page).

   - Use the Layout ➤ Breaks ➤ Next Page option to insert a Section Break (Next Page) and force the text to reflux again to the document's Section 2 first page (second document page, Figure 9-40).

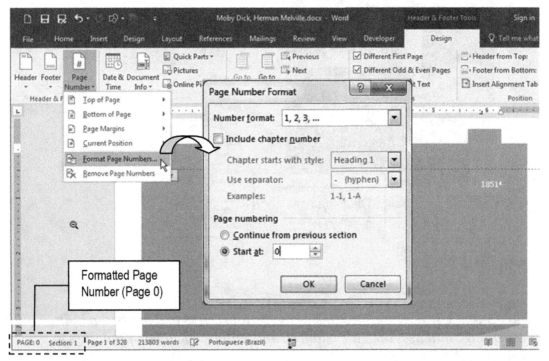

Figure 9-39. *Double-click the cover page Header area to show the Header & Foooter Tools Design tab and use the Page Number ➤ Format Page Numbers... command to show the Page Number Formats dialog box and note that it sets Section 1, Page numbering Start at = 0*

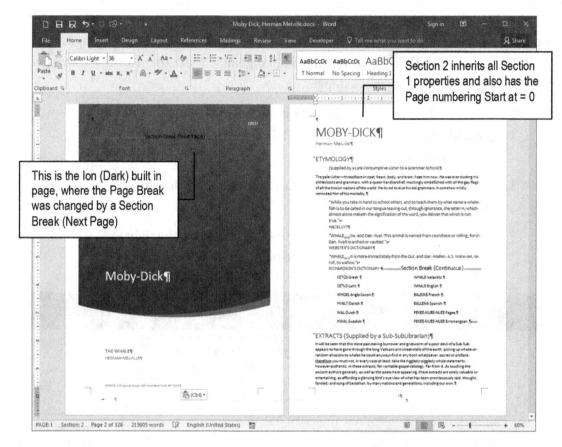

Figure 9-40. *The Ion (Dark) Cover Page received a Next Page Section Break, making Section 2 (book text) inherit all its properties, including first page numbered as 0 (zero)*

Attention   By inserting a Section Break (Next Page) on the Cover Page, the second document page is now in document Section 2, which received by default the Link to Previous option set and inherited all Section 1 properties: Number format = 1,2,3 and Start at = 0.

Make "Whale Definitions" Flow in Two Columns

Now that the document has a Cover Page that uses its Properties, it is time to further format it using columns and section breaks.

Note that the "Moby Dick, Herman Melville.docx" document has an "ETYMOLOGY" section on its second page that has twelve whale definitions in different languages (from "KETUS Greek" to "PEKEE-NUEE-NUEE Erromangoan"). Make them all flow into a two-column format by following these steps:

1. Select all these twelve whale definitions on second document page (drag the mouse from "KETUS Greek" to "PEKEE-NUEE-NUEE Erromangoan").

2. Use the Layout ➤ Columns ➤ Two command them flow in a two-column format.

3. Drag first column Left margin control on the ruler to the right to give it a bigger Left indent from the page Left margin (Figure 9-41).

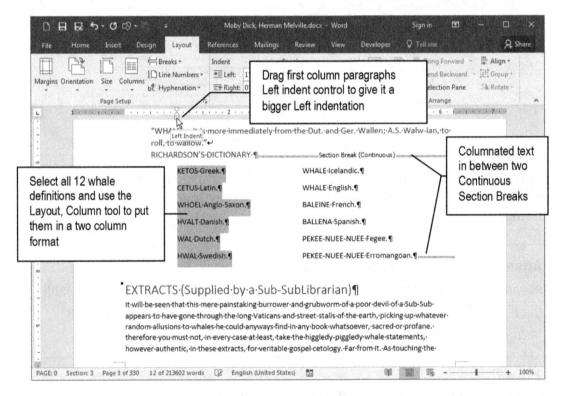

Figure 9-41. *Select the 12 whale definitions in different foreign languages and use the Layout ➤ Columns ➤ Two command to make them flow in a two-column format. Then select the six paragraphs of the first text column and drag it Left indent control on the ruler to increase its left indentation*

Attention   By inserting the "whale definitions" in a two-column format, Microsoft Word also inserted two new Continuous Section Breaks in the document, which now has Section 2 (columnated text) and Section 4 (remaining text).

Both Section 3 and Section 4 received by default the Link to Previous option set, and inherited all Section 2 properties: Number format = 1,2,3 and Page numbering Start at = 0 (cascade inherited from Section 1).

Add a Bottom Border to the Citation Style

Open the Apply Styles window (see Figure 5-2) and note that the "Moby Dick..." document "EXTRACTS..." section has some pages of "extract" paragraphs, which may have different numbers of sentences but always end with the author or source.

Each of these "extract" paragraphs were formatted with the Citation style, having as many Manual line Break characters as needed to separate each of its sentences from one another and from its author/source, located in the last paragraph line: a formatting technique that guarantees that all its sentences belong to a single Paragraph break, no matter how long they are (Figure 9-42).

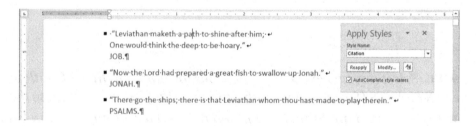

Figure 9-42. *The "Moby Dick..." document "Extract..." section has "extract" paragraphs formatted with the Citation styles. They have Manual Line Breaks inserted at the ends of sentences to separate them from one another and from its author/source.*

We must update the Citation style by adding a bottom border, so each "extract" paragraph be better separated from the next!

Follow these steps:

1. Select the first two Citation style paragraphs ("Leviathan..." and "Now the Lord..."), click the Border tool, and select Inside Horizontal Border to insert a border between them (Figure 9-43).

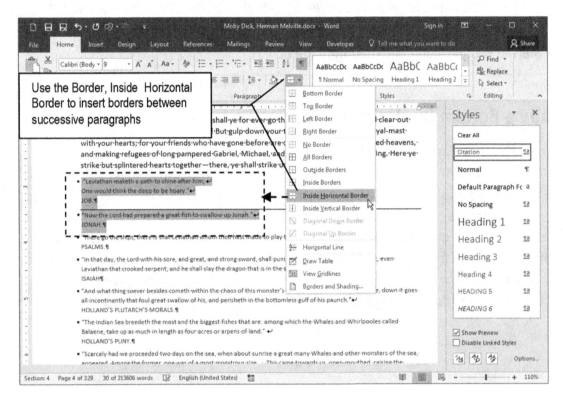

Figure 9-43. *Select any two extracts paragraphs formatted with the Citation style from the "EXTRACTS (Supplied by a Sub-SubLibrarian)" section, and use the Border ➤ Inside Horizontal Border command to insert a bottom border in between them*

2. Right-click the Citation style in the Styles window and choose Update Citation from Selection to update the style, adding a bottom border between every two consecutive Citation style paragraphs (Figure 9-44).

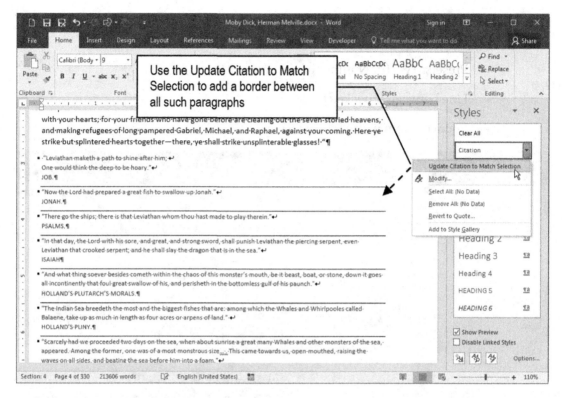

Figure 9-44.   After inserting the Inside Horizontal Border to the Citation style paragraph, right-click it in the Styles window and choose Update Citation to Match Selection

Make "Extracts" Flow on Two Columns

Now that each "extract" paragraph formatted with the Citation style has a border to separate it from the next, it is time to make them all flow through a two-column format by following these steps:

1. Click the beginning of the first Citation paragraph ("Leviathan..." on document page 3), press and hold Shift, and press Page Down successively until you reach the last Citation paragraph ("Oh, the rare ..." on page 9, right before "Chapter 1" text).

2. Use the Layout ➤ Columns ➤ More Columns... command to show the Columns dialog box and check these options (Figure 9-45):

- Presets: Two (or Number of columns = 2).

- Line between (checked).

- Equal column width (checked).

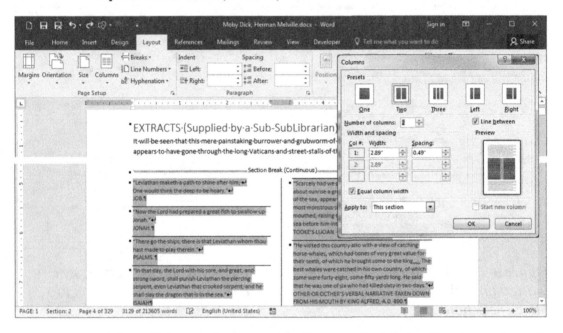

Figure 9-45. *Select all "extract" paragraphs formatted with the Citation style and use the Layout ➤ Columns ➤ More Columns... command to show the Columns dialog box, from where you can select Preset = Two, and check the Line Between option to make the text flow in a two-column format with a line in between them*

3. Close the Columns dialog box and press the Left arrow to return to the first Citation paragraph ("Leviathan...").

4. Use the Border toll to add a Top border (Figure 9-46).

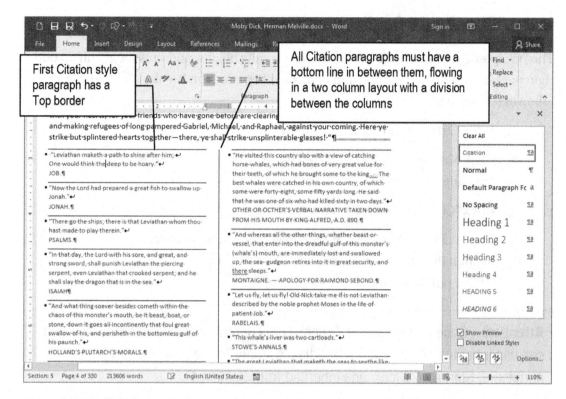

Figure 9-46. *Format all Citation paragraphs using a two-column layout with a line dividing them*

Attention   By inserting the "extract" paragraphs in a two-column format, Microsoft Word inserted again two new Continuous Section Breaks in the document, which now has Section 5 ("extract" columnated paragraphs) and Section 6 (remaining text).

Both Section 5 and Section 6 received by default the Link to Previous option set, and inherited all Section 4 properties: Number format = 1,2,3 and Page numbering Start at = 0 (cascade inherited from Section 1).

Make "Chapter 1" Begin on an Odd Page

The "Chapter 1" section is where the book text really begins, and must begin on an odd right page, which needs the insertion of an Odd Page Section Break right before it, by following these steps:

1. Press Ctrl+F to show the Navigation pane.

2. Click Navigation Pane Headings option, to show document Heading styles.

3. Click "Chapter 1" to select it in the document text.

4. Use the Layout ➤ Breaks ➤ Odd Page command to insert a Section Break (Odd Page) before "Chapter 1" paragraph (which will be put in document Section 7).

Attention   Once more, Section 7 received by default the Link to Previous option set, and inherited all Section 6 properties: Number format = 1,2,3 and Page numbering Start at = 0 (cascade inherited from Section 1).

Insert Page Numbers

The "Moby Dick… " document must have now seven sections divided by six section breaks (one on the cover, four to enclose the two columnated texts, and one before "Chapter 1"), and is time to number its pages.

This is a nice learning example because the document is now quite complex with its many Section Breaks, all of them inheriting Section 1 properties, defined by the insertion of the Cover Page as the first document page (Number format = 1,2,3 and Start at = 0).

Our intention is to apply different page number styles to this document:

• Cover page: not counted or numbered.

• Restart page numbering using Roman numerals on page 2 "Etymology", which must be numbered in its Footer area. All other pages before Section 7 ("Chapter 1") must be numbered in the Odd/Even Headers.

• Restart page numbering using Arabic numerals in Section 7, "Chapter 1" page in its Footer area. All other pages till the end of the document must be numbered in its Odd/Even Headers.

To correctly create and format these Footers, Odd and Even Headers using different numbering styles in such a complex document, you must use the tools found in the Header & Footer Tools Design tab and pay close attention to the text, the Formatted Page Number shown in the Status Bar, and the Section type you are formatting (first, even or odd section page).

Creating Section 2, First Page Footer

The "Moby Dick..." document must have the cover page not counted or numbered, and the first book page, inserted in Section 2, must be numbered in its Footer, using Roman numerals.

Follow these steps:

1. Press Ctrl+Home to go to the first document page (with the Ion (Dark) built-in page).

2. Double-click the first page and note that the Different First Page and Different Odd and Even Pages options are checked (see Figure 9-38).

3. Click Next command to go to Section 2, First Page Header (second document page).

4. Click Go To Footer command to go to Section 2, First Page Footer area.

5. Click Center alignment tool in the Home tab of the Ribbon (or press Ctrl+E) to center align the footer text.

6. Use the Page Number ➤ Page Number Formats... command to show the Page Number Format dialog box and set these options to Section 2:

   - Number format: I, II, III (uppercase Roman numerals).

   - Page numbering: Start at = I

   - Close the Page Number Format dialog box and look to the Status Bar: the Formatted Page Number must show Page I, Section 2, while Page number shows Page 2 of 328.

7. Use the Page Number ➤ Current Position ➤ Two Bars option to numbering Section 2, First Page Footer (Figure 9-47).

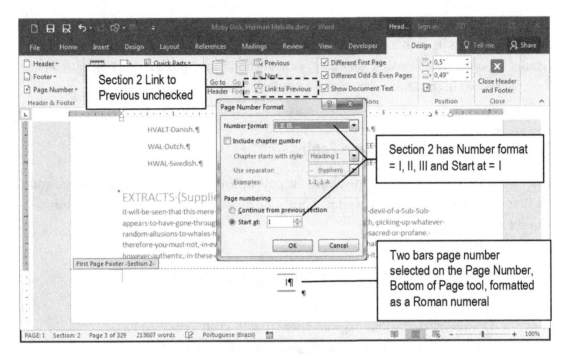

Figure 9-47. *Section 2, First Page Footer area, must have Link to Previous unchecked, Number Format = I, II, III; define its Page numbering to Start at = I, so its First Page Footer receive page number I (Roman uppercase numeral)*

8. Click the Link to Previous tool to uncheck it and break the link between Section 2 and Section 1, First Page Footer.

Attention   The order that you uncheck Link to Previous tool is important. If you uncheck it after set Section 2, Page numbering Start at = 1 (as proposed by this exercise), the Cover Page will inherit these options and it will be counted as Page 1, which will make the document page count go from 328 to 329.

---

9. Press the Go to Header button to select the First Page Header area, and if necessary, uncheck the Link to Previous option.

10. Press Next button tab to go to the next section header.

At this point, you may reach the third document page, an Even Page Header with Microsoft Word Status Bar indicating that it is Page II, Section 4, Page 3 of 329 (Figure 9-48).

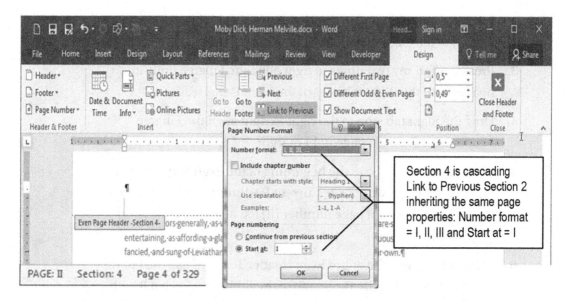

Figure 9-48. *The third document page is at Section 4 due to the two Continuous Section Breaks inserted in the 2ⁿᵈ document page (Section 2, Page I) to columnate part of its text. Since it has the Link to Previous option set, it cascade inherited all Section 2 page properties (Number format = I, II, III and Page numbering Start at = I), receiving an Even Page Header and Formatted Page Number = Page II*

Attention   When Section 2 received Number format = I, II, III and Page numbering: Start at = I, all sections after it will receive these same formatting options. Use the Page Number ➤ Format Page Numbers… tool to show the Page Number Format dialog box and see for yourself.

Creating Section 4, Even Page Header

The "Moby Dick…" document has Title, Subject, and Author properties set (using the File ➤ Info page) allowing use of Microsoft Word Header and Page Number tools to create nice page headers (as explained in "Exercise 2" of Chapter 8).

Since this document is formatted with Mirror margins with the Different Odd and Even Pages option set, even pages (left pages) must be numbered on its left (outer) margin, so follow these steps to create Page II, Section 4, Page 3 of 329 Even Page Header:

1. Click the Header tool found in the Header & Footer Tools Design tab and choose Filigree built-in header to insert the Author and Title document properties right aligned in Section 4, Even Page Header.

2. Click the Left align tool in the Home tab of the Ribbon (or press Ctrl+L) to left align the Filigree header text.

3. Press the Tab key two times to right align the Filigree built-in header with the Right tab stop of the Even Page Header.

4. Drag the Right tab stop to the right to right align the Filigree header with the even page right margin.

5. Press Home key to go to the beginning of the Even Page Header and use the Page Number ➤ Current Position ➤ Plain number tool to insert the next page number (ii) left aligned on the Even Page Header.

6. Optionally, select the entire Even Header Text and use the Font Color tool found in the Home tab of the Ribbon to format it with Automatic color (Black).

Figure 9-49 shows how the Section 4, Even Page Header must be defined and formatted after following these last steps.

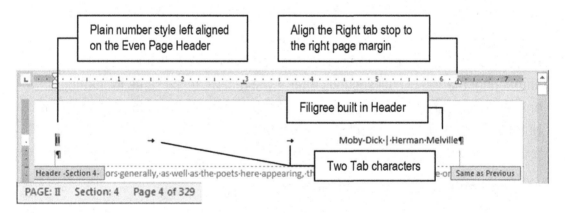

Figure 9-49. *Use the Header tool to insert a Filigree built-in header in Section 4, Even Page Header. Left align it and press Tab twice to align it to the Right tab stop. Press the Home key to go to the Even Page Header beginning and use the Page Number ➤ Current Position ➤ Plain number tool to insert a left aligned page number.*

Renumbering Section 5 First Page

Considering that the text cursor is still positioned in the now-formatted Even Page Header of Page II, Section 4, Page 3 of 329, press the Next button found in the Header & Footer Tools Design tab to reach the 5th document page header: it will be again an Even Page Header considered as Page II, Section 5, Page 5 of 329.

This fifth document page received Formatting Page Number = Page II because it has the Link to Previous option set, and had received by inheritance the same Section II page properties: Number Format = I, II, III and Page numbering Start at = I.

To make it appear with an Odd Page Header, receiving the Formatted Page Number = Page III, you must set Section 5 Page numbering = Continuous from last section.

Follow these steps:

1. Click Page Number ➤ Format Page Numbers… to show the Page Number Format dialog box for Section 5, Page 5 of 329.

2. Set these options:

   • Number format: I, II, III (uppercase Roman numerals).

   • Page numbering: Continue from last section.

3. Close the Page Number Format dialog box.

Attention   When you close the Page Number Format dialog box, Microsoft Word will go back to Page II, Section 4, Page 3 of 329 (Even Page Header). Click the Next button to now reach an Odd Page Header, with the Status Bar showing Page III, Section 5, Page 5 of 329.

Creating Section 5, Odd Page Header

Since this document is formatted with Mirror margins with the Different Odd and Even Pages option set, odd pages (right pages) must be numbered in its right (outer) margin, using the same information inserted in Section 4, Even Page Header text: it must left align the Filigree built-in header and right align the Page Number, Plain number.

Follow these steps to create Section 5, Odd Page Header:

1. Click the Header tool found in the Header & Footer Tools Design tab and choose Filigree built-in header to insert the Author and Title document properties right aligned in Section 5, Odd Page Header.

2. Click the Left align tool in the Home tab of the Ribbon (or press Ctrl+L) to left align the Filigree header text.

3. Press the End key twice to go to the end of the line and press the Tab key twice to insert two tab stops.

4. Use the Page Number ➤ Current Position ➤ Plain number tool to insert the next page number (III) right aligned in the Odd Page Header.

5. Drag the Right tab stop to the right to align the page number with the odd page right margin.

6. Optionally, select the entire Odd Header Text and use the Font Color tool found in the Home tab of the Ribbon to format it with Automatic color (Black).

Figure 9-50 show how the Section 5, Odd Page Header must be defined and formatted after following these last steps.

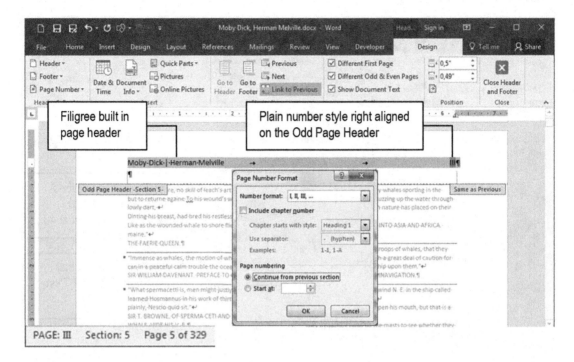

Figure 9-50. Use the Footer ➤ Filigree tool and the Page Number ➤ Current Position Plain Number to create Section 5 Odd Even Header. This time, since this is an odd (right) page, the page number must be right aligned.

Creating Section 7, Odd Page Header

Considering that the text cursor is still positioned in the now-formatted Odd Page Header of Page III, Section 5, Page 5 of 329, press the Next button found in the Header & Footer Tools Design tab until you reach the Even Page Header of Page VI, Section 5, Page 8 of 329, and note that you cannot go further using the Next button.

Microsoft Word gets stuck on this page and you will need to press the Page Down key to arrive at the First Page Header of "Chapter 1" text, located on Page 1, Section 7, Page 9 of 329.

Click the Go To Footer button (or use Page Down key) to select the First Page Footer area and note that, due to the action of inheritance, it received the same Section 2 First Page Footer, using the same page properties: Number format = I, II, III and Page numbering Start at = I (Figure 9-51).

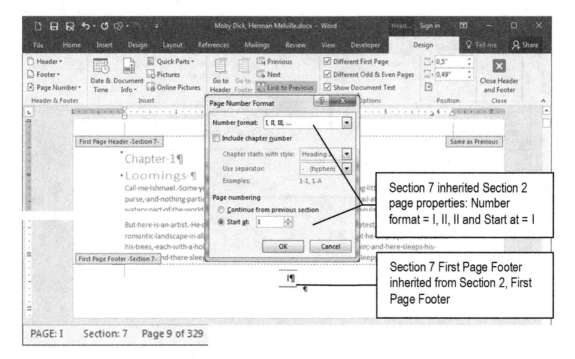

Figure 9-51. *"Chapter 1" begins on Page I, Section 7, Page 9 of 329. It received this Formatted Page Number because it inherited Section 2 page properties: Number format = I, II, III and Start at = I*

To make it appear as Page 1, Section 7, Page 9 of 329 you just need to change its Number format = 1,2,3. Follow these steps:

1. Click Page Number, Format Page Numbers... to show the Page Number Format dialog box for Section 7, Page 9 of 329.

2. Set these options:

   - Number format: 1,2,3

   - Page numbering: Continue from last section.

3. Close the Page Number Format dialog box and watch the Section 7, First Page Footer (Figure 9-52).

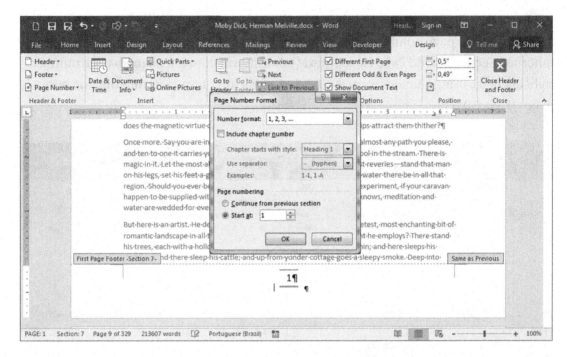

Figure 9-52. *Change Section 7 Number Format = 1,2,3 and note that will inherit Section 2, First Page Footer, but will use Arabic numerals to restart the page numbering*

Attention   When you close the Page Number Format dialog box, Microsoft Word will move the focus to the page First Page Header. Click the Go to Footer button and inspect the First Page Footer, with the Status Bar showing Page 1, Section 7, Page 9 of 329.

Inspecting Section 7, Even and Odd Page Headers

Considering that the text cursor is still positioned in the First Page Header of Page 1, Section 7, Page 9 of 329, press the Next button found in the Header & Footer Tools Design tab to reach Section 7, Even Page Header, which received the next chapter page number: Page 2, Section 7, Page 10 of 329. It inherited Section 2 Even Page Header text (page number left aligned, book information right aligned), using Section 7 Number format = 1,2,3 to correctly continue numbering "Chapter 1" pages.

Press Next button again to reach Section 7, Odd Page Header, which received again the next chapter page number: Page 3, Section 7, Page 11 of 329. Once more time, it inherited Section 4, Odd Page Header text (book information left aligned, page number right aligned), using Number format = 1,2,3 to correctly continue numbering the book pages (Figure 9-53).

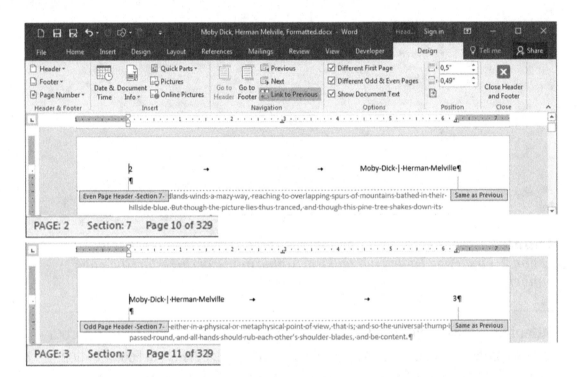

Figure 9-53. *Due to inheritance, Section 7 Even and Odd Page Headers received the same text used by Section 2, Even Page Header and Section 4, Odd Page Header. By using Number format = 1,2,3 it changes the document header number format*

Attention   The "Moby Dick, Herman Melville, Formatted.docx", which you can extract from Chapter09.zip file, contains a formatted version of this exercise.

Conclusion

This chapter gave the opportunity to learn and to use Section Breaks to create different page formatting options, considering the page number style, page renumbering, and columnated texts.

The exercises gave you a chance to learn how Microsoft Word uses inheritance to convey Header/Footer text and formatting between consecutive document sections. By using the Page Number Format dialog box (accessed just by the Page Number tool found in both the Insert tab and the Header & Footer Tools Design tab), you can use the Number format and Page numbering options to create different page number styles, restarting the document page numbering whenever be necessary.

Summary

In this chapter you learned:

- That Microsoft Word uses Section Breaks to allow creation of different pages inside the same document.

- That you can select between four different Section Breaks: Continue, Next Page, Even Page, and Odd Page.

- To change a section break it is better to use the Page Setup dialog box Section start option.

- That each Section Break can store the First, Even, and Odd Header/ Footer text, even though it is not being used in the document.

- Whenever you delete and insert another Section Break to change its type, you will lose the First, Odd, and Even Header/Footer information typed in the deleted Section Break.

- That Section Breaks have a strong inheritance that is passed for the next inserted Section Break.

- How to use the Header & Footer Tools Design tab Link to Previous option to set or break a Section Break text and properties inheritance from the previous section.

- That columnated text is always between two successive Continuous Section Breaks.

- That the bottom section break of a columnated text is the one that stores the column properties used in the text.

- How to use the Page Number Format dialog box and its Number format and Page Numbering options to insert different numbering styles or restart the page numbering in a document that uses Section Breaks.

In the next chapter, we will talk about Tables and Figures, and how you can use Microsoft Word tools to correctly manage these objects in your documents.

CHAPTER 10

Formatting Tables

In this chapter, we will have the opportunity to discuss how to manage the tables that you may need to insert in your documents.

We will start with very basic operations (insert and delete table, rows, columns, and cells), table formatting, and how to resolve misbehaving tables inserted in your documents, discussing how to take advantage of the many table format interfaces available in Microsoft Word.

All documents cited in this chapter can be found by downloading the Chapter10.zip file from this Internet address:

```
https://github.com/apress/msft-word-secrets
```

Inserting Tables

Microsoft Word tables are the modern way to tabulate text (tab stops were the typewriter way, and even today, tab stops have their place). Although there is more than one way to create a table (you can use Tab stops), I think that it is better to create it using the intuitive Table control found in the Illustrations area of the Insert tab of the Ribbon, which drops down a visual tool from where you can select the size of the table to be created: see the cursor's position in Figure 10-1.

© Flavio Morgado 2017
F. Morgado, *Microsoft Word Secrets*, https://doi.org/10.1007/978-1-4842-3078-7_10

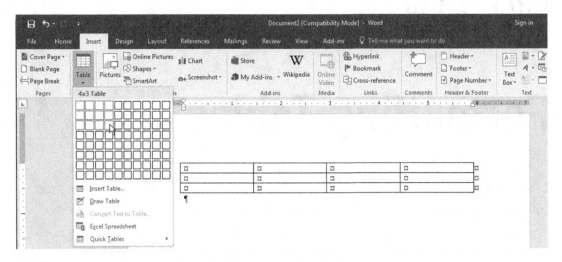

Figure 10-1. *To insert a new table in the document, use the Insert tab Table command to define the number of rows and columns that the table must have. This figure draws a 3-row-by-4-column table. Click the mouse to finish the operation.*

Figure 10-1 created a 3×4 table (12 cells) on the document page. Note that each of cell of the figure shows the "¤" hidden character, which defines where the cell text ends, because the Show/Hide command found in the Paragraph area of the Home tab of the Ribbon is checked.

Each table cell can hold any amount of text, and you can navigate through its cells by directly clicking it with the mouse, or using the Tab key: each time the Tab key is pressed, Word moves to the next cell.

Attention   To insert another table row, click the last table cell and press the Tab key. Inheritance will take care to copy the current row format to the new table row.

Typing Text in Table Cells

You can consider Microsoft Word table cells as minidocuments where you can insert and format paragraphs like you do in any other document area. You can press Enter and insert one or more paragraphs in any cell, or press Ctrl+Enter to insert a Line break, or even press Ctrl+Tab to insert one or more Tab characters inside a single cell. And for each of these paragraphs, you can define all available formatting options (alignment, indentation, line space, space before and after).

Now, with all the knowledge you have gathered so far in this book, think about the mess we can create in a single cell if we are not aware of such hidden characters...

Figure 10-2 shows what happened to the first table cell after I inserted a Tab, a Shift+Enter (Line break), and two Enter keys and changed the alignment of its last paragraph. Note that all other cells in the same row now have the same height. The figure shows the same table with the Show/Hide option checked and unchecked so you can draw your own conclusions!

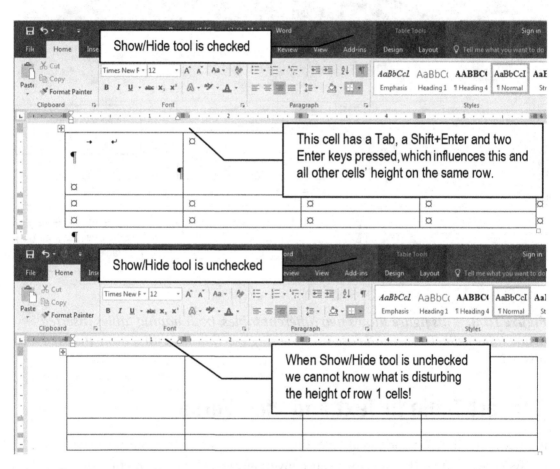

Figure 10-2. *Consider Microsoft Word table cells as minidocuments where you can insert paragraphs and hidden characters. This figure shows a cell with hidden characters inserted, which changed the height of that cell, affecting all other cells of the same row. Without the Show/Hide tool checked, one cannot anticipate what will happen to a table that gets such a high height row.*

And this is not all. Microsoft Tables are so versatile that you can also insert another table inside any of its cells. Figure 10-3 shows two tables: the first one is the same table used by Figure 10-1 that now has tables inserted inside two of its cells (cells (1,2) and (2,3)—the first number index describe the row number and the second the column number), while the second table is a more common problem: a one-cell table (external, which has two Enter keys so you can see it better) that received another table inside it.

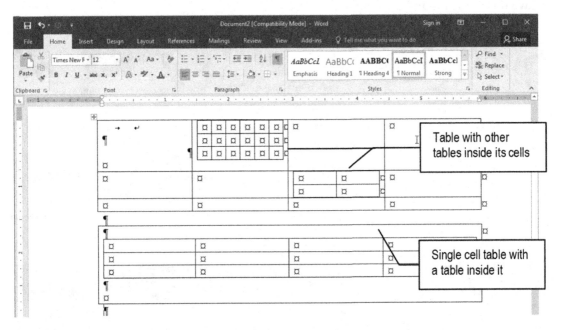

Figure 10-3. *This figure shows two different tables, both having tables inserted inside table cells. The second case shows a single-cell table with a table inserted inside it.*

Convert Table to Text and Vice Versa

It is necessary that you understand that once a table exists in the document, you can always convert it to text (and conversely convert any text to table), and this double conversion process may sometimes be the only way to correctly re-create a table.

To convert any table to text, follow these steps:

1. Click anywhere inside the table to select it (or click the "+" square in the top left table corner to select the entire table);

2. In the Table Tools ➤ Layout tab that appears on Ribbon whenever a table is selected, click the Convert to Text command;

3. Microsoft Word will show the Convert Table to Text dialog box, asking how you want to separate the table values;

4. Choose the separator character to be used as cell content delimiter and press Enter to finish the conversation process.

Figure 10-4 shows what happens when we convert to text an empty 5×4 table using Tab stops as cell separator. Note that Word inserts n-1 tab stops to delimit each table cell value (where n = the table columns count), using a pilcrow paragraph mark to separate each table row.

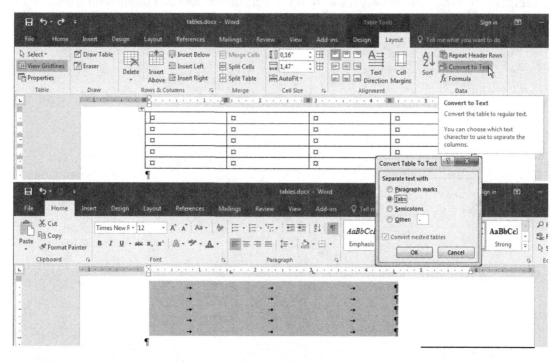

Figure 10-4. *You can convert any table to text selecting the table and using the Table Tools ➤ Layout tab ➤ Convert to Text command. Microsoft Word will ask to select the cell separator character that must be used to separate each cell content (default is Tab).*

You are now in a position to appreciate the need to understand what a Tab character means. Looking to Figure 10-4, you must clearly understand that, although no text was inserted in the table, the three tab stops of these five paragraphs can represent a 5×4 table (with the first cell content being at left of the first Tab character)!

To reconvert the selected text to a table, follow these steps:

1. Select just the text paragraphs that you want to convert to a table (no less, no more);

2. In the Insert tab of the Ribbon, click the Table ➤ Convert Text to Table... command;

3. Microsoft Word will show the Convert Text to Table dialog box, guessing the table dimensions and cell separator character it will consider to create the table, relative to the text you selected;

4. If everything is OK, press Enter to convert the text to a table.

Figure 10-5 shows how easy it was to reconvert the perfect 5×4 table, which was previously converted to text, using Tab stops as cell character separator.

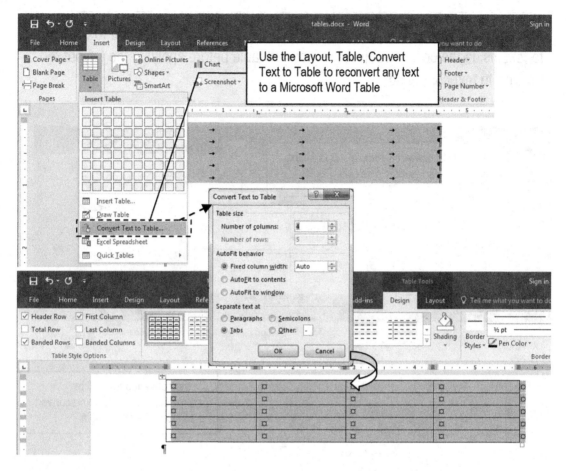

Figure 10-5. *To convert text to table, select just the paragraphs you want to convert (no more, no less), click the Insert tab on the Ribbon, and apply the Table ➤ Convert Text to Table command. Microsoft Word will show the Convert Text to Table dialog box, making a guess of which type of table it can create based on the selected text.*

But if the table is too complex, like the ones shown in Figure 10-3, where a cell has a table inserted in it, the conversion of table to text may create paragraphs with very different quantities of Tab characters (or any other text separator character chosen, Figure 10-6), so that it may become impossible to reconstruct the original table design using the Table ➤ Convert Text to Table command (Figure 10-7).

Attention   If you have a table inserted in another table cell and want to convert it to text inside the cell, select just the inserted table before applying the Layout ➤ Convert to text command.

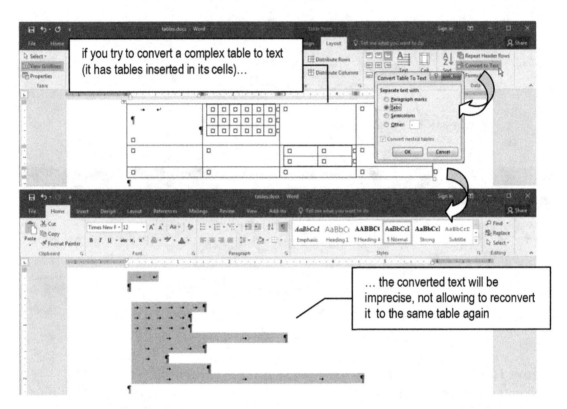

Figure 10-6. *Complex table designs may create very uneven text paragraphs, having different numbers of Tab stops (or any other text separator character used by the Convert Table to Text dialog box).*

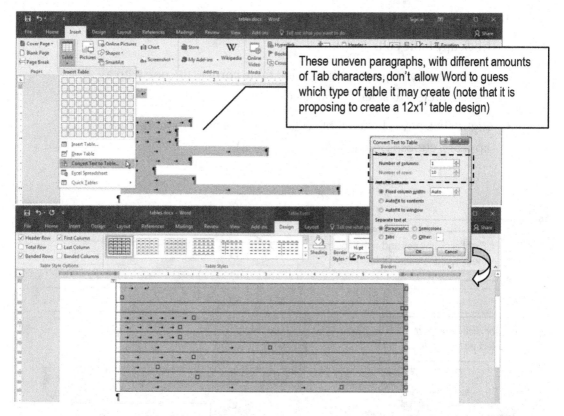

Figure 10-7. *When you try to reconvert uneven paragraphs to a table, the Convert Text to Table dialog box may not be capable of "guessing" which type of table you want to create, and the result may be a table quite different from the one that generated that type of text.*

Selecting and Deleting Tables and Cells

Once a table is inserted in any Microsoft Word document, it is not obvious how to delete it: it is very persistent in the document, neglecting to react to the so-obvious Delete key.

There are many strategies to delete a table from the document, using the mouse or the keyboard.

To delete a table using the mouse, you can follow these next steps:

1. Right-click any table cell, which makes a small floating toolbar appear above it.

2. In the floating tool bar, click Delete and select Delete table.

Or use another method:

1. Click any table cell.

2. Click the small square at the top left table corner (the one with a "+" character) to select all table cells.

3. Right-click any selected table cell, and in the pop-up menu that appears, choose Delete table (Figure 10-8).

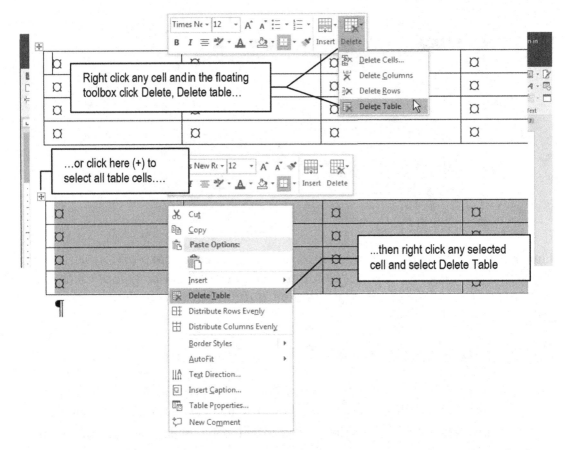

Figure 10-8. *To delete a table using the mouse, right-click any of its cells and select the Delete ➤ Delete Table command in the small toolbox that appears. Or you can click the small box with a "+" character in the top left table corner to first select the entire table, right-click any selected cell, and select Delete Table in the pop-up menu.*

To delete a table using the keyboard, you can

1.   Insert one empty paragraph after the table;

2.   Select the table and this empty paragraph;

3.   Press Delete key.

Selecting All Table Cells to Delete a Table

Another way to delete a table from any document is by first selecting all table cells and then using Shift+Delete.

Once again, you can select all table cells by using different strategies:

- Click the first table cell and drag the mouse to select all its cells;

- Click the first table cell, press and hold Shift, and click the last table cell;

- Click any table cell and then click the small square in the small box at the top left table corner (the one with a "+" character);

- Alt+Double-click at left of any table row (point the mouse cursor to the left of any table row until it becomes a normal mouse pointer before performing the operation).

Once the table is selected, you can easily delete it pressing Shift+Delete (or eventually convert the table to text and delete the associated text).

Try for yourself!

Selecting a Single Cell

Use the mouse to select any amount of contiguous table cells and apply a desired format to them:

To select a single cell, anywhere in the table;

1.   Point the mouse to the left of any cell (inside it) until the cursor turns into a small black arrow pointing up (indicating that just one cell will be selected);

2. Click to select just this cell (Figure 10-9).

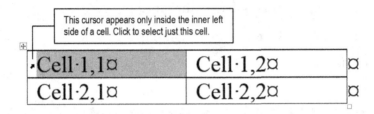

Figure 10-9. *Point the mouse inside any cell inner left side until it changes to a small black arrow and click to select it*

Selecting and Table Rows and Columns

You can select an entire row or column by dragging the mouse or using the right mouse cursor for the task.

To select a row or column by dragging the mouse:

1. Click first cell row/column cell.

2. Drag the mouse to left (or down) to select the entire row (or column).

To select an entire row using the mouse cursor:

1. Point the mouse to the left of any row (outside the table) until the cursor changes to a regular mouse arrow.

2. Click to select the entire row (Figure 10-10).

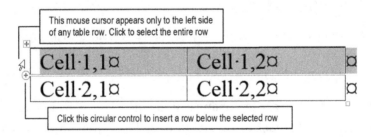

Figure 10-10. *Point the mouse to the left of the first table column until it changes to a normal mouse arrow and click to select the entire row. Displace it toward the bottom of the row to show the "add row" circular control and click to insert a new row below it.*

To select an entire column using the mouse cursor:

1. Point the mouse to the top of any row (above the table) until the cursor changes to a small black arrow pointing down.

2. Click to select the entire column (Figure 10-11).

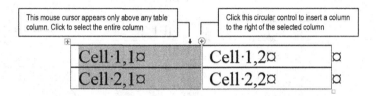

Figure 10-11. *Point the mouse to the top of any table column, above the first table row until it changes to a small black arrow pointing down and click to select the entire column. Displace it toward the right column border row to show the "add column" circular control that, when clicked, inserts columns to its right.*

Inserting Table Rows, Columns, and Cells

You can insert rows, columns, and cells in any Microsoft Word table by using different methods using the mouse and menu commands. Let's see them!

Using the Mouse with Table Handles

As Figures 10-10 and 10-11 explain, you can easily insert a new row or column in a table by selecting the desired row(s) or column(s), displacing the mouse to point to the bottom of the last row selected (or to the right of the last column border) to show the circular control with a "+" character, and clicking it.

The row(s) (or column(s)) will be inserted below (or to the right of) the last row (or column) selected (Figure 10-12).

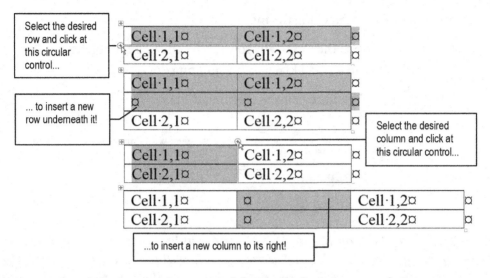

Figure 10-12. *Click the circular control (with the "+" character) that appears whenever you select one or more entire rows (or columns) and point to the bottom left (or top right) of the selection, to easily insert rows at the bottom (or columns to the right) of selection.*

Attention   The number of rows or columns selected is equal to the number of rows or columns inserted.

Using Table ➤ Insert Command

Microsoft Word will also insert new cells to left or right of the current cell, allowing you to create tables that have different numbers of columns among its rows.

To insert a new cell in any table:

1. Right-click the cell that will be neighbor to the cell to be inserted and choose Insert ➤ Insert cells to show the Insert Cells dialog box;

2. In the Insert cells dialog box, select Shift cells left or Shift cells right option to insert a single cell;

3. Choose Insert entire row to insert a row below (or Insert entire column to insert a column to the right);

4. Press OK to make the desired insertion.

Figure 10-13 shows how you can insert a cell to the left of a given cell using the Shift cells right option to create a table with an uneven number of columns.

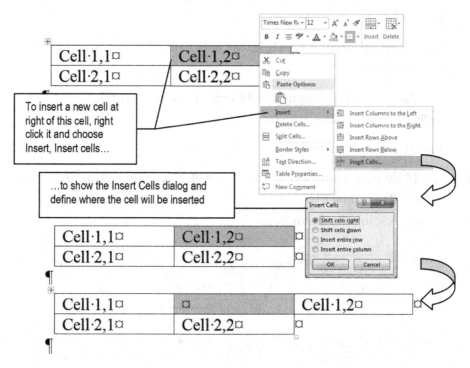

Figure 10-13. *Right-click any cell and select Insert* ➤ *Insert cells to insert a cell to the left or right of the selected cell (you can also insert a row above or a column to the left of it).*

Using Split Cells

Microsoft Word also allows inserting more cells in any table without displacing cells to the left or right by splitting a cell into the desired number of rows and columns.

If you split the cell into more than one row, all other cells of the same row will receive the same row height as the split cell.

Attention   If the text inside the split cell does not fit any more in the new cell width, the cell height will also be enlarged.

To split a cell into rows and columns:

1. Select the desired cell.

2. Right-click it to show the pop-up menu.

3. In the pop-up menu, select Insert ➤ Split cells to show the Split cell dialog box.

4. Use the Number of columns and Number of rows controls to define how the cell may be split.

5. Press OK to split the cell.

Figure 10-14 shows what happens when the table shown in Figure 10-13 (which received a new cell in its first row) has its first cell (cell 1,1) split into two columns and two rows using the Split cells dialog box.

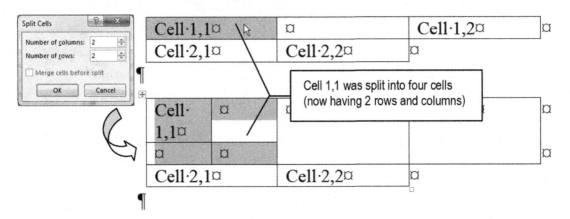

Figure 10-14. *Microsoft Word also allows inserting cells in a table using the Split Cells dialog box. In this case, the inserted cell will not displace the remaining cells' position, but may impact on the row height of the split cell.*

Attention   As explained before, by splitting a table cell into two or more rows/ columns, you will create a complex table that, if it's converted to text by using the Layout ➤ Convert Table to Text command, will not be able to be rebuilt it from its paragraphs using the Insert ➤ Table ➤ Convert Text to table command.

Merging Cells

You can also create tables having rows with different column counts by merging one or more of its cells into a single cell.

To merge table cells:

1.   Select the cells you want to merge;

2.   Right-click the selection and choose Merge cells.

If the merged cells had text inside them, the text of each cell will be separated by hidden paragraph characters, with each cell using text rows inside the merged cell.

Figure 10-15 merges the four cells produced in split cell 1,1 into a single cell again. It then merges all remaining row 1 cells and merges them again into one single cell again, creating a single, big cell in row 1 with two rows of text.

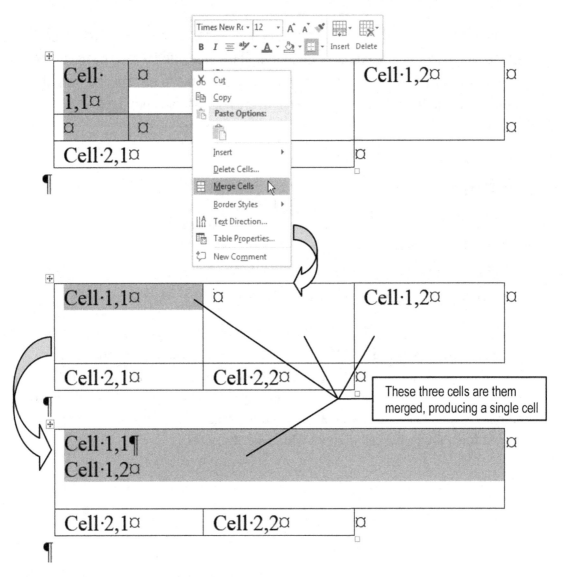

Figure 10-15. *Use the Merge command to join individual cells into one. If these cells have some text, the text will be separated by hidden paragraph characters inside the merged cell.*

Changing Cell, Column, or Row Dimensions

Once a table has been inserted in a Microsoft Word document page, you can use the mouse to change any individual cell, column, or row dimensions, independently or all at once.

Follow these simple rules:

- To change any cell width or height you must first select the desired cell. The width of all other cells in the same column *will not* be affected, but the height of all cells of the same row will be.

- To change any column width, you must select the entire column or no cell at all.

- Whenever you change any cell width, the entire row width will be changed.

Changing Cell Dimensions

To change any cell width, you must first select the desired cell (point the mouse to its inner left side and click). Then you can drag its right border to change just the selected cell width, or its down border to change the entire row height (Figure 10-16).

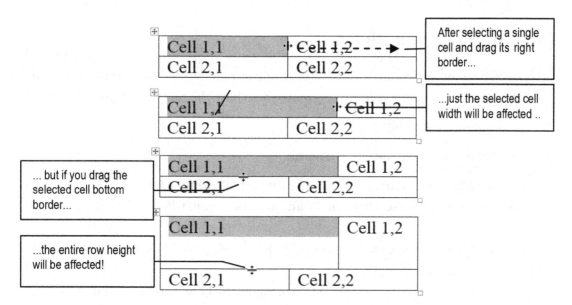

Figure 10-16. *To change any cell's width, select it by pointing the mouse to its inner left side (the cursor will change to a small black arrow) and then drag its right border to the desired dimension. Whenever you drag any cell bottom border, the entire row height will change.*

If you could not diminish the row height by dragging any of its cells' bottom border, it is due to one of these reasons:

1. There are one or more hidden characters (like Enter, Shift Enter, Tab, etc.) inserted in one or more of its cells.

2. Any cell line spacing is greater than 1.

3. Any cell has Space Before and/or After defined.

To correct issue 1, click the Show/Hide tool in the Home tab of the Ribbon, and remove all unnecessary hidden characters.

To correct issues 2 and 3:

1. Select the entire row (point the mouse to the left of the row and click).

2. Change all cells Line Spacing = 1.

3. Set the Space Before and After = 0.

Changing Column Width

You can change the any column width by dragging its right border to a new position, but to affect all cells of the same column and make them have the same width you must either

- Not select any cell; or

- Select all cells of the entire column.

But since Microsoft Word tables can have cells of different widths, you may first need to adjust some cell widths so Microsoft Word can understand which cells belong to the desired column.

Note however that you can't drag the right border of any cell or column past the left border of the column at its right.

Consider for example the complex table of Figure 10-17, which has different numbers of cells in each of its rows. Which cells belong to column 1, column 2, etc., according to Microsoft Word column counts?

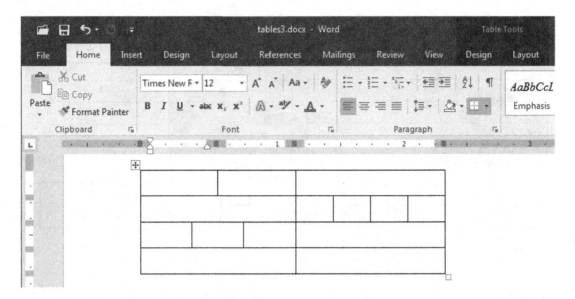

Figure 10-17. *A complex Microsoft Word table, made by splitting some of its cells to create rows with different numbers of cells. Which cell belongs to each table column?*

To determine this, you must first point and click the mouse over any column cell (over the first row cell of each column) to realize which cells are selected in column 1, column 2, and so on.

Figure 10-18 shows that when the mouse is over the first cell of the first row (supposedly selecting cells from the first table column), Microsoft Word selects cells from columns 1 and 2. By clicking over the second cell of the first row (supposedly selecting cells from the second table column), the selection may take cells from the third column. And when clicking over the third cell of the first row (supposedly selecting cells from the last table column), this column and all remaining cells below it will be selected.

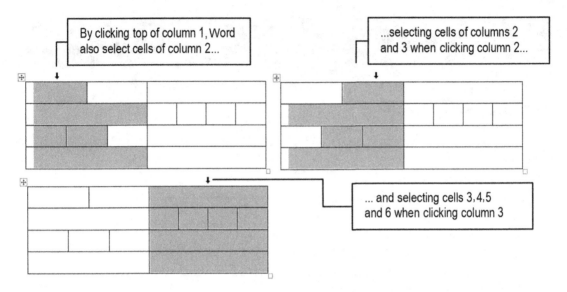

Figure 10-18. *When a table has uneven number of cells in its many rows, it may be difficult to select all cells of a column by just point-and-click. You need to first redefine some cells' width before selecting each column individually.*

Deleting Table Cells, Rows, and Columns

You can also delete a single cell, an entire row, or an entire column from a table. Note however that by deleting a single table you will create a *hole* in the table, which will oblige Microsoft Word to make a decision about what to do with the remaining cells of the row or column to which it belongs: shift all cells at its right to the left, or shift all cells at its bottom upward.

To delete a single cell, follow these steps:

1. Select the cell to be deleted (point the mouse to the cell's inner left and click).

2. In the small context toolbar that appears, click Delete ➤ Delete Cells… to show the Delete Cells dialog box.

3. Select the method that Microsoft Word must use to treat the remaining cells at its left or below (if any):

   • Shift cells left: all cells at left of the selected cell will be displaced to the left (leaving a hole at the right of the cell row).

   • Shift cells up: all cells below the selected cell will be displaced up.

Attention   By selecting the Shift cells up option, since Microsoft Word can just leave holes in the right table column, if the deleted cell is not at the last table column, a new empty cell will be created in the same column and last table row.

Figure 10-19 shows an example of what happens when you delete a single cell and select either Shift Cells Right or Shift Cells Up.

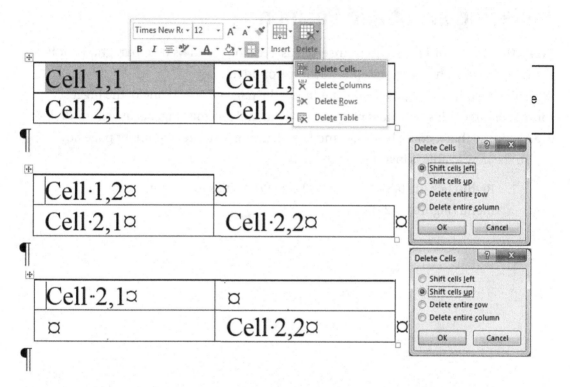

Figure 10-19. *To delete a single cell or an entire row or column, select the cell first and right-click it to show the small tool bar from where you can click Delete ➤ Delete cells... command to show the Delete Cells dialog box; once that has been done, you can take the desired action.*

To delete an entire row or column from a table, you can use one of these methods:

1. Select any cell from the row/column to be deleted.

2. Use the Delete ➤ Delete cells... command to show the Delete Cells dialog box.

3. Select either Delete entire row or Delete entire column to proceed.

You can also use a faster method:

1. Select the entire row or column (point the mouse over the column or at left of the row and click).

2. Right-click the selection and choose Delete Row or Delete Column options (according to selection).

Table Alignment and Position

Every Microsoft Word table can be inserted as a text object in its own paragraph, or float above the page with text paragraphs flowing around it.

This versatile way of positioning tables on the page is indeed one of the biggest sources of difficulties that most people have with table formatting, because they did not even suppose that it could be done, and keep fighting with the document page flow.

To see how a table is inserted on the page:

1. Right-click the table and select Table Properties in the context menu (Figure 10-20).

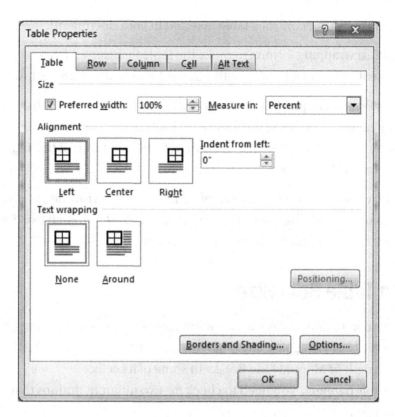

Figure 10-20. *Right-click a table and select Table Properties to show the Table Properties dialog box from where you can use Text Wrapping to define that the table is a text object (None) or floats over the page (Around).*

2. Use the Text wrapping area to define the table behavior regarding how the text wraps around it:

    - **None**: the table is inserted as a text element having it own paragraph.

    - **Around**: the table is floating over the document page, with text flowing around it.

3. Use the Alignment command to define the table position on the page (Left, Center, or Right aligned).

Note in the Table Properties dialog box that the Alignment option has an Indent from left option that is only enabled when Alignment = Left and Text wrapping = None, to allow defining the table distance from the page left margin.

Use these tips to better control a table inserted in your document:

- Use Text wrapping = None to make the table be inserted as a text element so you can better control the text that is above and below it.

- Click the small square at the top left table corner (the one with a "+" character) and drag the mouse to displace the table from the page's left margin (changing the Indent from left option of the Table Properties dialog box).

- To give a standard cell size to all or some table cells (row height and/or column width), select all desired table cells first and then use the other Table Properties dialog box tab controls.

Changing Table Row Size

It is not uncommon to find tables with different row heights—a formatting change that can be defined either by dragging any table row bottom border, or by inserting and removing Paragraph or Manual Line Breaks in some of its cells.

Whenever this happens, you need to check for two different options that can affect any table row height:

- Paragraph formatting options: select the entire table and check if all its cells have the same Line Spacing and Space Before and After options.

- The row height increase, defined in the Table Properties Row tab.

The Table Properties Row tab offers special controls that allow changing all selected rows' height at once and the way a table will behave whenever it's big enough to fit on a single page (Figure 10-21).

Figure 10-21. *Use the Table Properties Row tab to define the selected cells' row height and the way a table behaves when it is too big to fit on a single page*

Attention   Any table row height is first defined by any of its cells' Font and Paragraph properties. For better results use the same Font type and size, Line spacing = 1, and Space Before = After = 0 for all table cells.

- **Specify height**: this option defines the amount of vertical space added to a table cell.

  - **Row height is**: use At Least to define a minimum cell height; use exactly to define a fixed cell height.

- **Allow row to break across pages**: uncheck this option to make each cell appear on a single document page.

- **Repeat as header row at the top of each page**: check this option to make a table that is big enough not to fit on a single page, automatically repeat its first row at the top of the next page (tables that fit on a page will not react to this option).

Changing Table Column Size

Column widths can be easily controlled using by dragging the column right border, but to easily give to all column cells the same width, you will do better using the Paragraph Properties Column tab Preferred width control, which can be defined as table width percent or by specific inch value (Figure 10-22).

Figure 10-22. *Use the Table Properties Column tab to apply the same column width to all selected cells, using a table width percent value or a defined column width in inches*

Attention   To easily adjust a cell column width according to the column cells' content, use the same Microsoft Excel approach: double-click the column right border to make Microsoft Word adjust the column width to the widest column content.

Changing Cell Dimensions and Vertical Alignment

Use the Table Properties Cell tab to define selected cells' width and vertical alignment (since cell height may be defined by another cell of the same row or to the options set in the Table Properties Row tab).

Figure 10-23. *Use the Table Properties Cell tab to define selected cells' width and vertical text alignment*

Attention   These options can also be set using the Table Tools Layout tab controls, as you will see in the next section.

Use the Table Properties Alt Text to insert a table text description that can be used by people with vision or cognitive impairments.

Formatting Tables

Besides the Table Properties dialog box, Microsoft Word offers many different tools to format a table using the Table Tools Layout and Design tabs of the Ribbon that appears when a table is selected.

This section will try to make sense of many different ways of changing a table appearance—and some problems that may arise from tweaking these options—by using one of the default tables that can be easily created using the Insert ➤ Table ➤ Quick Tables... option (it will use the "With Subheads 1" quick table, Figure 10-24).

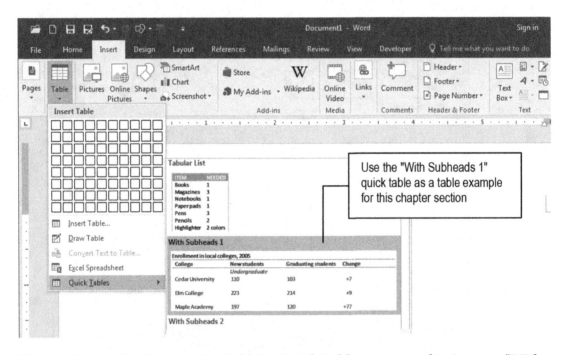

Figure 10-24. *Use the Insert ➤ Table ➤ Quick Tables command to insert a "With Subheads 1" table in any document to follow the next exercise.*

Attention   The Insert ➤ Table ➤ Quick Tables command has some interesting ready-made tables that are worth exploring to understand how to use the rich resources offered by Microsoft Word to format tables.

Table Styles

Figure 10-25 shows the "With Subheads 1" quick table selected in a Microsoft Word document page with the Table Tools Design tab selected. Note that it offers on its left side the Table Style Options area, which allows defining which type of table styles can be applied to the selected table, with the Style Gallery showing the default Table Style set applied to format it.

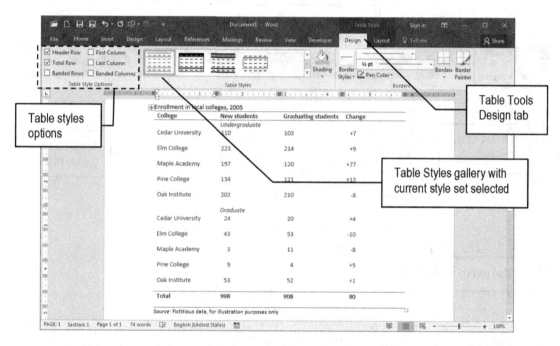

Figure 10-25. *This is the "With Subheads 1" quick table created by Microsoft Word using the Insert ➤ Table ➤ Quick Tables command.*

As you can see, any table can have different styles applied to specific rows and columns: the Header (first row) and Total row (last row), First and Last column, and Banded Rows and Columns (creating a vertical or horizontal "zebra" effect in alternating rows and columns).

This is possible because Microsoft Word allows you to create a Table Style that has these substyles (header and total row, first and last column, banded rows and columns) to allow an easy customization of any table, which is the work done by the Table Styles gallery.

Whenever you expand the Table Style gallery, what you see is an enormous variation in how these substyles can be defined so they can be easily applied to the selected table.

Note however that not every style set implements all substyles. Figure 10-26 shows how the "With Subheads 1" table became after it received the "Grid Table 2 - Accent 1" style set, which implements the Banded Rows and Columns, and had the Banded Rows option selected in the Table Tools Design tab.

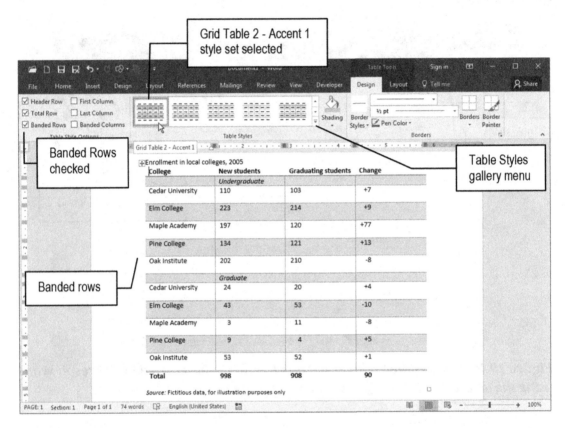

Figure 10-26. *By using the Table Styles gallery you can select different style sets that may use the substyles for header and total rows, first and last column, banded rows and columns. The Grid Table2 - Accent 1 style set implements the Banded Rows and Columns, which allow you to apply a shaded effect to the background of alternate table rows.*

You can inspect how this style set was built: click the small arrow located in the bottom right corner of the Table Styles gallery to expand it and select the Modify Table Style... command, which will open Microsoft Word Modify Style for the selected table style (Figure 10-27).

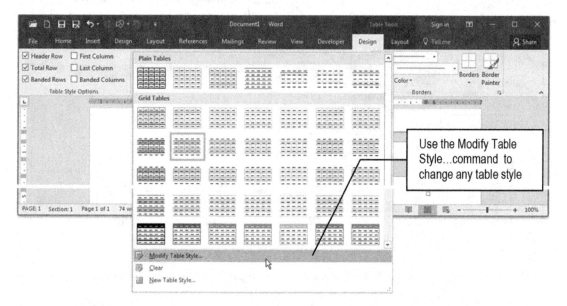

Figure 10-27. *Expand the Table Styles gallery and select Modify Table Style... command to show Microsoft Word Modify Style dialog box for the selected table style*

The Modify Style dialog box for a style set is the best interface to quickly format all table cells, because it offers the Apply formatting to list, from where you can select what must be changed in the table style (Figure 10-28).

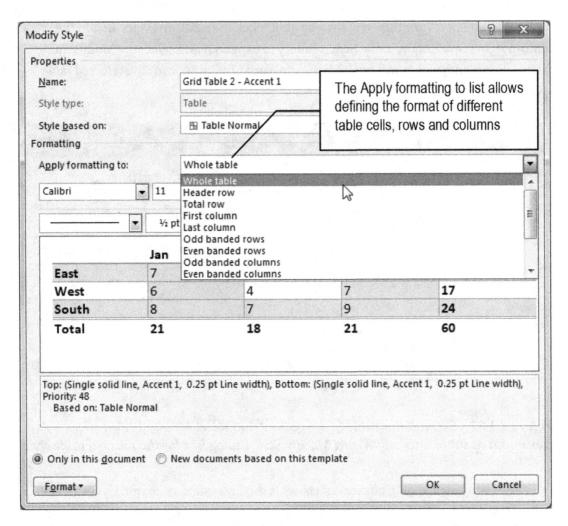

Figure 10-28. *Use the Modify Style dialog box "Apply formatting to" list to select what must be changed in the Table Style. You can define options for the Whole table, and for the format of specific rows and columns.*

Use these tips whenever you need to use the Modify Style dialog box to change any table appearance:

- **Whole table**: select this option to make adjustments to the Font and Paragraph options of all table cells.

- **Header row and Total row**: select these options to make adjustments to the first and last table rows.

- **Odd and Even banded rows and columns**: use these options to define the alternate color used in odd and even table rows and columns (if needed).

- **Top and Bottom Left and Right cells**: use these options to make specific formatting options for table corner cells.

Although you can use the Styles window, New Style button to create a new table style, you will do better by selecting an existing table style from the style pane, applying the desired changes, and then saving it with a new name.

Follow these steps to create a new table style:

1. Create a new empty table (which will be formatted with the Table Grid style set), or select any existing table in your document.

2. Expand the Table Style gallery and select the Modify Style... option to show the Modify Style dialog box (see Figures 10-27 and 10-28).

3. In the Modify Style dialog box, set these options:

   - **Name**: name the new style you want to create.

   - **Style based on**: select Table Normal for use an empty style or any other table style already saved (and available in the Table Style gallery).

   - **Apply formatting to**: use each option to define the appearance of header and total rows, first and last column, odd and even banded rows.

     Use the font, size, and Format button options to set each possible substyle (you will do better by making a single choice for Whole table option).

4. Close the Modify Style dialog box to save your new style.

The new table style create will appear in the Table Style gallery at the same table style group from which the Style based on option was defined (you may need to expand the Style Gallery and point the mouse for a similar preview to find it on the list).

Attention   Since the Modify Style dialog box Style based on option doesn't have a "No Style" option (as you found for paragraph, character or list styles), there is no way to create a new table style that is not based on the Table Normal style, because every table style has Style based on = Table Normal. This way, whenever you create a new style based on another style, you are indeed cascade inheriting Table Normal, which also inherits the Normal style.

Normal Style Inheritance

The most common disturbing effect in table formatting comes from Normal style inheritance.

Look to Figure 10-28 and note that the Grid Table 2 - Accent 1 table style is based on Table Normal style. And even if you could shake Microsoft Word upside down, you could not find any trace of the Table Normal style to change any of its settings, like the "Style based on = Normal" style.

Yes, it's true. Every table style inherits the Table Normal style which by itself inherits the Normal style, meaning that any change made to the Normal style will be instantly reflected in all table styles and consequently seen in all document tables formatted with them, respecting the previously explained principle that a global format change cannot change a local format change.

You can make a simple experiment about how a simple Normal style change can disturb the "With Subtitles 1" quick table, by following these next steps:

1. Right-click the Normal style in the Style Gallery found in the Home tab of the Ribbon and select Modify... command to show the Modify Style dialog box.

2. In the Modify Style dialog box for the Normal style, click Format button and choose Paragraph to show the Paragraph dialog box.

3. In the Paragraph dialog box Indentation area, set this option: **Special = First line = 0.49** (Figure 10-29).

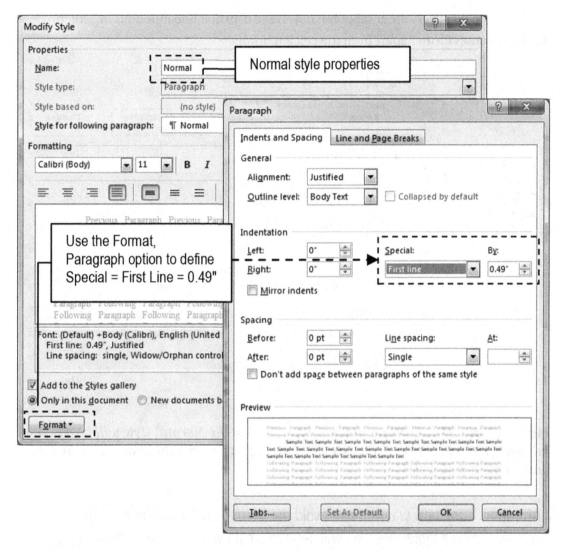

Figure 10-29. *Use the Modify Style dialog box to show the Paragraph dialog box and add an Indentation = Special = First line = 0.49*

4. Close the Paragraph dialog box and close the Modify dialog box to add a first line indentation to the Normal style and all paragraphs based on it.

Now, every "With Subtitle 1" quick table cell (and every other document table) has a First line indent = 0.49, which completely affected the table formatting options. Figure 10-30 shows how this simple change affected the table Header row (first row), where the third column header (Graduated students) doesn't fit anymore on a single row.

Also note that every other table cell now has a 0.49 first line indentation, which makes its values further apart from the cell left border.

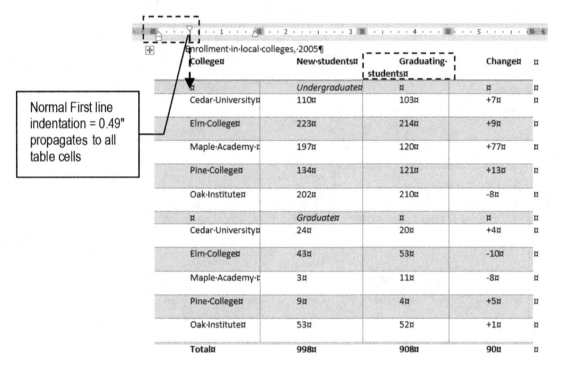

Figure 10-30. *The First line Indentation = 0.49 of the Normal style will be cascade inherited by any table style because they are all based on Table Normal (which is based on Normal style)*

Attention   The only way you can avoid the Normal style inheritance in table cells is by not using a table style. You will need to create your own Paragraph styles to be applied to specific table rows (like TableTitle, TableFirstRow, TableLastRow, and TableCells). All of them must set property Style based on = No style, and they must be manually applied to the desired table rows.

Formatting Row Height

Some formatting options applied to table cells—or the ones inherited from changes to Normal style—can pose difficulties in keeping (or changing) a table format, which is especially true regarding table row height, which can be affected by font or paragraph formatting, and must be manipulated to force the entire table to fit onto a single document page.

The "With Subheads 1" quick table can be used as an example because it has no Paragraphs or Line breaks inserted in any of its cells (check the Show/Hide tool in the Home tab of the Ribbon and see for yourself), but it does have widely spaced rows whose height cannot be lessened by dragging any row bottom border up or by changing the cell Height option found in the Cell Size area of the Table Tools Layout tab (Figure 10-31).

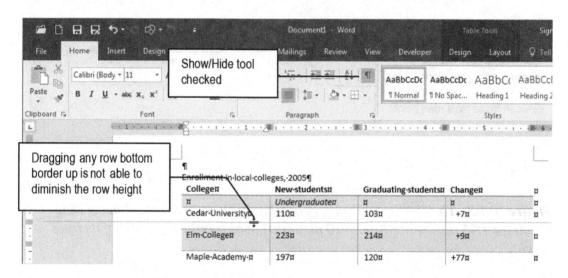

Figure 10-31. *You cannot lessen any "With Subheads 1" quick table row height by dragging any row bottom border up. It is an indication that at least one row cell has a different Paragraph Line Spacing or Space Before or After set.*

Whenever this happens, the problem you face to change the table row height resides in font or formatting options imposed on specific cells, which affect the entire row height, probably arising from changing some Paragraph options, like Space Before or After and Line spacing for one or more row cells.

By inspecting the "With Subheads 1" quick table column cells Paragraph options, you will realize that the first table column has no formatting options set (Line spacing = Single, Space Before = After = 0), but its second, third, and fourth columns have some cells with a Space before option set (Line spacing = Multiple = 1.15, Space After = 10 pt, Figure 10-32).

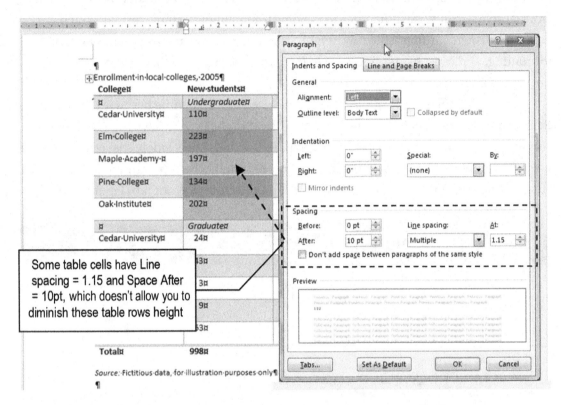

Figure 10-32. *The "With Subheads 1" quick table has some cells that set Line spacing = 1.15 and Space After = 10 pt, which avoids reducing some of its rows' height*

To have greater control over the table row height, you need to act on cell Paragraph formatting by following these steps:

1. Click the small square at the top left table corner (the one with a "+" character) to select all table rows.

2. Show the Paragraph dialog box and clear all the options that can produce such odd results:

   • Indentation Left = 0

   • Indentation Right = 0

- Indentation Special = None

- Spacing Before = 0

- Spacing After = 0

- Line spacing = Single

Figure 10-33 shows the final effect on "With Subheads 1" quick table, which now has all its rows with the smaller possible height for the font size selected.

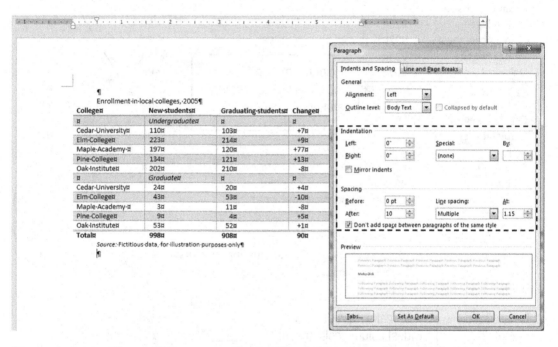

Figure 10-33. *The easiest way to diminish a table vertical length that has no unused Paragraph or Line breaks in its cells is to select the entire table and remove all Paragraph options that can disturb cell formatting: Indentation Left = Right = 0, Special = None, Space Before = After = 0 and Line spacing = Single*

Formatting Column Width

Another simple action commonly performed in table formatting is to change column width to make the table fit the page width, or to give it a better appearance.

You can make changes to the table column widths by using different techniques:

- Double-click the right border on any column width (to adjust the column width to the widest cell content).

- Drag each column right border to the desired width (Figure 10-34).

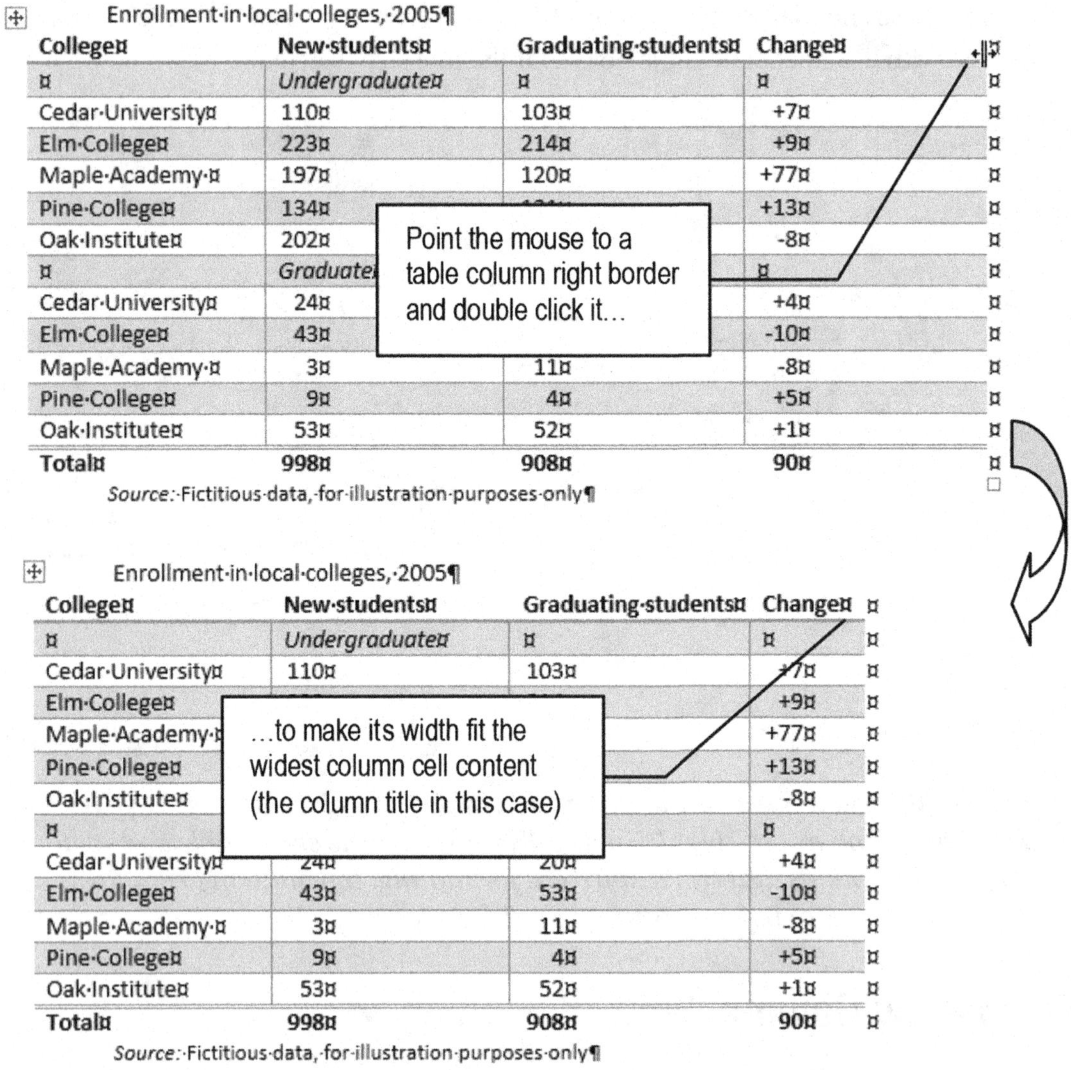

Figure 10-34. *Double-click a table column right border to make its width fit the widest cell content*

- Use the Cell Size area commands of the Table Tools Layout tab (Figure 10-35).

Figure 10-35. *Use the Cell Size area controls of the Table Tools Layout tab to define table column widths*

The Cell Size area of the Table Tools Layout tab of the Ribbon has five controls to allow you to adjust the column widths of a table:

- **AutoFit**: allows automatically adjusting column width and row height according to current font and paragraph settings:

  - **AutoFit Contents**: adjust column width, row height to the smallest possible values that fit cell content (Figure 10-36).

  - **AutoFit Window**: adjust table width to page width and distribute column widths.

  - **AutoFit Column Width**: same as double-clicking the column right border, adjusting column width to fit the widest column cell content.

- **Cell Height and Width**: show current cell height and width and allow defining a numeric value for both sizes (using the current ruler measurement unit).

- **Distribute rows and Distribute columns**: make the selected rows/columns receive the same width.

The easiest way to make a table adjust its columns and rows to use the smallest cell height and width is by using AutoFit ➤ AutoFit Contents command (Figure 10-36).

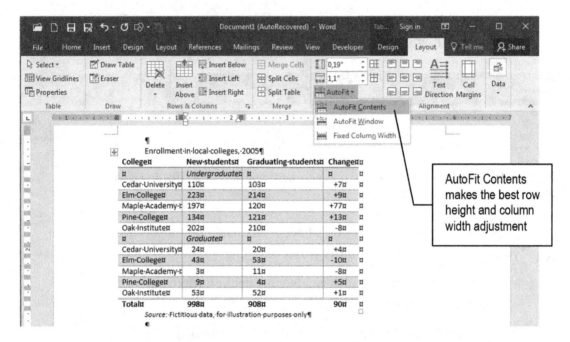

Figure 10-36. *Use the AutoFit ➤ AutoFit Contents command to make the best row height and column width adjusments possible to a table*

But if want your table to spread its cells across the entire page width (between page left and right margins), use AutoFit ➤ AutoFit Window command (Figure 10-37). The resulting table will have different column widths, according to the widest column content.

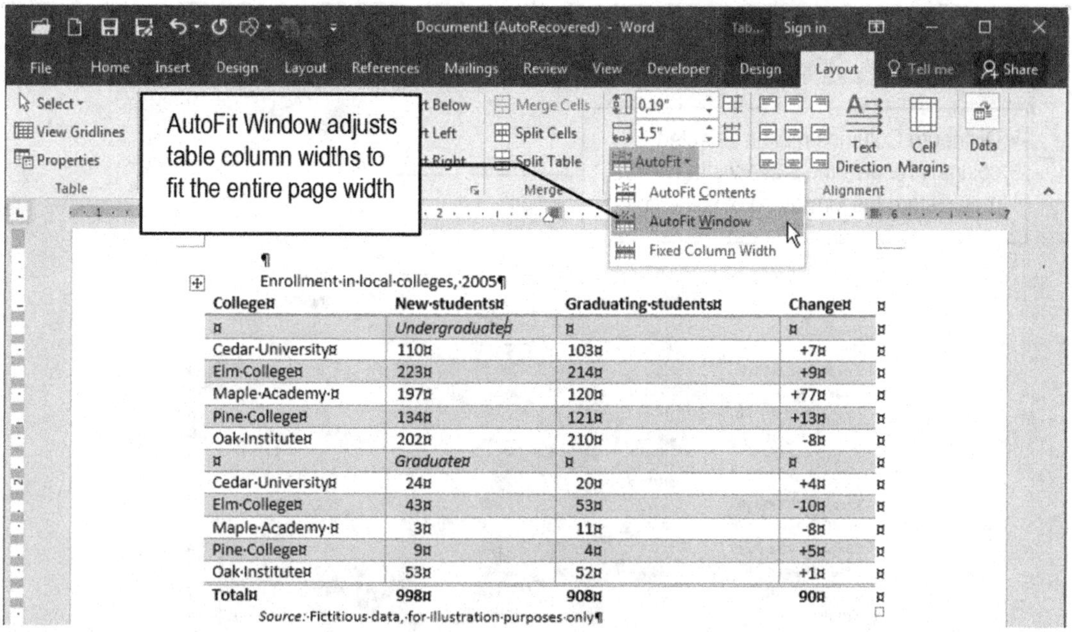

Figure 10-37. *Use the AutoFit ➤ AutoFit Window command to make a table adjust its content to the page width. Note however that it has different column widths.*

To make some table columns have the same width, select them all (point the mouse over the first column until it turns into a small black down arrow and drag through the columns) and use the Distribute Columns command found in the Cell Size area of the Table Tools Layout tab (or right-click selected columns and choose Distribute Columns). Note however that this command may not make the best width adjustment for all columns, as you can see in Figure 10-38, where the 3rd column title does not fit on a single row).

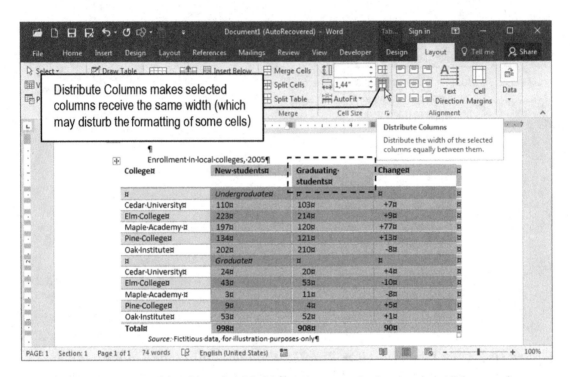

Figure 10-38. *To make selected table columns receive the same width, use the Distribute Column command found in the Cell Size area of the Table Tool Layout tab (or right-click selected columns and choose Distribute Columns)*

Fixing Tables That Don't Fit on a Page

Sometimes a table seems not to fit on a page, spreading its columns past the right page margin, and you don't know how to access these out-of-bounds cells to fix the table column widths (Figure 10-24).

College	New students	Graduating students	Chang
	Undergraduate		
Cedar University	110	103	+7
Elm College	223	214	+9
Maple Academy	197	120	+77
Pine College	134	121	+13
Oak Institute	202	210	-8
	Graduate		
Cedar University	24	20	+4
Elm College	43	53	-10
Maple Academy	3	11	-8
Pine College	9	4	+5
Oak Institute	53	52	+1
Total	998	908	90

Source: Fictitious data, for illustration purposes only

Figure 10-39. *This table column is hugging the right page margin. Which size does it have?*

Whenever such a problem occurs in a document you can easily fix it by using two different methods:

1. If the table is simple, without merged cells, convert it to text and reconvert the text to table (as explained earlier in this chapter).

2. For any table (especially the complex ones, full of merged cells), use Microsoft Word Draft view (located in the Views area of the View tab of the Ribbon) and then change the column size.

Microsoft Word Draft view is a special view that does not show the page document margins and the gray document area that surrounds it: the white page representation. It shows the text flowing as older DOS text processors, using a dashed line to indicate a page break, and allows viewing entire tables no matter how wide they are. Figure 10-40 shows Figure 10-39 table as it appears in Microsoft Word Draft view.

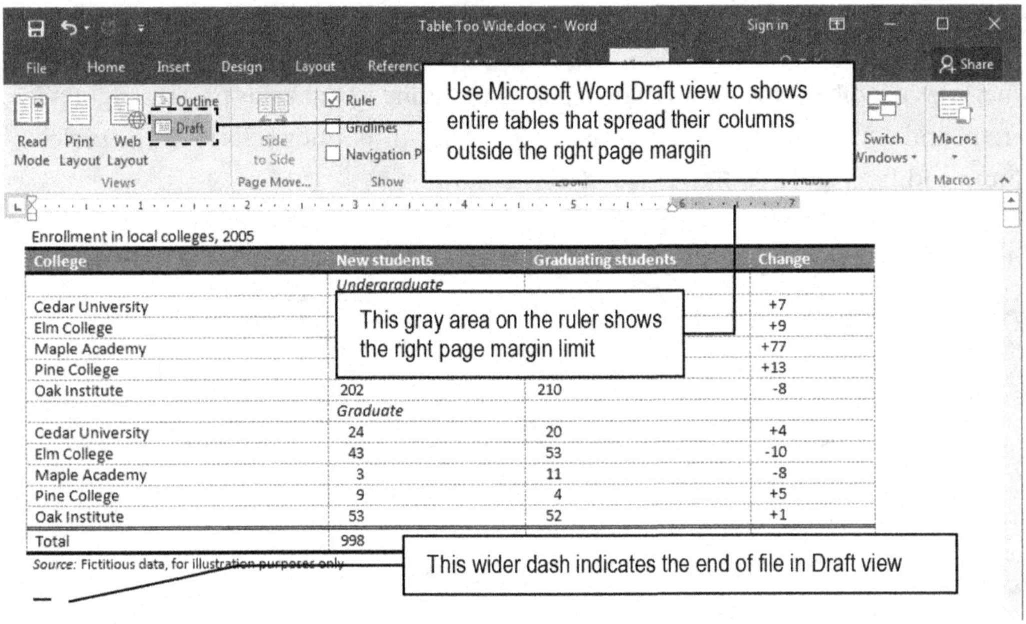

Figure 10-40. *Use Microsoft Word Draft view to show all document width (the real document width used by the table that do not fits on page width), disregarding the page margins. This figure show how the entire table in Figure 10-39 appears in Draft view.*

To fix the table width you need to interact with the table formatting, changing:

- each table column width (select the entire table and double-click any column right border line to make an autofit to the column content).

- the table font size and font (use a smaller font size so the text fits within the desired table limits).

You will need to begin changing the margins of the first columns to the left, one by one, until the right column right margin fits inside the page margin (inside the white scale of the ruler). Then use the tools discussed in the previous section to adjust the table width (Figure 10-41).

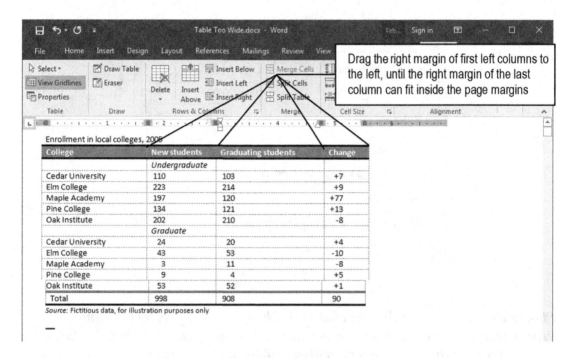

Figure 10-41. *To fix an overly wide table using Microsoft Word Draft view, drag each right border of the first left columns to the left, until you have space to drag the right margin of the rightmost column so it fits inside the page margins. You may eventually need to change font size.*

Cell Margins

Cell Margins is a command found in the Alignment area of the Table Tools Layout tab (see Figure 10-35) that allows adding margins and a second border to all table cells, which sometimes confuses the Microsoft Word user about where its odd formatting comes from (I myself have been confused by its strange effects at times).

Whenever you click the Cell Margins command, Microsoft Word will show the Table Options dialog box (Figure 10-42), which can be also evoked from the Table Properties ➤ Table ➤ Options... command button (see Figure 10-20).

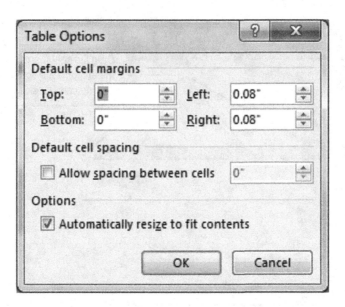

Figure 10-42.   *Use the Table Options dialog box, evoked by using the Table Properties dialog box Options… command button, or by clicking the Cell Margins control found in the Alignment area of the Table Tools Layout tab.*

- **Default cell margins**: use these options to add horizontal (Left and Right) and vertical (Top and Bottom) space from cell borders (by changing the Top and Bottom options you will increase the row height).

- **Default cell spacing**: check Allow spacing between cells and define a space amount to add a white border around each table cell.

- **Automatically resize to fit contents**: checked by default; table row height and column widths are automatically resized whenever you insert or delete text in a cell.

Figure 10-43 shows what happened to the "With Subheads 1" quick table after it received the AutoFit ➤ AutoFit Window and Distribute Columns commands and had the Allow spacing between cells = 0.08 checked in the Table Options dialog box. Note how the cell border now has a white space to separate each cell.

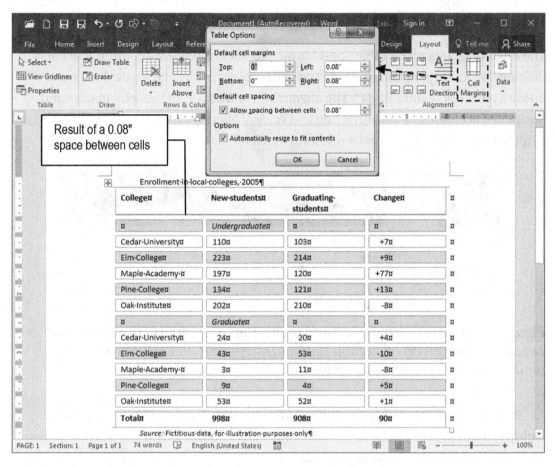

Figure 10-43. *The Table Options dialog box, evoked by using the Cell Margins command found in the Alignment area of the Table Tools Layout tab (and in the Table Properties ➤ Table ➤ Options… command button)*

Attention   The lesson here is quite simple: whenever you need to remove the odd white space found between table cells, use the Cell Margins command to evoke the Table Options dialog box and uncheck the Allow spacing between cells option.

Alignment and Text Direction

The Alignment area of the Table Tools Layout tab offers interesting controls that allow defining the text orientation and how text will be horizontally and vertically aligned inside a table cell (Figure 10-44). The alignment controls are all self-explanatory and positioned according to the horizontal and vertical effect they apply to the cells. The Text Direction just needs a click for its results to be seen.

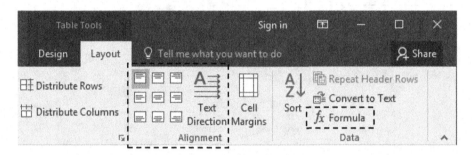

Figure 10-44. *Use the controls found in the Alignment area of the Table Tools Layout tab along with other table options (merge cells and column width) to produce nice table formatting options.*

By using these controls along with the Merge cells and controlling table column width, you can produce interesting table formatting options, which will be the objective of the exercise found in the next section.

Exercise 1

The objective of this exercise is to teach how you can use the knowledge gained so far with the aid of Microsoft Word Table Tools tab to quickly format a table so it can fit on a single page.

Extract the "Table Formatting Exercise.docx" document from the Chapter10.zip file and note that it has a single text page, whose first paragraphs were extracted from the US NCES (National Center for Education Statistics) web site (Figure 10-45), from this Internet address:

```
https://nces.ed.gov/programs/coe/indicator_cha.asp
```

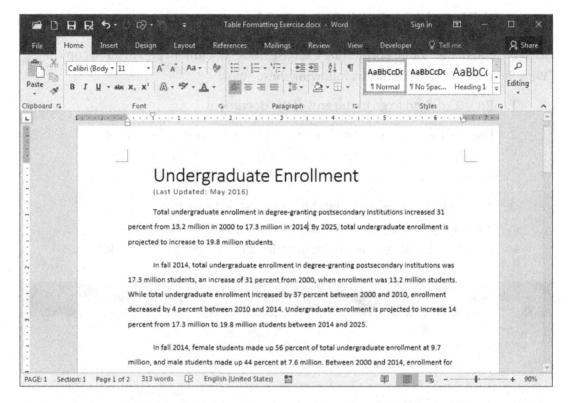

Figure 10-45. *This is the "Table Formating Exercise.docx" document that you can extract from Chapter10.zip file. It has some paragraphs extracted from NCES web site*

Inspect the Normal Style

Your first step in this exercise is to inspect the document Normal style, because it will be inherited by any table inserted in the document.

Follow these steps:

1. Right-click Normal style in the Style gallery in the Home tab of the Ribbon and choose Modify... command to show the Modify Style dialog box.

2. In the Modify Style dialog box, look to the Normal style description (or click Format ➤ Paragraph) and note that it has these properties set:

   - Indentation = Special = First line = 0.49.

   - Line spacing = 1.5

3. Close the Modify Style dialog box.

Insert "With Subheads 2" Quick Table

Go to the end of the "Table Formatting Exercise.docx" document and insert a copy of "With Subheads 2" quick table, by following these steps:

1. Press Ctrl+End to go to the end of the document.

2. Use the Table ➤ Quick Table command found in the Insert tab of the ribbon to insert a "With Subheads 2" quick table at the cursor position.

3. Note that the table inherited the Normal style formatting, applying it in all of its cells (First line indent = 0.49, Line spacing = 1.5), making the table spread to the next document page (Figure 10-46).

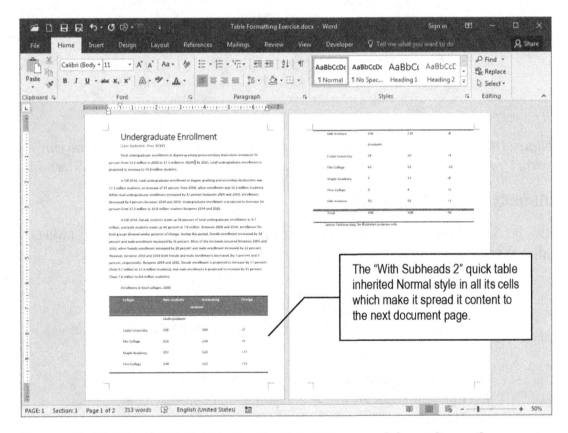

Figure 10-46. *The "With Subheads 2" quick table spread through two document pages because its cells inherited a First line indentation = 0.49 and Line spacing = 1.5 from Normal style*

Remove Table Paragraph Formatting

To try to make the "With Subheads 2" quick table fit on a single page, remove all paragraph formatting properties inherited from Normal style, by following these steps:

1. Click the small square at the top left table corner (the one with a "+" character) to select all table rows.

2. Show the Paragraph dialog box and clear all Normal style inherited properties:

   • Indentation Special = None

   • Line spacing = Single.

3. Close the Paragraph dialog box and note that the table now fits on a single document page (Figure 10-47).

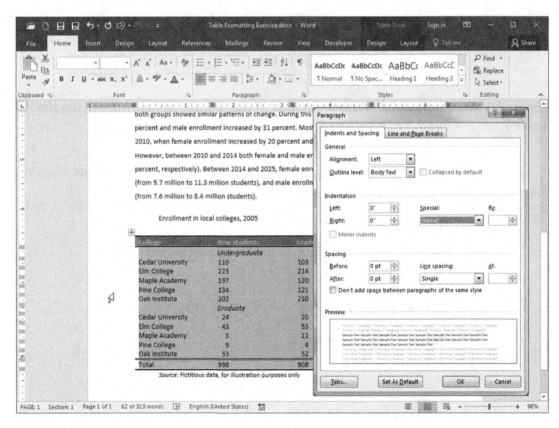

Figure 10-47. *Select all "With Subheads 2" table cells, show the Paragraph dialog box, and type a 0 (zero) value on all its properties to default values*

Format the Table

We will now format the "With Subheads 2" table by using the Table Tools Layout tab and some techniques approached in this chapter, by removing the subheads "Undergraduate" and "Graduate" from the original position (on a line above their contents), and putting them aside, rotated on the first table column at left of its content (Figure 10-48).

¤	College¤	New students¤	Graduating students¤	Change¤	¤
Undergraduate¤	Cedar University¤	110¤	103¤	+7¤	¤
	Elm College¤	223¤	214¤	+9¤	¤
	Maple Academy¤	197¤	120¤	+77¤	¤
	Pine College¤	134¤	121¤	+13¤	¤
	Oak Institute¤	202¤	210¤	-8¤	¤
Graduate¤	Cedar University¤	24¤	20¤	+4¤	¤
	Elm College¤	43¤	53¤	-10¤	¤
	Maple Academy¤	3¤	11¤	-8¤	¤
	Pine College¤	9¤	4¤	+5¤	¤
	Oak Institute¤	53¤	52¤	+1¤	¤
¤	Total¤	998¤	908¤	90¤	¤

Source: Fictitious data, for illustration purposes only¶

Figure 10-48. *Change the "With Subheads 2" quick table appearance using the Table Tools Layout tab to rotate its Subheads into the first table column*

To choose such formatting options, you will need to take these intermediate steps in the table:

1. Insert a new first table column.

2. Drag Subheads to a new position in the first table column.

3. Remove old subhead lines.

4. Merge and rotate subhead cells.

5. Make table cells fit their contents.

Insert a New First Table Column and Drag Subheads

To make table subheads appear rotated in the first table cell, we need to insert a new first table column by following these steps:

1. Point the mouse over the first table column (cursor changes for a small black arrow pointing down) and click to select it.

2. In the floating tool bar that appears, select Insert ➤ Insert Left (Figure 10-49) to insert a new first table column.

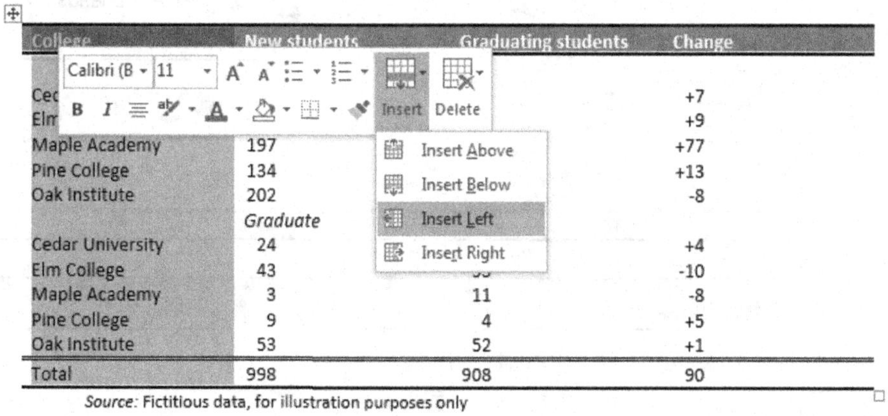

Figure 10-49. *Insert a new first table column by selecting the first column and using the floating toolbar Insert ➤ Insert Left command*

3. Click the View Gridlines option found in Table area of the Table Tools Layout tab to make Microsoft Word show the table cells.

4. Select the "Undergraduate" text in cell (2,2) and drag it to cell (3,1) (to the left of first cell "Cedar University" in cell (3,2)).

5. Select the "Graduate" text in cell (8,2) and drag it to cell (9,1) (to the left of second cell "Cedar University" in cell (9,2)) (Figure 10-50).

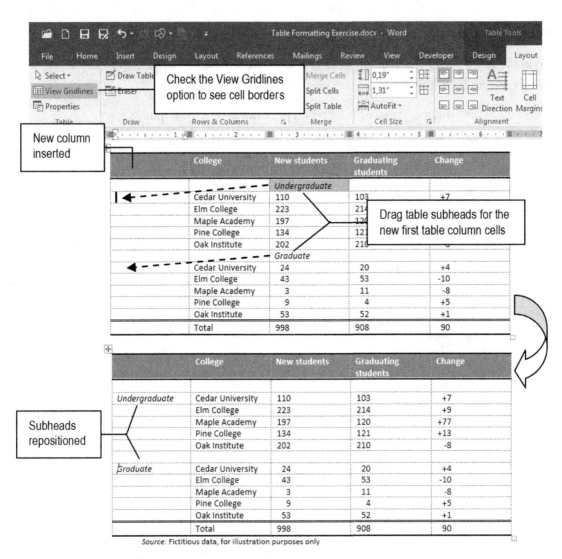

Figure 10-50. *Show gridlines and drag table subheads for new cells in the first table column*

Delete Unused Rows

After the subheads were moved to the new first table column, the "With Subheads 2" quick table has two empty rows (rows 2 and 8) that can be deleted, by following these steps:

1. Point the mouse to the left of row 2 first cell (mouse cursor will change to a normal pointing arrow) and click to select the entire row.

2. In the floating toolbar that appears, click Delete ➤ Delete Rows command to delete the selected row.

3. Repeat steps 1 and 2 to delete the empty row above the "Graduate" cell (row 7, after the row deletion) (Figure 10-51).

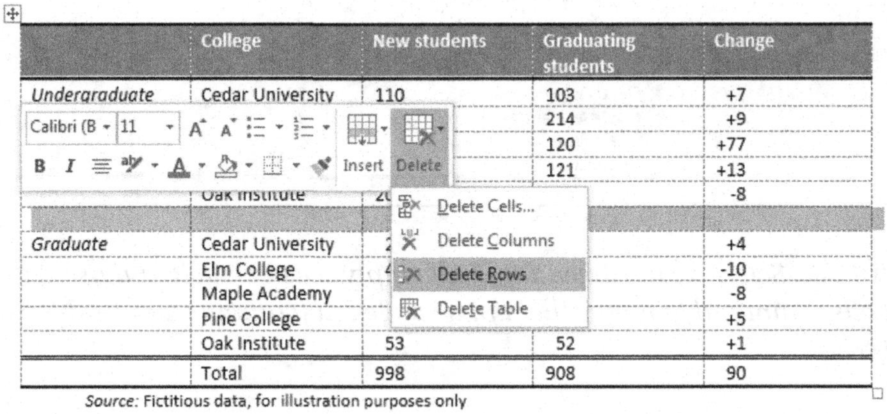

Figure 10-51. *Select the unused rows (point the mouse to its left side and click) and use the Delete ➤ Delete Rows command to remove them from the table*

Merge and Rotate Subhead Cells

The subhead cells positioned in the first table column must now be merged with all the empty cells below them, so the text can be rotated.

Follow these steps:

1. Click cell (2,1) with the "Undergraduate" text and drag the mouse down to select all empty cells below it (cells (2,1) to (61)).

2. Use the Merge Cells command found in the Merge area of the Table Tools Layout tab to merge them in a single cell.

3. Repeat steps 1 and 2 to merge the "Graduate" cell with all empty
    cells below it (Figure 10-52).

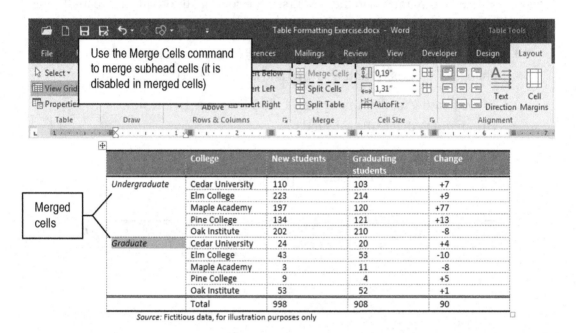

Figure 10-52. *Select each subhead and all empty cells below it and use the*
Merge Cells command to merge them in a single cell (command is disabled in
merged cells)

4. Select both merged cells and double-click the Text Direction tool
    to make them rotate 45 degrees upward (Figure 10-53).

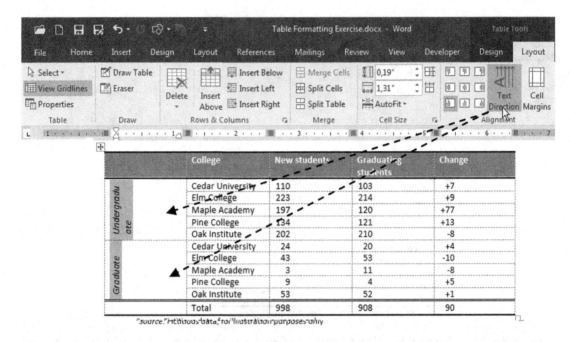

Figure 10-53. *Use the Text Direction tool to rotate upward the merged subhead cells in column 1*

Adjust Table Cells

The table is now produced but needs adjustment in its cells, which can be easily achieved by using the AutoFit and Cell Margins tools.

Follow these steps:

1. To quickly adjust all table cells for the best fit row height and column width, use the AutoFit ➤ AutoFit Contents command found in the Cell Size area of the Table Tools design tab (Figure 10-54).

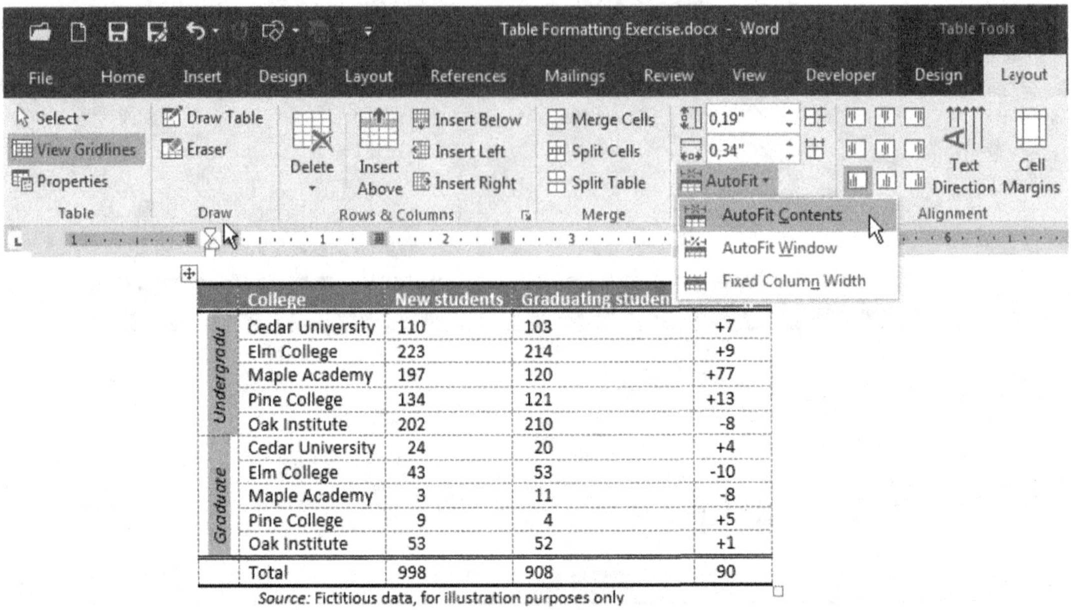

Figure 10-54. *Use the AutoFit ➤ AutoFit Contents tool to quickly adjust table cells for the best fit row height and column width*

2. Select the entire table and use the Cell Margins tool to show the Table Options dialog box and use the Top and Bottom options to add a 0.03 vertical space in each cell (defined by trial and error, Figure 10-55).

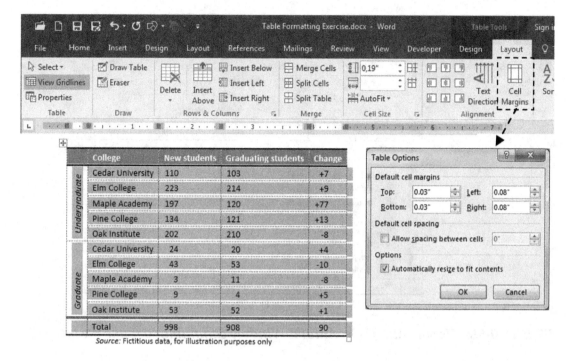

Figure 10-55. *Use the Cell Margins command to show the Table Options dialog box to add a vertical space to all table cells (Top and Bottom = 0.03)*

3. Apply the AutoFit ➤ AutoFit Window command to make the table spread through the entire page width (Figure 10-56).

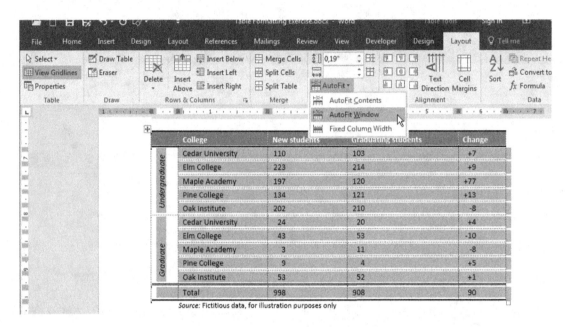

Figure 10-56. *Use the AutoFit ➤ AutoFit Window command to make the table fit.*

4. Use the Center Align Left tool to center align all table columns that have numbers (Figure 10-57).

	College¤	New students¤	Graduating students¤	Change¤	
Undergraduate¤	Cedar University¤	110¤	103¤	+7¤	¤
	Elm College¤	223¤	214¤	+9¤	¤
	Maple Academy¤	197¤	120¤	+77¤	¤
	Pine College¤	134¤	121¤	+13¤	¤
	Oak Institute¤	202¤	210¤	-8¤	¤
Graduate¤	Cedar University¤	24¤	20¤	+4¤	¤
	Elm College¤	43¤	53¤	-10¤	¤
	Maple Academy¤	3¤	11¤	-8¤	¤
	Pine College¤	9¤	4¤	+5¤	¤
	Oak Institute¤	53¤	52¤	+1¤	¤
¤	Total¤	998¤	908¤	90¤	¤

Source: Fictitious data, for illustration purposes only¶

Figure 10-57. *Use the Center Align Left tool found in the Alignment area of the Table Tools Layout tab to horizontally and vertically center all columns with numbers*

The table formatting is ready, and the table fits on the first document page!

Attention   Extract "Table Formatting Exercise, Done.docx" document from Chapter10.zip file for a final version of this table exercise.

Table Calculation

Most Microsoft Word users don't even imagine that it is possible to make calculations using data inserted in a document table cell using the Formula command found in the Data area of the Table Tools, Layout tab of the Ribbon (see Figure 10-44).

When the cursor is positioned in a table cell and you click the Formula tool, Microsoft Word will show the Formula dialog box, from where you can type a formula or use the Paste function list to select a common, predefined function to create a table formula (Figure 10-58).

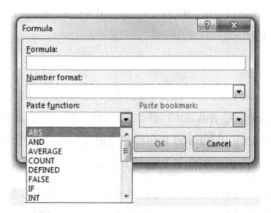

Figure 10-58. *Use the Formula dialog box to build a formula in any table cell with the aid of the Paste function list, from where you can select different and popular math functions*

The Formula dialog box has these options:

- **Formula**: must begin with the "=" operator (without the quotes) and operate over identifiable document cells or bookmarks.

- **Number format**: use to select the format to present the formula result.

- **Paste function**: use to select one of the functions available to insert it in the Formula control.

Attention   It is out of the scope of this book to approach each possible function available from the Paste function list. Perform an Internet search on the desired function to obtain more explanation about its syntax and return result.

Using Positional Arguments in Formulas

The formulas created by the Formula dialog box can relate one or all table cells, other formula results, and any field codes inserted in the document that can be mathematically evaluated.

You can use functions AVERAGE, COUNT, MAX, MIN, PRODUCT, and SUM to operate over table cells surrounding the formula using the self-explanatory positional arguments LEFT, RIGHT, ABOVE, and BELOW.

For example, the bottom right table cell (last table cell) can sum all cells in the same row above it using this formula:

=SUM(ABOVE)

Attention   Microsoft Word will sum all cells using positional arguments, discarding all non-numerical values found in the positional range direction. To avoid formula errors, it is advised to insert a 0 (zero) value in all empty cells.

You can use the Microsoft Word list separator ("," for United States Windows version) to sum different positional arguments. For example, the next formula sums all values to the left and above the selected cell:

=SUM(LEFT,ABOVE)

Using RnCn or A1 Reference Style in Formulas

Use the RnCn Excel style reference to relate specific table cells in a formula, where n is the row or column number. Table 10-1 show how to use the RnCn syntax to relate to different table cells.

Table 10-1. *Microsoft Word RnCn Syntax to Relate Table Cells in Formulas*

Reference	Syntax
Entire column	Cn
Entire row	Rn
Specific cell address	RnCn
Row that contains the formula	R
Column that contains the formula	C
All cells between two table cells	RnCn:RnCn

For example, you can sum all cells from row 10 using this formula:

=SUM(R10)

Or you can sum all cells from row 2, column 1, to row 10, column 4 using this formula:

=SUM(R2C1:R10C4)

You can also use Microsoft Excel A1 reference style in table formulas, where each table column is associated to a consecutive letter and each table row to a consecutive number. Table 10-2 shows how to use the A1 style to relate different table cells.

Table 10-2. *Microsoft Word A1 syntax to Relate Table Cells in Formulas in a 4×4 Table*

Reference	Syntax
First table cell (top left cell)	A1
Last 4×4 table cell (bottom right cell)	A4
The first two cells in the second row	A2,B2
All 4×4 table cells	A1:D4

For example, you can sum all cells in the first three columns (A, B, and C) of the first row (row 1) using this formula:

=SUM(A1:C1)

Or you can sum all table cells of a 4×4 table using this formula:

```
=SUM(A1:D4)
```

Updating Table Formulas

Whenever a formula is inserted in a table cell, Microsoft Word will try to update and present its value using the Number format defined by the Formula dialog box (if any).

If you change data in any cell that affects the formula scope, the formula will not be automatically calculated: you must manually update the affected formula(s) using the F9 function key.

To update:

- Just one cell: select the cell table that contains the affected formula and press F9.

- Entire table: select all table cells and press F9.

- Entire document: press Ctrl+A and press F9.

Attention   To show a cell formula instead of its value, use the same strategy explained before to alternate between Microsoft Word field values and field code: press Alt+F9 function key to alternate between cell value and cell formula.

Exercise 2

The objective of this exercise is to learn how to insert and copy formulas in a Microsoft Word document table to make data calculations.

Extract the "Table Formulas Exercise.docx" document from the Chapter10.zip file, open it in Microsoft Word, and note that it has a changed version of the "With Subheads 1" quick table which received a Total Students column to its right (Figure 10-59), where we must insert formulas to sum the New Students and Graduating Students columns for each row.

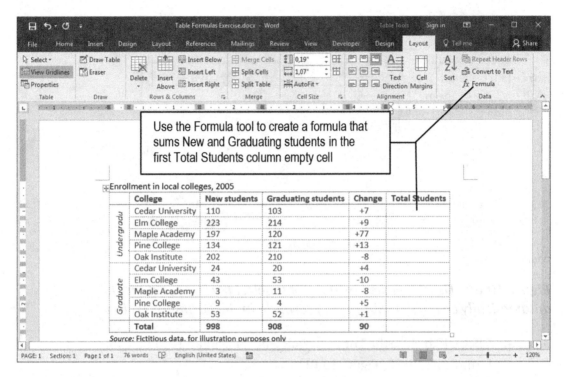

Figure 10-59. *This is the "Table Formulas Exercise.docx" document, which you can extract from Chapter10.zip file; in this file, you can practice inserting formulas in the Total Students column to add the New and Graduating students of each row.*

Follow these steps:

1. Click the first empty cell of the Total Students column (cell F2 or R2C6).

2. Click the Formula tool found in the Data area of the Table Tools Layout tab of the Ribbon to show the Formula dialog box and set these options:

    -   In Number format select #.##0 option (this format always shows a zero; add a thousand separator character, if necessary).

    -   In Paste function list, select SUM function. This will automatically create the =SUM(LEFT) formula that uses the LEFT positional argument to sum all left cells values (Figure 10-60).

Enrollment in local colleges, 2005

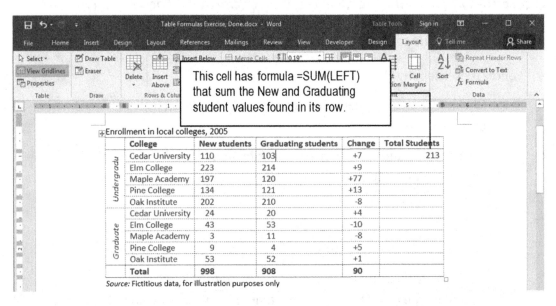

	College	New students	Graduating students	Change	Total Students
Undergradu	Cedar University	110	103	+7	
	Elm College				
	Maple Academy				
	Pine College				
	Oak Institute				
Graduate	Cedar University				
	Elm College				
	Maple Academy				
	Pine College				
	Oak Institute			+1	
	Total	99			90

Source: Fictitious data, for illust...

Figure 10-60. *Use the Paste function list to select the SUM function and automatically create the =SUM(LEFT) formula in the Formula text box*

3. Click OK to close the Formula dialog box; insert and evaluate the formula in cell F2 (Figure 10-61).

Figure 10-61. *Note that the =SUM(LEFT) formula inserted in cell F2 evaluates correctly because it just operates over the two numbers found in row 2: the New and Graduating students column cells.*

4. Press Alt+F9 to alternate cell value to cell formula and note that cell
    F2 has the { =SUM(LEFT) \# "#.##0" } formula (Figure 10-62).

	College	New students	Graduating students	Change	Total Students
	Cedar University	110	103	+7	{ =SUM(LEFT) \# "#.##0" }
	Elm College	223	214	+9	

Figure 10-62. *Press Alt+F9 to alternate from cell value to cell formula and note
that cell F2 now has the { =SUM(LEFT) \# "#.##0" } formula*

5. Press Alt+F9 again to return to cell value and reevaluate cell F2
    formula.

6. Select cell F2 value (213) and press Ctrl+C to copy it to Clipboard.

7. Select all other empty cells of the Total Students columns and
    press Ctrl+V to paste the same formula (the calculated value of
    213 will be repeated in each cell, Figure 10-63).

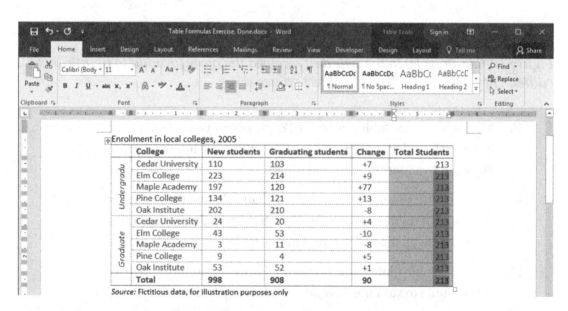

Figure 10-63. *Select cell F2 value, press Ctrl+C to copy to Clipboard, select all
empty cells of Total Students column, and press Ctrl+V to paste the same formula.
Values will not be updated.*

8. Considering that the cells where the formula was pasted are still selected, press F9 to force recalculation.

9. All but the last cell in the Total Student column will now recalculate to the right values (Figure 10-64).

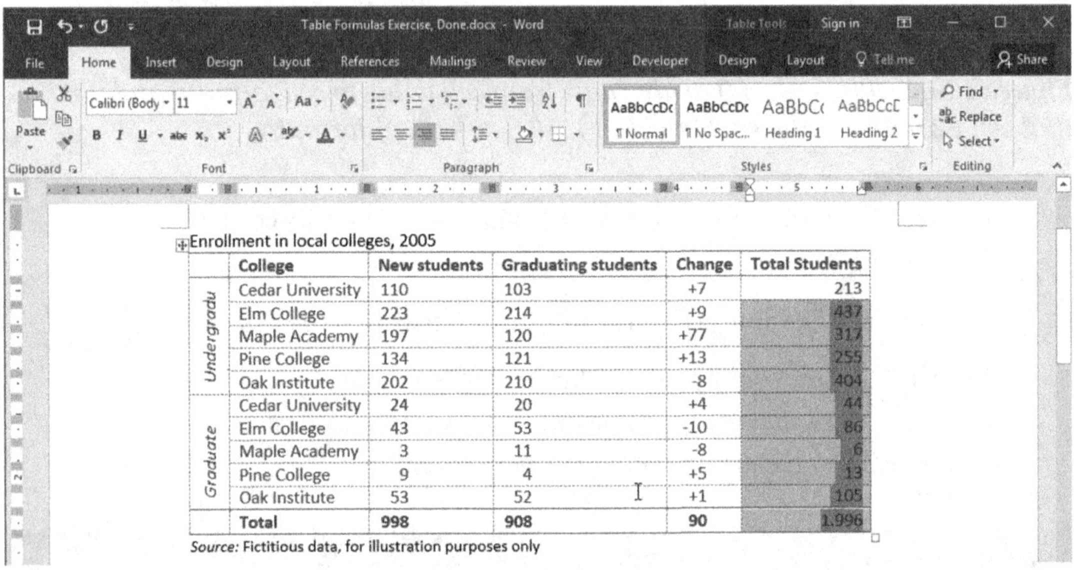

Figure 10-64. *Press F9 in the cells that received the paste formula to update their values. They will now reflect the correct values*

10. Note that the last table cell (cell F12, the bottom right cell) had incorrectly added the Change column (90) to the total number of New and Graduating students (1,998).

11. Click cell F12 to select it and click the Formula tool found in the Data area of the Table Tools Layout tab to show the Formula dialog box with the cell inserted in this table cell.

12. In the Formula dialog box, delete the Formula text box and insert this formula to sum the New and Graduating students for row 12:

    =C12+D12

13. Close the Formula dialog box to insert the new formula and evaluate the result (Figure 10-65).

Enrollment in local colleges, 2005

	College	New students	Graduating students	Change	Total Students
Undergradu	Cedar University	110	103	+7	213
	Elm College				437
	Maple Academy				317
	Pine College				255
	Oak Institute				404
Graduate	Cedar University				44
	Elm College				86
	Maple Academy				6
	Pine College				13
	Oak Institute	53	52	+1	105
	Total	998	908	90	1.906

Formula

Formula:
=C12+D12

Number format:
#,##0

Paste function: Paste bookmark:

OK   Cancel

Source: Fictitious data, for illustration purposes only

Figure 10-65. *Click cell C12 and click the Formula tool to evoke the Formula dialog box for this cell. Change cell F12 formula to =C12+D12 to correctly sum the New and Graduating students for row 12.*

The document table now has all formulas necessary to correctly calculate the sum of New and Graduating students for all its rows.

Try to change some values, select the entire table, and press F9 to recalculate it! Try for yourself!!!

Conclusion

In this chapter you have had the opportunity to understand how Microsoft Word inserts and formats tables in its documents.

Among other things, you learned how to convert a table to text (and vice versa), how to select, insert, and delete rows and columns, and how to use the many interfaces available to manage table properties.

Not all table formatting options were explored in this chapter, not only due to the huge number of tools offered by Microsoft Word in the Table Tools Design and Layout tab, but also due to the lengths of this chapter and book, which have already surpassed all initial expectations.

Among them we can cite the Borders area and the Shading tools found in Table Tools Design tab, along with the Draw, Rows & Columns, and Data area tools found in the Table Tools Layout tab.

I will leave these tools as an exercise to the reader to explore to master Microsoft Word table formatting.

Summary

In this chapter you learned:

- That Microsoft Word tables has cells that can be considered as small text processors, receiving Paragraph and Line break characters.

- How and why you must master the art of converting a table to text (and vice versa).

- How to select table elements (cell, row, column, entire table) using the mouse and the table handles.

- How to insert and delete cells, rows, and columns into tables.

- How to change the alignment and position of cell contents.

- That a table can be inserted as a text object, in its own paragraph, or floating over the page with text flowing around it.

- That you probably should choose to use tables inserted as text objects, unless you are creating complex page designs.

- How to format tables using table styles.

- That the TableNormal style is the base table style, which is based on the Normal style.

- How cell content inherits the Normal style properties.

- That Microsoft Word has the Quick Table command that can be used to inspire you about how you can create and format tables.

- How to change Row height and Column width.

- How Row height is impacted by Paragraph formatting options.

- How to use Cell Margins to insert or remove a white space between table cells.

- How to merge and rotate table cells.

- How to easily adjust table cells to make the best row height and column width that may fit each cell content.

In the next chapter, we will explore how to use Microsoft Word Templates to produce standardized formatted documents.

CHAPTER 11

Creating and Using Templates

A template is a special kind of file that allows you to start a new document using a predefined set of formatting options. Templates are available for the main Microsoft Office applications (Word, Excel, and PowerPoint), and you can also create them to allow customization of different documents with the same appearance.

In this chapter you will learn about how you can download, use, and create your own Microsoft Word Template files. All the documents cited in this chapter can be found by downloading the Chapter11.zip file from this Internet address:

https://github.com/apress/msft-word-secrets

What Is a Template?

A Microsoft Word template is indeed a common .DOCX document that has the extension changed to .DOTM to allow it to be treated differently by the program (the.dotm file extension means **DO**cument **T**emplate with **M**acros).

By default, Microsoft Word doesn't open a template: it uses its structure to create a new, unnamed document that is a perfect copy of the original. Yes! A template is a kind of document that can make copies of itself without disturbing its own content.

Whenever you open Microsoft Word 2016, it will show you the Start Up screen (also called New window) from where you can decide which template will be used to create a new, unnamed document (Figure 11-1).

© Flavio Morgado 2017
F. Morgado, *Microsoft Word Secrets*, https://doi.org/10.1007/978-1-4842-3078-7_11

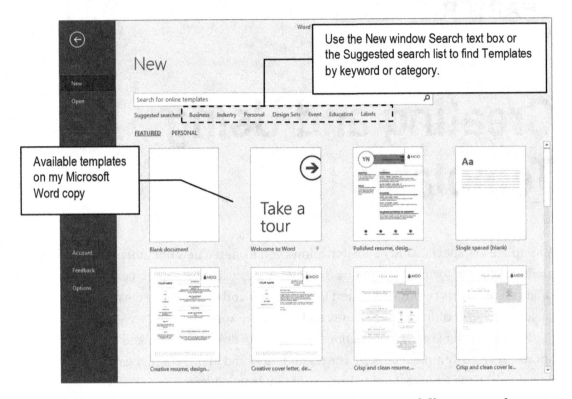

Figure 11-1. *The Microsoft Word New window shows many different templates from where you can create a new document*

This window is opened by default due to the Show the Start screen when this application starts option found in the General ➤ Start up Options area of the Word Options dialog box (displayed by the File ➤ Options command, Figure 11-2).

Attention   By unchecking the Show the Start screen when this application starts option, Microsoft Word will immediately show a new, empty copy of a blank document when it is opened.

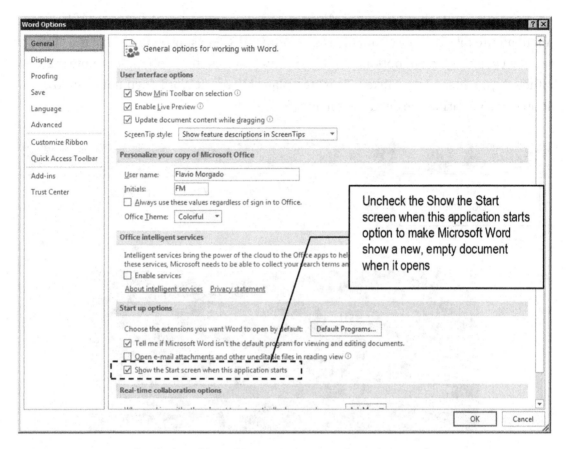

Figure 11-2. *Uncheck the Show the Start screen when this application starts option, which isfound in the General ➤ Start up option area of the Word Options dialog box (found using File ➤ Options)*

Types of Word Templates

The New window (shown by clicking File ➤ New command) offers different types of Templates that can be used to save time when you have a need to create well-formatted special-purpose documents. It is also a source of inspiration and possibilities that you can achieve by mastering Microsoft Word features.

Try for example the "Take a Tour" template: a document that gives basic guidance about how to take the most from Microsoft Word 2016, focusing on the use of the "Tell me what you want to do" option, which is always shown in the Ribbon. Also note that although you opened the "Take a Tour" template, Microsoft Word document window shows Document1 as the document name (Figure 11-3).

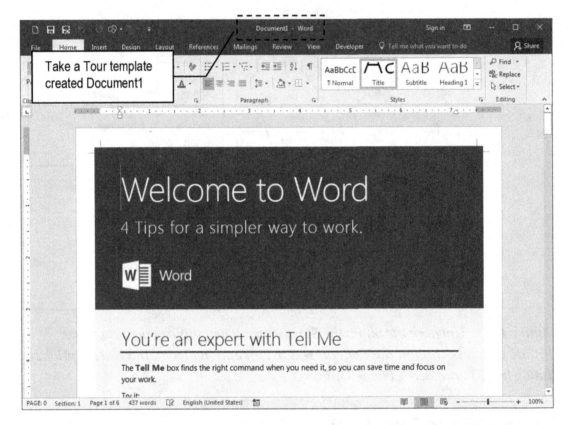

Figure 11-3. *The Take a Tour template is a simple document prepared to guide the user to make the most of the Tell Me tool always visible above the Ribbon's right corner*

There are a lot of different Microsoft Word templates to choose from, and they can be divided into three main groups:

- **Empty templates**: creates empty documents to work with (as the New Document.dotm and Single Spaced Blank.dotm shown in Figure 11-1).

- **Templates with page and style formatting**: shows special formatting pages, with graphic and design elements, from where you can type text.

- **Templates with formatting and Controls**: shows documents that have special page and style formatting options, and also have Controls that guide the user to where the information must be typed.

To understand the different types of templates, you must open and try them to see what they offer, how they were formatted, and how they work. Let's try.

Templates with Formatting and Controls

Many templates found in the New window have both page and style formatting and use Microsoft Word Controls to guide the user to insert the information in the right document places.

Since the New window changes the Templates as you select them, let's have a simple introduction about Controls using the Suggested Search: Design Sets ➤ Invoice (Red design) template (Figure 11-4).

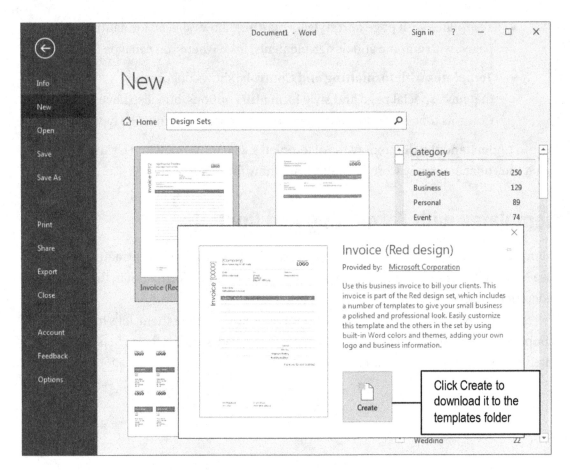

Figure 11-4. *Select different Microsoft Word templates using the Suggested Search option. This figure shows the Design Sets category, with the Invoice (Red design) template appearing as the first business template.*

By double-clicking the Invoice (Red design) template and clicking Create:

1. Microsoft Word will download it from the Office site and store it in the default Templates Folder

2. Will create a new, empty copy of it so you can work with the document, insert your own data, and save it wherever you want on your hard disk, leaving the original template untouched (Figure 11-5)

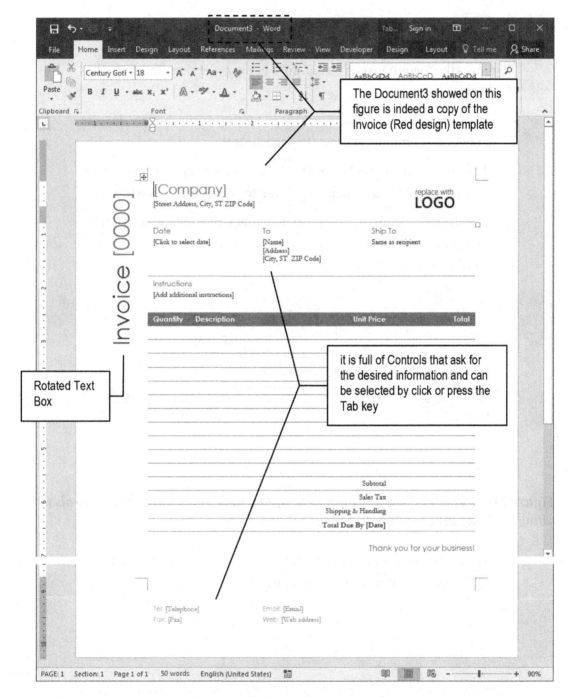

Figure 11-5. *The Invoice (Red design) template opened as Document3 (see the title bar) inside Microsoft Word. It uses tables to insert information in the page and footer.*

Explore the document using these tips:

- Press Tab key and note how the Invoice (Red design) document copy moves the focus between its controls, in the order they appear in the document.

- Check that document has three tables: for the invoice header, Invoice details, and company contact (in page footer).

- Click any document table and check the View Gridlines option in the Table area of the Table Tools Layout tab to see table cell borders.

- Click the red "Company" title and note that it becomes grayed as a clear indication that it is a Document Control, where you can insert text (the Company name, Figure 11-6).

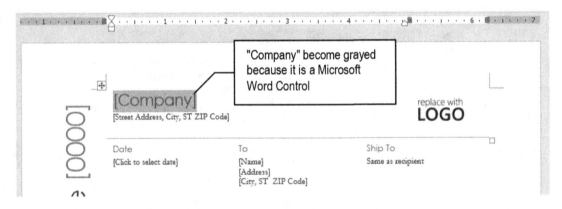

Figure 11-6. *The Invoice (Red design) template uses Microsoft Word Controls to allow inserting information, like the company name*

- Try the Date control and note that it expands and shows a Calendar control, from where you can select the date (Figure 11-7).

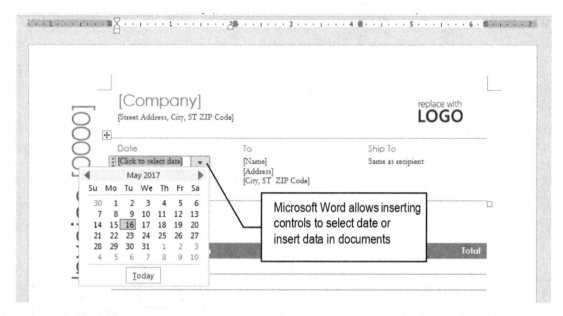

Figure 11-7. *The Invoice (Red design) template has a lot of Microsoft Word Controls inserted in the document that protect the document content leaving the user to use just the document controls to insert text*

How Microsoft Word Controls Work

The Invoice (Red design) template shown in Figures 11-6 and 11-7 allow to insert information in specific document places using Microsoft Word Controls.

Such controls are used to create what is called a "Microsoft Word Form", which must be used in Execution mode, and can be put in Design mode to allow inserting, deleting, formatting, and defining control properties.

To understand how this is done, you must first show the Developer tab on the Ribbon, by following these steps:

1. Use File ➤ Options to show Word Options dialog box.

2. Click Customize Ribbon option.

3. In the right list box, check the Developer option (Figure 11-8).

571

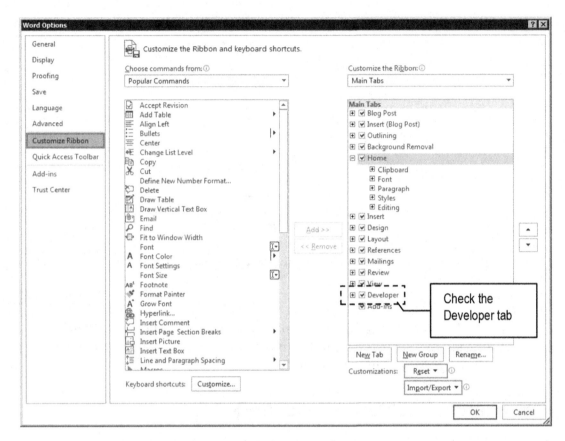

Figure 11-8. *Use the Word Options dialog box, Customize Ribbon option to show the Developer tab*

4.   Close the Word Options dialog box.

Now your Microsoft Word copy must show the Developer tab of the Ribbon (noted in many figures of this book), from where you will find the tools used to manage Microsoft Word Controls and Templates (Figure 11-9).

Figure 11-9. *Use the Developer tab Controls and Templates area tools to manage Microsoft Word Controls and Templates*

Controls Design Mode

The Controls area of the Developer tab of the Ribbon offers the tools needed to insert different types of controls in the document, plus the Design Mode, Properties, and Group commands.

The Design Mode command is the one responsible for switching Microsoft Word Forms view from Execution mode to Design Mode (when checked).

Check the Design Mode tool and note how the Invoice (Red design) template change its appearance and now shows the controls inserted in the document surrounded by tags with the control name (Figure 11-10).

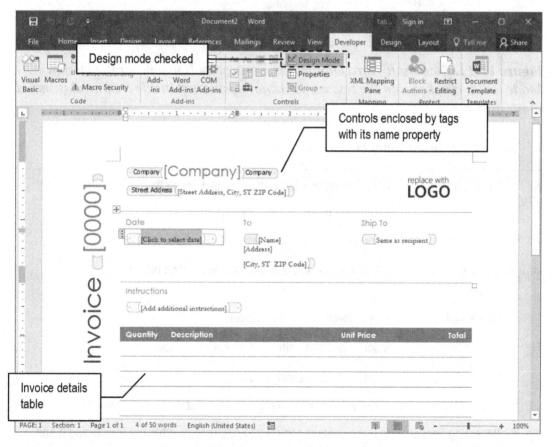

Figure 11-10. *When the Design Mode tool is checked, Microsoft Word shows all Controls inserted in the document, enclosed by tags that identify them by Name property*

Control Types and Basic Properties

Whenever the Design Mode tool is checked and the text cursor is not positioned inside the tags that enclose any Control inserted in the document, Microsoft Word 2016 enables nine Content Control tools plus the Legacy tools that give access to the old Forms and ActiveX control types used by Microsoft Office 2003 or older versions (Figure 11-11).

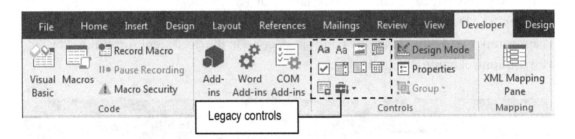

Figure 11-11. *Microsoft Word enables the Control tools whenever the Design Mode tool is checked and the text cursor is not positioned inside a Control inserted in the document*

You can use these Content Control types:

Aa	Rich Text	Allow typing and formatting the text inside the control
Aa	Plain Text	Allow typing text, but not formatting it
	Picture	Insert a picture in the document
	Building Block Gallery	Allow the user to choose specified building blocks
☑	Check Box	Insert check box in the document
	Combo Box	Insert a text box with a list of predefined values
	Drop-down List	Insert a list of predefined values
	Data Picker	Insert a calendar control to choose dates
	Repeating Section	Insert a content control that can receive other controls inside it and create copies of itself
	Legacy Tools	Insert Forms and ActiveX controls used by Microsoft Office 2003 or previous versions

Each control type has properties that allow controlling its appearance and the way it works when the Design Mode tool is unchecked, meaning that the Microsoft Word document is in Form mode.

Click any Control inserted in the document and click Properties (or right-click and choose Properties) to show the Content Control Properties dialog box (Figure 11-12).

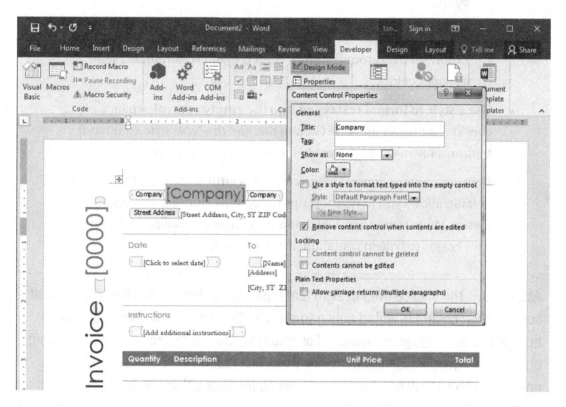

Figure 11-12. *Select any Content Control and click in the Properties tool found in the Controls area of the Developer tab to show its properties. Different control types can have different properties to set.*

Some of properties are common to all Content Controls, like the following:

- **Title**: specify the control name as appears inside the tags that enclose it.

- **Tag**: property used by VBA programmers, not available to the common user.

- **Show as**: define how the control will appear when Design Mode is unchecked:

    - **Bounding Box**: add a title and a border when control is selected.

    - **Start/End Tag**: show tags with control name enclosing the control.

    - **None**: (default value) hide control title, borders, and tags.

    - **Color**: set background control color (default is Automatic, same as paper color).

- **Use a style to format text typed into the empty control**: when checked, activates the Style Combo box and the New Style command button, allowing you to select or create a style to format control text.

- **Remove content control when control is edited**: checked by default; allows you to type text tips inside the Control tags when Design Mode is checked, which is automatically removed when the user begins to type information inside the control.

Attention   The invoice (Red design) template keeps checked the Remove content control when control is edited option to show to the user which information must be typed in each document control. For example, the red "[Company]" text (without quotes) was typed inside the Company Plain Text control with the Design Mode option checked. It will be removed as soon as the user selects the control and presses a key in it.

- **Content control cannot be deleted**: available only when property Remove content control when control is edited is unchecked, avoids having the control deleted by the user when Design Mode is unchecked.

- **Contents cannot be edited**: locks the control value when Design Mode is unchecked, avoiding its being changed by the user.

- **Allow carriage returns (multiple paragraphs)**: check to allow user to insert text with the Enter key breaking text lines.

Insert and Delete Controls

Is quite easy to insert and delete any of the Content Controls available in the Developer tab Controls area once the Design Mode option is checked:

1. Position the text cursor inside the document where the control must appear.

2. Click the desired control to insert it.

As soon as the control is inserted in the document, click the Properties command found in the Controls area of the Developer tab (or right-click it and choose Properties) to show the Content Control Properties dialog box and give a name to the control. This name will appear in the tabs surrounding the control that determine its limits.

Removing any control is even easier:

- Right-click the control and select Remove Content Control; or

- Drag the mouse over the entire control to select it (with its tag boundaries) and press the Delete key.

Restrict Document Editing

After formatting a Microsoft Word document using Controls and putting the document in Execution mode by unchecking the Design mode command, the document users may use its controls to type data, but they also has a chance to put the document in Design mode again, or even worse, delete the controls inserted in the document.

To make a Microsoft Word Form document protected against user changes, you can employ enforcement protection against changes, with or without a password.

This is done using the Restrict Editing tool found in the Protect area of the Developer tab, which shows the Restrict Editing pane to allow the user to select the kind of restriction that must be applied to the document when the Yes, Start Enforcement Protection button is clicked (Figure 11-13).

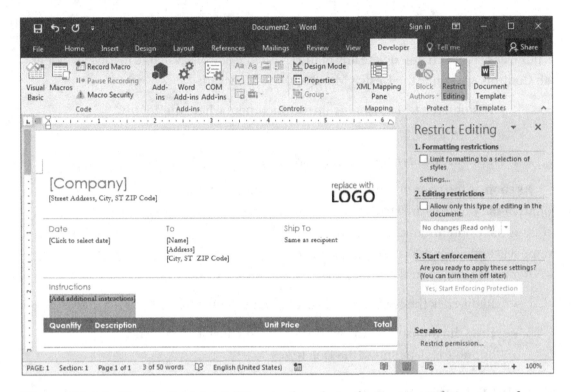

Figure 11-13. *Use the Restrict Editing tool to show the Restrict Editing pane from where you can select the restricions that must be applied to the document when the Start Enforcement button is clicked*

The Restrict Editing pane has three steps in the following sequence, which may offer some options:

- **Formatting restrictions**: check the **Limit formatting to a selection of styles** and use the Settings button to show the Formatting Restriction dialog box to select formatting options allowed.

- **Editing restrictions**: check the Allow only this type of editing in the document and use the list options to define which type of editing is allowed:

    - **Tracked changes**: allow users to turn on Track Changes in the document.

    - **Comments**: allow users to insert comments in the document (show the Exceptions list, which allows different users to add comments: allow by selecting Everyone).

- **Filling forms**: use this option to allow just Content Controls to be selected to insert data.

- **No Change (Read only)**: (default value) locks the documents against any change.

- **Start enforcement**: by selecting one of the two first options of restriction, you must click the Yes, Start Enforcement protection command button, which will show the Start Enforcement Protection dialog box, from where you can define a password to unlock protection (Figure 11-14).

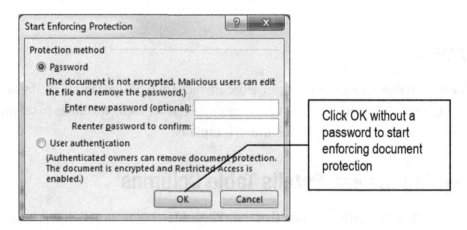

Figure 11-14. *Use the Start Enforcing Protection dialog box to start the document protection against the changes restriction selected. By typing and corfirming a password, Microsoft Word will ask for this password to allow changes to the document.*

By using a password to start the document editing protection, Microsoft Word will ask for this password to unlock the document again. Leave the password blank to start protection and test the document.

Attention   Well-designed Microsoft Word form documents that use Controls must enforce editing protection, with or without a password, to guarantee that the user will have access to just the controls content, without disturbing the document formatting options.

It is out of scope of this book to give a detailed explanation of how to use Microsoft Word Controls to create guided documents, but I am supposing that by now you will be very comfortable to explore and try such templates, exploring the Controls properties to allow you create your own documents that use such resources.

Exercise 1

The objective of this exercise is to improve the Invoice (Red design) template, by adding a Repeating Section control inside the Invoice details table, using formulas to calculate the invoice, and saving it as a new document template.

Formatting Invoice Details Table Columns

Before you begin, you must be aware that the =PRODUCT( ) table function does not work well with Positional arguments when it finds empty or text cells in the argument direction.

That is why the exercise proposes to put the Invoice details Description as the first table column.

Follow these steps to format the invoice table found in the Invoice (Red design) template:

1. Use Microsoft Word File, New window to select the Design Sets templates category and load the Invoice (Red design) template (see the section "Templates with Formatting and Controls").

2. Check the Design Mode command in the Controls area of the Developer tab of the Ribbon.

3. Delete all but the first Invoice details table empty row cells of
    column Quantity, Description, Unit Price, and Total (cell range
    R3C1:R12C4 or A3:D12, Figure 11-15).

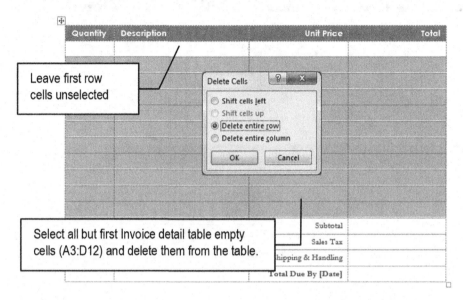

Figure 11-15. *Delete all but first row empty cells of Quantity, Description,
Unit Price, and Total columns of the Invoice details table found in the Invoice
(Red detail) template*

4. Select the Description column and drag it to the left, to the first
    table column position (Figure 11-16).

581

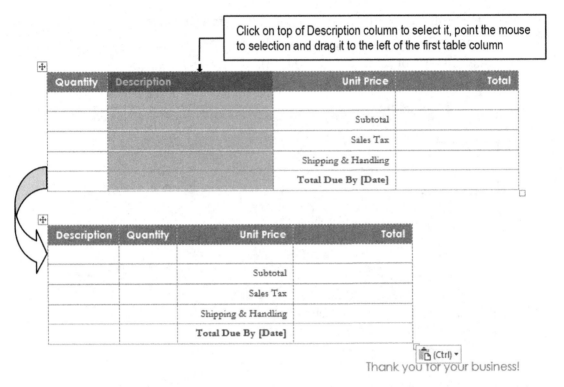

Figure 11-16. *Select the Description column, and click and drag the selected column to the left of the first table column*

5. Adjust the Invoice details table to the page width and adjust the Description, Quantity, Unit Price, and Total column widths:

- Apply the AutoFit ➤ AutoFit Windows command found in the Table Tools Layout tab.

- Drag Unit Price column right border to the right to straighten the Total column.

- Drag Quantity column right border to the right to straighten the Unit Price column (to fit the Total Due by [Date] text).

- Drag Description column right border to the right to enlarge it to the maximum value that fits Quantity column header column (Figure 11-17).

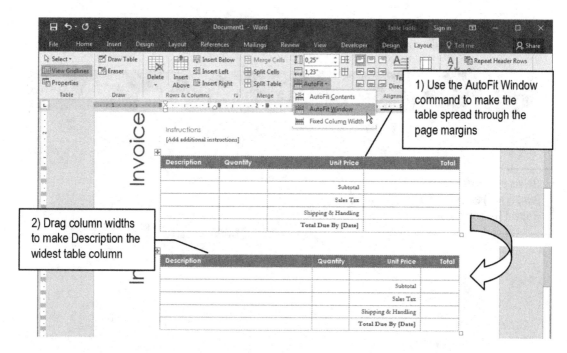

Figure 11-17. *Use the AutoFit ➤ AutoFit Window command found in the Table Tools Layout tab to fit the invoice table column to page width and drag its columns to give the maximum horizontal space to the Description column*

Insert Form Controls

Now that the numbering columns Quantity and Unit Price are side by side in the Invoice details table and it has just one, empty row to insert detail records, it is time to insert controls in the Invoice details table, so Design Mode can be unchecked and the users can use them as a guidance to fill the document with relevant data.

This first and unique empty row of the Invoice details table must first receive a Repeat Section Content Control, because this control can add copies of itself. And Description, Quantity, and Unit Price columns empty cells must receive individual Plain Text Content Controls, to guide the user where to type each type of information.

Follow these steps to insert the Repeating Section Control in the Invoice details table:

1. IMPORTANT: Uncheck the Design Mode command found in the Developer tab to stop the Execution mode.

2. Select all cells of the first empty row of the Invoice details table (cells A2:D2).

583

3. Click the Repeating Section control to insert it in the second, empty table row (Figure 11-18).

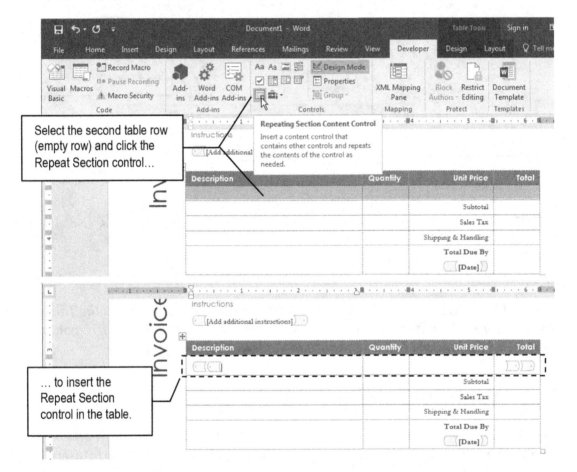

Figure 11-18. *Select the second Invoice table row and click the Repeating Section control to insert it in the table. Note that it has two tabs that show the cells it will repeat in the table when Design Mode is unchecked.*

Attention   The Repeating Section Content Control requires that entire rows be selected before being inserted in a table to represent its cells.

---

4. Insert a Plain Text Content Control in each empty cell of the Description, Quantity, and Unit Price columns (inside the Repeating Section control) and in the Total column cells at right of the Sales/Tax and Shipping and Handling cells:

- Click the desired empty column to select it.

- Click the Plain Text Content Control to insert it in each cell (Figure 11-19).

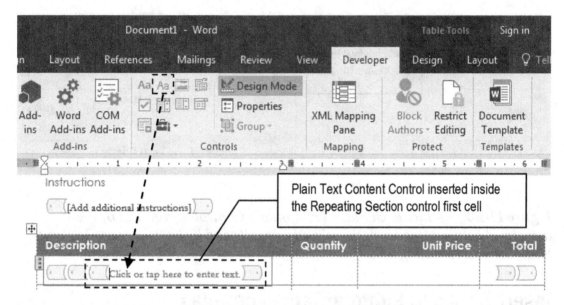

Figure 11-19. *Click inside the Repeating Section control Description column and click the Plain Text Content Control to insert it in the second row's first cell. Repeat this operation to insert other Plain Text controls in the Quantity and Unit Price columns.*

- Change the "Click or tap here to enter text" text inside each Plain Text control by the associated column header text for the second row cells and by 0.00 for the Sales/Tax and Shipping and Handling cells (Figure 11-20).

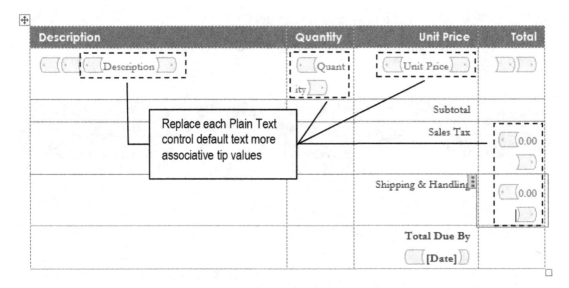

Figure 11-20. *Replace each Plain Text Content Control default text by the associated column Header in the second row cells and by 0.00 for Sales/Tax and Shipping and Handling cells.*

Insert Total and Subtotal Table Formulas

The Invoice detail table now has a Repeating Section control inserted in its first line, which has received inside it three Plain Text controls to allow the user to type information in the table cells.

The table is already prepared to receive formulas in its rightmost column, so it can correctly calculate the Total cell of each item, and the Subtotal cell:

- The Total cell inside the Repeating Section control must receive this formula:

  `=PRODUCT(LEFT)`

- The Subtotal cell, below the last Invoice Detail item must receive this formula:

  `=SUM(ABOVE)`

Follow these steps to insert these formulas:

1. Click the Total column empty cell (cell D2 or R2C4) inside the Repeating Section control, at the left of the control closing tag.

2. Click the Formula command found in the Data area of the Table Tools Layout tab to show the Formula dialog box and define these options:

    - Formula: =PRODUCT(LEFT)

    - Number format: #,###.00

3. Close the Formula dialog box to insert the Total cell formula.

4. Click cell D3 to select it (cell in Total column at right of the "Subtotal" cell).

5. Click the Formula command to show the Formula dialog box and define these options:

    - Formula (proposed by default): =SUM(ABOVE)

    - Number format: #,###.00

6. Close the Formula dialog box to insert the Subtotal formula.

Figure 11-21 shows these formulas inserted in the specified Invoice details table cells, after pressing Alt+F9 to alternate from cell value to cell formula view.

Description	Quantity	Unit Price	Total
((((Description))	((Quant ity))	((Unit Price))	{ =PRODU CT(LEFT) \# "#.##0,00 " })))
		Subtotal	{ =SUM(AB OVE) \# "#.##0,00 " }

Figure 11-21. *After inserting the cell D2 and cell D3 formulas, press Alt+F9 to alternate from cell value to cell formula to see how the Formula dialog box inserts them in these cells*

Bookmark Cells and Insert Total Due Formula

Since nobody knows in advance how many Invoice detail items will be inserted by the user in the Invoice details table, there is a technical need to Bookmark the Subtotal, Sales/Tax, and Shipping and Handling cells in the Total column, so the Total Due cell on the table bottom right border can correctly calculate using a formula like this:

```
=Subtotal + SalesTax + ShippingHandling
```

To bookmark a cell (or any text selection) means *to associate a cell to a name*, so you can easily return to it at any moment or refer to it in other Microsoft Word contexts.

Follow these steps to bookmark the Subtotal, Sales/Tax, and Shipping and Handling associated values in the Invoice details table Total column:

1. IMPORTANT: First select the entire cell value that you want to associate to a bookmark.

2. Click the Bookmark command found in the Links area of the Insert tab to show the Bookmark dialog box.

3. Type an associative name for the cell value (considering that Bookmark names can have up to 40 characters and must not contain spaces).

4. Click Add to add associate the cell value to the Bookmark name Figure 11-22) and insert it in Bookmark name list.

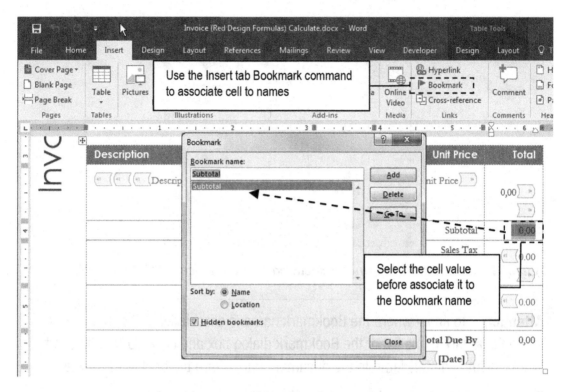

Figure 11-22. *Drag the mouse over the cell value to select it and use the Bookmark command to show the Bookmark dialog box to associate the value with a name*

5.   Click Close to close the Bookmark dialog box.

Figure 11-23 shows the Bookmark dialog box after associating cells D3, D4, and D5 to Bookmark names Subtotal, SalesTax, and ShippingHandling.

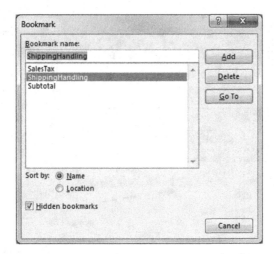

Figure 11-23. *Bookmark names associated to the Invoice detail table cells*

Attention   To know where the Bookmark name is associated in the text, select it in the Bookmark name list of the Bookmark dialog box and click Go To. Microsoft Word will immediately jump to the document part where the bookmark resides.

Bookmarks can be easily deleted when the text it refers to is deleted from the document. This is another reason to imply document protection by using the Restrict Editing tool.

Once the desired cells have been appropriately bookmarked, you no longer need to worry about how many Invoice items will be inserted in the Invoice details table so the Total Due cell formula (cell D6) can correctly relate to the Subtotal, SalesTax, and ShippingHandling cells.

Follow these steps to insert the Total Due formula in cell D6 of the Invoice details table:

1. Click cell D6 (bottom right corner table cell).

2. Click the Formula command found in the Data area of the Table Tools Layout tab to show the Formula dialog box and use the Paste bookmark list of the Formula dialog box to select bookmark names and create this formula:

   • Formula: =SubTotal+SalesTax+ShippingHandling

   • Number format: #,###.00

3. Close the Formula dialog box to insert the Total Due cell formula (Figure 11-24).

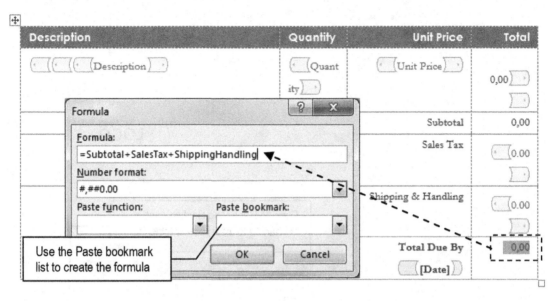

Figure 11-24.   *Click the last Invoice details table cell (cell D12, Total Due) and use the Formula command found in the Table Tools Layout tab to insert a formula to sum the SubTotal, SalesTax, and ShippingHandling Bookmarks*

Test and Save the Template

The document created by the Invoice (Red design) template that receives Controls and Formulas in its Invoice table details is ready to be tested and saved as a new template.

Test the Invoice Details Table Formulas

To test the document you must first prepare it to receive data from the user by following these steps:

1. Click the Invoice details table and uncheck the View Gridlines option found in the Table Tools Layout tab.

2. Uncheck the Design Mode tool found in Developer tab of the Ribbon. The Detail will show just one empty row to receive data (Figure 11-25).

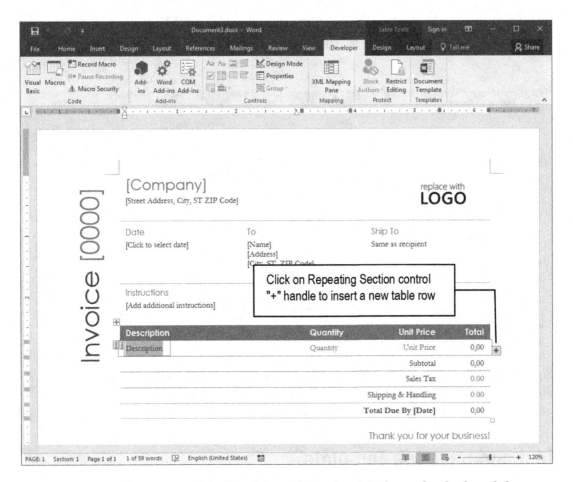

Figure 11-25. *The Invoice details table with Design Mode unchecked and the Description Plain Text Content Control selected. Note how each control inside the Repeating Section control inserted in the second table row now has its own tip (grayed); all Total columns show 0.00 values (returned from formula results or other Plain Text controls).*

3. Type these values for the first Invoice item (press Tab to move between fields):

    •   Description = Item 1.

    •   Quantity = 10.

    •   Unit Price= 1.28

4. Click the "+" handle of the Repeating Section control at the right of first Invoice detail item to insert another empty row in the Invoice details table with the same Plain Text controls and formula in Total column (Figure 11-26).

Description		Quantity	Unit Price	Total
Item 1		10	1.28	0,00
Description		Quantity	Unit Price	0,00
			Subtotal	0,00
			Sales Tax	0.00
			Shipping & Handling	0.00
			Total Due By [Date]	0,00

Item 1 was inserted and New table row inserted by Repeating Section control after type Item 1 invoice details

Figure 11-26. *After inserting the first Invoice detail item, press the "+" handle of the Repeating Section control at the right of the Total column to insert a new table row with the same set of controls and formula*

5. Insert a second Invoice detail item in the new row inserted in the table (Item 2, Quantity = 20, Unit Price = 2.15).

6. Repeat steps 4 and 5 one more time to insert a third Invoice detail item (Item 3, Quantity = 30, Unit Price = 4.77).

7. Press Tab on the last Unit Price invoice item to go to the Sales/Tax control and type 10.

8. Press Tab on the Sales/Tax control to go to the Shipping and Handling control and type 20.

9. Press Ctrl+A to select the entire document and press F9 to recalculate it (Figure 11-27).

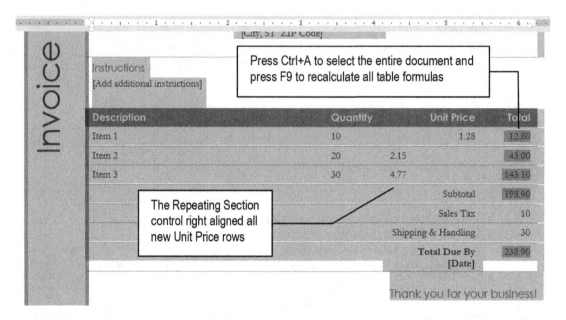

Figure 11-27. *To recalculate the Invoice detail tables, press Ctrl+A to select the entire document and press F9 to recalculate all its fields and formulas*

Attention   Note that new items inserted by the Repeating Section control "+" handle left align the Unit Price field—and there is not anything you can do about it!

Once the Invoice detail table is correctly calculating its formulas, you must remove all data from the Invoice detail table before you save the document as a new template. You can do this using two strategies:

- By removing all but the first Invoice detail table rows to leave it like Figure 11-25.

- By inserting a desirable number of empty rows in the Invoice detail table.

Either way, you must select each Plain Text Control (in Invoice details table, Sales/Tax, and Shipping and Handling) and delete its contents; press Ctrl+A and F9 to recalculate the table before saving it as a new, reusable Microsoft Word template.

Figure 11-28 shows how this table will look like after you clear the controls and use the Repeating Section control "+" handle to insert 10 new empty rows in the table (note how the Repeating Section control left aligned all new Unit Price controls).

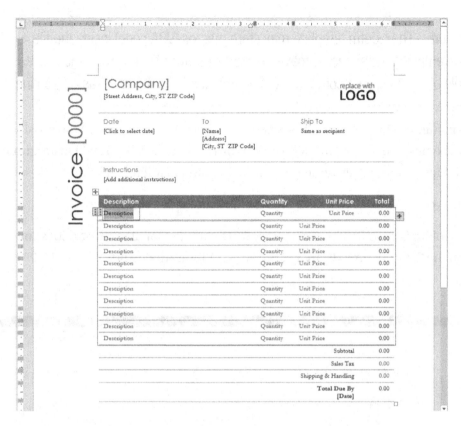

Figure 11-28. *Clear the Invoice details table controls and use the "+" handle to insert some new, empty new rows, before saving it as a new document template*

Saving the Template

To save a document as a template, use the File ➤ Save As command to evoke the Save as dialog box and type:

- File Name: the template name

- Save as Type: and select one of the two possible template types:

  - Word Template (*.dotx).

  - Word Macro Enabled Template (*.dotm).

Attention   The *.dotm template may store macros (VBA code) inside the file. Such type of templates with macros may be considered by antivirus programs as files capable of infecting your computer and be transferred to the antivirus quarantine folder.

No matter the folder you had selected, whenever you select one of the possible Template types (.dotx or .dotm) Microsoft Word Save As dialog box will instantly change to this folder (where <UserName> is your login name in Microsoft Windows system):

`C:\Users\<UserName>\Documents\Custom Office Templates`

This folder is specified by the Options ➤ Default personal templates location option found in the Save documents area of the Word Options dialog box (Figure 11-29).

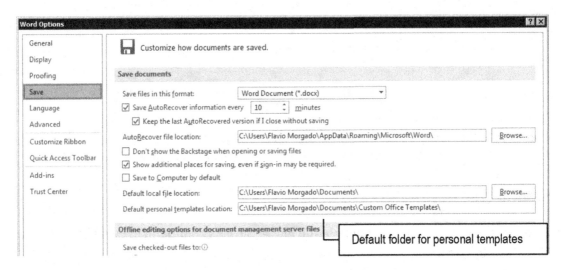

Figure 11-29.   *Microsoft Word defines the default location for all Microsoft Office personal templates using the Word Option dialog box (File ➤ Options, Save area ➤ Default personal templates location)*

Attention   The "Invoice (Red Design Formulas) Calculate.dotx" template document, which you can extract from Chapter 11.zip file, has a copy of Invoice (Red design) template shown in Figure 11-28, with Microsoft Word Repeating Section and Plain Text Content Controls and Formulas.

Open a Saved Template to Create Documents Based on It

To open a saved template, you must navigate to the folder where it is stored and use Microsoft Word Open dialog box to open it.

By opening the template you are indeed opening the file that should be used to generate copies of it, so be careful to save the changes you make in this file.

But whenever you want to create new copies of a personal template created by you, follow these steps:

1. Select File ➤ New.

2. Click the Personal option to show all templates stored in \Documents\Custom Office Templates folder.

3. Select the desired template and click the desired template to open a copy of it inside Microsoft Word (Figure 11-30).

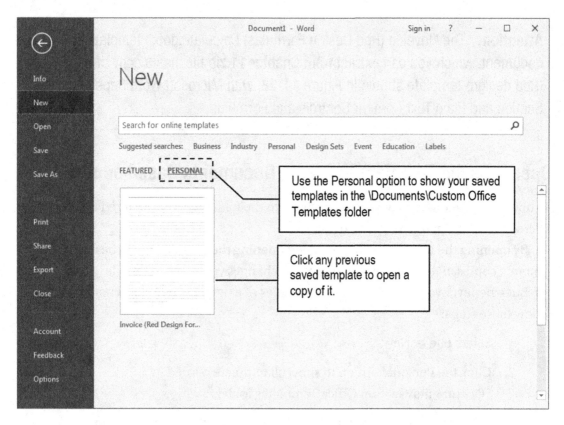

Figure 11-30. *Use the Personal option found in the New window (File ➤ New option) to show your templates and select the one that must create a new document copy of it*

Attention   All .dotx templates will automatically create new .docx documents, while all .dotm templates will automatically create .dotm (macro enabled) documents.

The Normal.dotm Template

Every time Microsoft Word opens and you click the Blank document option to create a new document, you are indeed creating a copy of the Normal.dotm template document, which is the file responsible to bring the default white page and all Recommended style formatting options (including Normal and Heading styles).

Without knowing it, you may have already changed the Normal.dotm template more than one time using some of this book's exercises and tips:

1. by clicking the Set as Default command button found in the Font and Paragraph dialog box to change the Normal style formatting options.

2. when you used the New Style dialog box to create a new style and selected the option "New documents based on this template".

3. when you associated a Style shortcut to Normal or Heading styles using the Customize Keyboard dialog box, which by default offers to store it in the Normal.dotm template (see Figure 5-16).

When you make such basic changes and they are propagated in the Normal.dotm template, you begin to notice that this special Microsoft Word Template can store more than just document formatting options like page properties and styles information. It can also store:

- AutoText and AutoCorrect entries.

- Macro codes.

- Shortcut keys.

- Toolbars and custom menu settings (when available).

As you can see, the Normal.dotm template is the file that stores your Microsoft Word preferences regarding formatting and personalization, which leads us to suppose that there is more than a single reason to know how to correctly manipulate it:

- to not to lose the hard defined personalizations made in your Microsoft Word copy.

- to copy your Microsoft Word preferences between computers.

- to change the appearance of new Microsoft Word documents.

Where Normal.dotm Is Stored

Although your personal templates are stored by default in \Documents\Custom Office Templates\ folder, the Normal.dotm and all templates downloaded or available in the File ➤ New window Featured option are stored in this deep, very hidden, almost secret folder:

C:\Users\<UserName>\AppData\Roaming\Microsoft\Templates

You can check or change this folder using the top-secret File Location dialog box found when you click the File Locations... command button found in the General area of the Advanced options of Word Options dialog box (Figure 11-31).

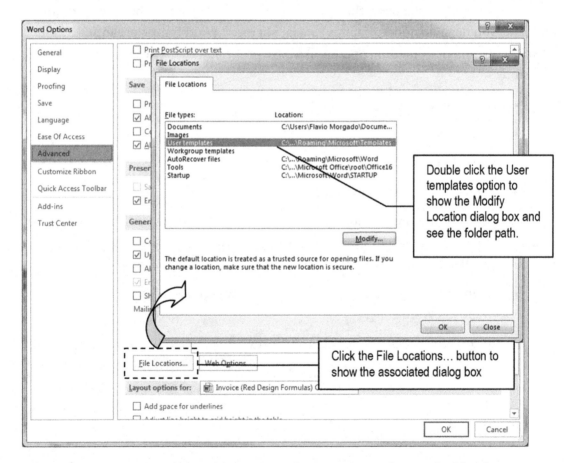

Figure 11-31. *Microsoft Word stores templates in the path specified by the User Templates options found in the File Locations dialog box (accessed using the File ➤ Options ➤ Advanced ➤ General ➤ File Location command button)*

Attention   The C:\Users folder and all folders inside it are hidden, protected system folders that may require you to log into Microsoft Windows with Administrator privileges to access its content.

Microsoft Word will always check for the Normal.dotm file when it opens. If it is not found in the specified folder, a new, empty default copy will be created.

Normal.dotm Is Protected

Since every time you open Microsoft Word it automatically opens the Normal.dotm template to load the user preferences for page, styles, autocorrection, and so on and eventually creates a new, empty document that is a copy of it, this template is locked against editing, and you can change its appearance.

Many people search for information on the Internet about how to change this default, empty document, and knowing that Normal.dotm template is locked against editing, you need to follow the next sequence to change it using Word, without losing your preferences stored inside it:

1. Make a Normal.dotm copy.

2. Change the Normal.dotm copy.

3. Replace the original .dotm copy with the changed version.

Let's see each of these steps with more detail.

Make a Normal.dotm Copy

Whenever you need to change the default Normal.dotm blank document, you must first make a security copy of it by following these steps:

1. Navigate to the Microsoft Word templates folder:

   `C:\Users\<UserName>\AppData\Roaming\Microsoft\Templates.`

2. Right-click the Normal.dotm file, drag it to an empty place in the folder, and select Copy here to save it in the same folder as Normal - copyedit file.

3. Open the Normal - copyedit file, format it to the way you want so that every new, empty document looks like it, and save it.

4. Close Microsoft Word.

5. Rename the original Normal.dotm file name to Normal2.dotm.

6. Rename the new Normal - copyedit file to Normal.dotm.

Exercise 2

The objective of this exercise is to produce a change in the Blank document template to make Microsoft Word always insert a watermark on its pages, and default header text (an operation that can be used to tag every document produced by a hypothetical office using its Microsoft Word copies and computers).

Follow these steps to create the Normal.dotm copy:

1. Navigate to the Microsoft Word templates folder:

    `C:\Users\<UserName>\AppData\Roaming\Microsoft\Templates`

2. Right-click the Normal.dotm file, drag it to an empty place in the folder, and release the mouse button.

3. Select Copy here to create the Normal - copyedit file in the same folder.

Attention   Now your Microsoft Word folder will have a security copy of the Normal.dotm file.

---

4. Open Microsoft Word, and select Open Other Documents ➤ Browse to show the Open file dialog box.

5. Navigate to the Microsoft Templates folder:

    `C:\Users\<UserName>\AppData\Roaming\Microsoft\Templates`

6. Select Normal - copyedit file produced in Step 3 and click Open.

Attention   It is important to note that you cannot use the File ➤ New option, nor double-click the Normal - copyedit template, because you will create a copy of the file structure, and will lose the personal data inserted in Normal.dotm. You MUST open the file copy.

7. Use the Watermark tool found in the Page Background area at the right of Design tab to insert any of the available watermarks in the Normal - copyedit page.

8. Double-click the page Header area to show it.

9. Verify that the watermark is a WordArt object inserted in the Header, and vertically aligned on the page (Figure 11-32).

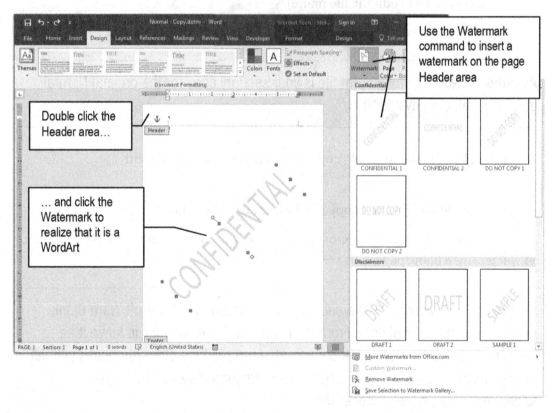

Figure 11-32. *Use the Design tab Watermark command to insert one of the available watermarks in the Normal - copy.dotm file. Double-click the page header and note that the watermark is a WordArt object inserted in the Header page area and vertically centered on the page.*

10. Save Normal - copyedit document again on the Microsoft Templates folder.

11. Close Microsoft Word.

At this point the Normal - copyedit file stored in Microsoft Word secret Templates folder already has all changes needed to use the company formatting options (we add just a watermark, but you can also make changes to page size, styles formatting, headers etc.).

Follow these steps to replace Normal.dotm by the Normal - copyedit file:

1. Supposing that Microsoft Word is closed, use Windows Explorer to navigate to the secret Templates folder located in

   `C:\Users\<UserName>\AppData\Roaming\Microsoft\Templates`

2. Right-click the Normal.dotm file and choose Rename (or click it a second type to edit the file name).

3. Change the Normal.dotm file name to Normal2.dotm file name.

Attention   Now Normal2.dotm file is your security copy for the original Normal. dotm file, without any changes.

---

4. Right-click the Normal - copyedit file (the one changed) and choose Rename.

5. Change the Normal - copyedit file name to Normal.dot.

Now, every time you open Microsoft Word and select the Blank document template, you will receive a blank page with a watermark. Try it!

Attention   I personally dislike such approach of tag the Microsoft Word Blank document with personal data. From my point of view, it is better to leave it as is—a new, empty, normal blank document—and produce other templates with all desired formatting, that can be saved in the \Documents\Custom Office Templates folder and used whenever necessary.

Always make copies of your Normal.dotm file to quickly adapt any Microsoft Word copy to your needs.

Creating Your Own Templates

Whenever you need to create and distribute your own templates, begin with a new, empty document derived from Normal.dotm (or from another template that has all the formatting you need).

Then follow this checklist to define the document standards:

- Use the Page Setup dialog box to define page properties (size, margins, multiple pages, position and type of headers and footers).

- Define the style set to be used.

- Define the first page formatting.

- Define the headers/footers formatting (for first, even and odd page).

- Save the document as .dotx or .dotm format.

Attention   Remember that some antivirus programs may incorrectly interpret .dotm files (Word Macro Enabled Templates) as treats because they have the potential to carry VBA code that may produce damage.

Use Your Template

Once a template is created and saved, you can use its formatting options two different ways:

- Use all its formatting options (page and styles formatting), by creating a copy of it using one of these methods:

    - Selecting it using the File ➤ New ➤ Personal option (that shows the \Documents\Custom Office Templates folder).

    - Double-click the .dotx or .dotm file in the folder it resides in.

- Use just the template styles (ignoring all its page setup formatting), by associating the document to the desired template using:

  - The Document Templates command found at the right of the Developer tab (see Figure 11-9).

  - Any .dotx document template saved using the Save as New Style Set... command found in the Style Set Gallery menu of the Design tab (see Figure 6-5).

  - Any Microsoft Word document that can be selected by the Browse for Themes... option of the Themes tool found at left of the Design tab (see Figure 6-9).

Insert a Document Text in an Empty Template

To use all the formatting options of any Microsoft Word Template (page and styles formatting) you must begin to type in a copy of this template, or more commonly insert any other document text inside a new, empty copy of this template.

There are two different ways that you can insert a document text in a new, empty document based on any template:

- By using the Object ➤ Text from file option found in the text area of the Insert tab of the Ribbon (Figure 11-33).

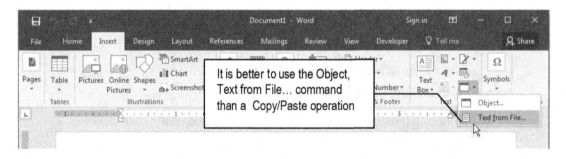

Figure 11-33. *Use the Insert ➤ Object ➤ Text from file tool to select all the text of another Microsoft Word document and inserting at the current cursor position*

- By selecting the entire document text (Ctrl+A), copying it to clipboard, and pasting it into the new document based on the desired template.

All styles used in the original document (Normal and Recommended styles, if any), will automatically become formatted with the same style used in the destination template.

Attention   Since the Section Break holds all page information, the document you insert in the template must not have any Section Breaks to avoid that template page properties being overidden by other document page properties.

You may eventually need to make an advanced Find and Replace operation using the same style in the Find what and Replace with options to reapply each template style to the document text pasted inside the template copy.

Most publishers—Apress included—use such methods to make their book templates available. They offer a template file from where you must delete the text and insert your own text to send the document to an expected format, so the book page count can be anticipated with accuracy.

Associating a Document with a Template

You can also associate a document to an existing template, which will update equivalent document styles to the same template styles formatting while also making available all template styles to the document. The template page formatting options will not be used.

You can do such operations using the Document Template command found at right of the Developer tab, which will show the Templates and Add-ins dialog box from where you can select a template file to be attached to this document (Figure 11-34).

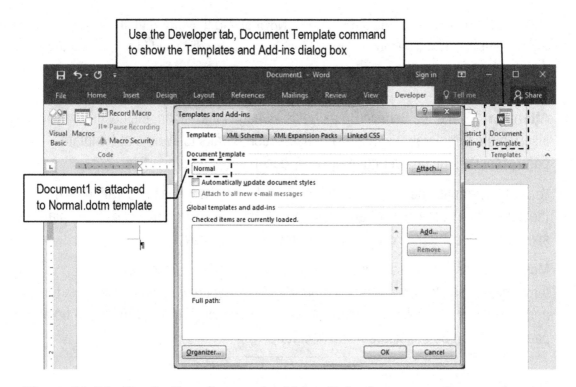

Figure 11-34. *Use the Templates and Add-Ins dialog box to attach a template to a document. By doing this, all template styles becomes available and active in the current document.*

As Figure 11-34 shows, the Document1 opened by the Microsoft Word is attached to Normal.dotm template. And the same way that most styles inherit the Normal style formatting options, by attaching a document to a template you make it permanently inherit all template styles formatting.

Any changes made to the template styles will be automatically applied to the document whenever it is opened, which is a quite good formatting rule to quickly change documents based on the same template.

Attention   Any Microsoft Word .dotx or .dotm template cannot be attached to another template. Both the Document template and the Attach button will become unavailable in such file types.

Using the Template and Add-ins Dialog Box

The Template and Add-ins you see on Figure 11-34 allows you to

- attach a document to a template;

- indicate to which template a document is attached to;

- automatically update the document styles to the current template styles formatting;

- define which template—and its styles (besides Normal.dotm)—must be loaded whenever Microsoft Word starts.

The Templates and Add-ins dialog box controls are as follows:

- **Attach**: click the Attach button to show a File Explorer window from where you can select a new template to be attached to this document.

Attention   Any Microsoft Word document can be attached to just one template at a time.

- **Automatically update document styles**: Check this option to automatically update all document styles to the same styles that may exist in the attached template.

- **Global Templates and Add-ins**: Click Add button to select all templates whose styles you want to be available whenever Microsoft Word is opened (you need to check the templates so its styles become available in the Styles pane).

- **Organizer**: Show the Organizer dialog box (Figure 11-35) from where you can copy styles from one file/template to another.

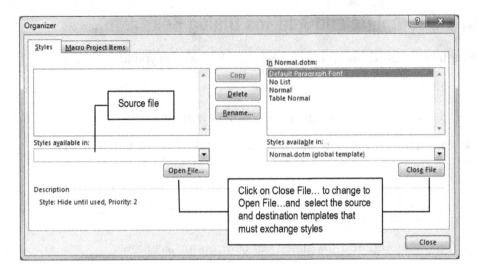

Figure 11-35. *Use the Organizer dialog box to transfer styles (and macros) from the source (left list) to the destination (right list) document. You can use the Close File button to close and open documents from where you want to exchange macros and styles.*

Attention   Whenever you need to use one or more styles that already exist in a Microsoft Word template or document, you don't need to recreate it: just use the Organizer dialog box to copy them between the selected documents. Use the Styles available in list and the Close file button below each list to open the source (left list) and destination (right list) files and the Copy, Delete, and Rename buttons to manage the styles.

Use the Macro Project Items of the Organizer dialog box to transfer macro codes between Microsoft Word documents.

Exercise 3

The objective of this exercise is to show how a document text with section breaks inserted in a Template overrides the Template page properties.

Follow these instructions:

1. Extract the "6x9 Book.dotx" Microsoft Word Template document from Chapter11.zip file to this folder: \Documents\Custom Office Templates

2. Use the File ➤ New ➤ Personal templates options to show all Custom Office Templates and click the "6x9 Book" template to create a new, nonempty .docx copy of it (Figure 11-36).

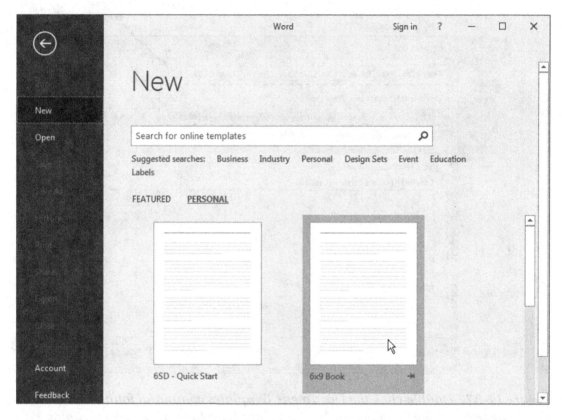

Figure 11-36. *After extracting the "6x9 Book.dotx" Microsoft Word Template document to the \Documents\Custom Office Templates folder, use the File ➤ New ➤ Personal option to click it and open a new, empty .docx copy of it.*

Attention   The "6x9 Book.dotx" template has text inserted in it, so it creates new documents with text already inside them.

---

3. Click the Document Templates command found in the Developer tab of the Ribbon to show the Templates and Add-ins dialog box and note that this document is attached to the "\Documents\ Custom Office Templates\6x9 Book.dotx document" (Figure 11-37).

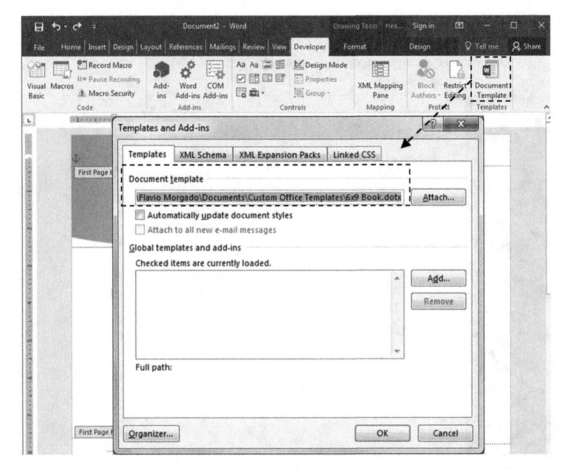

Figure 11-37. *Double-click the Document Templates command found in the Templates area of the Developer tab to show the Templates and Add-ins dialog box from where you can verify to which template the document is attached*

4. Explore the Microsoft Word document created from this template and note that it has

- Different first page, with a semi-ellipsis inserted in its First Page Header (double-click the Header/Footer area to select it).

- Different first page, odd and even page headers and footers.

- Page Size of Width = 6 and Height = 9.

- Examples of each main style inserted as text (Chapter Number, Chapter Title, Heading1 to 4, BodyFirst, BodyCont, and Note, Figure 11-38).

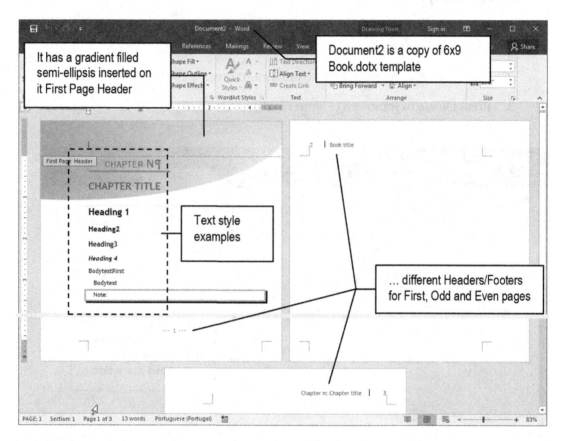

Figure 11-38. *The "6x9 Book.dotx" template has a different first page (with a semicircle inserted in its First Page Header), different First, Even and Odd Headers/Footers, and text examples of its main styles (Chapter Number, Chapter Title, Heading1 to 4, BodyFirst, BodyCont, and Note).*

Attention   The semi-ellipsis was inserted in the First Page Header using the Insert ➤ Shapes control, and formatted using the Shape Fill tool with a Gradient fill from 50% black to white. Study it!

Insert Another Document Text

To use this document you first need to remove all its template example contents and then use the Insert ➤ Object ➤ Text from File command to select the desired document text.

Follow these steps:

1. Double-click the text area to close the Header and Footer area and select the document text.

2. Press Ctrl+A to select the entire document text.

3. Press Delete to remove it (Figure 11-39).

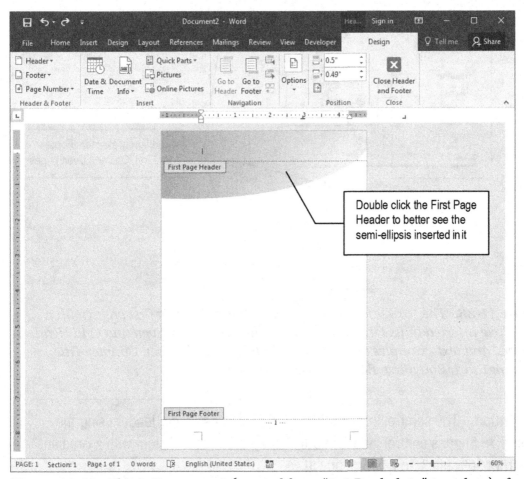

Figure 11-39.   *This is Document2 (created from "6x9 Book.dotx" template) after removing all its text (its First Page Header is selected so the figure can show the semicircle inserted in it)*

4. Extract file "Moby Dick, Herman Melville, Formatted.docx" document from Chapter11.zip file.

5. Use the Insert ➤ Object ➤ Text from File tool to show the Insert File Microsoft Windows Explorer dialog box and select the "Moby Dick, Herman Melville, Formatted.docx" document.

6. Press OK to insert all document pages in the empty document based on "6x9 Book.dotx" template. Document will receive about 630 pages.

7. Press Ctrl+Home to move to its beginning and note that it lost the template First Page Heather and there is at least two different page sizes (Figure 11-40).

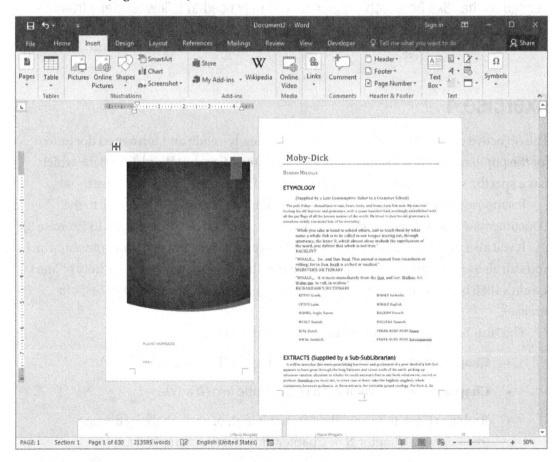

Figure 11-40. *The "Moby Dick, Herman Melville, Formatted.docx" document has six section breaks, each one carring its page formatting. When it is inserted in an empty document based on the "6x9 Book.dotx" template, its Section Breaks override the template page formatting.*

Attention   Since the "Moby Dick, Herman Melville, Formatted.docx" document (created in "Exercise 2" section of Chapter 9) has six different Section Break types, each Section Break used its own page formatting option.

Remove all section breaks from the source document before inserting it in a new template. The reader is invited to remove all Section Breaks from the source document before trying to reinsert it in the empty document based on the "6x9 Book.dotx" template.

You can also extract the "Moby Dick, Herman Melville, No Section Break.docx" document from Chapter11.zip file to this exercise. After inserting it in the document based on the "6x9 Book.dotx" template, you may need to follow all steps from "Exercise 2" section of Chapter 9 to reformat it!

Exercise 4

The objective of this exercise is to easily adapt a ready-made and formatted document for the popular 6×9 book format using its associated Microsoft Word Template, which has a specific style set and different page layouts for first, even and odd pages.

It supposes that you had already extracted the "6x9 Book.dotx" template to the \Documents\Custom Office Templates folder (as specified by the first steps in Exercise 3).

It will also use "The Adventures of Tom Sawyer, Mark Twain.docx" document, which you can also extract from the Chapter11.zip file; this document has the entirety of Mark Twain's 1876 book, formatted in a 134 Letter page size document (without Section Breaks).

The "6x9 Book.dotx" template has these special styles:

- **Chapter Number**: to format each "Chapter N" paragraph (if any).

- **Chapter Title**: to format each chapter title text (if any).

- **BodytextFirst**: to format the first paragraph of each chapter (the one that follows a Chapter N or Chapter Title style paragraph, if any).

- **BodyText**: to format all other body text paragraphs.

Since "The Adventures of Tom Sawyer, Mark Twain.docx" document uses Recommended styles to format its paragraphs (Heading1 for "Chapter N" titles and Normal for body text), the strategy that must be used to apply these Template styles to the text is to execute successive Find and Replace wildcard operations.

Base a Document on the "6x9 Book.dotx" Template

As usual, we first need to create a new, empty document based on the "6x9 Book.dotx" template, in which we must insert "The Adventures of Tom Sawyer, Mark Twain.docx" document text.

Follow these steps:

1. Use the File ➤ New ➤ Personal command to show the contents of the \Documents\Custom Office Templates folder, and click the "6x9 Book.dotx" template to create a nonempty copy of it (see Figure 11-38).

2. In the new .docx document based on the "6x9 Book.dotx", press Ctrl+A to select the entire text and Delete key to clean the document (see Figure 11-39).

3. Execute the Insert ➤ Object tool ➤ Text from File command to show the Insert File dialog box and select "The Adventures of Tom Sawyer, Mark Twain.docx" document to insert it in the new, clean document based on the "6x9 Book.dotx" template.

4. Since the source document has no Section Breaks, it will adapt to the empty document page formatting options, which will flow the text to fit on 227 pages using a single section (Figure 11-41).

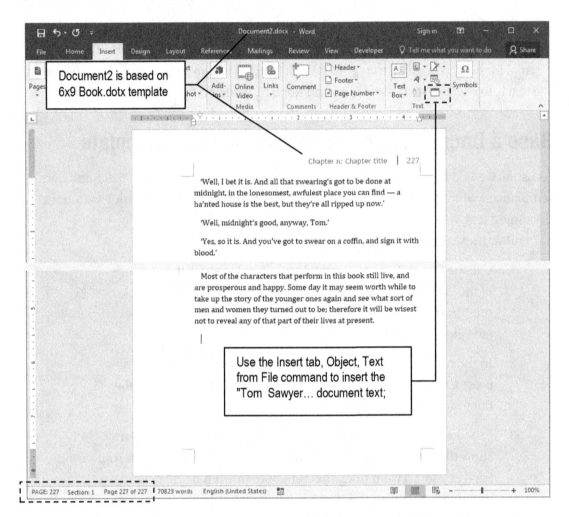

Figure 11-41. *In a clean, empty copy of the "6x9 Book.dotx" template, use the Insert ➤ Object ➤ Text from File command to insert the "The Adventures of Tom Sawyer, Mark Twain.docx" document text*

5. Press Ctrl+Home to go to the text beginning and note that the first two paragraphs are formatted with the Title and Subtitle Recommended styles, and that all pages received the document page formatting and headers (Figure 11-42).

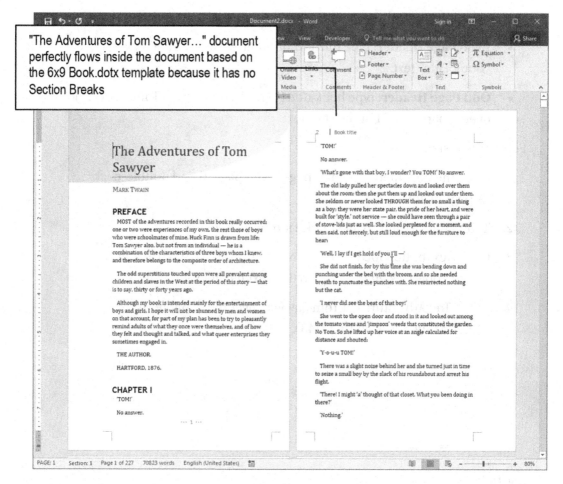

Figure 11-42. *These are the first pages of Document1.docx based on "6x9 Book.dotx" template, which received the text from "The Adventures of Tom Sawyer, Mark Twain.docx" document*

Changing Odd and Even Headers

The "6x9 Book.dotx" template has default text inserted in its First page footer (page number), even and odd page Headers. You must first change the default Even and Odd Page Header texts so whenever you insert Section Breaks in the document, the new section inherits the appropriate Headers.

You must apply these changes:

- **Even Page Header**: type the author name ("Mark Twain") over "Book Title" text.

- **Odd Page Header**: type book title ("The Adventures of Tom Sawyer") over "Chapter n: Chapter title" text.

Follow these steps:

1. Go to the document's second page (even page 2) and double-click its page header;

2. Type "Mark Twain" over "Book Title" indicator.

3. Click Next button located in the Navigation area of the Header & Footer Tools Design tab to go to the next header (odd page 3).

4. Type "The Adventures of Tom Sawyer" over the "Chapter n: Chapter title" text (Figure 11-43).

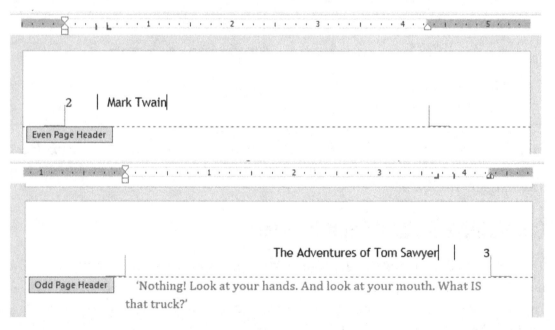

Figure 11-43. *Type the author name (Mark Twain) and the book title (The Adventures of Tom Sawyer) into the Even and Odd Page Headers of the document based on the "6x9 Book.dotx" template that received "The Adventures of Tom Sawyer, Mark Twain.docx" document text*

Changing Text Styles

Now you must apply the Template styles to the document text. Since it has the BodytextFirst style that must be applied to the first paragraph that succeeds each "CHAPTER N" text (formatted with Heading1 style), we can make such formatting using two successive Find and Replace operations:

- First Find and Replace will format each "CHAPTER N" and next paragraph with a blue color.

- Second Find and Replace operation will search for every Normal style with blue color and change it to the BodytextFirst style.

Apply BodytextFirst Style to Each First Chapter Paragraph

Follow these steps to format the desired text with a blue color:

1. Double-click the document text to close the Header page area (if still opened).

2. Press Ctrl+Home to go to the document begin, click the first paragraph of "Preface" section, and apply the BodytextFirst style using the Styles Gallery.

3. Press Ctrl+H to show the Find and Replace dialog box with the Replace tab selected (or select the Replace command in the Home tab of the Ribbon).

4. Click More ➤ to expand the Replace dialog box and check User wildcards option.

5. In the Find what text box type:
   (CHAPTER*^13)(*^13)

Attention   The wildcard search is case sensitive. The (CHAPTER*^13) will select every paragraph that begins with "CHAPTER" and has any other text (*) and a Paragraph Break (^13). The (*^13) will select the next paragraph that succeeds it. The parenthesis pair ( ) allows you to use the \n option in the Replace with text box.

Always use the Find Next button to verify if the desired text is being selected by the wildcard operation.

6. In the Replace text box, type click Special ➤ Font to show the Font dialog box and use the Font color tool to choose a blue color.

7. Click Replace All button to change 35 occurrences (Figure 11-44).

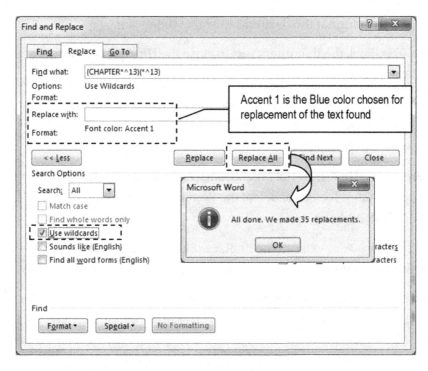

Figure 11-44. *Use the Find and Replace dialog box Replace tab*

At this point, all "CHAPTER N" paragraphs formatted with the Heading 1 style and the Normal style ones that succeed it must be formatted with the selected blue color in the text. It is time to search for every Normal paragraph with a blue color and change it to the BodytextFirst style.

Now follow these steps to change all Normal style blue paragraphs to a BodytextFirst style:

1. In the Find and Replace dialog box, uncheck the Use wildcards option.

2. Click the Find what text box and select as follows:

   - Click Special ➤ Style to show the Find Style dialog box and select Normal style.

   - Click Special ➤ Font to show the Font dialog box, and click Font Color tool select the same Accent 1 blue color used in the last search operation.

3. Click the Replace with text box and set these options:

   - Click No Formatting button to remove the previous formatting options:

   - Click Special ➤ Style to show the Find Style dialog box, BodytextFirst style.

   - Click Special ➤ Font to show the Font dialog box and click Font color control select Automatic (or Black).

4. Click Replace all to change 35 occurrences, applying the BodytextFirst style to each first chapter paragraph (Figure 11-45).

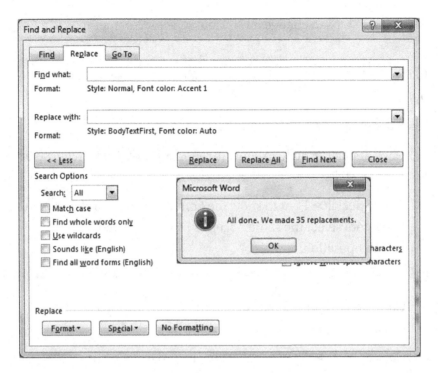

Figure 11-45. *Once all first paragraphs after a "CHAPTER N" paragraph have been tagged with a blue color, use another Find and Replace operation without wildcards to search for each Normal, Font color = Accent 1 paragraph and change to BodytextFirst, Font color = Auto (black)*

Apply Bodytext Style to All Normal Styles

Now that all first paragraphs of each chapter are correctly formatted with the BodytextFirst style, it is time to change each remaining Normal style to a Bodytext style.

Follow these steps:

1. In the Find and Replace dialog box, click Find what text box and set these options:

    • Click No Formatting to remove all previous Find what formatting options.

    • Click Special ➤ Style to show the Find Style dialog box and select Normal style.

2. In the Replace with text box, set these options:

    •   Click No Formatting to remove all previous Replace with
        formatting options.

    •   Click Special ➤ Style to show the Find Style dialog box and select
        Bodytext style.

3. Click Replace all to apply the Bodytext style to all Normal style
    paragraphs (Figure 11-46 shows that Microsoft Word shows an
    erroneous number of replacements).

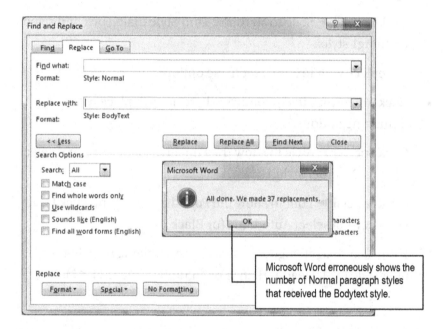

Figure 11-46. *After applying the BodytextFirst style to each first chapter*
paragraph, use the Find and Replace dialog box to search for every Normal style
and replace it with a Bodytext style

Apply Chapter Number Style to All Heading1 Styles

Now that the body text received the BodytextFirst and BodyText styles, let's change each Heading1 style to the Template Chapter Number style.

Follow these steps:

1. In Find and Replace dialog box, click Find what and set these options:

    - Click No Formatting to remove all previous Find what formatting options.

    - Click Special ➤ Style to show the Find Style dialog box and select Heading1 style.

2. In the Replace with text box, set these options:

    - Click No Formatting to remove all previous Replace with formatting options.

    - Click Special ➤ Style to show the Find Style dialog box and select Chapter Number style.

    - Click Special ➤ Font to show the Font dialog box and click Font color control select Automatic (or Black).

3. Click Replace all to change 35 occurrences, applying the Chapter Number style to all Heading1 style paragraphs (Figure 11-47).

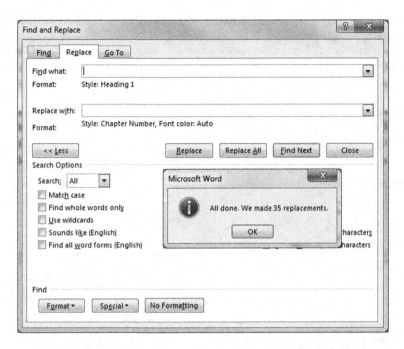

Figure 11-47. *The last Find and Replace operation must search for each Heading1 style and change it to a Chapter Number style with Font color = Automatic (since all "CHAPTER N" Heading1 styles are still formatted with the Accent 1 blue color)*

At this point, the document based on the "6x9 Book.dotx" template that received "The Adventures of Tom Sawyer, Mark Twain.docx" will be formatted like Figure 11-48.

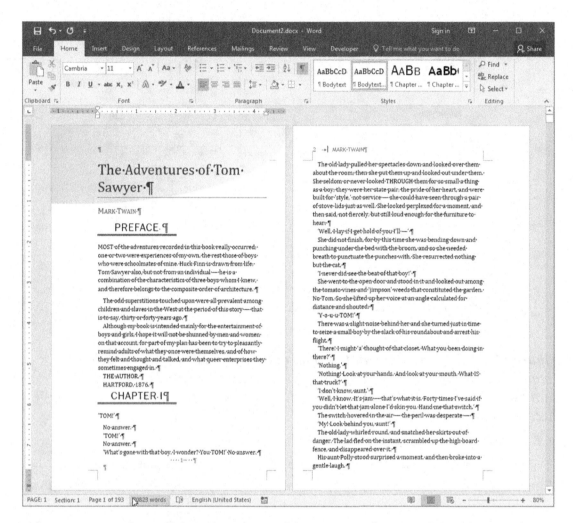

Figure 11-48. *This is "The Adventures of Tom Sawyer" inserted in a document based on the "6x9 Book.dotx" template, after receiving the right Even and Odd Page Headers and the ChapterNumber, BodyTextFirst, and BodyText styles*

Insert an Odd Page Section Break Before Chapter

To finish this exercise we must insert an Odd Page Section Break before each "CHAPTER N" text paragraph, formatted with the Chapter Number style, so each chapter receives the First Page Header formatting, with the semi-ellipsis in its First Page Header and page number in its First Page Footer (see Figure 11-38).

As explained before you can automatically do this by first inserting an Odd Page Section Break in the document, cutting it to Clipboard (Ctrl+X), and using a Find and Replace operation.

Follow these steps:

1. Check the Show/Hide tool in the Home tab of the Ribbon.

2. Click anywhere in "CHAPTER I" text on the document's first page and press Home to position the text cursor at the beginning of this paragraph.

3. Use the Layout ➤ Breaks ➤ Odd Page command to insert a Section Break (Odd Page) hidden character before this paragraph.

Attention   Since you inserted an Odd Page Section Break, the "CHAPTER I" text will now begin on document page 3, automatically receiving a First Page Header (Figure 11-49).

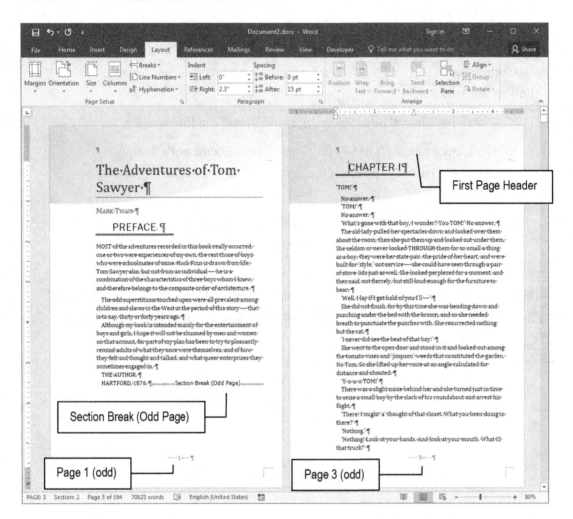

Figure 11-49. *When you insert an Odd Page Section Break before "CHAPTER I" text, it makes this chapter begin on the next odd page number (page 3), and a First Page Header style is applied*

4. Click the Section Break (Odd Page) and press Shift+End (or Shift+Right arrow) to select it and press Ctrl+X to cut it to Clipboard.

5. Press Ctrl+H to show the Find and Replace dialog box, click More>>, and unselect Use wildcards.

Attention   There is no need to use a wildcard search in this Find and Replace operation.

6. In Find what text box, set these options:

    - Click No Formatting to remove all previous Find what formatting options.

    - Click Special ➤ Style to show the Find Style dialog box and select Chapter Number style.

    - Type this search string: CHAPTER

7. In the Replace with text box, set these options:

    - Click No Formatting to remove all previous Replace with formatting options.

    - Click Special ➤ Clipboard Contents to add a ^c as replacement string.

    - Click Special ➤ Find What Text to add a ^& to the replacement string, which must become (Figure 11-50): ^c^&

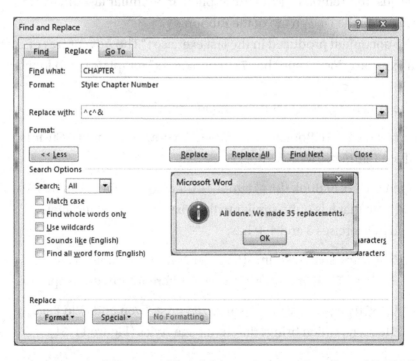

Figure 11-50.   *Once you have cut the Odd Page Section Break to the Clipboard, use the Find and Replace dialog box to search for every "CHAPTER" text in a Chapter Number style paragraph, and use Special ➤ Clipboard Content (^c) and Special ➤ Find What Text (^&) to precede each chapter with an Odd Page Section Break*

631

8. Click Replace all to change all 35 occurrences.

The document will now have an Odd Page Section Break preceding every "CHAPTER" text formatted with the Chapter Number style, with the first chapter page formatted using the "6x9 Book.dotx" template First Page Header. I end up having 235 6×9 pages (considering that you manually inserted an Odd Page Section Break before its last chapter, "Conclusion").

Attention   The file "The Adventures of Tom Sawyer, Mark Twain 6x9 Book.docx" has this exercise done for your appreciation.

Exercise 5

The objective of this exercise is to demonstrate that by attaching a document to a new Template file, just the Template styles are applied, in a similar fashion used by the Style Set Gallery found in the Design tab of the Ribbon.

It uses the document produced in the last exercise ("The Adventures of Tom Sawyer, Mark Twain 6x9 Book.docx") and the "7x10 Book.dotx" template (both found inside Chapter11.zip).

Follow these steps to inspect the "7x10 Book.dotx" template:

1. Extract the "7x10 Book.dotx" template to the \Documents\Custom Office Templates folder.

2. Open the "7x10 Book.dotx" template (or a document based on it) and note that it is quite similar to the "6x9 Book.dotx" template used in Exercises 3 and 4. It has:

    •   The same style set name (Chapter Number, Chapter Title, BodytextFirst, and BodyText) with different formatting options.

    •   A 7×10 page size with personalized First, Even and Odd Page Headers, which brings different page styles (Figure 11-51).

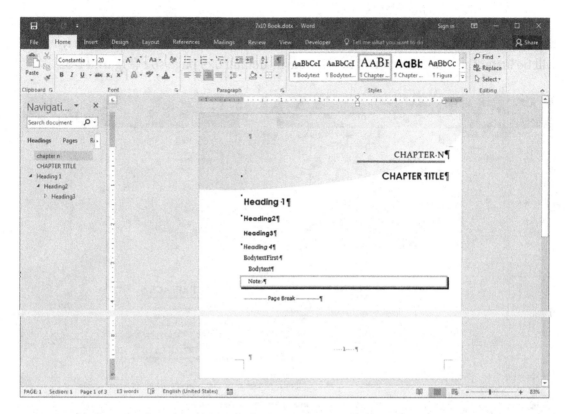

Figure 11-51. *The "7x10 Book.dotx" template has the same style set name found in the "6x9 Book.dotx" template, using a different font set and formatting options. It also has a 7×10 page size with its own First, Even and Odd page footers and headers.*

3. Open "The Adventures of Tom Sawyer, Mark Twain 6x9 Book. docx" document.

4. Use the Document Templates command found in the Templates area of the Developer tab to show the Templates and Add-ins dialog box.

5. Click the Attach button of the Template and Add-ins dialog box to show the Attach Template Windows Explorer dialog box.

6. Navigate to the folder where you extract the "7x10 Book.dotx" template, select it, and click OK to close the dialog box and point to the desired template association.

7. Check the Automatically update document styles option and click OK to close the Templates and Add-ins dialog box.

Since "The Adventures of Tom Sawyer, Mark Twain 6x9 Book.docx" document has the same style set name found in the "7x10 Book.dotx" template, the document styles will be instantly updated, but will not update its default 6×9 page size (Figure 11-52).

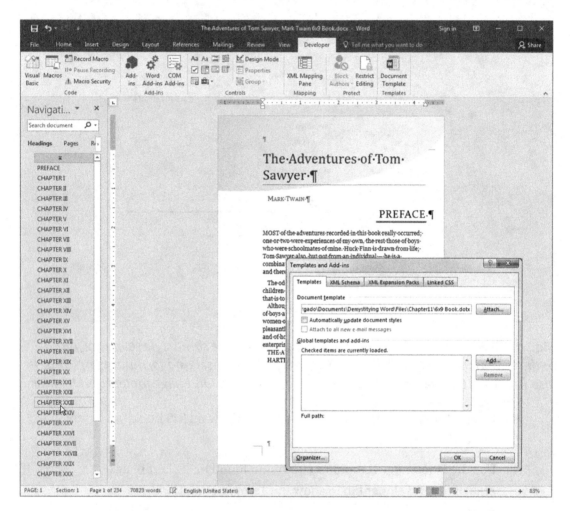

Figure 11-52. *Whenever you attach an existing document to a new template, all template styles become available for the document, and the ones with the same name will be automatically updated to the template formatting standards. The document page properties will not be changed.*

Exercise 6

The objective of this exercise is to prove that whenever you have a document formatted with the appropriate style set, having no Section Breaks, you can easily change its appearance by inserting it in another template and updating both its styles and its page formatting.

It uses the document produced in the last exercise ("The Adventures of Tom Sawyer, Mark Twain 6x9 Book No Section Break.docx") and the "7x10 Book.dotx" template (both found inside Chapter11.zip).

Follow these steps, supposing that you have placed a copy of the "7x10 Book.dotx" template in your \Documents\Custom Office Templates folder:

1. Create a new document based on the "7x10 Book.dotx" template using one of these two strategies:

    •   Click File ➤ New ➤ Personal to show the \Custom Office Templates folder and click the "7x10 Book.dotx" template.

    •   Double-click the "7x10 Book.dotx" file wherever you had stored it.

2. Since the new document based on the "7x10 Book.dotx" template is full of style examples, press Ctrl+A to select the entire text and Delete to clean the document content.

3. Use the Insert ➤ Object ➤ Text from File command to show the Insert File dialog box from where you must select "The Adventures of Tom Sawyer, Mark Twain 6x9 Book No Section Break.docx".

Attention   It is important to insert the right document version—without Section Breaks—so the document can inherit all template page and styles formatting.

---

4. Press Ctrl+Home to go to the document begin and note that it now has 144 7×10 pages (Figure 11-53).

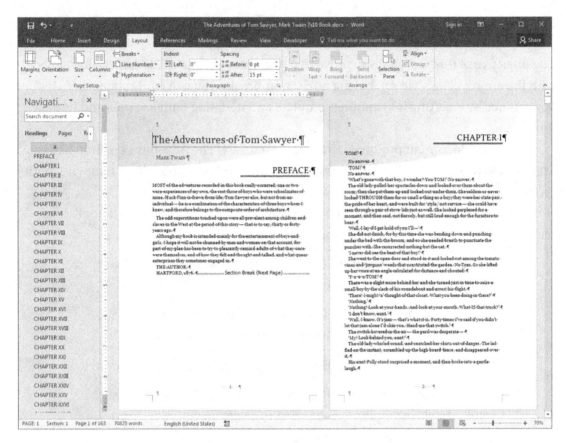

Figure 11-53. *This is "The Adventures of Tom Sawyer, Mark Twain 7x10 Book. docx" document, which you can extract from Chapter11.zip file, offering Mark Twain's famous book in 164 formatted pages using the popular 7×10 book format*

5. Double-click the document's second page header and type "Mark Twain" over "Book Title" indicator.

6. Click Next button located in the Navigation area of the Header & Footer Tools Design tab, select the Odd Page Header, and type "The Adventures of Tom Sawyer" over the "Chapter n: Chapter title" text.

7. Check the Show/Hide tool in the Home tab of the Ribbon and use the Layout tab, Breaks, Odd Page command to insert an Odd Page Section Break before "CHAPTER I" text.

8. Click the Section Break (Odd Page) character, and press Shift+End to select it and Ctrl+X to cut it to Clipboard.

9. Press Ctrl+H to show the Find and Replace dialog box and make a replacement operation to automatically insert the Odd Page Section Break on Clipboard before each "CHAPTER" text formatted with Chapter Number style using:

    -   Find what: "CHAPTER" (click More>>. Format ➤ Style and select the Chapter Number style).

    -   Replace with: ^c^& (click Special ➤ Clipboard Content and Special ➤ Find What Text).

    -   Press Replace All to change all 35 occurrences.

After manually inserting an Odd Pager Section Break in the last book chapter (Conclusion), the document will have 163 7×10 pages, with each chapter beginning on an odd page with a different page style.

Figure 11-53 shows the appearance of "The Adventures of Tom Sawyer, Mark Twain 7x10 Book.docx" (which you can extract from Chapter11.zip file); this now reflects the state of the document after undergoing all these exercise steps. It now has the template formatting options, including page formatting and styles.

Attention   The reader is invited to study to "7x10 Book.dotx" template format, including the fonts used in the text (styles, headers and footers) and the Header/ Footer text formatting.

Conclusion

In this chapter, you have seen how to take the best from Microsoft Word Templates offered by the File ➤ New window and how to use your own Templates to quickly format long text documents using the same formatting standard for similar text paragraphs (document title, subtitle, chapters, body text for the first and other paragraphs).

You also learned about how Microsoft Word can also use the Developers tab Controls and Form mode, and how to use Formulas in its tables to make rudimentary—and not so trustworthy—calculations, which require manual recalculations.

Summary

In this chapter you learned:

- That a Template is a special kind of document that automatically creates copies of itself.

- That Microsoft Word has different types of templates (empty templates, templates with one page formatting, templates for long documents).

- That you can create a document based on an existing Template by using the File ➤ New windows or by double-clicking the template in the folder it resides in.

- How to use Microsoft Word Controls and the Design Mode option to insert and use Controls in documents.

- How to restrict document editing using the Restrict Editing tool found in the Developer tab.

- How to change an existing Invoice template adding its Controls and Formulas so it can have a better usage.

- That every time Microsoft Word starts and brings you an empty page, it is indeed bringing you a copy of the Normal.dotm template.

- That the Normal.dotm template is hidden in this system folder:

  `C:\Users\<UserName>\AppData\Roaming\Microsoft\Templates`

- That the Normal.dotm template cannot be changed while Microsoft Word is opened.

- How to change the Normal.dotm template, so every new empty document created with Word has a defined appearance.

- That you must insert text examples of the formatting styles used in your own templates.

- How to insert text in a document template.

- How to attach a document to another template.

- That documents attached to other templates inherit just the template styles and none of the template page formatting.

- How to use the Insert ➤ Object ➤ Text from File command to insert another document text inside a template.

- That you must remove all Section Breaks from source documents before insert them on another template (or you may run the risk of ruining the template formatting).

- That by using the same style set name in templates and documents, you can easily change the document appearance by inserting it in another document based on such a template.

In the next chapter, you will learn about how to use Microsoft Word Master/Sub documents feature to work on a collaborative way with a writing team to quickly produce superb documents with the same formatting options.

CHAPTER 12

Master and Subdocuments

In this chapter you will learn about Microsoft Word Master and Subdocuments feature, which allows you to manage independent documents (called Subdocuments) in a single file (called Master documents), to produce a final document that constitutes the essence of the collaborative work of different people enrolled to pursue the same task, such as the production of a book that contains independent chapters from many different authors.

Using the Master and Subdocuments approach, you can define a template of chapter and section names and from there create, split, and merge the subdocuments needed to compose the final product.

All documents cited in this chapter can be found by downloading the Chapter12.zip file from this Internet address:

```
https://github.com/apress/msft-word-secrets
```

The Master and Subdocuments Approach

Microsoft Word's Master and Subdocuments feature is implemented by the Outline view option, which has already been introduced in the section "Using the Outline View" of Chapter 7.

There, you learned that whenever you turn on Outline view, you can best manage the Heading style paragraphs of your document, collapse and expand Heading paragraphs, and promote or demote the Outline level of one or many Heading style paragraphs with a click of the mouse, and easily change the position of big blocks of text by dragging one or more collapsed Heading style paragraphs to a new position (or moving them with the Move Up or Move Down tools and its associated shortcuts Alt+Shift+Up or Alt+Shift+Down arrows).

© Flavio Morgado 2017
F. Morgado, *Microsoft Word Secrets*, https://doi.org/10.1007/978-1-4842-3078-7_12

Microsoft Word also uses the Master document area of the Outlining tools tab to store the tools needed to deal with the Master/Subdocument approach of managing different files as a single one.

To show these tools, you must

1. Click the Outline tool found in the Views area of the View tab.

2. Select the Outlining tab that appears at the beginning of the Ribbon.

3. Click the Show Document command of the Master Document area of the Outlining tab (Figure 12-1).

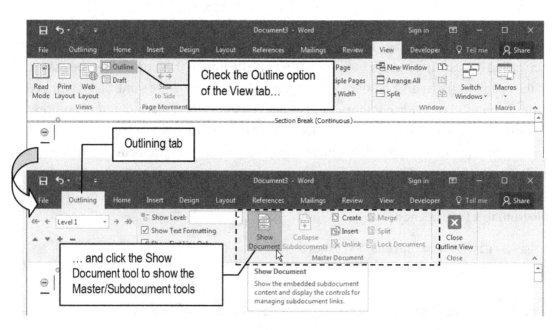

Figure 12-1. *Use the Ouline view to show the Outlining tab, from where you can click the Show Document option of the Master Document area to show all available Master/Subdocument tools*

Master Document Commands

By inspecting the Master Document area of the Outlining tabs you may note that it has different commands to deal with the Master/Subdocuments relationships (see Figure 12-1).

They are as follows:

- **Show Document**: expand the Master Document area to show other commands to deal with Master/Subdocuments.

- **Collapse Subdocuments**: alternate the Outline view (and Print Layout view) between file path (Collapsed Subdocument mode) and content (Expanded Subdocument mode).

- **Create**: allow creating a subdocument for any Heading paragraph style. The entire Heading branch (including its subheadings) will be included in the subdocument.

- **Merge**: allow merging one or more selected subdocuments in Outline view Expanded Subdocument mode into a single subdocument.

- **Insert**: show the Insert Subdocument dialog box from where you can navigate to the folder that contains the Microsoft Word file that must be inserted as a subdocument.

- **Split**: the inverse of the Merge command, allows splitting the current subdocument in Outline view Expanded Subdocument mode from text position to its end, in two different subdocuments.

- **Unlink**: load all subdocument content into the master document, breaking the Master/Subdocument link.

- **Lock Document**: lock the Master document from changes in any subdocument. Just the Master document text can be changed.

Establishing Master/Subdocument Relationships

The Master document is an empty main document that may (and probably will) have text inside it, and to succeed using Microsoft Word Master/Subdocument tools you must also follow these two basic rules:

- All documents (Master and Subdocuments) must be based on the same Template, to guarantee that they use the same style set and page sizes.

- All documents must use Heading styles to format their chapter and section paragraphs (or styles that have the Paragraph dialog box Outline level option set to any level different from Body text).

You can establish Master/Subdocuments relationships by first creating the Master document based on the desired template and then use one of those two methods:

- Use Heading styles to create the first approach to the final document structure, defining chapter and section names (formatted with Heading1 to Heading9 styles).

- Insert the links to subdocuments that represent the document chapters.

The first approach is used when you can anticipate in advance how the final document must be, and then distribute the subdocuments created by it. The second approach is used when you already have the document chapters made in independent Microsoft Word files and need to join them together to assemble the final document.

Let's see them both in more detail.

Creating Subdocuments from a Master Document

If you need to produce a document—like a book or manual—that is written by different people, or produced with a given "Table of Contents" structure, you will do better by first creating a document (called Master) that defines the final document content structure, and then creating the subdocuments from it.

You will need to follow these steps:

1. Create a new, empty document based on the same Template that all subdocuments are also based on.

2. Type each chapter name in its own paragraph (Chapter 1, Chapter 2...), formatting them with Heading 1 style (Outline level = 1).

3. Optionally, type inside each "Chapter n" Heading 1 style the section names, formatting them with Heading2 style.

4. Check the Outline command found in the Views area of the View tab of the Ribbon to show and select the Outlining tab.

5. Use the Create command found in the Master Document area of the Outlining tab to transform Heading1 style paragraph in an independent subdocument.

Exercise 1

The objective of this exercise is to create a Master/Subdocument relationship based on a predefined document structure based on Heading styles.

Follow these simple steps:

1. Open a new document in Microsoft Word.

2. In the first paragraph type "Master Document" and format it with the Title style found in Style Gallery.

3. Insert three successive paragraphs, each one identifying a chapter number (Chapter 1, Chapter 2, and Chapter 3).

4. Apply the Heading1 style to each "Chapter" paragraph.

5. Click View ➤ Outline to show the Outline view and the Outlining tab.

6. Click Show Document button to show the Outline tools.

7. Select all three "Chapter" Heading1 paragraphs and click the Create command found in the Master Document area of the Outlining tab.

8. Close the Outline view.

Microsoft Word will transform each "Chapter" Heading1 style paragraph into a subdocument, surrounding it by a rectangle, with a subdocument icon placed at its left, using what is considered as Expanded Subdocument mode (Figure 12-2).

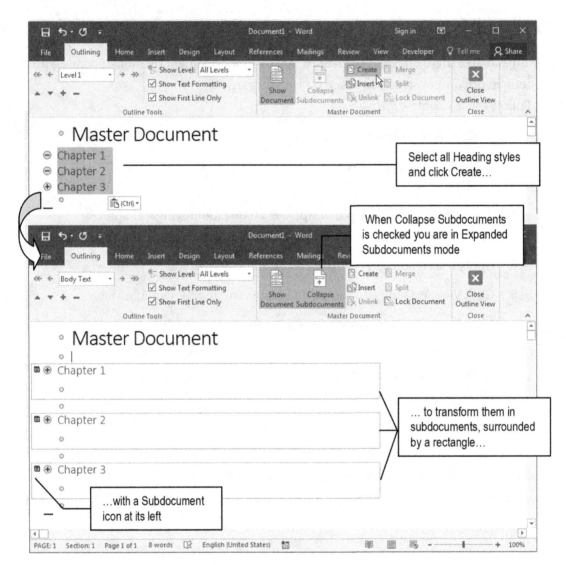

Figure 12-2. *Type the Heading1 styles that will identify the final document structure, check the Outline view, and use the Create command found in the Master Document area of the Outlining tab to transform each Heading paragraph into a subdocument*

After the Heading1 paragraphs have been transformed into Subdocuments, use File ➤ Save as command to choose an adequate folder to save the master document. Microsoft Word will propose the first document paragraph text ("Master Document") as the file name for the Master document, and when you save it, it will also create independent Microsoft Word .docx files to identify each subdocument, naming them with their first Heading1 style paragraph text (it will save the Master Document.docx file and will also create Chapter1.docx, Chapter2.docx, and Chapter3.docx in same folder).

Using Collapsed Subdocuments Mode

To verify where each subdocument was saved, click Collapse Documents to uncheck this option to enter Collapsed Subdocuments mode (which will turn into Expand Subdocuments) and show each subdocument file path instead (Figure 12-3).

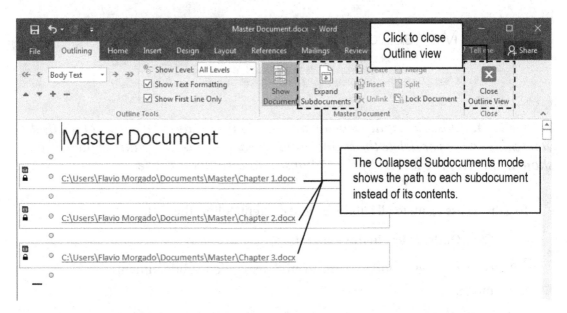

Figure 12-3. *Uncheck the Collapse Subdocuments command found in the Master Document area of the Outlining tab to enter the Collapsed Subdocuments view and see the path where each subdocument was saved*

If the Outline view is in Collapsed Subdocuments mode and you close the Outline view (by clicking the Close Outline View button or selecting another view mode in the View tab), Microsoft Word will lock the subdocuments and will not show subdocument contents—just the path to them. Microsoft Word will also lock each subdocument, avoiding their deletion (Figure 12-4).

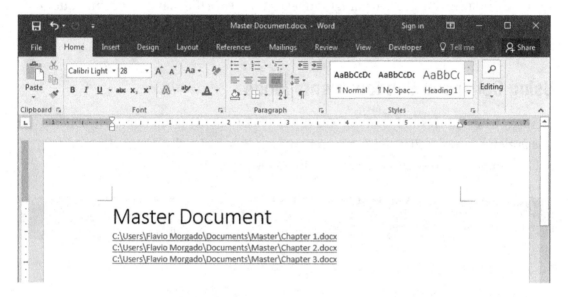

Figure 12-4. *Close the Outiline view to return to Print Layout view and note that you cannot access or delete the subdocument contents: just the paths to them are shown, and they are locked by the Collapse Subdocuments mode*

To gain access again to all subdocument content, follow these steps:

1. Click Outline view in the View tab.

2. Click Expand Subdocuments to enter Expanded Subdocuments mode.

Whenever you enter again in Expanded Subdocument view, you can gain access to each subdocument content and close the Outline view to return to the Print Layout mode and work on the text as if it were a single file (Figure 12-5).

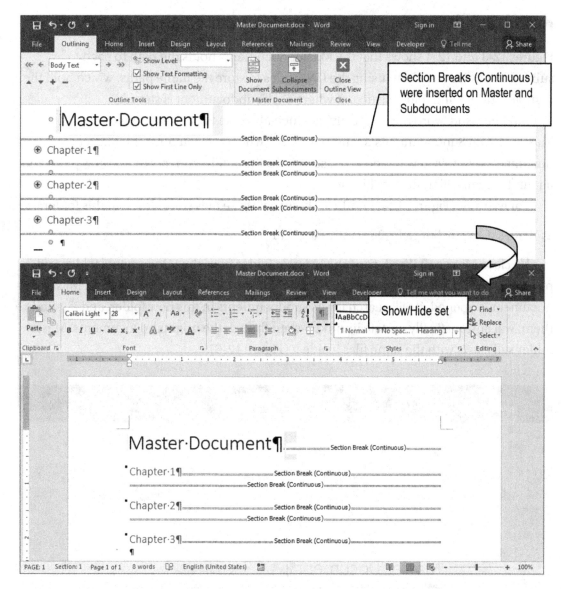

Figure 12-5. *To gain access to the subdocuments inserted in a Master document, you must show the Outline view and click the Expand Subdocuments option to enter Expanded Subdocuments mode. Close the Outline view and note how the document is now formatted when the Show/Hide tool is checked*

Attention   The file Master.zip found inside Chapter12.zip has the Master Document.docx, Chapter1.docx, Chapter2.docx, and Chapter3.docx files. Extract them to a new folder and open the Master document to try it.

How Are Subdocument Paths Saved in the Master Document?

Figures 12-3 and 12-4 shows that the Master documents holds the path to each subdocument inserted in it, using the UNC rules to store file name paths, which hold the complete driver and folder structure where each subdocument is stored.

But Microsoft Word doesn't really use such absolute file paths. If you move the Master and all Subdocuments to another folder, whenever you open the Master document from this new folder, it will search for the subdocuments in this new path, and if it finds them, will update its file path.

For example, Figures 12-3 and 12-4 show that these files were stored in this folder:

`C:\Users\Flavio Morgado\Documents\Master`

If I close Microsoft Word, copy the \Master folder from the \Documents folder and paste it in the C:\ root folder, whenever the C:\Master\Master Document.docx Master document is opened, it will search for its subdocuments in this new folder, and if it finds them, will automatically update its links—even though the original \Documents\Master folder still exists with the same files inside it (Figure 12-6).

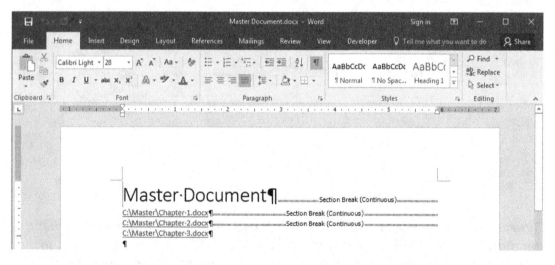

Figure 12-6. *If the Master and Subdocuments are moved to a new folder in your drive or network, whenever you open the Master document, it will search for its subdocuments in the path it resides in, and if it finds them, it will automatically update its links*

The lesson here is quite simple: Microsoft Word always stores the subdocuments as a relative path to the Master document, expecting that the Master/Subdocuments are always stored in the same folder.

Attention   Try not use different folders to store copies of your Master/ Subdocuments files. It may trick you into using an incorrect version of the final, updated subdocument files.

Section Breaks Inserted in Master/Subdocuments

Did you notice in Figures 12-2 to 12-5 that after changing Microsoft View from Outline to Print Layout and back again to Outline view, many Section Breaks suddenly appear in the document?

They were automatically inserted by Microsoft Word to keep the Master document page properties, while also keeping each subdocument page's properties.

It works this way: whenever you select a Heading style and click Create command of the Outlining tools tab, Microsoft Word first adds a Section Breaks before the Subdocument, to guarantee that it can hold the Master document page formatting. It then inserts the subdocument, and inside the Subdocument, adds another section break, so the Subdocument can hold its own page properties.

Attention   When you use the Create command found in the Outlining tab, every Section Break automatically inserted by Microsoft Word inherits the page properties of the Master document.

Look again at Figure 12-5 and realize that there is a first Section Break (Continuous) after the "Master Document" text paragraph (inserted in the Master document), right before "Chapter 1" text.

Also note that immediately after "Chapter 1" appear two successive Section Break (Continuous) characters: the first one inserted inside Chapter1.docx Subdocument.

Attention   The second Section Break was indeed inserted before "Chapter 2" text, repeating the same formatting rule for every Subdocument automatically created by the Create command.

To confirm where these Section Breaks were inserted, to enter Collapsed Subdocument mode (click Collapse Subdocuments), close the Outline view again to return to Print Layout mode and, having the Show/Hide tool checked, observe how each Subdocument is preceded by a Section Break (Continuous) inserted in the Master document (Figure 12-7).

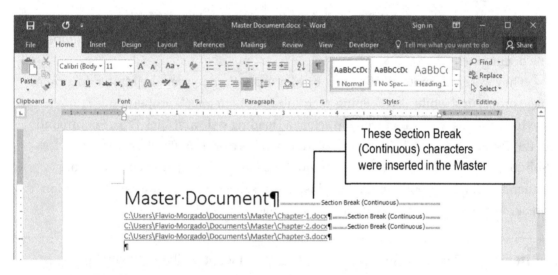

Figure 12-7. *Close again the Outliine view to return to Print Layout view and note that the Master document received a Section Break (Continuous) hidden character before each Subdocument*

To further realize how each subdocument received a Section Break at its end, Ctrl+Click its link in Print Layout view to open it in its own Microsoft Word window (Figure 12-8).

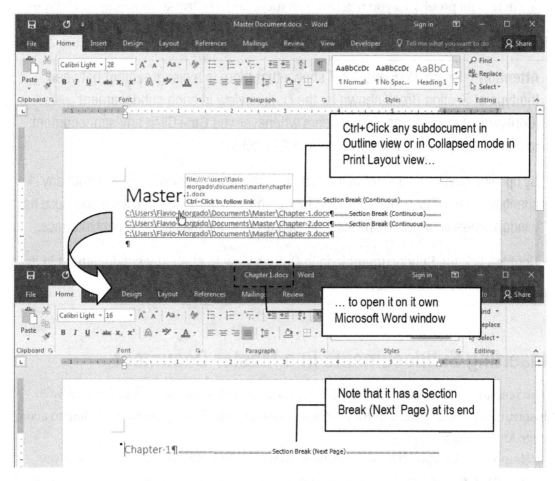

Figure 12-8. *Ctrl+Click any Subdocument in Outline view or Print Layout view and Collapsed Subdocuments mode to open it in its own Microsoft Word window*

Yes, it is true! By imposing Master/Subdocuments relationships, Microsoft Word inserts a lot of Section Breaks that you must manage to not lose control over your final document formatting.

There is no problem if you delete any of these Section Breaks, or change their type (using the Section Start option found in Layout tab of the Page Setup dialog box).

Attention   Figure 12-5 and 12-7 shows that there is a disagreement between the type of Section Break shown by the Outline view in each subdocument (Continuous) and the one that appears whenever you Ctrl+Click any subdocument to open it in Microsoft Word window (Next Page).

By opening any subdocument in its own Microsoft Word window, you can make any changes to the subdocument text and formatting, and whenever you save and close its window, these changes will be instantly perceived in the Master document interface.

Double-click the Subdocument icon in Outline view to open any subdocument in its own Microsoft Word window.

Inserting Subdocuments in a Master Document

The second way by which you may create Master/Subdocument relationships is by inserting Subdocuments in another document—all based on the same Template to avoid page formatting problems.

Supposing that you have already defined where the subdocuments are stored on your computer or network, follow these steps:

1. Create a new, empty document based on the same Template that all subdocuments are also based on.

2. Save this document in the same folder where the subdocuments are stored, using the "Master" prefix—or name—to identify it.

3. Check the Outline command found in the Views area of the View tab of the Ribbon to show and select the Outlining tab.

4. Click the Show Document option found in the Master Document area of the Outlining tab to show the Outline tools.

5. Click the Insert tool found in the Master Document area of the Outlining tab to show the Insert Subdocument dialog box from where you can select and insert the desired subdocument.

6. Repeat step 5 for every other subdocument that must be inserted inside the Master document.

Whenever a Subdocument is inserted in a Master document, Microsoft Word will also insert a Section break before it and another Section Break inside—as the Create command does.

Note however that if the Master and Subdocuments have different page layouts, these many Section Breaks may create a document with different types of page formatting. To fix this problem you will need to delete all inserted section breaks and insert them again, so they can receive, by inheritance, the same page formatting used by the Master document.

Exercise 2

The objective of this exercise is to show how Microsoft Word reacts when you insert Subdocuments in a Master document and they have different page formatting options.

Extract MasterSubdocuments.zip file from Chapter12.zip file and extract its contents to a new folder. It has the Master.docx, SubDocument1.docx, Subdocument2.docx, and Subdocument3.docx documents based on the default Normal.dotm template.

The Master.docx document has a 5×4 page size and the "Master Document" text followed by an Odd Page Section Break (Figure 12-9). It also has two empty paragraphs in its second, blank page.

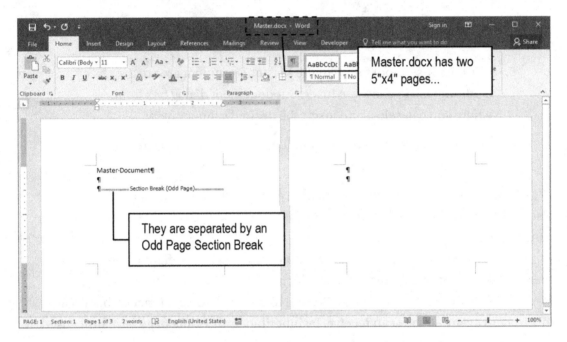

Figure 12-9. *The Master.docx file that you can extract from MasterSubdocuments.*
zip file is formatted with a 5×4 page. Its first paragraph identifies the document
and its two pages are separated by an Odd Page Section Break

The Subdocument1.docx, Subdocument2.docx, and Subdocument3.docx have texts
that identify their contents followed by an empty paragraph, and all three documents
were formatted with a 5×6 page size (Figure 12-10).

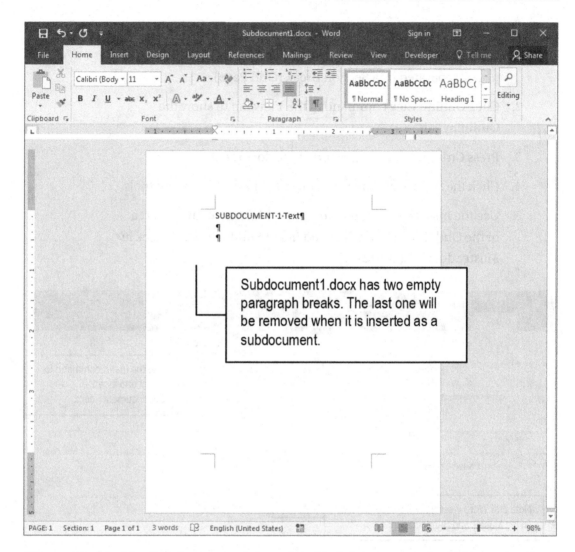

Figure 12-10. *The Subdocument1.docx (and Subdocument2.docx) has a 5×4 page size and two empty paragraph breaks. The last one is always removed (or exchanged) by a Section Break when the document is inserted as a subdocument*

Attention   The Next Page Section Break inserted at the end of any subdocument always removes the last paragraph break to avoid inserting a new document page. This is why Subdocument1.docx, Subdocument2.docx, and Subdocument3.docx have two paragraph breaks on their second pages—the last one will be removed.

Follow these steps to insert its three subdocuments using the Outlining tab:

1. Open the Master.docx document and note that it has two small pages, separated by a Section Break (Odd Page).

2. Click Outline view command of the View tab to show the Outlining tab.

3. Press Ctrl+End to go to the end of the document.

4. Click the Show Document to show the Master Document tools.

5. Use the Insert command found in the Master Document area of the Outlining tab to select and insert Subdocument1.docx in Master.docx (Figure 12-11).

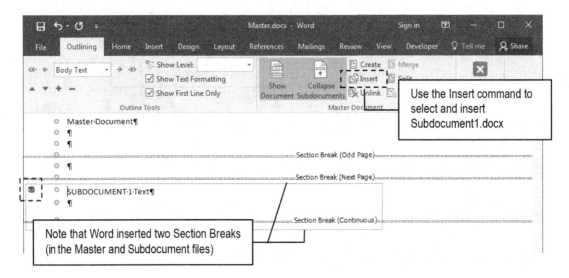

Figure 12-11. *Use the Insert command of the Outlining tab to select and insert Subdocument1.docx as a subdocument of Master.docx Master document*

Attention   According to Figure 12-11 Microsoft Word inserted two Section Breaks: one in the Master document (Next Page) and other in the Subdocument1. docx (Continuous).

---

6. Double-click the Subdocument1.docx Subdocument icon to open Subdocument1.docx in its own Microsoft Word window (Figure 12-12) and note that the Continuous Section Break shown by Figure 12-11 is indeed a Next Page Section Break.

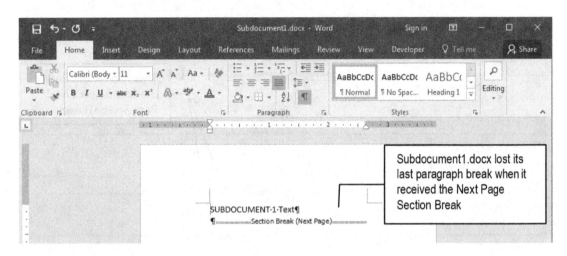

Figure 12-12. The Subdocument1.docx exchanges its last paragraph break with a Next Page Section Break, which disagrees with what is shown by the Outline view of the Master.docx document shown in Figure 12-11

7. Close Subdocument1.docx to return to Master.docx document in Outline view.

8. Press Ctrl+End to go to the end of Master.docx document and use again the Insert command to select and insert Subdocument2.docx and Subdocument3.docx as subdocuments of Master.docx document (Figure 12-13).

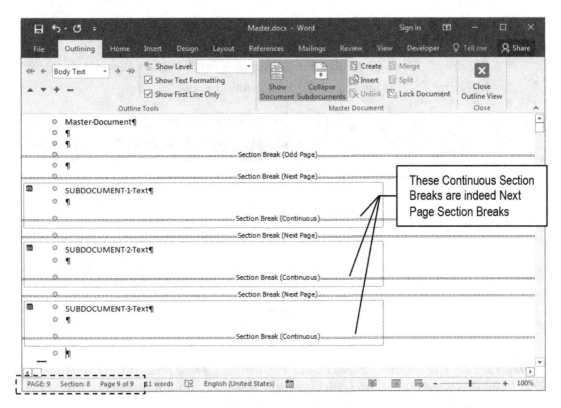

Figure 12-13. *After inserting the three subdocuments in Master.docx, the final Master document will become full of Next Page Section Breaks. The total number of pages shown in the Status Bar reflects the page count for the Master and all Subdocuments it points to*

Attention   Double-click Subdocument2.docx and Subdocument3.docx icons to show each file in its own Microsoft Word window and note that each lost its last paragraph break, having now a Next Page Section Break in its place—although the Outline view keeps showing that each one has a Continuous Section Break at its end.

Looking to Figure 12-13 status bar you may note that the Master.docx document now has nine logical pages (eight physical sheets of paper, because it has an Odd Page Section Break on its first page that increases page counting by one, missing logical Page 2).

Close Outline view mode to return to Print Layout view and note that Master.docx document preserves its 4×5 page size for each Next Page Section Break inserted in it, while the Next Page Section Break inserted in each subdocument makes it preserve its own page size, just as it should (Figure 12-14).

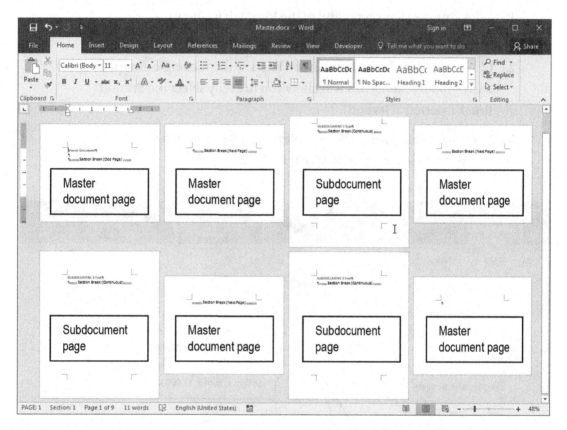

Figure 12-14. *By closing Outline view, you will return to Print Layout view, from where you can use the Zoom tool to inspect the Master.docx document. Note that it kept its 4×5 page size in each page before the Next Page Section Breaks inserted in it, and also kept each Subdocument page size by inserting Next Page Section Breaks inside each subdocument*

Restoring Master Page Settings in Subdocuments

You can easily restore the Master.docx 5×4 page size in all subdocuments inserted in it by manually removing the Next Page Section Break inserted inside each subdocument file, leaving the Next Page Section Breaks inserted in the Master.docx document untouched.

After removing them you can change all Master document Section Breaks to a desired standard (Odd Page Section Break, for instance), to guarantee that each subdocument text will begin on an odd page.

Follow these steps:

1. Click Outline view command of the View tab to show the Outlining tab.

2. Check the Show Document option to show the rectangle around each subdocument (this will allow you to easily select the Section Break inserted at its end).

3. In each subdocument, click the Next Page Section Break at its end and press Delete to remove it (Figure 12-15).

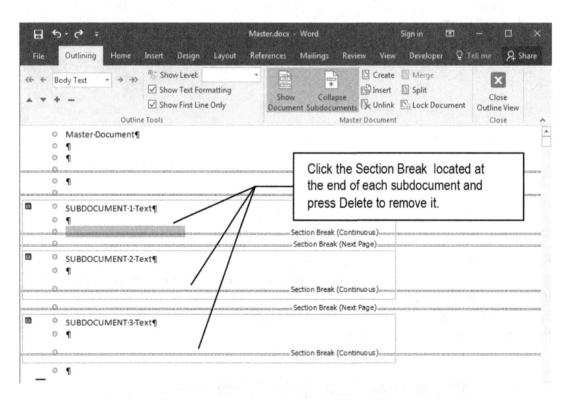

Figure 12-15. *Click the Section Break located at the end of each Subdocument and press Delete key to remove it*

4. When all subdocuments no longer have Next Page Section Breaks at their ends, close the Outline view to return to Print Layout view and the Master.docx document will now have just one page.

5. Also remove the Next Page Section Break inserted before the first subdocument (the one inserted below the Odd Page Section Break that already existed in the document).

Attention   In a real situation, to easily move to the end of each subdocument text and find the Section Break you want to remove, you may need to select Show Level = Level 1 in the Outline Tools area to show only the Heading1 styles, collapsing the document text.

Alternatively, you may also double-click each Subdocument icon to show it in its own Microsoft Word window, press Ctrl+End to go the subdocument end, and remove its last Section Break.

As each subdocument has the Section Break at its end removed, it inherits the page properties of the section above it; these properties are stored by the Section Break inserted in the Master document. When you finish, the Master.docx document in Outline view will be like Figure 12-16, having just the Next Page Section Breaks inserted in the Master document, after the end of each subdocument.

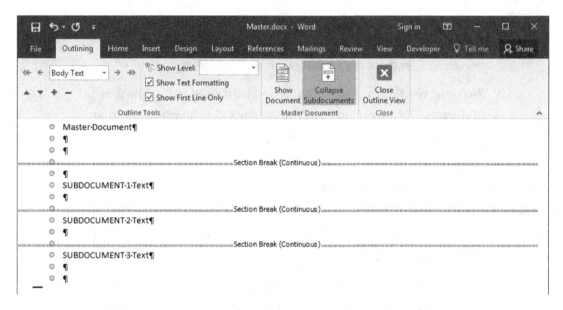

Figure 12-16.   *This is how the Master document will look like after all Next Page Section Breaks have been removed from inside each subdocument*

Close the Outline view to return to Page Layout view and note that now Master.docx Master document has just two pages that uses its default 5×4 size, with all subdocument paragraphs printing on its first page (Figure 12-17).

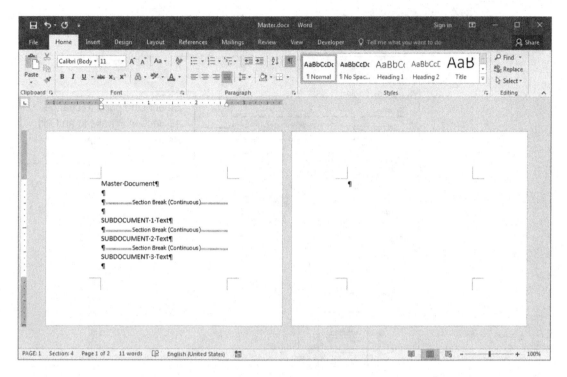

Figure 12-17. *After all of the subdocument's Section Breaks were removed, the Master.docx Master document recovers its default 5×4 page size for all its pages!*

Attention   I do not have a decent explanation for why the Master.docx Next Page Section breaks were changed to Continuous Section Breaks as the subdocument section breaks were removed. It is a very unexpected Microsoft Word behavior…

Making All Subdocuments Begin on an Odd Page

To make all subdocuments begin on an odd page, with all the formatting options imposed by the Master.docx document (including header/footer area, if any), just change each Section Break type in the Page Setup dialog box.

Follow these steps:

1. Press Ctrl+A to select the entire Master.docx document (including all subdocuments text).

2. Double-click the ruler to show the Page Layout dialog box.

3. In the Layout tab, select Section start = Odd Page (Figure 12-18).

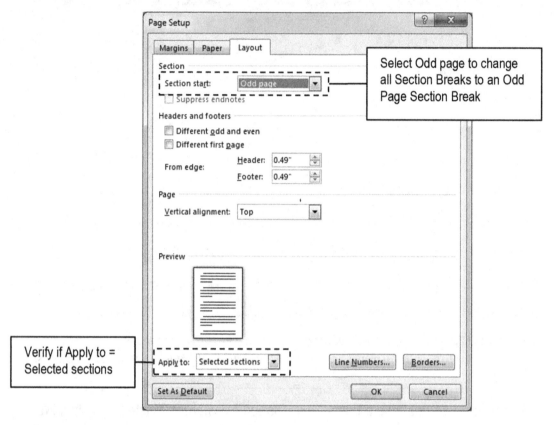

Figure 12-18. *Press Ctrl+A to select the entire document, use the Selection start option to define the type of Section Break, and verify that Apply to = Selected sections*

4. Verify if Applies to = Selected Sections and press OK to close the Page Setup dialog box.

Now, Master.docx Master document has four physical pages (seven logical pages, because some even pages are missing due to each Odd Page Section Break): one for its cover, and one to begin each subdocument inserted in it (Figure 12-19).

Attention   The MasterSubdocuments (done).zip file, which you can also extract from the Chapter12.zip file, has these exercise documents as shown in Figure 12-18.

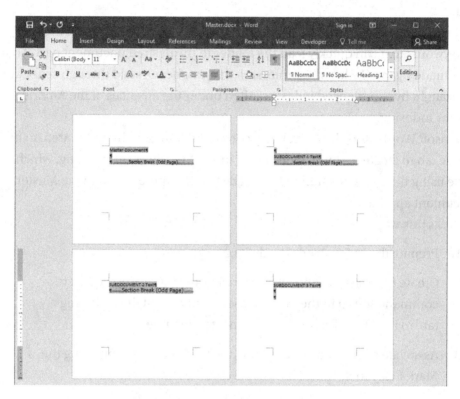

Figure 12-19.   *The Master.docx file with just Odd Page Section breaks at the right position*

Attention   The reader is invited to try the other Master Documents tools, like Split (to break a subdocument in two), Merge (to merge two subdocuments into one), and Unlink (to break the Master/Subdocument relationship and insert the subdocument text in the Master document).

Creating an Index

Index is the name given to the list of words, terms, and topics that is often found in the last pages of technical documents, along with the page numbers where they appear in the text.

To be correctly built, its terms must capture the essence of the issues they represent using keywords that can quickly lead the reader to the desired document part. That is why it is made by the "Indexer," a profession that can be pursued through self-study courses taught by experienced indexers, often under the auspices of the American Society for Indexing.

Microsoft Word offers the Mark Entry command found in the Index area of the Reference tab to create a simple index using up to three levels of indexing, which must be made using the entire document text—a task that is quite suited to the Master/Subdocument approach.

It works this way:

1. Prepare the Index words in advance.

2. Create the Master/Subdocument relationships, using the Insert command found in the Master Document area of the Outlining tab, to insert all chapter files in a master document.

3. Associate all desired words to the appropriate Index tem using the Mark Entry tool.

4. Generate the Index at the desired place in the document (usually in a new subdocument inserted at its end, or at the end of its very last chapter).

How to Tag an Index

The first step needed to create an Index is to prepare in advance the words that must be tagged in the text, either alone or under a given keyword that represents a set of similar words.

Attention   Although Microsoft Word can easily tag the words for you to create an index of sorts, it's practically guaranteed to be substandard.

Knowing in advance that this is a profession, you may take a look of some book Indexes to realize how they were prepared, and then try to create your own, which is not an obvious or easy task.

The Apress technical team of editors asks for every one of its authors to create such a list of terms or words, offering a very well-prepared Index Keyword document which has a section called "How to Capture the Information." Among other things, this document states that

- Related concepts that should be grouped together, like:

```
Formatting
        Font
        Paragraph
        Styles
```

- Use no more than two levels of subentries

```
Formatting
        Font
                Font Dialog box
                principles of use
                Home tab
```

- Information should be indexed under a main noun (or compound noun) and not under adjectives. For example, instead of using these three Index terms:

```
Formatting characters
Formatting paragraphs
Formatting styles
```

use instead:

```
Formatting
        characters
        paragraphs
        styles
```

They also offer some general rules to tag entries and subentries:

- Main entries begin with capital letter (do not use numbers or symbols).

- A subentry must be indented and begin with lowercase, unless it is a proper noun.

- If a keyword has an abbreviation and a long form, use the more prevalent one.

Quite simple rules, very well prepared for a good orientation from where to start.

So, before making your index, you should also know in advance that by using Microsoft Word and the Master/Subdocuments approach, you can browse all the independent chapters of a book, one page at a time, to find and tag the words that may compose the book Index.

And once you find them, you can tag the Index entries in two ways:

- **Manually**: using the Mark Index Entry dialog box.

- **Automatically**: creating a concordance table file.

The Mark Index Entry Dialog Box

Whenever you click the Mark Entry command found in the Index area of the Reference tab of the Ribbon, Microsoft Word shows the Mark Index Entry dialog box, from where you can define how each Index entry must be tagged (Figure 12-20).

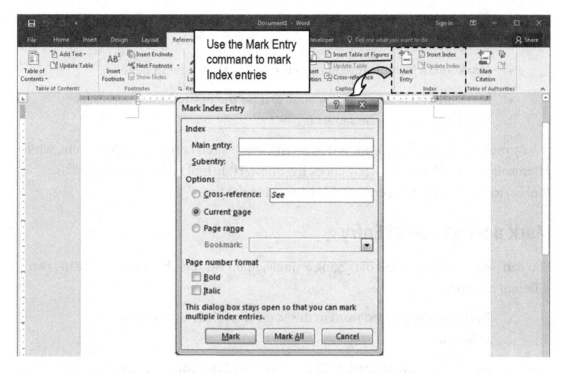

Figure 12-20. *Use the Mark Entry command found in the Index area of the References tab to show the Mark Index Entry dialog box, from where you can tag all desired document words as they may appear in the document Index*

The Mark Index Entry dialog box has these options:

- **Main entry**: to type a single Index entry or a noun that will aggregate other related terms.

- **Subentry**: to insert the second-level word that will be tagged in the text, under the noun that is typed in the Main entry.

Attention   To insert a third-level subentry, type in the Subentry text box the subentry text followed by a colon (:) and the third-level subentry text.

- **Cross reference**: to insert an Index entry like "see <word>".

- **Current page**: to tag the desired entry with its own page number.

- **Page range**: to tag the desired entry associated to a page range.

- **Bold, Italic**: allow tag the Main entry or its subentry using bold, italic, or both.

- **Mark**: mark just this reference in the selected document page.

- **Mark all**: run through all the book text for the desired word and mark all references with the same tag.

By pressing Mark or Mark all, you will mark the desired entry in the document, while Microsoft Word will automatically check the Show/Hide tool in the Home tab of the Ribbon to show the hidden entry fields inserted in the text.

Mark a Single-Level Entry

You can perform this process of tagging a single, main word in the document using two different methods:

1. By typing the desired word in the Main entry, leaving the Subentry field blank.

2. By selecting the desired word in the text and clicking the Main entry text box to automatically copy the selected word while also clearing the Subentry text box.

Both methods will insert a hidden Microsoft Word field in the document that uses this syntax (where <Main word> is the word you typed)

{ XE "<Main word>" }

Mark a Two-Level Entry

To tag a two-level Index entry, using a noun in the Main entry and a term as subentry, you need to follow a different approach:

1. Select the desired word to be tagged in the text.

2. Click the Main entry text box to automatically copy the selected word while also clearing the Subentry text box.

3. Cut the word from the Main entry text box and paste it into the Subentry text box.

4. Type the desired Noun in the Main entry text box.

5. Press Mark (to mark a single entry) or Mark all (to mark all document entries).

Whenever you do this type of tagging, Microsoft Word will insert a hidden field in the document that uses this syntax (where <Main word> is the word you typed in Main word, and <subentry> is the word selected in the text, separated by a colon).

{ XE "<Main word>:<subentry>" }

Mark a Three-Level Entry

To tag a third-level Index entry, follow the steps used in previous section to tag a two-level entry.

Then press a colon at the end of the Subentry word and type the third-level entry. Microsoft Word will insert a hidden field in the document that uses this syntax (where <Main word> is the word you typed in Main word, <subentry> is the second-level entry, and <sub-subentry> is the word typed for the third-level text), each one separated by a colon:

{ XE "<Main word>:<subentry>:<sub-subentry>" }

Tag Index Words

Before you begin to tag words in the document, it is desirable for you to aware that

- By pressing Mark all, Microsoft Word will tag all equal words found in the document (meaning that some entries may appear with too many page references on the Index).

- You can always press Ctrl+Z to undo the last Mark entry made.

- You can always check the Show/Hide tool in the Home tab of the Ribbon to show the Index fields inserted in the text, removing or changing its content (which appears between double quotes inside the { XE ... } hidden field).

Insert the Index

Once the Index fields have been inserted in the document, use the Insert Index command found in the Index area of the References tab to show the Index dialog box (Figure 12-21).

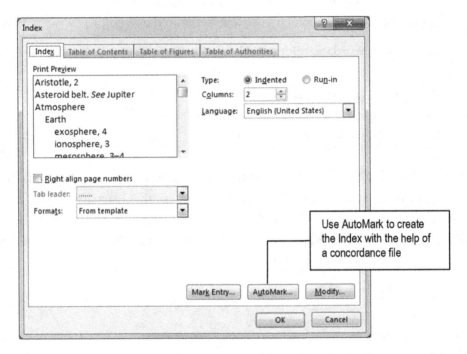

Figure 12-21. *Use the Insert Index command found in the Index area of the References tab to show the Index dialog box. Click OK to create the Index in the selected point of the document*

Whenever you click OK in the Index dialog box (or click AutoMark button and select a concordance file), Microsoft Word will

- Alphabetically sort the Index entries.

- Reference them by their page numbers.

- Find and remove duplicate entries found in the same page (considering the current page size).

- Display the index in the document.

The Index dialog box has these options:

- **Type**: specify type of the two-level entry to be created:

  - **Indented**: insert each Main entry sublevel in its own row.

  - **Run-in**: insert all Main entry sublevels in the same row, separated by a comma.

- **Columns**: define the number of columns for the Index that will be created (default is two columns);

- **Language**: define the language to be applied to the Index entries, so the Spelling Checker can verify them (all current installed dictionaries will appear on the list).

- **Right align page numbers**: adds a Tab character after each Index entry, aligning the page number to the right column border.

- **Format**: choose the desired format for the Index that will be created.

- **Mark Entry**: show the Mark Index Entry dialog box.

- **AutoMark**: select a concordance file, from where Microsoft Word will find the words and Index entries you want to use.

- **Modify**: show the Style dialog box, from where you can modify Index1 to Index9 styles used to format the Index.

Using a Concordance File

A concordance file is a Microsoft Word file that has just a two-column concordance table:

- the first column indicates the word to be searched in the text that must be tagged as an Index entry (case sensitive).

- the second column specifies the Index entry text.

Attention   To specify a second-level Index entry, separate the Main entry and the Subentry by a colon; to specify a third-level Index entry, type another colon after the Subentry and type Sub-Subentry.

Concordance tables are great to tag the same word as different Index entries. For example, the "Font dialog box" term can be tagged as a Main entry or as a Subentry of the "Dialog Box" entries.

Figure 12-22 shows a simple concordance table that shows in its first column examples for double-tagging the "Font dialog box" text either as a Main entry (Font) or as a Subentry (Dialog box:Font), and the "Paragraph dialog box" text either as a Main entry (Paragraph) or as a subentry (Dialog box:Paragraph). The last row shows an example of how tag the "Page break before" text as a third-level entry (Formatting:Paragraph:Text flow).

Font·dialog·box¤	Font¤	¤
Font·dialog·box¤	Dialog·box:Font¤	¤
Paragraph·dialog·box¤	Paragraph¤	¤
Paragraph·dialog·box¤	Dialog·box:Paragraph¤	¤
Page·break·before¤	Formatting:Paragraph:Text·flow¤	¤

Figure 12-22. *Example of concordance table to automatically tagged Index entries. The first column has the word that must be searched in the text (case sensitive). The second column has the Index entry text. Use a colon to separate a Main entry from a subentry (or a subentry from a sub-subentry)*

Once you have built and saved the concordance table in a given file and folder, use the Insert Index command to show the Index dialog box, click the AutoMark button, and select the file with the concordance table.

Microsoft Word will tag the text very quickly for you!

Removing Index Field Codes

Once a document is tagged with Index field codes, Microsoft Word offers no simple way to remove them and start again, unless you do a Find and Replace operation using the Special ➤ Field option (which adds the ^d find code to the Find what text box).

Since the Index field codes always begin with { XE, follow these steps to find any Index field code and remove it from the document:

1. Press Ctrl+H to show the Find and Replace dialog box with the Replace tab selected.

2. In Find What text box:

    - Click Special ➤ Field option:

      Find what: ^d

    - Type a space character and XE:

      Find what: ^d XE

3. Press Find next to find and select the first Index field code.

4. Keep the Replace with option empty, and use either Replace or Replace all to remove the Index entries.

Attention   Since the Index entry is inserted between double quotes, to find an specific Index entry, use ^d XE "<WordInitials>", where <WordInitials> are the letters that begin the Index entry. For example, to find all Index fields that tag the word "Home", search for ^d XE "Home".

Exercise 3

The objective of this exercise is to show how you can use the Mark Index Entry to tag words in a text and generate the Index of words at the end of a document.

To perform this exercise, extract the "European Convention of Human Rights Headings.docx" document from Chapter12.zip file and open it in Microsoft Word.

Attention   Note that this is not a long or technical document that deserves an Index at its end. It is used just as a source for this exercise.

Marking Single-Level Index Entries

Go to the document's Table of Contents and note that it has basic words formatted with Heading2 styles and used as chapter titles that deserve to be tagged as Index entries. Following the directions to create an Index, I will propose tagging these words as main index entries (the ones that are chapter titles):

- Dignity
- Freedoms
- Equality
- Solidarity
- Citizens rights
- Justice

Follow these steps to mark each of these words in the text as Index entries:

1. Press Ctrl+Home to go to text beginning.

2. Press Ctrl+F to show the Navigation pane, and click Headings to show the Heading styles.

3. Click Mark Entry command of the Index area of the References tab of the Ribbon to show the Mark Index Entry dialog box.

4. Click "DIGNITY" Heading2 style in the Navigation Pane to select this paragraph in the text.

5. Double-click the word "DIGNITY" to select it in the text and click the Main entry text box of the Mark Entry dialog box to automatically copy the selected word.

Attention   The Mark all button of the Mark Index Entry text box is just enabled when you first select the desired word in the text before clicking the Mark entry text box.

---

6. Click Mark all command to mark all occurrences of the word "DIGNITY" in the text (Figure 12-23).

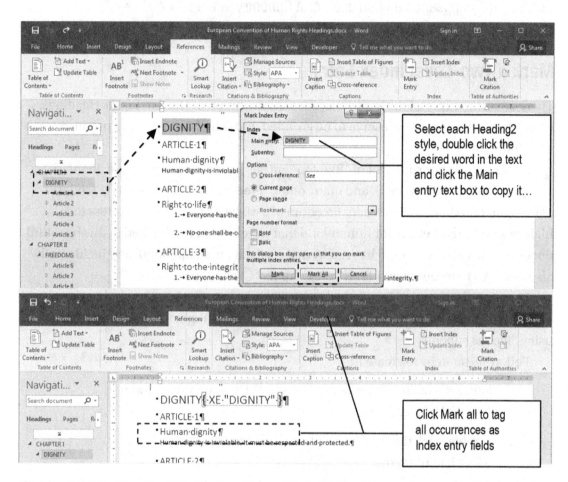

Figure 12-23. *Use the Navigation Pane (Ctrl+F) Headings view to easily select the text that must be tagged as an Index entry. Select the desired text, click the Mark entry text box to copy it, and use the Mark all command button to mark all its ocurrences in the text*

The "DIGNITY" keyword will be marked with the { XE "DIGNITY" } hidden field right next to each occurrence in the text.

Repeat steps 4 to 6 to also select and mark all other chapter title words found in the text (FREEDOMS, EQUALITY, SOLIDARITY, CITIZENS RIGHTS, and JUSTICE).

Attention   The same text in the document can receive more than one Index field code. It may appear as a Main entry or a Subentry in the Index.

Mark a Two-Level Index Entry

There are some expressions in the "European Convention of Human Rights Headings. docx" document that may deserve to be grouped under the same noun to produce a two-level index entry.

For example, there are a lot of "Right to" entries in the text (Right to life, Right to integrity, Right to liberty, etc.), and many other "Freedom of" expressions (Freedom of thought, Freedom of expression, Freedom of association, etc.), that express the highest standards of ethics for humankind that were so well established in this beautiful document, which deserves to be read by and realized for all mankind, and incidentally also deserves to receive a two-level index entry.

For example, note that inside the "DIGNITY" chapter, "Article 2" entry has the expression "Right to life", which should be put inside the "Right to" main Index entry using "life" as subentry.

Follow these steps to create it:

1. In the Navigation Pane, select "Article 2" Heading3 style under "DIGNITY" Heading2 style.

2. Double-click the "life" word of the "Right to life" expression to select it in the text.

3. Click the Main entry text box of the Mark Index Entry dialog box to automatically copy it and clear the Subentry text box (Figure 12-24).

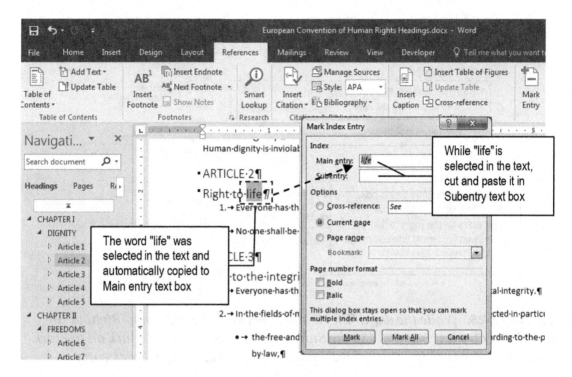

Figure 12-24. *Double-click the entries that you want to group in a two-level Index entry and click the Main entry text box of the Mark Index Entry dialog box, to automatically copy it and clear the Subentry text box*

4. Select the "life" word in Main entry text box, and press Ctrl+X to cut it to Clipboard.

5. Click Subentry text box and press Ctrl+C to paste it.

6. In Main entry text box, type the "Right to" expression.

7. Press Mark all to mark all its occurrences in the document as a second-level Index entry (Figure 12-25).

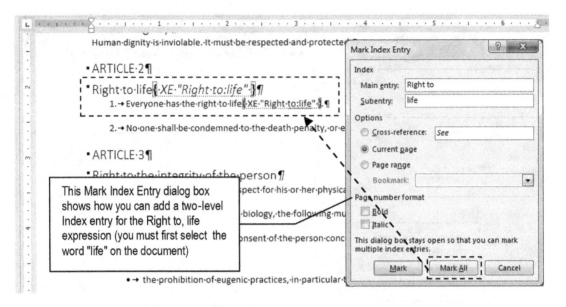

Figure 12-25. *While the word "life" is still selected in the text, type "Right to" in the Main entry text box, "life" in the Subentry text box, and click Mark all to mark every ocurrence of "life" as a sublevel under the "Right to" main index entry*

The "life" keyword will be marked as a second-level index entry of the first-level "Right to" index entry with the { XE "Right to:life" } hidden field right next to each word occurrence in the text.

Repeat the last steps to also mark "Right to integrity", "Right to life", "Right to marriage", and all other "Rights" that each human being deserves in his or her time on Earth and are so well established in the document.

Attention   To mark an entry like "Right to respect", you must select the entire expression "Right to respect" in the document and click the Main entry text box to copy it. Then cut just the Respect option of the Main entry and paste it in the Subentry text box, producing markup as in the following:

```
Main entry = Right to
Subentry = respect
```

By pressing Mark all, all "Right to respect" entries will be tagged in the text (the "respect" word alone will not)!

Use the Find what text box of the Navigation page and the Previous and Next buttons below it to quickly find what you want to tag in the text. For example, type "right to" to select all such expressions in the document.

Inserting the Index

When all Index entries are tagged in the text, it is time to generate the Index by following these steps:

1. Press Ctrl+End to go to the end of the file.

2. Press Ctrl+Break (or use the Layout ➤ Breaks command to insert the desired page break), so the Index begins on a new page.

3. Type "Index" and apply Heading1 style.

4. Press Enter to insert a paragraph after the "Index" heading.

5. Use the Insert Index command found in the Index area of the References tab of the Ribbon to show the Index dialog box (Figure 12-26).

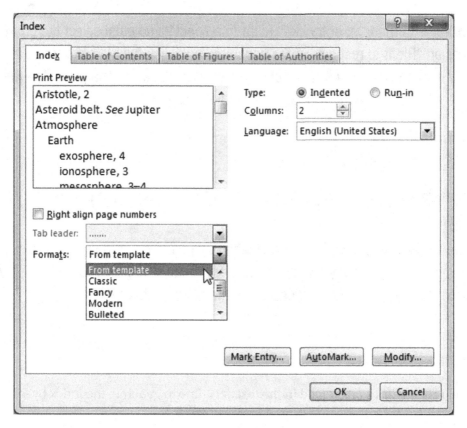

Figure 12-26. *Use the Insert Index command found in the Index area of the References tab to show the Index dialog box, from where you can select the format of Index to be inserted in the document*

6.   Press OK to insert the Index at current text position.

Figure 12-27 shows the Index created by the default options shown in Figure 12-24 for the "European Convention of Human Rights Headings.docx" document, after it had been tagged by the proposed Main and Subentries. Note that some entries appear on many different page numbers (like "life", "security", etc.).

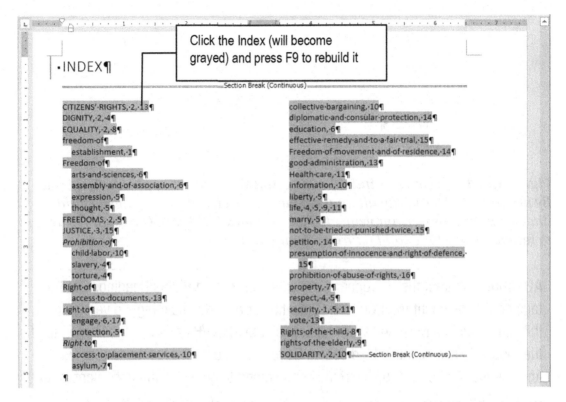

Figure 12-27. *This is the From Template Index format created at the end of the "European Convention of Human Rights Headings.docx" document, after it had been tagged by the proposed Main and Subentries*

As with the Table of Contents object, you can click any of its Index entries to select it (all entries will become grayed) and press F9 function key to update it.

Attention   Note that Microsoft Word enclosed the Index between two Section Breaks so it can be printed in a two-column format (the Continuous Section Break below the Index holds this column information).

To see that the Index inserted is indeed a Microsoft Word object created by a Field, press Alt+F9 to activate the Field code view (Figure 12-28). Press Alt+F9 again to return to Field value view and regenerate the Index.

Figure 12-28. *The Index is indeed a Microsoft Word object created by Field code. By pressing Alt+F9 you can alternate to Field code view and see how the Field dialog box options were implemented for the Index Field code (press Alt+F9 again to regenerate the Index and return to Print Layout view)*

Attention   Extract the "European Convention of Human Rights Headings - Index tags.docx" document from Chapter12.zip file for an Index field tagged version of this file. Open it in Microsoft Word and check the Show/Hide tool in the Home tab of the Ribbon to see its Index field codes. Go to the document's last page (Ctrl+End) and use the Reference tab, Insert Index command to generate the document Index.

Uncheck the Show/Hide tool in the Home tab of the Ribbon to hide the Index hidden fields inserted in the text.

Fix Index Field Entries

After an Index is inserted, you must analyze it to see if the Index fields inserted in the text lead to the desired final result. There's a good chance that you will find some defects and need to fix some Index field codes inserted in the text to produce a well-formatted Index.

The following are some of the common defects found in an Index:

- Duplicate Main entries: Index entries are case sensitive ("Right of" and "right of" typed in the main entry will create different Index nouns).

- Too long Index entries that must be separated.

- Too many successive pages for the same Index entry.

- Bad word chosen for a Main entry that must be changed.

And many other types of Index defects that may need to operated over the Microsoft Word fields used to generate the Index.

Look again to Figure 12-27 and note that some of these errors are present in the Index created. For example, it has three similar Main entries that can be changed to just one ("Right of", "right to", and "Right to" can be changed to just "Right to") and also has some overly long entries that could be broken in two (in the "Right to" Main entry you find "effective remedy and to a fair trial", " Freedom of movement and of residence", " presumption of innocence and right of defence").

To fix these Index defects you must

- Keep an eye on the Index (you may print it or split Microsoft Word window).

- Check the Show/Hide tool in the Home tab of the Ribbon so you can see the Index fields.

- Use the Navigation Panel Find to search for the field that represents the Index entry.

- Edit the Index entry in the text.

Let's see how you can do these changes in the Index using just Microsoft Word tools.

Split Microsoft Word to Fix Index Field Code Entries

Since the Index entries have no hyperlinks to the text position that they represent (they do not act like the Table of Contents entries for which you can use Ctrl+Click to jump to where they are in the document), to change Index field entries you must know the page number where the Index field code was inserted.

And the best way to do this is to use the Split command found in the Window area of the View tab to split the Microsoft Word document window into two areas: the upper area will be used to fix the text, while the bottom area will be used to show the Index.

Figure 12-29 shows the Microsoft Window for the "European Convention of Human Rights Headings - Index tags.docx" document in a split Microsoft Word window after receiving the Index on its last page: the upper part is at the text beginning (page 1) while the bottom part is at the document Index (page 18).

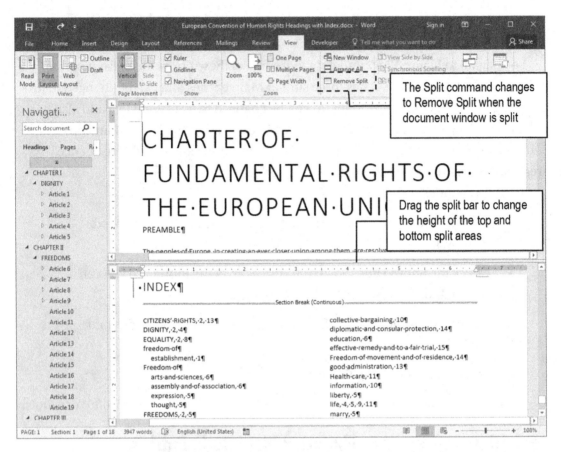

The Split command changes to Remove Split when the document window is split

Drag the split bar to change the height of the top and bottom split areas

Figure 12-29. *Use the Split command found in the Window area of the View tab to split the Microsoft Word document window in two areas that can show different document parts*

Attention   The Split command changes its name to Remove Split when the Microsoft Word document window is split. To return the document window to its original single area, double-click the split bar, drag the split bar to the top or bottom areas of the document window, or click the Remove Split command.

After the Microsoft Word window is split into two areas, to find and correct an Index field entry, follow these steps:

1. Scroll to the bottom document area that shows the Index to find the page number for the Index field that you want to fix.

2. Click the upper document area to select it.

3. Press F5 to show the Go to dialog box.

4. Type the page number and press Enter to move to that page.

5. Locate the Index field on the page and change the text inside the double quotes of the { EX "..." } Index Field code.

Changing an Index Field Code Entry

Looking one more time to Figure 12-27 you will note that the "Right of" and "right to" Main entries have just one Index entry each; they can be changed to a "Right to" entry so the Index has just the "Right to" Main entry.

Supposing that the document window is split in two areas, with the bottom area showing the Index, and that the Show/Hide command is checked in the Home tab of the Ribbon, follow these steps to make this change:

1. Use the scroll bar of the bottom document area to locate the "Right of" index entry page number (page 13, see Figure 12-27).

2. Click the upper document area to select it.

3. Press Ctrl+F to show the Navigation Pane.

4. In the Search text box of the Navigation Pane type "right of:" (the colon is important, because it is used in the Index Field code to separate the Main entry from the Subentry, Figure 12-30).

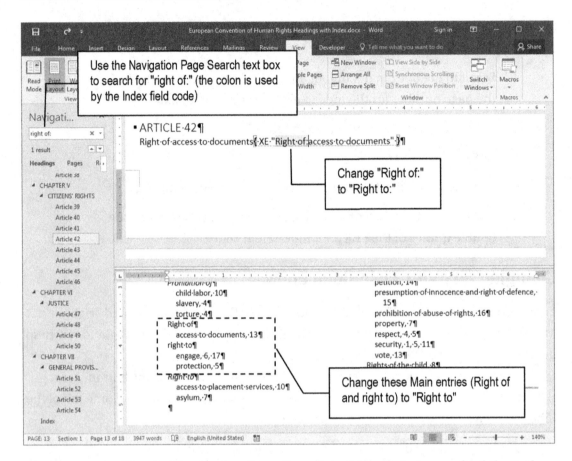

Figure 12-30. *Use the Navigation Pane Search text box to help you find the Index field codes that must be changed. Remember to type a colon for the search string, because Main entries always use it to separate it from the Subentry in the Index field code*

5. Change the { XE "Right of:access to documents" } field code to {
    XE "Right to:access to documents" }

Attention   Whenever a Microsoft Word document window is split, you can apply different Zoom factors to each document part.

To change the three occurrences of "right to" in the Index to "Right to" (uppercase), follow these steps:

1. Click the upper area of the split document window to select it.

2. In the Navigation Pane, click the Search type box arrow to expand it and select Options to show the Find Options dialog box.

3. Check Match case option and close the Find Options dialog box.

4. In the Navigation Pane Search text box type "right to:".

5. Microsoft Word will find four occurrences. Use the Previous and Next buttons to select each one and change each Index field code to "Right to:" (Figure 12-31).

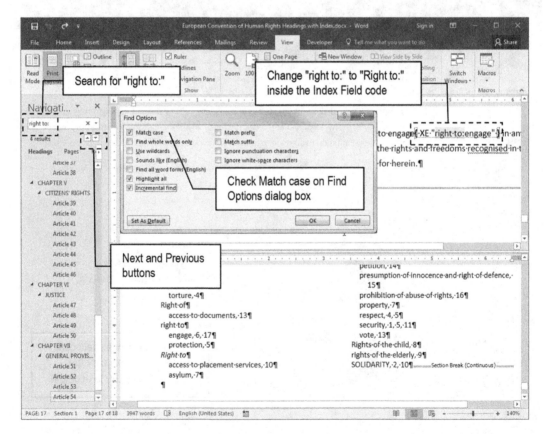

Figure 12-31. *Expand the Navigation Pane Search text box, select Options to show the Find Options dialog box, and check Match case option. Close the Find Options dialog box and search for "right to:" (note the colon) to find four ocurrences (use the Next and Previous buttons to change each Index field code to "Right to:")*

Update the Index

After the changes have been made in the Index field codes, is time to update the Index to verify if the changes made in the Index field codes inserted in the text generated the desired results.

Follow these steps:

1. Click the Index located in the bottom area of the split document window (it will become grayed).

2. Press F9 to update it.

Now, the document Index will have just one "Right to" main entry index (Figure 12-32).

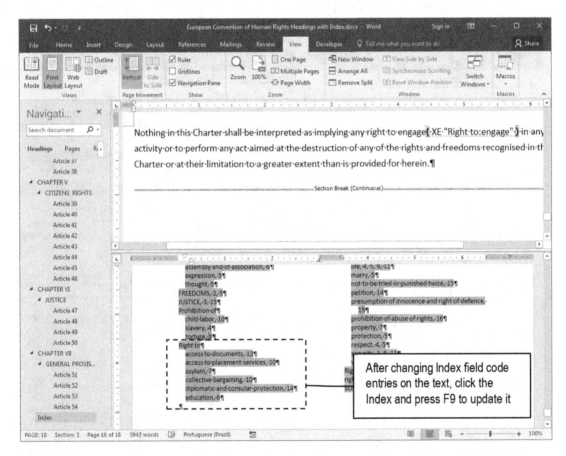

Figure 12-32. *To update the Index after making changes to the Index field code inserted in the text, click the Index and press F9 function key. This figure shows that the "Right of" and "right to" main entries were removed from the Index*

Dividing an Index Field Code Entry

To divide a long Index field code entry (one that deserves to appear as two different Index entries), you must

1. Select the desired Index entry in the text.

2. Press Ctrl+C to copy it to Clipboard.

3. Press Ctrl+V to paste a copy of it right next to the same Index field code.

4. Change both Index field codes to reflect the new desired entries.

Let's see how we can change the Index "Right to" subentry "presumption of innocence and right of defence" to these two subentries: "presumption of innocence" and "right of defence". Follow these steps:

1. Click the upper area of the document window.

2. Click the Navigation pane Search text box and type ":presumption" (note the colon that begins the search string, which will appear just in the Index entry).

3. Select the entire Index field code in the text and press Ctrl+C to copy it to clipboard.

4. Press Right arrow to go the end of the Index field code and press Ctrl+V to paste a second copy of it.

5. In the first copy, change the Index field code text to this:

   { XE "Right to:presumption of innocence" }

6. In the first copy, change the Index field code text to this (Figure 12-33):

   { XE "Right to:right of defence" }

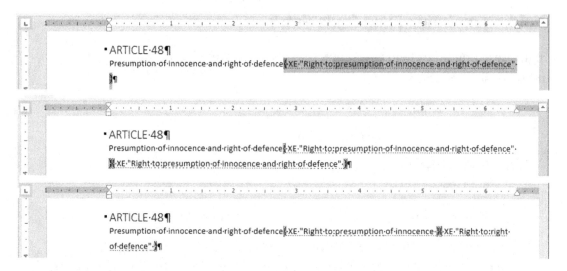

Figure 12-33. *To divide an Index entry, duplicate it in the document and change both entries to the desired text. This figure shows how the "Right to" subentry, "presumption of innocence and right of defence" was changed to two new subentries Index field codes: "presumption of innocence" and "right of defence"*

7. Click the Index to select it (it will become grayed) and press F9 to update it.

Figure 12-34 shows the Index after such a change has been made in the Index field code in the text.

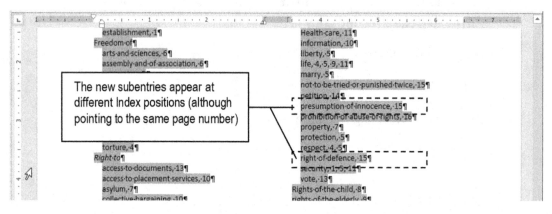

Figure 12-34. *The Index updated after breaking one subentry into two*

Attention   The "European Convention of Human Rights Headings with Index fixed. docx" document that you can extract from Chapter12.zip file, has the final version of the Index, as proposed by previous sections.

Exercise 4 (the Last)

The objective of this exercise—the last in this book—is to show how to use the Outlining tools to assemble a long document using Master/Subdocuments relationships and many other formatting tips previously discussed in earlier chapters of this book.

It will produce the "Book of Tales" using tales and fables from Aesop, Andersen, and the Brothers Grimm, spread in three different Microsoft Word documents formatted with the same Fables.dotx Template, based on a 6×9 page size.

You must extract the Tales.zip file from the Chapter12.zip file, and then extract all its documents to a single folder of your choice. Table 12-1 details the Microsoft Word document you must extract from Tales.zip and its contents.

Table 12-1. *Microsoft Word Document Inside Tales.zip, Its Contents, and the Number of 6×9 Pages Each File Contains*

File name	Contents	Pages
Fables.dotx	Template used by all documents	5
The Book of Tales Master.docx	Master document	3
Aesops Fables.docx	Aesop's fables subdocument	84
Andersen Fables.docx	Andersen's fables subdocument	178
Grimms Fairy Tales.docx	Grimm's fairy tales subdocument	316

Attention   As explained in the section "Associating a Document with a Template" of Chapter 11, if a Microsoft Word document is associated to the Fables.dotx template, and this template is found in the same document folder file, the Templates and Add-ins dialog box (found in Developer tab, Document Templates command) will always show it associated to this local template. In other words, if you want to change the appearance of all documents extracted from Tales.zip file, you just need to change the Fables.dotx template styles.

Inspect "Fables.dotx" Template

Begin by opening the Fables.dotx template in Microsoft Word, so you can understand how it was formatted.

Figure 12-35 shows its first three pages.

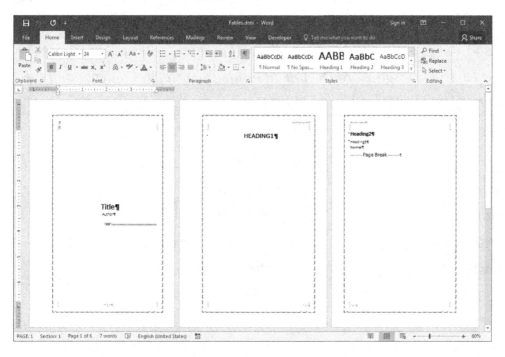

Figure 12-35. *The Fables.dotx template, which you can extract from the Fables. zip file, has six pages to allow you note how it uses Vertical aligment = Center in Section 1 to automatically align the cover page, along with the way it formats the Title, Subtitle, Heading1, Heading2, and Normal styles and the First, Even and Odd page headers*

Considering that you have selected the first document page, double-click the ruler to show the Page Setup dialog box and note that it has these formatting options:

- **Page size tab**: Height = 9"; Width = 6"; Multiple pages = Mirror margins.

- **Layout tab**: Vertical alignment = Center (for first page only),

The Mirror margins options allow you to alternate the inside margin from left (to an odd page) to right (to an even page), giving space to bind the document correctly. The Vertical alignment option = Center applied to Section 1 allows the first document page (which will hold the book title, author name, and date of publication) to automatically center align on the page.

The Fables.dotx uses a modified version of the Black & White (Classic) style set, showing formatting options examples for the Title, Subtitle, Heading1, Heading2 (which has the Page Break Before option set), and Normal styles, alternating the alignment of the author name (Header) and page number (Footer) on the odd and even pages.

Also note that each document page has a border surrounding it, created by the Borders and Shading dialog box (Figure 12-36), which you can show using the Borders command found in the Page Background area of the Design tab.

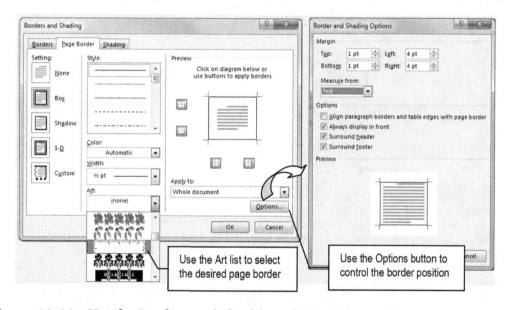

Figure 12-36. *Use the Borders and Shadding dialog box to select an Art that can be applied to all pages of the document, the Options command show the Borders and Shadding Options dialog box from where you can define the border margins, its position (from page borders or pabe margins - Text), and other options*

> **Attention**   Although not deeply approached in this book, the Borders and Shading dialog box allows you to define the background paper color and a border to be applied not just to text paragraphs, but also to the document page. The reader is invited to explore its usage to further improve the appearance of the documents. Just remember the basic rule: less formatting is more efficient!

Inspect "The Book of Tales Master.docx"

Open "The Book of Tales Master.docx" document in Microsoft Word and use the Document Templates command of the Developer tab to realize that it is attached to the Fables.dotx document (which must reside in the same document folder).

Note that it has a different border on the first document page, which already has a book title, author names, and dates of publications, all paragraph center aligned on the page by using the Vertical align = Center on Section 1 page properties (this effect is achieved by using the Borders and Shading dialog box to select the desired border and using the Applies to = This Section option, Figure 12-37).

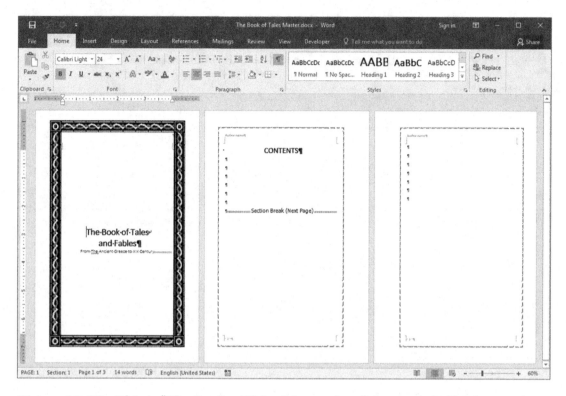

Figure 12-37. *This is "The Book of Tales Master.docx" document, which you can extract from Tales.zip file. It is based on the Fables.dotx template but had its Section 1 page border changed to create a better effect for the book cover page. It also has a second page where the Table of Contents must be inserted*

Note that this document also has a "Content" title on page 2, which will receive the document's Table of Contents.

Inspect "Aesops Fables.docx"

Open "The Aesops Fables.docx" document in Microsoft Word and use the Document Templates command of the Developer tab to confirm that it is attached to the Fables. dotx document (which must reside in the same document folder).

The "Aesops fables.docx" document is based on the Fables.dotx document and also uses all template formatting page properties (a 6×9 page size with same page borders, using Mirror margins and a Section 1 with Vertical align = Center). The book title ("Aesop's Fables") is shown on the page Header (left aligned on even pages and right aligned on odd pages, as page numbers do on the footer, Figure 12-38).

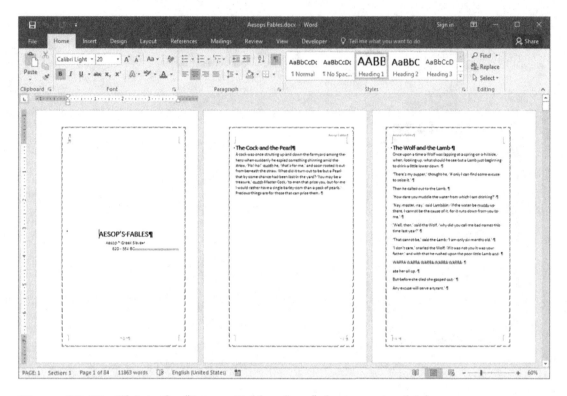

Figure 12-38.   *This is the "Aesops Fables.docx" document, which you can extract from Fables.zip*

Attention   Explore the "Andersen Fables.docx" and "Grimms Fairy tales.docx" documents to realize that they all obey to the same formatting options.

Create the Master/Subdocument Relationships

We will use "The Book of Tales Master.docx" document as the Master document in which we will insert "Aesops Fables.docx", "Andersen Fables.docx", and "Grimms Fairy tales. docx" as subdocuments to compose the final book.

Supposing that you have "The Book of Tales Master.docx" document opened in Microsoft Word, follow these steps to make it the Master document and insert the desired subdocuments:

1. Check the Show/Hide command in the Home tab of the Ribbon, so you can see all Section Breaks.

2. Check the Outline option in the Views area of the View tab to enter Outline view and show the Outlining tab.

3. Click Show Document to expand the Master Document area of the Outlining tab and show its tools.

4. In the Outlining tab, click the paragraph below the Section Break (Odd Page) (inside the Contents heading, Figure 12-39).

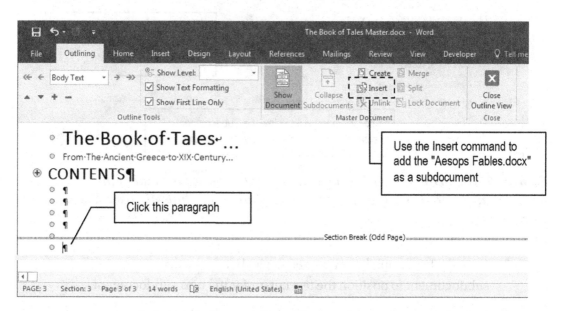

Figure 12-39. *Show the Outline view for "The Book of Tales Master.docx" document, click the paragraph below the Section Break (Odd Page), and use the Insert command to select the "Aesops Fables.docx" document as a subdocument*

5.   Use the Insert command found in the Master Document area of the Outlining tool to select the "Aesops Fables.docx" document and insert it as a subdocument.

6.   Delete the Section Break (Next Page) that Microsoft Word inserted at the end of the subdocument file (Figure 12-40).

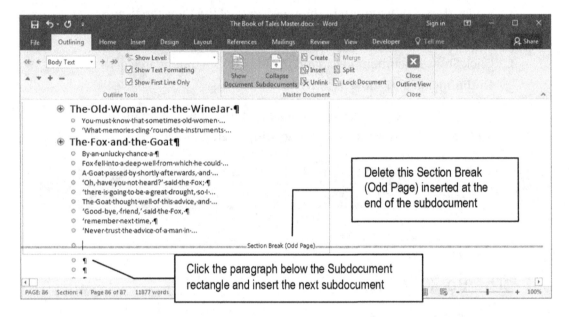

Figure 12-40. *Scroll the outline view down until you see the end of the subdocument and delete the Section Break (Odd Page) that Microsoft Word inserted in it*

7.   Click the paragraph below the rectangle that shows the subdocument to position the text cursor for the next subdocument.

8.   Repeat steps 5 to 7 to also add "Andersen Fables.docx" and "Grimms Fairy Tales.docx" as subdocuments.

Attention   If Word's find any disagreement among the Master and Subdocument styles, it will show you a dialog box for each style disagreement, asking if you want to rename the subdocument style. Whenever this happens, select the No to All option, so all subdocument styles are updated by the Master subdocument style formatting options (Figure 12-41).

Figure 12-41. Whenever Word's find disagreements between the Master and Subdocument style formatting, it will show this dialog box asking what to do. Select the No to All option to apply the Master style formatting options to the subdocument

Play with the Outline Tools

After inserting all three subdocuments ("Aesop fables.docx", "Andersen Fables.docx", and "Grimms Fairy Tales.docx") in "The Book of Tables Master.docx" Master document, try to use Outline Tools commands to limit which paragraphs appear—and how they appear—in the Outline view.

Try these exercises:

- Use Show Level tool found in the Outline Tools area of the Outlining tab to limit the Outline level of the paragraphs shown by the Outline view.

Attention   Since Title style in the Tales.dotx template was changed to Outline Level = 1, whenever you select Show Level = 1, just the Title and Heading1 styles will show up in the book outline (Figure 12-42).

- Set Show Levels = 2 to show Title, Heading1, and Heading2 styles (this last one associated to the tales title).

- Set Show levels = 3 to show up to Heading3 styles.

- Set Show levels = all; keeping the Show First Line Only option checked will show the first line of each Normal style paragraph.

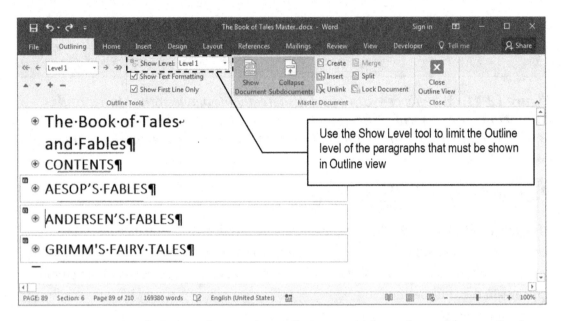

Figure 12-42. Set Show Level = Level 1 to show just Title and Heading1 styles in Outline view (both have the Paragraph, Outline level = 1)

- Select Show Levels = 2 and drag Heading2 styles (tales titles) to a new place inside a subdocument (or even between subdocuments) you can move entire tales to a new position inside the book.

- Uncheck Show Formatting option to show the outline text of each paragraph.

- Collapse an entire branch of styles (like the title of each subdocument, formatted with Title style), and use the Demote tool to change all Heading styles affected to the next Outline level.

Attention   You can move Heading2 styles wherever you want, but avoid saving the Master document, because it will also change each subdocument, meaning that you can inadvertently exchange authors' tales.

Close Outline View to See the Final Document

Click Close Outline View to return to Print Layout and press Ctrl+End to go to its last page and force Microsoft Word to recount its pages (the "Book of Tales" should now have 587 pages).

Press Ctrl+Home to return to the document's beginning and uncheck the Show/Hide tool in the Home tab of the Ribbon and note how the Master document seems to be a unique, very long document.

Press Ctrl+F to show the Navigation Pane and click Headings to show all its Heading styles. Try to expand and collapse the Heading1 styles in the Navigation Pane to see how easy it is to quickly select any tale title in such a big document (Figure 12-43).

Figure 12-43. *Close the Outline view to return to Print Layout view, press Ctrl+F to show the Navigation Pane, and use the Heading styles to quickly select any document tale (try to collapse any Heading1 style to easily show another author's tales)*

Insert the Book's Table of Contents

Now it is time to insert the book Table of Contents in the Contents section located on page 2.

Follow these steps:

1. Use the Navigation Pane to select the CONTENTS Heading and click the first empty paragraph of this section to define the place where the Table of Contents must be inserted.

2. Expand the Table of Contents command found in the References tab and select the Custom Table of Contents... option to show the Table of Contents dialog box.

3. In the Table of Contents dialog box: Set Show Levels = 2 (to use just Title, Heading1, and Heading2 styles, as shown by the Print Preview list, Figure 12-44).

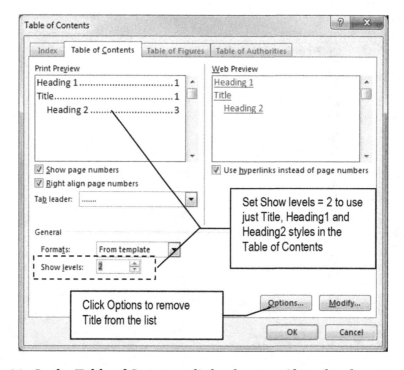

Figure 12-44. *In the Table of Contents dialog box, set Show levels = 1 to use just the Heading1 and Title paragraphs (the ones that have Outline level = 1)*

4. Click the Options button to show the Table of Contents Options dialog box, scroll the Available Styles list, and clear the Title style TOC level text box to tell Microsoft Word that you don't want to include it in the Table of Contents (Figure 12-45).

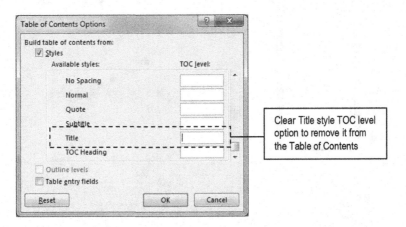

Figure 12-45. Use the Table of Contents dialog box Options button to show the Table of Contents Options dialog box, scroll the Available styles list, and clear the Title TOC level column to remove it from the Table of Contents styles

5. Close the Table of Contents Options dialog box to return to the Table of Contents dialog box and note that the Preview Options now show just Heading1 and Heading2 styles.

6. Click OK button of the Table of Contents dialog box to generate the book Table of Contents at the current text cursor position (Figure 12-46).

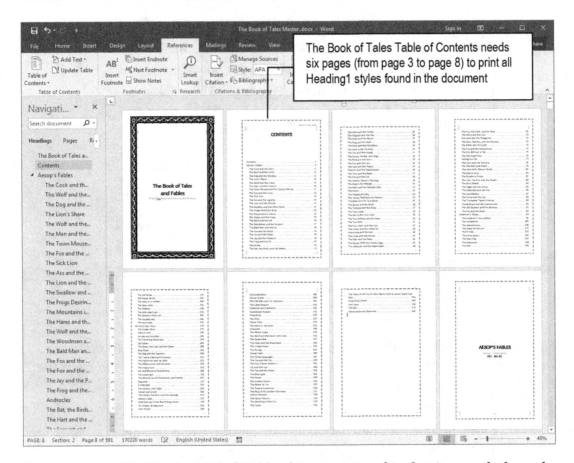

Figure 12-46. *The "Book of Tales" Table of Contents is so big that it spreads through six document pages. Change the TOC1 style font size and use a two-column format to use fewer pages*

Shrink the Table of Contents

The "Book of Tales" Table of Contents needs six document pages to print all Heading1 paragraphs found in the document, spreading itself from page 3 to page 8: too much for a TOC!

Follow these steps to change the Table of Contents formatting options:

1. Select the entire Table of Contents paragraphs.

2. In the Home tab of the Ribbon set these options in the Font and Paragraph areas:

   - **Font size** = 9

   - **Line spacing** = 1

3. In the Layout tab of the Ribbon set these options in the Paragraph
    area:

    • **Spacing Before** = 0

    • **Spacing After** = 0

    The Table of Contents will be reduced to five pages (Figure 12-47).

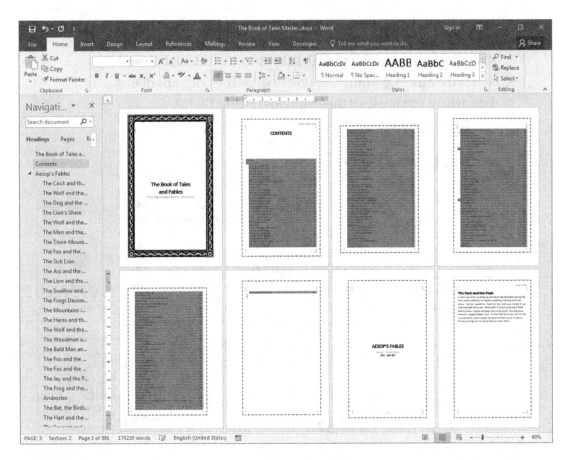

Figure 12-47. *Select the entire Table of Contents (it will become dark grayed)*
and change the text formatting options: Font size = 9 pt, Line Spacing = 1, Spacing
Before = After = 0. This will reduce the Table of Contents to five pages

Attention   Since the Table of Contents applies the TOC1 and TOC2 styles to format each Heading1 and Heading2 style text found in the document, and both TOC1 and TOC2 have the Automatically update option set (in the Modify Style dialog box), anytime you change any TOC1 or TOC2 paragraph format you will indeed change the associated style affecting the entire Table of Contents length.

4. With the Table of Contents paragraphs still selected, expand the Columns command found in the Layout tab of the Ribbon and select the More Columns... option to show the Columns dialog box, where you must set these options (Figure 12-48):

   - **Number of Columns** = 2

   - **Line Between** = Checked

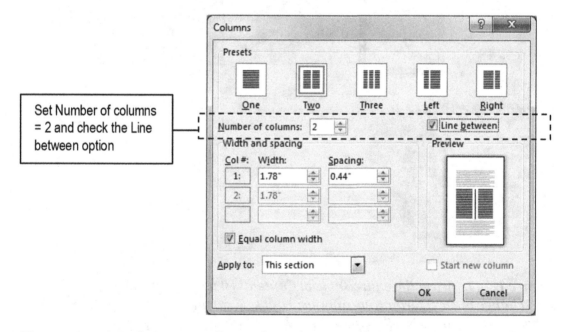

Figure 12-48. In the Layout tab, use the Columns tool, More Columns... option to show the Columns dialog box and set Number of columns = 2 and check Line between

When you press Enter, Microsoft Word will format the Table of Contents using a two-column format, and the TOC page number will shrink to just two and a half pages (Figure 12-49).

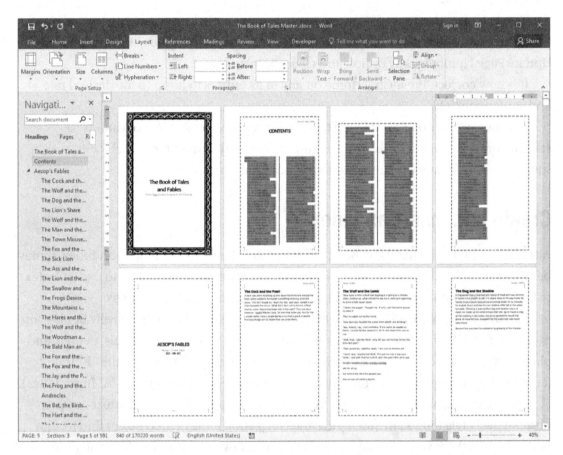

Figure 12-49. *By using a two-column format, formatted with Calibri 9 pt, Line spacing =1 and Spacing Before = After = 0, the Table of Contents size shrinks to two and a half pages!*

Recalculate the Table of Contents

Since the Table of Contents changed its own length, the page numbers it currently shows are no longer valid.

To recalculate the Table of Contents page numbers, click any of its entries and press the F9 function key to show the Update Table of Contents dialog box. Accept the default Update Page Numbers only option and click OK to update it.

It is now correct. Press Ctrl+Home on any of its entries to jump to the desired tale and see for yourself!

Use the Save button found in the top left corner of Microsoft Word window to save not only "The Book of Tales Master.docx" Master document, but each of its subdocuments (watch the status bar saving each subdocument).

Create and Insert an Index

Although a child book like "The Book of Tales and Fables" does not need an Index, it may be still desired for didactic reasons, just to teach children of all ages how to use an Index to find information—and to also expand your practice of creating an Index!

Looking to the Navigation Pane—and for the very essence of such a lovely book—you may note that children may be interested in three main categories: animals, people, and places, which should be easily found in the Index by name (like "Fox" in the "F" Index letter) and by aggregate (as a subentry of the Animals, Fox, located in the "A" Index letter).

To create such an Index, you may first list what must be tagged in the text—or just observe the Navigation Pane titles—use the Navigation Pane Search box to find its first occurrence in the text, select the text, and then tag it twice: once as a Main entry index and again as a Subentry of the desired aggregation noun.

Let's see how you can make such double Index entries in practice.

Creating a Concordance Table to Create the Index

Looking to the Navigation Pane Headings found in the Aesop's Fables (first book inserted as subdocument), you will note that the first tale is "The Cock and the Pearl," which has two entries: Cock (which can be tagged twice as Main entry and as an "Animals" subentry) and Pearl (which can also be tagged twice as Main entry and as a "Things" subentry).

This is a great time to experience how to use a concordance file to automatically tag the document text for all desired words that you want to appear in the Index.

I created the concordance table for the "Book of Tales and Fables" using these steps:

1. The "Book of Tales Master.docx" document was kept opened in Microsoft Word, showing the Navigation Pane Headings view.

2. A new Microsoft Word document was created, and a single column table was inserted in it.

3. Keeping both windows opened, I searched for each animal, thing, or character in the Heading2 paragraphs of the Navigation pane, inserting its name in the table (one name for row).

Attention   All beings from the animal word (including reptiles and insects) were considering as Animals (like Fly and Serpent). Some nonliving things were considered as Characters (like Wind and Sun). Others were considered as Things (like Crown).

The "Fables Index Concordance Table1.docx" document, which you can also extract from Fables.zip file, has such an initial table, in the order they appear in the Navigation Pane (it may have duplicate entries, Figure 12-50).

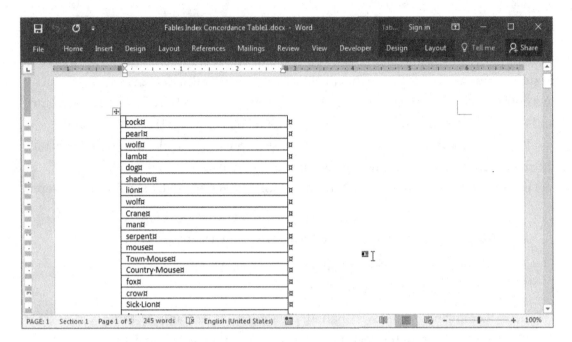

Figure 12-50. *This is the "Fables Index Concordance Table1.docx" document, which you can extract from Tales.zip file. It has the names of animals, characters, and things noted in the tales and fable titles that appear as Heading2 styles in the Navigation pane*

Since Microsoft Word will make a case-sensitive search to AutoMark the index entry, once this one-column table was created, every one of its items was searched (using Options, Match case, and Single word only options checked), fixing their upper- and lowercase presentation in the table (it gave me a lot of work to check it...).

Since the concordance table must have two columns (the first column is the item to be searched for in the document, and the second column is the Index entry to be created), after the words inserted in this single column table were checked and corrected, the column content as selected, copied, and pasted at its right to create a two-column table with the same content (intended to create Main key Index entries).

The "Fables Index Concordance Table2.docx" document, which you can extract from Tales.zip file, has this two-column table ready-made for an Index AutoMark operation (Figure 12-51).

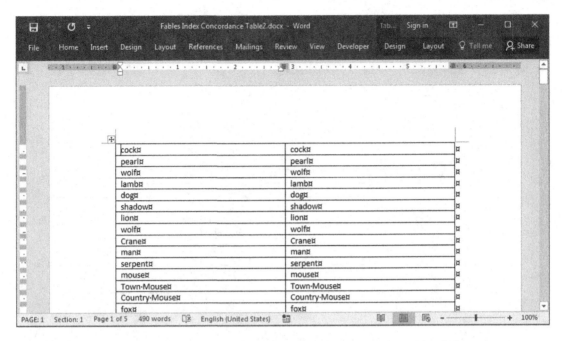

Figure 12-51. *This is the "Fables Index Concordance Table2.docx" document, which you can extract from Tales.zip file. It duplicates the first column to create the concordance table used by an AutoMark operation for the creation of Main key Index entries*

And to allow you to double-tag each Index entry as a subentry of "Animals", "Characters", and "Things", the "Fables Index Concordance Table2.docx" second column was modified by prefixing each of its items by the desired Master key ("Animals:", "Characters:", and "Things:"). The "Fables Index Concordance Table3.docx" document, which you can extract from Tales.zip file, has this concordance table for tab Index sub keys (Figure 12-52).

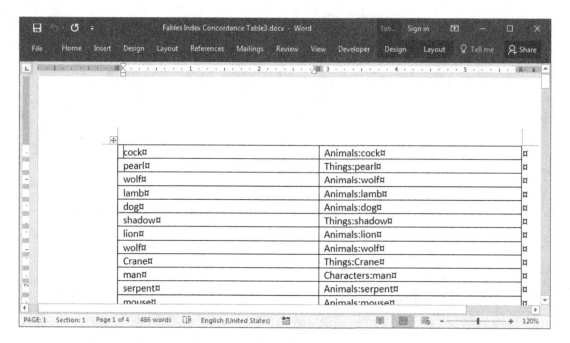

Figure 12-52. *This is the "Fables Index Concordance Table2.docx" document, which you can extract from Tales.zip file and use to tag Index subkeys. It prefixes each second column item by the desired Master key prefix ("Animals:", "Characters:", or "Things:")*

Using AutoMark with Concordance Tables

Now that we have that concordance tables to use AutoMark to tag the document with Index field codes (Master and Sub keys), it is important to know that, by an anticipated reason, you have to first mark the Main keys and then mark the Sub keys: by changing this order, the Main keys will not be marked.

To add all desired Index Main keys from "Fables Index Concordance Table2.docx" document, follow these steps:

1. In the "Book of Fables Master.docx" document, into which you have inserted the subdocuments, select the Insert Index command found in the Index area of the References tab to show the Index dialog box.

2. Click the AutoMark button to show the Open Index AutoMark File dialog box (see Figure 12-21).

3. Select the "Fables Index Concordance Table2.docx" document and press OK to close the dialog box.

4. Repeat Steps 2 and 3 to select "Fables Index Concordance Table3. docx" and press OK to also tag the desired Index sub keys.

Microsoft Word will use the two-column concordance tables to mark the Master key and Sub keys Index entries (watch the Status bar, which should say "Word is searching for index entries to add page... Press ESC to cancel", Figure 12-53).

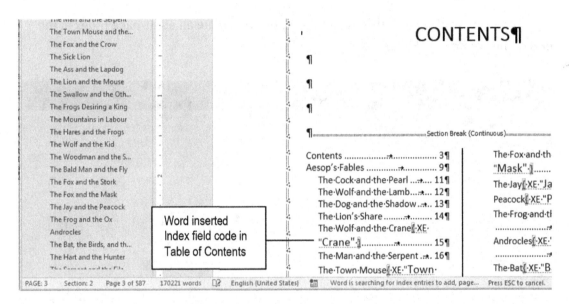

Figure 12-53. *Watch Microsoft Word status bar to note the "Word is searching for index entries to add page... Press ESC to cancel" message that appears whenever you use the AutoMark button of the Index dialog box to select a concordance table file*

Generate the Index

Once you had used the AutoMark feature to automatically tag the Index field codes in the Master document, it is time to generate the Index.

Follow these steps:

1. Press Ctrl+End to go the end of the Master document (you may reach page 587).

2. Use the Insert Index command found in the Index area of the References tab to show the Index dialog box.

3. Select the desired Index format and press OK to generate the Index.

Microsoft Word will run through the text and will create an eight-page Index at the end of the document (Figure 12-54).

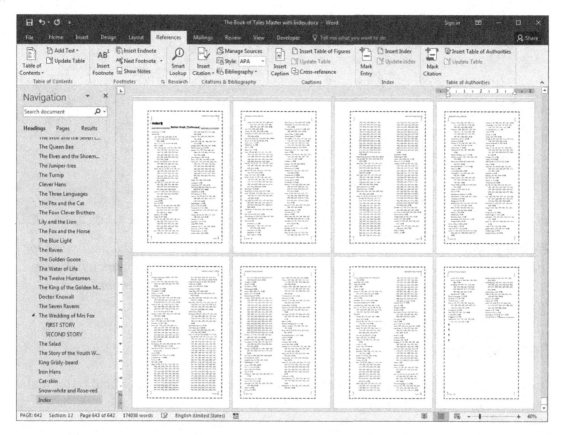

Figure 12-54. *These are the eight pages needed to generate the Index of "The Book of Tales Master.docx" Master document, as proposed by the concordance tables found in "Fables Index Concordance Table2.docx" (Master keys) and "Fables Index Concordance Table3.docx" (Subkeys) documents*

Inspect and Fix the Index Keys

Go ahead and inspect the Index created. You will notice that it doubled all Index entries (they all appear as an individual Master key or under the Animals, Characters, or Things master keys, Figure 12-55).

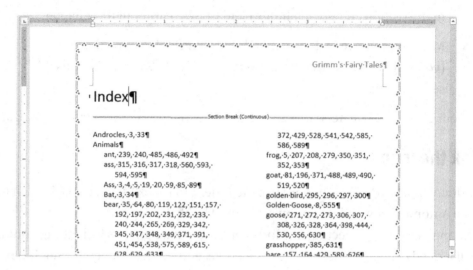

Figure 12-55. *The two concordance tables generated double index entries for most Index items. Note that it begins with "Androcles" and "Animals" main entries, and then begins to show all "Animals" subentries. Also note that some entries (like "bear") have a lot of page references.*

Note that the Index begins with "Androcles" and "Animals" main entries, and then begins to show all "Animals" subentries. Also note that some entries have a lot of page references (like "bear"). Others, like "king", "mother", and "man", have tenths of page number references, which appear in duplicate in their Master and Sub keys.

Now you may begin to understand that although Microsoft Word gave all the tools you need to create an Index, this is a very specialized task (indeed, it is a profession unto itself), and it needs greater attention to produce a final good result.

To fix this Index entries you can

- Remove them from the Index with the Delete key.

- Correct the concordance tables, remove the Index entries, remove the Index, and insert it again.

The first option is the easiest, as long as the Index isn't updated again.

The second option is the most professional one, and needs a more technical approach, so let's see it in more detail.

To correct the index entries you can

- Remove them all from the document (use a Find and Replace operation to search for ^d XE and replace with nothing), as explained in the section "Removing Index Field Codes" earlier in this chapter.

- Manually remove just the desired Index entries from the document (you will need to search for them using ^d XE "<WordInitials> as the search string).

In both cases, you will need to select and delete the Index and then insert it again.

Shrink the Index

The Index created by Microsoft Word use the Index1 to Index9 special styles: all of them have the Automatically update option set in the Modify Dialog box.

This means that, by selecting any Index entry and changing its formatting options, you will indeed change the associated Index style, automatically changing all Index entries that use it. To make an Index shrink its size, you just need to change its styles Font size by following these steps:

1. Select the first index entry ("Androcles" a Master key entry formatted with Index1 style).

2. Use the Font Size tool located in the Font area of the Home tab of the Ribbon to format it with a 7 pt or 8 pt size. All Master key entries will also be affected.

3. Repeat Steps 1 and 2 to also format the first "Animals" Sub key ("ant") to a 7 pt or 8 pt size.

At the end of this process, the Index will now use fewer document pages to print itself. I will leave to the reader the task of fixing and shrinking the Index as a last book exercise!

Conclusion

Microsoft Word Master and Subdocuments are a powerful way to deal with large documents, where each chapter belongs to a different document, sometimes written by different people all using the same template.

Using the Outline view, you can transform a document into a Master document, and insert its links in the subdocuments, using the Master as the text that holds all the subdocuments.

With the Master/Subdocument approach you can easily generate the Table of Contents, use the Navigation Pane to easily jump to any Heading style, and also tag all subdocuments at once with Index field codes to generate the final document Index.

Summary

In this chapter you learned:

- How to use the Outline view to create a Master document.

- How to produce the Subdocuments from a list of Heading styles.

- How to insert Subdocuments in a Master document.

- How to deal with the multiple Section Breaks inserted by Microsoft Word in the Master and the Subdocuments.

- How to create a document Index.

- How to manually tag Index words.

- How the Index words are tagged with hidden Index field codes.

- How to fix, search, and remove these Index field codes using the Find and Replace dialog box.

- How to produce Concordance Tables to use the AutoMark Index features.

Final Words

Now, we have come to the end of this book. In it you had the opportunity to realize that Microsoft Word is a sophisticated typographic tool that, to be correctly used, depends on having some basic typographic knowledge. Essentially, these chapters have shown that:

- There are several hidden characters used to represent nonprinting keys or control characters (like Enter and Tab, Shift+Enter, Ctrl+Enter, and Section breaks) that can impact the way text flows in and between document pages.

- Text flow control is very well done as long as certain ground rules are met:

    - Correctly use the Enter, Tab, and Space keys,

    - Make use of the paragraph alignment controls,

    - Apply the Line and Page Breaks tab options of the Paragraph dialog box.

- Make extensive use of Styles—notably the Recommended styles—to get the most out of the Microsoft Word tools that are based on them (Navigation Pane, Design Tab, Table of Contents, Outline view, Index formatting, etc.).

I sincerely hope you have enjoyed the book, and from now on, have most of the answers to any problems you may encounter when using Microsoft Word to format any type of text document you have created or edited.

Index

A

Advanced Find option, 167
Aesops Fables.docx document, 699
A1 reference style, 553
Ascender line, 21
AutoFit, layout, 529–531
AutoMark button, 674, 716–717

B

Baseline, 21
Booklets formatting
    design tab's Style Set gallery, 406
    document to booklet conversion, 408
    Even and Odd Page Headers, 408
    four-page sheet signatures, 401
    Page Setup dialog box, 401, 407
    rules, printing, 404
    sheets per booklet options, 402–403
BookTitle Style, 238–240
Borders and Shading
    border style, color and width, 55
    data formatted, 58–59
    dialog box, 58
    formatting changes, 57
    Home tab, Ribbon, 56, 58
    inheritance, 57
    page borders command, 54
    paragraph background color, 55
    text paragraph, 56

Bullets and Numbering
    changing levels, 66
    changing paragraph numbers, 66, 68–69

C

Capital line, 21
Cell Margins command
    automatic resize, 536
    default cell spacing, 536
ChapterTitle style, 230–236
Character attributes
    change case
        all caps, 116–117
        Shift+F3, 116
        small caps, 117
        strikethrough, double strikethrough and hidden, 118
    drop cap, 135, 137–138
    Find and Replace dialog box, 138–142
    font and font size, 111
    Font dialog box, 110
    kerning, 124
    Microsoft Word Font area controls, 110
    OpenType features
        contextual alternates, 130
        ligature, 126–127
        number form, 128–129
        number spacing, 128
        stylistics set, 129–130
        text effects tools, 130–131

© Flavio Morgado 2017
F. Morgado, *Microsoft Word Secrets*, https://doi.org/10.1007/978-1-4842-3078-7

I, J

T, U

Get the eBook for only $5!

Why limit yourself?

With most of our titles available in both PDF and ePUB format, you can access your content wherever and however you wish—on your PC, phone, tablet, or reader.

Since you've purchased this print book, we are happy to offer you the eBook for just $5.

To learn more, go to http://www.apress.com/companion or contact support@apress.com.

Apress®

Printed in the United States
By Bookmasters